The Sociology of Child Development

Harper's Social Science Series

Under the Editorship of F. STUART CHAPIN

Harper & Brothers, Publishers, New York

The Sociology of Child

Development

THIRD EDITION

JAMES H. S. BOSSARD

Late William T. Carter Professor of Child Development
University of Pennsylvania

AND

ELEANOR STOKER BOLL

Assistant Professor of Sociology and Child Development
University of Pennsylvania

To Barbara and Constance

Contents

21 Parents with Problem Attitudes   389
22 Homes with Conflict Situations   406
23 Families Under Stress   429

Part VII   Child Development and Nonfamily Groups

24 Growing Out of the Family   453
25 Children Who Reject Their Parents   474
26 The Peer Group—Preschool Playmates   498
27 Later Age Peer Groups   518
28 School Situations and Child Development   540

Part VIII   The Larger Social Setting for Child Development

29 Children as a Population Element   573
30 The Historical Status of Childhood   585
31 The Changing Status of Childhood in the United States   609
32 Child Development: Retrospect and Prospect   641

    Bibliography   663
    Index of Authors   695
    Index of Subjects   703

Foreword

Childhood is a universal human experience. A book about child development is therefore a book about all of us. The factors and problems involved in this process of growing up may be considered from different points of view: in this book the approach is primarily sociological. Its chief emphasis is upon the social situations in which children live and grow from infancy to maturity. Since all of us grow up with other persons, these social situations, too, are a part of our common experience.

A book of this kind should be readable. I have tried to make it so. The number of footnote references has been limited, so far as seemed advisable. The bibliographical appendix includes only a selected number of related books and articles, which made it necessary to omit many valuable references. Also, I have tried to write in a simple manner, and to avoid the use of technical terms. I hope that the esoteric will forgive this, and that other readers will like it.

I have received so much help in the preparation of this volume that my acknowledgments are almost certain to be inadequate. To Professors Ernest W. Burgess of the University of Chicago and Kingsley Davis of Princeton University, I am indebted for reading parts of the manuscript and for helpful suggestions. Professor F. Stuart Chapin, of the University of Minnesota, indicated additions to the original outline which have been included in its final form. Mrs. Frances C. Allen, of Philadelphia, contributed a revealing case study which is identified at the point of incorporation. Mr. Bradford Chambers has been most gracious in permitting me to examine his unpublished material on conflict gangs. Mrs. Eleanor S. Boll, Research Associate at the William T. Carter Foundation, has been a source of constant help. Specific contributions by her to the volume are noted on subsequent pages, but I am indebted to her for much more than such acknowledgments will indicate. The facilities of the Carter Foundation for Child Helping at the University of Pennsylvania have been utilized at every turn, a debt which it is a pleasure to owe. Generous adjustments in my teaching responsibilities, made by the administrative officers of the University of Pennsylvania, have permitted the completion of the manuscript much earlier than would have been possible otherwise. *The American Sociological Review, The American Journal of Sociology, The Annals of the American Academy of Political and Social Science,* and the University of Pennsylvania Press have permitted the reproduction of material previously published by them. Finally, my two daughters have taught me so much about children that it seems only proper, for professional as well as for affectional reasons, to dedicate this volume to them.

JAMES H. S. BOSSARD

Philadelphia, Penna.
March 15, 1947

Foreword to Revised Edition

Child development continues to be a challenging and rewarding area for scientific inquiry, and the steady production of valuable studies during the years since 1947, when the first edition was completed, presents a number of problems concerning the selection of material to be included. However, since the approach of this volume is a distinctly sociological one, only studies pertinent to that approach have been drawn upon in the preparation of this second edition. For summaries of other aspects of child development, such as the physical, psychological, or educational, the reader is referred to the excellent texts which devote themselves to those approaches. It is hoped that this brief comment will make clear both the continued emphasis of the sociological approach of this volume and the lack of specific mention of recent studies which fall outside of this province. Specific structural changes from the first edition include the addition of parents' occupations and family rituals as facets of child development.

For helpful suggestions incorporated in this revised edition, I am indebted to Professor Reuben Hill, of the University of North Carolina; Professor Jessie Bernard, of Pennsylvania State College; Dr. Evelyn M. Duvall, former Executive Secretary of the National Council on Family Relations; Dr. Eleanor S. Boll, of the department of sociology at the University of Pennsylvania; and Mrs. Bernece W. Shalloo, of the staff of the William T. Carter Foundation. For permission to reproduce earlier publications, I am indebted to the *American Sociological Review, Social Forces, Mental Hygiene, Child Development,* and the University of Pennsylvania Press. Finally, the facilities of the William T. Carter Foundation continue to be of the greatest help.

JAMES H. S. BOSSARD

Philadelphia, Penna.
June, 1953

Foreword to Third Edition

This third edition not only brings chapters in the earlier editions abreast of recent developments, but also makes changes in the structural organization of the volume. Chapters 1 and 2 of the revised edition are condensed into one; and Chapters 29 and 30 are combined into a single chapter. There are six new chapters: one on Families by Size (Chapter 3), one on The Empathic Complex and Child Behavior (Chapter 8), one on Domestic Animals: Their Role in Child Development (Chapter 11), one on Mothers' Role and Functions (Chapter 17), one on Fathers' Role and Functions (Chapter 18), and another on The Peer Group—Preschool Playmates (Chapter 26). The last three of these chapters have been contributed by Dr. Eleanor Stoker Boll. It is hoped that this new edition will increase the usefulness of this text.

JAMES H. S. BOSSARD
ELEANOR STOKER BOLL

Philadelphia, Penna.
December, 1959

Part I

Introduction

Chapter 1

The Sociology of Child Development

This is a book about children. Its central theme is the sociology of child development. In this respect it differs from either a psychological or pedagogical or psychiatric point of view. Since it is a book about children, the role of the child in contemporary thought needs to be considered; since it is written from the sociological point of view, the relation of child development to sociology and the meaning of the sociological approach should be explained. To these purposes the introductory chapter of this volume is devoted.

From Welfare Objective to Scientific Concept

The child came to the serious attention of the modern world as an object of tender solicitude and of organized welfare endeavor. It was as such that the child was first regarded by sociologists. This was wholly natural, for the desire for social uplift was the background out of which sociology arose. With this original primary emphasis upon social amelioration, the welfare of the child became an obvious and logical objective. The emphasis in the scientific approach to human welfare was upon prevention; and the prevention of social problems, if it meant anything, meant the promotion of the well-being of children. Thus naturally, in the course of time, the child became the largest concern in the field of social work, both in the number of workers employed and in the amount of money expended. Thus, too, courses in sociology which dealt with the child were of the problem kind, and emphasized ameliorative measures. They have been referred to customarily as courses in child welfare.[1]

In recent years, a newer approach to child study and problems has

---

[1] Cf. Raymond Kennedy and Ruby Jo Reeves Kennedy, "Sociology in American Colleges," *American Sociological Review*, October, 1942, pp. 661–675, for the relative importance of such courses.

come to be made by social scientists, and sociology has shared in this development. This newer approach can be summarized most tersely, perhaps, by saying that the child is regarded as a focal concept for scientific study rather than as a welfare objective. In other words, the child is seen as a human reality in whose development are combined the various specialized problems of particular groups of scientific students. The child, in short, serves as a project study, drawn from life rather than from the laboratory, in which may be observed the various processes of human growth and development. To say, then, that the child emerges as a focal concept for scientific analysis does not imply an approach that is theoretical or academic, as the phrase might indicate, but an intensely practical one, especially for the purposes of sociological analysis and research. It makes the child's social development a distinctive and legitimate scientific area for sociologists, just as it has been for psychologists and psychiatrists.

Sociology and the Area of Childhood

To think in terms of the realities of a functioning society, there are a number of reasons for sociologists to center much of their work around the child. Whether one begins from the point of view of group processes and analyzes them in terms of their simple beginnings, or whether he makes a lengthwise historical approach to the processes of personality formation and development, he is led in either event directly to the area of childhood. Some of the more obvious relationships between this area and the scope of contemporary sociological thought will be indicated in brief form.

THE SOCIOLOGICAL CONCEPTION OF PERSONALITY

Contemporary sociologists conceive of the human personality as a product of social conditioning. In this process, two sets of conditioning factors are recognized as of outstanding importance. One of these is the interactive experience of life within the group. Sociologists discuss this currently under the heading of "social interaction" or "the role of the group." But the influence of relationships with other persons is modified or qualified constantly by what these other persons have learned, that is, their cultural heritages. Thus we identify the second set of conditioning factors as cultural ones, comprehending the more or less accepted group ways of doing and thinking. These, of course, are sociological commonplaces today. They are recalled here because of their implications, not fully recognized as yet by many contemporary sociologists. Two of these implications are emphasized here. The first is the obvious fact that the social conditioning of the personality during the first years of life is of primary importance. Not only are the factors operating during this period the first to condition the individual, but there are few or no counter-influences to overcome. All this is but another way of stating that the basic patterns of personality are laid during the period of childhood.

The second implication is that the sociological processes of personality formation can best be studied during the earlier stages. There are a number of reasons why this is so. The relative lack of counter and complicating factors has been referred to. There is a simplicity and directness about the process during the first years that is apt not to be duplicated later on. The process takes place on a smaller scale; the groups within which the child interacts and the culture-transmitting process operate on a smaller scale than is found in the later stages of life. Something akin to controlled conditions can be set up for children, an opportunity likely to be lacking when the subjects studied are older. In other words, the whole range of experimental studies in personality formation is confined in large measure to the area of child life.

In short, the social development of the personality is in large degree the story of the social development of the child. This is the inevitable implication of the sociological approach to personality—a conclusion similar to that of the psychiatrist and psychoanalyst. In this approach, the role of the family is predominant, and the family is the one institution whose scientific study falls most clearly within the province of the sociologist.

CULTURAL CONTINUITIES AND DISCONTINUITIES

Viewed in retrospect, the culture of any society is a changing stream in which cultural continuities and discontinuities are occurring constantly. The more precise study of these, in their varying aspects and respective roles, falls ordinarily within the province of the culture historians and students of social processes. The point of emphasis here is that the child is the focal point of this recurring relationship between the cultures of successive generations.

Turning to cultural continuity, we see that the child is the carrier and connecting link between the cultures of succeeding generations. This is a fact of great importance; for, in terms of social process, it makes the relation of adult to child as important as, if not more so than, that of adult to adult. Groves has already emphasized this in these words: "When society is conceived as a functioning process, a continuous on-going in a way suggestive of the individual consciousness which carries the past into the present and establishes purposes directed toward the future, it is certain that the relationship of adult with child has in this cultural flow a more pregnant meaning than the contact of adult with adult."[2]

[2] Ernest R. Groves, *The Family and Its Social Functions*, J. B. Lippincott Company, Philadelphia, 1940, p. 16.

BEHAVIOR PROBLEMS AND THE SOCIALIZATION OF THE CHILD

The longer the sociologists' concern with crime, delinquency, and behavior of all sorts continues, the more one comes to be disturbed by the suspicion that our past approach has been from the wrong direction. We have, in times past, started with problem cases and worked back to general processes, and we have selected picturesque and intriguing factors and attempted to assess their role; whereas all the time we might have started more intelligently with the child and studied the normal processes of his development, ultimately coming to an understanding of deviant behavior in social relationships. In the medical field, the study of disease follows and is built upon an understanding of bodily structure and process; a similar procedure in sociology would make the study of juvenile delinquency a postscript to the study of the socialization of the child.

GROUP RELATIONS AND THE CHILD

The sociology of child development is an important part of the science of group relations. Children are a definite population element. All societies recognize the distinctive existence of groups organized on an age basis. Anthropologists have shown the prevalence and importance of the age classificatory device in primitive cultures,[3] and more recently sociologists have come to emphasize its role in contemporary society.[4] The ascription of the child's status and the ways for the child and youth to achieve status—these are the heart of the class system of any society. The status of the child element in the population, the factors affecting its status, and its relationship to other population elements—these are a major part of the problem of group relations in sociology.

There are other and important phases of a sociology of childhood. The foregoing discussion is intended to be suggestive and illustrative rather than exhaustive. The essential fact to be emphasized is the child as a challenging pattern of operating actuality, thus making his social development a major area for scientific exploration and an intriguing project for pedagogical exploitation. For this is the stimulating challenge of the child as a scientific concept, that in it so many of the basic principles of sociology and of the unexplored problems of sociological research are

[3] Ralph Linton, "Age and Sex Categories," *American Sociological Review*, October, 1942, pp. 589–603; and Ralph Linton, "A Neglected Aspect of Social Organization," *American Journal of Sociology*, May, 1940, pp. 870–886.

[4] Leonard S. Cottrell, Jr., "The Adjustment of the Individual to His Age and Sex Roles," *American Sociological Review*, October, 1942, pp. 617–620; Talcott Parsons, "Age and Sex in the Social Structure of the United States," *ibid.*, pp. 604–616; Earl H. Bell, "Age Group Conflict and Our Changing Culture," *Social Forces*, December, 1933, pp. 237–243.

combined into an operating pattern at a time in the life of the individual, and in a stage of simplified development, when they can be most readily understood.

Factors Favoring the Study of Child Development

One of the driving forces toward an emphasis upon the sociological study of child problems is what may be called the philosophy of the modern mind. The essence of this philosophy is the belief, so characteristic of the industrial-urban American culture, that man can in large measure control his own destiny. The contemporary American worships at the shrine of progress, meaning by that concept a controlled development of society in a direction believed to be desirable. Supremely sure of himself, he deems himself the master of his fate, contends that he need not submit, and that there really is no virtue in continuing to submit, to the limitations imposed upon him by the forces of nature or the follies of man.

This philosophy is deeply imbedded in our national way of thought because almost our entire history has been a living proof of its soundness. Three hundred years of continuous experience has made us the most confident and optimistic people in the world. We believe we can go to Heaven because, metaphorically speaking, for several centuries we have been doing so. We have occupied, exploited, and remade a very large and a very rich continent. As that process has gone on, civilization has repeatedly been reborn on its advancing frontier. The political philosophy which initiated our separate existence revolutionized the political tenets and structures of much of the world. Our own political ideas and forms have been repeatedly recast, always with the fond belief that the latest revision would just about usher in the millennium. Our industrial history is a dazzling record of miracles. What, in view of all this, could the philosophy of the American mind be but what it is? How else could we proceed but in our confident roistering fashion?

The implications of such a philosophy for children are obvious. If society is to control and direct its development—call the process social planning, postwar reconstruction, or what you will—then the place to begin is with the oncoming generation. The remaking of the world can never hold much point or hope of reasonable success if it is conceived in terms of the immediate present. It is essentially a process of trading in social futures, if the terminology of the market is permitted. Controlled and directed social movement implies a forward-looking philosophy with its eyes and its values focused on the future. And the future is the child. The child is the hostage which each generation gives to destiny, as a token of its behavior and its hopes.

The Plasticity of Human Nature

A second basic factor profoundly influencing contemporary thought in regard to the child has been the widespread acceptance of the idea of the plasticity of human nature. This idea, or principle, is the product of recent work in a number of sciences—principally psychology, anthropology, and sociology—and it is significant that the unorganized and originally unrelated efforts in these sciences have fitted together so aptly into the same pattern of conclusion.

One group of studies has emphasized the modifiability of human nature, how from the very beginning of life the original responses are modified by the particular requirements of the group in which the child lives. Moreover, this is a continuing process. Responses to stimuli in the environment are constantly in the process of formation and modification. Reinforcing these conclusions are the results of the accumulated material from anthropological sources revealing the diversity of group ways of living and thinking, i.e., the variety of cultural patterns into which children are born and by which they are conditioned. These studies have in turn been supplemented by the work of the sociologists, showing the relationship between culture and personality in a degree which led them to speak of personality as the subjective side of culture. In other words, modern scholarship has made it very apparent that everywhere throughout the world individuals are constantly being modified and conditioned for participation in their culture, that cultural unities vary from one group to another, as do the methods of cultural conditioning or the role of the respective agencies and persons who do the conditioning.

This principle, now an accepted foundation stone in the social sciences, is a revolutionary concept, once one turns to its implementation. It brings to the forefront, first and foremost, the whole process of child rearing and training, in both its individual and collective aspects. The meaning of education now comes to be reinterpreted to include the whole process whereby the child is inducted into his culture, that is, the whole transformation of the newborn infant into membership in a specific society with a specific culture. It comes to include, too, the transmission of the cultural heritage from one generation to another, and the process by which a society perpetuates and renews itself.[5]

Whether these contemporary convictions prove ultimately to be merely airy dreams in the realms of delusive grandeur, or the sterner stuff out of which better human beings and better worlds are destined to come, it must be clear that in all these efforts the child is the major objective;

[5] For a complete exposition of this point of view, read John Dewey, *Democracy and Education,* The Macmillan Company, New York, 1916; and collected papers in the *American Journal of Sociology,* May, 1943.

and an understanding of the child—his personality development, his socialization, his role as carrier of the culture, his cultural induction and his indoctrination—is the enduring basis of any possible successful achievement. The modern mind, wrestling with the problems of human and social well-being, finds them where Plato dreamed his ideal state— in the directed development of the next generation. Science now dictates what our tender sympathies long have counseled. Society's "acre of diamonds" lies revealed in the cradle within the home, and social statesmanship finds its task in the rearing of the child.

The Study of Human Behavior

Human behavior is a fascinating field for study. Understanding it has always intrigued human interest. Through the ages, man has observed the conduct of his fellows and utilized his generalizations as a guide for his experience. Thus must one interpret the fables, legends, myths, proverbs, sagas, sacred writings, literary tales, etc., which constitute the accumulated wisdom of the ages; they involved and reflected man's observations on what people did, and why. And this is the substance of human behavior.

With the passage of time, such observations grew in range and complexity; with the advent of writing and printing, they came to be recorded; with the growth of human learning, they became naturally more specialized. These developments coincided in point of time with the use of the modern sciences. The result was a natural one, no matter how slowly the logic of thought might move to its destined end; the study of human behavior came to be recognized as a legitimate field of scientific study. The point to be recognized (and it seems important by way of proper perspective) is that the modern sciences concentrating upon the problems of human behavior represent, then, so many current phases of man's abiding and age-old aspiration to understand his fellows and ultimately himself.

The scientific study of behavior did not begin as such. That is to say, there was no conscious recognition among the early scientists of the scope of the study of human behavior as a whole. The period of beginning was one of specialized sciences attacking some one particular field or group of problems involving human reactions, often working independently of other sciences in related fields, and at times having no appreciation of such relationships or of the larger implications of their work. Each of these specialized sciences staked off its own claim, as it were; developed its own tools and techniques; and, in course of time, arrived at its own conclusions. It is only in recent decades that an appreciation of the underlying field of human behavior has been recognized as the common core of these sciences.

Two Fundamentally Different Approaches

When one surveys the various sciences studying human behavior, two fundamentally different approaches can be identified. One concerns itself with the individual who behaves, focusing attention upon his physical make-up, his biological heritage, his psychological traits, his personality trends, and the like. But all behavior is related to situations, in which the personality is developed and to which behavior is a response. The scientific study of the situations related to behavior is, then, the second fundamental approach to be noted.

The first of these is the one that has been followed generally by professional and scientific groups concerned with human behavior. Included here are the physical and biological sciences which have gathered a mass of information about the mechanism of the body—its structure, its physiological processes, the chemical role of the endocrine system, and the hereditary equipment of the organism. These foundation studies are highly important: first, because of the light they throw upon the physical equipment of the individual; and, second, in their emphasis upon behavior as the result of adjustment to the enveloping situation.

Second are the psychological sciences which occupy a central position in the studies of human behavior. The plural number is used because there are different approaches to the behavior of man which come properly within the scope of psychology, just as there are many systems of psychology. The scientific study of the child, from the psychological side, has been made in large measure via the psychometric approach, concerning itself with studies of capacity and thinking of behavior as a correlate or function.[6] Another group of psychologists have made what might be called the personality-testing approach. Their studies grew out of an interest in the correlation between intelligence and performance (i.e., behavior). The discovery that this correlation was not high led to an emphasis upon other traits and factors, such as temperament, character, and so on. Psychiatry may be included as one of the psychological approaches, even though it began as a branch of medicine. Concerned originally with the clinical treatment of the physiological causes of mental disorder, psychiatry represents today a framework of reference for behavior as a whole, with a variety of interpretations in sociopsychological terms and factors. The contemporary psychiatric point of view of mental disturbance as a failure of the organism as a whole to adapt to the conditions of life can have no other meaning but that psychiatry becomes an applied science (or an art?) of human behavior. Similarly, one must include psychoanalysis in the psychological group. Like psychiatry,

[6] W. I. and Dorothy S. Thomas, *The Child in America*, Alfred A. Knopf, New York, 1928, Chap. 8.

it began as a specialized therapeutic approach. As time has gone on, it too has become increasingly a study of the human personality, contributing concepts, emphases, and techniques, as well as conclusions distinctly its own.

Finally, there are the social sciences, which have turned increasingly in the past few decades to the study of human behavior. It is easy to understand the reasons for this development. In the first place, much of the work of the groups of sciences already mentioned has reached into, or has implications for, the social sciences; in the second place, the more one delves into the study of behavior, the more one sees that it is something which develops in relation to and with other people. Human personality is a product of social contact and communication, and its scientific study leads directly and inevitably to the study of the background situations to which behavior is a response.

The Sociological Conception of Personality

Among the social sciences, sociology in particular has been interested in the general study of human behavior. This interest grows directly out of the sociological conception of personality. Such a conception naturally is conceived in terms of those social traits and relationships which distinguish the individual and differentiate him from other members of society. Virtually all sociological definitions of personality go back to that of Park and Burgess, who identify it as "the sum and organization of those traits which determine the rôle of the individual in the group."[7] Since such a role grows out of the ideas, attitudes, traits, and habits of the individual, these too must be included in the sociological meaning of personality.

The sociological insistence is that personality, thus defined, is not inborn but is acquired or achieved. On the basis of the individual's native or innate equipment, the human personality is a product of social conditioning. In the process of personality formation, two sets of conditioning factors operate. One of these is the interplay of person with person, which we term social interaction. Of outstanding importance in this connection, then, are the experiences of the person in his or her social contacts. But the influences of relationships with other persons are constantly modified or qualified by what these other people have learned. Here is the second set of conditioning factors, namely, the cultural, embracing the more or less accepted ways of group doing and thinking. Hence personality is determined also by the conditioning power of the cultural heritage and by the social patterns of behavior which social groups develop, approve, preserve, and transmit from generation to

[7] Robert E. Park and Ernest W. Burgess, *Introduction to the Science of Sociology,* University of Chicago Press, Chicago, 1921, p. 70.

generation. What this means, in substance, is that the sociologist sees personality as a reflection of the social situations in which the individual has been reared and to which he reacts. The self is a social looking glass.

The Situational Approach to Behavior

For many years, references to the background factors in human behavior utilized the general term *environment,* and earlier applications of scientific methods to the problems of human behavior gave ample recognition to its importance. Thus Gabriel Tarde, one of the first students of crime to employ positive methods, championed the idea that the criminal was entirely a social product.[8] Among the earlier psychologists, John B. Watson had an almost complete disregard for inborn or constitutional traits.[9] William A. White, among the psychiatrists, early stated a clear and marked emphasis upon environmental factors in the causation of mental disorders.[10] Similarly, Alfred Adler, in the psychoanalytic group, wrote more than a generation ago of the relative importance of environmental conditioning.[11]

With continued progress in methodology, it became evident that some term other than environment was needed to identify specific combinations of environmental factors, and gradually the word *situation* came into use. This specificity of combination became evident in the work of such physiologists as Loeb, Jennings, and others, in their work with "tropisms," that is, reactions of organisms to light, electricity, heat, acids, and so on. Next it was applied by psychologists—Thorndike, Yerkes, Watson, Köhler—in their experiments with rats, dogs, monkeys, and babies. The procedure of both of these experimental groups was the same: they prepared situations, introduced the subjects into a situation, observed the behavior reactions, changed the situation, observed the changes in the reactions, and so on.

It was a logical next step to apply this procedure to the study of human behavior, and much of the emphasis in recent years has been in this direction. Although the methodology was developed by comparative physiologists and psychologists, the foundation for its extension to human behavior was laid by Pavlov, Krasnogorski, Bekhterev, Watson, and others, in their work on the conditioned reflex. What this means is usually

[8] Gabriel Tarde, *Penal Philosophy,* translated by Rapelje Howell, Little, Brown & Company, Boston, 1912.

[9] John B. Watson, *Psychology from the Standpoint of a Behaviorist,* J. B. Lippincott Company, Philadelphia, 1919.

[10] William A. White, *The Mental Hygiene of Childhood,* Little, Brown & Company, Boston, 1924.

[11] Alfred Adler, *Understanding Human Nature,* Garden City Publishing Co., Inc., Garden City, 1927. Consult his *The Neurotic Constitution,* Dodd, Mead & Company, Inc., New York, 1917, for his explanation of how the individual compensates for his organic deficiencies.

explained in terms of Pavlov's classical first demonstration with dogs. A dog is shown a piece of meat. His mouth waters in anticipation of eating it. The meat may be thought of as the original stimulus; the mouth watering, as the dog's reaction. Pavlov's experiments showed that repeated association of other stimuli with this original stimulus in time brought out the original response. The reaction to the associated stimulus is called a conditioned reflex.[12] Applied to children, these experiments had similar results, and made it clear how "fears and prejudices and prepossessions are produced, especially by the behavior of other persons. A single association may be sufficient to produce the reflex. There is on record, for example, the case of a youth who was the subject of an experiment with odors. The odor of roses produced a feeling of fear, and investigation disclosed that the subject had been injured in an automobile accident near a rose garden. A whiff of lavender may recall mother, and tuberoses remind us of death. We have here [concluded the Thomases] a most important approach to the formation of personality traits as dependent on situations.[13]

Meanwhile the sociologists, recovering from their earlier inoculations of biological analogy, economic interpretation, and instinct psychology, saw in the situational approach very great opportunities for sociological emphasis. The sociologists' situational approach to behavior rests, of course, upon the striking concepts developed by the late Professor Cooley. His ideas of "the self as a social product," "the looking-glass self," and "individual and society as two aspects of the same thing" had appeared as early as 1902, but it was destined to be another decade and more until the implications of these concepts began to be realized for purposes of sociological study.[14]

Following Cooley, the next major step in the development of the sociological approach to behavior problems came with the publication of Thomas and Znaniecki's monumental work on the Polish peasant.[15] In this, the peasant is studied in the process of moving from a European to an American situation, thus approximating the controlled change of situation with which, as has been pointed out, the physiologists and psychologists had been working experimentally. Throughout their entire work runs the fundamental theme of the relationship between personality and the environing culture. "Personality is always a constitutive element of some social group; the values with which it has to deal are, were and will be common to many personalities, some of them common

---

[12] I. P. Pavlov, *Conditioned Reflexes*, translated by G. V. Surep, Oxford University Press, London, 1927.

[13] W. I. and Dorothy S. Thomas, *op. cit.*, p. 507.

[14] Charles H. Cooley, *Human Nature and the Social Order*, Charles Scribner's Sons, New York, 1902.

[15] W. I. Thomas and Florian Znaniecki, *The Polish Peasant*, Richard G. Badger, Boston, 1919.

to all mankind. . . . Personal evolution can be understood only in connection with social life. . . . Personal life records, as complete as possible, constitute the perfect type of sociological material. . . . A social institution can be understood only if we . . . analyze the way in which it appears in the personal experience of various members of the group and follow the influence which it has upon their lives."[16]

Of particular significance in its effect upon subsequent sociological thinking was the emphasis upon the individual's definition of the situation. On the basis of his cultural and social conditioning, the individual meets the various social situations which confront him, and defines them with reference to his own behavior. Thomas further distinguishes between those definitions of the situation which are laid down for the individual by his culture—which Thomas calls the moral or public definition—and those which represent the individual's own conception— which he terms personal or hedonistic. The interplay between man and his culture is well stated in these words: "The human personality is both a constantly producing factor and a continually produced result of social evolution, and this double relation expresses itself in every elementary social fact; there can be for social science no change of social reality which is not the common effect of pre-existing social values and individual attitudes acting upon them. . . ."[17]

Following his work on the Polish peasant, which Burgess identifies as "the starting point for the sociological explanation of personality and culture,"[18] Thomas carried forward his analysis of the cultural conditioning of personality in his paper presented to the American Sociological Society in 1926, with particular emphasis upon the role of "critical experiences." "Behavior traits and their totality," he wrote then, "are the outcome of a series of definitions of situations with the resulting reactions and their fixation in a body of attitudes or psychological sets. Obviously, the institutions of a society, beginning with the family, form the character of its members almost as the daily nutrition forms their bodies, but this is for everybody, and the unique attitudes of the individual and his unique personality are closely associated with certain incidents or critical experiences particular to himself, defining the situation, giving a psychological set, and often determining the whole life direction."[19]

Two years later, in his presidential address to the American Sociological Society, he made a clear distinction between different approaches to the study of behavior:

[16] *Ibid.*, Vol. III, pp. 6, 10, 6, 7.

[17] *Ibid.*, p. 5.

[18] Ernest W. Burgess, "The Cultural Approach to the Study of Personality," *Mental Hygiene*, April, 1930, p. 310.

[19] W. I. Thomas, "The Problem of Personality in the Urban Environment," *Publications of the American Sociological Society*, 1926, Vol. XX, p. 31.

In approaching problems of behavior, it is possible to emphasize—to have in the focus of attention for working purposes—either the attitude, the value, or the situation. The attitude is the tendency to act, representing the drive, the affective states, the wishes. The value represents the object or goal desired, and the situation represents the configuration of the factors conditioning the behavior reaction. . . . The situations which the individual encounters, into which he is forced, or which he creates, disclose the character of his adaptive strivings, positive or negative, progressive or regressive, his claims, attainments, renunciations, and compromises. For the human personality also the most important content of situations is the attitudes and values of other persons with which his own come into conflict and cooperation.[20]

Reinforcing Thomas' point of view were the conclusions of Faris, Bernard, and others. In 1921, Faris indicted the explanation of behavior in terms of instincts,[21] and three years later Bernard's book on instinct appeared, followed by his analysis of environments in 1925.[22] In his paper for the American Sociological Society in 1925, Faris foreshadowed the later sociological dictum of personality as the subjective side of culture in these words:

Individuality may then, from one standpoint, be thought of as character, which is the subjective aspect of the world the individual lives in. The influences are social influences, but they differ in strength and importance. When completely ordered and organized with the conflicting claims of family, friends, clubs, business, patriotism, religion, art and science all ordered, adjudicated, and unified, we have not passed out of the realm of social influence, but we have remained where the social group, taken separately, can be invoked to explain the behavior. Individuality is a synthesis and ordering of these multitudinous forces.[23]

Meaning of the Term Situation

One of the few organized efforts to define the term was made at the meetings of the Section on Sociology and Social Work of the American Sociological Society in December, 1930. In this symposium, Mrs. Ada E. Sheffield presented the idea of family case work as dealing, not with a client, but with "a dynamic field of experience, a field in which the individual or the family figures within an aggregate of interactive and inter-

[20] W. I. Thomas, "The Behavior Pattern and the Situation," *Publications of the American Sociological Society,* 1928, Vol. XXII, pp. 1–2.
[21] Ellsworth Faris, "Are Instincts Data or Hypotheses?" *American Journal of Sociology,* September, 1921, pp. 184–196.
[22] L. L. Bernard, *Instinct: A Study in Social Psychology,* Henry Holt & Company, Inc., New York, 1924; "A Classification of Environments," *American Journal of Sociology,* November, 1925, pp. 318–332.
[23] Ellsworth Faris, "The Nature of Human Nature," *Publications of the American Sociological Society,* 1926, Vol. XX, p. 29.

dependent factors of personality and circumstance . . . a segment of interactive experience involving clients in complex relationships with their physical and social setting." This new unit she spoke of as a *situation.*[24]

In defining the term for purposes of sociological analyses, Queen says: "A situation consists in relationships between persons viewed as a cross section of human experience, constantly changing in kaleidoscopic fashion, and affected both by material conditions and by relationships to other persons. Thus we made of the concept 'situation' an intellectual tool similar to the anthropologists' concept 'culture complex,' in that both are quite flexible as to content, both are capable of subdivision, both are something more than the sum of discrete elements, both convey the idea of relationships, both present nuclei about which configurations gather, and both are constantly changing."[25]

When one turns from formal definitions of the term, such as those just cited, to its actual use in the recent scientific literature, he finds that at least three general basic ideas seem to be included in the concept of the social situation.

The first is the idea that the stimuli included are all external to the organism. This implies at once that the term situation is not, properly speaking, synonymous with the word *environment*. As Mead points out, environment means all the factors to which the responding unit responds.[26] This obviously would include certain acquired internal aspects of the organism which would obviously operate as stimuli. These internal stimuli are not included in the concept of the situation; we are concerned only with those that are external to the organism.

The second basic idea involved in the term *situation* is that of the reciprocal relationship of these stimuli. In other words, they do not just operate; they operate with, upon, and in relation to, each other. In other words, a situation is an organization of stimuli in which each stimulus has a given relationship to every other one. It is the particular relationship of these stimuli to one another that gives them their meaning in any specific situation.

This basic principle, that any fact derives its attributes and meaning from its relation to other facts, is pertinent to all scientific study. The failure to realize this in regard to social facts has greatly handicapped sociological analysis in the past. An example of this principle from the mechanical field will serve as a simple illustration. A watch lies on the desk in the office wherein this is written. The time is night. The building

[24] Ada E. Sheffield, "The 'Situation' as the Unit of Family Case Study," *Social Forces*, June, 1931, pp. 465–474.

[25] Stuart A. Queen, "Some Problems of the Situational Approach," *Social Forces*, June, 1931, p. 481.

[26] George H. Mead, *Mind, Self, and Society*, University of Chicago Press, Chicago, 1934, pp. 245–247.

is almost empty of human occupants. There is no other watch or clock in it. In relation to this particular office and its furnishings, this watch has a certain meaning, and the possible questions concerning the watch tend to be limited by the other facts which inhere in the situation. At this point I leave the office to visit a friend's home. This friend has a large and varied collection of watches, clocks, sundials, hourglasses, and the like. Here and now, the watch appears in a new situation. New questions arise concerning it. Its significance is totally different from what it was an hour ago. It is, of course, the same watch intrinsically, but its meaning has been profoundly changed. So it is with the facts which serve as stimuli in a given situation. From the standpoint of the situation, the stimuli included exist in relation to one another, and from this obtain their meaning in the particular situation under consideration.

The third characteristic of the situation is that it is organized about, or in relation to, some focal point or person. It is this aspect of a special relatedness, with reference to some person or object, that has come to be the essence of the scientific use of the situation concept. On the basis of this specific unity of organization the situation becomes an emergent, by which we mean that this special relatedness becomes in itself an additional and effective factor.

The simplest illustration of the idea of an emergent is water—a combination of hydrogen and oxygen, in the very definite proportions of two parts of hydrogen and one part of oxygen. This special relatedness forms the liquid emergent known as water, which has quite different properties, that is, behavior, than either of its gaseous components. Concerning its reality, Mead speaks in these general terms: "Anything that as a whole is more than the mere form of its parts has a nature that belongs to it that is not to be found in the elements out of which it is made."[27]

The existence and importance of this factor of special relatedness were recognized by a number of thinkers in the nineteenth century. Such men as John Stuart Mill, Lester F. Ward, Spaulding, Wundt, and others were aware of it; and various terms, such as "creative synthesis," "evolutionary naturalism," "organicism," "holism," and "heteropathic causation" were used to identify it. C. L. Morgan's term *emergent* has, however, found most favor among contemporary philosophers, biologists, sociologists, and the like, who utilize the concept.

By way of summary, then, a situation consists of a number of stimuli, external to the organism but acting upon it, organized as a unit and with a special relatedness to one another as stimuli of the specific organism involved. It thus becomes, as Lundberg suggests, a "field of force,"[28] or a segment of life to which the organism reacts as a whole.

---

[27] *Ibid.*, p. 329.
[28] George Lundberg, *The Foundations of Sociology*, The Macmillan Company, New York, 1939, pp. 217 ff.

Thus conceived, it becomes a tool of precision for the scientist in studying the behavior of the organism, as definite and specific as the situation
of the experimental physiologists and psychologists.[29]

Three Aspects of Social Situations

Social situations having been defined in terms of the basic ideas included, it is pertinent next to indicate the distinctive points of view
from which they may be regarded. In speaking of these approaches for
purposes of study, reference is intended not to the methodology to be
employed, but rather to the nature and range of the phenomena considered. To clarify the distinction between these different ways in which
social situations may be regarded, an illustration may serve to advantage.

On the desk on which this chapter is being written there stands a Royal
typewriter. Let us suppose that we are Martians engaged in an exploratory study of typewriters, rather than Earthians similarly interested in
social situations. In all probability we should begin our study by regarding the typewriter as a mechanical structure made up of many separate
parts. We would proceed to consider these parts—keyboard, letters,
platen, ribbon, frame—inquiring and observing how they are related to
each other, always coming back to a recognition of the basic structural
unity. Our questions, our problems, the facts we observe, the generalizations we make, are those which bear upon the parts of this machine, their
organization and special relatedness that is the essence of a Royal typewriter.

An operator of this machine, or structure, now approaches and begins
typing. Immediately a whole new series of questions, observations,
facts, and conclusions come to the fore. These have to do with the function of the parts of the structure. The field of study now centers basically
around process, the process of operation. Each part of the machine is
performing its role, a role which at the same time is related functionally
to the role of every other part. This is a wholly new approach, distinct
from the first-mentioned line of inquiry, yet a pertinent part of our study
of the phenomena of typewriters and typing.

Sooner or later, in the course of our study, there will come the discovery that the typist is not simply operating a machine but is using the

---

[29] The reader should compare this characterization of the situation with that of
Leonard S. Cottrell, Jr., in his article, "The Case Study Method in Prediction," *Soci-
ometry*, November, 1941, pp. 358–370. See also Leonard S. Cottrell, Jr., and Ruth
Gallagher, "Important Developments in American Social Psychology During the Past
Decade," *ibid.*, May and August, 1941, for a statement of the main currents of change
in contemporary social psychology. Another contribution by Cottrell is his "Analysis
of Situational Fields—A Theoretical Orientation for Social Psychology," *American
Sociological Review*, June, 1942, pp. 370–383.

machine to record and convey letters, words, sentences, and ideas. The typed page may be a report on research, part of a Presidential message, or a kidnaper's demand for ransom. It may be written in English, French, Latin, or American slang. The ideas expressed may be simple or complex, and the style may be direct or involved. Peculiarities of sentence construction and vagaries of punctuation and spelling attract our attention. In other words, an entirely new set of problems, facts, and interests engross us. We are now concerned, not with the structure of the machine or the processes of operation, but with the material or content of the process.

The three ways of regarding the phenomenon of typewriting may be identified under the headings of *structure, process,* and *content,* and the illustration just used serves to indicate the argument of the present chapter concerning the fundamental ways of approaching the study of social situations. The thesis here advanced is that social situations, just like social institutions and various other organized data in sociology, can be regarded and studied from the three distinct points of view identified by the terms *structure, process,* and *content,* and that much clarity and progress in understanding them will ensue if this distinction is recognized and maintained.

STRUCTURE

A social situation is, from one point of view, a structure. Its analysis and description as such might be spoken of as a still-life picture. When we structurize a social situation, we see it in repose. Our interest is in the structural elements, their characteristics, and their position and relationships to one another. We are concerned chiefly with the relationships that are relatively continuous. What distinguishes a structure is the fact that it has form and that it is an organization, and the essense of both is continuity of relationship.

In the scientific study of a social situation structurally conceived, we take it apart, examine each part as to its nature, and inquire into the way these parts are organized into a unit. This is one separate but important step in understanding the situation. If I understand him correctly, it is this that Lundberg had in mind when he wrote: "After the field, i.e., situation has been selected, the problem is to structure it so that the relationship of the elements in the field can be accurately shown. The method of doing this with which we are most familiar is, of course, to name with words certain elements or factors in the situation and then by use of the adjectives or adverbs of ordinary language we attempt to give an accurate statement of the relationships within the field."[30] Similar would appear to be Mrs. Sheffield's thought in her paper

[30] Lundberg, *op. cit.,* p. 108.

of three decades ago: "The identifying of a pattern that is relatively constant helps us to bring order into our thinking about the variables which appear. It should clarify causative relations, should help us to follow social process, and to raise significant questions."[31]

PROCESS

A second way in which a social situation may be viewed and studied is in terms of process. If the structural approach is a still-life picture, this second is a motion picture. We are concerned now with the interaction of the elements of the situation. The term *social interaction* is used constantly by contemporary sociologists, currently as the generic name for a whole set of processes taking place between individuals; thus, social interaction denotes the set of processes by virtue of which society exists. Here, however, we are using the term *interaction* as a category of analysis, to identify the reciprocal or interdependent relationship among the elements in a situation. The basic idea involved is not one of a mere meeting or collision of these component elements, but something more pervasive and subtle, in the course of which each acts upon or somehow changes or modifies the other. Such interaction may take place between individual organisms, between persons, or between persons and their stimulating environment. Conceived thus in terms of process, the situation becomes an immediately related and functioning segment of human experience, as both Mrs. Sheffield and Queen have indicated in their definitions cited earlier in this chapter.

CONTENT

Finally, from the third point of view, both structure and process are but vehicles or channels through which are transmitted a content of ideas, attitudes, words, and the like. This content we speak of as "culture."

The cultural content of the interactive process is confined to the human level. Before me on the floor, as I write, are puppies engaged in play. Here is an interactive process most assuredly; there are gestures, grimaces, growls, with an evident role of attitudes, dispositions, emotions, and the like. This is process, but there is no cultural content. Culture is exclusively a human product, and the culture content of the interactive process is confined to human relationships. The interactive process may be thought of, then, as a series of functioning operations conveying cultural items. Through this interactive process these cultural items are molded into a pattern which becomes the central core of the situation.

It is this cultural, or distinctively human, element in social situations which is apt to be overlooked by students who approach the subject from the background of certain disciplines whose point of view is es-

[31] Sheffield, *op. cit.*, pp. 471–472.

sentially organismic. An excellent illustration of this appears in a recent and in many ways an excellent volume.

Some phenomena of nature exist in the form of static structures, others in the form of reversible or irreversible processes. Examples of the first are geometrical forms, of the second, waterfall, wind, combustion, etc. The existential form of the organism is dynamic. This has been formulated by Jennings in his much quoted statement that "The organism is a process." In the last analysis, "organism" and "life" are identical concepts. The first term places the emphasis on the structural, the second on the dynamic aspect. The two aspects are inseparable from each other. The essential characteristics of the organism are, however, more clearly revealed in its function than in its morphological features.[32]

This cultural content, however, is a very specific thing in the case of any given social situation, in spite of what has been said about its pervasiveness. Although culture is comprehensive, like the air we breathe, nevertheless the human personality is constantly selecting items and elements from the current culture, and is channelizing them through the interactive processes, so that any given social situation represents both a cross section and a cross selection of the contemporary culture organized about a given focal point.

The distinction between process and content, as well as the specificity of the cultural content, is well set forth by Anderson in his analysis of family situations.

The examples set for the child by his parents, older persons, and associates operate from birth onward. Older persons transmit a variety of techniques and attitudes. . . . Two problems can be distinguished: first, the actual content of the pattern which is imitated. Thus the child observes his parents greeting neighbors or friends, hears the comments made by his parents on individuals, organizations, and activities, and is given examples of either good or poor sportsmanship when he plays with his parents. A boy sent to a clinic because of his unpopularity was socially isolated among his fellows because of his many caustic comments and criticisms. It was found that his father was known throughout his community for similar behavior. Here what seemed abnormal in the boy had been learned in the normal manner directly from a parent. Next, we may distinguish the effects of these patterns as transmitted upon the child's adjustment. If parents quarrel frequently in the presence of the child, he not only acquires quarreling as a mode of approach to others but may react with uneasiness and frustration. A child is sensitized to some social actions and hardened to others. Whether he becomes hardened or sensitized depends upon his total makeup and the character of his previous experience quite as much as upon the intensity or character of the stimulation given.[33]

[32] Andras Angyal, *Foundations for a Science of Personality,* Commonwealth Fund, New York, 1941, p. 20.

[33] John E. Anderson, "The Development of Social Behavior," *American Journal of Sociology,* May, 1939, p. 849.

Implications of the Situational Approach

Once the full meaning of the situational approach to behavior problems is recognized, it becomes important to consider the implications of such an approach, and it is to this discussion that we turn next.

1. It seems necessary to begin by emphasizing that the situational approach is distinct and separate, commensurate with the study of the personality that reacts to the situation. This fact would seem to require emphasis because such status has not been given to it in the past. Almost without exception, situations and situational factors in behavior have been referred to as though they were of secondary importance, a sort of by-product of the primary concern with the behavior of the organism. Studies of situations have been incidental studies, often casually made, and with secondary status ascribed to them. This has been true even when the avowed purpose was the study of the situation. Few studies of social situations have gone far without shifting consideration from the situation to the way in which the individual defines the situation and reacts to it.

Obviously, this has not made, nor can it make, for any considerable progress in the understanding of situations themselves. What has just been said is not to be interpreted, of course, as a criticism or depreciation of the emphasis in behavior studies upon the organism and its responses; the sole insistence here is that, once the role of the situation in behavior is recognized, the situational response must be recognized as distinct and separate, commensurate with studies of the organism and its behavior.

2. The second implication of the situational approach to behavior problems, and complementary to the first one, is a recognition of the situation as a *separate* field for scientific investigation. In other words, situations need to be studied, inductively and by themselves, without any reference to the way in which organisms react to them. This is said with particular regard to social situations, with which we are primarily concerned.

Emphasis upon this second implication again is necessary because of the past failure to recognize it. The reasons for this failure are easy to understand; they are natural products of the history of the situational approach. Recognition in scientific circles of the role of the situation in behavior began, as has already been pointed out, with the physiologists in their work on tropisms. In these studies, simple situations were created and the reaction of simple forms of life to them was observed; in these cases, there would have been little or no point to any major concern with the situation. The experimenters created them, and the elements involved were few and simple. For example, when a specific acid is dropped into water in order that the reaction of the amoeba may be observed, the situation created is the combination of two liquids with specific chemical formulas. The situation was not only simple, it was also thoroughly understood. Naturally, the investigator's chief concern was with the reaction of the amoeba. The case would be similar with the application of heat or of light. The resulting situation was simple and could be expressed with the precision of a mathematical formula.

Following the physiologists, some of the psychologists utilized the situational approach. The situations employed by them were more complex, it is true, than those created by the physiologists. But the fact remains that they too were relatively simple, and that they were created by the experimenters. Moreover, the elements involved in their creation were physical elements whose nature was known precisely and whose relationship was a tangible and constant reality. Naturally again, the psychologist, once having created or established his situation, was concerned with it only incidentally, as a vehicle to his investigation of the subject's responses to this situation. This remained true of scientists like Pavlov, Krasnogorski, Bekhterev, and so on, in their work on the conditioned reflex. One who goes through the reports on their work finds but scant reference, other than brief, simple explanation, to the situations employed. All the emphasis is upon the reactions to these situations, and the possible meaning of the observations.

This is perhaps the place to recall that most of the studies of child behavior have been made by persons trained in the biological and psychological sciences. Even the sociological studies of young children have been carried out by psychologists, psychiatrists, and educators. It involves no untoward criticism of their work to point out that, in their approaches to child behavior, they have shown the effects of their scientific backgrounds. Nor does it seem difficult to understand how such students would be prone (a) to minimize the role of the situation, or (b) to assume that social situations are understood adequately, and that the important fact is to see how the individual defines the situation and reacts to it. Most of them, naturally enough, have therefore been disposed to think primarily in terms of persons and their reactions; and when they have spoken of the situational approach, it has been with one eye turned toward it and the other toward the behavior reaction to it.

It is the emphatic insistence of this volume that a situational approach to human behavior is an entirely different matter. Social situations differ from mechanical or physical situations, and in a number of respects. In the first place, social situations are not created artificially as are those of physiologists and psychologists; they are accepted by the student as they are found. This changes the whole relationship of the student to the situation. In the one case, he creates a situation to see how the organism will react; in the case of social situations, he finds them ready-made and must learn to deal with them as they are. Second, social situations are more complex than the physical, nonhuman situations which have been dealt with prevailingly in behavior studies. The physiologists and psychologists customarily combine a small number of elements to create their situations. In the case of social situations, the very nature of the human personalities involved excludes any such simplicity. The human personality is a very complex product; hence the simple combination of a man, a woman, and a child, in a family situation, would be far more complex than the combination of three chemical agents, for example. Again, the elements involved in a social situation cannot always be identified with clarity, nor can their role in the situation be expressed with the precision of a mathematical formula. For instance, the degree and nature of tension between the father and mother may be an integral part of a family situation and have profound significance for the child; yet these aspects may be difficult to identify or express with any kind of satisfactory accuracy. The emotional quality of a social relationship is as real a social fact as the temperature of water, but no statistical thermometer has yet been devised to measure and express it. Finally, social situations differ from nonsocial situations in the inexorability with which they change. Most of the situations utilized by students of prehuman behavior were fixed, or they changed slightly or slowly or both. This is not true of social situations; they are constantly changing, at times with considerable rapidity. From one point of view, social situations are functioning processes, which places them in a category quite different from standardized psychological tests, for example.

The scientific study of social situations is possible only if they are regarded as objective and separate realities. This is the first step in their scientific investigation. We must begin by disregarding the ways in which individuals define situations or react to them. Further progress involves their analysis with regard to the nature and range of the stimuli involved, the ways in which these stimuli operate, the cultural content of the interactive processes in situations, and the manner of organization, or special relatedness of all the stimuli involved, with special reference to the object or person considered. Each of these must be defined with precision and analyzed with an appreciation of all the complexities present. Only after social situations have been thus studied, with the slow laborious technique of the scientist, are we in a position to consider adequately their role in the behavior of the individual. He who would study social situations would do well to analyze carefully the procedures of scientists who have dealt with situations at the prehuman level, and note the detailed precision with which they work. From the standpoint of methodology, consider the following quotation from Pavlov:

While, as we have seen, very strong and even specialized stimuli can under certain conditions acquire the properties of conditioned stimuli, there is, on the other hand, a minimum strength below which stimuli cannot be given conditioned properties. Thus a thermal stimulus of 45 degrees C. applied to the skin can be made into an alimentary conditioned reflex, whereas at 38 or 39 degrees C. (approximately 2 degrees C. above the skin temperature in the dog) a thermal stimulus is ineffective. Similarly, while with the help of a very strong unconditioned stimulus it is possible to convert a very unsuitable stimulus—for example, one which naturally evokes a different unconditioned reflex—into a conditioned stimulus, it is exceedingly difficult or even impossible with the help of only a weak unconditioned stimulus to transform even a very favorable neutral stimulus into a conditioned stimulus. Even where such a conditioned reflex is successfully established, its occurrence results only in a very small reflex response. Some unconditioned stimuli may be permanently weak, others may display a weakness which is only temporary—varying with the condition of the animal.[34]

It will be noted, in the above description, that the difference of a few degrees in the temperature of the stimulus determines whether it has conditioning properties or not. This is highly suggestive to students dealing with social stimuli, both in its implication of accuracy and in the importance of the degree of strength or weakness of a specific stimulus.

3. This is perhaps the place to emphasize the interdependence of the sciences which the careful study of situations involves. This is a matter concerning which clear thinking has not always prevailed. The point of view presented here can best be explained through the use of examples. The physiologists, in their studies of the responses of organisms to varying situations, obviously drew upon the data of chemistry, bacteriology, physics, and the like, in order to create and describe accurately the situations to which the organisms were submitted; and quite as obviously, no question concerning such a procedure would be raised. Similarly psychologists, in creating situations or tests of a physical or mechanical sort to which their subjects are submitted, drew without the slightest hesitation upon the underlying physical sciences. That is to say, these earlier groups who utilized the situational approach to the study of behavior called upon all the scientific disciplines necessary in order to understand, as accurately as possible, the nature of the elements which they combined to create the situations they utilized for their own specific purposes. When, now, one turns to the much more comprehensive, complex, and difficult task of dealing with social situations to which human behavior is a response, it ought to be clear that the sciences which must be called upon and whose findings must be utilized are far more numerous. Hence in utilizing the situational approach, sociologists should have no hesitance or compunction in drawing upon the work of physiologists, physiological

[34] Pavlov, *op. cit.*, p. 31.

chemists, endocrinologists, psychologists, psychiatrists, psychoanalysts, historians, economists, political scientists, cultural anthropologists, horti-culturalists, statisticians, and the like, as the need may arise. The most extensive, and at times the most complete, utilization of the data of the complementary sciences by sociologists in developing the situational approach is entirely in keeping with the scientific folkways, and in this case peculiarly proper because of the difficulties of the material involved.

Summary

1. The child came to the serious attention of the modern world as a welfare objective. In recent years, the emphasis in our thinking has changed the child into a scientific concept, as it were, making it a project study in which the processes of human growth and development may be observed and studied.

2. Two factors particularly have favored the scientific study of child development. One has been the modern belief that man can direct the development of the society in which he lives, as well as of its members; the second is the belief in the plasticity of human nature.

3. Two fundamentally different approaches to the study of human development can be identified. One concerns itself with the individual who behaves, the other with the situations to which behavior is a response.

4. The term *situation* is used in this volume to mean (a) a number of stimuli, external to the organism, but acting upon it, (b) organized and operating as a unit, and (c) bearing a special relatedness to one another as stimuli of the specific organism involved. It is, thus, a "segment of life to which the organism reacts as a whole."

5. Social situations can be studied from three distinct points of view. These are identified by the terms *structure, process,* and *content.*

6. The objective analysis of behavior along the lines just indicated constitutes an approach to behavior problems commensurate in importance to the study of the individual and his traits. It is a separate, distinct, and highly important approach, and needs to be recognized as such.

7. Social situations need to be studied objectively, and without reference to the way in which organisms react to them. This has not been done in the past because, for the physiologists and psychologists who first dealt with the role of situations, such situations were simple, ready-made, and thoroughly understood. Social situations, however, are not created as a rule by experimenters; they are accepted as they are found.

Part *II*

*The Child
and His Family Setting*

Chapter **2**

Family Structures and the Child

A social situation was defined in the preceding chapter as an organization of stimuli, external to an organism and acting upon it, and having a special relatedness to one another as stimuli of the specific organism involved. Furthermore, it was pointed out that social situations, thus conceived, could be studied from three points of view, identified by the terms *structure, process,* and *content.* The present chapter is devoted to (1) the meaning and importance of family situations in child development; (2) types of family structures and their varying significance for the child; (3) recent changes in family structural forms; and (4) the significance of the predominance of the immediate family form in our contemporary society.

Family Situations: Their Meaning and Importance

The term *family situation,* as utilized in this book, involves the application of our definition of the phrase *social situation* to the specific family group. A family situation may be defined, accordingly, as a unit of stimuli operating within the confines of the family circle, and organized in relation to the person or object which serves as the focal point in the particular case being considered. Stated another way, the term *family situation* means a group of family stimuli operating as a unit with reference to some polar point. This polar point may be an outside object, a member of the family group, or a nonmember observer or student of the family. It is important to keep in mind the role of this focal point, for what is implied is that the family situation changes as the polar point is changed. To speak in general terms, the family situation of a child is the unity of existing stimuli within the family circle as they operate upon the child; that of the husband or wife in the same family will be quite different. The change in the polar point changes the entire situation, its involved stimuli, and the relationship of these stimuli.

There are two basic reasons for beginning the situational approach to child behavior with the study of family situations. One is their primary importance in the determination of behavior patterns; the second is their prior value for purposes of scientific analysis.

The importance of family situations in the formation of personality is emphasized today by all the sciences which are participating in the study of human behavior. Much of the recent advances in the fields of psychology, psychiatry, psychoanalysis, sociology, criminology, education, and social work reveals with striking clarity the early and pervasive role of the family in conditioning the behavior of its child members. The family is a society, the first in which the child lives, and the most powerful in changing original nature into the socialized personality.

This emphasis upon the family's primary importance in the socialization of the child must not be taken to mean, as frequently happens, that the personality is wholly and irrevocably formed during the first few years of life. Brown contends, for example, that far too much emphasis has been placed upon childhood experiences per se, that subsequent experiences determine the importance of these early activities, and that the individual, instead of being a product of his childhood, is the result of what adolescence, youth, and adulthood do to childhood experiences.[1] Similarly, Folsom points out that no one has yet proved that the total rate of personality development is faster in childhood than in later life.[2]

The prior value of family situations for purposes of scientific analysis derives from at least three characteristics. The first of these is the relative size and simplicity of family situations. In many cases, family situations include only two persons. Three-person family situations, particularly where very young children are concerned, are quite common. Current census data reveal the general prevalence of the small-family system. To speak in quantitative terms, family situations involving only a few persons are a normal feature of our life. In the second place, family situations are of a continuing and recurrent nature. The interacting personnel remain normally the same, at least over considerable periods of time. Many of their characteristics, as well as many of their relationships, are relatively permanent and stable. Particularly is this true in the study of social situations with the child as polar point. Ordinarily, changes in personnel are limited in number, particularly when compared with such changes in other social situations; changes in the characteristics and relationships of this personnel tend to occur slowly and often imperceptibly. Finally, the relationships in family situations are peculiarly frank

---

[1] Lawrence G. Brown, *Social Pathology*, F. S. Crofts & Co., New York, 1942, p. 11.
[2] Joseph K. Folsom, *The Family and Democratic Society*, John Wiley & Sons, Inc., New York, 1943, p. 323.

and intimate. Customarily there is less dissembling in the family than in other human groups, certain occasional and conspicuous instances to the contrary notwithstanding. Because of its intimacy, frankness, and privacy, the family provides a unique opportunity for the free expression of personality; it is these characteristics which facilitate equally well the scientific study of family situations. In short, one is led to conclude that family situations are the most important of the social situations which determine behavior, and relatively the easiest to study.

The Family as a Structure

Since the time of Sumner, sociologists have recognized that a social institution consists of a concept and a structure, and that this structure is a framework which consists not of physical realities but of relatively permanent relationships.[3] The family is a social institution, and, as such, it is a social structure, consisting of a framework of relatively continuing relationships. More specifically, this means that the family has an over-all form, a size, a given number of parts, i.e., members with a relatively stable nexus of determined roles.

To study the family as a structure is to view it in repose, that is, to consider it as a form of organization. Thus approached, there are many lines of inquiry which may be pursued. One aspect of the family as a structure is selected for analysis in this chapter. This is the structural form, or overall organization, of the family unit. Attention is directed primarily to the different types of structural form, to recent changes in emphasis regarding these structural forms, and to their significance in the child's social development.

Structural Forms of the Family

People constantly use the word *family* as though no question concerning its meaning could possibly arise. Even experts in the field of family study tend to do this. There is, of course, some justification for this because, as Linton has pointed out, "all societies recognize the existence of certain close-knit, internally organized cooperative units intermediate between the individual and the total society of which he is a part";[4] and to some one of these every person is assigned on the basis of a biological relationship clustering around a common ancestry. When the word *family* is applied to such a unit, there is general agreement as to its meaning. When one proceeds beyond this point, however, the term *family* comes to mean something quite different from one culture to another. What

---

[3] William Graham Sumner, *Folkways*, Ginn & Company, Boston, 1906, pp. 53 ff.
[4] Ralph Linton, *The Study of Man*, D. Appleton-Century Company, Inc., New York, 1936, p. 152.

begins as a rather standardized biological or reproductive unit comes to take diverse forms as a socially institutionalized phenomenon. Anthropologists have shown considerable interest in this problem of the structure of the family in the various cultures which they have studied. Sociologists, concerned more with contemporary culture, have given less emphasis to it, despite its great importance in our own societal organization. It will be desirable, therefore, to consider briefly, by way of background, some structural forms of the family in our contemporary Western culture, with special reference to the child.

When we consider the family from this point of view, it is necessary, first, to draw a line between the immediate household unit and the larger body of related kinsfolk. The distinction is a real one, and the term *family* has been applied in different cultures to each of these to the exclusion of the other. The student from a middle-class American home today, where the word *family* is synonymous with the reproductive unit of society, finds it difficult to realize that there have been many societies in which such units have not been so designated and in whose everyday life such a domestic structure has played a rather minor role. In translating the documents used in his study of the Polish peasant, Znaniecki found it wholly impossible to use the word *family* in the sense in which American students use it. The family, to the Polish peasant, was a social group which included all the blood and law relatives up to a certain variable limit, usually the fourth degree. To designate the smaller grouping which we call the family, Znaniecki used the term *marriage group.*[5] It is well to remember that in our own culture the transition in the concept of the family as a larger kinship group to that of the smaller household unit is rather recent. It is still found most typically in the urbanized areas of our large metropolitan centers, with their apartments, their small row-houses, and their residential hotels, all lacking the old-fashioned "spare bedroom" as the most convenient defense against invading relatives.[6]

Thinking in terms of the contemporary American child and adapting our terminology to this point of view, we find that the following family structural forms stand out. First, there is the child with his father and mother. This is the biological and reproductive unit; in normal times and circumstances the parents are married and have established a home, where they live with their child or children. (In ordinary times, about three-fourths of American men under twenty-five years of age who marry establish a separate home.)[7] Thus the biological and reproductive unit

[5] W. I. Thomas and Florian Znaniecki, *The Polish Peasant,* Richard G. Badger, Boston, 1919, Vol. I, p. 87.

[6] Ernest W. Burgess, "The Family as a Unity of Interacting Personalities," *The Family,* March, 1926, p. 3.

[7] Paul C. Glick, "Family Status of Men of Military Age," *American Sociological Review,* April, 1943, p. 157.

becomes also a social unit in which develop the community and intimate features of social life. We shall call this the child's *family of procreation.*

In a great many households, however, the child grows up in a family which differs from the above. Often one and occasionally both of the parents may be missing; on the other hand, an aunt or uncle or grand-parent or other kin, friend, boarder, etc., may be a continuing member of the child's family. This group is the household unit in which and through which the child receives his orientation in the social world. This it seems most pertinent to call the child's *family of orientation.* In many cases, the child's family of procreation and the family of orienta-tion are the same; but often this is not the case. In either event, both of these forms may be thought of as the child's *immediate family* in the sense of comprising the circle of his immediate, intimate, and con-tinuing family contacts.[8]

Each child as he grows up discovers that he is also a member of a larger kinship group to which the term *family* is applied. William Brown, for example, is one of the Westchester County or one of the South Caro-lina Browns. This group contains all the relatives by blood or marriage up to a certain degree of relationship, a degree which varies from one family or culture to another. Here again it is necessary to identify two subdivisions. Some of these kinship group families develop primarily through or around the male line; some, through the female line. The terms *patrilinear* and *matrilinear* are applied here, the reference being not so much to the line of descent that is utilized as to the degree of social adhesion or isolation that follows the marriage. For example, when Mary Jones marries William Smith, are she and her children regarded as Jones or as Smith kinsfolk by each group and by both? The answer to this question varies considerably from one family to another, and in dif-ferent regions of this country. The distinction is important, particularly again with reference to the child and to the family's functioning in the development of his personality. For this larger circle of kinsfolk, as con-trasted with the immediate family, the phrase *kinship group family* is used.

The basis of this larger kinship group is a blood fiction, that is, all mem-bers consider themselves to be related by blood. It is obvious, however, that this form of family is something more and different. Although the basic implication is that of common blood or descent, there are other and highly important factors in its formation. These include as a rule

---

[8] Some of the concepts here used are to be attributed to W. Lloyd Warner, of the University of Chicago, The reader should also consult J. L. and J. P. Gillin's text-book, *An Introduction to Sociology,* The Macmillan Company, New York, 1942, Chap. 9, for a summary of family-type groups. Such a comparison will reveal our preference for the term *kinship group family,* rather than "extended family," as used there. Also, our use of the terms *family of procreation* and *family of orientation* is slightly different.

commonness of point of view, community of rearing, a sense of intimate familiarity, and the sharing of a common place or status in society.

This seems the proper place to emphasize a point so often overlooked: that the biological basis of the family is secondary and that the primary factors in creating its unity and importance are the social bases which have just been enumerated. There are, let it be added, several lines of evidence which warrant such a conclusion. First is the work of the anthropologists which shows that kinship groups exist and kinship is reckoned in societies which know nothing of the biology of procreation. Second, there is the almost universal rule which permits adoption into the kinship group, thus clearly indicating that the social rather than the biological relationship is the important thing. Again, it must be obvious that kinship reckoning in unilateral lines ignores a great many of one's blood relatives, another instance of social acceptance given precedence to the blood bond.[9] This conception of the family as a social rather than a biological fact, emphasized by contemporary sociologists, is particularly significant in the study of the child's social development.

An obvious but by no means insignificant fact about the kinship group family, when descent follows through the male line, is the sharing of a common name. This serves to bring together people with the same name, leading them often to think of themselves as a common group and also having other persons regard them as such. In past times, the family name frequently was a distinctive label, indicating a person's association with a place or occupation.[10] This is less true today, but it still serves as an index of status.[11] The more self-contained and powerful a family is, the more its name takes on a social significance. This will be discussed more adequately in a subsequent chapter.

The hold of this kinship group family upon its individual members usually depends in this country upon the strength of the "we" feeling which it has developed. This depends in turn upon a number of factors. One of these is the spatial distribution of its members. In earlier times, kinship groups generally lived closely together, with constant interrelationships among the members; this is still true in some areas. When such a condition obtains from infancy, persons are conditioned from birth to accord much more importance to contacts with their kinsfolk than when they are apt to be scattered over wide areas and when mobility may make their present whereabouts uncertain. A second factor is tradition. What has been the past history of the family in this respect? Some families have a history of close interdependence over long periods

---

[9] J. L. and J. P. Gillin, *op. cit.*, Chap. 9.

[10] For a brief summary, consult the article on "Names" in the *Encyclopædia Britannica*, 14th ed., 1937, Vol. XVI, pp. 63–64.

[11] Clarence Schettler, "Does Your Name Identify You?" *Social Forces*, December, 1942, pp. 172–176.

of time, and conscious effort tends to maintain this under changing contemporary conditions; other families have never "made much over their kin." This is affected in turn by a third factor: the reputation or prestige of the kinship group. There are family lines whose prestige has been such through the years as to confer distinction upon every individual within the range of its membership. No one is likely to ignore his inclusion among the Cabots of Boston. Families like these tend to be "closed corporations" in many of the affairs of life. On the other hand, there are families which have been discredited, perhaps repeatedly, by the behavior of one or more members, with the result that the hold upon their kinsfolk is weakened correspondingly. In still other cases, crises within or involving the kinship group call forth a sense of solidarity otherwise lacking. Between the extremes of the Cabots on the one hand and the misfit families on the other, there fall a large number of kinship group families whose members come in some way to identify themselves with some particular traits or qualities, and come to be so regarded by their friends and associates.

Perhaps something should be said here about the status of the kinship group family. There are societies in which the term *family* means only this particular type; but this is not true as a rule in our contemporary Western culture, for here its importance has been much reduced in recent years and its role tends to be secondary or supplementary. Perhaps most American children today are thought of as members of two types of families, the immediate and the kinship group, the word *family* being applied somewhat indiscriminately to both types.

The Significance of Family Structural Forms

These structural forms of the family represent fundamental distinctions in the study of the family. In varying degrees they loom in the background of most children. What is their meaning for child development?

Very early in life, the child comes to sense that there is not one but several families with which he has some kind of relationship, that these families differ from one another in certain respects, that his relationship with them is not always clear, and that often they are contradictory and conflicting. Thus the distinctions that have been drawn between the different types of family structure are clearly and closely related to the child's personality growth; one does not have to accept *in toto* the psychoanalytic developments of the past generation to realize that many of the internal, and often quite hidden, conflicts of the individual derive from his relations with his several family groups.

First, the child comes to learn that there are differences in many things between the family of procreation and the family of orientation. What problems are created for children when the family of orientation differs from the family of procreation? The significance of the presence in the home of adults, usually relatives, on husband-wife relationships has received considerable attention. Far less attention has been given to what it means to children to be reared in homes where adults other than the parents live. Analyses of census data[12] show a considerable number of households in which "other adults" are living, dependent markedly upon the stage in the life cycle of the family. Such percentages, large as they are, show but the extent of such cases at the time of the census enumeration; they do not indicate how many children pass through this experience in the course of their formative years.

The coming of another adult into the family of procreation changes the structural form of the family in that it enlarges the series of continuing relationships which comprise it, as well as alters the whole form of the structure. Novelists and dramatists have shown repeatedly how the addition of one person to the family group changes the entire situation in the home. Most such representations, however, are confined, as in *Ethan Frome*,[13] to adult relations, but the same is equally true in the case of child relations.

Perhaps the basic fact about the presence of "other persons" in the home is that they are not acceptable equally to all members of the family of procreation. They may be acceptable to the child, or to the parents, or to one parent and the child, and so on, but not to the other or others. The presence of an adult relative, particularly if childless, invariably means the presence of an active competitor with the parent of the same sex as the relative for the child's affection. This competition may be overt or it may be subtle and insidious. Or the adult relative is not included in the rules or regime which the parent imposes upon the others in the family; hence this adult, no matter how circumspect his behavior may be, appears to the child as a challenge to the parent's authority, or as a refuge or comfort which the child may seek. A good many domestic situations might be summarized in the statement that the presence of a younger adult in the family means a potential competitor for the affection of the child; and the presence of an older person, a potential competitor for his control. The problem, of course, is often less simple than such a summary suggests. Adults who live with other families often tend to be problem adults. A parent's brother or sister who is not married, or who has been married but not successfully, or who cannot get along with other people, or who does not earn enough to support himself, or who is too sick or too feeble to live by himself—these constitute a good proportion of the adults who live with "their" families. Taking in a relative

---

[12] Paul C. Glick, *American Families*, John Wiley & Sons, Inc., New York, 1957, pp. 46, 80.

[13] Edith Wharton, *Ethan Frome*, Charles Scribner's Sons, New York, 1911.

is often the assumption of a burden and a problem. Parents may assume such an obligation with the philosophy of maturity or the resignation of despair, but to the child the newcomer is as he is, without the comfort of compensating philosophy.

There are, of course, cases in which the problems created for the child are obvious and serious. Here is a 9-year-old boy who is taught to practice sex relations with his 26-year-old aunt, who lives with the family. The boy alternates between a sense of guilt after each such episode and his fear of his aunt, with serious consequences for his school work and his personality. In other cases an uncle seduces his 14-year-old niece; a boarder practices masturbation with two young sons in the household; grandpa assumes the right to discipline the grandchildren, with whom he lives, as well as to set their parents "straight"; the friend of the mother subtly stirs up the children against their father. Such cases are all too frequent, especially in that area of family life which textbooks generally ignore.

The addition of adults to the family of procreation alters accordingly the age and sex structure of the child's immediate family. An example will serve to illustrate this point. In a family of procreation, with a father, a mother, a son, and a daughter, the age and sex structure is evenly balanced. There are two adults and two children, two males and two females. This family is now joined by two male adults. There are now four adults and two children, and three adult males to one adult female. In this case the whole form and structure of the family change; also involved is a shift in the center of gravity in the predominating subjects of conversation, play, activities, and all the other pursuits of the family.

The family of orientation at times includes boarders and lodgers who may share the family's life. In an earlier day, when the sociological literature was moralistic and reformist in tone, much was said as to how their presence imperiled the moral and social fabric of the home. In more recent years, despite the emphasis upon housing problems, there has been but little reference to their effect upon home life; despite our new insights into the processes of behavior formation, there has been only a slight analysis of their role in the formation of child personality. The following paragraph, taken from a life-history document, suggests interesting implications about the role of a lodger in a normal home. The writer is a 22-year-old boy; the family, a white-collar clerical one, living in a small eastern town. Although religious by profession, the family enjoyed occasional lapses from the standards of their religious group, the mother having a taste for a drink now and then, and the father enjoying a bawdy story. The story concerns Norman B., a lodger who lived with the father, mother, and son for about eight years, from the son's ninth to his seventeenth year.

I still distinctly remember that man. I distrusted and hated him then, and I do so now. When I ask myself why, I think it is because of what he did not say. He would always sit at home and seldom spoke unless spoken to. But you could feel what he thought, that he disapproved of what we were doing. He seemed so smug and self-righteous that even as a boy I felt that I wanted to hit him. Sometimes, if we had a particular bit of fun at home, he would get up silently, perhaps sigh, and prepare to leave. When father or mother asked if he was going out, he would answer in a quiet superior way, "I am going to church," or "I am going to prayer meeting." Soon I began to take a curious delight in being naughty just because I felt his eyes were on me. As I think back to my home life during those years, I keep on thinking about him and I am sure that the way he antagonized me stimulated me toward misbehavior more than anything else in my youth.

This reference to the lodger is incidental in the history from which this excerpt is taken, and for that reason is particularly suggestive of the role of a lodger in a normal family situation. A survey of the information available on the lodger and boarder problem indicates that many of the behavior developments are more serious, quite a few involving sex contacts between children and lodgers or boarders, usually between opposite sexes and often spanning unusual age differences. Parents at times close their eyes to such implications, unwilling no doubt to curtail the family income derived from these sources.

Another fact of significance for child development is the child's discovery of and experience with the conflicts between the immediate family and the larger kinship group.[14] There is considerable sniping among relatives in many families, as most everyone knows, and contact with children indicates that this is not lost upon the child. Often relatives visit a home and deliberately sabotage parent-child relationships. The mother's sister may dislike the children's father and make slyly derogatory remarks about him; the father's brother may cast slurs at the mother or her sister; another relative adroitly suggests that the father is cruel to the mother. In the case records of the William T. Carter Foundation is the following story related by Henry K.:

The family consists of a father, mother and child. The home was comfortable with two servants in constant attendance. The mother's brother, a not too industrious person, made extensive visits during his lengthy periods of unemployment. Another brother, newly married, brought his wife for lengthy visits. Henry remembers distinctly the impression he received from these relatives. His father, being away from home at work to maintain this establishment, was a recurring subject of conversation of these less occupied and economically strained relatives. Their attitude was that Henry's father was not friendly, that he was a hard and cruel man, that he was not cordial to a great many nice

[14] For a study of the relationship between the immediate family and the larger kinship group, consult James H. S. Bossard and Eleanor S. Boll, "The Immediate Family and the Kinship Group: A Research Report," *Social Forces,* May, 1946, pp. 379–384.

people, and that in all of these ways he somehow was doing a very mean thing to Henry's mother. Henry recalls how distinct this impression was, and how it bothered him, because to him his father was kind and generous. Henry reports that for several years he was greatly confused about his father.

A certain degree of conflict between the child's patrilinear and matrilinear kinship groups is inevitable, frequently it is serious, and on occasion it comes to the child's attention and has great meaning. The case of Richard K., taken from the files of the Carter Foundation, suggests the implications of such conflict for a normal boy in a normal home.

Richard K. remembers that his mind was in considerable turmoil as early as his fifth year because of the conflict in his mind between the two kinship groups of his parents. It bothered him a good deal until past his adolescent years. His father was a Brown, the oldest child in the Brown family. The Brown family was a compact group, with strong loyalties, positive convictions and quick tempers. It was semi-patriarchal in form. Each Sunday it gathered at the grandfather's house, where all matters of interest and importance to three generations of Browns were discussed. The Browns knew they were Browns, were proud of it, and made much of it. Before his fifth year, Richard was conscious of the Brown label on himself.

Somewhere around his fifth birthday, he spent a week during the summer vacation with his mother's aunt, an older woman who loved children and was said to have a way with them. From her he sensed that his father had done wrong to his mother (he learned that this was the fact that his father had a temper and spoke crossly to his mother at times), that this vague something was common to the Browns. Later the aunt told him that she hoped he was not like the Browns. Several days after that, the aunt looked at him fondly and said, "You really are a Smith (mother's family) instead of a Brown." Several days later, he returned to his home; he remembers it was as a somewhat heavy-hearted and even more preoccupied boy.

At Christmas time, the issue was revived. His mother, her brother, and he, with horse and sleigh, visited Grandfather Smith. He was a jolly, pipe-smoking, happy, placid old man. There was much happiness abounding in the Smith home. Richard particularly remembers a sleigh ride on a moonlight night, with the singing of old favorite songs. It was good to be with the Smiths, but the next week in school he remembered that he signed his name as Richard Brown.

A year or two seemed to pass, when the whole conflict was reopened when Mrs. Smith's brother died following an appendectomy. Richard cried bitterly, as he walked about the grounds surrounding his home. His quick-tempered father was irritated. "Stop your crying. Uncle Edwin is better off dead than alive. He was too lazy to work anyway." Later, in calmer vein, his father tried to explain that Uncle Edwin had never gotten very far, and that this was a reference to the easy-going, happy-go-lucky living of all of the Smiths.

Gradually, as he grew older, the basic conflict took this form—the Smiths are likable people. It is pleasant to be with them; I like to visit the Smith relatives; I always enjoy myself there; they do interesting things; I like the Smiths better than the Browns; I want to be a Smith; I am a Smith. But the Smiths haven't gotten very far in the world. And my name is Brown; people call me Brown; to all outside people, I am a Brown; I am my father's son; he dominates me; when I marry, my children will be Browns; the Browns have money, attractive homes, horses to ride; it has many advantages to be a Brown.

Finally, there are the conflicts and tensions among kinsfolk in the child's background, and the question of their meaning for subsequent mental conflicts, as emphasized in the psychoanalytic approach. This raises problems which require careful exploration. Mead suggests,[15] for example, that the true patriarchal family is much more troublesome in this respect than the American system of the immediate family.

In the true patriarchal family, where the child's attention is focused in upon his parents, where all his intense childish effort is directed towards becoming part of their relationship, the type Oedipus conflict is often intense and terrible. There a brother is either an ally against the father or else a surrogate for the father, and the child's deep repressed hatred of his father as a rival shapes any hatred of his brother as a rival—in an absolute sense—for his mother's love. But in the American family, the child's eyes are focused upon the outside world. He wins praise and approval as he displays that he "loves mother" not by loving her, but by eating his carrots and growing to be the tallest boy of his age on the block. He and his father are not measured against each other on the same scale for his mother's personal love—they aren't in the same class.

There is, too, the question of the extent to which the experiences of early childhood coincide with kinship ties. In the kinship group family, the child plays with relatives—cousins, nephews, nieces, etc. Even when visiting nonkinsfolk, the fiction is maintained; the children visited are called cousins and their parents are addressed as "Uncle John" and "Aunt Harriet." As a result, the emotional feelings connected with early child experiences come to be associated with kinship, thus possibly intensifying the conflicts and feelings of guilt which are involved. Childhood is a period of experimentation with life, with mingled emotional results; and it would seem of basic importance for mental analysis whether these experimental associations are with the children of your mother's sister or the unrelated children around the corner three blocks down the street.

Social Change and Family Structural Forms

Two changes in the structural form of the American family stand out clearly in recent decades. One is the growing emphasis upon the immediate family rather than the kinship group family; the other is the declining size of the immediate family. The latter development will be

[15] Margaret Mead, *And Keep Your Powder Dry*, William Morrow & Company, Inc., New York, 1943, p. 110.

given extended discussion subsequently in this volume; attention here is directed to the growing importance of the immediate family.

Students of the family will agree without hesitation that the role of the kinship group family has been declining in importance in our contemporary Western culture. Any short history of the family will make clear the contrast between the kinship family pattern of the Chinese, the patriarchal form of western Europe, the pre-twentieth-century American semipatriarchal form, and the metropolitan family of procreation of the present day. It will also be obvious from such a survey that anything like the current form would have been completely incomprehensible to our forebears through the long centuries of the past. One may illustrate the extremes of this historical development by contrasting the historic Chinese family, with its several generations living under one roof as a matter of course, of pride, and of religious devotion, and the American woman who asks for and receives a divorce because after her marriage her husband's relatives moved into their home and her husband refused to ask them to leave. "What in China," says Groves in commenting upon such a case, "would seem commonplace appears to the western reader an impossible matrimonial situation."[16]

The process of change to the predominance of the immediate family structure is still going on. This is particularly true among the more recent arrivals in America. The earlier immigrants came to this country often as large family groupings; later, individuals or parts of families predominated, but carried with them the tradition of this concept of the *Grossfamilie*. As a result, the first or immigrant generation frequently established in America the kinship group family; whereas the second generation, born in this country, accepting its different family tradition, and eager to exemplify it "without stain of foreign origin," has accepted the immediate type. This relatively sudden change involves elements of tragedy, with neither generation able to understand the point of view of the other. The depression decade of the nineteen thirties brought to the forefront many such family crises, with the adherents of the older order expecting to share the earnings of an employed kinsman, who, steeped in the American tradition, saw no reason or justice in such an expectation.

The causes of this changing predominance in the structure of the American family seem clear. In part, it is the result of the marked horizontal mobility of our population, often involving transfers over long distances. The average American kinship group tends to sprawl all over the continent. Earlier, American families scattered over great distances under the stimulus of economic opportunity; more recently, because of the facility of transportation. Vertical mobility has played an important

[16] Ernest R. Groves, *The Family and Its Social Functions*, J. B. Lippincott Company, Philadelphia, 1940, p. 19.

role, because with so large a proportion of the population raising its status, it was inevitable that the smaller units within the kinfold should progress at unequal rates, with a resultant avoidance each of the other. Another factor undoubtedly has been the concentration of the population in urban areas, with its apartment-house separate living and the inevitable curtailment of rooms to the barest requirements of the immediate family. Then, too, the establishment of social security systems means that the insurance features of the old kinship group system are no longer vital to the individual. Finally, the emergence of the immediate family unit as the dominant and often the only form of family structure recognized is only a phase of the large shift in our society from a primary to a secondary group basis.

Today an increasing number of children, particularly in our urban centers, know only, or mostly, their immediate families. What contacts they have with other kinsfolk are of a secondary rather than a primary nature. To have relatives live with one leads to comment in many urban circles today and calls forth condolences from one's intimate friends. It is considered in the light of an unnatural situation inevitably resulting in hardship, from which husband, wife, and child may be expected to hope secretly but fervently to be relieved at the earliest possible moment.

Although this may seem entirely natural to the present generation, it is well to emphasize that this is a distinctly new, and very recent, experiment in human history. Its development is limited largely to the present century, and is still characteristic largely of our urban culture. Moreover, it has been happening at a time when the immediate family has been decreasing in size. (The declining birth rate will be considered in a later chapter.) The fact pertinent here is that the decline in the birth rate has involved primarily the extension of the small-family system. All the data available today indicate that in recent decades there has been a steady and appreciable decrease in size, both in the family of procreation and in the family of orientation. The extent of the decrease varies considerably from one area to another, being smallest among farm and small-town populations and largest in the metropolitan centers. Such a decline in size throws into even bolder relief the growing emphasis upon the immediate family structure and its role in the processes of child development.

Significance of the Predominance of the Immediate Family

The increasing shift to the immediate family form involves a change in the size, nature, and complexity of the child's primary socializing group. Viewed as a socializing agency, the earlier kinship group family within which the child was largely reared was a good deal of a world within itself, with its own variety of personnel and its own framework of values, maxims, jokes, judgments, and attitudes. Mangione has given us a picture of this kinship group world in his description of life in a "little Sicily" in a contemporary American city. He writes: "There were seldom less than fifteen men, women and children at those Sunday sessions; on the Sundays when it rained, there would be as many as thirty. It was obvious that no one else in Mount Allegro had as many relatives as I did; it was also true that no one else's relatives seemed to seek one another's company as mine did. Sundays or weekdays, they were as gregarious as ants but had a far more pleasant time. There were always relatives and friends present or about to arrive. And when they finally left for the night, they occasionally came back for a surprise visit which they called a sirinati."[17]

Into this world the child was thrust and to it his earlier adjustments were made, no matter how uncongenial these contacts and requirements were. Years ago, Chesterton, the English essayist, in writing of the family, said: "Of course the family is a good institution because it is uncongenial. It is wholesome precisely because it contains so many divergencies and varieties. It is, as the sentimentalists say, like a little kingdom, and, like most other little kingdoms, is generally in a state of something resembling anarchy. It is exactly because our Uncle Henry does not approve of the theatrical ambitions of our sister Sarah that the family is like humanity. The men and women who, for good reasons and bad, revolt against the family, are, for good reasons and bad, simply revolting against mankind."

In the smaller, immediate family of today, and against the background of other social changes, the child's early contacts, being less dictated by the kinship circle, permit a greater degree of selection. Very early, the child moves with his clique rather than with his clan. This brings with it elements of selection, of freedom, and of more enriching experience. It results, too, in the greater importance at an early age of other groups, like the play, nursery, and kindergarten school groups.

There can be no doubt that family relations in general and parent-child relations in particular are intensified in the immediate family. A number of years ago, W. I. Thomas pointed out that with the dissolution of the larger kinship group the small family "has become introverted, and turned upon itself, and has taken a pathological trend in the direction of demanding and conferring response."[18] More recently, Margaret Mead, in her stimulating interpretation of our changing American culture,[19] refers to the intensification of relationship that follows from the limitation in the number of family personnel. Many a contemporary child having only a parent or parents as anchors in a world that is other-

[17] Jerre Mangione, *Mount Allegro*, Houghton Mifflin Company, Boston, 1942, p. 22.
[18] W. F. Dummer, *The Unconscious*, Alfred A. Knopf, New York, 1927, p. 157.
[19] Mead, *op. cit.*, pp. 83 ff.

wise vague and shifting, naturally places great emphasis upon these ties. The results of this vary from the enrichment of parent-child relationships on the one hand, to a pathological inversion on the other.

This relatively exclusive dependence upon the immediate family means that the quality and continuance of these family relationships become correspondingly vital to the child, as well as to all the members of the family. If the immediate family ceases to function, the child's family anchorage is gone. We recall here how frequently siblings in present-day homes are admonished to get along with each other because "you are all that each has got."

The passing of the kinship group family and its scattering over a continent means that many children have no relative to turn to when the immediate family passes or fails to function. The child passes to the care of strangers and comes to be considered, as such children do in our contemporary society, as being a bit peculiar because he "has no family." What makes all this of such great importance is that along with it has developed the increasing breakup of immediate families through desertion, separation, and divorce. One of the peculiar tragedies of the child of today is, then, that there is a greater reliance upon the immediate family at the very time when it is increasingly breaking up under the impact of modern life.

The immediate family makes for much greater positiveness, and possibly promptness, in family control and direction of the child. This is true chiefly because there are fewer persons to consult and fewer points of view to reconcile. Particularly is this manifest in the case of important family issues. Shall Mary stop school and help her mother? Shall Jim go through college? Shall Elinor go to business college?

The younger generation of today, in its immediate family life, will find it difficult to appreciate how complicated such problems are in a kinship group family system, where so many more persons have to be consulted, family precedents have to be considered, and family jealousies have to be avoided. Current decisions by the immediate family tend not only to be more prompt but may also be more intelligent. The situation in regard to the child's discipline is similar. The child in the larger family group was often insulated by four or five layers of kinsfolk before contact with an irate parent was established; on the other hand, the erring child, provided his conduct was considered sufficiently reprehensible, might be chastised four or five deep. Most often, however, these intermediaries would disagree or conflict, rather than reinforce each other. All of this naturally made for confusion, inconsistency, and that lack of promptness which is the essence of effective discipline. Decision is a virtue, even if the decision is bad; and the decisiveness in child rearing and development made possible by the immediate family is a fundamental even if not spectacular factor in the background of the contemporary child.

In many ways the most significant result of the dominance of the immediate family is that it results in a constant measurement and comparison of the child, his traits, his problems, and his development with children in other nonrelated families, also immediate in structure, rather than with the children in his own kinship group. The contemporary immediate family has become standardized; it compares itself with other standardized families as they appear in magazine advertisements, on the radio, on the screen, and as sensed in social contacts. This constant tendency to take a sidewise view of life has a number of significant results. First, there is a great deal of emphasis upon conformity. The parent wants the child's home, clothing, toys, activities, etc., to be like and at least as good as those of "other children." The ancient legend of the doll that grew a soul and became a human being after having been the play friend of a dozen generations in the same nursery gives way to the contemporary parent's fear that his child's toys do not conform to those in the latest issue of *Life*. "From the day when self-conscious fathers stand outside the glass-walled hospital nursery and anxiously compare the shape of their own babies' heads with those of the other babies, the child is valued in comparative terms, not because he is of the blood and bone and 'name' of his parents, but because of his place on some objective (but undefined) rating scale of looks and potential abilities."[20] This constant comparison, not with his own kinsfolk but with "other people's children," creates in turn a tremendous drive toward achievement. From the beginning of his life, the child senses that his place, even in his own family, depends on his achievement and on how he compares with other children. At the same time, he is learning that this is true of his family. On these two levels, child and adult, operates the American pressure to get ahead, by way of both material achievement and social status. In short, the immediate family system paves the way for our accepted pattern of upward vertical mobility.

It is the consensus that many Americans suffer from a sense of insecurity, and there can be little doubt that this is in part a heritage of the immediate family form. The very size of the family unit is important to the child in this respect for the same reason that the size of the ledge from which we view the precipice below affects our sense of security. The American child who lives and matures in a father-mother-child family unit stands on a very narrow family platform, even if it is in no way imperiled. To this is added the constant danger for the child that the few persons he must rely on may falter or fail. Reinforcing these implications of a small family unit is the fact that as the contemporary child grows older his life diverges from that of his parents—a common and inevitable fact because the child does not follow the occupation or status of the parents. Moreover, such a condition is particularly pronounced and

[20] *Ibid.*, p. 88.

serious in the large number of immigrant homes where the child is educated beyond anything his parents can comprehend, and where he must
early adjust to sailing an uncharted sea, so far as they are concerned. In
these cases, the immediate family does not understand the activities and
achievements of the child, nor can the parents offer him any guidance
or stability or security. The situation makes for insecurity for both parent
and child.

Summary

1. A family situation may be defined as a unit of stimuli operating
within the confines of the family circle, and organized in relation to the
person or object which serves as the focal point in the particular case.

2. Family situations should be studied with all possible scientific objectivity, first, because of their great importance in determining personality patterns; and, second, because they offer the best opportunities
for the development of scientific techniques in the situational approach
to behavior problems.

3. The family may be viewed as a structure. Thus considered, and
from the standpoint of the child, one can distinguish between the immediate family, comprising the household family unit, and the kinship
group family, including relatives up to a variable degree of relationship.
The immediate family may be the family of procreation or the family
of orientation.

4. The difference between these two subtypes has great significance
in child development. The coming of another adult into the home alters
the whole form of the family structure and creates many problems for
the child.

5. The immediate family has come to be the characteristic American
type, although the process of its ascendancy is still going on. This is a
new development and experiment in child history.

6. The predominance of the immediate family form instead of the kinship group type has great importance for the child. It means that his
primary socializing group is smaller and less complex. Greater selection
of child contacts is possible. Parent-child relationships are intensified,
but the child's family anchorage is more limited. There is apt to be
greater promptness and positiveness in child rearing. The child is compared chiefly with other people's children rather than with those of his
kinsfolk. There results a passion for conformity and a tremendous drive
toward achievement. The child's feeling of insecurity may be heightened.
The "adoption fantasy" becomes more pronounced.

7. Many conflicts in the child's mental life can be understood if viewed
against the background of the tensions and conflicts in the family structure.

Chapter 3

Families by Size

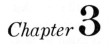

The importance of the size of an interacting group has long been recognized in a general sort of way. A large industrial plant, one is told, presents problems of labor relations different from a smaller one. Small classes, as every pedagogue knows, permit teaching methods that are not feasible with larger ones. There is an optimum size for discussion groups. Small memberships in college fraternities result in fraternal relations not customarily found in larger chapters. Military leaders have given much thought to the most effective size of operating unit. The British House of Commons meets in a room kept small deliberately, in order to permit a higher quality of public debate than would prevail in a larger chamber. The size of the group *is* important.

Recently, the study of small groups has received a great deal of attention in the sciences concerned with human behavior. Particularly has the output of published articles increased since 1945, and even more so since 1950. Claims for the practical values of studies in this field include the military, hospital, prison, food use, alcoholic consumption, and many other areas.[1] It seems wholly in order to think of the family as a group, differing in size, and with resulting consequences for child rearing. The present chapter is a tentative step in this direction. Since research in this direction has been rather limited, what is herein presented must be viewed chiefly as hypotheses for further study.

The Small-Family System

The phrase "small-family system" was made a part of the sociological literature with the appearance in 1913 of a small book by that title, writ-

---

[1] Cf. the December, 1954, issue of the *American Sociological Review* for a collection of suggestive and useful articles on small groups, as well as for an extensive bibliography.

ten by C. V. Drysdale.[2] It was used originally to identify families with some degree of contraceptive sophistication who were utilizing their knowledge to limit the number of offspring, and students of population still emphasize mainly the characteristic of size, and its relation to problems of the birth rate and population change. Subsequent studies of family life, however, have shown that size is correlated with various other phases of family behavior, until now the term has come to mean a way of family living with definite characteristics, practices, and values.

In this chapter, the term *small family* is used to mean any family with three or less children, and data on fertility and family size show these to be the most common types of American families. A special report of the United States Census Bureau shows that, of all women who, in 1940, were between 45 and 49 years of age, and who reported the total number of children ever born, one out of six (16.7 percent) had borne but one child; one out of five (20.0 percent) had borne two children; and one out of six (15.3 percent) had borne three. More than half (52 percent) of all women reporting had borne three or less children.[3]

A summary by Glick of census data on number of families and percentage distribution of families by size shows that in April, 1953, 56.9 percent of all families consisted of three, four, or five members. Comparing changes in recent years, Glick writes: "The mean size of family tended to stabilize at about 3.5 persons between 1950 and 1953."[4] Utilizing the census data on number of families and percent distribution by number of members under 18 years of age, one finds that in April, 1953, 42.9 percent of families had no member under 18, and 49.6 per cent had one, two, or three members under 18.[5] Finally, recourse to the 1950 census report on fertility shows that of women ever married, 40 to 44 years of age, 46.5 percent reported one or two children ever born, with 14.1 percent reporting three children. For the age group 45 to 49 years, 41.7 percent had one or two children, and 13.8 percent reported three children; for women 50 to 54, the percentages were 38.9 and 14.3, respectively.[6]

Selected Features of the Small-Family System

Many of the characteristics of the small-family system are matters of general agreement. First is its overall theme. The term "theme" is used here in the sense of a dominant affirmation (or attitude value) which

[2] C. V. Drysdale, *The Small Family System*, B. W. Huebsch, New York, 1913.
[3] U.S. Bureau of the Census, *Differential Fertility, 1940 and 1910*, Special Report of the 1940 Census, Tables 1–4 and 15–18.
[4] Paul C. Glick, *American Families*, John Wiley & Sons, Inc., New York, 1957, p. 31.
[5] *Ibid.*, p. 37.
[6] U.S. Census, 1950, *Special Report on Fertility*, p. 5C–182.

tends to control behavior or stimulate activity in a society.[7] In the small-family system, the overall theme is planning. Planning is the substance of its procedure and its thinking—planning of size; of the spacing and timing of the birth of the children; of the emphases and programs to be followed in child rearing; of the main objectives in education, with careful attention to its status-achieving and promoting possibilities; and of preparation for subsequent careers. From this point of view, the family is a consciously controlled and directed experiment in living, performed by man, rather than an experiment performed by nature on man, as is the case in more passive and fatalistic cultures.

Second is the fact that parenthood in the small family is intensive rather than extensive. This emphasis begins at the onset of pregnancy, as the mother receives continuing prenatal care. After the child is born, the pediatrician is consulted on matters of diet, immunization, as well as the slightest sickness. Later on, the "child psychologist" may be consulted on the "everyday problems of the everyday child." Should Junior show symptoms of deviant behavior, the psychiatrist is called in. All this marshaling of scientific aids is utilized so that each pregnancy may eventuate in a normal child, that every possible child shall survive and develop to the utmost of his capacities. Such a history of intensive care is today the common lot of the child in the small family, in marked contrast to another and an older system of extensive parenthood in which many children were sired in the hope that some would survive.

Another characteristic has to do with the type of interaction that prevails within the small family. Recent studies have shown that size determinant is an integral part in group interaction.[8] In a small group, according to Bales and others, for example, if the participants "are ranked by the total number of acts they initiate, they will also tend to be ranked by the number of acts they receive."[9] These and other more abstract and generalized studies give full warrant to the idea that the small family tends to make for a coöperative and democratic type of relationship. Each member, and especially the child, can receive a good deal of attention and consideration. Each is given a voice in group discussions, or at

[7] Morris Edward Opler, "Themes as Dynamic Forces in Culture," *American Journal of Sociology*, November, 1945, p. 198.

[8] Robert F. Bales, *Interaction Process Analysis: A Method for the Study of Small Groups*, Addison-Wesley Press, Cambridge, Mass., 1950, and "A Set of Categories for the Analysis of Small Group Interaction," *American Sociological Review*, April, 1950, pp. 257–263; Robert F. Bales, and others, "Channels of Communication in Small Groups," *ibid.*, August, 1951, pp. 461–468; John James, "A Preliminary Study of the Size Determinant in Small Group Interaction," *ibid.*, August, 1951, pp. 474–477; A. Paul Hare, *A Study of Interaction and Consensus in Different Sized Groups*, University of Chicago dissertation, 1951; William M. Kephart, "A Quantitative Analysis of Intragroup Relationships," *American Journal of Sociology*, May, 1950, pp. 544–549.

[9] Bales, and others, *op. cit.*, p. 468.

least has the opportunity to be heard. It may be more than a coincidence that the democratic and the small family have appeared together in point of time. Furthermore, family planning, motivated so largely by hopes for the future of its child members, naturally emphasizes the importance of coöperative relationships between parent and child. The child is the hope of the family plan. The essence of good parent-child relationships is to have the child coöperate voluntarily rather than be high-pressured into the family program. Here is another reason for small-family parents to take recourse to books and courses on child psychology, the better to understand children and to promote such coöperation.

Coupled with this greater freedom and democracy of expression in the small family is the individualizing of the activities and roles of its members. Small-family living makes for individual emphasis, in development and in thinking. The family members are noncompeting: father, mother, and child each goes his own respective way.

This lack of competition within the family turns its "green" eyes outward, accounting for what Margaret Mead[10] has called the sidewise look by the parents, meaning that they compare and measure their children primarily with children in other families in the same residential area, the same social class or clique, or the same school. This reinforces the pressure by the parents on the child, already inherent in the planning procedure which underlies small family living.

This sidewise look applies characteristically to kinsfolk and certain other close associates. Relatively little attention is given to kinsfolk unless they fit into, and can contribute to, the planned goals of the small family. A study made of the attitudes toward kinsfolk of 68 university students revealed that much importance was attached by them to the fact that relatives live at different economic and social levels.[11] This attitude on the part of the students obviously is a reflection of that of the parents.

The planning emphasis in the small family; the sidewise view which characterizes its thinking, particularly in regard to its child members; the relative lack of contacts with kinsfolk: all combine to lead the small family to make an appraising selection of homesites and residential areas, on the basis of their contribution to family plans. School facilities, recreational opportunities, social contacts, are three of the important considerations which underlie these selections. To a very large extent the contemporary suburb, with its standardization of some specialized pattern of living, is the product of these selections. Small families tend to group themselves on the basis of their family plans and ambitions.

The small-family system is essentially a quality system. It prevails pri-

---

[10] Margaret Mead, *And Keep Your Powder Dry*, William Morrow & Company, Inc., New York, 1943, p. 109.

[11] James H. S. Bossard and Eleanor S. Boll, "The Immediate Family and the Kinship Group," *Social Forces*, May, 1946, p. 383.

marily at the middle- and upper-class levels. Its driving force is one of ambition, in an open-class system, in which a large proportion of the population aims at raising the status or pretends to have a status higher than is actually attained. Small families invariably are under stress, stress to achieve and to get ahead. This stress or pressure falls with particular heaviness upon the children, who are the potentials of the family's status-raising program. Most children in small families grow up under the shadow, so to speak, of the family level of expectation. Because the parents do so much for the children, they expect a great deal from them in turn. Children are pushed to the utmost, often without regard for their capacities, limitations, interests, or needs. Because of the small number of children, the parents allow no margin of error or failure, as tends to be the case in the larger family.

An added factor here is that the parents tend to impose not only their own ambitions, but also their unfulfilled desires, upon their children. The man with a lifelong but unfulfilled wish to be a doctor drives his son toward the medical profession, willy-nilly; the mother who never rated socially when a girl now grooms her daughter for a social career, regardless of the latter's abilities or interests. The drive of these unfulfilled desires of the parents, and how they may complicate the lives of their children, are particularly obvious to educators at the college and university level.

Significance for Child Development

The literature on child development in the small family tends to fall into two main parts. The first part deals specifically with the problems of the only child; the other, with the more general results of the small-family system. Since the only child is dealt with in Chapter 5, attention is confined here to a summary of the more general results.

1. There is no doubt that children in small families enjoy advantages beyond those available to children in large families at corresponding economic and social levels. Furthermore, they receive more individual attention from their parents. With fewer to consider, their value seems greater; their health and safety and security seem more important. These general considerations, when translated into specific opportunities and services, comprise many of the factors that are important in child development, and, to the contemporary parent, they outweigh other considerations, as the birth statistics of Western culture clearly show. Mature reflection and long-continued study of the small-family system suggest, however, additional problems which must be considered.

2. The small-family child's earliest social experiences (that is, with other persons) is in a small group. This is an obvious fact, but its implications would seem to be of very great importance. These implications grow out of the size and composition of the small family group as compared

with the characteristics of most other groups in which one lives and works. A small family consists ordinarily of two or more adults, and from one to three children. Life within this group tends to be organized so that the child or children occupy the center of the stage. Their efforts tend to be eased and encouraged by adults. They enjoy "protected" competition. Much is done for them by their parents. Parents often have to double as parents, as playmates, and as friends. On the basis of these early experiences, the child forms his conception of himself, his role, and his importance in the group. He grows up in a world that largely revolves around him, and he thinks of himself accordingly.

A somewhat exaggerated illustration of the point in mind is found in the following excerpt from a life-history document in the files of the William T. Carter Foundation:

I grew up as an only child. In our house lived my father, my mother, two uncles, and two servants. Until I was 12 years old, this was our household. A great many other adults came and went, as visitors or in some other capacity. Always, I was the center of attraction, and the main recipient of attention. This was the situation in which my habit patterns developed, habits which created so many problems for me as I grew older, for, unless I could always be the center of attention in a group, I would either sulk, behave conspicuously, or withdraw from the group.

Compare situations of this kind with those which obtain today in group life outside of the family. Let us begin with his school groups. Whereas most children in earlier years in the history of this country grew up in a large family and then entered a small school, today an increasing number of children leave a small family to enter a large and complex school situation; where once he went to school through quiet lanes and streets in company with other siblings in his family, today he may go alone through a maze of heartless and hectic traffic. Warren S., for example, is 12 years old. He has a sister aged 6. To reach his school, he walks a mile and a half, crossing three heavily traveled lanes of traffic, only one of which has police supervision. When he arrives at school, he is one of 918 in his class. He is in Section 37 in English. His mother cannot understand why he cries and asks not to go to school.

Or consider the industrial situation which the small-family child enters today. The chances mathematically are that he goes to work in a large plant or office building, along with thousands, or even hundreds of thousands, of other persons. He is a single cog in a huge machine, a role diametrically the opposite of that he enjoyed in the small family.

Another type of situation which a large proportion of young men, and an increasing proportion of young women, are compelled to enter, is service in the armed forces. Stouffer and others have called attention to the problems of adjustment of American youth during World War II. In

5 years, from 1940 to 1945, the American army grew from 16,624 officers and 249,411 enlisted men to 772,863 officers and 7,305,854 enlisted men. Army life involved a totally new way of life for most of these people, with its authoritarian organization, its demand upon rigid obedience, its highly stratified social system, and its emphasis upon traditional ways of doing.[12] Small wonder that one out of five came to be rejected for psychiatric reasons.[13]

It is not meant to imply that the small-family child always finds himself a problem at school, in industry, or in military service. What is being emphasized here is the disparity between the small-family life situation and those which most young people enter today as they leave home; as well as between the individualized dominating role they enjoy in a small-family setting, and that which most of them are destined to play at school, at work, and in the armed forces. There seems to be, then, this curious paradox about the small-family system, that, while it represents an adjustment to the high expectancies and ambitions of modern living, it is a correspondingly inadequate training ground for performance in the realities of its everyday work. In short, people have small families in answer to the demands of modern life, but small families provide a poor kind of training to meet its requirements. To the extent that this is so, one finds here an illustration of how some civilizations tend to be self-destructive.

3. One of the most important features of child development in the small family is the undue pressure upon the child or children. Everything that has been said about the small-family characteristics underscores the high level of expectation of the parents. Most every parent is ambitious for his children: the small-family parent is so to an exaggerated degree, both because there are so few children on which he can focus his ambitions, and also because the whole family life is organized around the children's future development. Because these expectations and pressures often disregard the actual capacities, interests, and limitations of the children, they are the source of many serious strains and corresponding problems. Ambitious parents may complicate the lives of their children, too, and it is no secret that they often do.

There are many concrete aspects around which these family pressures cluster. Some of them center around the interest in family continuity, with undue solicitousness over the health or marriage of a child. Perhaps the mother has refused to bear more than one child, she may have aborted one, she may have tried to avoid having the child but failed; all these and other circumstances may create feelings of guilt, of undue

[12] Samuel A. Stouffer, and others, *The American Soldier,* Princeton University Press, Princeton, 1949, Vol. I, p. 54.

[13] Edward A. Strecker, *Their Mothers' Sons,* J. B. Lippincott Company, Philadelphia, 1946.

anxiety, of abnormal apprehensions. The result invariably is an unhealthy and unnatural concern with and for the child. Not all interest in family continuity is conditioned by circumstances of this kind; obviously, much of it is a wholly normal concern, focusing heavily upon children in small families only because there are so few of them.

Or consider families in which there is an established business, or where the family history shows a succession of generations represented in the same profession or social position. Here is a family which has held an honored position for several generations in the law, or medicine, or the armed forces, or social circles. Naturally parents and grandparents who achieved such positions want their descendants at least to maintain such status, if not to raise it. Pressures of this kind often come, not only from members of the immediate family, but also from the larger kinship circle. When the child's capacities and interests coincide with those of his family, there is only the tension of intense pressure; it is when they do not, when the child either cannot or is not interested in functioning at the level of family expectancy, that more serious problems are created. The late William A. Percy wrote with great poignancy of such a situation in his own case, pointing out his father's (onetime United States Senator from Mississippi) disappointment in a son whose interests ran in a different direction.[14]

4. The size of the small family creates, or intensifies, a number of emotional problems, four of which will be summarized briefly. There is, to begin with, a high degree of emotional concentration in the contemporary small family, owing not only to the limited number of members, but also because the immediate family has become so largely the sole important kinship unit. So far as the children are concerned, this means that the love and solicitude of the parents are centered on very few persons: in the case of the only child, on but one person. In any particular family, the intensity of such concentration depends upon the emotional output of the parents and the number of the children.

This accentuation of the problem of relations of members to each other in small-family groups is particularly apt to lead to difficulties if the size of the group is three (the one-child family), for it raises inevitably a two-against-one issue. Most often this means that one parent and the child combine against the other parent. Especially do such situations obtain when one parent is antagonistic to another.

The Vernons have been married for 19 years. Mrs. V. frankly states that she never has loved her husband. They have one child, a son of eleven, whose birth was the result of an unwanted pregnancy by the mother. During the son's entire life, the mother has clung closely to him, and has cultivated, subtly to be sure, a latent antagonism in the boy toward his father.

[14] William Alexander Percy, *Lanterns on the Levee*, Alfred A. Knopf, New York, 1941.

In other instances, a husband shows signs of jealousy of a child, and visits his displeasure upon both mother and child, with a resultant common resentment against him. In still other cases, the husband and child may compete with each other for the attentions of the mother. Such was the case in the Laird family:

Mr. Laird married a woman three years older than himself, after having been much "spoiled" by his mother. When their one child was born, and the mother gave normal attention to the child, the husband became petulant and resentful. Soon he began to increase his demands upon the mother, as though vying with the baby for attention. As the child grew older, and began to sense the pattern of behavior of the demanding father, she, too, became more and more demanding. As a result, by the time the child was 13, the mother's health was impaired by the increasing demands of the father and daughter competitors. Mrs. Laird was a highly conscientious and motherly person, who sought to be both a good mother and a dutiful wife.

Again, there is the frequency with which competition develops for the affection of the children in small families. This competition ordinarily is of two kinds: one where the parents compete with each other; second, where other kinsfolk are involved. Both kinds of such rivalries may grow out of personality clashes in the child's family background, but they are most apt to be pronounced and serious when cultural differences obtain, such as religious, class, economic, or national group differences. In cases of this kind, the child becomes a pawn in a game between conflicting cultural groups, with his affection, loyalty, or possession the symbol of victory or defeat.

The emotional problem in the small family probably most emphasized in the literature is that of the child's social weaning. By "social weaning" we mean here the readjustment of parent-child relationships in keeping with the child's growing maturity. This is a part of the normal process of growing up, and occurs usually between the twelfth and the twentieth year. While it presents some difficulties for both child and parent, in the large family any reluctance that parents may have to seeing their child grow up and away from them is limited because of the ease with which parents can transfer their possessive feelings to the younger children. In the small family, such transfer is more difficult or impossible, so that the process of weaning often is delayed, if not prevented entirely.

Finally, there is the relation of the small-family system to the discipline of the children. The emotional implications here are of very great importance. In small families, the overwhelming proportion of the disciplining must be done by the parents. If the child needs a lot of disciplining, or the parents are unusually dominating, or both, an undue amount of disciplining of one child is done by one or both parents. The result is a concentration of deeply conflicting emotions: of deep devotion and love by parents who do so much for their children, and of marked resentment by children against extensive disciplining. This antithesis in the child's intimate background may well be the source of many of the deep-seated conflicts that characterize the current generation. It is in these respects in particular that the small family stands in such striking contrast to the large family system where the children largely discipline each other.

5. People are prone to identify themselves with the groups to which they belong. Size of group is an obvious group characteristic, and it means a great deal to its individual members. Students in a large university, members of a large fraternity, soldiers in a large army, and citizens of a large country, tend to consider themselves important because they are a part of a large organization. Conversely, members of a small group, particularly of so meaningful a group as the family, may feel, even if not wholly at the level of consciousness, a certain insignificance. This is perhaps the larger background of those feelings of loneliness and insecurity which are generally attributed to the small-family child. He is a chronic victim of loneliness, of intimate contact with peers at odd moments when one can "take down one's hair." This lack of intimate contacts with peers is, in turn, a part of a larger isolation. Gruenberg has written of this:

> In the small city family, the child grows up in relative isolation. He may perhaps see many people of all sizes and ages. And under present crowded conditions, the household may include various relatives or a grandparent. But the child has direct and vital dealings with very few persons.[15]

Perhaps the basic act here is that the child in the small family views the world from a very narrow ledge. His insecurity grows out of the smallness of his group, the limited group of dependable peer supporters, the lack of feelings of nearness to kinsfolk, and the uncertain durability of his immediate family. There is nothing perplexing about the widespread prevalence of people with feelings of inferiority and insecurity. Many of them are small-family people, reared in relative isolation: lonely folk, almost faceless and nameless, in the lonely crowd.[16]

The complement to this relative isolation from peers is the fact that small-family children spend so much of their earlier years in the company of adults. Adults play with them, walk with them, study with them, educate them, and discipline them. They see much of life through adult eyes; they sense the nature of adult pressures and tensions; they adjust to adult demands. And the adjustments made by children to adults differ from those made to other children. The literature on the oldest child has revealed this: how the child assumes the tolerance of elders yet thinks of them as aliens; how the element of power comes to be emphasized unduly; how it means association with persons who are preoccupied with

---

[15] Sidonie Matsner Gruenberg, "Changing Conceptions of the Family," *Annals of the American Academy of Political and Social Science*, May, 1947, p. 130.

[16] David Riesman, *The Lonely Crowd*, Yale University Press, New Haven, 1950.

other problems, and who will agree to patterns of behavior which relieve them of attention and responsibility.

6. A final point, often overlooked, is that the impact of crises often varies in seriousness with the number of persons who can share them. "Misery loves company" is not only a trite old saying but also points toward a valid sociological principle. The shadow which divorce casts over the lives of children in our contemporary culture has received considerable emphasis; rather less emphasis has been given to the impact of other family crises, particularly if there are but one or two children. Nine-year-old Beatrice summarized the situation rather aptly in the following conversation with her mother:

BEATRICE: Mother, can we adopt another little girl?
MOTHER: I don't know, but I doubt it.
BEATRICE: I wish we had another girl living with us.
MOTHER: Why?
BEATRICE: Well, if there was another little girl, it wouldn't be so bad when father and you go yackety-yack all the time. If there was another little girl, we could comfort each other when daddy and you do that.

In the small-family system, experiences tend to be shared with so few people. The child in the small family has so few people, particularly peers, to talk over his problems and to help him over a psychological hurdle. The important fact about so many life experiences is that they need to be shared, if their true meaning is to be assessed. This is as true of joys as of sorrows; of achievements as well as of failures; of triumphs as well as of disappointments. It is at this point that one wonders to what extent the size of the group helps to determine whether one becomes an extrovert or an introvert, whether one finds life's truest meanings in contacts with other people, or whether one is driven within one's self for these satisfactions. Obviously, other factors are important in the development of these contrasting types; our question here is one of the identification of a contributing cause.

The Large-Family System

The large family as such has received very little attention from students of family life and child development. One need not search far for some of the reasons for this. Most families are small in size, and the trend for many years has been in this general direction. Moreover, current thinking about child and personality has been so family-minded that it has counted its tasks in terms of families rather than of children: this in spite of the obvious fact that a family with 12 children is 12 times as important statistically as the family with one child—if one thinks in terms of children.

An examination of United States census reports reveals data which underscore the importance of the large family in the study of child development. First, taking a sidewise view, a total of 1,147,937 or 3.1 percent of all primary families in the United States in 1950 consisted of eight or more persons.[17] Next, a more lengthwise view reveals that in 1950, of 11,176,350 women ever married, 45 to 59 years of age, 8.6 percent had 7 or more children.[18] Allowing an average of 8 children for these mothers who had 7 or more children, it would appear that 2 out of 5 of all children ever born to women, 45 to 59 years of age, were born in families of 7 or more children. Finally, there are the federal reports on the number of live births by birth order which show that, for the year 1950, close to 8 percent of all live births were the sixth or higher child in birth order.[19] On the basis of the foregoing data, it seems reasonable to conclude that the large family is of considerable importance, as a type of family situation, in the rearing of American children.

A pioneer study of large-family life and of selected child-rearing practices has been made by the authors of this volume. It included 100 families, unselected save for one stipulation: at least six children must have been born to the parents. A total of 879 children were ever born in these families. In 60 of the families, both parents were native-born whites of native-born parentage; another 17 reported both parents as native-born white of foreign or mixed parentage; in 10 families, both parents were foreign born; 8 were Negro families; and in 5 cases, one parent was foreign born and the other was native born. By religious preference, 63 were Protestant; 26 were Roman Catholic; three were mixed, with Roman Catholic fathers and Protestant mothers; and 8 were Jewish. A wide variety of occupations was represented, but middle- and upper-class levels predominated. Most of the families were small city, town, village, or farm families, although 24 big city cases were included. One-half of the families came from Pennsylvania and New York, but 21 additional states were included. Information was obtained chiefly from the children who grew up in these families. Questionnaires, life-history documents, and repeated interviews were utilized.[20]

As a pioneer study, the chief efforts were directed toward the exploration of new grounds and the opening of new vistas, which could be used subsequently in the formulation of hypotheses for more comprehensive

[17] U.S. Census of Population, *General Characteristics of Families, 1950,* p. 2A–10.
[18] U.S. Census, 1950, *Special Report on Fertility,* pp. 5C–17, 18.
[19] National Office of Vital Statistics, *Births by Age of Mother, Race, and Birth Order,* 1950.
[20] For the completed study, see James H. S. Bossard and Eleanor S. Boll, *The Large Family System,* University of Pennsylvania Press, Philadelphia, 1956. For a contrast between large and small families, see also James H. S. Bossard, "Large and Small Families—A Study in Contrasts," *The Journal of the American Society of Chartered Life Underwriters,* Summer, 1959, pp. 221–241.

and specific research projects. Some of the tentative conclusions of this study are presented then as selected hypotheses.

1. There is a large-family, just as there is a small-family, system. This is to be interpreted to mean that large-family living is for its child members a way of life, a series of practices, a pattern of attitudes, procedures, and values that are characteristic of and peculiar to families of larger size. These characteristics of the large-family system are in many ways the direct opposite of those of the small family, as will be seen in the summary which follows.

2. The large family is not as a rule a planned family in the sense that that term is used in the current literature. True, there are large families that are planned for size, but the plan is general rather than specific. There are other families that are large by consent, usually because moral, religious, or other beliefs forbid interference with "the processes of nature." There are families that are large for other reasons, but the large family as a type is not a planned family in the sense that a specific number of children are scheduled, to be born at the time and intervals that the parents desire.

3. Parenthood in the large family tends to be extensive rather than intensive. This does not mean that parents of large families love their children any less or are less concerned with their welfare and development. It simply means that, under sheer weight of numbers, there is often not the concentrated care of the large-family child, nor the solicitous anxiety over him, nor the officious oversight, nor the pervasive possessiveness, that are the more common lot of the small-family child. Large-family children are left on their own, to care for themselves, to meet life's little problems, both earlier and to a greater extent: there just isn't enough parent to reach around and leave as large a piece of parent for each child as is possible in the small family.

4. Large-family living makes for an early acceptance of the realities of life. To put it another way, being reared in a large family makes for an early and a continuing adjustment to the changing vicissitudes of a realistic world. Things are always happening in a large family, its members live in an ever-changing milieu, minor crises are constantly arising. Moreover, they are shared in by so many more people. The large-family member learns therefore to take minor disturbances in stride: it is almost as if one developed an immunity against them.

Furthermore, the large family is peculiarly vulnerable to major crises, especially when the children are young. Such vulnerability grows not out of the prevalence of divorce or separation, as is the case in the small-family system, but out of other developments. One of these is drunkenness, which was prevalent in our families and which, as always, has serious repercussions for the children. Drinking fathers tend to be harsh and cruel parents. Death of one parent or both parents is the most serious hazard: almost a third of the families were thus afflicted during the years when as many as four of the children were under 14 years of age.

Major crises of this kind are serious for any family; they are particularly so for large families, many of which have previously been under economic pressure. These crises have to be met, through the sacrifices of the older children often, and through the "sticking together" of all of the family. The latter is the most common device in the large family for weathering family crises.

5. Inherent in every fact and impression that one gets from the study of the large family is its emphasis upon the group rather than the individual. This group emphasis expresses itself in a number of ways. First, from childhood on, children in large families play together, and their play is confined as a rule to the family group. Second, and almost from the start, the children work together. There are a great many things that need to be done. Each has his or her allotted task, and one must stay in line. You work as a member of a team or group. Third, problems must be solved and crises have to be met by sticking together, as has been pointed out in the preceding paragraph. Fourth, decisions must be made on a group, i.e., family basis. What one can do, as a large-family member, depends upon what others do, and plan to do. Most large families operate on a close economic margin, if margin at all, which means that economic necessity makes coöperation a virtue. At every turn, it is not only one's own efforts, but the modifying forces of the behavior of other family members, that determine what one can do or cannot do. The condition of the hand-me-down that must be worn, the acquiring of a new dress, the use of the living room for your date, of being able to go to town alone, of getting to sleep early, of taking a night-school course—all these are grist of the group mill.

Another factor that emphasizes the group is the feeling of family awareness that large-family members develop. Various circumstances contribute to this. Size calls attention to itself per se, and this makes for an awareness of itself. There is the constant reminder of the family because of the deprivations and limitations, as well as of the joys and satisfactions, which it brings. There are the continuing comments of friends and neighbors. This apparently begins early in life for the children reared in large families. Their schoolmates tease them, the teacher refers to it, their friends joke about it. Feelings of shame, and at times of pride too, were frequently referred to in the course of the study. Nor were the parents immune. All of this combines to create an awareness of the family as a group and as a distinct and unique aspect of one's experience. Needless to say, such feelings of family awareness are lacking in the small family.

6. Group existence and awareness make for group functioning, and this in turn calls for organization and leadership. A large number of persons, of differing ages and sexes, living within a limited space, on a

limited income, and with limited living facilities of various kinds, make organization, administration, authoritarian control, and executive direction inevitable to some degree, and our judgment is that the larger the family group becomes the more such developments will appear. This naturally makes for a dominant role of the father, the mother, and/or the elder siblings.

Many of the problems and values that characterize large families are those involved in group leadership and group functioning. The data of the present study make it abundantly clear that the good father is the wise executive director, the effective mother is the able household manager, and the older brother or sister most respected is the good leader. Conversely, the bad father is the too autocratic one, who tries to handle all problems by the ordering-and-forbidding technique, and the mother most criticized by the siblings is the ineffective one. Favoritism is a frequent cause of trouble. These are all aspects of faulty administration.

7. With large-family living go emphases on qualities of behavior which are group essentials. Conformity is valued above self-expression. Listening is the rule rather than talking: at least one learns to give and take turns in conversation. Earlier forms of heating houses, with their open hearth around which the family gathered to keep warm, aided and abetted this tendency. Modern methods of heating, which make all rooms of even temperature, permit a cell-like type of existence, with a radio in every cell. All this suggests, and there is nothing facetious in this comment, that the current cocktail-party pattern of everyone talking and no one listening may be the result of family conditioning rather than a psychopathic group emergent.

Another necessary group virtue is coöperation. What siblings most complain about each other is not doing one's share, failure to do teamwork, "getting out of line." The family must function as a group to do its group chores, and that calls for coöperation. The material of this study contains little mention of the child that excels at large, as is so common with small-family children; there is little comparison with the neighbor's children; the emphasis is upon duty, not spectacular achievement.

8. Whenever any considerable number of people function together, rules of conduct and procedure become necessary, and, as a rule, the greater the number of persons in the group the more numerous and stringent the rules. Applied to the present study, this means that discipline is stressed in the large family.

Discipline is not only the inevitable accompaniment of large-family living, but its proper exercise is much stressed. Much of it is exercised in the name of the paternal constitutional monarch, but its execution often is left to the siblings. Children in a large family discipline each other, adjustments must be made to peers, not primarily to adults. And discipline of children by children has its own distinctive features. First of all, it **is** realistic, not ideological; it is practical, not theoretical. Children understand each other, and their minds are not yet cluttered with theories of child rearing. They "see through" each other, they realize the implications of each other's behavior better than adults do. And, what is more, they know how to deal with each other. It is often said that children are diabolically cruel to each other, and this is true: first, because they know what is important—to children; and second, they know what to do about it. Significantly, then, the disciplinary measures they use are often more subtle than overt. For the nonconforming member, there are obvious indications of impatience; for the odd one, there is ridicule; for the vexing transgressor, there is disdain.

The complement to this sibling-rearing-by-sibling is a pattern of parental behavior quite different from that which obtains in the contemporary small family. The oversolicitous mother is strangely out of place in a family of 12. The nagging parent, the type who says, "Mary, go out and see what Johnny is doing and tell him to stop," is too much occupied in a large family to "ride" any one child. Both parent and child in a large family are apt to be less demanding and less possessive in their attitudes toward each other. The stark realities of large family living laugh to scorn the neurotic sins of the small family. In short, our hypothesis here tends to agree with George Bernard Shaw's comments years ago:

> The old observation that members of large families get on in the world holds good because in large families it is impossible for each child to receive what schoolmasters call "individual attention." The children may receive a good deal of individual attention from one another in the shape of outspoken reproach, ruthless ridicule, and violent resistance to their attempts at aggression; but the parental despots are compelled by the multitude of their subjects to resort to political rather than to personal rule, and to spread their attempts at moral monster-making over so many children, that each child has enough freedom, and enough sport in the prophylactic process of laughing at its elders behind their backs, to escape with much less damage than the single child.[21]

9. Ten children born in the same family are not going to behave alike any more than they are going to look alike. Differences of behavior manifest themselves early in life, on the basis of age, sex, abilities, interests, duties assigned, and conceptions of role developed by both individual and group alike. Particularly important is the specialization in the tasks assigned customarily to different members. On the basis of these assignments, and the siblings' adjustment to them, emerges the unity of larger patterns of behavior which constitute the core of personality.

Specialization of role and function among the children is another characteristic of the large-family system. Obviously, this takes many forms. Earlier, it was quite customary in large families to direct the chil-

[21] George Bernard Shaw, *Misalliance,* Brentano's, New York, 1914, pp. xix, xx.

dren, particularly the sons, into different occupations. Thus, one son might be given to the church, another to the army, another to the law. If today there is less practice of routine occupational assignment, the distinction between personality patterns is no less pronounced.

This specialization of role among the siblings is particularly important in the large family. First, there is the principle that the degree of specialization correlates with increases in the size of the group. Emile Durkheim, the French sociologist, first developed this in his analysis of the division of labor, pointing out that the larger the number of people living together the greater the division of labor and specialization of function there are apt to be.[22]

A second important fact in this connection is that the number of siblings limits the range of choice of those lower in the order of birth. Only the oldest child has a relatively unlimited choice. Since no one wants to duplicate the role of another sibling, each succeeding child's choice is limited by the choices of his predecessors in the order of birth. Specialized roles are preëmpted by the older siblings: they come to be firmly held with the progress of time. Thus the younger children in a large family may have greater difficulty in finding satisfactory roles within the family group. Also, they may be under greater temptation to develop patterns of rebellion. At any rate, our hypothesis is that such specialization of role, and the individual response to it, come early in life for members of large families; that such experience is of importance in shaping the patterned form of adjustment to life; and that both the early acceptance of assigned role in the group, or rebellion to it, are important determinants in shaping the personality. Often, the subsequent effort to escape an early assigned role and transfer to another becomes one of life's basic drives.

10. Durkheim points out still another principle of value in the study of the large-family system. The greater the degree of specialization, he says, the greater the degree of interdependence that comes about. This in turn demands *consensus*, a term and idea which Durkheim has contributed to sociology. It is this *consensus* which gives unity to the group, binds the members together, and "the greater the diversity of relations . . . the more it creates links which attach the individual to the group."[23] It is our hypothesis that the larger the family group, that is, the more persons that are living together in a family, the more family consensus tends to develop, the stronger its hold upon individual members becomes, and the stronger the position of the father as its directive symbol becomes.

11. Other things being equal, the large-family system makes for a certain balance and sanity in child rearing. Our material tends to show that

[22] George Simpson, *Emile Durkheim on the Division of Labor in Society,* The Macmillan Company, New York, 1933, Book II.

[23] *Ibid.,* p. 109.

having many children makes for an extended accumulation of parental experience, which in turn results in a certain detached and objective attitude toward child problems. The large-family parent, instead of rushing to the doctor or psychologist or psychiatrist about Mary's present annoying behavior, has seen the same symptoms with Mary's three older sisters, and knows that nothing is so helpful as a liberal dose of judicious neglect. Parents of small families often act neurotically about these phases and tend to communicate their neurotic concern to the child; parents of large families, viewing similar problems from the vantage point of historical perspective, learn to take them in patient stride. One wonders, too, of the effect of this upon the older children. They, too, see the younger children go through the same stages that they did, and they likewise come naturally by an objectivity toward human behavior which cannot be expected of the small-family child.

It is at this point that one becomes aware of the need of long-range studies of the large family. Only recently has the importance of historical studies of individual families come to be appreciated. Such observations as have been made have revealed the existence of a family cycle, with distinct stages, each with its own crises, preoccupations, and problems. Parenthood is one of these stages, with child bearing, child rearing, and child launching as clearly defined substages. This concept of the family cycle has proven to be very helpful in the analysis of family life and child development.

Unfortunately, these studies and the concept of the family cycle as thus far developed have been based almost wholly on the small-family system, in which each stage of the cycle tends to be distinct, and where the various stages follow each other in a rather clear-cut sequence. This is far from the case in the typical large family, where the last children may be born or be in the preschool period at the same time that the first born are leaving home and embarking on their adult careers. Thus one finds in such families, not a succession, but an accumulation, of stages.

What is the significance of this for the older children? Our case material suggests that the fundamental problem of the older children in large families lies in the fact that, by the time they reach the need-to-be-launched stage, their parents are still occupied with the tasks of the child-rearing and child-bearing stages. There are, to be sure, those few remarkable parents, so energized or financed, that they can bear, rear, and launch a dozen children with noticeable effectiveness, but they are non-existent thus far in our study. Mostly, the older children in large families launch themselves, if indeed they are launched at all, or, in recent years, they are launched in and by the armed forces of their country.

Similarly, one wonders what are the special problems of the younger children in those cases where all of the substages of parenthood are present at the same time in the family history. Is there a jaded parent, surfeited with an undue prolongation of the joys of parenthood? Is there a foolish parent, bent on prolonging parenthood with the last-born? Is there a tired parent, worn out with the tribulations of the years? A preliminary study of children of overage parents suggests a wide variety of complications for the child of such parents.[24]

12. To grow up in a large family is to come to terms with life. This seems the best way to designate the almost inevitable socializing process of large family living. There are many aspects of this process—learning to live with people, learning to play with them, to work with them, to share with them, to endure and enjoy with them. To grow up in a large family means that one must accept people, not as a pleasant interlude from which one can withdraw as fancy dictates, but as a constant bill of fare. It is this fact of constancy which seems basically important. From infancy, the large-family child (except the first one for a limited time) is surrounded by other children, always. One wakens with one or several in the same room, perhaps in the same bed. One lives with them before breakfast and in the disarmed moments at bedtime. One shares with others constantly, and thus one just comes to accept the presence of other persons. It is on this basis, of the acceptance of the constant presence of other persons, that the patterns of adjustment are formed.

This suggests a problem of great import. Is there any relation between the size of the family group in which a person is reared and the size of the working group in which he or she makes his best occupational adjustment?

Tentative data gathered by the authors over a period of several years seem overwhelmingly positive in the answer they indicate. Persons reared as only children or in small families are happiest in jobs where they work alone or with one other person. Similarly, it seems that persons reared in large families make better occupational adjustments when working in larger groups. It is hoped that a more pretentious research study will be made to answer the question, for its answer would be of great help in placement and personnel work.

13. As a system, the large family seems not to perpetuate itself. Rates of marriage and of reproduction are relatively low, as compared with the population as a whole. Many reasons for this appeared in the course of the study. Economic pressure resulting from the mere fact of numbers; the crises, often major ones, that appeared in so many families; the problems that arose from incompetent or unwise parenthood; the stresses and strains of limited space—all of these and others often overshadowed the other compensations of the large family. In only 30 percent of the families were parents and informants agreed that it was wholly good. Most often, the overall attitude of siblings could be expressed in the words of

[24] James H. S. Bossard, *Parent and Child: Studies in Family Behavior,* University of Pennsylvania Press, Philadelphia, 1953, Chap. 10.

one informant: "It was nice, it was fun, but—" It is the *but* which is the key word in interpreting the failure of the large family system to perpetuate itself.

Medium-Sized Families

Studies of medium-sized families, with respect to their distinctive features, particularly so far as child-rearing practices are concerned, are lacking. An initial project of this kind, including 100 three-child, 100 four-child, and 100 five-child families, has been undertaken by the authors of this volume, with the aid of a number of family sociologists throughout the country. No conclusions based on these studies are as yet available. There is a strong general impression, based on the data thus far gathered, that each size tends to have certain distinctive features. Size of family group seems to be a fundamental and important determinant of family life and child rearing.

Summary

In this chapter an attempt has been made to emphasize size of family group as a determinant of family life and child rearing.

1. The small-family system constitutes, then, a distinct type of family situation for the rearing of children. Such children are likely to enjoy certain superior advantages and opportunities, particularly in so far as individual care and relative economic resources are involved. On the other hand, they have to pay a price for all this, chiefly in the form of problem-creating circumstances. There is the danger, purely on the basis of the arithmetic of the situation, of acquiring an exaggerated opinion of their importance in group life. There is the continuing factor often of an undue pressure to achieve, and to excel. There is the atmosphere of concentrated emotions, as well as the necessity of dealing unduly with adults, preoccupied with the weight of their pressures in their own lives. Finally, there is the comfort or the inadequacy of sharing life and its experiences.

The small-family system is a quality system. It is based on the idea of achievement. It is an upward, climbing system, adapted to the requirements and opportunities of an open-class system. It is a rationalized system, giving sway to long-range planning rather than a passive hopefulness or a careless disregard. It is a system of prudence, based on the insecurities of a rapidly changing culture.

2. Preliminary studies suggest that there is a large-family system. Characteristically, the large family is usually not a planned family. It tends to be extensive rather than intensive in regard to its children. Large-family living makes for an early acceptance of the realities of life, it is peculiarly vulnerable to major crises, it emphasizes the group rather

than the individual, group leadership and organization are stressed, discipline and conformity are essential, specialization in role and function among the children is inevitable, and there is a relative balance and sanity in child rearing. There is some reason to think that the large family does not perpetuate itself.

3. Studies now under way of medium-sized families suggest that families of differing sizes between small and large-sized ones each have their distinctive pattern of family life and child development.

Chapter 4

Family Process and the Child

A family is more than a structure. It is a vibrant functioning reality, a group of persons living together in intimate continuing relationships. A second approach, then, to the study of family situations may be made through the objective analysis of the interactive processes which take place between the elements (chiefly persons) comprising the family structure. The purpose of the present chapter is to consider the family as a form of social interaction, with particular reference to the significance of these processes in the social development of the child. Accordingly, the emphasis here is upon the processes that are involved, the role of these processes, their more important constituent elements, and the nature of their operation. Specific problems created for the child and reports on research findings concerning these problems are reserved for a later chapter.

The Meaning of Social and Family Interaction

Sociologists speak a special language, as Waller reminds us,[1] because it facilitates precise communication in their specialized field. In this scientific jargon, the term *interaction* has the sanction of frequent usage and great emphasis; hence it seems necessary to say something more about its meaning. "The notion of interaction is not simple, but very complex," says Ormond.[2] It "involves, not simply the idea of collision and rebound, but something much more profound, namely, the internal modifiability of the colliding agents." For a complete analysis of interaction as a sociological process, the reader is referred to any standard work

[1] Willard Waller, *The Family,* The Dryden Press, Inc., New York, 1938, p. 15.
[2] A. T. Ormond, *Foundations of Knowledge,* Macmillan & Company, Ltd., London, 1900, p. 196.

on systematic sociology.[3] For an interpretation of family life in terms of the interactive process, the reader will find most helpful Waller's book *The Family,* already cited. An even more intensive application of the interaction concept to social phenomena is found in Brown's book *Social Pathology,* for the author makes this concept the central frame of reference for the problem of personal and social disorganization.[4] Each or all of these books will provide an adequate grasp of the many aspects and ramifications of the interactive process, as well as proof of its fundamental significance in the field of sociology.

For our purposes, it will be enough to identify the term as the generic name for the range of contacts between persons through which each influences the other, to the end that every new experience becomes part of a new totality. The term *family interaction* is used to include these reciprocal relationships between the members of a family in their continuing life with each other; and the results of this interactive family process, so far as the child is concerned, may be thought of as the child's familial sociopsychological heritage.

The Peculiar Nature of Family Interaction

Family interaction is, as has just been pointed out, one form or area of social interaction and, as such, is part of the more comprehensive field of personal interrelationships. It is important, however, to point out that the family is also something more; it is a unique and distinctive kind of interaction. A family is a set of peculiarly intimate relationships, such as one finds perhaps nowhere else in the field of social interaction. Its intimacies are of many different kinds and degrees. They are mostly continuing in character. With few exceptions, they have the full sanction of society. They come to express themselves in a terminology which has meaning to the family members and to no one else. These intimacies and their peculiar tokens exist regardless of the degree of harmony within the family; in fact, family discord and tensions precipitate their own distinctive varieties of expression. Even when the family breaks up, some of these intimacies persist as do the tokens of their expression, so that this aspect of family interaction often continues long after the family's corporate existence.

Another reason for the distinctive peculiarity of family interaction is to be found in the composition of the family. The family community is made up of units dissimilar in age and sex, complementary in their na-

[3] Excellent here is Leopold von Wiese and Howard Becker, *Systematic Sociology,* John Wiley & Sons, Inc., New York, 1932. See also Robert E. Park and Ernest W. Burgess, *Introduction to the Science of Sociology,* University of Chicago Press, Chicago, 1921, Chaps. 5, 6.

[4] Lawrence G. Brown, *Social Pathology,* F. S. Crofts & Co., New York, 1942.

ture, mutually responsible, and with the unifying bond of kinship for all but husband and wife; in the latter case there is the compensating bond of other relationships. Perhaps no one has described this phase of family life better than Bosanquet did almost sixty years ago:

As with all organic wholes, its parts are admirably fitted by nature to subserve each other's needs, and to supplement each other's efforts. The need of the weak for protection finds its correlative in the pride of the strong in protecting; the clinging appeal of the child for affection elicits a response which might otherwise remain dormant for ever. The authority which all adults like to exercise finds a beneficent outlet in guiding the action of immature wills; and children who weary when left to the caprices of their undisciplined natures, find strength and contentment in a rule which is autocratic without having the impersonal rigidity of external law. And the man, again, who would prefer solitude to the constant clashing at close quarters of his own will with that of another man, finds it completed instead of thwarted when its functions are supplemented by those of the woman."[5]

Despite all this, the formal existence of a family does not, as everyone knows, guarantee a "condition of continuing harmony." There is about family interaction this additional distinctive feature: its naked incisiveness. One can dissemble only little in most phases of family interaction. Indeed, from more than one aspect, family interaction is a brutal process, the more so because of the very likenesses of the family members and the intimacies of the relationships between them. Here again it is worth while to quote Bosanquet at some length.

A plain person finds no attraction in a mirror; and a person sensitive to his own defects of character may be inexpressibly jarred by seeing them reflected in another. I have known mothers whose irritation at the faults of their children was greatly enhanced by the fact that they recognized them as merely the faults of their own childhood recurring once again. And we fear no critic as we do the critic of our own Family, for has he not the key to all our weaknesses within himself? The stranger may be hostile and severe, but we can always console ourselves with the thought—which in nine cases out of ten will be perfectly true—that he does not really understand us. It is not being misunderstood which hurts most; it is being understood at our weakest, just as what helps the most is being understood at our best. And the member of our Family understands us literally "down to the ground," for it is the same ground upon which he himself stands.

Here, too, we may perhaps find an explanation of the strange bitterness which so often seems to attach to differences of opinion between members of the same Family. When an outsider differs from us we can accept it as something to be explained away by differences of experience, of surroundings, of education, above all of inherited temperament and disposition; in a sense it is possible to think of each being so far right that his opinion is the natural out-

[5] Helen Bosanquet, *The Family*, The Macmillan Company, New York, 1902, p. 242.

come of the sort of person he is. But when our brother differs from us there is no such escape from discord; this, we feel uneasily, is the same sort of person as ourselves, his opinion proceeds from the same nature as our own, and we cannot see any reason for the conflict. It is as if one's own judgment were divided against itself.[6]

Levels of Interaction

It will help, perhaps, in clarifying further the nature of the interactive process in the family to point out that it takes place on several levels. Speaking generally, it may be said that interaction operates on as many levels as there are levels of communication; some idea of what this involves may be gathered from the fact that Sapir, in his analysis of speech as a personality trait, identifies at least five different levels of speech alone.[7] For our purposes, it will be sufficient to distinguish three main levels. The first is sensory interaction, a comparatively simple form confined to reciprocal reactions through the various senses—the sound of a voice, the sight of a gesture or facial expression, or a tactual contact between one person and another.

Nonverbal communication is of the highest importance in human interaction. Especially is this true in the more intimate forms of interaction such as one finds in the family. Much of the love-making between husband and wife is nonverbal, and certainly many of the signs of affection or the reverse between family members are of this kind. Many, perhaps most, signs of intimacy in long-continuing relationships are unspoken. It seems quite obvious that interaction on this level plays a particularly important role in the early life of the child, both because of the continuing emotional relationship between parent and child and also because of the child's lack of linguistic equipment for the first years. We wish to advance here the concept of *the facial personality of the parent* as a useful device to emphasize the child's first impression of the parents.

Second is emotional interaction, as in reciprocal joy, fear, love, hate, etc. Everyone is familiar with the fact that the feeling reaction of one person, communicated to another, modified and returned to the first person, tends to intensify the original emotional condition. This process is revealed most clearly in the development of mob psychology. In its saner and simpler forms, it is going on constantly between the members of the family group; it constitutes that intimate emotional responsiveness which is so uniquely the characteristic of family life.

Finally, there is interaction at the intellectual level, the process taking the form of a reciprocal exchange of sentiments, ideas, abstractions, judgments, evaluations, and the like. Here one person expresses an opinion or

[6] *Ibid.,* pp. 249–251.
[7] Edward Sapir, "Speech as a Personality Trait," *American Journal of Sociology,* May, 1927, pp. 892–906.

states an idea, to which another person reacts; this calls forth a reaction from the first, and so on. This process is clearly revealed in arguments, debates, and "bull sessions," but again the most common form of it is found in rational conversation such as recurs constantly in the normal relationships of family life.[8]

The distinction between differing levels of interaction is particularly important when considered in relation to the child. It shows, first, that the interactive process begins long before the child has learned to speak. The foundations of parent-child relationships, therefore, precede verbal interaction. The implications of this are profound, both for child development and for mental hygiene problems. Second, the differing levels of interaction emphasize the variety and the subtle scope of the interactive process. Parent-child interaction is far more comprehensive than rational discussion based on the child's developing ability to participate. Third, the natural history of parent-child relationships, which remains to be written, must be based upon an understanding of the sequence in the differing levels of the interactive process.

General Importance of Family Interaction

The constant interaction between the members of the family constitutes one of its fundamental features and gives it such great importance in the development of the personality of its members, especially its younger members. Moreover, it is this aspect of family life that is being emphasized by contemporary students, both because of an increasing appreciation of its importance in the study of personality and also because, in a rapidly changing society constantly becoming more complex, personal relationships within the family become increasingly important. Recent literature on the family emphasizes this, particularly in the case of its adult members, chiefly husband and wife. The growing prevalence in our society of specialized groups into which one puts but part of his personality, the increasing formality and impersonality in our social relations, make the family virtually the one place where one may be at ease. This is particularly true in regard to the emotional aspects of our lives. Man is not a perfunctory, rational animal. It has been said that what distinguishes man from other animals is drinking without being thirsty and making love at all seasons. The essence of both, obviously, is emotional.

It is the general importance of family interaction for the child that chiefly concerns us here. It is in this unit of interacting personalities that the child learns to live, in which his personality first takes form, and in which this personality continues for a number of years to be confirmed

[8] Cf. Park and Burgess, *op. cit.*, Chap. 5; Edward W. Gregory, Jr., and Lee Bidgood, *Introductory Sociology*, Prentice-Hall, Inc., New York, 1939, pp. 55–56.

and enriched. There are at least three reasons why this family experience is of such overwhelming importance in molding the child's personality. In the first place, the family gives the child his earliest or first experience in living, and first things always have a special significance. A girl's first beau, a boy's first kiss, an author's first book—these always have a peculiar meaning. Second, family experiences are repeated over and over again. By the fifteenth birthday, for example, a boy or girl may have spent as many as 5,475 days or parts of days with his or her family. This repetitive aspect alone is enough to give the family an overwhelming importance. Third, family interaction is tinged from the beginning by an emotional coloring that places its interrelationships in a distinctly specialized class. This is particularly true in the case of parent-child or intersibling relationships.

Common Contributions of Family Interaction to the Child

Extended consideration has been given to the interactive aspect of family life, not only in the recent literature on the family and on parent-child interaction, but also in the more generalized studies of interpersonal relations. These studies tend to be divided into two main groups. In the first group are those which are concerned with family interaction, primarily from the point of view of determining what it is that the child gets from this interactive experience, and particularly as far as his sociopsychological needs and development are concerned. The second group of scientific studies have centered about certain generic processes in interpersonal relations, with reference to family interaction. To turn here to the first group, a survey of the literature on child development reveals that at least seven contributions have been emphasized in recent years, and these will be summarized briefly.

1. One of the basic things which the family gives its members is the satisfaction of what W. I. Thomas has called "the desire for intimate response." Every normal human being—and this includes every normal child—wants to be wanted, to be understood, to be appreciated, to be loved. This desire can best be satisfied in the family. Children get this satisfaction from their parents, and it is because of this that so much of their experience with their parents is so meaningful. It is this that is so instrumental in creating the bond which binds the child to his family emotionally, even where there are other unattractive and unfavorable aspects of the relationship. Persons who take children away from sordid surroundings and homes where they are badly and even cruelly treated, and place them in better homes or more attractive surroundings, are frequently chagrined to find these children longing to return to the parental hand that abuses them. What the child is apt to miss in such cases is the emotional tie-up with people who share this intimate reciprocal re-

sponsiveness. This affectional bond between members of the family, particularly between parent and child, is of vital importance under any circumstances of family life; it is increasingly and correspondingly important as other bonds—economic, protective, educational, and religious —become less effective.

There is some reason to think that this aspect of the family interactive process has increasing meaning for the child in contemporary culture. This observation is based on the growing complexity and impersonality of social life, particularly in urban centers. We recognize that these changes have great meaning for the adult members of the family. The recent literature on the family, with its emphasis upon the role of the family as a cushioned retreat for its members, leaves no doubt of this. Little thought, however, has been given to the significance of these changes for the child. The urban child's life is complex and impersonal, too. A 7-year-old, for example, may be in a second-grade class of 50 members in a school with hundreds of pupils. To get to that school means coping with many persons and running the gauntlet of incessant traffic. If a boy, he may have to fight his way to school and back. Obviously, such a child needs a home as a "cushioned retreat" from his activities outside the family even more than the adult. It may be that the most important need of a school child under 10 years of age is to have a mother awaiting his return home, and that the lack of this maternal presence is one of the most serious costs of the gainful employment of women with young children. Because they are less tangible than needs of feeding and discipline control, requirements of this kind are overlooked.

2. The family sets the stage to develop and utilize the child's abilities. Through its selection of toys, games, and playmates, the family establishes the first situations in which the child performs. At first these situations are apt to be centered around him, to encourage and stimulate him alone; later, the element of competition is allowed to enter. Usually the earlier forms of competition are artificial or protected in character, devised for the purpose of showing what the child can do. Later this may be changed, and the children may be introduced gradually to, or left to wander into, a natural or unprotected competition. It is the art of parenthood to manage these changes deftly and aptly, and for the best development of the child. Obviously the difficulties of many children are due to the fact that they have grown up without being "emancipated" from a protected competition.

3. A desire for the approval of one's kind is a basic human need. Here again the family is important because it is our first audience. The giving or withholding of the approval of this audience operates as a powerful selective force in determining the goals upon which the child concentrates and around which he develops skills.

A generation ago, Alfred Adler called attention to the "talent-finding" effect of proper parental encouragement, as did also John Anderson. Both pointed out how a parent's encouragement of the child's efforts in a particular activity, or the lack of such encouragement, determined the child's interest and application, thus resulting in a given skill or the lack of it. The differentiating effect of practice, the role of the family audience in his development, may be shown easily in regard to manual skills; and there seems no reason why the same is not true of other forms of behavior. The parable of the talents is apparently the statement of a fundamental principle.[9]

4. The child receives from the family his first lessons in living with other persons and in making adjustments to them. The family is a miniature society in which the child comes slowly to discover that there are other persons whose presence, needs, and rights have to be considered. Gradually he finds that he must limit his demands in the presence of others, and must adjust to them. The transition from the egocentric to the socialized stage takes place gradually and at varying times and rates in different children. Sometime, between the eighteenth and thirty-sixth month, true social behavior develops, and chains of response of both the linear and the circular type described by Allport put in their appearance.

Certainly the child receives plenty of practice in this process of adjustment. He has to adjust, first of all, to the adults in his family group—parents, relatives, servants, etc.—and each of these adults is apt to be a good deal of a law unto himself. Then, if there are other children in the family, adjustment must be made to them on the basis of their personalities, age, and status in the family group. In other words, the young child has to learn early to shift gears continually, as it were, in dealing with the other persons in the family group.

Part of this experience is the child's introduction to the study of human behavior. He learns how people act, how they react, how they differ. He learns that one adult talks much and does little, another is exactly the reverse; one threatens but does not punish, another does neither, a third does both. It is amazing to discover at how early an age children classify their elders on the basis of their behavior types. "My daddy don't spank, he just be cross," a 2½-year-old told her governess when the latter threatened to report the child's conduct to her father and made the added threat that he would punish her. Then, too, children sense early how members of the family group differ in the ways in which they meet situations and deal with other persons, which techniques succeed and which do not. Mother has her own ways of dealing with Daddy when he is an-

[9] Alfred Adler, "Character and Talent," *Harper's Magazine*, June, 1927, p. 68; John Anderson, in W. F. Dummer, *The Unconscious*, Alfred A. Knopf, New York, 1927, Chap. 3.

gry; this is what Grandma did to her neighbor; Sister manages to win usually, because of her technique; brother Charles seems to lose out so often because he acts thus and so. The family, in other words, is a psychological laboratory and a school which is always operative, and in which human nature and relationships are most often seen in the raw, that is, on the basis of that intimate and uninhibited responsiveness which is the essence of family life.

5. It is perhaps here that the role of the family in the determination of personal attitudes should be discussed. The reality and importance of attitudes, as well as the prior and basic importance of the family in their determination, have been much emphasized in recent years by the social sciences. Among the attitudes formed through family experience are those which its members develop toward each other on the basis of their intimate and emotional relationships. Each member of the family group comes to develop an attitude toward every other member—child toward child, parent toward parent, parent toward child, and child toward parent. It is in this way that the child obtains his patterns for a varied number of later personal relationships.

The attitude of the child toward the parent has been particularly emphasized by students of behavior problems, chiefly because it has in it more than a person-to-person relationship; it involves also the relationship of one person to another who has greater powers. The parent, in other words, is not only a person but also the symbol of authority, and the child's attitude toward the parent becomes his attitude toward authority.

The importance of adjustment to authority as a pattern of behavior can best be appreciated when we remember that every individual lives his life constantly in the presence of forces greater than he. These forces may be cosmic, such as the forces of nature; or political, such as the state; or occupational, such as the employer; or domestic, such as one's mate; they may be all of these, and others, existing at the same time. All of us must adjust all through our lives to persons and forces greater than we.

Modern psychiatrists who contend that much adult behavior is the result of childhood patterns formed through family experience have emphasized greatly the role of the family in the creation, through parent-child relationships, of patterns of reaction to authority. This does not involve a full acceptance of the claims of the Freudian and other psychoanalytic schools regarding the importance of infant training. Careful empirical studies, like that of Sewell, on 162 farm children, show that none of the infant disciplines was related significantly to childhood personality adjustment. "Such practices as breast feeding, gradual weaning, demand schedule, and easy and late induction to bowel and bladder training, which have been so much emphasized in the psychoanalytic literature, were almost barren in terms of relation to personality adjustment as measured in this study."[10]

6. We are on more objective ground when we proceed to point out that the child gets from the family interactive process many of the tools with which he acquires his beyond-the-home education. Particularly important here is the acquisition of language. The role of language is recognized in the sociological literature primarily as a vehicle (a) in the accumulation and transmission of culture, and (b) in the development of personality. Basically, language is a symbolic technique that permits communication among individuals. The ability to use this technique is the key to contacts, interactions, and relationships which are involved in social organization. To express it in another way, words are the symbolization of experience; and the number, variety, and adequacy of the words the young child learns through his family experience, and the meanings which are fixed upon these words, become the tools of his subsequent instruction. A more extended discussion of the child's linguistic acquisitions in the family, and their importance, will be found in a later chapter.

7. Finally, the child obtains through his family experience his first living habits; and because so many of these first habits remain through later life, this acquisition is of great importance in the development of the person. Living habits are specific things, both as to the area of life they comprehend, and as to the particular procedures involved. That is to say, eating habits revolve around the food needs, and they include the foods relished and eaten, how and when eaten, with what regularity, in what combinations and amounts. We are dealing here not with vague general notions but for the most part with very definite, concrete aspects of living. John develops the habit of gulping down his food; it is Mary's habit to eat a scanty breakfast, or none at all; Bill never eats liver.

It must not be assumed that these living habits have to do only with eating, sleeping, bathing, bowel movements, and the like. They include many other things, such as manner of walking, manner of speaking, gestures, grimaces, carriage, way of sitting, use of eyes and hands, care of personal appearance, etc. Detailed studies of human interaction reveal the surprising importance of many such matters, which unfortunately are often considered trivial by parents.

Out of the vast amount of scientific data of recent years, two facts stand out in clear relief. One is that the foundations of human personality are laid in early childhood; the second, that the chief molder of personality

[10] William H. Sewell, "Infant Training and the Personality of the Child," *American Journal of Sociology,* September, 1952, p. 158. See Harold Orlanksy, "Infant Care and Personality," *Psychological Bulletin,* January, 1949, pp. 1–48, and William H. Sewell and Paul H. Mussen, "The Effects of Feeding, Weaning, and Scheduling Procedures on Childhood Adjustment and the Formation of Oral Symptoms," *Child Development,* September, 1952, pp. 185–191.

thus becomes the family. It is in family experience that we find the origin and fixation of the reactions of one individual to another. As Anderson has put it, "The behavior of the adult toward persons has its genesis in the behavior of the child toward persons. Social behavior is of a piece with all other forms of behavior and is governed by the same laws."[11]

Family Interaction and the Family Cycle

Family life is never static. It is always changing, and, presumably, in certain predictable stages. This idea utilizes the natural history method, so successfully applied in the biological sciences, and involves the concept of the family life cycle, now utilized in some form by most contemporary students of the family. The concept is fundamental to a consideration of family interaction.[12]

In the early years of this century, Rowntree described a regular economic cycle in the life of the British working family. Its financial status went down with the arrival of several children and remained low until the children were of working age, at which time the family income increased and remained higher until the children left home. After this, at a later age, the family was again left in reduced circumstances. Later studies substantiated the concept of a family economic cycle, and showed that it is not restricted to British working families. For sociologists, these researches became significant for the deeper fact that lay behind them: that the family goes through successive stages of development as it progresses from youth to old age, and that this means successive changes in family relationships, needs, and interaction.

Glick, considering the history of the family from the demographic point of view, notes seven stages: (1) first marriage, (2) birth of the first child, (3) birth of the last child, (4) marriage of the first child, (5) marriage of the last child, (6) death of husband or wife, and (7) death of wife or husband. He points out that changes in these stages involve changes in the ages of the persons, size of families, residential shifts, family income, home ownership, and employment for husband and/or wife.

Out of this dynamic point of view has come the division of the family cycle into certain stages. The first National Conference on Family Life

[11] Anderson, *op. cit.*, p. 90.

[12] For more complete discussion, see B. S. Rowntree, *Poverty*, The Macmillan Company, London, 1901; Edgar Sydenstricker and W. I. King, "The Income Cycle in the Life of the Wage Earner," *Public Health Reports*, Washington, 1924, pp. 2133–2140; Evelyn Duvall and Reuben Hill, *Report of Committee on the Dynamics of Family Interaction*, National Conference on Family Life; Paul C. Glick, "The Family Cycle," *American Sociological Review*, April, 1947, pp. 164–174; James H. S. Bossard and Eleanor S. Boll, *Ritual in Family Living*, University of Pennsylvania Press, Philadelphia, 1950, Chap. 7; Paul C. Glick, *American Families*, John Wiley & Sons, Inc., New York, 1957, Chaps. 3, 4, and 5; Evelyn M. Duvall, *Family Development*, J. B. Lippincott Company, Philadelphia, 1957.

took this cyclic concept as its fundamental frame of reference, identifying (1) the founding family, (2) the expanding family, and (3) the contracting family. Duvall and Hill, in their report to this Conference, subdivided these into: (1) Early Marriage and the Expectant Family stage, (2) the Child Bearing stage, (3) the Preschool stage, (4) the School Age Family, (5) the Family with Teen-agers, (6) the Family as a Launching Center, and (7) the Family in the Latter stages.

Obviously, the history of the life of a family is a continuum, even if changing ceaselessly. But the stages thus far identified do serve as a convenient framework for the analysis of family life, and particularly of family interaction. Each stage has its own preoccupations and tasks, its own peculiar satisfactions and frustrations. Even now, it is doubtful whether students of the family are sufficiently articulate about these dynamic processes within its larger organization, in which each member is contributing to a constantly changing pattern.

The concept of the family cycle is, like all other conceptual tools, a useful and meaningful device which nevertheless has its limitations. Families do not always develop through these six stages, nor at times fit into any one of them. 1. Obviously, the childless family reaches the first stage only and develops its changing relationships on an entirely different basis. Even when it ages, it does not fit into the defined classification of the aging family. 2. Again, children are not all born at once, nor reach the subsequent stages together. In large families, all stages are often represented at the same time. Even in small modern families, age spans are great in certain cases. 3. Some families are formed when the parents-to-be are middle-aged. This is not "cricket" so far as the concept of the family cycle is concerned. But it happens frequently that this sort of marriage produces children. 4. Finally, there is the make-up of the aging family. This includes homes in which married children, with or without their spouses, are still, or again, living with their parents.

Family Habits of Interaction

The family life in which one grows up consists to a considerable extent of a series of habit patterns. Families do many things invariably in the same way. There are family patterns of eating, talking, greeting people, and behaving toward each other. In fact, most aspects of family living come to be routinized, and this applies to social interaction as well as to other forms of behavior.

Families differ decidedly in the nature of these living patterns. In one family, for instance, there may be much light-hearted banter; in another, quarreling is the rule. One family fosters free and easy conversation; the members of another family tend to be preoccupied; in the third, there is a consistent pattern of tight-lipped silence. The Jones family is noted for good-humored teasing; the Browns are known as a sensitive group that explodes at the drop of the hat. There are families that do things together; in other families, activity consists of a series of individual appearances in public with a petulant domestic recovery from such appearances.

It is these patterns of interaction that the child absorbs in the course of his or her family experience. Many of these habits are taken over, through a process much like osmosis in the world of plant life, with little or no awareness of what is going on; others are modified as the growing child evaluates them on the basis of experience; some, perhaps a relatively few, come to be rejected, with substitutions of a quite different kind. It is this process which ingrains the family patterns of interaction into the growing child, which explains in large measure the emphasis that predictive studies of marriage success and failure place upon the total configuration of reactive tendencies. Stated simply, young people who grow up in happy families form happy families in turn. Equally simple is the explanation. Persons who grow up habituated to patterns of interaction making for happy relations carry over such habits to the families they form in turn.

Attitudes Toward Parenthood

A second basic factor affecting family interaction, particularly so far as the child is concerned, consists of the attitudes of the parents, first, toward parenthood, and second, toward children.

It is one of the pleasing fictions of our culture that every baby is a "bundle of joy," brought to eager, loving parents; fortunately the fiction becomes fact often enough to justify the retention of this pretense. Proceeding into the realm of reality, one finds that parenthood often is not voluntary, as the recurring role of infanticide and the age-old search for effective contraceptives so clearly prove. Recently, there have been a good many references to parents' acceptance or rejection of the child after its birth, and undoubtedly such reaction is a basic factor affecting the interactive process in the family as well as the child's personality development. However, the matter is by no means so simple as is implied in most of these references, and it is suggested here that the larger question is actually that of the parents' whole attitude toward parenthood.[13]

[13] For suggestive studies bearing on attitudes toward parenthood, the reader is referred to Harold T. Christensen, "Mormon Fertility: A Survey of Student Opinion," *American Journal of Sociology,* January, 1948, pp. 270–275; Lemo Rockwood and Mary Ford, *Youth, Marriage, and Parenthood,* John Wiley & Sons, Inc., New York, 1945, Chap. 8; Robert R. Sears, Eleanor E. Maccoby, and Harry Levin, *Patterns of Child Rearing,* Row, Peterson and Company, Evanston, Ill., 1957, Chap. 2; E. E. LeMasters, "Parenthood as Crisis," *Marriage and Family Living,* November, 1957, pp. 352–355; Community Service Society, *The Family in a Democratic Society,* Columbia University Press, New York, 1949, Chap. 3; and Hilde Bruch, *Don't Be Afraid of Your Child,* Farrar, Straus and Young, New York, 1952.

This attitude derives from at least five distinct sources. The first is the acceptance or rejection of the idea of parenthood. This question is precipitated most often by the coming of the first child. It is the common experience of married couples that their life together begins with a marked sense of fulfillment and release. Both may be slipping out from under the domination of their parents for the first time. There is often a first sense of satisfactory erotic experience. Sex fulfillment affects one appreciably, both physically and psychically. Feelings of frustration, carried through youth, may pass. There is the stimulating sense of new responsibilities. The personality blossoms, the ego expands. Both mates are experimenting with new aspects and areas of life, and as these experiments are successful, life as it seems complete and satisfactory. Now comes the actuality of pregnancy and the portended arrival of a child. By its very nature this is prone, even under the most favoring circumstances, to produce elements of psychic shock. The child may be wholly wanted, and there is only the shock of responsibility. Or the child may come too soon, so that it breaks in, as it were, upon what the couple had looked upon as a happy, carefree time together. In other cases, the couple has not made a wholly satisfactory adjustment in marriage, and the coming of the child is resented as a permanent commitment to a contract not yet so accepted by both parents. There is at times a deep-seated reluctance on the part of one mate to "mix our blood" with that of the conjugal partner's family. This is often indicated in intercultural, racial, or internativity marriages. Again, a number of students steeped in psychoanalytic lore point out that the coming of a child crystallizes the mother's attitude toward her biological destiny, and that the woman who harbors a lifelong resentment toward being a female is apt per se to resent and reject her child. Finally, in the deepest sense, the acceptance of parenthood involves the acceptance of the idea of self-continuity in the existing world of the individual. To become a parent involves one's acceptance of the world, in all of its stark realities; it means one's projection into the future. The child is the parent's hostage to fortune, a belief in a future worth-whileness.

A second element in the attitude toward parenthood is the attitude toward the individual child. Is the child of the sex that was wanted? What is the parent's reaction to the child's appearance? Does the child suggest, in feature or later in attribute, someone whom the parent likes or dislikes? The answers to these questions have a fundamental bearing upon the acceptance or rejection of the child, not as they affect the assumption of overt parental responsibilities, but as they bear upon the emotional reaction to the particular child. There is a cold, calculating acceptance of a child, based on economic or personal advantage, a wanting of children because it is the thing to do; and there is a warm, personal, innermost acceptance of them, the essence of which is love. There is a difference, and a very meaningful difference, between the emotional acceptance of a child and the acceptance of parental responsibility, to which we turn next.

The responsibilities of parenthood are enormous and exacting, and the attitude toward the child is influenced by the nature of the parents' reaction to these responsibilities. The particular challenge of these responsibilities has been changed considerably by the growing predominance of the immediate family form, reference to which was made in the preceding chapter. In a kinship group family, the child is reared in the traditional manner, and the mother shares with, and absorbs from, her kinsfolk the necessary knowledge. So, too, there is at least a partial kin group pooling of the material resources required. All this is far different from present-day responsibilities. The science of child rearing has been revolutionized and is still changing. "Handouts" from relatives are not acceptable. The school requires the child's attendance, and the conventional requirements of school life translate themselves into many dollars. The law forbids child labor. Urban housing facilities place sharp limitations upon the size of the family. In other words, whether the family can afford to have another baby is a live question which must be faced with the birth of each child. There is the question of disposition, too. Are the parents willing to accept the demands upon their time, their energy, their financial means, and their pleasure, which parenthood makes? It is significant to note here that clients of birth control clinics largely seek contraceptive aid to limit the number of children rather than to avoid them altogether.

A fourth source of the attitude toward parenthood is to be found in the parent's reaction to the changes in family life which result from the coming of children. The completeness of this change is indicated by the frequency with which one hears parents say: "What did we ever do before the children came?" The coming of a child is like the advent of a new sun or planet into the solar system. The center of family life shifts. A reorientation of relationships follows. The relationship between husband and wife changes. Part of the affectional output is transferred from mate to child. This is particularly likely to happen with the mother, as the common complaint of husbands indicates. If the erotic relationship suffers, there may be a compensating increase of feelings of respect. Many couples vow never to do so, yet they invariably address each other as Father and Mother after they have children. Each comes to see the father or mother stereotype in the other. Everything in the home comes to be viewed in relation to the children. Conversation is changed as to objectives, inclusions, and avoidances. In the home there is increasing pressure upon the parent to live up to the stereotype of the parent. To all these changes and demands each parent reacts, and this reaction runs deep into the ultimate attitude toward the child. Such reactions may vary from an almost self-persecuting acceptance to a complete unwillingness to accept; they may result in a parent who is intensely jealous of his child or a genial-appearing one who sits by and in reverie recounts the trips he could take "if it weren't for the children."

Finally there is the parents' willingness or unwillingness to accept the social aureole of parenthood. This term is used to identify society's projection of the idealization of parenthood upon the individual father or mother. The mother and her child in the park, the father and his sons at the football game, the matron and her daughters at the opera—these arouse a distinctive reaction from onlookers. These parents are regarded quite differently from what they would be if they were alone. There is something in the appearance of parent with child that calls forth the warming glow of our approval. We accord them the pathos of the mores.[14]

To this social aureole of parenthood there is a reaction of the individual parent. Some parents simply revel in it and take advantage of the "privileges and immunities thereunto appertaining." "Many women," says Waller, "base their whole claim to consideration in this world and the next on the process of parturition."[15] On the other hand there is the young mother who resents being a *jeune fille* no longer, and there is at least one taproom keeper who said to his 8-year-old daughter: "Don't call me Daddy when there are ladies about."

Here, then, are five variables in the complex of parenthood. Each of these is a distinct element; each is subject to change, and often does change. Each is approached with a preconception which yields to the modifying force of experience. Moreover, there are two parents, each with his own attitude, and there emerges from their combination yet another which is different from either one in isolation. The pattern of the attitude toward parenthood is not a simple thing; indeed, it is quite complex.

The Attitude Toward Children

There is an attitude toward children, distinct from that toward parenthood, which operates to affect the family interactive process. This attitude again is a complex product, but some of the threads in its creation are quite clear. First is the parents' experience with their own parents. It is often emphasized that parents treat their children the way they were treated by their parents. There is much truth in this statement. Early in life, as the child plays, first perhaps with pets and dolls and then with other children, the game of "papa and mamma" is very popular. In this play, there is much conscious imitation and unconscious retention, and this is largely retained as the child grows older, to reappear when he in turn becomes a parent. There is, however, a more central fact to be

[14] Waller, *op. cit.*, p. 462.
[15] *Ibid.*, p. 463.

noted: The parent repeats the treatment which he received from his parents, as modified in the crucible of experience. For example, many parents make every effort to give their children what they themselves never received, and to use methods that are the opposite of those used with them. The drive in parents to avoid the mistakes perpetrated on them by their parents is often a powerful one, leading them to treat their children far differently from the way their parents treated them.

Perhaps all this is part of the larger pattern of one's philosophy of life. Philosophy follows experience and seeks to justify it. One's philosophy of life may be defined, therefore, as one's personal rationalizations upon the facts of life. In other words, it is a more or less well-defined and -developed system of beliefs, values, principles, etc., which we hold, through which we unify life and give it meaning. It is this philosophy that orients us toward the polar star by which we steer the course of our lives.

Part of this philosophy consists of our conception of people—what they are like, what motivates them, how to deal with them, and so on. Children, of course, are people; hence the philosophy of life, and particularly of human nature and of childhood, which the parents hold is a powerful factor in the creation of their attitude toward children. Does the parent think that children are little animals or that they should be treated like young adults? Does the parent harp constantly on the virtue of obedience, or does self-control seem the higher good? Can the child be molded according to plan, or is what "is in the blood" his irrevocable destiny?

Important, too, is the parent's adjustment to his own philosophy of life. The simplest way to express this is in terms of the parent's conscience. Glueck wrote about one aspect of this a number of years ago:

> Individuals who bring into the marital and parental relation a too rigid and inflexible conscience, whose neurotically exaggerated sense of guilt and need for expiatory punishment exposes them to a life of mean and purposeless denial and asceticism, create a domestic atmosphere that distorts and scars those who are obliged to live and grow within it. A parent of this type is apt to instill in his children a form of perverse morality and ethics that is destructive of happiness. His notions of the duties and privileges of parenthood are of a kind to exclude from the child-parent relationship any possibility of naturalness, of a free interchange of trust and confidence, and to breed secretiveness, distrust, and deception.[16]

One of the most powerful determinants of the attitude toward children is to be found in the emotional needs of the parents. There is much psychological exploitation of children in the world, chiefly because they are utilized so often to satisfy what the parent does not find elsewhere in life. The love-starved mother who sublimates her need in solicitous devotion to her son; the unhappy mother who watches hawklike over her daughter's relations with boys; the disillusioned husband whom the neighbors

[16] Bernard Glueck, "The Significance of Parental Attitudes for the Destiny of the Individual," *Mental Hygiene*, October, 1928, p. 734.

speak of as "such a good father"; and that most solicitous parent in the world, a maiden aunt—these can be observed at every turn, even if what they are doing to the children in their charge is less obvious. Moreover, these more conspicuous cases serve to illustrate what is seldom absent in the parent-child relationship, i.e., the temptation to utilize the tender dependence of the child so as to satisfy the deficiencies in the recesses of one's own being.

One special aspect of this is of particular importance, and that is the degree of life's satisfaction that the parent finds outside the home. Parents who feel frustrated because of their out-of-the-home experiences are apt to seek diligently for compensating satisfactions within their family circle. Glueck calls this the transposition of satisfactions. He writes:

Life offers certain satisfactions that affect primarily our sense of self-esteem, our pride and sense of achievement. These satisfactions are bound up with the personal returns we get from our membership in the social group. They define the degree of esteem in which we are held by our fellow men and the imprint of our ego upon the world about us. Now the sources of these satisfactions lie predominantly in spheres less intimate than in the home circle, and the nature of these satisfactions is different from those that we naturally expect from the family circle.

But sometimes it happens that as a result of certain personality difficulties, specifically those related to the presence of an undue sense of inferiority and timidity, of a general sense of insecurity, an individual feels a strong need for the transposition of these values. His happiness and efficiency as a member of society outside of home relationships are dependent to an undue extent upon getting a kind of return from his business or professional relations which one can expect only from the home circle. Unless his business relations reach a certain degree of warmth, unless he is constantly given evidence by his superiors or associates that they think well of him as a person, that they value him as a friend as well as a business associate, he has a keen sense of privation. Such a person is not apt to promote his opportunities for getting out of life sufficient ego satisfactions. In consequence, he is apt to seek compensatory satisfactions of this type in the circle of the home. He is then apt to exaggerate the virtue and the importance of obedience and submissiveness on the part of the children; he is apt to be unduly tyrannical and egotistical in the exercise of parental authority; and he will in consequence either transmit his own sense of inferiority and timidity to his children or provoke in them a negativistic and rebellious attitude toward sources of authority. Moreover, the marital relations between two people one or both of whom are disposed in this manner are apt to be unhealthy and ineffectual and conducive to an unhealthy home atmosphere.[17]

The Spirit of Family Interaction

"It is within the family emotional climate," writes Sheldon Glueck in a summary of the work of the Gluecks on juvenile delinquency, "that the

[17] *Ibid.*, pp. 733–734.

most deeprooted and persistent character and personality traits and distortions of the growing child are developed."[18] This observation calls attention to the fact that, underlying all the other factors in family interaction is the spirit or atmosphere of family life. This is one of the intangibles of life which students, preoccupied with scientific analysis and measurement, tend to avoid. And yet it is far too important a reality to pass by. It is something so real that it strikes the observer almost as soon as he appears upon the family scene. The sacred writings of various people, as well as the masterpieces of literature, have not overlooked these realities of the spirit, and neither should sociologists studying the intimacy of family life. In recent years, students of problem children have said much about the effects of troubled and strained and disturbed "psychic atmosphere" in the family backgrounds of their cases. If psychic atmosphere is important in the study of nervous or delinquent children, it seems equally important to emphasize the role of family spirit in normal child development.

Santayana, the philosopher, writing at the close of his life, gives us an excellent illustration of this.

After my mother and sisters left, my uncle Santiago, with his wife Maria Josefa and his daughter Antonita, came to live with us, and a new and distinct chapter begins in my experience. The scene, the persons, the events are still present with me most vividly. I didn't feel deeply or understand what was going on, but somehow the force of it impressed my young mind and established there a sort of criterion or standard of reality. That crowded, strained, disunited, and tragic family life remains for me the type of what life really is: something confused, hideous and useless. I do not hate it or rebel against it, as people do who think they have been wronged. It caused me no suffering; I was a child carried along as in a baby-carriage through the crowd of strangers: I was neither much bothered nor seriously neglected: and my eyes and ears became accustomed to the unvarnished truth of the world, neither selected for my instruction nor hidden from me for my benefit.[19]

The spirit of family life is compounded of many ingredients, some obvious and clear in the consciousness of the members of the family, but others buried in the unawareness of a deep mental hinterland. The turned-up nose of daughter Sue, the son's mischievous brown eyes, the mother's forgotten experience with a brown-eyed lover, the deepness of father's voice, sister Kay's lilting laughter, the wiggling stump of the tail of the family's cocker spaniel, the peaceful glow of candlelight at the evening dinner table, a roaring fire in the grate, father's deep satisfaction with his work, and Mother's patent satisfaction with Daddy—to some

[18] Sheldon Glueck, "The Home, the School and Delinquency," *Harvard Educational Review*, Winter, 1953, p. 25.

[19] George Santayana, *Persons and Places,* Charles Scribner's Sons, New York, 1944, p. 119.

these may appear as incidental minutiae of family life. Clearer insight may recognize them as of the greatest importance. Moreover, it is not only the persons and elements which are present in the interactive process, but each is the focal point of past experience. As Dollard has reminded us, to the concept of the family as a unity of interacting personalities should be added the phrase, "each with a history."[20] It is, then, out of this miscellany —of persons and things, present and past, obvious and subtle, remembered and forgotten—that there emanates from and pervades the family interactive process a certain essence which is the spirit of the family process. It is one of the basic realities of family life.

The Specificity of Family Interaction

It is often assumed that a single or unified family pattern of interaction exists which is the same for all its child members. Manifestly this is not the case. The interactive process within the family group is an individual one, varying from one individual to another. Each member has a specific relationship to every other member. Particularly is this true of each parent to each child, and some of the reasons for this are quite obvious.[21] Father has one attitude toward his son, another toward his daughter. Mother, who detests her mother-in-law, and her daughter, who is the image of her paternal grandmother, develop patterns of interaction quite different from those existing between Mother and her son, who is the image of Mother's father, whom she reveres. Little Jane, who has red hair and a temper like her father, clashes with him, while sister Sue, with the conciliatory passiveness of her mother, never squabbles with her daddy. Obviously sex, physical appearance, temperament, and other differences between the members of the family play their respective roles in the determination of these specific patterns. Moreover, the life of any family is a changing stream, so that its patterns of interaction would change from one stage to another in the family cycle.

Summary

The salient points in this chapter may be summarized briefly as follows:

1. Family life may be viewed as an interactive process between its members. As such, it is a peculiar form of social interaction, distinguished by the intimacy, deep community, and brutal incisiveness of its relationships.

2. Family interaction proceeds not only at the intellectual but also at

[20] John Dollard, "Needed Viewpoints in Family Research," *Social Forces,* October, 1935, p. 110.

[21] For an interesting study of mother-child interaction, see Barbara Merrill Bishop, "Mother-Child Interaction and the Social Behavior of Children," *Psychological monographs,* Vol. LXV, No. 11, 1951.

the sensory and the emotional level. This tripartite nature is responsible for its fundamental importance.

3. In the constant interplay between family members, the child's personality takes form. Common contributions of the interactive process to the child are (a) satisfaction of the desire for intimate response, (b) a stage for the development of the child's ability, (c) the approval of one's kind, (d) the first lessons in living with other persons, (e) determination of personal attitudes, (f) tools for the acquisition of an education, and (g) living habits.

4. Family interaction varies from one stage to another in the family cycle.

5. Parent-child interaction is greatly influenced by the attitudes of parents toward parenthood and children.

6. Underlying all other factors in family interaction is the spirit or atmosphere of family life—subtle, difficult to measure, but all-pervasive in scope and fundamental in importance.

7. Patterns of family interaction are individual and specific, varying from one child to another, and changing often in the course of the life cycle.

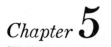

Chapter **5**

Interaction Between the Siblings

The family is a miniature society. In this society there are three sets of relationships: those between the adult members, usually the parents; those between parents and children; and those between the children. Each of these is distinct, even though they overlap and modify each other. In the preceding chapter, family interaction was considered primarily in terms of parent-child relationships; the present chapter is devoted to interaction between the siblings.

Distinctive Features of Sibling Relationships

The relations between children in the same family are much like the relationships of the adult world. The children of the family, then, are fellow citizens of this miniature world, and in it they receive from each other experience in human living together. Stated in this general manner, the family shares this function with all the other agencies in which children meet with each other. All the child's life—at home, visiting in another home, in school, etc.—is experience in living with other people. There are, however, in the sibling relationships within the family certain features which are unique and important, and which make such experience within the family unlike in character and importance the experience gained elsewhere.

One of these distinguishing features of the relations between siblings is their inclusive character. This inclusiveness has, for example, a time aspect. Children in the same family may play together, work together, be together for longer periods of time per day, week, and year, than is the case with most other relationships. This fact, and its meaning for children, is generally overlooked by adults. Parents are prone to gloss over, as a pleasant surcease from responsibility, the hours their children play together. When the inevitable quarrels arise, the parents think of them as a problem of jealousy, casting its shadow over what should be a juvenile Eden. What parents fail rather generally to appreciate in such cases are the facts from the standpoint of the children: that such quarrels and disagreements arise between two personalities, even if juvenile, who are forced to spend many long hours with each other, usually with definite limitations of space, object, and interest. It would be an interesting problem in research to compare adults and children in this respect. Suppose, for example, one were to observe 3 children at play for 500 hours, on a sun porch, with 8 toys. The number and duration of quarrels should be noted carefully. Then repeat the experiment with three unselected adults, for an equal period and under similar limitations of space and object, and again note the number and duration of quarrels. This might be an enlightening study in the relative behavior problems of children and adults.

A second aspect of the inclusiveness of the sibling relationship is the range of contacts included. Depending upon circumstances, children in the same family eat together, bathe together, share the same room, play with the same toys, wear each other's clothes, and have various other contacts. This suggests the third aspect, i.e., the peculiar intimacy of the contacts between siblings. They cover, in other words, every aspect of life. Here again a study in comparisons might yield intriguing results. It would be enlightening to study the relationships of adults compelled to live together for long periods of time, in the most comprehensive and intimate contact, and without the redeeming bond of romantic attraction. Certainly such studies would enable us to see "the problem of the jealous child" in a proper perspective—and possibly our own.

Next to its intimate nature is the stark frankness of the sibling relationship. It is not one of company manners, with doting parents hovering near to smooth out tangles and irregularities. Relationships between siblings permit little or no dissembling. In the parlance of the baseball world, each solves the delivery of the other early in the game. No tricks will suffice, no deception will work. Siblings come to know each other like a book. They come to live largely with each other—to use the vernacular again—"with their hair down." Life among siblings is like living in the nude, psychologically speaking.

Living in this miniature society with fellows of one's own relative age and status does much for the child. To begin with, it serves to bring him into, and to keep him in, the world of reality. It is easy for children who play alone and with inanimate objects to live in a world of make-believe, to invent companions with whom to play. Many only children do so. This is far less likely to happen when there are other children of a near age in the family. Such siblings serve as a constant crude awakening. The reality of an annoying younger brother crowds out the imaginary pal. The introvert tendency is not apt to be encouraged, for example, in a family of 6 children born within 10 years.

The negative side of this service might be noted: the fact that siblings act as substitutes for parents. To put the matter with blunt directness, they save each other from being with parents and other adults too much. When there are several children in a family, they will inevitably spend much time with each other and less with the parents. The significance of this is that they are kept from the unnatural environment which the adult furnishes. Parents and other adults are less satisfactory companions for children than are other children because children treat each other more like equals. Parents and other adults are apt to be oversolicitous, less understanding, more condescending, less interesting, more tired and abstracted, to offer a protected form of competition, and in many ways to afford a less healthy environment for a child's normal development.

Other possible advantages are obvious. Children may stimulate each other's creative interests. It is always true that two minds are better than one, and that in their interplay each stimulates the other. There are, of course, the inevitable rivalries between siblings. They may be friendly and wholesome, or they may be of the frankest bitterness. The turn which these rivalries take is likely to depend upon the larger family situation, upon the wisdom of the parents and their relations with each other. In some families, such rivalries are utilized and maintained at a stimulating level; in others, whole family groups may be divided into two camps, with the children lining up on one side or the other.

Living with other children in the home from the earliest days insures an abiding appreciation of the rights of others. This appreciation comes in large measure through conflict. Parents are annoyed often, and quite distressed at times, by these conflicts, but conflict is to a great degree the inevitable accompaniment of the process whereby the child learns to live and work with others. There may be many squabbles before the taking of turns is established, but in the end the child will have learned the lesson of limiting his demands in the presence of others. It is unfortunate to have brother break the choicest doll, and some hours of warfare may result; but how better can be achieved a vivid sense of the doll's value and of responsibility for the care of someone else's choice doll?

Educational Aspects of Sibling Relationships

The family is a miniature school in which the children, particularly the older ones, act as teachers to each other. There is much reason to think that, as far as instruction in the ways of meeting child life problems is concerned, the older brother or sister is often a more effective and wiser teacher than the adult. Children understand each other, often better than adults do; their interests and problems are common; they speak the same language, as it were; and they have the same general kind of experiences. Thus it comes about that an older brother's or sister's estimate of parent, teacher, policeman, or grandparent is keener than that of the parents, and is almost invariably more likely to be accepted by the other child or children. One of the distinct advantages enjoyed by younger children in a family is to be "tipped off" or "taught the ropes" by the older siblings. This takes the form of practical and concrete information on how to meet life's problems.

As this is being written, the author had the privilege of reading a verbatim report of a conversation between two sisters, aged 9 and 7 years respectively, and recorded without their knowledge. The conversation had to do with a controversy raging on the school playground and involving second- and third-grade children. This intersibling discussion covered the following points: (1) analysis of the issue and how it arose; (2) a characterization of the chief personalities involved; (3) reasons for the existing line-up; (4) questions of strategy; (5) what would be involved if the sisters took opposing sides; and (6) a final compromise, as the result of which both agreed to delay decision for the time being. Throughout the entire conversation, which took place over a lengthy period while both were playing in their sandbox at home, the older child was contributing constantly to the younger child's knowledge both of the issues and of human nature, drawing on her longer experience in the school.

The family is a school of mirrors, often. Children are apt to see themselves in their brothers and sisters. "Your nose is like Bill's." You mouth your words like sister." "Jimmy and you both look like the Brown side of the family." Children who hear statements like these from infancy on early come to realize that a brother or sister is enough like one so that one can see and hear oneself. This is a helpful device, particularly at the time one begins the process of making oneself over. It is an excellent help for purposes of self-correction and self-discipline. Possibly those modern teachers who would develop personal traits and habits in students through the use of moving pictures first got the idea from living in a large family where the children were much alike and where they could see themselves reflected in their next of kin.

Life among siblings is a school of many lessons. Not only is each child teacher, pupil, and supervisor, but each one differs from the other in age, sex possibly, interests, temperament, and range of activities. Each makes his or her own contributions, each presents distinctive problems. Moreover, each one is growing, and rapidly at that. The result is that the contributions and problems of each are constantly changing. All this demands constant adjustments and readjustments. Living comes then to involve a whole series of little crises and of adjustments in small things. Developed as a habit, facility in the making of adjustments makes correspondingly easier the solution of the more serious problems of adolescent and adult life. The old adage, "Practice makes perfect," holds good here.

Life among siblings may be a hard school, with long hours of apprentice-ship, a great range of possible conflicts, and demands for constant appli-cation, but facility in the arts comes in just this way.

Emotional Satisfactions

Some of the contributions of children to each other within the family fall in the field of subjective satisfactions. These are difficult to put into objective form and any effort to describe them may expose one to the charge of not being objectively scientific. But it *is* pleasant for most chil-dren to have other children in the home; it is satisfying to know that there are others of your kind; it is a comfort to have another person of your rela-tive age and status and bound to you by bonds of blood, available in your home to share your thoughts if not your toys. Perhaps much of this may be reduced, in the final analysis, to the much-discussed and -empha-sized factor of a sense of security. Children in the same family give each other a sense of security.

Apparently the feelings of security, and their source, that come from family living vary considerably on the basis of the size of the family. In the study of large families summarized in Chapter 3, one of the specific questions asked of the children reared in these families was: "Do you think a large family makes for a sense of security among its members: (a) economic security; (b) emotional security?" Informants were asked to write out their thoughts on this, and the question was discussed with those who were interviewed personally. Relatively adequate responses were obtained from 90 sibling informants in as many different families, and their verdict seemed clear. (1) Seventy-three of the 90 agreed that large family living produces feelings of security; 17 appeared to dis-agree. The ratio was more than 4 to 1—81.1 percent to 18.9 percent. (2) Emotional rather than economic security was stressed. Only 4 in-formants stressed economic security alone; 26 wrote or spoke only of emotional security; the others, while speaking of both, emphasized the emotional as the more important. (3) Siblings in these large families found security in other siblings rather than from their brother or sister. Differences in the sex and age of siblings become particularly important in smaller families, it would appear.[1]

In contrast, an intensive study of 100 unselected families with two children each, now being made by the authors, shows a marked differ-ence. While this study is not complete, it appears that siblings in these families think of security, and particularly emotional security, primarily in relation to their parents.

[1] James H. S. Bossard and Eleanor S. Boll, "Security in the Large Family," *Mental Hygiene*, October, 1954, pp. 530–531. Cf. also *The Large Family System*, University of Pennsylvania Press, Philadelphia, 1956, Chap. 11.

Speaking generally, one would expect, under favoring circumstances, a sense of support, of consolation, of spiritual renewal to come from a fellow sibling, the opportunity to talk things over, intimately, frankly, with one's own kind—at odd moments, late at night, or incidentally while at play. There is a feeling of belonging, of not being isolated, of being fellow members of a group whose interests are irrevocably bound up together. And it is this sense of security, this feeling of belonging, this conviction of the certainty of support which builds itself through succeeding days into the foundations of mental hygiene.

The Only Child

What children in the same family contribute to each other may be brought out in a reverse manner by considering the problems of the only child, who, by way of contrast, receives no such contributions. Approximately one out of six completed families (wife 45 years of age or over) today has only one child. The only child thus not only presents a valuable study by way of contrast but represents per se an important aspect of child behavior.

Both popular comment and scientific studies agree that the only child differs in various respects from other children. This is perhaps the first distinctive fact about the only child: that he is so often identified as different and singled out for discussion. There is an extensive literature on the only child, with some considerable differences of opinion. But through this literature there is a continuing recognition of him as a problem. Fenton, one of the students of the problem, concludes that one may expect a priori that all only children will be problems of one kind or another.[2] Both popular and scientific comment agree in general on the nature of the problem. Popular opinion, speaking in terms of overt behavior, identifies two types: children who are "spoiled," egocentric, difficult, and unsocial; and those who are sensitive, isolated, hesitant, and unduly dependent upon their parents. The scientific literature, thinking in terms of causative factors, emphasizes, first, that the only child lacks necessary association with other children; and, second, that he receives too much attention from his parents.[3]

Concerning the traits and types of behavior usually considered of social importance, there is somewhat less agreement. The nature of the studies which have been made and the shift in the conclusions reached can best be revealed by brief summaries of six of these studies. (1) In 1898, on the basis of 481 cases, Bohannon concluded that only children were below average in health and vitality; suffered more frequently from

---

[2] N. Fenton, "The Only Child," *Pedagogical Seminary*, December, 1928, pp. 546 ff.
[3] Anne Ward, "The Only Child," *Smith College Studies in Social Work*, September, 1930, p. 41.

physical or mental disorders; entered school later, were more irregular in attendance, did below-average work; joined less in group work; and were noticeable for peculiarities, precocities, selfishness, and affectations.[4] (2) Neal, writing in 1927 on the basis of the experience of the Los Angeles Child Guidance Clinic, affirmed this characterization. The only child is usually a problem child, is "jealous, selfish, egotistical, dependent, aggressive, domineering or quarrelsome."[5] (3) Fenton in 1928 published studies whose conclusions were rather different. His investigations were based on 193 unselected elementary-school children, of whom 34 were only children, and 512 university students, of whom 73 were only children. His method was to use teachers' ratings on 12 traits of these individuals. He concludes that only children were only little more selfish and unsocial, more unpopular with their schoolmates, slightly less obedient, somewhat more inclined to be leaders, to be self-confident and aggressive. On the whole, while recognizing their handicaps and behavior, he insists that the picture has been magnified in the past.[6] (4) Bellerose, studying 25 only, youngest, oldest, and middle children referred to a habit clinic, concluded that only children were not unique, although they showed a larger occurrence of food fads and temper spells.[7] (5) Ward, analyzing 100 case records of only children living with their parents and referred to child guidance clinics in large cities, found that the only children were notably younger than clinic children as a whole; ranked higher in intelligence; were less subject to stealing, lying, and truancy; were more restless, overactive, and had more school difficulties.[8] (6) Cutts and Moseley, in their study of 498 only children, are distinctly more encouraging. They found, in their lengthwise approach, utilizing case histories extending over periods of time, that (1) the problems of only children are complicated often by family circumstances, such as late marriage, which are responsible for their being only children; (2) most of their cases grew up to be well-adjusted adults; (3) there is evidence that they did not achieve their success without a struggle. "People who overcome handicaps grow strong in the process. But there is always the danger that an obstacle will prove insurmountable."[9]

What these and other studies agree on is that the only child tends to be characterized by certain attitudes and traits which handicap his adjustment to his fellows and result in behavior that naturally follows such

[4] E. W. Bohannon, "The Only Child in a Family," *Pedagogical Seminary*, April, 1898, pp. 306–310.

[5] Eva Neal, "The Only Child," *Mental Hygiene Bulletin*, November, 1927, pp. 1–3.

[6] Fenton, *op. cit.*, pp. 546–556.

[7] Dorothy Bellerose, *Behavior Problems of Children*, Smith College School for Social Work, thesis, 1927.

[8] Ward, *op. cit.*, pp. 41–66.

[9] Norma E. Cutts and Nicholas Moseley, *The Only Child*, G. P. Putman's Sons, New York, 1954, p. 234.

handicaps. What they do not agree on is how frequent and how serious these traits are. Why they disagree in this respect is probably to be explained in terms of differences in the data upon which they worked. There obviously were differences in the bases used for selection of the cases; the identification and tabulation of traits varied; and the times and places of the studies were different.

Going beyond the statistical judgments of tabulated cases, one finds rather general agreement on the elements in the domestic background which are peculiar to only children. In other words, whatever the outcome in the case of any individual child, the existence of certain common hazards or handicaps is generally recognized; five of these will be summarized briefly. (1) The only child does not have other children with whom to play and compete, within the intimate world of the family. He lacks, say all students of him, just those experiences and lessons emphasized in our preceding summary of what children in the same family give each other. He is not schooled in the lessons of living with his kind, i.e., with other children of his age, ability, and type. (2) There are hazards to his emotional development. The psychoanalytic school emphasizes this point. The emotional demands of the parents converge upon the only child—an unnatural emotional demand upon an immature person. Also, the only child never has anybody to threaten the security of his libido fixation on the parent of the opposite sex. (3) His parents are apt to be overly solicitous. Part of this oversolicitude for the only child is that which is ordinarily focused upon the first-born. Parents with several children who will remember their concern for their first-born in contrast with that for the subsequent children, will be particularly able to appreciate this fact. But a good deal of this oversolicitude grows out of circumstances peculiar to the case of the only child. Only children are often born to marriages contracted late in life; or to women, who, after several miscarriages, have finally had a child and face the impossibility of having another; or who, after years of sterility, have achieved motherhood, but with no promise of additional children. In these and other cases, the natural anxiety for the first-born combines with the exaggerated concern for the only child. This oversolicitude may take many forms. There often is an abnormal concern about the health of the child. Not infrequently there is too much praise for any minor achievement. Or there may be interference with the most minute activities of the child's life. The oversolicitous parental situation will be discussed more adequately in a subsequent chapter. (4) Just as parents of only children are thrown too much with and upon the child, so the only child is thrown too much with and upon his parents. There is too early a shift to adult activities and interests, because no childish activities and interests are available in the home. This fosters precocity and explains the frequency of leadership, as well as unpopularity, among only children. (5) It must be recognized, on the other hand, that the only child has certain distinct advantages. Ordinarily, his economic position is better than it would be if there were other children. This may mean more toys, better educational opportunities, more and better clothing. Parents of such a child have more time to devote to his supervision and guidance. They show in many ways that they expect a great deal from him, since he is the only one.

Variations in Contributions of Children to Each Other

In a preceding chapter it was pointed out that what the child gives his parents is a highly individual matter, depending upon a great many factors that operate both on the parents and on the child. Obviously, the same is true in regard to the contributions of children in the same family to each other; the discussion of such contributions would be incomplete without reference to the more important of these factors. Accordingly, five such factors are selected for brief analysis at this point.

THE NATURE OF THE CHILDREN

Just as the contributions which the adults with whom we live can make to us as personalities vary with the persons concerned, so what siblings contribute to each other is dependent upon the siblings—their nature and how they regard and affect each other. Each child is a distinctive person, responding in his own ways to life. Siblings may be so different in ability, appearance, and temperament that the very laws of heredity and social interaction seem capricious. Many people, including parents and students of family-child relationships, seem to act as if the Smith children, like Ford automobiles in an assembly plant, are all alike originally, only at some later time beginning to show differences on the basis of the "wear and tear of life." This, of course, is not true. The children in the Smith family, like those in any other, are distinctive individuals to begin with, and their conditioning experiences only accentuate these differences. Once this individual character of every child in the family is kept in mind, it follows as a matter of course that each sibling will have his own distinctive relation to, and effect upon, every other sibling. Not infrequently, one outstanding trait may color the whole relationship. The dull child is ridiculed by the brighter sibling. The sensitive child is teased by a cowardly brother. The stronger child is expected to fight the other's battle, the more daring one is looked up to to pull the filial chestnuts out of the paternal fire, the "cuter" of the sisters begs for nickels and dimes for both. Illustrations of the significance of conspicuous traits like these serve to emphasize how in lesser degree and in more subtle manner facts about the nature of children are important to an understanding of their relations with each other.

THE NATURE OF THE HOME SITUATION

Situations in the home affect intersibling relations in many ways. First of all is the obvious role of living arrangements. These may be of a kind to minimize friction and irritation. Each child may have his own room, toys, play space, and shelves and closets for his own clothing and possessions; on the other hand, four children may share the same room, and even the same bed, creating a situation which is bound to complicate and render sibling relationships difficult. Again, living arrangements may be wholesome in character and in consequence; conversely, they may be unhealthy to the core. Often children sleep with siblings of the opposite sex, for example. A good many behavior problems that come to clinics have this background, and analyses of the facts indicate that such living arrangements are not always due to the compulsion of poverty.

Favoritism on the part of a parent or adult member of the household may put the relations between siblings on an entirely different basis than would otherwise obtain. The literature on parent-child relationships is replete with evidence on this point.[10]

Favoritism need not be forthright and overt; it may be unconscious and confined to incidental and indirect expression. Children are uncanny in their discernment of the subtleties of preference. Again, relations between children in the same family are influenced greatly by the attitudes of the family as a whole toward the particular siblings involved. Mother, for example, tells Mrs. Brown, who lives next door, that Jack is neat and orderly and puts the blocks back in their box when he has finished his play, but Bill never does. Sister Penelope, aged 16, hears this and repeats it. Aunt Martha tells the cook, the cook tells the laundress, and finally Daddy hears it, too. Meanwhile, Jack and Bill have been hearing it, and acting accordingly. The family attitude is definite on this point, now: Jack is orderly, and Bill is not. Whatever the degree of fact originally, as the attitude was crystallizing, the fact kept pace with it. Soon Jack assumes a responsible role about the blocks, and a protective one toward Bill. A relationship now crystallizes, as did the attitude underlying it. Whatever the concrete circumstances, the central point to be emphasized here is that a child is apt to adopt or be influenced by the family attitude about the other sibling. In some cases, both the attitude and its absorption may be quite unconscious; in other cases, it is definite and consciously arrived it.

DIFFERENCES IN AGES OF SIBLINGS

Child spacing has been emphasized primarily in relation to the infant mortality rate, the health of the mother and child, and the convenience of parents; one of the distinct advantages claimed for the birth control

[10] For a discussion of the role of favoritism in large families, see Bossard and Boll, *The Large Family System*, pp. 98–99.

movement is its contributions to these designated ends. Not much attention, on the other hand, has been given to the relationship between child spacing and sibling relations. The question is important, and is destined to receive increasing attention with progress in family planning. Is it better, from the standpoint of sibling harmony, for children in a family to come one, or two, or three, or more years apart? Many parents discuss this as a problem, speculate about it, have decided ideas about it, and proceed to have their families accordingly; but concrete and objective evidence is lacking. Certain aspects are fairly obvious. The range and extent of contacts vary inversely with the time span between the birth of siblings. All other things being equal, children born 10 months apart will have more in common than those born after a 10-year intervening period. Close companionship is more likely between siblings near in age; those separated by too long a period tend to grow up in separate worlds, as it were.

Confirmation of this comes from the study of large families, previously referred to. This shows, at first glance, that happiness, as reported by the children, increases as the size of the family increases. A careful reading of the case material, however, suggests that the reason for this is that, with increase in family size, the time interval between birth of siblings decreases. Shorter intervals between births make for happier children, it would appear.[11]

DIFFERENCES IN THE SEX OF SIBLINGS

It must be obvious that differences in the sex of the children in the same family constitute an important factor in determining their possible contributions to each other. The consequences of this factor are mostly of two kinds. In the first place, there is the effect upon the range of common interests. Early in life, boys and girls become interested in different games, contacts, and activities of all sorts. The objectives of the sexes begin early to differ, as do also the kinds of training to which they are submitted. Perhaps distinctions of this sort become less pronounced with the equalization of opportunities between the sexes in our schools and in other socioeconomic pursuits, but many differences in the lives and interests of the sexes remain and continue to evidence themselves early in life. The second way in which sex influences the interrelationships between siblings is through what Adler calls the masculine tradition of our culture. This tradition, says Adler, acts as a definite impulsion toward certain attitudes organized principally around the assumption by the male of his own superiority, and the acceptance, however grudging and reluctant, by the female of her own inferiority of position.[12] Here is an illustration, in other words, of how society and the family influence re-

---

[11] *Ibid.*, pp. 84–85.

[12] Alfred Adler, *Individual Psychology*, Harcourt, Brace & Company, Inc., New York, 1925, pp. 322 ff.

lations between siblings through the attitudes which they create. There are, for example, one set of standards for boys and another for girls. The distinction is made openly, with the knowledge of all concerned, and on the basis of the sex difference. Boys are indulged in privileges which are denied to girls, they are exposed to realities in life from which girls are sheltered, the distribution of opportunities and facilities in a family is often decided on a sex basis.[13] Such distinctions, and the attitudes which accompany them, influence the relations between siblings and what they are going to give each other as fellow members of the family.

DIFFERENCE IN ORDER OF BIRTH

The importance of the individual's position in the family on the basis of order of birth has been recognized by students of behavior. In part, this importance grows out of the differences in the parents' attitudes toward children on this basis, but much of it grows out of its effect upon relationships between the children themselves. No one who has had the experience of living as a child in a family in which there are other children will deny that their relations with each other are influenced at every turn by the order of their appearance in the family. Family conversation is replete with references to it. Adults, speaking of their earlier experiences, constantly refer to it. Similarly, recognition by scientists of its role in the development of behavior is growing. In recent years a creditable literature has developed in this area. The next few pages seek to summarize the essence of these studies.[14] To facilitate presentation, reference will be made to the first-born, the in-between, and the last or youngest child.

1. The first child has per se certain unique experiences. One of these is that he begins life as an only child. All the other children miss this

[13] Blanche C. Weill, *The Behavior of Young Children of the Same Family*, Harvard University Press, Cambridge, 1928, pp. 34–35.

[14] Studies of the significance of birth order in child behavior include the following: E. M. Abernethy, "Further Data on Personality and Family Position," *Journal of Psychology*, April, 1940, pp. 303–307; Dora E. Damrin, "Family Size and Sibling Age, Sex, and Position as Related to Certain Aspects of Adjustment," *Journal of Social Psychology*, February, 1949, pp. 93–102; Helen L. Koch, "Some Personality Correlates of Sex, Sibling Position, and Sex of Sibling among Five- and Six-Year-Old Children," *Genetic Psychology Monographs*, Vol. LII, 1955, pp. 3–50; Helen L. Koch, "Some Emotional Attitudes of the Young Child in Relation to Characteristics of His Sibling," *Child Development*, December, 1956, pp. 393–426; Joan K. Lasko, "Parent Behavior Toward First and Second Children," *Genetic Psychology Monographs*, Vol. XLIX, 1954, pp. 97–137; J. P. Lees, "The Social Mobility of a Group of Eldest-Born and Intermediate Adult Males," *British Journal of Psychology*, July, 1952, pp. 210–221; J. P. Lees and A. H. Stewart, "Family or Sibship Position and Scholastic Ability," *Sociological Review* (British), July, 1957, pp. 85–106; Robert R. Sears, "Ordinal Position in the Family as a Psychological Variable," *American Sociological Review*, June, 1950, pp. 397–401; I. S. Wile and A. B. Jones, "Ordinal Position and the Behavior Disorders of Young Children," *Journal of Genetic Psychology*, Vol. LI, 1937, pp. 61–93. For a more complete bibliography, consult Edith G. Neisser, *The Eldest Child*, Harper & Brothers, New York, 1957.

experience. Until other children arrive, the first-born is alone, in the center of the stage. His adjustments are only to adults. He learns to accommodate only to older persons. These older persons are apt to be pliant and tolerant. Usually it is their first experience with parenthood. Their behavior is prone to be tentative. They proceed experimentally. The first is the practice child.

Then comes the arrival of the second child. This presents a crisis, and it occurs usually with devastating suddenness. All his life the oldest child has ruled as king or queen; and then, one day, in the midst of tense excitement, he is dethroned. "The king is dead. Long live the king." Most often, all this happens, as far as the first child can understand, without warning. There is no preparation, but suddenly a *fait accompli.* It is in this connection that the time interval between births becomes important. Reference has already been made to this factor. It is particularly important in the case of the oldest child, because it determines the severity of the crisis. It is in this connection, too, that the whole process of sex education of young children, and of adroit manipulation of family situations by the parents, becomes important. There are families in which, as has been pointed out, the second and subsequent children arrive without any preparation in the minds of the prior-born. On the other hand, there are families in which the children, when quite young, have an understanding of the processes of birth and are led, skillfully and sympathetically, to await and accept the changing physical condition of their mother in pregnancy as well as the arrival of the new brother or sister. Unfortunately, such cases are relatively rare; in most families the oldest child faces dethronement and the coming of a rival with inadequate preparation.

The oldest child must adjust to this situation, and the effort to do so furnishes the key to many behavior problems which afflict the family in subsequent days. His first effort generally is to regain the attention that has been diverted from him to the new arrival. This may take the form of intensifying past performances or developing new techniques. What the dethroned child early senses is that it is the very helplessness of his rival that seems to account for his extraordinary success in gaining attention. This is a technique the older child understands. He, too, succeeded when he utilized it. He will try it all again. There is, for example, the food technique. His parents were once so concerned that he eat well and regularly. Now they are devoting much effort to the feeding of his rival. Suddenly, he does not eat. Many parents immediately become alarmed. The child may be ill. He will not grow if he does not eat. He will become restless and cry if he does not eat. They plead, threaten, scold, argue, tempt. Ah, sweet victory. Attention has been regained. The faithless parents have been shown the error of their way. The food tyranny technique is but one of many. The struggle to establish toilet habits delivers another weapon into the hands of the young warrior. He cannot but notice the considerable attention that is devoted to the new arrival because of his lack of such habits. Why, questions an awakening intelligence, should he be exemplary in his toilet habits when their absence in his rival has such attention-getting powers? Thus may arise enuresis, another solution for outraged babyhood.

Food, toilet habits, crying, temper tantrums are ready tyrannies for the dethroned child to use. But the possibilities do not end with such obvious weapons. There is a good deal of reason to think that less simple devices are utilized, such as the anxiety symptoms which loom so large in the literature of child behavior. These symptoms include nightmares, nail biting, restless sleep, stammering, excessive shyness, neurotic vomiting, negativism, fantasies, and the like. It is not implied that these are to be explained solely on this ground, but they do all have this common element: they are effective in attracting attention from other children and centering it upon the subject with the symptom.

With the passing of time, this situation with its aspects of displacement and jealousy changes to one with possibilities of an entirely different sort for the oldest child. This new situation is replete with elements which make for the development of leadership. With the coming and growth of younger children, the oldest child naturally assumes such a position. Ordinarily he is older, bigger, stronger. And what is of outstanding importance in the eyes of the younger children is that he is the one who does things first. It is he who is first allowed that prime adventure of contemporary urban children—crossing the street alone. He goes to school first, contacts the teachers, learns the ropes. He is the pioneer, the pathfinder, the trail blazer. He sets the pace. More than that, he comes to be a sort of top sergeant in the familial company, assuming a certain oversight of the behavior and disciplinary problems of the younger children. He regards his superiority over his brothers and sisters often as his natural right. It is this situation which explains, possibly, his higher rate of achievement and success, indicated in various studies of data in *Who's Who* and other compilations.

Studies of large-family living suggest that increase in family size tends to intensify the eldest child as a type. Characteristics of the type in such families are marked patterns of responsibility—for the care of the younger children, for their management and discipline, for their adjustment to parents and other adults, and for the development of their capabilities. Patterns of sacrifice and service also manifest themselves early in life. Being the oldest means doing things for the younger ones, and this can be as habit-forming as other patterns of behavior. It is upon this child often that an undue share of the family burdens fall. Especially is this true in the case of household chores. In fact, in large families much of the rearing of the younger children falls upon the older ones, and particularly upon the first-born. Sibling sacrifice is no empty phrase for many eldest children.[15]

There is reason to think that the oldest child in a family of some size is peculiarly schooled in certain specific traits. There comes early a growing sense of responsibility for the younger children as they arrive, and a sense of power, too, augmented and intensified with each new addition; but more than these, there seems to come also a certain perspective in viewing life and its processes. There is the oldest child's own poignant experience when the second-born arrives, to which adjustment must be made; as time goes on, this is repeated in a sense in the case of each succeeding child as it is dethroned. From the repetition of these experiences, once shared and then observed in others within the intimate relationships of the family, there comes an insight into life and an ability to view it with objectivity and understanding that is found more frequently possibly in the oldest child in larger families than elsewhere.

Finally, the oldest child receives from the younger children in the same family certain incentives of both a stimulating and a restraining sort which, operating often in involved and subtle fashion, tend nevertheless because of their persistence to be of considerable importance. These grow out of the fact that, while priority in order of birth confers a position of leadership, this leadership must be maintained, not only against the younger children but against children in other families. The oldest child is expected to jump farther, climb higher, draw better houses, spell more words, etc., than the other children in the family; and he dare not, if he is to retain his prestige, he outclassed in these things by children of comparable age and status in other families. It is not implied that the oldest child always succeeds in doing all these things, it is not even likely that there is much conscious appreciation of the situation; the whole point is that the situation is there and that its implications, consciously felt or not, tend to encourage and stimulate such performances on his part. But there are also certain restraining elements in this situation. The oldest child is expected to excel, but in good deeds only. He always carries in the minds of his younger brothers and sisters, and possibly in his own, a certain responsibility for the behavior of the younger children. "Bill did it, so I thought it was O. K.," says Robert, who is two years younger. The younger children like to "get something" on the older ones, particularly on the oldest one. Such information can always be used to advantage. In summary, then, the oldest child is generally "on the spot," as is the leader of any group, to perform a little better and to act a little more circumspectly than his younger followers.

[15] For a more complete discussion of these points, consult Bossard and Boll, *The Large Family System,* Chaps. 8, 9, and 12, and J. P. Lees, *op. cit.,* p. 216. For a readable and suggestive book in this area, cf. Neisser, *op. cit.*

2. The in-between child, as such, encounters situations different from those of the first-born, and from the very beginning. The parents have a different attitude, because they have had a child before him. On the basis of their experience with the first-born, certain very definite ideas about child rearing may have taken form. Many parents begin rearing the second child with no other idea than repeating their experiences with the first one. In some cases, this view is not modified; in other cases, only slowly and almost resentfully. On the whole, then, the in-between child has less of a trial-and-error rearing than the first; his parents are less tolerant, more confident, more positive and sure about themselves.

In the next place, the in-between child enters a more complex family situation than did his predecessor, for he finds not simply the parents but also the personality of the first-born. This other child whom he finds and with whom he must henceforth live, with no choice of his own, is and invariably continues to be bigger and stronger than he, with greater liberty of action and with constant priority in life's experiences. To make matters worse—and it is a matter of no small moment—so many of his dearest possessions come to him second-hand. The first-born got the play pen when it was new; the other children also use it subsequently. Mary had the doll when it was new; Helen, a year and a half younger, gets it minus a leg, some hair, and the left eyebrow. Jack wore the overcoat when it was new; Bill, two years younger, will get it this fall if Jack has surely outgrown it. Thus, through the span of childhood and over a range of possessions, the second and subsequent children in most families get the used, the soiled, the made-over, the second-hand toys, clothing, beds, books, and the like. In many families the children born after the first one grow to maturity with only few new articles of play or attire. Obviously, we have as yet but little appreciation of what this means to the children involved, and its role in the molding of their personalities.

Another specific factor in the lives of children other than the first-born grows out of the fact that the oldest child blazes the trail and sets the pace for the other children in matters educational.[16] The nature and school work of Mary, the first of the Tweed children, set the original pattern of association in the minds of teachers between the name Tweed and the behavior and performance of their children. Helen, the second of the Tweeds, comes to be spoken of as Mary Tweed's sister. She does as well as Mary, or better, or not so well. Henceforth, all the Tweed progeny are measured by the yardstick of Mary's performance. (And woe for the subsequent Tweeds if Mary set a high standard of measurement. Here is the genesis of many behavior problems.) Moreover, this is repeated as the Tweeds pass from grade to grade. Years later, Helen has graduated from college and is herself a teacher. One day, she presents

[16] Alice Leahy, "Emphasis in Psychiatric Social Case Work," *Mental Hygiene*, October, 1926, pp. 743–750.

herself to the dean of the graduate school. "Oh, yes," says the dean, "I'm pleased to see you. You are Mary Tweed's sister." And absent-mindedly he calls her Mary several times during their brief interview.

Meanwhile, there comes the in-between child's dethronement, when the next baby comes along. He now experiences what he precipitated for the oldest child. And yet his experience is different, for he is being attacked from both the front and the rear. The new baby comes from behind to steal his status of being the baby of the family, with all the rights and privileges thereunto appertaining, while in front of him is this older, bigger, stronger, more experienced child.

And so it is throughout all his life as a member of the family. Always in front is this child with whom he never catches up, who always assumes this lordship or oversight over him as a matter of unquestioned right. Always, behind, is this other child, younger, smaller, more helpless, the "baby" of the family. What a struggle the in-between child has, just to be somebody, to be a distinct person instead of just a later edition of the eldest sibling or a transitional link between someone above and someone below in the upward climb of family life.

Caught thus between an upper and a lower millstone, as it were, three possible choices are open to the in-between child. One is to drive himself forward, hard, relentlessly, to catch up with or to overcome the oldest child. Given an in-between child with energy and a certain capacity for development, this is very apt to be the line followed—continuous endeavor under full steam. It is this which leads Adler to remark that the restless neurotics are, to a preponderant degree, second-born children.[17] A second possibility is to criticize and depreciate the older child, and thus attempt to equalize the struggle. Envious depreciation is the weapon of the less competent. You build yourself up by tearing down your competitor. Thus arise those lasting animosities, that guerrilla type of warfare, that prevails in some families between siblings. This subject of sibling rivalry is significant. Mead terms it the typical expression of the American attitude toward success. In the prevailing type of small, immediate family, the American child is constantly being compared with other children on the normal frequency curve of community statistics; hence the competition between siblings is not for the mother's person or the father's money, but for approval of one's achievement on the community rating scale.[18] The third possible course of behavior is for the in-between child to drop back and affiliate with the younger ones. This solution may be accompanied with varying attitudes. There may be the

[17] Adler, *op. cit.*, p. 322.
[18] Margaret Mead, *And Keep Your Powder Dry*, William Morrow & Company, Inc., New York, 1943, p. 109. See also David Levy, "Sibling Rivalry Studies in Children of Primitive Groups," *American Journal of Orthopsychiatry*, January, 1939, pp. 205–214; and David Levy, *Studies in Sibling Rivalry*, Research Monograph No. 2, American Orthopsychiatric Association, New York, 1938.

attitude of defeatism, a loss of initiative. There may be a sadistic turn, with the in-between child becoming a tease and a bully, taking out on the younger children the venom of his spite toward the oldest one. There may develop, however, an almost tender care for the younger children, the extreme opposite of the privileged despotism of the oldest child.

The last child grows up in a more complex family situation than do any of the other children, for there are not only the parents, but also the personalities of the other children, the interplay of their personalities, and their attitudes, singly and collectively, toward him. In a family with several children, and with only the ordinary differences in personal traits, one can appreciate readily how complex such a situation may become. There are distinguishing features in the attitudes of the parents toward the last-born. "Even with wise parents," writes Weill, "there is a tendency to prolong the last babyhood. The parents are older. Their financial position is generally stronger. The cultural opportunities open to this child are consequently greater than those afforded the older children. Discipline may break down with him largely or completely."[19]

One of the most important facts about the last-born child is that he is never dethroned. The significance of this is that he grows up in a peculiar and meaningful sense as the baby of the family; and much of what has been said or written about the status, experience, and problems of the last-born is comprehended by this fact. This tendency to regard him as the baby not only is characteristic of the parents, but comes to be shared, especially in many larger families, by the older children. In some large families, the situation is particularly favorable to the "spoiling" of the youngest one. The older children perhaps are at work. Earning money, they remember the privations of their childhood and seek to prevent them for their younger brothers and sisters. The older children fight the battles of the youngest one. They intercede for him with the parents. They make contacts for him. They steer him in advantageous directions. Life for him becomes a relatively easy matter.

It is not uncommon for the oldest child, especially in a larger family, to become a parent substitute for the youngest one. The parents being older by the time the youngest is growing up, they may be less able to be adequate parents; they may be prone to be less sympathetic with the problems of childhood; they may be blasé, having gone through the experience a number of times. Thus the youngest turns to the oldest child, who is so much nearer the problems involved and yet has, in the eyes of the youngest child, the necessary experience and opportunity.

Of course, something much the reverse may happen. If the last-born arrives a number of years after the birth of the oldest and older ones, there may arise considerable resentment against the newly born mem-

---

[19] Weill, *op. cit.,* p. 37.

ber. Especially is this apt to be true if the older children are charged with much of the responsibility of rearing the new one. As this is being written, there comes to light a case from a social agency in Philadelphia. A 17-year-old boy, the oldest of four in a Lithuanian family, is given the responsibility for the care of a newborn brother. Among other duties enjoined upon him is the changing and washing of the baby's diapers. This he resents exceedingly. He broods over his predicament. He longs for surcease from his sorrows. At the depth of his degradation there comes an invitation to join a gang of counterfeiters. To him it seems like an answer sent from heaven. Success with the counterfeiters means freedom from his brother's diapers; failure, but a few years in jail at the worst, by which time his youngest brother will have grown out of the stage of his toilet dependencies.

Two possible roads are open most widely for the last-born to take in his adjustments to his family situation. One is to accept the situation and exploit it. Be the baby, and make the most out of it. Utilize the position to the utmost. Why try to develop your own powers? Why try to secure things for yourself? Simply wait, and someone in the family group, mindful of the fact that you are the baby, will secure it for you. The other alternative is again, as for the in-between child, to drive restlessly forward, to catch up and even surpass the others. It is not without significance that "both in the Bible and in fairy-tales, people's knowledge of mankind has generally given to the youngest the greatest gifts, especially the 'magic boots' which enable him to surpass his brothers."[20] This kind of person is sometimes referred to as the "Joseph type," and the story of Joseph (Genesis: 37–50) is particularly revealing in this connection. Joseph, it is noted, was the second last-born of his father, the son of his old age, beloved above his other children. His brothers, jealous of this, hated him so they could not even speak peacefully to him. Planning originally to kill him, they sold him to the Ishmaelites for 20 pieces of silver. But in the wake of their success against their brother came a series of spectacular developments to his advantage. Everything came to him, even the wife of Potiphar, and the ultimate triumph of this dreamer over his older, more practical brothers was complete.

Personality Roles in Large Families

Whenever a number of persons are in continuing association with each other, specialization of function of the individual members tends to occur. Sociologists use the word *role* to designate this. Some such specialization of role obviously occurs within the family; and the larger the family, the greater the degree and number of specialization in these roles. By way of illustration is a study of sixty-four large families in which

[20] Adler, *op. cit.*, p. 322.

each child in the family was characterized by a sibling informant. These characterizations, when imposed upon each other, fall into eight rather distinctive groups, suggestive of eight family group roles. A brief description of each follows:

1. Every family identifies at least one of its siblings as the responsible type, the one that is looked up to, the one that assumes direction or supervision of the other siblings, or renders service to them. The word *responsible* is the one used most frequently in referring to these siblings, but in some cases such words as *dutiful, bossy, drudge, leader, helpful, martinet,* and *policeman* are also used. These seem to identify chiefly the way in which this position of responsibility is exercised.

2. The second most frequently identified is the popular, sociable, well-liked sibling. This quite often is the second-born, or the one that follows in order of birth the responsible sibling. It seems in many cases as if, finding the post of responsibility preëmpted, he or she (and most often it is a he) proceeds to gain recognition and self-esteem through personal charm rather than personal power.

3. The third is the socially ambitious type. The term *social butterfly* is often used by the informants in describing this type. The picture is quite clear. Whereas the preceding type was described chiefly in terms of appeal to the other siblings, this third group directed its social interests mostly to persons outside of the family. Most of these siblings were women, mostly third, fourth, or fifth in the order of birth.

4. Fourth of the types by order of frequency were the studious ones. These apparently sought and found recognition within the family and outside by doing well in school, or withdrew from sibling activities to find surcease in books. Male and female siblings appear in about equal proportions, and are usually described as quiet, hard-working, and, in some cases, as methodical.

5. The self-centered isolate appears as the fifth of the types identified by our informants—this in spite of all that has been said about the socializing effects of large family living. Descriptions of this type vary from references to their secretiveness to stubborn antisocial attitudes toward the other siblings and/or life. In some instances the chief fact noted is an unwillingness to participate in family activities; in others, a withdrawal from the family and an organization of life on an away-from-home basis.

6. Many large families report at least one member who is largely or wholly irresponsible. These siblings seem to withdraw from the family life, but in ways that differ from the family isolates. They do not withdraw their physical presence or their participation in group activities; they simply sit back, as it were, and withdraw from the responsibilities which the others accept.

7. There were the siblings who were not well. Some of these had physical defects, sufficient to set them apart and to create special problems; some had to carry the burden of chronic or long-drawn-out illness; and still others seemed hypochondriacal, and learned to utilize their illness to gain them special favors or to justify their failures.

8. Not many large families escape having a "spoiled" sibling. Most often this is the last-born child, although there are cases, like that of Joseph of Old Testament fame, where it is the second youngest. What apparently happens in this latter type of case is that the parents, and particularly the mother, conceive of the second-last one as the last one, and proceed to "spoil" that one. Then, perhaps several years later, perchance as an accident, another child is born. Possibly the mother resents the coming of this last child, and having started to spoil the second-last one, continues to do so. This was pointed out as particularly true in two of our families where it was common knowledge among all the other siblings that the mothers resented the coming of the last-born and doted unduly (in one case, the rest of her life) upon the second youngest.

These eight types fall into an intriguing sequence, suggesting a theory of specialized personality roles and behavior patterns in the large family that is breath-taking in the challenging leads which it opens up. Keeping in mind always the constancy of the individual child's drive for recognition and status, let us consider the eight types in the order of their presentation, which is essentially the order of frequency of identification. The first ones to appear develop patterns of responsibility because they are first and are followed by younger and more helpless siblings. The next ones, finding this role preëmpted, seek recognition by making themselves agreeable. They do not seek to wrest control from the older children; they compete with it or supplement it with their personal charms. The next children, finding these two roles preëmpted, turn from the family to the community. They become social-minded and socially ambitious. Those that follow in turn have to turn to a new avenue of achievement. These turn to the schools. They become the scholars, the studious ones, the sophisticates, the intellectuals. Finding all of these avenues under active cultivation, the next child withdraws from competition. This is the family isolate. Or he may not withdraw his presence, only his sense of responsibility—these are the irresponsible ones, who participate but let others hold the bag. Both the isolate and the irresponsible are patterns of withdrawal and often of failure to find a satisfactory avenue of achievement. The physically defective, the sickly, and those who pretend to be—they have their excuse for relative failure to find their roles, if they wish to use it. Finally, at the end of the line is the terminal child, either pampered into relative ineffectiveness or wearing the "magic boots" to overtake the older ones.

The Individuality of Sibling Interactions

In the preceding pages it was pointed out that the contributions of siblings to each other vary on the basis of certain factors, five of which were selected for discussion. These five were the nature of the child, the nature of the home situation, the age of the siblings, differences in sex, and order of birth. These factors, it will be appreciated, influence not only the relationships between siblings, but also those between parents and siblings. It is possible for the purposes of discussion to consider these factors separately and to point out their possible roles. In the reality of life situations, however, no such isolation prevails. In any one family, all of them operate and affect each other in all kinds of ways—now one reinforces the other; here one counteracts the other; there the two combine to negate, stimulate, or avoid the third. For example, the status and role of the oldest child may be completely negated by the sex factor and the home situation. The oldest child is a daughter. The home is one in which the masculine tradition is strong. The mother wants very much to have a son. The second child is a son. The result of this situation is apparent. The oldest daughter has at best only part of the eldest child's customary prerogatives.

We come then to point out—and the fact cannot be emphasized too much—that the interaction between the siblings in any one family is a distinctly individual one. Our understanding of the role of any one factor is at best only relative, suggestive of the possibilities for which to look. How they operate, with every other factor, in any particular family, must always be regarded as an intriguing field for careful study, and with a driving appreciation that each case will have its own special variants and yield its own special returns in human understanding to students who proceed in the best traditions of the scientific method.

Summary

1. Interaction between siblings constitutes a fundamental aspect of family life. The distinctive features of sibling relationships are their inclusive character, the extensiveness of the contacts included, and the frankness of the relationships.

2. Siblings are effective teachers for each other, both through word of mouth and by serving to mirror each other. The family is a miniature school, and a hard school offering many lessons as siblings live constantly with each other.

3. Siblings give emotional satisfactions to each other, often with particular emphasis upon a sense of security which has basic implications for mental hygiene.

4. The problems of the only child—his egocentrism, his sensitiveness, and his emotional isolation—illustrate in reverse the importance of sibling interaction. The only child lacks the things that siblings give each other.

5. What siblings contribute to each other varies considerably. Differential factors are (a) the nature of the children, (b) the nature of the home situation, (c) differences in the ages of the siblings, (d) differences in their sex, and (e) order of birth.

6. The size of the family seems to affect the crystallization of types among the children, as well as the personality role which each develops.

Chapter 6

Family Culture and the Child

A third approach to the study of family situations concerns itself with their cultural content. Although family structure and family process are distinct social entities, each with its own significance, from the larger point of view both are but means to an end, and that end is the content which they serve to convey. This content is culture, and it is in many ways the most significant aspect of a family situation. Accordingly, the present chapter is devoted to a consideration of the meaning of family culture, its relation to the larger culture system, the differing versions of this larger system, the cultural role of the family, and the nature of the contemporary problems precipitated for children by these cultural factors and processes.

The Sociological Emphasis upon Culture and the Family

Culture is another of the words which sociologists have come to accept as part of their scientific terminology, investing it with rather precise meaning. In contrast to popular parlance, which uses it as synonymous with good manners, proper etiquette, or refinement of artistic taste, it is defined by sociologists and other social scientists as "that complex whole which includes knowledge, belief, art, morals, law, custom and other capabilities acquired by man as a member of society."[1] Expressed more simply and tersely, culture is the sum total of the ways of doing and thinking, past and present, of a social group.[2] From the standpoint of the child, culture is the social heritage to which he is born and in which he is reared. This social heritage includes the answers which his group has made and is making to the problems of life.

[1] E. B. Tylor, *Primitive Culture*, 7th ed., Brentano's, New York, 1924, p. 1.
[2] Emory S. Bogardus, *Contemporary Sociology*, University of Southern California Press, Los Angeles, 1931, p. 68.

It is an accepted sociological principle that culture, thus conceived, is one of the chief determinants in the formation of personality. In fact, so great is the relative importance which sociologists attach to the conditioning power of the cultural heritage that personality is continually spoken of as the subjective side of culture. Equivalent in meaning is the other frequently cited dictum of the self as a social looking glass. The foregoing principle was emphasized in Chapter 2 and is recalled here because of its background importance to the discussion in the present chapter. Stated usually without reference to or qualification for age, the application of this principle to the child would seem to be particularly obvious. In other words, if culture determines personality, certainly it does so with particular force and effectiveness in that period of life when it is accepted and absorbed with little or no hesitation or questioning.

Along with his emphasis upon cultural data and the principle that personality is culturally determined goes the sociologist's concern with the family. The insight into social relations which sociologists have obtained thus far all points unmistakably to the primary importance of the family; courses on the family are among the few given by sociology departments everywhere, and much of the research work done by sociologists centers about the family. In brief, both by what they say and by what they do, sociologists reveal their great emphasis upon and preoccupation with the social role of the family, a fact which again seems most applicable and pertinent in the area of the social development of the child.

Combining these emphases in sociology, one must conclude that the cultural content of family situations has marked importance for personality studies in general and for the social development of the child in particular. If, on the one hand, sociologists have been slow in appreciating this, it is due to facts other than the logical sequence of their thinking; if, on the other hand, students of child behavior have not recognized the primary role of cultural factors, it would seem to be due to their preoccupation with other contributing circumstances.

The Family Culture Pattern

In making a cultural approach to the study of family situations, it is important to distinguish between family life as part of the culture system and the family as a medium through which the larger cultural heritage is transmitted to the child. These are two distinct social realities; it is important to identify and remember the difference between them.

The pattern of family culture is our first concern. Speaking generally, this consists of the ways of living and thinking which constitute the family and sex aspects of group life. This is one of the patterns which is part of the culture system of all societies. It includes marriage and courtship procedures, sex mores, husband-wife relationships, status of men and women, guardianship, parent-child relationships, divorce, disposition of the children's earnings, family solidarity, responsibility toward aging parents, attitudes toward unmarried mothers and children born out of wedlock, and various other matters. In short, there exists in each society a series of socially accepted attitudes and forms of behavior centering around the sex, procreative, homemaking, child-rearing, and family relationship activities of the group which social scientists today speak of as the family and sex culture pattern.

SELECTED FAMILY CULTURE PATTERNS

What family patterns are and how they differ from one culture to another can best be shown by presenting several brief descriptions of such patterns as they have been observed in widely different cultural areas.[3]

1. The first is summarized from the available data on southern Italian family life.[4] Family life here is strongly knit, and is dominated by the father, in whose name authority is exercised. Control by the father is rigorous and comprehensive. It includes the management of the household, the right of control over the children's occupation, and selection of their marital partner. The children are expected to accept the mates selected for them. Property considerations in marriage still prevail. The family is a closely bound economic unit. Children go to work early, and the wages earned by each member of the family go into a common fund. This fund is controlled by the parent and utilized for the needs of the family members. In return for their coöperation in this, the children are given an allowance, are maintained when unemployed, and are given aid when they are married. The strong unity of the southern Italian family shows itself in other ways. Respect for parents and relatives is much emphasized. Fear of the father and love of the mother are twin principles in family life. Overt acts of hostility against one member become the concern of the entire group. Violent quarrels may occur within the family but are not to be talked about to persons outside the family group.

Marriage is consummated at an early age. Girls particularly have a short childhood. The emphasis in their early training is upon becoming good wives and mothers. Girls are taught to feed and bathe and clothe

[3] There is a considerable literature on family culture patterns in various parts of the world. For a summary more extended than the plan of this volume permits, the reader is referred to Joseph K. Folsom, *The Family and Democratic Society*, John Wiley & Sons, Inc., New York, 1943, pp. 1–54, 84–145; Stuart Queen and John B. Adams, *The Family in Various Cultures*, J. B. Lippincott Company, Philadelphia, 1952; International Issue on the Family, *Marriage and Family Living*, November, 1954; International Issue on Services to the Family, *ibid.*, August, 1955; and Norman D. Humphrey, "The Cultural Background of the Mexican Immigrant," *Rural Sociology*, Vol. XIII, 1948, pp. 239–255.

[4] Irvin L. Child, *Italian or American?* Yale University Press, New Haven, 1943; Celena A. Baxter, "Sicilian Family Life," *The Family*, May, 1933, pp. 82–88; Jerre Mangione, *Mount Allegro*, Houghton Mifflin Company, Boston, 1942; Caroline Ware, *Greenwich Village*, Houghton Mifflin Company, Boston, 1935.

babies, make beds, and do the family washing. The younger girls in lower-class families are generally placed in domestic service. A girl's place is understood to be in the home, and consideration for a girl in the family takes the form of selecting a good husband and providing her with a fine wardrobe and a well-filled hope chest. The male, by way of contrast, must play a superior role, and therefore is given special educational opportunities in his youth.

The distinction between men and women is also evident in their recreational life, for each sex remains separate. Italian men engage in drinking, playing games, arguing, and discussing public affairs. Games with small stakes are popular; clubs and societies are relatively prevalent. By contrast, women are not expected to drink much or to play games, their social life being confined to visits with neighbors or socializing at the neighborhood store. There is some seclusion of women from public activities. A good wife is one who bears many children and works harder than her husband, leaving to him the management of family affairs and its leadership in communal relations.

There is little discussion of sex within the family, yet children are present constantly when parents speak of it and the small homes make inevitable some observation of parental sex behavior. There is a fairly frank acceptance of a double standard of sex behavior, but a young man does not make sexual advances to unmarried girls whom he respects. There is a high value upon a girl's virginity until her marriage. Daughters particularly are jealously guarded by their fathers. In Sicily, the sex mores are enforced by fear of the vendetta. Chaperonage still flourishes, especially in the upper classes. Infidelity of the wife is considered extremely seriously; male jealousy and possessiveness are institutionalized. Rates of illegitimacy are relatively low, but natural children are the responsibility of the father and must be given the same treatment as though born in wedlock. Marriage and the family are under the special control of the church, which, for most southern Italians, means the Roman Catholic Church. Although Roman Catholic by profession, there is much criticism of the church and antagonism toward the clergy. This is particularly true of the men, who incline to think of the church as intended chiefly for the women, children, and aged.

2. The family pattern of Sweden may be described briefly by way of contrast. Here is a country with a long history of continuous peace, a homogeneous population with no problems of minority groups, a long tradition of public education and democratic processes, and well-established patterns of normality and lawfulness.

Relatively speaking, there is equality between the sexes in Sweden. "During the rapid industrialization of Sweden the status of Swedish women has been revolutionized. Their economic standard, their legal status, their civil rights, their daily work environment, and their general attitude to life for all closer to a complete equality with those of men than in most other countries."[5] The marriage rate in Sweden is lower than in most countries. This is due in part to the age structure of the population, in part to the industrial structure which separates men-employing industries from those which employ women, and in part to a certain prudence in founding a family which is so widespread as to make it a definite social characteristic. Long engagements are common; the average age at marriage is high, as is also the percentage of unmarried persons. Virtually half the adult population of Sweden is unwed. Before the time of a mobile, industrially employed population, there was widespread acceptance of the pattern of premarital sex relationships, and a relative tolerance of them continues down to the present day. The double standard of sex conduct, more prevalent during the nineteenth century, has been giving way rapidly to the acceptance of the same standard for both sexes. This obviously is a phase of the equality of the sexes, previously mentioned. The rate of illegitimacy is high in Sweden. During the decade 1921–1930, almost one child in every six was born out of wedlock. Sweden is also noted for its advanced legislation on the care and status of children thus born.

There is secular rather than church control of marriage and divorce. Divorce is approved in preference to the toleration of extramarital relationships. In fact, the theory of divorce is more liberal in Sweden than in the United States, although recourse to it is less frequent. Divorce by mutual consent, and without specific cause, is obtainable. Divorce risks have increased approximately tenfold during the lifetime of recent generations. During the years 1861–1870, an average of 4.9 marriages were thus dissolved, as against 1,000 new marriages; but during 1931–1935, the corresponding figure was 56.[6]

There is a great deal of emphasis upon scientific infant and child care. Some of this is confined to the home, particularly during the preschool years. Swedish mothers take charge of their children during this period more than do American mothers. Beyond these years, the child-caring and -training functions of the family have been transferred to a great extent to communal institutions. There is a long tradition in Sweden of public services of this kind, and the feeling of group responsibility for child welfare is very strong.

3. A third example of a family culture pattern representative of still another section of Europe in the years before the Second World War, is the one found in the Soviet Union. Drawing heavily upon the summary

[5] Alva Myrdal, "Swedish Women in Industry and at Home," *Annals of the American Academy of Political and Social Science,* May, 1938, p. 216. For a discussion of the socioeconomic status of Swedish wives in relation to that of husbands, cf. C. Arnold Anderson, "Employment, Occupation, and Socio-Economic Status of Swedish Wives in Relation to Occupation and Status of Husbands," *Statistical Review* (Stockholm), No. 1, 1957, pp. 3–15.

[6] *Ibid.,* p. 221.

presented by Fairchild, we may note the following main features:[7] (a) Equality of husband and wife is emphasized. Women have equal status with men in all "spheres of economic, state, cultural, social and political life."[8] (b) There is separation of property owned by husband and wife respectively. Mutual responsibility of each for the support of the other and of the children is accepted. (c) Marriage and divorce depended on the simple process of registration. Beyond social control by way of protecting the mother and child, the relation between the sexes was a matter of private concern only. There was considerable freedom in sex relations. Divorce was frequent, with a considerable changing of marriage partners. Toward the end of the period under consideration, an increasing stability of the family came to prevail, and there was a rise in divorce requirements.[9] (d) Freedom of abortion prevailed from 1930 to 1936, when it was restricted to cases in which the mother's health was threatened by pregnancy or when the parent had a serious disease which could be transmitted. (e) The primary purpose of marriage regulation was the obligation for the care of children. By the code of 1926 the support of children was obligatory and strictly enforced, in accordance with ability to pay. (f) Responsibility for the maintenance of children included those born out of wedlock, no distinction between legitimate and illegitimate children being recognized. (g) The state accepted a large measure of responsibility for the care and education of children. A comprehensive network of agencies to deal with the problems of pregnancy, childbirth, and infant care developed. Public education began at the age of 4, and continued, according to the child's ability, through a university. (h) Russian parents carried the primary responsibility for the nurture and upbringing of their children. The various auxiliary and supplementary child-caring services which developed were based on the idea that the essential function of women in the family went beyond those of cooking, washing the clothes, and bathing the children. (i) Complete freedom of dissemination of contraceptive knowledge and material guaranteed the child's right to be wanted. (j) The general picture seems to have been one of personal freedom in family and sex relations, consonant with the stability of reproduction and child care, as the Russians interpreted it.

The Primary Importance of the Family Culture

No part of the entire culture system seems quite so important for the child as the family culture pattern. It is peculiarly the child-centered aspect of the culture; in fact, the child is what gives meaning to the pat-

[7] Mildred Fairchild, "The Status of the Family in the Soviet Union Today," *American Sociological Review*, October, 1937, pp. 619–629. See also Rose Maurer, "Recent Trends in the Soviet Family," *ibid.*, June, 1944, pp. 242–249.

[8] Fairchild, *op. cit.*, p. 624.

[9] Sweeping changes in divorce legislation were decreed as of July 9, 1944.

tern as a whole. The family culture consists of all the stages involved in the child's birth and rearing; it includes virtually every feature of the child's life for a number of years. Other aspects of it can be viewed from the child's standpoint with a certain objectivity: the child is introduced to those parts of the culture. But he lives the family culture, and thus one must regard it as the most subjective, the most deeply embedded part of the cultural heritage: the one which carries over longest in the life span. With these general thoughts in mind, the reader is asked to consider again the three family patterns which have just been presented. They are representative of three cultural systems in an old, relatively developed, and socially mature continent. The differences are striking. The family life of each is distinctive, and different from the other. They differ in their minutiae, in combination, in values, in point of view; and these differences are the essence of what the children in these respective cultures absorb with such intimate completeness as to seem the nature of human nature.

The Family and the Larger Culture System

The family culture is, of course, only a part of the larger culture of society. This larger culture is made up of a number of patterns involving the fundamental aspects of the communal life. Recent students of culture have identified thirteen patterns as generally present in the cultural system or configuration of a society. They are as follows:

1. Patterns of communication: gestures and language.
2. Methods and objects for providing for man's physical welfare.
   a. Food getting.
   b. Personal care.
   c. Shelter.
   d. Tools, instruments, and machines.
3. Means or techniques of travel and transportation of goods and services.
4. Exchange of goods and services: barter, trade, commerce, occupation.
5. Forms of property: real and personal.
6. The sex and family patterns.
   a. Marriage and divorce.
   b. Forms of kinship relation.
   c. Guardianship.
   d. Inheritance.
7. Societal controls and institutions of government.
   a. Mores.
   b. Public opinion.
   c. Organized state: laws and political officers.
   d. War: institutional form of conflict of tribes, societies, or states.
8. Artistic expression: architecture, painting, sculpture, music, literature, dancing.

9. Recreational and leisure-time interests and activities.
10. Religious and magical ideas and practices.
11. Science (in civilization chiefly).
12. Mythology and philosophy.
13. Cultural structuring of basic interactional processes, such as competition, conflict, cooperation, differentiation, stratification, accommodation, and assimilation.[10]

THE FAMILY AND THE TRANSMISSION OF CULTURE

A second cultural role of the family is its service as an agent in the transmission of this culture system or configuration to the child. This is one of the fundamental roles of the family in relation to the child. It is through the family that the child gets his first introduction to the culture of his era and area. And for a number of years the family remains the chief agency through which he has contacts with the cultural milieu.

Varying Versions of the Culture Configuration

THE ETHOS, OR NATIONAL CULTURE

Children are born customarily into a particular system or configuration of culture patterns, usually national in scope, and of a definite historical epoch. The distinguishing culture system of a particular society was called the *ethos* by the ancient Greeks; and William Graham Sumner, pioneer American sociologist, utilized the term to apply to the totality of characteristic traits by which a society is individualized and differentiated from other societies.[11] It is in the ethos, then, that the United States differs fundamentally from Nazi Germany, modern Persia, ancient Judea, or the interior of China in 2000 B.C.

A few comparisons will reveal how comprehensive these differences are in our contemporary world. Consider, for example, the United States and India in recent decades. The differences in the material culture of the two countries are well known and require no comment here. Less emphasized are the differences in their nonmaterial culture, which really are the characteristic features of the two countries. As suggested by Young, they are as follows:[12] Our American culture is dominated by (1) belief in individual material success and national progress; (2) belief in universal literacy and education as the means of solving social and personal problems; (3) acceptance of the idea that there is advantage and virtue in rapid movement through space; (4) faith in the virtue of constant change in all, or most, aspects of life; (5) confidence in man's ability to control and direct his destiny, in both a personal and a social

[10] Kimball Young, *Sociology—A Study of Society and Culture*, American Book Company, New York, 1942, p. 39.
[11] William G. Sumner, *Folkways*, Ginn & Company, Boston, 1911, pp. 37–38.
[12] Young, *op. cit.*, pp. 42–43.

sense. In India, by way of contrast, there is less belief in progress, or none, in our sense of the word; mere bigness has no special merit; there is no virtue in rapid movement; calm deliberation is the height of desirability; and the desire for forgetfulness of the self and of the wish to be somebody is the ultimate good, rather than material success.[13]

To this ethos, or national cultural pattern, the child is introduced by his family. This introduction is in part formal, but much more it is incidental and imperceptible. The ethos surrounds the child at every turn; he learns it because he knows no other. It is like the air he breathes or the landscape he sees. To him it is but a natural part of the scheme of things. And all the time, as he learns the culture he absorbs the family attitude toward it. He shares this attitude with his parents, and because of his emotional relationship to them his attitude toward the culture becomes emotionally tinged. Thus originate those feelings toward one's country, and about other countries whose cultural pattern is different, with which we have been so much concerned in recent years. One recalls here Sumner's remark that the ethos furnishes the point of view from which one group criticizes the ways of another group.

The identification of the family version of this natural culture pattern is highly important in any country; it is peculiarly so in the United States because of the heterogeneity of our population. In 1930, one-third of the population of the continental United States consisted of persons who were either foreign-born or native-born of foreign parents. Included in these two elements were 29 nationality groups consisting of more than 100,000 individuals, 16 of more than 500,000, and 11 of more than a million. In many cases, considerable numbers of people in one nationality group have lived together in a relatively compact manner so as to maintain various features of their alien culture, despite many years of American residence. In studying family situations from the point of view of cultural content, it becomes important to ask questions such as those which follow. Is the family version of the ethos of this American-reared child an American version, an American-Sicilian one, or an American-Bulgarian one? Do the father and mother represent the same national culture? Are the versions held by the immediate family and that of the larger kinship group family the same? Here, concretely speaking, is a young man, born and reared on the lower East Side of New York, son of an Italian father and an Irish mother. What is his national culture pattern as transmitted by his family?

THE REGIONAL CULTURE

Recently, social scientists have broken down the nation into regions. The region is a unit part of the larger society, identified first in geographical terms, subsequently on the basis of trade and other economic con-

[13] K. Shridharani, *My India, My America*, Duell, Sloan & Pearce, Inc., New York, 1941.

siderations, and now increasingly on cultural bases. Much of the research work on the region today is based on identifying selected traits which lend themselves to statistical treatment. Howard Odum has made a noteworthy contribution by dividing the states of the nation into six groups on the basis of outstanding similarities of culture. Zimmerman and Du Wors, in an excellent study, have identified seven geo-social areas in the United States, each with its own peculiar social system, significant for family life and child development.[14]

These cultural areas are not mere academic distinctions. Under one name or another, they have long been recognized in popular parlance as well as in more intellectual discussions. The Southerner differs from the Maine Yankee, and the Iowan in Hollywood is unlike both; the Prussian and the Bavarian have never "spoken the same language"; the northern Italian is different from the Sicilian in many respects in his ways, his speech, and his ideas. The region has its distinct cultural features. It carries "certain dominant motifs which serve as selective norms and as centers with reference to which conduct is directed. . . . It is this complex regional culture which produces the personality patterns of its inhabitants through the stimuli which it radiates, the preferences and choices which it offers, and the distinctive placement of persons or groups of persons, which constitutes its structure."[15] The region, in other words, is a distinctive social system that supplies a plan for personality patterning. It is this regional or sectional variant of the national cultural pattern that is imposed on the child through the family.

A considerable number of studies of family culture patterns in particular regional areas in the United States have been made.[16] These show significant variations within the same nation. When to these studies of family culture are added the available analyses of the larger regional culture, the scope of the cultural differences between regions within the United States becomes apparent.[17] Moreover, the reader will remember

[14] Howard Odum, *Southern Regions of the United States,* University of North Carolina Press, Chapel Hill, 1936; H. W. Odum and H. E. Moore, *American Regionalism,* Henry Holt & Company, Inc., New York, 1938; Carle C. Zimmerman and Richard E. Du Wors, *Graphic Regional Sociology,* The Phillips Book Store, Cambridge, Mass., 1952.

[15] J. O. Hertzler, "Some Notes on the Social Psychology of Regionalism," *Social Forces,* March, 1940, pp. 331–332.

[16] Nels Anderson, "The Mormon Family," *American Sociological Review,* October, 1937, pp. 601–608; C. C. Zimmerman and M. E. Frampton, *Family and Society,* D. Van Nostrand Company, Inc., New York, 1935; Howard W. Beers, "The Farm Family in Central New York State," *American Sociological Review,* October, 1937, pp. 591–600; Horace Miner, "The French-Canadian Family Cycle, *ibid.,* October, 1938, pp. 700–708; D. Sanderson and Robert Foster, "A Sociological Case Study of Farm Families," *The Family,* June, 1930, pp. 107–114.

[17] Consult, for example, the studies of the culture of contemporary rural communities made under the direction of the United States Department of Agriculture and published in its Rural Life Study Series. For a glimpse of regional nonmaterial culture, see John Walker McCain, Jr., "Some Small-Town Folk Beliefs of the Carolina Piedmont," *Social Forces,* March, 1934, pp. 418–420.

that ours is a nation which throughout its history has been free of barriers in the interchange of populations between its respective regions, and that the foregoing cultural variations were identified at a time in its history when there prevailed the utmost facility in the mobility of population. Cultural variations on a regional basis are not only extensive but highly persistent.

The large-scale movement of people from one region to another within the United States has been studied from the standpoint of population changes, the social effects of mobility, its relation to employment, its effect upon school facilities, and various other aspects. For this reason it is striking to notice how little appreciation has been given to its meaning for child behavior, although it is obvious that its significance in this respect must be marked. The child is inducted into the regional culture. This regional variant is in many respects more intimately meaningful to him than the national culture. When the family moves from one region to another, the transition for the child may be very difficult. Consider, for example, the child of North Carolina piedmont parentage who is thrust overnight, as it were, into the school and social life of a second-generation Irish or Portuguese section in New England. Such a child appreciates, if parents and child behavior students do not, the reality of differences in the regional culture.

THE CLASS CULTURE

The population of any national and regional society is divided in turn into class and other interest groups, and the more these groupings become distinct and fixed, the more prescribed and predictable are the patterns of attitudes and behaviors associated with them. These class culture patterns have become so important in the social development of the contemporary American child that a separate chapter is devoted later in this volume to their analysis. The one point to be emphasized here is that the family transmits to the child the culture pattern of its own class, together with the class attitudes toward other classes. The family influence upon the child is particularly significant in its rating of social classes, placing its own class in the scale and determining its attitudes toward other classes. Here one finds marked emotions, for these matters of class distinctions go far below the surface. Prejudice and appreciation, antagonism and coöperation, pride and a rankling sense of injustice— these develop as by-products of the transmission of the class culture. Class bias has its roots in the family setting of the child, and it has taken form before the family turns him over to other culture-transmitting agencies.

In other words, the child gets from the family pattern a way of living, based on the fact that he is born in a certain class in a given region in a particular nation. He learns the life of Boston rather than of Burma; of the flat or the farm; of the slum or the suburb; of the Sicilian concrete mixer or the Fifth Avenue surgeon. In short, the child gets from the family his class cultural orientation. Thus as a functioning element in the cultural content of any given family situation, there must be considered the family version of the class culture which has been transmitted to the child.

THE FAMILY VERSION

The culture to which the child is born is too vast, too comprehensive, too diverse, to be transmitted in its entirety, either by the family or by other agencies subsequently assisting it. This is particularly true of ideas, beliefs, and values in the culture. From the beginning of the child's induction into the culture, the family does more than merely transmit the culture. To speak more precisely, the family customarily performs three additional or supplementary functions: (1) it selects from the existing surroundings what is transmitted; (2) it interprets to the child what is transmitted; and (3) it evaluates what it transmits. In other words, the child sees the cultural heritage through the eyes of his family; he learns of it through the symbols which the family uses; and he shares the family's feelings toward it.

There are a number of factors which in turn determine this selective and evaluating process. Obviously, the family is limited in these respects to the culture which it has come to know; in part, it depends on what in the culture it has access to; third is the effect of its experience with different aspects of the culture; and, finally, there is the influence of the family's hopes. Each family is prone to see its children as its future, so that domestic hopes and ideals are imposed upon the children, often with more emotional accompaniment than are the realities of the culture. In other words, every family transmits the cultural heritage in its own way. More than that, it transmits its own version, compounded out of what it can see of the culture, how it sees it, and how it wants to see it.

The result of this selective and evaluating process on the part of the family is the formation of the child's sense of values, in regard to both personal pursuits and social behavior. The culture to which the child is born has its folkways, its mores, and its scale of rewards for differing schematizations of living. But it is within the bosom of the family that judgments are formed, conflicts of culture are resolved, choices are made or at least influenced. Life is varied and complex, infinitely full of possibilities. Personality development is a constant series of choices. These choices represent the person's values, and modern scholarship concludes that these values are in large part the result of family conditioning.

So fundamental is the role of the cultural values transmitted by the family and operating in any given family situation that the fullest consideration must be given to their identification and operation. Unfortunately, sociologists have shown a reluctance to deal with values, apparently on the ground that their intangible and subjective nature makes their objective study impossible. Being relative newcomers to the study of behavior problems, sociologists seem to have leaned over backward in their desire to confine themselves to data and methods similar to those of the older and more established natural sciences. It is an implication of the outline of study proposed in this chapter that culture values can be studied objectively.

The Family and the Child's Place in the Culture

As the child is being introduced to his cultural heritage, there arise other questions of a more personal nature. Who am I? What am I? What is my own particular relation to this cultural situation in which I find myself? What is my peculiar place in it? What is my status?

These questions arise early, and are insistent. Parents may sense them before children develop to the point of formulating them. Social workers recognize the craving of adopted and foster children to learn about their own parents—who they were, what sort of people they were—regardless of how they were treated by them. The press is replete with stories of grown persons seeking knowledge of parents they never knew. The study of genealogy is a very human and understandable quest.

Sociologists and psychiatrists have made much of the concept of status. They define it to mean position in society, the standing accorded the individual by his fellows. Status, in other words, is one's place on a prestige scale. Linton defines it in terms of polar positions in the patterns of reciprocal behavior between individuals and groups.[18] Perhaps we might summarize by saying that status involves one's personal orientation in his cultural setting. A more extended discussion of the subject of status will be found in subsequent chapters.

One of the most important things which the family does for the child is to give him status. Rather, one should speak of the statuses which he gets from the family. There is, first of all, his status in the family of procreation. With the coming of another child, this status is modified, often quite materially so. Again, the child has his status in the family of orientation, if that differs from the family of procreation. In these statuses in the immediate family, sex, age, and age relationship are the determining factors.

It is with reference to the child's status in the large society that the family serves a most important function. In this connection both the immediate and the kinship group types may be of great importance in giving the child his status in the world of his fellows. The family does this

[18] Ralph Linton, *The Study of Man*, D. Appleton-Century Company, Inc., New York, 1936, Chap. 8.

by means of two things: it gives him a name and a social position. Without a name, the child is only an undifferentiated human organic unit. When he is named he becomes "somebody." Then, by virtue of his family, he obtains a place in the social group. He is now what sociologists call a "person," that is, an individual with status.[19]

What has just been said suggests the tremendous role of the family name and tradition in the development of a child. Nimkoff contrasts in this connection the histories of several well-known American families. As an example on the positive side is the famous Adams family, which for two centuries has been distinguished for its record of public service. John Adams (1735–1826) was the second President of the United States. His cousin, Samuel Adams, was an outstanding leader in the American Revolution. His son, John Quincy Adams, was our sixth President. His son, Charles Francis Adams, was U.S. Minister to England. The latter's son, Henry Adams, became a distinguished historian; and his son, Charles Francis Adams, was Secretary of the Navy in the administration of President Hoover. As illustrations on the negative side may be cited the Juke and Kallikak families, so well known to students of American social problems. It requires but little imagination to appreciate the tremendous handicap imposed by these family names upon successive generations.[20]

The family name is particularly important in the United States, with its many large population groups of recent foreign extraction. These family names quickly identify the child as a member of a particular group, and since these groups are apt to have a distinctive status, the child is assigned that status. What may result from this is described by Schettler. "Persons of minority nationality groups learn through experience that certain names always awaken certain prejudices. These persons realize that it is their names that constitute the common enemy for them as well as for members of the majority group. Evaluation of themselves stops with the judgment placed upon their names. Without consideration, much of their personality has been thereby discarded. These persons act upon the lesson learned, and they decide that a new or false name is an effective mask for disguising themselves. They change their names. Taraskevicia is translated as Rasko, Strakovsky is recast as Stark, Berkovitz evolves as Burke, Trofinov turns up as Travis, and Keidansky is shortened to Kay."[21]

This factor of status is related closely to two other concepts much emphasized in the recent literature of social psychology and psychiatry. One of these is the matter of security. We all seek security throughout

[19] Robert E. Park and Ernest W. Burgess, *An Introduction to the Science of Society*, University of Chicago Press, Chicago, 1925, p. 35.

[20] Meyer F. Nimkoff, *The Family*, Houghton Mifflin Company, Boston, 1934, pp. 68 ff.

[21] Clarence Schettler, "Does Your Name Identify You?" *Social Forces*, December, 1942, p. 172.

life. Very early in life the child senses security or insecurity as a member of the family group. He feels that he was wanted or not wanted; that he was a boy when his mother wanted a boy, or the reverse; that he came too soon, or when he was wanted. Later on, he seeks security through membership in secondary groups, through achievement of one sort or another. Many a personality pattern of extreme aggressiveness or incessant restlessness or an insatiable drive for power results from deep-seated insecurity formed during this period. Still later, people seek security in marriage. The pattern of many marriages is not one of romance, but of a drive for the security which the chosen mate may give. Part of the quest for security is for physical and economic safeguards against the threats of an external, foreboding world; but much of it is psychosocial —a wanting to belong.

Status has a great deal to do with conduct through its effect upon one's conception of oneself. The role of the conception of oneself has been grasped by many students of human nature. William James used to remark that a man had as many selves as there were persons who recognized him and carried an image of him in their minds. The poet Masefield writes:

> And there were three men went down the road,
> As down the road went he.
> The man they saw, the man he was,
> And the man he wanted to be.

Status is a factor in the determination of a person's conception of the self, and this conception in turn is a determinant in his behavior. This, then, is another element in the cultural content of a family situation which should be considered.

Social Change and the Family's Transmission of Culture

The culture-transmitting role of the family has been growing in importance in recent times and in a number of ways. First, the culture to be transmitted has been accumulating rapidly. Cultural expansion in the past century and a half has been phenomenal, and the rate of growth shows no signs of abatement. Rather, all the evidence points to its acceleration, particularly the part which is the result of modern science. During the past century or more, there has developed a pattern of science, invention, and discovery which has become thoroughly embedded in our cultural configuration and which has resulted both in very rapid cultural change and in its cumulation in precise and available form. All of this means not only that there is much more for the family to transmit to the child, but also that the task of selecting and interpreting and evaluating the culture has grown correspondingly.

This expanding task of the family in turn necessitates a longer period of time, so that with the accumulation of culture there needs to be a corresponding lengthening of what has been spoken of traditionally as the period of infancy. Actually, what is meant is the period of preparation for life during which the child remains under the supervision of the family. It is obvious, too, that the lengthening of this period is primarily a social fact, rather than a biological one as has been assumed so often. The lengthening of this period of the child's dependence upon the family is a change of outstanding significance, both in the history of the family and in the social development of the child. This will be discussed more adequately in a later chapter; we seek here only to identify it as an accessory to the expansion of modern culture and the tasks of the contemporary family.

This longer period and the more extensive culture markedly change the culture-transmitting role of the family. Time was when the culture was simple and the time available for its transmission was short. What the family did was largely to impose this culture upon the child. Today, the family increasingly becomes the manager or administrator of the child's induction into the culture. A part, and a highly important part, of its function remains what it has always been, but in addition there are increasingly the tasks of selecting parts of the culture to be emphasized, establishing necessary and advantageous contacts with specialized cultural agencies, detouring around some aspects of the culture, depreciating others—in short, manipulating and assessing the expanding process of inducting the child into an accumulating culture.

Our rapidly changing and accumulating culture places other responsibilities upon the family. Several of these will be identified.

1. The family must play its role in preparing the child for change. In times past, the time span of change, especially for important changes, was longer as a rule than a generation or even a single human life. As a result, man was trained to adapt himself to fixed conditions. This meant emphasis upon the acceptance of the family culture. Today, this time span is very short. Important changes, even epoch-making changes, are frequent; a number occur within the period when the individual is being reared. What this means is that part of the culture-transmitting role of the family is to prepare the child for change, i.e., for novelty of circumstance. If the family is too backward and resistant to change and transmits this attitude to the child, he may grow up to live in a world of unreality. There are such families, and their children often pay the price of continuing maladjustment.

2. On the other hand, not all changes are important or desirable. The death rate of changes is high. Their life span is short. A certain resistance to them is both essential and wholesome. The family, in other words, needs to play a stabilizing role in a rapidly changing culture. Groves

has written understandingly of this particular function of the family. "Human nature," he says, "by its use of the family has organized its best defense against the risk of having all its values placed outside itself. This, of course, does not mean that it is possible for the family to cut itself away from its surroundings, or that it can safely ignore changing conditions. It does, however, indicate that adjustment is a two-way process, and that the family by its guardianship of profound human motivation saves itself from merely registering in favorable fashion the inflow of physical and social circumstances."[22]

3. In a rapidly changing world, the family must give the child a sense of stability and security. There are other institutions and agencies which tend to play a stabilizing role, but they do not afford the comprehensiveness and the intimacy of the family relationship. Change, confusion, and uncertainty have their psychic aspects and implications, and the insurance and insulation against them need to be in kind. The family, it will be recalled, has always served as a refuge and an insurance. In times past, it has been the physical and economic side of this that has been emphasized, first because those were the chief hazards confronting its members, and second because no other agency afforded adequate protection against them. Today, both of these circumstances have changed; it is against the hazards of the spirit that the family offers its chief protection. A child's home still is his castle, even if the light within it has become more important than the moat and wall without. Thus conceived, the family is today more than ever before "the final refuge for those who can find little sense of security elsewhere. This is why the instability of the family becomes so greatly significant. It is not that it is more vulnerable than other social institutions, for on the contrary it is more resistant, but rather that its getting into difficulty demonstrates how serious and widespread general social instability has become."[23]

4. Finally, mention must be made of the fact that the relationship between culture and family is reciprocal. During periods of marked cultural changes, or cultural maladjustment, the family, as a primary agency in cultural transmission and continuity, tends to be weakened and to be rejected by its individual members. "Periods of violent change," writes Zimmerman, "are those in which the family is lifted from its former influence, so that the individual and the older culture can operate on principles independent of each other . . . the illusion arises that the culture of the age has no family necessity."[24]

[22] Ernest R. Groves, *The Family and Its Social Functions*, J. B. Lippincott Company, Philadelphia, 1940, p. 448.

[23] *Ibid.*, p. 454.

[24] Carle C. Zimmerman, *The Family of Tomorrow*, Harper & Brothers, New York, 1949, p. 69. For a more complete elaboration of this point of view, see the same author's *Family and Civilization*, Harper & Brothers, New York, 1947.

Summary

1. A third approach to the study of family situations concerns itself with their cultural content. This, in many ways, is the most significant aspect of family situations; it is the aspect which contemporary sociologists emphasize.

2. The pattern of family life is part of the larger culture system of society. These family patterns differ markedly from one group to another, as studies of selected patterns clearly reveal. From birth, the child is inducted into his particular family culture.

3. Another cultural role of the family is to serve as agent in the transmission of the larger culture systems to the child. For a number of years, the family remains the chief agency through which the child has his contacts with the cultural milieu.

4. There are varying aspects of the larger culture configuration: (a) the national culture; (b) the regional culture; (c) the class culture; and (d) the individual family's version.

5. The family fixes the child's place in the larger cultural configuration through the ascription of status, the assignment of a name and traditional place, the bestowal of a sense of security and a conception of one's role.

6. The culture-transmitting role of the family increases in importance in a changing society. With the rapid accumulation of culture in the contemporary age, the family tasks of selecting, interpreting, and evaluating the culture grow correspondingly.

Chapter 7

What the Child Gives the Parents

The joys of parents are secret, and so are their griefs and fears. They cannot utter the one, nor will they utter the other. Children sweeten labours, but they make misfortunes more bitter. They increase the cares of life, but they mitigate the remembrance of death. The perpetuity by generation is common to beasts; but memory, merit and noble works are proper to men. . . .

He that hath wife and children hath given hostages to fortune, for they are impediments to great enterprises, either of virtue or mischief. Certainly, the best works, and of greatest merit for the public, have proceeded from the unmarried or childless men, which, both in affection and means, have married and endowed the public. Yet it were great reason that those that have children should have the greatest care of future times; unto which they know they must transmit their dearest pledges.[1]

RELATIVE NEGLECT OF THIS APPROACH TO THE STUDY OF THE FAMILY

Students of family-child relationships, being adults usually and parents in some cases, emphasize mostly how parents are responsible for the development of children, how they condition child reactions, how they are the agents which transmit to children the prevailing culture. Relatively little attention is given to a consideration of what the child gives the family and to his role in family development. What makes this omission all the more striking is that common observation reveals constantly the most amazing and obvious changes in the lives and attitudes of a married couple after the arrival of a child.

It is an intriguing exercise for the imagination to speculate on what the literature on the family and child development would be like if it could be written by very young children. When children are encouraged to discuss situations instead of being merely subjected to them, one is amazed at how differently the same situation can look to two generations, this in spite of children's obvious difficulty in analyzing situations and

[1] Francis Bacon, *Essays*, E. P. Dutton & Co., Inc., New York, pp. 60, 63.

verbalizing their ideas. Failure to appreciate the contributions of the child to the development of family life is an excellent illustration of man's egocentric approach to human problems of all sorts, and his relative inability to regard himself objectively and in proper perspective. It suggests the question, occasionally and pertinently raised, as to whether adults can ever understand children. "Most of us are adultcentrics: we cannot even for a moment step outside the sphere of adult interests and concerns or set aside the grown-up way of thinking."[2] In fact, it raises the question how much scientists studying the child really want to understand child behavior, and to what extent their "scientific" conclusions are verbal projections growing out of their own emotional needs. This point is somewhat different from but is related to the conclusions of Dorothy Thomas, namely, that any observation or series of observations is likely to be a distortion of reality in directions predetermined by the personality make-up of the investigator.[3]

SOME PRELIMINARY OBSERVATIONS

What a child contributes to the family is, of course, a highly individual matter. Many facts about the child and the family have their importance in this connection. Most of these can be grouped, however, under three main headings.

1. The child's characteristics are of obvious importance, varying in degree with the family reaction to them. There is, for example, the sex of the child. Is it the sex which was wanted by the family, and how strong and united was the preference? What are the physical features and traits of the child? Is he considered to be attractive or not? Which of the parents or grandparents does he resemble, and what are the family conceptions of the person resembled? Is the child normal or not? Is he alert, phlegmatic, coy, mischievous, or stupid? At what achievement level does he function? Is the child the kind that parents are proud of, and for what reasons? What are his particular capacities or limitations? In other words, what kind of child is it that has joined the family group, measured by the particular criteria which that family group value or customarily employ?

2. The attitudes of the parents, both toward parenthood and toward children, will also be significant. These have been discussed in Chapter 4, and it is suggested that the reader review those pages, in the light of their bearing upon the specific theme of this chapter.

Involved in the attitudinal pattern of the parents, with particular ref-

[2] George Lawton, "Can Adults Ever Really Understand Children?" *Childhood Education*, April, 1940, p. 341.

[3] Dorothy S. Thomas, Alice M. Loomis, and Ruth E. Arrington, *Observational Studies of Social Behavior*, Institute of Human Relations, Yale University Press, New Haven, 1933, Vol. I, p. 244.

erence to any one child, is the time or stage in their life when the child arrives. Did he come too early in their lives? Obviously, parenthood means something quite different to a 16-year-old boy and girl, all other things being equal, than to a couple of 28 or 40. Even more important than age in years is degree of emotional maturity. How well are parents prepared emotionally for parenthood and its responsibilities? There are parents but little older emotionally than the children they are rearing, for emotional development does not always conform to chronological age. Complementary to emotional readiness is educational and economic preparation for parenthood. Again, there is the arrival of the first child in relation to the time of marriage. Did the child arrive too soon to accord to the mores of the group? Did he come too early, measured by the wishes and convenience of the parents? Finally, there is the relation of each additional child to the number and birth dates of the children already born. What a child brings to a family depends then, in large measure, on what the family will permit him to bring, on how the parents accept parenthood, and on how they assess or define each new experience of parenthood.

3. Basic to the attitudes of individual parents is the culture of the society to which the parents belong. The advent of a child takes its meaning in part in terms of the larger cultural determinants. There is, for example, the Hebrew conception of parenthood as a form of life fulfillment. There is the Roman Catholic emphasis upon parenthood as the essential purpose of marriage. In certain social classes, children are valued because they mean family continuity; they serve as agents for the perpetuation of family fortunes and prestige. To the creator of a successful business enterprise, children, and particularly sons, embody the founder's hope for its continuance and family control. In many national groups, children are a symbol of the parents' patriotism—the parental contribution to the national reservoir.

This is perhaps the place to refer to the question of a maternal instinct. Is love of one's own child instinctive? It is part of the mental orientation of many persons to think so. Particularly has it been customary during the past to refer to the existence of such an instinct, the idea implied being that there is a deeply embedded something, hereditary in character and universal in existence, which leads women to have a tenderly solicitous regard for their offspring. There is much, on the basis of a common-sense approach to life processes, to justify such a conclusion, but the tendency of many modern scholars is to be rather skeptical about it. It is their custom to point out the widespread existence of infanticide among many primitive folk, as well as among more advanced groups; and it is their argument that whatever the role of hereditary factors may be, parental interest in children is to a large extent acquired after the birth of the child.

THE DYNAMIC CHARACTER OF THE CHILD'S CONTRIBUTION

One further preliminary observation is in order. The child's contribution to the family is a constantly changing one. Parent-child relationships, on both the interactive and cultural bases, represent a continuing, developmental process. Family life is an experience which is going on constantly, in which adults, as well as children, are undergoing personality development. It is important to emphasize this because the widespread acceptance of the idea that the child's personality is relatively determined in the first few years of life has carried with it the implication that parent-child relationships become fixed during that same period. This, of necessity and fortunately, is not true. Obviously, the relationship between the parents is changing constantly. As Plant put it, "Marriage may itself be described as a childhood experience in which with the aid of certain sophistications one can manage rather comfortably to show the development of family life for the adult as quite as changing and adapting an affair as it is for the child."[4] Similarly, parents change their attitudes toward their children. Many a parent, extremely resentful of a child in the beginning of married life, reacts later on as far and as vehemently in the opposite direction. A 21-year-old bride, thoroughly frightened and bitter because of her pregnancy, seeks vainly for someone to commit an abortion on her. Ten years later, with three children, she pleads with her childless friends to "settle down and live." Unmarried parents who in the first throes of their desperation will do anything to be relieved of their child will seek, with equal desperation, traces of this child ten years later. Of course, the reverse may happen. A child that is welcomed today may be rejected three years later. The father may become jealous of the child, or at least irritated or restless because of the mother's preoccupation with it. A woman who thrilled to her first experience with motherhood may resent the tiring wear of the toddler stage.

Common Contributions by Children to Parents

Recognizing the individual and changing character of the child's effect upon the family, we shall attempt to set forth here some of the contributions which are apparent to the objective observer.

THE CHILD AND FAMILY INTERACTION

The coming of children increases the number of personal relationships and thus the range and complexity of the interactive processes within the family. This touches upon a subject of fundamental sociological importance. The relationship between the size of a group and the nature

---

[4] James S. Plant, "Mental Hygiene Aspects of the Family," a pamphlet reprinted from the April, May, June, 1932, issues of *The Family*, pp. 17–18.

of the interactive processes within it has been a social problem of perennial interest. Perhaps no people have been more aware of its importance than were the ancient Greeks. The Greek concept of the city-state, which was but a village community in an advanced stage of development, was the result of their judgment as to the best available political compromise between the two conflicting demands for social order and individual liberty. A smaller unit than the city-state would make it insecure; a large one would prove to be tyrannical. Both Plato and Aristotle showed an awareness of this problem and advanced definite ideas concerning the most desirable size of the group. Plato's ideal city was to be limited to the conveniently divisible number of 5,040 free citizens, plus their families and slaves; Aristotle, advocate of careful study rather than of wishful thinking, concluded that a state with more than 10,000 citizens would be impractical. "A state," he insisted, "can begin to exist only when it has attained a population sufficient for a good life in the political community . . . but there must be a limit. And what should be the limit can be easily ascertained by experience."[5]

In more recent times, Simmel has emphasized the quantitative determinants in social forms and processes. "To every definite number of elements there correspond . . . a specific sociological form, a characteristic organization, and a definite degree of firmness of texture."[6] Becker and von Wiese have touched upon the matter at various points—the dynamic interaction of relations, types of plurality patterns, and the systematic classification of groups on the basis of size.[7] Similarly Wirth, in analyzing urbanism as a way of life, emphasizes the significance of the size of the population aggregate in relation to the interactive process between its members.[8]

THE LAW OF FAMILY INTERACTION

Quintilian, the famous Roman rhetorician of the "Silver Age," once remarked that "for exploring human nature, one household is large enough." In keeping with this observation, the thesis is here presented that the relation of the size of the group to the complexity of its interrelationships may be stated with the precision of a mathematical law. This law is presented under the name of the Law of Family Interaction.

By way of preliminary explanation, what happens within the family with the coming of each child may be stated simply and graphically as follows:

[5] *Politics,* translated by Benjamin Jowett, The Clarendon Press, London, 1920, pp. 267–268.

[6] Nicholas J. Spykman, *The Social Theory of Georg Simmel,* University of Chicago Press, 1925, p. 129.

[7] Howard Becker and Leopold von Wiese, *Systematic Sociology,* John Wiley & Sons, Inc., New York, 1932.

[8] Louis Wirth, "Urbanism as a Way of Life," *American Journal of Sociology,* July, 1938, pp. 10–14.

The relations of husband and wife are like this:

Those of a husband, wife, and child can be diagramed like this:

Those of a husband, wife, and two children look like this:

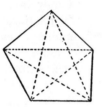

Those of a husband, wife, and three children look like this:

Within every family, there are two variables which submit to precise mathematical determination. One of these is the number of members in the family, i.e., the size of the group; the other is the number of personal relationships between its members. If these two variables are considered mathematically, what happens with the addition of each new member of the family group may be set forth in the following two sets of numbers:

Number of persons 2, 3, 4, 5, 6, 7, 8
Number of personal relationships 1, 3, 6, 10, 15, 21, 28

Family life begins customarily with two members, husband and wife, and one set of personal relationships. The advent of a new member, such as a child, increases the number of persons by one, to a total of three, but the number of personal relationships by two, i.e., from one to three. The coming of another member increases the size of the group from three to four, but the number of personal relationships from three to six, i.e., by three.

Considering these two series of numbers, the first is a series of ordinary numbers, changing in the simplest arithmetic progression in whole numbers; the second is a series of triangular numbers. The law may be stated, then, as follows: *With the addition of each person to a family or primary group, the number of persons increases in the simplest arith-*

metical progression in whole numbers, and the number of personal interrelationships within the group increases in the order of triangular numbers.

The mathematical formula involved may be set forth as follows:

$x =$ the number of personal interrelationships
$y =$ the number of persons
$$x = \frac{y^2 - y}{2}$$

The basic implication of this law is that every increase in the number of members of a family (or other primary group) results in more than a corresponding increase in the number of personal interrelationships, and that the larger the group becomes, the more disproportionate is the increase. It seems obvious that this fact should have great meaning in a study of the interactive process, with applications not only for the family but for various types of group functioning. We shall concern ourselves, however, with its meaning for family life.

1. Applying this law to family relationships, one is impressed with the actual complexity of life in families of even moderate size, especially for the young child. Consider, for example, a family of five, consisting of father, mother, and three children. A total of ten sets of personal relationships prevails within this family; and because of the close proximity and intimate nature of family life, there is a continuing awareness of each of them on the part of all the members of the family group.

One is apt to overlook the significance of the mere size of the household for the young child. The writer has recently studied the case of Helen K., who at 5 years of age is nervous, high-strung, and overstimulated, with spells of nervous vomiting. Helen is an only child; but in her two-and-a-half-story home of moderate size there live, in addition to her father and mother, two grandparents, one paternal, the other maternal. Two servants are also in the home daily. With 7 persons in the home, there are 21 sets of personal relationships. In at least 10 of the 21, there is some emotional strain and tension. Helen is the person most constantly present in the household. It seems apparent that the size of this household unit, when translated into the number of personal relationships, tells much about Helen's problem.

2. On the other hand, the proposed law clarifies what the loss of one member may mean to the interactive process of a family. Just as the addition of one member increases the number of relationships in exact keeping with the number of members already in the group, so does the withdrawal of one member similarly decrease the range and complexity of the interactive process. This becomes particularly significant in a small family. In a family of three, the loss of one member reduces the number of relationships by two-thirds of the former number; in the case of a family

of four, the reduction amounts to one-half. The law has peculiar significance, then, in analyzing the effects of the loss of a parent, for example, in
military service, or through death, divorce, desertion, and the like. The
family's loss of one of its members has its quantitative dimensions, dependent upon the size of the group.

3. The Law of Family Interaction throws peculiar light upon the nature and role of the larger families of former days. Consider, for instance,
some families of colonial America. Benjamin Franklin came from a Boston family of 17 children. In a family of 19 members, there would be 176
sets of interrelationships. One wonders whether Franklin was led as a
young man to leave his family to seek a career or to escape the complex
life of his primary group setting. Patrick Henry was one of 19 children. If
all these and both parents were living, there were 210 sets of interactive
relationships in the Henry household; and again one is led to wonder if
this complex setting may not have conditioned his vehement insistence
upon liberty. There is Chief Justice John Marshall, who was the first of 15
children. May not his judicial temperament have developed through
his experiences as the oldest son in carrying adjudicating responsibility
for the 105 relationships which existed among the Marshall children?

4. The larger family of former generations is often compared with the
small, immediate family of today. Usually, such comparisons are vague
and expressed in rather general terms. The proposed Law of Family
Interaction enables a precise mathematical comparison between the two
in terms of the exact number of interactive relationships. In a family of
4 members, which is a typically sized contemporary family, there are 6
sets of personal relationships; in a family of 12, such as was characteristic
of a century ago, there are 66 sets. Such a comparison reveals the precise
nature of the revolutionary change in the intimate response pattern of the
average family member which has come about as the result of the small-
family system.

The enormity of such a change in the intimate life of the individual
precipitates questions of great importance. What is its significance for the
social development and needs of individuals? What is the significance of
the small-family system of today, thus mathematically appraised, in the
socialization of the child? What is its meaning in terms of the socioemo-
tional security of the individual family member? Does this revolution in
the intimate interactive life of the individual explain the devotion of contemporary youth to the larger economic and political associations? Does
it explain the eagerness of the emotionally isolated person of today to
participate in mass emotional movements?

5. Finally, the Law of Family Interaction emphasizes the fact that
with each child there is an increasing extension and complexity of social
experience within the family, with more possibility, on the one hand, for
satisfactory stimulus and response. What this means for the individual

member of the family depends on his ability to enlarge the capacity for such intimate relationships as the family makes possible. Some persons have this ability to a great degree, others almost wholly lack it. This is why the coming of children enriches the life of one family and results usually in the disorganization or disintegration of another.

Supplementing this law is a second formula as determined by Kephart. This concerns the total number of potential relationships within a group, as compared with the number of person-to-person relationships considered in the foregoing law. The total possible number of relationships, according to Kephart, that can exist in a given group at a given time is always mathematically determinable, and is represented by the formula $\dfrac{3^n - 2^{n+1} + 1}{2}$. Concretely, this means that in a family of 5 there are 90 potential relationships.[9]

THE EXPANSION OF FAMILY INTERESTS

Just as the coming of children broadens and complicates the interactive processes within the family, so there occurs a similar development in regard to its interests. With the birth of the first child, parents become attentive to a number of matters they had not considered before; or, if they have considered them previously, they do so now with new meaning and intentness. One is reminded here of Popenoe's statement that a man who does not marry is only one-third alive, that married people may be two-thirds alive, but that only those who experience parenthood may be alive fully.[10]

First to arise are often problems of family finance, with particular emphasis upon future prospects. Occupational ambitions of the father may be sharpened, and long-range plans for careers may be made for the first time. Interest in life insurance often becomes vital at this stage of a family's history, or enlarged insurance programs may be undertaken. What kinds of insurance should be purchased—for immediate protection, for the future education of children, to meet the ordinary hazards to life and limb? Next to receive attention are questions concerning the home. Is home ownership desirable? Is it feasible under existing conditions? What kind of home is it best to purchase? What financing plans are most desirable?

Interests like these quickly shade into questions concerning the community. What kind of community is this? Is this the place to rear children?

---

[9] William M. Kephart, "A Quantitative Analysis of Intragroup Relationships," *American Journal of Sociology*, May, 1950, pp. 544–549; see also, Ernest Beaglehole, "A Critique of 'The Measurement of Family Interaction,'" *ibid.*, September, 1945, pp. 145–147; and V. A. Graicunas, "Relationship in Organization," *Bulletin of the International Management Institute*, March, 1933, pp. 39–42.

[10] Paul Popenoe, *Modern Marriage*, The Macmillan Company, New York, 1927, p. 26.

To buy a home? What, if any, are the zoning restrictions? What kind of people live in this community? Who are the people that dominate it? How politician-ridden is this place? What is the tax rate? What is the status-conferring rating of this area? One particular aspect of the organized life of any community, which many parents consider of great importance, is its educational facilities. Are there nursery schools in the neighborhood? Is there a publicly maintained kindergarten? What is the quality of the instruction in the school system? How do the schools of the particular district rate educationally? Roman Catholic families will consider the availability of parochial-school instruction. Upper-class families may be interested in private-school facilities. In addition to the school system, many parents will want to know about Sunday School and church facilities, provisions for playgrounds, public libraries, community sports programs, and a great variety of other community resources and facilities.

These and many similar questions become vital to adults when they achieve parenthood. The answers at which they arrive become the essence of the forces which distribute and segregate our contemporary populations. A large proportion of the movement of families within large cities, between city and suburbs and from one suburb to another, represents choices and plans for the children in these families. Studies of one suburb in the Philadelphia area show that more than 80 percent of its families located there "for the sake of the children." They come more specifically, writes Jones, "because their children will have better opportunity for satisfactory educational and recreational lives, and because these things contribute to better health."[11]

Moreover, it is not simply the local community and the larger society of the present which become of interest and importance to parents with the birth of their children; it is also their future development and welfare. The child is the future of the family; and no parent with the slightest interest in his child can ever be wholly unconcerned with the world of tomorrow, for it is in that world that his child will become, like the parent, an adult member. "After me the deluge" may be the philosophy of a cynical bachelor; it can never be the sentiment of a normal parent.

EMOTIONAL SATISFACTIONS OF LONG DURATION

The child not only broadens the interests of parents in community and social matters of all kinds, but gives to most parents emotionally satisfying interests of lifelong duration. Nothing is perhaps more essential to a happy life than such interests. Many people are fortunate in acquiring an interest or interests of this kind. They may be of many different kinds. One person may find such an interest in the quest for political power, climbing from one post of political preferment to another; the next person

[11] Arthur H. Jones, *Cheltenham Township,* University of Pennsylvania Press, Philadelphia, 1940, pp. 51–52.

may find it in the winning of wealth and its use for the acquisition of a few selected objectives; a third may find it through his creations on an artist's canvas, the pages of a book, the test tube of the laboratory, or in the ability to drive an automobile on the sand dunes of Utah faster than any other person. For vast numbers of people, life interests of a satisfactory sort are difficult or impossible to obtain. Great masses of men are condemned perforce to monotonous labor and to a rather drab existence. Such persons may find, as can all others and as many do, abiding life interests in the careers of those whom they conceive to be like themselves—their children and their children's children. Of a truth are such interests lifelong in duration and emotionally satisfying in kind.

It is true that there is much exploitation of children to satisfy the emotional needs of parents and other related adults; more extended consideration will be given to the resulting problems in a later chapter. But such cases, let it be emphasized here, are pathological or problem-creating only in the degree or the form of development of what in other families is a wholly normal relationship. Emotional exploitation of children is news; behind the news are innumerable parents who find in their interests in children deep and abiding satisfactions without exacting any crippling bondage. This is the essence of normal and happy parenthood. Particularly do these emotional satisfactions tend to grow in importance as parents and children grow older. Earlier in life, parents are more active, more concerned with their own achievements and hopes. Life's compensations tend to come more adequately from the range of one's own activities. It is only with the passing of time, the hardening of circumstances, the reconstruction of values, and the greater need for emotional satisfactions from without that one turns normally to the developing careers of one's own children.

THE OPPORTUNITY TO RELIVE LIFE

This acquisition of lifelong interests suggests another of the child's possible contributions to his parents. It is the opportunity, in a sense, to live their lives over again. This is something which most persons, including those who will not admit it, would like to do; it is something which, in the literal sense of the phrase, is obviously impossible. What every modern student of parent-child relationships emphasizes, however, is that the parent sees in the child his nearest approach to such an opportunity. As Plant says:

> Early sensing that there is no living over life with the advantages of learning from mistakes of the first trial, we quickly find the next best outlet—that of living out these dreams and unrequited hopes in the lives of the children to come. Indeed, those in children's work would be quite without clients if children could live "de novo"—instead of being expected to live out the lives of their parents. Every social worker is acquainted with this problem and what it

means to children—these moldings of the child's life to bring it into conformity with what the parent has been looking for in the way of picking up the lost thread. As soon as we know that a child is coming in the family, we "hope that it will be a boy" or "hope it will be a girl"—not having the courtesy even to await the child's birth before beginning to fix upon it the pattern we expect it to fill. Early in the childhood of the parents this pattern was being formed— the tom-boy child dreaming that her child would be a butterfly, the shy child that his boy would be a football hero. We enter here so sincerely one of the great and intriguing fields of conduct disorder. . . . There are few matters so common and impelling as the need that the individual has for mending the broken threads of his own life in the growing lives of those over whom he has a feeling of control. It is for this that the adult looks to the family experience.[12]

This tendency of parents to seek to relive their lives in those of their children leads inevitably to a foisting upon the children of activities and pursuits not of their own choice. This practice is spoken of in mental hygiene circles as projection. It is a practice extensively indulged in by parents, and it has much meaning for educators and for students of behavior problems. A definite factor in parent-child relationships, it will be discussed more fully in a subsequent chapter.[13]

THE CONTROL OF HUMAN DEVELOPMENT

The parents' effort to relive their lives through the careers of their children is in turn but part of a much larger story. This is the fact that the child gives to the parent control over another person, and of a most intimate and comprehensive kind. It is a control that is all-pervasive. Arising as a form of physical control because of the infant's complete helplessness, it comes, as time goes on, to cover every aspect of the child's life and to be supported by the entire range of society's sanctions.

The acquisition through parenthood of control over another person is one of life's major experiences, and its significance may be considered from various points of view. There can be no doubt, for example, of its emotionally satisfying nature. Control of a child satisfies the parent's will to power. This is a deeply rooted desire. All persons have it, and they seek to satisfy it in many ways. We begin to seek it as children in playing with dolls and animal pets. Courtship is, in more ways than meet the eye, a search for power. Much of our adult life involves its quest. It is this age-old, universal desire which is satisfied in the parent with the coming of children, and the entire range of parenthood is from one angle a constant exercise of the power of control over another person.

A good deal has been said in recent years about the fact that some parents utilize this power over their children to secure relief from per-

[12] Plant, *op. cit.,* pp. 13–14.
[13] Kimball Young, "The Projection of Parental Ambitions," *The Family,* May, 1927, pp. 67 ff.

sonal thwartings and maladjustments in their lives outside of the home. In other words, the disgruntled parent can come home and take it out on his child. The father who is forced into insignificance and obscurity in his job returns home to restore his ego in an exaggerated obedience from his son. The employee who is "barked at by the boss" all day can compensate at night by "laying down the law" to his little William. The mother who was "cut" at her bridge club in the afternoon takes it out on her daughter that night. In these and in many other similar cases, the child becomes for the parent a vehicle for the transposition of satisfactions, as discussed in Chapter 4.

This control over another person, particularly of a relatively helpless individual and one's own flesh and blood, brings with it inevitably some sense of responsibility for the obligations involved. For many people, the responsibility that children bring is the first really vital and continuing one which they have been called upon to assume. The reaction to this responsibility is, of course, individual; there is involved essentially a test of the individual character. Parenthood, in other words, sets the stage for the development of parents. It is a testing of the potentialities of personality. If people have the possibilities of growth within them, what better can call them forth than the experience of parenthood?

To those who see in their control over a child an opportunity to direct the development of a human being, this responsibility may lead to a deep and continuing search for life's values. What do I want my child to be? So far as I can influence and direct his development, what are the important and worth-while goals to be sought? These questions arise with the birth of the first child; they persist throughout infancy, adolescence, and into early manhood and womanhood. Reference has been made on an earlier page to the tendency of parents to answer these questions on the basis of their own unfulfilled dreams and ambitions. Important as the role of such projections may be, even allowing for all the unconscious manifestations of them which the psychoanalyst may find, there is more to the story than that. Parents are constantly being confronted in their experience as parents with questions of life's values. Parenthood is a daily round of decisions on the question of what things are important, and in what order.

The child's questions arise early. "Daddy, what is God?" "Mother, why are people poor?" "Is what the Sunday School teacher tells us true?" "Daddy, our neighbor says we shall not walk on her grass." "May we go to the carnival?" "Is there a Santa Claus?" These and literally a million other questions are asked. Many of them are answered, sometimes in direct spoken words, often in glances, grimaces, or gestures. The simpler the answer, the clearer the thought behind it; the clearer the thought, the more clear-cut the decision or judgment of the values involved.

Beyond the almost endless stream of questions arising as the child is adjusting to his cultural setting are the plans made by parents for their children. These involve choices—in expenditures of time and effort, in schools, in social contacts, in occupations, in forms of behavior, in spheres of activity. All of these involve decisions, and these decisions represent value judgments. From one standpoint, all life is a constant series of choices of life values. These choices come to be made more definitely as they are the more consciously imposed upon those for whom we have assumed responsibility.

INSIGHT INTO LIFE'S PROCESSES

This survey of the child's contributions to his parents would be incomplete without reference to the fact that children give parents an intimate insight into the processes of life—its appearance, growth, and development. Because of our inability to consider ourselves with sufficient objectivity, we need to see this process at work in other persons and in other forms of life. Through the long centuries of "man's rough road," he has seen it constantly in the seeds he sowed, the harvests he reaped, the animals he domesticated, as well as in the abundant progeny he brought into the world. Today, an increasing percentage of people live in cities where they neither sow nor reap—crops; where a cow can be seen only in the zoological garden, and where even a pup is a luxury, and a nuisance, to be spayed or boarded out periodically in order to keep domestic and neighborly peace.

This change in the range of many people's contacts with living things resulting from the widespread substitution of urban for rural life makes experience with the birth and rearing of children all the more important if the processes of life are to remain part of the content of conscious thinking. Let it be emphasized here that there is a difference between an abstract understanding of a process, and constant contacts with its concrete manifestations. The insight into the processes of life development which the nurture of one's own children gives covers much of what in academic circles constitutes the substance of biology, psychology, and the related life sciences. Constant contact with growing children gives meaning to the findings of scientists in these fields; also, such experience acts as a corrective for much of what passes as scientific achievement.

INSIGHT INTO THE MEANING OF LIFE

What parenthood brings to one, in the ultimate analysis, is some comprehension of the meaning of life and of the individual's role in the cosmic scheme of things. Stated in its simplest form, it is this: Each person is but a temporary trustee of the life stream.

One comes to sense this first, perhaps, with one's possessions. Yesterday, you owned them absolutely. You gave them the care that such absolute possession deserved, for their preservation was as signally important as your own life; they became as vital as the maintenance and development of your own personality. Today, your child uses them carelessly, and destructively perhaps. You squirm a bit at first, but, after all, it is *your* child violating *your* possessions; and you resolve the conflict finally so that the violation of what was yours dissolves into the development of your child that is. These possessions may be your old toy, your book, your chair, your watch, or your house. Somewhat later, you experience the same changing evaluation of your energy. Originally, your energy was yours, to expend for your pleasure and your development. It was so insensibly a part of you that your use of it could not be conceived of except in terms of yourself and your interest. With continuing parenthood, this, too, shades gradually into the feeling that every parent knows, where your energy and even your life blood become the small change you pay to satisfy the passing needs of your children. It is at such moments, when a parent has given his all to the insatiable demands of his child, that there comes the true meaning of one's relation to life: that each generation is but a trustee of life, for all its values and all its possessions. Thus, in the larger sense, we never own anything; for everything that can be owned belongs to time, and time is endless. This, then, is the real end of life, that we receive, as it were, the torch from one generation, to carry it and perchance to brighten it, but ultimately always to turn it over to the next generation. This it is that the child brings, in some varying form of expression, to each parent who has the capacity to perceive it.

Summary

1. Studies of family-child relationships, being made by grownups, are adultcentric. This is another illustration of man's difficulty in studying himself in the proper perspective. This chapter represents an effort to show what the child contributes to the parents.

2. What a child contributes is, of course, a highly individual matter, dependent chiefly upon (a) the child's characteristics; (b) the attitudes of the parents, both toward parenthood and toward children; and (c) the larger cultural determinants.

3. The child's contribution to the parents is constantly changing. Family life is a living, growing thing, in which attitudes and evaluations are constantly changing.

4. Common contributions of children to parents include (a) an increase in the range and complexity of family interaction, (b) an expansion of family interests, (c) emotional satisfactions of lifelong duration, (d) the opportunity to relive life, (e) the control of human development, (f) insight into life's processes, and (g) insight into the true meaning of life.

Part *III*

Facets of Family Life

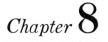
The Empathic Complex
and Child Behavior

Various studies of child behavior, and conferences of workers dealing with particular cases, focus attention chiefly upon the mother, as though she were synonymous with the child's family background. In still other instances, the child's family is interpreted to mean father and mother. Obviously the mother and/or the father customarily are the key persons in the child's family situation. According to the federal census, of all children under 18 years of age and living with one or both parents, 89 percent were living with both parents, 10 percent with the mother only, and 1 percent with the father only. However, when one is concerned with the role of the family in an understanding of the child's behavior pattern, the parent or parents are by no means the whole, or even at times the major, part of the family situation. It is the purpose of the present chapter to examine the larger meaning and scope of the term *family situation*, and its relation to child behavior.

The Family of Orientation: Its Composition

The child's family of orientation was defined in Chapter 2 as the circle of his immediate, intimate, and continuing contacts. Utilizing this concept, of whom and what may this family of orientation consist?

First, there are the other children in the family. In more than four-fifths of the completed families in this country, two or more children grow up together. It is but emphasizing the obvious to point out that children influence each other, and particularly when growing up in the same family. Chapter 5 has indicated the ways of interaction among siblings.

A quantitative indication of the extent of the role of teen-age siblings in selected child-care and control activities is found in Johannis' analysis of 1,027 nonbroken white families in Tampa, Florida. Among the categories included are "teaching children right and wrong" (teen-age sons, 7.8 percent, teen-age daughters, 8.0 percent); "sees children have fun" (teen-age sons, 23.4 percent, teen-age daughters, 22.6 percent); "teaches children facts and skills" (teen-age sons, 13.7 percent, teen-age daughters, 11.4 percent); "sees children have good table manners" (teen-age sons, 11.2 percent, teen-age daughters, 18.3 percent); "helps children with school work" (teen-age sons, 25.1 percent, teen-age daughters, 30.9 percent); "sees children eat the right foods" (teen-age sons, 12.3 percent, teen-age daughters, 14.7 percent); "sees children wear the right clothes" (teen-age sons, 25.1 percent, teen-age daughters, 35.4 percent).[1]

The role of siblings varies a great deal with the size of the family. The matter of sibling discipline might be taken as a case in point. Discipline of younger by older children seems more prevalent in larger than in smaller families. A study of 100 families, each with 6 or more living children, revealed that in one-fifth of the families the older siblings were the chief or sole disciplinarians of the younger children, and in 91 of the families there were references to some discipline from this source.[2] Tentative figures for a companion study of 100 two-child families, now in progress, indicate a much lower percentage of sibling discipline.

Second, there are the other adults in the family background, by which we mean adults other than the parent or parents.

Stepparents might be singled out as a special group of these. In many ways, they could be grouped with the parents, and yet, in various ways, they may differ. The role of stepparents is a phase of child development increasing in extent but as yet relatively unexplored.[3] A brief factual summary will indicate the proportions of this problem. One out of every 5 marriages in the United States in recent years has been a remarriage for one or both of the spouses; in approximately 1 out of every 14, both have been married before. Moreover, remarriage has been increasing in extent in all age groups, but particularly in the ages from 25 to 34, inclusive. These, it will be noted, are the likely years of parenthood. Then, too, the previous conjugal condition of those remarrying has changed considerably in the past two generations. Formerly most persons remarrying had been widowed; today more than one-half have been divorced. How many children are involved in these remarriages is not known. Scattered state reports show that more than one-half of the divorced persons who remarry have children, and it seems safe to assume that the proportion among the widowed remarrying is somewhat higher.[4]

---

[1] Theodore B. Johannis, Jr., "Participation by Fathers, Mothers and Teenage Sons and Daughters in Selected Child Care and Control Activity," *The Coordinator*, December, 1957, p. 31.

[2] James H. S. Bossard and Eleanor S. Boll, *The Large Family System*, University of Pennsylvania Press, Philadelphia, 1956, p. 131.

[3] For a valuable study in this area, cf. William C. Smith, *The Stepchild*, University of Chicago Press, Chicago, 1953.

[4] For a summary of the data on remarriage and its significance in child development, see James H. S. Bossard, *Parent and Child*, University of Pennsylvania Press, Philadelphia, 1953, Chap. 8.

Kinsfolk are the largest group of other adults that the child contacts during the early and more formative years. Despite changes in the relationship between the immediate and the extended families in recent years, kinsfolk still come to each other's aid, particularly in the sharing of living quarters. Census data reveal to some extent the presence of relatives in the household at any one time, but these show the situation only as of the day of the given survey, and hence do not answer our question: How many children grow up with relatives living in the home as the child is growing up?

To throw some light on the question as stated, a study of 410 university students may be of interest. Only one item of information was called for: List all the persons who lived as members of your household prior to your tenth birthday. The results follow:

1. An even 100 were families which had consisted of parents and children only. This is roughly one out of every four.

2. In 30 cases, or 7 percent, there had been but one parent or a stepparent, for at least a part of the time.

3. In 50 cases, or 12 percent, servants, but no other persons, had lived in during that period.

4. In 230 cases, or 56 percent, relatives and/or other persons had lived in the household as members of it. Families, with servants living in, and other persons, have been listed in this category.

It may be pointed out at once that university students represent a selected group, and this is true. There can be little doubt, however, that the number of families with only parents and children living in the household would be larger than in the general population. Unfortunately, too, this sample, while suggestive, is too small to be definitive.[5]

Equally restricted in scope but indicative within those limits is the study of 100 large families, previously referred to. This shows that, in 24 of the 100 families, relatives living with the family interfered in the discipline of the children.[6]

Kinsfolk need not live in the same household to have importance in the child's development. Despite certain individualizing influences affecting the modern family and the rising predominance of the immediate family, a study of 68 students at a large eastern university suggests that there is a marked degree of identification with kinsfolk as such, regardless of what they are like or how well one has known them previously. Two aspects of this are particularly noticeable. First are the differences in allusions to relatives and to friends. Although there are many references to friends, there are no suggestions of identification with friends or neighbors at all comparable to those with any or all relatives. This seems significant in that our friends are of our choosing, but we are born to our kin. Close identi-

---

[5] *Ibid.*, p. 49.
[6] Bossard and Boll, *op. cit.*, pp. 133–134.

fication, then, was with the people "inflicted" upon the informants. In cases where the relatives were acceptable people, this was a source of satisfaction and ego-inflation. Many wrote of talented relatives who visited and glamorized their very homes with their presence. On the other hand, those who were immoral, peculiar, faddish, infantile, the shabby, the uncouth, and the uneducated—these are sources of deep shame, personally.

A second aspect of this identification with kinsfolk is evidenced in the references to their special treatment. No matter whether they were loved or hated, whether they lived next door or across the ocean, they were a part of the family and had special prerogatives as such. This acceptance of special prerogatives worked in two directions. The relatives felt it their right to drop in unexpectedly; to stay as long as they chose; to walk into the kitchen to find themselves something to eat; to rearrange the guest-room furnishings; to use the personal belongings of the family members; to make comments upon the clothing, household management, behavior, and discipline of the family.

Relatives also regard each other as custodians of the family reputation. Because the reputation of any family member is a part of the composite reputation of the whole family kinship group, relatives often take on voluntarily and sincerely a responsibility for each other in matters of social etiquette, general education, and occupational or professional guidance. Sometimes this partially self-protective obligation is assumed in such a way that it can be called only "interference." But often the gentle, well-meant suggestions and advice of intelligent and mature relatives, who want to see each generation a credit to the family, are of invaluable help especially to children, but also, sometimes, to adults.[7] Obviously the degree of cohesion of the kinship group varied considerably from one family to another.

It would be to ignore the obvious to overlook the role of members of the family group now deceased. They are gone, to be sure, but no one who knows family life would say that their influence has ceased. Specifically, one hears in many homes statements like these: "What would your Aunt Ellen say if she were alive?" "What do you suppose Mother would do?" "You know what Grandfather Jones always said." Snatches like these show how the memory of deceased family members survives, how their remembered attitudes continue to influence behavior patterns. At times, too, it is not so much an attitude that is remembered as a figure that is built up against the horizon of the past. This happens often when a parent died during the infancy of the child. The deceased parent may be made into a paragon of virtues, or, as unfortunately happens at times, as a scapegoat responsible for all the present problems of the family.

Children normally contact still other persons within their homes with a

[7] Cf. Bossard, *op. cit.*, pp. 67–81.

frequency and/or under circumstances which make them a definite part of the family scene. These include guests, family friends whom the child and his family visit, servants, other caretakers of the child, and, as we shall attempt to show later, also domestic pets within the household. Because these receive separate consideration in later chapters, mere mention of them will suffice at this point.

Two Concepts: The Family Complex and the Empathic Complex

To assume, as is often done, that the child's family which molds his behavior consists wholly or mainly of his parents, seems rather remote from reality. Actually the child ordinarily contacts, from infancy on, a wide array of persons within his home or through family contacts. Besides the parents, there are the other siblings, kinsfolk, guests, servants, and others, all of whom are a part of the family environment and may, and ordinarily do, play a role in influencing the child's behavior. To designate this larger group, we shall employ the term *family complex*. The word *complex* is used here to mean a whole made up of integrated parts, a system of particulars like, for example, the B complex in vitamins. When, therefore, we shall refer henceforth to the child's family background we shall do so as meaning this broader concept of the family complex.

A second complex we shall use is that of the *empathic complex*. This has particular reference to the child's relation to the family complex. The word *empathy* is defined in current dictionaries as "the imaginative projection of one's own consciousness into another being," or "the ascription of our emotional feelings to the external object which serves as their visual and auditory stimulus." It was the late Harry Stack Sullivan, a psychiatrist, who sparked the term into use in connection with the study of human behavior. "Empathy," he wrote, "is the term that we use to refer to the peculiar emotional linkage that subtends the relationship of the infant with other significant people."[8] Sullivan primarily utilized the term *empathy* in connection with the subtle process whereby certain emotional states, like anxiety, are transferred from mother to infant, but he did recognize that as the child grew older he came to perceive through this same emotional linkage more overt manifestations in regard to behavior. In fact, he sensed the role of this emotional linkage throughout the life of the individual. "We do not know much about the fate of empathy," he wrote, "in the developmental history of people in general. There are indications that it endures throughout life, at least in some people."[9]

We shall define the term *empathic complex* to mean the particular or specific emotional linkage between a child and the significant persons in

[8] Harry Stack Sullivan, *Conceptions of Modern Psychiatry,* The William A. White Psychiatric Foundation, Washington, D.C., 1947, p. 8.
[9] *Ibid.*

his background. For a number of years, this means primarily persons who live in the same household, and the range of his family's contacts.

The Theory of the Empathic Complex

The theory of the empathic complex is presented in three parts.

1. As the child grows out of infancy and his more or less exclusive contact with the mother, he develops close relations with a selected few other persons. Some of these are members of his immediate family; some, of his kinship group; still others are selected from family contacts, such as guests, servants, and the like. Data presented later in this chapter suggest the possible number and range of such persons.

2. These persons are selected by the child, within the limitations that his situation imposes. In doing so, he considers primarily the total personality of these "other persons," and only secondarily the details of his relations with them, that is, their methods of child rearing. Behrens, in a highly significant study, has shown this in the case of the mother. "The study indicates that evaluations of child-rearing practices are of little value unless understood as aspects of a dynamic process of socialization dependent on the social interaction of those individuals concerned." The results of this study show that "the child's adjustment to socialization was significantly related to the 'total mother person' and specifically to her character structure, but insignificantly related to the mother's specific rearing techniques."[10]

In selecting "total persons," the child does so on the basis of his needs of them, and not as they are viewed by other persons. For example, a quiet, serious, hard-working father, whom adults characterized as a good father, a good husband, and a good provider, appeared to the child as a cold and forbidding total person. In another case, an impressive-looking, vigorous lawyer, coming to the home to visit, impresses a lonely, day-dreaming boy with the way other persons kowtow to him.

To illustrate still more concretely the nature of this process of selection, we cite a case from a considerable collection of similar cases, as yet unpublished.

Marcia is the youngest of four children. She is 4 years old. Helen, next to her, is 6 and has started school. Tom, her brother, is 10, looks with disdain upon all females, and spends as much time as possible away from home. Jane, the oldest of the four, is 13, old enough now to be companionable with her young and attractive mother. Marcia is lonely. Time drags for her. Meanwhile Mrs. Adams, a charming widow, has moved next door. She and Marcia's mother quickly become friends, visiting back and forth. Mrs. Adams lives alone, has no children of her own, but is very fond of them. Marcia begins with

[10] Marjorie L. Behrens, "Child Rearing and the Character Structure of the Mother," *Child Development,* September, 1954, pp. 225–238.

short visits to Mrs. Adams. Then they become longer and more frequent. Soon Marcia stays for dinner with Mrs. Adams, and a little later stays overnight. Mrs. Adams has a way with children. Soon Marcia spends as much time as possible "next door." She has "taken over" Mrs. Adams completely.

Above all, and pervading all, influencing the child's selection is the emotional rapport which develops between him and these "other persons." And this, be it emphasized, is a two-way relationship. Children, because of their dependence, want to be loved, to be recognized for themselves, but they also want to love in return. Years ago, Charles Dickens expressed this latter factor, so often overlooked, we believe, in contemporary studies. In *Great Expectations*, Pip, who had been reared by Mr. and Mrs. Joe, has just been freed of the guilt for having stolen Mrs. Joe's pie. "I do not recall," he says, "that I felt any tenderness of conscience in reference to Mrs. Joe. But I loved Joe—perhaps for no better reason in those early days than because the dear fellow let me love him."[11]

3. These "other persons," or empathic complex, become the primary factors in the child's behavioral development, and for three main reasons.

a. They serve as the polar points around which the details of child rearing are organized. The theory of the empathic complex is not meant to ignore or to depreciate the constant repetitive processes that go on in the child's life, the multitude of continuing details of family life and habits of child rearing, but to add to their consideration the idea that there are polar points, highly magnetized as it were, around which they tend to swirl and become organized.

b. They become the motivating forces which strengthen or weaken the methods of child rearing. The child decides that he wants to be like one or more of these other persons, and, to become so, will respond cooperatively to certain aspects of his rearing. Or he will think, as a young person said to us recently, "the key to my behavior is the strong desire not to be like my older sister."

c. They serve as the mediating agents between the child and his environment. Zimmerman and Broderick have shown how family friends serve this purpose with families as a whole.[12] Our theory contends that a similar function is served by his empathic complex for the child.

It should be made very clear that the thesis advanced in this chapter is supplementary and not opposed to the cultural study of patterns of child rearing and development. Each culture and subculture has its distinctive modes of child rearing and personality formation. Our thesis suggests that, within the cultural configuration of the area of the family, it is the empathic complex which accounts for the selective aspects of the in-

[11] Charles Dickens, *Great Expectations*, Rinehart & Company, New York, 1955, p. 6.
[12] Carle C. Zimmerman and Carlfred B. Broderick, "Nature and Role of Informal Family Groups," *Marriage and Family Living*, May, 1954, pp. 107–111.

dividual child's behavioral development, thus explaining the wide variations that obtain within a seemingly common background. Simply stated,
what we are proposing for the study of behavior is that it is people, and
not methods of child rearing, that are significant in explaining the differentials within a culture or subculture. It is on this basis, too, that the
negative findings of Sewell and his associates may be explained.[13]

Some Suggestive Lines of Evidence

In support of the thesis which we have advanced, we submit four lines
of evidence, selected from our studies in the sociology of child behavior.

1. In the analysis of autobiographies, which we have used extensively
in our work, we have found that almost without exception the authors explain their own development in terms of a relatively few persons toward
whom they developed marked feelings of like or dislike when quite
young. The number of such persons usually is limited, ranging from two
to perhaps as many as seven. As a recent example of such writing by a
distinguished author, there is the analysis made by Arnold Toynbee, the
historian. He identifies the following major influences in his early formative years: (a) mother, (b) great-uncle, (c) uncle, (d) a tutor, and
(e) selected books, chiefly of a historical nature.[14]

2. In a collection of 300 life-history documents which we are preparing
for publication, we find, virtually without exception, that in writing of the
factors believed to influence the behavior of the writers the references are
to a selected few persons, and that the clearest and fullest descriptions
are in terms of the personalities and values of these persons. It is also
evident, in this material, that the writers have strong emotional attitudes
toward these persons, either of appreciation or of aversion, so that the persons referred to, and their character structures, stand out as vivid impressions in their experience history.

3. In one of the tests of our theory, we sought to ascertain how many
such persons were confined to the family group of a given number of
persons. Accordingly, we asked a total of 150 persons to (a) list all persons in their immediate family, (b) all persons in their paternal kinsfolk's group, (c) all persons in the maternal kinsfolk's group, and (d) to
indicate all those with whom they had close emotional ties (those they
liked very much), those toward whom they had opposite feelings (dis-

[13] William H. Sewell, "Infant Training and the Personality of the Child," *American
Journal of Sociology*, September, 1952, pp. 150–159; William H. Sewell and Paul H.
Mussen, "The Effects of Feeding, Weaning, and Scheduling Procedures on Childhood Adjustment and the Formation of Oral Symptoms," *Child Development*, September, 1952, pp. 185–191; and William H. Sewell, Paul H. Mussen, and Chester W.
Harris, "Relationships Among Child Training Practices," *American Sociological Review*, April, 1955, pp. 137–148.

[14] Arnold J. Toynbee, "I Owe My Thanks," *Saturday Review*, October 2, 1954,
pp. 13 ff.

liked very much), and those toward whom they had neutral feelings. Sixty of these were undergraduate students in a large eastern university, and 90 were members of an evening adult education group. Table 1 represents the answers in summary form.

TABLE 1. Empathic Complex Data
(150 cases—41 males, 109 females)

Immediate Family	Males	Percent-age	Females	Percent-age	Total	Percent-age
Total Immediate Contact	154	100.0	499	100.0	653	100.0
Close	109	70.8	401	80.4	510	78.1
Disliked	28	18.2	51	10.2	79	12.1
Neutral	17	11.0	47	9.4	64	9.8
Total Paternal Kinsfolk	442	100.0	899	100.0	1341	100.0
Close	195	44.1	379	42.2	574	42.8
Disliked	43	9.7	92	10.2	135	10.1
Neutral	204	46.1	428	47.6	632	47.1
Total Maternal Kinsfolk	408	100.0	1045	100.0	1453	100.0
Close	157	38.5	403	38.6	560	38.5
Disliked	52	12.7	123	11.8	175	12.0
Neutral	199	48.8	519	49.6	718	49.4

It will be noted that the average number of persons in the immediate background that elicited positive (not neutral) responses was approximately four per person; of the paternal kinsfolk it was about the same; and only fractionally higher for the maternal kinsfolk group. Clearly, the emotional responses to the members of the family group are limited in number and highly selective.

In our detailed analysis of this material, there are some marked variations on the basis of the size of the several family units, the physical nearness to one or both kinship groups, and relationships between groups on the basis of past history. On the whole, however, most replies fell within a range of three to five persons in each of the three groups, including both those actively liked or disliked.

4. Another experimental study made with 38 advanced university students in the field of human behavior is presented in summary form. They were asked (1) to identify the chief influences which conditioned their own behavior up to the fifteenth year; (2) if these were persons, to write out brief characterizations of such persons. Care was taken to explain that attitudes of hate or aversion might be significant, as well as love, admiration, or respect. Finally, thumbnail characterizations of the 38 persons who contributed such information were obtained.

The number of cases is, of course, too small to have anything but suggestive value. It is with this acknowledgment that selected aspects of this material are presented.

1. The influences identified by all 38 cases center around persons: persons they liked and persons they disliked.
2. It is equally clear that all had pronounced emotional attitudes toward these persons.
3. The number of such persons identified ranged from 3 to 8. The most frequent numbers were 5 (8 cases) and 6 (18 cases).
4. The person mentioned most frequently was the mother, also the most emphasized. Father and other sibling followed in that order.
5. Kinsfolk mentioned, in order of frequency, were aunts (usually maternal aunts), grandparents, uncles, sisters-in-law.
6. Other persons, in order of frequency, were nurse (governess, Negro mammy), teacher (in kindergarten or primary grades), guest, neighborhood personage.

Finally, we compared the characterizations of the influencing persons, as given by those coöperating in the study, with the thumbnail characterizations given to us of those coöperating. The results here are striking. In 34 out of 38 cases, the sketches of those coöperating identified, wholly or largely, the traits and values mentioned by the coöperators, as existing in the persons whom they mentioned as major influences in their lives. Our studies here are too limited in number and, as yet, not developed sufficiently in method to merit more than mention as an area for future investigation.

Each of these studies, however limited in number of cases and superficial in character, suggests that adults who analyze the outstanding influences in their earlier behavioral development emphasize a selected few persons whom they contacted in those early years: toward whom they developed strong emotional attitudes; who came to personify certain traits, values, habits, occupations, and behavior patterns; and whom they more or less consciously sought to emulate or, in the case of feelings of aversion, to develop opposing traits, etc. On the basis of these contacts, the boy or girl reacts toward the methods of child rearing that constitute his or her experience, and evaluates other conditioning factors encountered.

Summary

1. In studying the role of the family in the development of the child's behavior, the family must be conceived to include more than the parents.

2. The family of the child's orientation to life includes, in addition to the parents and possible stepparents, siblings, kinsfolk, guests, servants, and household pets.

3. To comprehend this broader range of family personnel and influences, the term *family complex* is suggested.

4. For the peculiar emotional linkage between the child and significant

persons in his background, the concept of the empathic complex is suggested.

5. The theory of the empathic complex holds that (a) as the child grows out of infancy he develops close relations with a few other persons, mostly adults; (b) these persons are selected on the basis of the child's felt needs of them; and (c) these other persons become the primary factors in the child's behavioral development.

6. Suggestive lines of evidence include autobiographical material, life-history documents, data on personal contacts within the family complex, and an experimental study in coöperation with 38 graduate students in a large university.

Chapter 9

Family Guests
and Childhood Visiting

It has been pointed out in the preceding chapter that the child's family background actually consists of the whole segment of life that is organized around the immediate family. Two aspects of this family complex, of obvious importance in the child's development, are family guests and early childhood visiting, particularly to kinsfolk and family friends. The present chapter is devoted to a consideration of these two, with suggestions of their role in child development.

I. Family Guests

In the absence of other empirical data, chief reliance regarding the role of family guests is placed upon a study made under the auspices of the William T. Carter Foundation at the University of Pennsylvania.[1] Included are certain methodological observations concerning the study and a summary of the present conclusions on the data assembled.[2]

Descriptive Summary of Autobiographical Material

INCIDENCE OF GUEST NARRATIVES IN AUTOBIOGRAPHIES

The first outstanding fact is that in a group of 200 autobiographies selected at random, but including the author's childhood, 117 contained direct references to guests entertained at home. Eighty-three made no mention of any visitors.

The authors who did write about guests varied considerably in the ex-

[1] Part of this chapter is taken from our article, "The Role of the Guest: A Study in Child Development," which appeared in the April, 1947, issue of the *American Sociological Revew*. Reproduction here is by courtesy of the *American Sociological Review*.

[2] More complete discussion of methodology is included in the foregoing article in the *American Sociological Review*.

tent to which they included experiences with guests as important parts of their history. These variations ranged from a two- or three-line reference to whole chapters devoted to visitors and their entertainment. In only two cases, though, did the author mention guests in such an incidental way as to make the reader assume that neither the fact of the entertaining nor the guest himself had made upon the child an important, conscious impression which lasted into adulthood. All the other 115 authors related such experiences as vivid, lasting impressions, worthy of record as part of a family or of a personal history.

AMOUNT OF ENTERTAINING

The amount of entertaining by the authors' families also varied a great deal. Half the writers gave their readers no clue as to the frequency of visiting in their homes. The other half were specific. Forty-five mentioned that their parents had guests frequently, or almost all the time. Eight wrote that there were very few visitors, and three mentioned times in their lives when their family's entertaining habits changed radically, from often to seldom, or the reverse.

The amount of entertaining had no marked correlation with the importance given to guests in the life story. One of the merely incidental references was made to let the reader know that the author's father had many visitors, whereas some of the authors who stated that their families had few guests devoted pages to the description of those few.

Analysis of Guest Narratives

A number of the observations in the autobiographies about the role of the guest in the family were echoed almost identically by author after author. These are assumed to be common features of the entrance of visitors into a family circle, at least for this group of writers. They are classified below, and are described by selected examples from the autobiographies.[3]

THE GUEST AS A STANDARD FOR MEASURING PARENTS

A frequent common memory of guests mentioned by these autobiographers involved a comparison of the guest with a parent. The newness of a guest's behavior, as contrasted with the familiarity of the parent's personality, sometimes made children very sensitive to traits which they had either taken for granted or had not been aware of before. Here are some examples:

Vivian Hughes used to listen to her mother entertaining. She was pleased and amused by her mother's intelligence and sense of humor as

---

[3] For a complete summary of the autobiographical part of this study, the reader is referred to "The Role of the Guest," *op. cit.*

compared with the stupidity of the "usual female visitors" who enjoyed only worries and grievances.[4] Edgar Lee Masters was much gratified by the frequent visits of his school teacher to his mother, who had had no great amount of formal education but had read widely and was a match for the schoolmistress.[5] But another writer went through agonies watching his father "show off" and "tell tall tales" to the very respectable men he brought home.[6]

THE GUEST AS A MEASURE OF FAMILY STATUS

A family has status only in comparison with the status of others. Small children are often well insulated from a recognition of their family's standing by a lack of that comparison. But sometimes, the guest serves to indicate the family's place, socially, religiously, or morally. The daughter of a well-to-do Russian patriarch reveals that she did not know she was living in luxury, so accustomed to it was she. But on Christmas, when all the peasants from her father's estate came to be entertained and to receive gifts from him, the girl gained a conception of her family's position in that country.[7] A farm boy, though, tells of his resentment over the yearly visits of his town aunts, because they let it be seen that their sister had married beneath her. He disliked to see his mother put on airs for them, and then become subdued in spirit before their superiority.[8]

THE GUEST AS A MEANS OF EXTENDING THE HORIZON OF BELIEFS AND CUSTOMS

Most young children seem to be strongly convinced that there is only one true religious faith, one honest political party, one right code of ethics, one "proper" way of doing a certain thing, and they believe that people who believe and do differently are not themselves "proper." Often, this is not so much the result of personal smugness or of deliberate parental indoctrination as it is of a lack of intimacy with people whose beliefs and customs are unlike their own. The guest who is accepted by the parents as a "proper" person often discloses to the children during his visits a point of view different from, or directly opposite to, that which the family entertains. Sometimes the children are much shocked by these revelations, but nevertheless they come to see that people they know and like act differently and hold views different from theirs.

---

[4] Vivian Hughes, *A London Child of the Seventies*, Oxford University Press, London, 1934, p. 89.

[5] Edgar Lee Masters, *Across Spoon River*, Farrar & Rinehart, Inc., New York, 1936, p. 66.

[6] *Sherwood Anderson's Memoirs*, Harcourt, Brace & Company, Inc., New York, 1942, p. 45.

[7] Princess Catherine Radziwill, *It Really Happened*, Dial Press, Inc., New York, 1932, pp. 28–29.

[8] Cyrenus Cole, *I Remember, I Remember*, State Historical Society of Iowa, Iowa City, 1936, pp. 67–69.

THE GUEST AS A MEASURE OF THE CONSISTENCY OF ADULTS IN PRECEPT AND PRACTICE

Children often have the opportunity to observe in the privacy of the family circle that parents do not always practice what they preach. But the social gathering together of adults can increase the opportunity for such observations when those adults are being companionable or convivial, and forgetful of the penetrating scrutiny of the younger generation. In both morals and manners, guests revealed adult inconsistencies to the authors of the autobiographies. An actor's daughter writes about the night that she was wakened by the noise of a party, got out of bed, and slipped in among the guests unnoticed. Beer and rye were abundant. Members of her family were dressed in their wrappers. A man was holding Mamma's hand. Another was trying to kiss Nana, a favorite aunt; he was "nosing" into the lace cascade on the front of her wrapper.[9] One autobiography tells of a boy watching a series of scenes between the Jewish stepfather-in-law and his mother. The man, who had come to visit, had to have his food prepared in the orthodox manner, which made a lot of trouble for the lady of the house. After a time, he suspected that she was only *pretending* to prepare his food properly. The youngster knew that these suspicions were correct—his mother was only pretending.[10]

THE GUEST AS A MEDIUM FOR TEACHING CERTAIN RULES OF SOCIAL BEHAVIOR

In the informal atmosphere of the family, a considerable laxity of manners and a wide choice of conversation topics are permitted that are not suffered outside the family circle. A mother can hardly anticipate *all* these differences for her young child. Yet most children somehow attain that knowledge by the time they reach their early teens. One of the roles of the guest seems to be to help clarify for the child what is, and what is not, expected in "polite society" at his own particular social level. Sometimes dismissal from the scene, because of the parents' inability to cope with the situation before guests, marks the lesson indelibly. Also, before the arrival of guests, harangues between parents who do not approve of each other's behavior before guests make children particularly keen to see who will win out when the guest does arrive. Autobiographers describe instances of all these kinds of lessons on how to behave when an outsider joins the family.

A number of writers remembered being sent from the room for behavior which they had not known would get them into trouble. One, when a little boy, was absorbed in listening to some breezy gossip of his mother's

[9] Aline Bernstein, *An Actor's Daughter*, Alfred A. Knopf, New York, 1941, pp. 142–149, 108–110.

[10] John Cournos, *Autobiography*, G. P. Putnam's Sons, New York, 1935, pp. 26–30.

when the vicar came to call. He waited patiently for the vicar to be welcomed and seated and then asked his mother to go on with the story
about _____. He was promptly sent upstairs.[11] Another, when a small
child, found her baby chamber pot hidden away in a closet. She was
ecstatic over finding her old friend and thought that her mother and the
luncheon guests would be too. So she ran into the room and displayed it.
Her mother fainted, and the girl was banished to the attic.[12] A third tells
of hearing the cook say that if the vicar came to tea much oftener he
would eat Auntie out of house and home. The girl thought the vicar ought
to know, so she told him. But she was sent to bed without any supper.[13]
The impressions made by these experiences were deep and long-lived.
They probably brought the dawning of a consciousness of conversational
taboos.

THE GUEST MAY CHANGE THE NORMAL FAMILY REGIMEN AND OCCASION
SPECIAL PRIVILEGES FOR THE CHILDREN

Some of the authors remembered how enchanted they had been with
the changes in the usual family regimen when guests came. The "room,"
a parlor-bedroom, was used in the daytime only when guests came;
special company cups and saucers were used instead of the usual dinner-
ware; a beautiful white tablecloth was put on the table instead of the
red-checked one used for the family. "Company towels" instead of meal
sacks, "company soap" instead of the yellow kind, "company tissue" instead of leaves from a mail-order catalogue—all were exciting differences
in home life when a guest came.[14]

GUESTS, THROUGH THEIR DISCUSSIONS WITH EACH OTHER AND WITH
PARENTS DURING VISITS, MAY BE AN INTELLECTUAL STIMULUS TO CHIL-
DREN

A common observation in these autobiographies is that their authors,
as children, loved to listen to the conversations of grown-up guests, and
were stimulated by them. The exact kind of stimulus depended upon the
kind of people entertained and the type of entertainment offered.

In the homes represented here, there were five noticeably different
habitual ways of entertaining guests. First, there was the home in which
the adults sat in a group and indulged in aimless gossip and in telling

[11] Charles Finger, *Seven Horizons,* Doubleday, Doran & Company, Inc., New York,
1930, pp. 10–11.

[12] Mara Millar, *Hail to Yesterday,* as told to Page Cooper, Farrar & Rinehart, Inc.,
New York, 1941, pp. 22–23.

[13] Jeanette Gilder, *The Autobiography of a Tomboy,* Doubleday, Doran & Company, Inc., New York, 1901, p. 91.

[14] Frazier Hunt, *One American,* Simon & Schuster, Inc., New York, 1938, pp.
8–9; Zora Neale Hurston, *Dust Tracks on a Road,* J. B. Lippincott Company,
Philadelphia, 1942, p. 34; S. B. McClure, *My Autobiography,* Frederick A. Stokes
Company, New York, 1914, pp. 5–6.

anecdotes. Here the children were eager to learn the latest tales about people whom they knew. They struggled to keep well posted. Also, they loved to hear any simple anecdotes and remembered many of them. Second, there was the home in which guests were entertained by cards, games, and stunts. Several writers mentioned their own prowess in beating guests at the games played. Conversation was restricted during these visits, but one writer says that she was proud of entering into the spirit of the games her father's friends played, and when Mr. Fitch won a hard hand she called out, "Good for you, Fitch!" much to the amusement of the men, who thought it a spontaneous remark. It was, instead, well calculated to produce just the effect it did produce.[15] A third type of entertainment was very formal: formal teas, dinners, and balls. Conversation here took place in little groups. The children were stimulated by the sense of rank, by social finesse, by styles of dress, by grace in dancing, and by personal popularity.

A fourth kind of entertainment was mentioned by two of the authors.[16] Both had come from peasant homes across the sea. In these homes the villagers all gathered together, and the old men of the village told stories —either folk tales, or historical stories about their country. These youngsters, listening as they sat on the floor of their homes, looked up to the wisdom of the old men, and knew their country's past. The fifth kind of entertainment was give-and-take discussion between intellectuals on topics of mutual interest, particularly the arts and sciences and current events. It is not surprising that this type was prevalent in the great majority of the homes of boys and girls who grew up to write their autobiographies.

THE GUEST MAY PRODUCE CONFLICTS AND INCREASE FAMILY TENSIONS

Often members of the family disagree in their estimates of a guest or of his behavior. In some cases, in these narratives, such differences became acute and caused family conflict. Harriet Munroe used to enjoy watching the games of the men who came to play cards with her father. But her mother did not approve of these people, who filled the house with smoke and required spittoons. The poet writes that she noticed the men came less and less often and that finally her father went out in the evenings to the home of a widower instead of bringing his friends home.[17] Two of the authors tell of their jealousy of the men who came to visit their mothers. The boy was sullen and angry.[18] The girl decided upon action

[15] Gilder, *op. cit.*, pp. 34–35.

[16] Feodor Ivanovitch Chaliapin, *Pages from My Life*, Harper & Brothers, New York, 1927, p. 3; and Michael Pupin, *From Immigrant to Inventor*, Charles Scribner's Sons, New York, 1926, pp. 5–7.

[17] Harriet Munroe, *A Poet's Life*, The Macmillan Company, New York, 1938, p. 24.

[18] Leo Lania, *Today We Are Brothers*, Houghton Mifflin Company, Boston, 1942, p. 17.

and told her mother's suitor that it was time to go home. Her mother was cross and scolded the child, who was thus doubly hurt.[19]

THE GUEST MAY UNITE THE FAMILY IN A MILD CONSPIRACY AGAINST HIM

The family often has a heightened sense of solidarity in the presence of an outsider, but at times circumstances make the family members more like fellow conspirators. Vivian Hughes tells of the time a guest came to call in the afternoon and stayed and stayed. Her hostesses grew uneasy. Finally, Mrs. Hughes rose and said that though she liked to sit in the dusk without lights, she hardly expected her guest to share that enthusiasm. The guest chuckled and left. Vivian and her mother turned to each other, smiled, and relaxed. The gas company had turned off the gas, and the lights could not be lighted.[20] The young man who always brought useless gifts to the family, necessitating a written thank-you note;[21] the uncle who always wanted to help, but who instead got in everyone's way;[22] the pastor who invariably turned up on housecleaning day;[23] the members of the clergyman's congregation who felt free to drop in at any time and comment on the behavior of his children;[24] the man who *would* appear just at mealtime—all of these inspired in the families of the writers the same feeling of conspiracy against them that drew the members of the family, for a time and on occasion, closer together.

THE GUEST MAY BE A SOURCE OF ANECDOTES AND CUE WORDS THAT BECOME PART OF ANY FAMILY'S COMMON HERITAGE

W. B. Maxwell's family had a word all their own. They would say, "May I Bynge you?" and would speak of being "Bynged." To outsiders it was just nonsense, but to the Maxwells it was full of meaning. It was coined from the name of a man, Mr. Bynge, who often stayed through dinner but would not share the family meal; he therefore sat in a corner and watched every mouthful his hosts ate, until the custom became annoying. Mr. Maxwell says that his own children use this word and know its connotation, but probably have no idea whence it came.[25] Cue words like this, that have no meaning to others but which instantly recall to the minds of the members some commonly shared experience, are rich pos-

---

[19] Marguerite Harrison, *There's Always Tomorrow,* Farrar & Rinehart, Inc., New York, 1935, p. 32.

[20] Hughes, *op. cit.,* pp. 19–20.

[21] *Ibid.,* pp. 95–96.

[22] Selma Lagerlof, *Memories of My Childhood* (translated by Velma Swameton Howard), Doubleday, Doran & Company, Inc., New York, 1934, pp. 181–184.

[23] *Ibid.,* pp. 149–152.

[24] John Andrew Rice, *I Came Out of the Eighteenth Century,* Harper & Brothers, New York, 1942, pp. 45–46.

[25] W. B. Maxwell, *Time Gathered,* D. Appleton-Century Company, Inc., New York, 1938, pp. 22–27.

sessions of family life. Guests, at least those in the homes of these auto-biographers, seem to supply a good share of such words.

A Further Note on the Use of Autobiographical Material

In view of other discussions of the use of autobiographical material in studying behavior and personality development, further comment suggested by its use in the present study may be in order. Four distinct values seem to inhere in this specific experience.

First, it has a "prospector" value; that is to say, it can be used to reveal the presence of "ore," which obviously is the first step in mining and refining it. It will be recalled that, in the present study, 117 out of the 200 authors referred to guests. Some 232 times these writers chose to delineate entertaining guests at home as moments of consequence in their early family histories. This certainly would serve to indicate that here is a subject significant enough to deserve further study. Not only the presence but also the richness of the "ore" is implied in these facts.

Second, the use of autobiographical material in the present study suggests specific leads for investigation, and it does so in two ways. In the first place, the authors mention a wide variation of guest influence, ranging all the way from the bringing out of the best tablecloth to the eruption of serious conflict between parent and child. In the second place, the kinds of experiences remembered during the visits of guests were common to many of these writers, so that they could be grouped in different categories according to their special kind of influence. In other words, this reveals preponderances, or areas of concentration.

Third, it is highly significant that all this information is derived from sources unrelated to the present study, and compiled without reference to the particular interests of the present project. No organized research unit suggested the subject of guests or their role in personality development to the authors of these autobiographies. In this sense, the information furnished is both objective and spontaneous. For the uses indicated above, this makes it particularly valuable.

A fourth possible value is that, for the most part, the persons furnishing the autobiographical case material have had some experience and facility in expressing their ideas. They write well and verbalize readily—at least in comparison with people not so trained, from whom most material bearing upon behavior problems must be secured. Furthermore, they have had experience in thinking through the processes of human development and expressing them effectively, which is one of the basic requirements in writing an acceptable autobiography. It must be admitted that this involves also a possible defect, as far as the scientific value of the material is concerned, for it may result in a striving for effective expression, possibly at the risk of truthfulness. In writing human material, there is at times the temptation to add "the fictional touch." By way of defense, it might be said that this would be less true in recalling childhood impressions of family guests than in certain other areas of life.

General Observations on Contemporary Case Material

In addition to the autobiographical material, 200 case records were gathered from contemporary sources, and their analysis is presented as the second main division of this study. First to be considered are certain general observations on the case material.

1. In terms of family interaction as a whole, the arrival of a guest brings new personnel into the family group. This means the introduction of new factors into the interactive relationships of the family. As the interactive process continues henceforth, all the members are affected. Their interactive relationship can never be the same again, which implies that the persons involved will be different. It is similar to adding a new chemical to an existing chemical solution: Things happen, and a new compound is formed. It is well to remember in this connection that the historic conception of the family as a domestic community, shared through the centuries by such students as Aristotle, Thomas Aquinas, and others, included the idea of the larger concentric circle of the household group, and that in this the guest was an integral even if temporary part.[26]

2. Another outstanding impression gained from the study as a whole is the importance of family experiences with guests as source material for the learning process that goes on within the family, with particular reference to its child members. In an earlier chapter it was pointed out that life in the family group is, for a child, a sort of laboratory process of experimentation in the field of behavior. In this process guests have a peculiar importance. They come into the home, generally with some, and often with the complete, acceptance by the parents. They are outsiders, yet less so than other persons. They constitute, in other words, a sort of intermediate stage between the child's confined family contacts and the more formal contacts with people from the world outside. Furthermore, they come to the child's attention on a distinctive plan. They are adults from the outside world who have the attractiveness of novelty, and often an interpretive coloring given them by the adults in the family group. Particularly is this true of the approved guest in upper-class homes, where family entertainment has a relatively selective character. That is to say, guests are invited into the home because the family wants them, and their

---

[26] For certain expressions included in this summary I am indebted to Professors L. Guy Brown and Franz H. Mueller, whose discussions of our paper, "The Guest in the Family," at the meetings of the American Sociological Society, December 28, 1946, were highly stimulating.

contacts with children result from the conscious sanction of the parents.

3. The elders in the family function, in large measure, as the manipulators of this use of guests in the learning process. This begins with the selection of the guests who come habitually to the home. How these may differ among families whose circumstances are relatively similar in many respects can be shown by the following contrast between the seven most frequent contacts with male guests of two boys before their tenth birthday. A's contacts, in order of frequency, were with an attorney, a judge, an attorney, a business executive, an attorney, a university professor, and a gentleman farmer. B's contacts, in order of frequency, were with a realtor, a salesman, an advertising solicitor, a sales manager, the owner of an electrical supply store, an automobile salesman, and a newspaper reporter. In both instances, the boys were in the habit of sitting about and listening to the conversation with these visitors. It must be obvious that, in the language used, as well as in the whole complex of ideas and allusions involved, these guests created wholly different situations in the home life and development of these two boys.

Again, parents often manage guest situations for their own conscious purpose. Guests with definite ideas on pertinent subjects are "drawn out" in front of the children. Conversations are often staged for specific purposes. Clever parents may be quite adroit about this. Guests "offer" advice about child rearing and adolescent behavior, or children are called upon to perform before them. The American fashion of having children "show off" before guests still persists, and the children are either thrilled or bored now as in colonial days. The coming of guests may serve as an opportunity or occasion for parents to impart to the child his conception of his role. The child may have been developing a certain pattern of activities, like helping the mother with the preparation of the meals. This may have been developing gradually. Then comes the important guest, and the mother puts into words what has been crystallizing, when she says to the visitor: "Helen is fast becoming mother's little helper." Further conversation ensues, with the result that both Helen and her mother become more aware of the role that has been in process of formation. Thus one hears constantly before guests and children such references as: "Mary is becoming quite a musician"; "Joe is our camper-outer; we never know where he is"; "Gloria has no interest in homework"; or "Bill is much interested in chicken raising."

Finally, after the guests have left, post-mortems follow. There may be analyses, comments, and evaluations concerning many things relating to the visitors: their behavior as guests, their occupations, plans of living, patterns of expenditures, or attitudes expressed. Sometimes this family appraisal may be made "in front of the children" and with their participation; often it proceeds without consciousness of their presence until Junior stops to inquire: "Daddy, why do you think Mr. Blank's job is a racket?"

In other words, parents may use guests as pawns in the child's learning process, or the same results may accrue as incidents in the family's accommodation to the guest.

4. The role of the guest in child development obviously varies a great deal from one family to another. Some of the differentiating factors can readily be identified. First is the size of the family. Children in small families tend to welcome guests much more than when there are a number of siblings and guests are taken more in their stride as part of the complex life of the household group. The only child in particular may be very happy and enthusiastic over guests who break the relative quietness of life in a small family. On the other hand, only children were observed in the course of the study whose possessive attitude toward the parents and the home led them to resent a guest as an intruding irritant.

Second, and closely related to the first factor, is the relative social accessibility or isolation of the family. In the latter case, the guest more often is a sparkling innovation or a breath of fresh air, whereas in the first situation the coming of a guest may just be another passing incident. The case of Ruth illustrates how the isolation of the family, together with other factors, creates a situation in which the child looks forward with great anticipation to the arrival of guests. Ruth lives in a country village containing about 15 houses; it is almost 30 miles to the nearest town. She has one sister, 7 years older. Her parents were 36 and 37 when she was born. Ruth says that neither of them is affectionate. "Guests in my house," she says, "were a grand and glorious occasion. I always looked forward to company for days ahead, and enjoyed every minute of their stay, except the few whom I disliked."

A third factor is the quality or tone of the personal relationships of the family which the guest enters. The case material includes some instances in which the intrafamily relations were none too cordial, and the arrival of a guest led to an almost immediate increase in tensions. In several cases, the guest was the friend of one member of the family, which led to his reception by the other members with unfriendliness; in others, his arrival was the signal for the beginning of a series of rival maneuverings, the object of which was to tell him the different sides of family bickerings or to "capture" his loyalty. Tension and maneuvering of this kind may not always be recognized and assessed by the child at their true meaning, but they are nevertheless part of the family milieu, sensed by the child and assimilated by him in various ways. Not infrequently, of course, guests reveal family tensions to the child, especially when they are relatives.

Fourth is the number of guests. Here, as in the economic realm, supply becomes a factor in the determination of value. Reference has already been made to the welcome extended to a guest in the relatively isolated home. Similar is the "feel" one finds in the well-managed, upper-class family where there are considerable selection of guests and a definite limitation of their number. Guests in these homes are managed; they do not overrun the family. In contrast are those homes revealed by the study in which there are constant streams of visitors—all kinds of people for all kinds of purposes. The home partakes somewhat of the nature of New York's Grand Central Station. There is no privacy, particularly for the child; his main impression may be one of "neglect in the midst of plenty." Children in such homes often reveal considerable resentment against people, or a callous disregard of their presence.

In contrast to such cases are those socially minded families who entertain a great many guests and treat them with open-handed tolerance and generosity. The life of the family group shades almost imperceptibly into the life of the neighborhood. Here one senses a family of extroverts, whose life seems to be lived in the open, whose problems are talked over with whoever is about—and guests seem to be about most of the time.

Fifth is the kind of relationship established between the guest and the child. Obviously many things are important in this connection, and some of them will be touched upon in subsequent pages; but two kinds of influences are clearly revealed in the case material. One has to do with the attitude of the guest toward children; the other, with the interests of the children. The attitude of the adult guest is particularly stressed in the material gathered from the young children. Their comments center constantly around certain types. There are the guests who "make over" the children unduly, until they shy away or become definitely antagonistic. Other guests ignore children, because they either do not like children or do not like their parents. Then there are the guests who fail to realize that children grow up and who treat William, who is now all of 12, as if he were still in the diaper stage. Again, there are the guests who do not approve of the children's behavior, and show it in a variety of ways. Children apparently are quick to sense these attitudes; guests often make them vocally and patently clear. The range of guest attitudes toward children is wide, and their existence and particular nature are very real and very important to children.

Complementary to the attitudes of the guests are the interests of the children. Such interests are highly important because they determine what Dollard and Miller have called the cues of the child,[27] that is, how he will respond to the guest. A simple illustration will suffice. Included in the case material is the account of the visit of a well-known novelist to two different homes with children. In the first home lives a 12-year-old boy. His interests are wholly mechanical, and what small interest he

[27] John Dollard and Neal E. Miller, *Social Learning and Imitation*, Yale University Press, New Haven, 1941, p. 21.

showed in the author apparently grew out of the fact that he owned a large power mower which cut the grass on his estate. In the second home was a 14-year-old daughter who read extensively, including some published stories by the author. Her interest in this guest was enthusiastic and almost boundless. Obviously, the respective attitudes of these two children reflected their specific interests. It is these two—the attitude of the guest and the interest of the child—which unite to create the *modus vivendi* between guest and child on the basis of which specific influences tend to operate.

Finally, the more one peruses the case material, the more one is impressed with the fact that the role of the guest varies with the child's age and stage of development. Provided a satisfactory relationship has been established, the child tends to take from the guest according to his need. Rosamond Lehmann, the novelist, grasped at the underlying principle when she wrote: "When we are children, we do not see the people close to us as themselves—only as our need for them, our habit of them. When something happens to make us realize that they have an enormous life going on apart from us, we feel rather resentful."[28]

In the early days of the child's life, the guests to which he is exposed tend to influence him in an impressionistic rather than a rational sort of way. Some vivid impression—a spectacular act, a striking word or story, the warmth of a smile—constitutes the child's recollection. Kay is 17 years old. She recalls that when she was about 4, a guest came to her home and in the course of the conversation referred to some man who drank himself to death. From this remark she developed in her mind the picture of a man standing near a store and drinking water until he burst. This scene, constantly recalled as time went on, became virtually a nightmare to her.

At a subsequent stage, perhaps from the tenth to the fourteenth year, the child may not be much interested in family guests. This is the age of shyness and withdrawal from the company of adults. Children are gawky and awkward; because of constant association, parents show no awareness of this, but guests are less successful in their dissembling. It is now that children rebel against appearing before them. When the visitor appears, the child retires to his room or leaves the house. The process of social weaning has begun, and in the earlier phases of it guests are part of the adult-family personnel of whom the child tends to be rather critical.

As the child grows older and becomes concerned with attaining adolescent and adult status, the most frequently voiced comments about guests relate to the age and developmental status which the guest projects upon the child. These comments fall into two groups. First, and more frequent, are those which criticize guests for not realizing the present age of the

[28] Rosamond Lehmann, *The Ballad and the Source,* Reynal & Hitchcock, New York, 1945, p. 100.

younger members of the family. "He thinks I am still a child." "So this is the baby. My goodness." " 'How big you've gotten,' she said over and over, and then ignored me the rest of the evening." "He never notices me when he talks, as though I still were a child." In contrast are the comments of appreciation because guests accept children at their own conception. "He treats me naturally." "He doesn't act as if I were a baby." Few of the case documents of younger persons are free of comments of one or the other kind. No other aspect of the behavior of a guest seems more important to the teen-ager.

In later adolescence, and with the transition to adulthood, boys and girls become more interested again in family guests, but perhaps on a more rational and selective basis. In this stage there is a growing consciousness of social behavior, and guests are evaluated with reference to the emerging needs of the younger members of the family. Most of the comments now refer to the guest's social graces or their lack. "He was a most interesting person." "I loved to hear him talk." "She had lots of pep and would pull all of us out of the doldrums." "He was full of fun and stories about Oklahoma where he came from." And there are statements like these: "He forgot to act his age." "He [the minister] always played and sang, 'There is a tavern in the town,' which isn't exactly a hymn." "He thinks he is always right, the big blabbermouth." "She is such a complaining person." "The ham he had promised for seven years finally arrived." "She always monopolized the conversation." It is in this stage that the most critical as well as the most appreciative comments upon the social behavior of guests appear, again an apparent identification of the prevailing interests of the youths in the family.

Some Specific Conclusions on the Contemporary Case Material

VERIFICATION OF THE AUTOBIOGRAPHICAL CONCLUSIONS

All the specific conclusions drawn from the autobiographical material presented earlier in this chapter are further emphasized by the other case documents. This is more particularly true of the histories secured from adults; this is natural, since the autobiographical statements, too, came from adults. One difference, however, is apparent. The authors of the autobiographies, having experience and facility in self-analysis and expression, more readily verbalize their experiences and insights than the other persons interviewed, who yield their conclusions by inference rather than in the more direct statement. And yet one finds striking flashes of insight from very young persons included in the study. Selecting, for example, the first conclusion from the autobiographical material that the guest becomes a standard for the measure of the parent, one finds Vivian, aged 12, pointing out that everyone who visits at their house "treats Daddy with great respect, except Betty (age 27) and Mrs. Teller." Similarly, Dorothy at 13 tells how her father "always makes a fool of himself when that blonde woman comes to the house."

THE GUEST AS THE PERSONIFICATION OF TRAITS, OCCUPATIONS, AND PERSONALITY TYPES

One of the most frequent references, direct or implied, is to the guests as the personification of some trait, occupation, or personality type. The child's conception of the guest is usually rather simple and is expressed in terms of some unitary summary, such as the doctor, that silly woman, the complainer, a good storyteller, etc. Often it is this one trait or characteristic that stands out, and on the basis of which the guest is favored or not. In the adolescent stage, guests with some one or more desired traits are set up as a model. Helen, past 13, when asked to tell about the guests in her home, placed Peggy at the top of the list. When asked what it was about Peggy that attracted her, she called attention to her good "sportsmanship and her friendliness." Helen, who is described by her associates as a very friendly girl and noted for her sportsmanship, said that she tried to "model herself after Peggy."

In the descriptive accounts secured from younger men and women, chiefly of university age, guests are identified generally in terms of relatively simple social personality types. Those most commonly found include the following: wives who tyrannized their husbands, couples who made a real marriage with little in the way of worldly goods, well-groomed career women without an ounce of maternal warmth in them, little wrinkled old ladies of youthful spirit and animated conversation, rollicking bachelors who took on sobriety with married life, relatives who fought each other and fawned on the uncle who had a large fortune, good sports in adversity, persons who had little or nothing to complain about but did so unceasingly, fair-weather visitors, those who used you for their own selfish ends, self-absorbed bores, conversational extroverts, "snobs and democrats," those who never imposed upon hospitality and those who always did, the pretenders, and the genuine.

Boys come early to note the occupations of guests, and how particular occupations are regarded by their parents and the other guests. What happens in the home before a guest's arrival may be the initial part of a subtle but effective process of occupational selection. Mother may slave in the kitchen, extra help may be hired, father is concerned over the preparations. Then Comes Dr. Thomas, the family physician. Everything that happens impresses Junior with the fact that Dr. Thomas is an important person and that his visit is an event in the life of the family. Perhaps Mother or one of the other guests drops a few judicious words about Junior becoming a doctor like Dr. Thomas. The prospect of becoming a doctor brings a warming glow; an occupational choice has been formed.

Years later, the young interne may say he cannot remember when he decided to become a physician.

THE GUEST AS THE PERSONIFICATION OF PET AVERSIONS AND DISLIKES

One aspect of the foregoing process reserved for separate discussion is the guest's personification of pet aversions and dislikes. Just as there are guests who impressed children so favorably that they accepted them as models to follow, so there are those who came to be identified as the living image of what the children wanted to avoid being.

In a good many cases, these dislikes involved some one or more mannerisms of the guest which the child or the family, or both, found offensive —garrulousness, incessant complaining, inconsiderateness, insincerity, grasping manner, and so on. Grace C., the most feminine-appearing woman interviewed, will serve as an illustration. In talking over the role of family guests, Grace said that two guests stood out above all the others. One was a woman who had been a counselor in the camp to which her sister had gone for the summer. This woman had a very mannish appearance; her hair was cut like a man's and she wore mannish clothes. Apparently, Grace's sister was fond of this woman, a fact which Grace resented. Whenever she came to the house, Grace would leave the room as soon as possible. Meanwhile, another guest who came frequently was described by Grace as being very feminine; she wore feminine clothes and had very feminine mannerisms. Grace said that this woman was very beautiful and treated her like a grownup, and that her visits were happy occasions.

Another series of pet dislikes seem to grow out of the visits of relatives and the bickerings that attended their presence. In a number of cases, strong resentments developed against relatives in general, leading to resolutions to avoid them in later life. Robert K. was such a person. His father was one of 12 children; his mother, one of 13. Both families visited back and forth a good deal. A series of rather difficult family problems seems to have arisen during Robert's coming of age, and he "grew heartily and irrevocably sick of the whole business." Now, at 32, and married for 9 years, he has had two visits from relatives and has made one such visit himself.

THE ROLE OF THE DRAMATIC IMPRESSION

In working over the source material of this study, one is impressed over and over again with the great importance of some striking, dramatic impression made by the guest upon the child. This is the same technique which the skillful criminal lawyer has long followed in dealing with juries: that one big impression, dramatically staged, may offset the accumulated weight of more prosaic details. A considerable number of persons who were included in this study emphasize, often to what seems a disproportionate extent, the importance of some one guest who was colorful and intriguing or had some outstanding feature or trait—the lawyer, with "the brusque manner and large head who always dominated our household"; "the perfectly groomed and poised woman, whose every little movement I watched and tried to emulate"; the handsome "singer-actor whose gleaming teeth were responsible for the faithfulness with which I brushed my teeth for years"; the actor with "the flowing tie and the story of the lion-taming act"; the mayor of the town who "got down on the floor and played with me." By way of contrast, another good proportion of these subjects singled out the guest who dramatized their dislikes and ever afterwards served as the personification of all that was to be avoided. As the flashing light reveals more sharply the figure against the sky, so the vivid colorful guest, with his glamour and his dramatic grip upon the child, brings into bold relief the model that is henceforth to be accepted or rejected.

THE GUEST AS A PRACTICE PERSON

Another phase of the guest-child relationship is the role of the guest as a practice person for the growing child. Since relationships between the child and his parents are more or less crystallized, it is the guest who offers the child an opportunity to try out procedures in meeting new situations. Mary, for example, has been told by her mother how to greet visitors, how to make introductions, how to improvise conversations. From the movie magazines and other sources she is learning about being glamorous and interesting and intriguing. Comes now the guest, and here is someone on whom to try out her newly acquired techniques. Furthermore, the guest offers the challenge and lure of new situations. The more one appreciates this particular aspect of the young person's interest in a family guest, the more can one understand the nature and intensity of the child's reaction to many guests. With some, the new techniques have a chance to function, and do so successfully. Those guests "treat me like a grownup"; with others, there is no opportunity and failure ensues. It is evident from the implications, and also from the expressions in the case material, that one of the most rankling memories is that of the guest who ignores the young boy or girl. Several varieties of this ignoring process are mentioned repeatedly—the guest who "just doesn't notice you," the one who is laudatory and "sickeningly sweet," the one who greets you effusively and then with an impatient expectancy assumes your prompt disappearance, and again the one who acts as though you were 5 instead of 15.

A "crush" on the older person of the opposite sex appears a number of times in the case material. Many boys and girls become interested in guests of the opposite sex, sometimes seriously, perhaps more often in a playful, practice sort of way. It would seem that girls are more willing to speak of this than boys; yet, on direct questioning, many men admit having been enamored, while in the adolescent stage, of women guests, often much older than themselves. Marion's story, told with frankness, serves as an illustration of the "crush" on an older male guest.

When I was about 8 years old, I fell in love for the first time, with a lad who frequently visited my family. He must have been about 20, a handsome fellow, and one who liked children and knew how to interest them. When he came, I wore my heart in my eyes. He neither took advantage of nor laughed at my affection. He gently called me his little fiancée and said that when I grew up we might be married. With me it was deadly serious. I told all my young friends that I was engaged, and meant it.

After I had been "engaged" for some time, I can't remember how long it was, Raymond came to the house one day and, while the family was assembled, looked at me in such a way as to say, "I hope you will understand" and told us that he was going to be married. I fled from the room, and went to my bedroom and sobbed. Various members of my family ascended to me and started to tease me. That's what I got for being so "forward" with men. Did I really think that Raymond could be serious about a baby like me? Etc., etc.

Then Raymond arrived and shooed them all away. He dried my tears, sat me down, and told me the facts—not of life—but of love. He told me that boys and girls love many different people before they grow up enough to find the one they want to marry, and that it was normal and nothing to be ashamed of nor to hide. Loving, he said, was the important thing, not being loved. Sincerity in showing one's feelings was what would make one grow into a person who would be very much loved.

Raymond's lecture to me gave me a new slant on the way to behave toward the opposite sex as I grew older and came to know boys of my own age. No one else had ever given me such direction. And from my own family I would only have gathered the notion that the proper behavior for young ladies was a flirtatious coyness, resulting in the wrapping around the finger of any eligible male, and with no compromise of affection on the part of the girl. Because I trusted Raymond, and his philosophy suited me, I adopted it,—to the disgust, many times, of my family. So far, I seem to have gained much, and gotten into no trouble, as a result of this infant "engagement."

THE PARENTS EMERGE AS ADULTS

In the ordinary course of family life, the child sees the adults in the family group function primarily in the role of parents, grandparents, uncles, aunts, and the like, and he comes to know them primarily in that relationship. This is particularly true of the parents. The presence of a guest often changes this situation completely. The parents now function as adults in relation to other adults, with the children as witnesses to the change in roles.

The case material brings out many phases in this process. Some subjects speak of their parents as coming to life, changing from drab to interesting and colorful persons. The whole family scene may change, as if the canvas of life were suddenly splashed with vivid colors. Edgar C., now 31, recalls that the conversation in his home usually was rather trite and commonplace, with no reference to public or international affairs. But when guests came, his father would wake up as out of a dream, and actually sparkle in his discussion of public events. He remembers that he would look at his father in amazement and think of him as an entirely different sort of person. Gradually it dawned on him that his mother never participated in these talks, would even act bored while they were going on, and would at times seek to divert the conversation away from these topics. As time went on, he began first to sense and then to see clearly that his father, a brilliant and widely read man, had married a rather domestic woman who had no intellectual interests whatever.

Apparently, in a number of cases, the children, seeing this transformation in their parents and in their relations with each other that occurred with the arrival of guests, realized for the first time the boredom or strain that existed between their parents. Often this came as a by-product of conversation between the adults—the mother complaining about her inadequate kitchen allowance; the father, about her unwise expenditures; the mother dropping some remarks about his interest in other women; he suggesting that if she stayed at home sometimes she could get some sewing done for the children.

The revealing significance of conversations between parents and guests is emphasized a good deal, with frequent references to the fact that they became "less adorned" than when the family talked by itself, that the father swore, that the mother told a risqué story, and that "they" said all kinds of things in front of the child. Eva's case is an interesting illustration. Eva was 5 when a college mate came to call on her mother. As the two women talked, Eva was relegated to the next room, supposedly out of earshot. The next day, Eva suddenly said to her mother: "Frances, you are a g— d— old nut," for which she was promptly and severely punished. It was not until weeks later that her mother realized that the classmate had made that remark to her, whereupon both women had laughed heartily. Eva, who had heard the remark and noted her mother's laughter, repeated it the next day, obviously to call forth the same happy laughter from her mother.

One fundamentally important phase of this whole process is that the child sees the parent in a new light, as an adult in relationship with other adults. Thus, as a by-product of the guest's coming to the home, the child learns the real nature of his parents, often for the first time. At times, he gathers from the behavior of guests his first appreciation of the excellent repute and high status of his parents; but more often the comments are far from complimentary. The mother is seen as a social climber, and parents are seen pretending in ways that the children realize are obvious falsehoods. Several children spoke of their parents telling lies in front of guests, and when they (the children) corrected the misstatements, punishment was meted out to them. Or the children were instructed to deceive guests about certain matters, either through positive misrepresentation or by withholding the truth.

By far the most frequent complaint of children about their parents' behavior in front of guests concerns their "showing off." Here is a patriarchal Italian father who insists that his children march up to him in front of guests to ask for money to go to the movies. First he subjects them to a lengthy catechizing, after which the money is given with a grand flourish of generosity or a long preachment on economy, each intended for the benefit of the guests. The disciplining of children before guests is common in practice and in the complaints of the case material. There is Esther, whose father constantly made fun of her "in front of company." He would ask her to play the piano for the guests, or to read a poem; then, Esther having done so, he would criticize her performance or ridicule it until, time after time, she rushed from the room in tears. If she goes out with a boy friend and comes home after 9:30, her father insults her and the boy, regardless of who else is in the house. Esther hates her father but has a "guilty feeling about this, because nice girls don't hate their fathers."

Another rather basic aspect of the parent's emergence in the role of adult involves a comparison, in the eyes of the child, of the parent with other adults. That children are constantly making such comparisons is evidenced in a number of ways. In interviews with the younger age group, questions about guests continually called forth statements such as "he was taller than my father," "she was not as fat as Grandma," "she wore her hair like sister Jo," etc. From physical comparisons of such kinds, it is an easy step to an appreciation of other contrasts—clothes, grooming, manner of speech, range of interests, complex of attitudes. Most children approach such situations emotionally tilted toward the parent; and if he compares favorably with the guests, children are quick to note it, apparently often with comforting assurance. On the other hand, discussion of this matter with various children indicates that often the child's first feelings of antagonism to, or shame of, the parent appear with the advent of a guest. It is then that so many parents seem to fail their children, through uncomplimentary comparisons, through the discovery that the parents are not wholly and exclusively concerned with them, by seeing the parent in an adult role inconsistent with his parent role, or by indicating to the guest a conception of the child different from that ordinarily revealed. Family guests seem to serve like a turning table which reveals the parent to the child and the child to the parent in new, and often strange and startling, lights. The story of Florence is interesting in this connection.

"I don't remember," said Florence, "the guests that came to my house so much for themselves as for the ways in which they gave me new pictures of my parents, or strengthened the ideas that I already had about them. I learned very early that when guests came to visit my mother it was the time for her to reveal and laugh over all the serious little confidences that my older brother had given to her, things that I had heard her promise never to mention to a soul. I was glad that these visitors had given me that chance to find her out. Otherwise I might have learned to confide in her, with the same result."

GUESTS AS A PREVIEW OF ADULT LIFE

The arrival of guests, usually adults, results in the establishment of a segment of adult life in the home, in which the child plays the role of participant observer. Several distinct aspects of this process are identified in the case material.

First, the child sees adults in action. "You see what grownups are like," commented one 18-year-old. Here, in other words, is a preview of the behavior types and patterns of adult society. Adults are on exhibition, and the child's reactions are usually positive, and at times far from complimentary. Guests in the home personify adult traits and the types one will encounter in later life. They afford the child a transitional experience preparatory to later full-time adult living, and one senses from the material contributed by the younger children especially how wise parents utilize a guest as a device for the social education of the child.

Second, the guest serves as an agent for passing on certain phases of the larger group culture to the child. Several aspects of this can be identified. First is the guest who is brought into the home to strengthen some parent-selected aspect of the culture. This was evident in the case of Josephine, who, at 16, was reluctant to fall in with the family plan for university training. Josephine, steeped in the movie magazines, was of the opinion that a college education was only for girls who lacked the charms necessary for women to achieve their ends. Her mother, alert to the situation, invited to the home, for repeated visits, the very glamorous daughter of a friend who had won two prizes for scholarship at the neighboring university. The guest entertained Josephine at her sorority house and at several university affairs. Josephine now is eager to go to the university.

Another is the case where the guest is of another race or nationality. One of the guests at Helen's home was a Chinese student. Helen remembered him because he wore Chinese dress and taught her some Chinese words. After his visit, she read *Moment in Peking, Dragon Seed, Our Family*, and *My Country and My People*. She took two dollars of her own money and sent it as a contribution to Chinese relief. She wishes that she might visit China. She still reads everything about China that she can secure.

Other aspects involve the entertainment of guests from other regions in the United States, the revelation through guests of social and economic differences of which the child was not aware before, the identification of marital problems and the various sexual involvements outside the marriage bond. The guest, in other words, is not merely a person, but a cultural product, and he brings into the home his cultural background as surely as he does his clothes and the possible dust on his shoes.

II. Childhood Visiting

Consideration of the role of guests in the home in child development tends to emphasize the complementary experience of childhood visiting in other homes. Life-history documents, autobiographies, and interviews contain frequent reference to its importance. Here, obviously, is another area of behavior analysis calling for extended research.

A pioneer study of childhood visiting, based upon a hundred records, selected from 234 case histories obtained from boys and girls, will be presented as an indication of its possible importance. The methods utilized in the gathering of the information consisted of free-associational writing, supplemented by personal interviews in 22 of the cases. Selected conclusions of the study are presented in summary form.[29]

1. About one out of six of the cases report little or no visiting away from home as children. In a few of these cases there were understandable circumstances, such as chronic illness of a family member or recent arrival of the family, which limited social contacts, but in most of the other cases the controlling factor was the attitude of the parent or parents. These are the parents who have warped dispositions which lead them to distrust other persons and who, in their capacity as parents, force their attitude upon their children or manage their children's social relations on the basis of that distrust. Children of these parents seemed to show a definite resentment against the elders responsible for it.

2. The extent of visiting away from home during their early years varied a good deal, from a few scattered visits to near relatives to almost daily trips to homes and families other than their own.

3. Visiting away from home began early in life in a majority of cases, meaning as early as memory could push back the limits of recall. Most of these early visits were to relatives—grandparents, uncles and aunts—and close friends of the parents, in the order of their frequency. Because of the mobility of contemporary families, relatives are more scattered geographically than formerly, but modern facilities of communication and transportation have more than kept pace with this fact, with the result that kinship groups today, while often scattered over a considerable area, will visit each other with considerable regularity.

4. Visiting away from home in the early years seems for most children to have been a major social experience, involving new contacts, new experiences, the challenge of new problems, calling forth new adjustments, now conscious and now unconscious, to other people and other places than those found at home. Visiting away from home, in other words, was

[29] The entire study is presented in James H. S. Bossard, *Parent and Child*, University of Pennsylvania Press, Philadelphia, 1953, Chap. 13.

a definite phase of the growing-up process, involving experience with the larger world outside of the family.

5. One phase of this process was the feeling of achievement that came from the conquest of distance. Reference to the distances traversed in these early visits is constant, and such references are accompanied by expressions of vividness of memory. Such accounts invariably begin with words like these: "The one visit that stands out in my mind," or "The visit that I remember most clearly," or "When I was 9, we really went visiting, all the way to California."

6. A second distinct impression gained from the case material was that for most of the children these early trips away from home were experiments in freedom, like the short flights of fledglings away from the nest. True, the sweetness of freedom might sour quickly, often the freedom craved was only temporary, but it was a unique experience in any event.

7. These visits gave varied insights into life—the nature of adults compared with your parents, dissentions among relatives, "queer" people, new food, different home surroundings, "strange" family customs, new ideas and values in family living. Evaluated in terms of the learning process, these insights were of two different kinds. First there were those that were disillusioning—people, relatives, families, playmates were not as you thought they were. One-quarter of those who visited as children saw or had experiences of a sexual nature which they apparently had difficulty in assimilating. The other kind were more constructive in nature, teaching something useful later on—ways of dealing with people, of entertaining, of handling difficult situations, and, what was equally important, how not to do certain things.

8. Visiting away from home invariably led to comparisons between one's home and family and those visited. We human beings early learn to make comparisons, and when young children go visiting they see how "the other half" lives, metaphorically speaking. It is interesting to note that the majority of informants in the study had experiences, still fresh in their minds after a period of years, which led them to appreciate their own homes and parents more than they did before they went visiting. "We had a nicer life at home." "In our family we had better manners." "I discovered there were parents who didn't speak nicely to their children." The most-emphasized feature of home life was food and Mother's cooking. The stress in present-day pediatric care would seem to produce a strong emotional complex about food in the later years. In a minority of cases, the comparisons were not favorable to the home base. These experiences seem to have been particularly well remembered.

Summary

1. This chapter is based upon an original study of the role of the guest in child development. The study includes 400 case records, 200 of which

are autobiographies; 40 were obtained from children ranging from 10 to 15 years; 100 are autobiographical accounts from young people between 18 and 23 years of age; and 60 are records of interviews with adult persons, chiefly of middle age.

2. The published autobiographies emphasize the following conclusions: (a) The guest is a standard for measuring parents; (b) he is a measure of family status; (c) he extends the horizon of beliefs and customs; (d) he is a measure of the consistency of adults in precept and practice; (e) he serves as a medium for teaching certain rules of social behavior; (f) he may change the normal family regimen; (g) through their discussions with each other and with parents, guests may be an intellectual stimulus to children; (h) they may produce conflicts and increase family tensions; (i) the guest may unite the family in a mild conspiracy against him; and (j) he may be a source of anecdotes and cue words that become part of the family's common heritage.

3. Four distinct values inhere in the use of autobiographical material. First, it reveals the presence, and to some extent the richness, of the "ore"; second, through the areas of concentration revealed, it suggests specific leads for investigation; third, the information obtained is both objective and spontaneous; and, fourth, the material is usually well thought out and well written.

4. General observations on the contemporary case material emphasize that the guest adds a new factor to the family interactive process, furnishes source material in the learning process for the child, and is manipulated by the parents in this learning process. Obviously, the role of the guest varies a great deal from one family to another, depending upon the size of the family, its relative accessibility or isolation, the nature of intrafamily relationships, the number of guests, their relationship with the child and family, the interests of the child, and his age and general development.

5. Some specific conclusions on the contemporary case material include: the importance of the guest as the personification of some trait, occupation, or personality type; the similar personification of pet aversions and dislikes; the role of the dramatic impression; the guest as a practice person; the emergence of the parent as an adult in the eyes of the child; and the role of the guest in presenting a preview of adult life.

6. Early childhood visiting, or the lack of it, seems to be equally significant in adding to the child's experience history. Those who did not visit resented the lack, blaming parents for a pathological distrust of people. Those who did visit ranked it as a major social experience, enumerating a number of specific contributions to their development.

Chapter 10

Domestic Servants
and Child Development

Present in a large proportion of homes, and participating within limitations in the domestic routine, is the family servant. Although thus far unhonored in scientific studies, the servant is a definite part of the child's family world, operating in a relatively silent, subtle, but rather pervasive manner, and playing a role in his social development. This chapter is a pioneer attempt to analyze the role of the domestic servant in family situations, with particular reference to the young child. The chapter begins with an analysis, by way of background, of the main types of domestic servants and the chief varieties of servant-family relationship. Next there follows an explanation and a brief appraisal of the sources of information utilized in this study. The main body of the chapter is devoted to an inductive summary of the data on the ways in which domestic servants affect family relations and child development.

Types of Servants

Each servant-family-child relationship is in many ways a case unto itself. In considering a number of cases, however, one finds certain recurring variables. One set of these consists of the kinds or types of servants; another, of the nature of the relationships between family and servant. In part, these two overlap; but they are sufficiently distinct to be separated for purposes of general discussion.

One of the most obvious and significant distinctions in types of servants is between those who "live in" with the family and those who do not. This difference is important in its effect upon the extent to which the servant shares in the family life. Servants who "live in" are apt to become a more intimate part of the family routine, particularly so with reference to the life of the younger children. The U.S. Census of 1940 reports a total of

1,033,772 such servants living in private households. This figure does not include the servants who work in a household but live out, which means that they maintain a home elsewhere that is utilized chiefly for sleeping and leisure-time purposes. Some of this latter group work regularly in homes, and achieve a status close to that of the servant who "lives in"; others work irregularly or on a part-time basis, with resultant modifications in their relationship to the family.

Domestic servants can be grouped on the basis of race and national-origin differentials. In certain countries, such as England and Spain, and in some areas, perhaps chiefly rural, in the United States, most servants are of the same race and nationality as the families they work for. In this country, however, for the most part this is not the case. In the South and East, most household domestics are Negroes or members of earlier immigrant groups. In these cases, the employer-employee relationship is reinforced by considerations of racial attitudes and minority group status.

Finally, servants may be classified by the nature of their jobs. There is, for example, the household manager, found in larger homes with a staff of servants; there is the general utility maid who does all kinds of housework; there are the specialized jobs—nursemaid, governess, cook, upstairs girl, laundress, etc. The nature of the job has much to do with the relationship developed between servant and family, and particularly between servant and child. This is equally true of the other distinctions between kinds of servants that have just been summarized.

Servant-Family Relationships

The nature of the relationship which prevails between family and servant is highly important for the purposes of this chapter. Obviously, the variations here are endless, but six general aspects can easily be identified. First are the cases in which the servant has some social or kinship relation to the family. This includes the distant relative whom the family takes over; the reputed relative, where a myth of kinship is maintained to soften the servant status; and the impoverished "friend of the family" who came as a guest and stays on "to help out." In these and other cases, the relationship may be described as somewhat more than an employer-employee one, with a limited social and kinship aspect.

Second are the cases where the servant comes to be spoken of as a member, or almost a member, of the family, but where there is no kinship or family bond. For the most part, in these situations the service has been of such long duration and so satisfactory in character, and the family's social position is so secure that it can afford to assume the paternalistic tradition, with but slight emphasis upon the ordinary symbols and distinctions. The phrase "member of the family" usually means that the servant has a higher status than domestics in general, that less deferential behavior is required, and that she may share in some of the family's common activities.

Another relationship is that in which the mistress and the servant work side by side. These cases are most numerous on farms or where large families make necessary heavy household duties; hence the servant is more of a helper or fellow employee than one who "waits upon" the family.

In marked contrast are the homes where the "help" have a distinctive servant status. There may be the symbols of distinctive dress or "uniform," a servants' entrance, separate living quarters, and the like. These and other symbols bespeak a formality in the relationships between servant and family, and usually indicate a distinct cleavage between the two.

The socially distant but personally friendly relations between Negro servants and white families, found in the old South and elsewhere, is another type of relationship which appears as natural in certain areas of this country as it seems incomprehensible to persons from other areas. "Colored domestics who have worked for upper-class white families for many years are often allowed not only a wide province of authority with regard to the house, the children, and the choice of foods, but also a semi-familial relationship with their white employers."[1]

A final type of relationship to be identified here includes those servants who come from the same race or national-origin group as the employer, or even from a different group of a higher status. Here one is apt to find deep resentment and a sense of frustrated pride which may express itself in a highly impersonal relationship, or in intermittent sniping, particularly at the younger and more defenseless members of the families.

These differences in the type of servant and of family-servant relationship are very important in any analysis of the servant's role in child development. Two general kinds of situations are particularly significant. One is where the servant has the specialized task of child care. This ranges from the young girl, perhaps of high-school age, who comes to play with the child in the afternoon, serve his dinner, and put him to bed, to the full-time nursemaid who, in addition to supervising the children, cleans their room, washes their clothes, and the like. In the other type of situation the more trusted domestic servant is given some authority over the children, may discuss with the parents the problems of child rearing, or be given specific instructions to apply policies formulated by the parents.

Although such situations stand out as of obvious importance, the fact to be emphasized here is that domestic servants as a group, simply through their presence if in no other way, are part of the family life in which the

---

[1] Allison Davis, B. B. Gardner, and Mary R. Gardner, *Deep South*, University of Chicago Press, Chicago, 1941, p. 445. This book contains much interesting information on domestic servants in the South, with some references to their relationship with children.

child is inducted into his culture. Much of the relationship between children and servants consists of the minutiae of family life, ignored because of their repetitious triviality yet significant for that very reason. The simple fact is that many mothers, and fathers, have no conception of the importance of what goes on in the child's home life, other than formalized instruction, and they tend to "shed" much of the child-caring process as a bothersome detail. The mother who does not trust her "help" to wash and dry her best set of china but does trust her to spend the afternoon with Junior in the park; the clubwoman who leaves her children with a semi-illiterate Polish nursemaid while she attends such "interesting" meetings; the bridge fiend who cannot be bothered with the incessant questions of her 5-year-old daughter and leaves them to be answered by a superstitious old mammy—these and others like them are no figments of the imagination.

Sources of Information—A Methodological Note

The remainder of this chapter presents the results of a "first" study that sought to find the ways in which domestic servants affect the social development of the child. The information upon which this study is based was obtained from two sources. The first is an analysis of 100 autobiographies selected on the sole basis that the author must have written of his earlier life. Of these, 44 autobiographies contained references to the domestic servants in the home in which the author lived as a child. Of these 44, 5 were merely incidental references; that is, a servant was mentioned only as being present during a certain scene, and there was no suggestion of her having had any influence on the child's personality formation or on his family life. Nevertheless, three of these five references were to the author's earliest memory of his life, and they all included a family servant's presence. In the 44 autobiographies there were two other references to earliest memories which also included a family servant. Thirty-nine of the authors who wrote about servants described them as real people, as being closely associated with them in their early years of development, as having considerable influence upon them personally, and as being an integral part of their family life. Several of the autobiographers devoted as much as a whole chapter to one or two servants, or to the part all the servants played in the early family situation.

Most of these 39 writers seemed to consider family servants as definite members of the early family circle—not quite on a par with parents and siblings, but more intimately connected with the family situation than anyone else outside the immediate family. One author voices the attitude that many suggest: during childhood, there were two worlds of which one gradually became conscious—the inside world and the outside world. The core of the inside world was Mamma and Papa, the dispensers of necessities and the final court of judgment. The rest of the inside world consisted of nurses, governesses, cooks, maids, housekeepers, who did everything for one and who were with one all the time. Another author writes: "They were more than the friends of the family. They were *us* as much as ours." And still another: "These faithful creatures did indeed move in and out amongst us like shadows. We were not aware of them. In their presence we dressed and undressed. To them we unbosomed ourselves more freely than to our own parents."

Any fair appraisal of this autobiographical material must emphasize both its values and its weaknesses. On the credit side is the fact that these references to servants were made spontaneously. No questionnaires were submitted to the authors, no leading questions were asked, no suggestions were made. In fact, the situations were rather "loaded" against it; yet nearly half of this unselected group of a hundred successful persons, writing about the recollections of their childhood, included references to the role of servants in their lives. In their comments, they represent no school of academic thought, nor are they tarred by the brush of any theory of interpretation of personality development. On the other hand, these authors are successful persons, writing in a genial mood and with nice manners for popular consumption. Naturally, under these circumstances, there will be a tendency to be interpretive in a friendly rather than in a critical vein. One other possible criticism must be acknowledged, and this has to do with the general time span covered by these autobiographical references. The childhood of most of these authors covered the years at the turn of the century. They are writing, therefore, about servants and family-servant relationships as they existed during that general period, and not today when these situations are admittedly different in at least some respects.

The second source of information utilized in this study is a series of what may be termed interactive interviews. This term is applied to interviews in which the subjects are asked to tell about their early experiences with servants in the home, to recall acts, sayings, attitudes, relationships, etc., in as much detail as possible; and where, in addition, the interviewer asks pointed questions and suggests various leads. Information of this sort was gathered from a total of 21 persons. Of these, 15 were men and 6 were women; they ranged in age from 10 to 54 years. Obviously, the number and dispersion of cases call for extreme caution in the use of the material gathered.

Comparing the interview material with that derived from the autobiographies, we see that in many respects they agree with or tend to supplement each other. On the other hand, the interview material tends to be franker, more critical, less nice as it were. After all, people will say in frank conversation many things which they would hesitate to publish in a book, particularly when discussing certain aspects of their lives. These contrasts will appear a number of times in the summary of the material which follows.

Domestic Servant—Family Life—Child Development— An Inductive Summary

THE DOMESTIC SERVANT MAY BE A MOTHER-SURROGATE

In the life stories of some autobiographers, a woman servant is remembered as a real mother-substitute. One writes: "Our 'Fraulein,' who had come to us shortly before I was born and stayed with us 17 years, was the most cherished soul in the household. We called her 'Liebe' (which means Love) and there was no worse catastrophe than if she refused to kiss us good-night." Another spoke of Lucy, a Negro servant: "As for us little ones, Lucy was our all-in-all. She mended our clothes, tucked us in our cribs when we went to bed, knit our socks, held our noses when we took castor oil, and occasionally heard our prayers." And still another: "She [my nurse] was more to me than the usual mother would have been or could have been who had any other responsibilities."

Usually, this kind of servant filled the early physical and affectional needs of the child whose mother was too busy, too social, too formal, or who just did not care to perform such duties for her child. Usually, too, this type of servant was the sort of woman who had chosen her position because of her instinctive maternity, and who gave to the child a sincere love and understanding that grew out of her own warm nature and that is not inherent in every woman who happens to bear children. One sensed, in some of the cases, that the child was saved from affectional insecurity by having had the good fortune to include in his family circle a mother-substitute as well as his own mother.

The effects upon family relationships of this devotion between servant and child varied. There were children who greedily absorbed the affection of both servant and parent and felt the richer for having both. There were those who considered their mothers as beautiful ladies, and the servants as menial but nevertheless dearer. One writer remembered with gratitude the girl who stayed with the family for a time and made the home run smoothly at last. His mother was a very poor housekeeper and his home had been in turmoil. Finally, there was one young child, who, when his mother took him from his adored nurse's lap to show him off to her company, slapped her in the face with lusty resentment against her.

Only two cases in the interview material fall into this category, but both support the autobiographical record in this respect. In one of the cases in particular, the mother is represented as stern and cold, and the child found an affectionate haven in a highly maternal servant. In the other, the mother's employment and obvious preoccupation with her business left the child to make the servant her surrogate.

THE DOMESTIC MAY ACT AS A GO-BETWEEN AND MITIGATOR OF THE HARSHNESSES OF FAMILY LIFE

A great many writers remembered the family servants who interceded for them and acted as conspirators with them against the vicissitudes and stern regulations of family life. They stood somewhere halfway between child and parent and helped in small ways to spare them from each other. Susie, who heard her charge's screams when his father was beating him, ran for her Madam to tell her that the Master was killing the boy. The beating stopped and the boy remembered. Children who were not allowed sweets or evening snacks were treated to them secretly by friendly servants. Susan, who knew her little charge would be punished for losing his silver cup, helped him make up an elaborate lie about what had become of it, and stoutly corroborated his story when he told it. Nurse Kelly was always extracting her young master from scrapes, and when she could not do that she would sit outside the room in which he was confined for punishment, and feed and console him. To still his curiosity, another servant conspired to let a youngster peek into a room which had been forbidden to him, with the well-remembered result of finding an occupied coffin in the room and causing subsequent confession to Mother. The frequency with which this kind of act on the part of a servant was mentioned leads one to believe that the relaxing of regulations, the assuaging of punishments, and the sharing of secret pleasures were comfortable contributions to early home life. One suspects that some parents are a bit warier of their treatment of children in the presence of such servants.

There are constant references to this in the interview material, with additional information which suggests that servants are not above a bit of conniving in this respect—reporting the child to the parent for discipline and then seeking to soften the punishment that follows. Particularly stern parents, as hard in their dealings with servants as they are rigorous in disciplining their children, may well unite servant and child in the solace of conspiracy.

SERVANTS PROVIDE COMPANIONSHIP FOR THE YOUNG CHILD

There is much evidence that these autobiographers depended a great deal upon servants for companionship when they were quite young and at home most of the time, and when the parents and older siblings might be off visiting or at school. These good companions whose presence the children constantly sought included page boys who taught them to play soccer, a butler who told jokes and sang songs, a footman who gave lessons in the *Savatte*. A gamekeeper let his master's sons practically share with him his woods and wild life. Tony, the gardener, engaged in "important conversations" with his young master. An old French servant and his dog

"Mouche" were Sir Henry Layard's earliest companions. These servants were pretty much confined to the home grounds, as was the young child. They were accessible. They were, ordinarily, the simple, hearty kind of folk who enjoy children, and their duties were full of interest for the youngsters because they were not part of their own inner family life, and so seemed glamorous and adventurous.

The interview material and other supplementary data indicate that the amount of the time shared by servant and child tends to be determined in large measure by the age of the child, the factor of sex similarity, the mother's role and attitude in the child-caring process, and the special type of servant involved. An adult male, included in the interviews, tells of his devotion, from about his seventh to his tenth year, to a rather colorful Irish cook, which led him to spend countless hours in her company, even at the cost of running errands for her and otherwise helping in her work.

THE SERVANT MAY ENLARGE A CHILD'S KNOWLEDGE OF MANY ASPECTS OF LIFE WHICH ARE ALIEN TO HIM IN HIS OWN IMMEDIATE FAMILY, OR FROM WHICH HIS PARENTS HAVE CAREFULLY PROTECTED HIM

Two of the authors wrote about the delight they had as children in the literature that they found "below stairs." One of them recalls, "As one may read of strange customs in far lands, I learned of the exploits of contemporary murderers, the daily business of police courts and policemen and prisons, thrilling shipwrecks and railroad accidents, accepting all without horror as a part of the oddity of life. If I wondered at all, the wonderment ended in a conclusion to the effect that my parents and their friends were strangely unadventurous, intellectually."

One boy remembers visiting the cabin of a Negro servant and being enchanted with all the photographs of colored girls that adorned the walls. There are several references to parties in the servants' quarters which fascinated the children with new pictures of adult behavior. Poultney Bigelow, whose butler escorted him around Paris, writes, "My father was in my eyes the wisest man living, but as I retrospect at this moment, I feel sure that before I was eleven years of age I had experienced many phases of Parisian life about which he knew nothing save possibly through books."

Another aspect of this enlarging of horizons came about from the fact that the behavior of servants was revealed and discussed by the family in instances where the same behavior on the part of a family member would have been kept hidden. Children learned, for instance, through family discussions, that the faithful and loved woman servant was a laudanum addict; that all the maids were sooner or later dismissed for sexual irregularities; that a nurse was fired for meeting a sailor at night; that "after the third time father had staked James to the Keeley Cure he gave up the effort to rid him of the curse of intemperance. . . . Today, at 76, James still puts in a 12-hour day, 7 days a week, 'helping out' on the place, and proves that his stamina has not been undermined by the Demon Rum. A great lesson to us all"; that all the women servants in the home were periodic drunkards taken from a women's prison in an effort to help them save their own souls.

The interview material is particularly clear in regard to this second aspect. All but three of the subjects have rather vivid recollections of family discussions of the vagaries of the servants' behavior. Mary, the unmarried maid, terminates her employment because she is going to have a baby. Sarah, the cook, has been on a spree for the past two days. Katie has not been to work this week because she had to move after her "husband's" wife made a scene. Helen's husband has been arrested for being in the numbers racket, and Helen wants two weeks' advance salary. These and other incidents in the interview material are recalled as the occasion when as children these subjects had their first contacts with illegitimacy, drunkenness, adultery, and petty crime.

SERVANTS MAY INFLUENCE THE SEX LIFE OF CHILDREN

The autobiographies reveal three different aspects of the servants' influence upon the children's sex life.

First, there was instruction in the facts of sexual reproduction. "Youth was carefully 'guarded' in those days, and neither my father nor my uncle ever gave me any information as to the 'facts of life' either in connection with animals or humans, but I acquired them from the farm hands."

Second, two of the men writers speak of having had sex relations with girls employed by their family. One of them was taught the art as a small boy by a hired girl; the other "managed very well on the matter of natural gratification through the compliance of servingmaids about town and in my mother's service without any disaster either of body or of mind, so far as I can see even to this day."

A third aspect of this influence upon sex life came through the first awakening of the romantic urge in the small boys, by their awareness of their nurses and governesses as desirable women. Many men write about these domestic servants as their first ideal marriage-partner choice. Their awareness of the women varied with their individual natures and the responsiveness of the particular women. Some of the boys fell in love at a purely ideal level. Others were smitten with more profane love. One describes his juvenile passion for his nursemaid, and his very sensual delight in being drawn across her knees to receive an easily tolerated smacking.

One effect of these infant love affairs for nursemaids would seem to be a by-passing, or a mitigating, of the Oedipus complex in the normal family situation. A small boy can fall in love with his nurse without experiencing the heavily guilty incest feelings which would be provoked by a similar passion for his mother, and also without experiencing the deep hatred toward his father which such a situation produces.

The interview material not only reveals the three aspects indicated by the autobiographies, but suggests other facts which may be of considerable importance. One is the role of the sex differential in this respect. All of the men and none of the women interviewed acknowledged at least some implications for sex behavior resulting from the presence of servants in their home during their youth. Most of the servants referred to by the men were women, and at least one in each home was not too old or too plain to be of interest as a woman.

From all that one can gather, it has been a very old and not altogether uncommon practice in times past, and in many parts of the world, for male children to have their first, or at least a very early, sex experience with a domestic servant. Apparently, this has been true also in this country, especially where white domestics are employed, and where they live in. This seems to have been particularly true in rural areas in the case of farm boys. Although these women servants were much older than the boys, often by from 10 to 20 years, it is significant that most of the men speak of these as helpful experiences which served to lay the foundation for an early development of normal reactions to sex experiences. Several of the men interviewed, who reported sex relations with domestic servants, said they thought that it focused their attention too much and too early upon sex but agreed that it emphasized heterosexual rather than homosexual development.

There are indications that this particular role of the domestic servant has been changing in recent years. Several factors are involved. One of these is the increasing employment of Negro servants in white families. While Negro females are not without attraction for white males, as a great wealth of evidence attests, the color line may be crossed sexually less often when there is a marked age differential on the female side. Second is the increasing practice of the servants' living out, which often removes the occasion or opportunity. Third is the child's earlier exodus from the home to the school.

One other fact seen between the lines of these data is the sharp differences on a sex basis in the mores concerning servant-child sex relationships. When a young boy gains sex experience with an older servant woman, the mores at best indicate only slight disapproval, and rather frequently a mild approval. For the young boy it is considered fair game, and the older woman is thought of as having done him somewhat of a good turn by initiating him into his masculine prerogatives. But any semblance of the contrasting situation, with an older male servant suggesting or achieving sex relations with a young daughter in the family, would be universally condemned. He would be considered to have taken advantage of a minor, and accused of rape.

SERVANTS IN THE HOME CAN GIVE CHILDREN AN INTRODUCTION TO THE
MEANING OF CLASS STATUS, CLASS CULTURE, AND CLASS STRIFE, AND HELP
TO MOLD THEIR ATTITUDES ABOUT THESE THINGS

Several of the authors of these autobiographies indicate that early in
life they became aware of the status of the servants in relation to that
of their family, and seemed to be troubled with a sense of injustice about
the difference. One child was sensitive to the fact that his tutor ate his
meals with him as if he had never before had good food. Some mentioned
the hard work and small pay, and sometimes tried to help the servants
with their work. But what bothered them more was that their parents controlled so completely even the private lives of their servants. A man remembers with distaste the time a cook asked permission to spend the
night with her husband and was refused. The fact that she spent the
night with him in the barn anyway was considered indecent. When a relative of one of the maids in the same family was dying, the child's mother
told him that "the lower classes" make a great fuss about these matters
but do not feel them as "we" do. The injustice of this remark, to a boy who
knew the servants well and loved them deeply, remained with him all his
life. We can assume that among those authors who did not mention servants were those who came to a consciousness of class without any feeling of
injustice, and permanently ceased to think of servants as human beings
about whom one writes stories, or who in any way affect one's private life.

The children also noticed a way of living quite different from their own
when they entered the servants' quarters or visited the homes of married
servants, and they reacted variously. At one extreme a child was charmed
by the wholesome simplicity, warmth, and lack of formality and regulation in the home of his nurse, and was never so happy as during his visits
with her. At the other extreme, a young lady was appalled at all the evidences of the lower-class lack of adornment and begged her mother
never, never to let her become poor. One boy was pretty continuously perplexed, but was made thoughtful, by the scullery boy's discussions about
the behavior of the "upstairs folks." Some of this boy's remembered comments were: "You people upstairs stuff like pigs. That's what. You'll want
some of that bloody grub one of these days"; and, in regard to his own
type of reading material, "It don't lower any self-respec' in me to hear
that someone killed someone. But it'd make me blush like the devil to enjoy what some of 'em upstairs enjoy talkin' about."

One aspect of class consciousness experienced by children who lived
during the Civil War was class strife, and the relationship between the
political world and racial groups. They remembered the helplessness of
their families as they watched the conflict among their own Negro servants as they wondered whether to leave the families they loved and who
had treated them well, or to stand the scorn of other Negroes by remain-

ing and not taking the offered freedom. These writers also recall the return of some of the servants after an absence in the North. Some were obviously less well off than before, but were clinging sternly to "freedom." Others had turned haughty and were useless as servants. Still others ignored the whole business of emancipation and remained with their families, unchanged.

THE SERVANT OFTEN PERSONIFIES A SOCIAL TYPE TO THE CHILD

Among the persons interviewed there was not so much overt reference to class differences as to minority group implications. This was due probably to the fact that the people included in the study had lived as children in the northeastern part of the country where domestic servants were recruited chiefly from immigrant groups and more recently from the Negro race. All but three of the subjects agreed that their concept of selected minority groups as types was first formulated on the basis of their contacts with domestic servants from those groups. Among the younger persons these were chiefly Negroes, but among the older individuals the references were to the Irish, Polish, and Swedish. Further exploration of this point suggests the larger principle involved: that the servant often comes to the attention of the child as the personification of a type, not only of a minority group but of all kinds of social and personality types. For example, one of the case records reveals that the first nursemaid was spoken of by the parents as an orphan, and the subject remembers that as late as her thirteenth birthday she conceived of an orphan as a nursemaid with blue eyes and dark hair. This identification of the domestic servant with a social type is most likely to occur where the type is outside the range of the family's experience.

SERVANTS, IN IGNORANCE, CAN INSTILL DEEP FEARS IN CHILDREN, WHICH MAKE FOR INSECURITY AND TIMIDITY

There were nine separate references in the autobiographical material to deep fears that affect personality and which were implanted by foolish servants. The locking of a brother in a dark closet produced terrible fears of the dark in one child. Threats of hellfire permanently disturbed the early years of other youngsters. Stories about ghosts and witches and smugglers, which some children loved, nevertheless made shivering cowards of them. One boy was "perfectly terrified when the chimney-sweep arrived with his attendant coal-black imps, for the usual threat of foolish nurses to their charges when they proved refractory was, 'If you are not good I shall give you to the sweep, and then you'll have to climb up the chimney.'"

The interview material makes only incidental reference to such matters save in one respect, and this has to do with the servant as a source of superstitions. Apparently one of the ways in which busy domestic servants "entertain" the young members of the household in many cases is to recount colorful bits of folklore, superstitions, old wives' tales, and odd bits of proverbial wisdom. Naturally, these reflect the cultural background and level of the servant. Here, again, the racial and national origin identification of the servant becomes significant.

THE PRESENCE OF SERVANTS CAN REVEAL PERSONALITY TRAITS OF FAMILY MEMBERS MORE CLEARLY TO EACH OTHER

Many of the writers of the autobiographies mentioned their early attitudes about their parents' behavior toward servants, and the servants' toward their parents. In general, the children resented any unfair, harsh treatment by their parents to loved servants, admired their skillful and imaginative handling of them, and were awed by the deep devotion which often existed between their parents and long-time domestics. Gossip in the servants' hall about family members was revealing to the children. One youngster became a bit less frightened of his pompous father because his old Negro servant always laughed till she cried at the Master's nasty temper tantrums—and got away with it.

One particular aspect of the servant's role in revealing the parent's character to the child is mentioned in the interview material. One record refers at some length to a stepfather's romantic interest in a comely governess. Apparently, this employer found many occasions to spend time with his stepdaughter and nursemaid, and the relationship which developed between him and the maid seems not to have been lost upon either the child or her mother. This situation, in substance, is one that has frequently been used by novelists.

SERVANTS OF LONG DURATION CAN SERVE AS INFORMAL FAMILY HISTORIANS, AND GIVE THE CHILD AN "OUTSIDER'S" VIEW OF THE FAMILY. ON THE CREDIT SIDE, FAITHFUL OLD RETAINERS MAY EARLY GIVE THE CHILD A SENSE OF FAMILY CONTINUITY AND PRIDE

A number of the authors of the autobiographies spoke of old servants as considering the family, through successive generations, as their own family. Two of them were described as family historians, who knew all the experiences and anecdotes of the family and handed them down to the children. Another servant impressed a very young child, who cried when stuck by a pin, with the fact that he had a brave and noble family to live up to, and made him vow to be a more courageous and fitting member of his family.

The servants' role as family historian, however, may take a less pleasant turn than has just been indicated. Two of the people interviewed mention experiences which illustrate this. In one case, Chester, a general handyman in the family's employ for many years, apparently had stored up a good deal of resentment against his employer, and he "took this out" on the young boy, when no one else was about, by reminding him of his father's business failure years ago, as well as the reputed adulterous habits of the boy's aunt. In the other case, a garrulous cook would remind her employer's daughter, when they were alone, of the general reputation of the maternal branch of the family as "hard to get along with, and not worth the trouble at that."

SERVANTS, BY ADDING MERE NUMBERS OF PEOPLE TO THE FAMILY CIRCLE, CAN INCREASE THE COMPLEXITY OF FAMILY LIFE. THEY CAN ALSO RELIEVE COMPLEXITY, AND FURNISH EXTRA RESOURCES FOR SMOOTH FAMILY RELATIONSHIPS

The autobiographical material reveals that turmoils in family life were caused by inefficiency among, and problems with, servants. The physical and psychological management of a train of servants was the cause of one mother's constant fretting and weariness and of the irritation of her husband at having to pay the bills and yet never having the household running quite smoothly. Children who took delight in driving their governesses into leaving them, one after another, created family problems. Overbearing domestics struggled for supremacy over their employers and sometimes gained it, reducing the members of the family to a group of bewildered puppets dependent on a servant for their general scheme of life, and causing a sense of inadequacy or inferiority in the family.

Yet, there were other situations in which one or a group of servants took over the reins of the household in such a way as to relieve the family of all the ordinary physical stresses of living, thus leaving them free to cultivate a harmonious home life. Particularly in the relationship between parent and child was this kind of servant valuable. He spared parents the irritation caused by the difficult parts of child rearing, and at the same time he offered entertainment to the child at times when the latter might have become a trouble to his family; he also acted as a buffer between parents and child and sibling, as well as an extra person to go to for consolation when irritations did arise.

Servants in the home, by adding to the number of persons there, increase the number of sets of personal relations, in accordance with the Law of Family Interaction set forth in an earlier chapter. The interview material contains no reference to this, except in two cases where the large number of family members and servants early impressed the child with a certain hecticness of life. In fact, the comments of one of the persons interviewed were strikingly similar to the statement quoted in Chapter 4 from Santayana's autobiography.

THE PRESENCE OF SERVANTS IN THE HOME PERMITS MORE LEISURELY PARENTHOOD AND FAMILY LIFE IN GENERAL

Both the autobiographical and the interview material fail to emphasize the leisure resulting from the presence of servants, but it appears constantly between the lines. These are facts which obviously are more apparent to the outside observer than to the participant in the family situation. More extended consideration will be given to this aspect in the next chapter.

The restraint caused by servants is another point not mentioned in the autobiographical or volunteered in the interview material. In answer to direct questioning, all the persons interviewed agreed that the presence of servants makes for a certain restraint in personal relations within the home, particularly between parents and children. No matter how favored his position, the servant is still a servant. From this standpoint, he is an outsider, an audience, before whom you restrain yourself. The parent must not forget his role of employer, especially in the presence of the employee. Punishment, for example, may be postponed or softened; admonition is tempered with dignity; petty annoyances caused by the child must be dealt with in a manner befitting the entire witnessing personnel. The presence of the servant, like that of the guest, turns the private, dual relationship of parent and child into a triangular, semipublic one.

Some Unexplored Aspects of the Role of the Servant in Child Development

In addition to the foregoing, there are other aspects of the role of the servant in child development which call for exploration, three of which will be referred to briefly. First, how does the presence of servants affect the amount and duration of the waiting-upon which the child receives? This includes being waited on not only in the more elemental phases of living, but also in such matters as care of one's room, clothes, money, toys, and the like. This undoubtedly has significance for the child's development not only of habits of responsibility and self-reliance, but also of his scale of work values.

Again, there is the child's passage from protected to unprotected competitive situations. In most families, competitive activities involving young children are arranged and manipulated so as to show them off to advantage; i.e., the competition is "protected" so as to let them win. As the child grows older, parents gradually cease this manipulation so that he must compete on terms of equality, or of "unprotected" competition. What is the effect of the presence of servants, of their participation in the child's activities, of the relative leisure which their presence gives to parents, on this transfer in the life of the child? Is protected competition prolonged unduly so that the "young master" may continue to appear to advantage? Some children are driven to school by a chauffeur; others have to fight their way there. Some children play games with servants;

others, with the neighbor's children. These may be significant differences in the child's development.

Akin to this is a third aspect, the effect of the presence of servants upon the child's conception of the self. Two contrasting situations are apparent in the cases of Neal and Paul. Neal lives in a home in which there are four servants—a cook, an upstairs girl, a chauffeur, and a gardener. Three of the four seem devoted to him, and fetch and carry for him at his slightest command. Neal is seldom seen on the six-acre estate without two or three "retainers," as it were. At 13 he is accustomed to the habit of command. His situation is quite different from that of Paul, who lives with his father and mother in a modest five-room war-emergency home. His father is away much of the time, his mother is not in good health. There are no servants. Since he was 2 years old, Paul not only has looked after himself but has constantly served as a "mother's helper." One senses, as a result of the presence or absence of servants, not only the early crystallization of patterns of being served or of serving oneself, of distinguishing the tasks which one does and those which one delegates, but also of the larger matter of one's whole conception of oneself.

Summary

1. In homes employing domestic help, the servant is a definite part of the child's family world.

2. Servants may be classified or typed on the basis of whether they "live in" or not, of their racial and national origin, and of the nature of their job.

3. Six definite kinds of family-servant relationships are noted: (a) where the servant bears some kinship or social relation to the employer; (b) where service has been of long and satisfactory duration, so that the servant may be referred to as "a member of the family"; (c) where the servant is really a fellow employee; (d) where the help has a distinct servant status, with the customary symbols of service status; (e) where the servant has a socially distant but personally friendly status; and (f) where the servant bears a marked resentment toward the employer based on relative minority group status.

4. Published autobiographies and records of interviews are two available sources for studying the role of the servant in child development. Forty-four out of 100 autobiographies and 21 interview records were utilized in the study summarized in this chapter.

5. From the material assembled, 13 conclusions are drawn. (a) The domestic servant may be a mother-surrogate; (b) the domestic may act as a go-between and mitigator of the harshnesses of family life; (c) servants provide companionship for the young child; (d) the servant may enlarge a child's knowledge of many aspects of life which are alien to him in his

own immediate family, or from which his parents have carefully protected him; (e) servants may influence the sex life of children; (f) servants in the home can give children an introduction to the meaning of class status, class culture, and class strife, and help to mold their attitudes about these things; (g) the servant often personifies a social type to the child; (h) servants, in ignorance, can instill deep fears in children which make for insecurity and timidity; (i) the presence of servants can reveal personality traits of family members more clearly to each other; (j) servants of long duration can serve as informal family historians, and give the child an "outsider's" view of the family; (k) by adding mere numbers of people to the family circle, servants can increase the complexity of family life; they can also relieve complexity and furnish extra resources for smooth family relationships; (l) the presence of servants in the home permits more leisurely parenthood and family life in general; (m) the presence of servants may make for a certain restraint in family interaction.

Chapter 11

Domestic Animals:
Their Role in Child Development

Mythology and folklore, fables and fiction, interrelate man's life with dogs and other animals. In contrast, relatively few social scientists have done so, even those who specialize in the areas of family life and child rearing: this in spite of the obvious and observable role of domestic pets in both areas. Even the psychoanalysts, in their emphasis upon the role of the unconscious, have attributed much importance to animals.[1] In the earliest psychoanalytic paper on the role of animals in the unconscious, Jelliffe and Brink pointed out that their study was inspired by the astonishing revelation in psychoneurotic dreams of the use of animal material and the effective importance of it in the history of neuroses. "Psychoanalysis," they go on to say, "finds indeed an enormous rôle played by animals in symptoms as well as in dreams, an importance which is borne out by the place occupied by this same material in all other manifestations of the unconscious."[2]

Particularly is this omission by social scientists difficult to understand in the case of the dog, who has been man's companion since prehistoric times and the comfort and playmate of innumerable children through the ages. Even today, one in every four big-city families has a dog, despite certain difficulties that his care may involve. Among farm families, the proportion is three out of four, and for all families in the United States roughly two out of five have a dog. The dog population in 1957 in this country was placed at 25 million. In the same year, the American Kennel Club registered 112 different breeds, for a total registration of 5 million pure-bred dogs.

[1] For an interesting article, upon which we have drawn in this connection, the reader is referred to Marcel Heiman, "The Relationship Between Man and Dog," *Psychoanalytic Quarterly,* Vol. XXV, 1956, 568–585.

[2] Smith Ely Jelliffe and Louise Brink, "The Role of Animals in the Unconscious with Some Remarks on Theriomorphic Symbolism as Seen in Ovid," *Psychoanalytic Review,* July, 1917, p. 254.

There are many other family pets in addition to dogs—cats, rabbits, turtles, snakes, skunks, monkeys, hamsters—in fact, the list comprehends an almost endless array of animals. Their housing, feeding, medical treatment, and other forms of care are well-established forms of modern business. It has been estimated that the American people spend a half-billion dollars a year on their dogs alone, to say nothing of some 20 million fish tanks needed to house 120 million tropical fish.[3]

The present chapter seeks to call attention to possible ways in which domestic pets may affect family life and child development. The material that may be drawn upon in this connection concerns primarily the role of the dog, but what may be said about the dog would seem to be true in a general way about other domestic animals. It is hoped that further studies may test the suggested, as well as other, leads in this area.

Some years ago, the senior author of this volume made a series of case studies, 55 in all, of families with children and dogs, in an effort to ascertain the ways in which dogs entered family life and the child-rearing process. The main conclusions of this study follow.[4]

1. The dog is an outlet for our affection. This is its basic service and the chief reason for its presence in most homes. Repressed persons tend to disguise or to deny this interest, or to explain it on other than affectional grounds. "I'm afraid to be without a dog," "It's lonely without a dog." "He eats the scraps." Again, the manifestations of this interest in the dog vary from an occasionally kindly cuff to the most tender solicitude, dependent upon the nature and needs of the person involved. In most families, however, affection for the dog is open and frank, with general agreement that the dog receives more attention and affection than any other member of the family. The therapeutic significance of this seems very obvious and very great, and the growing conventionality and impersonality of contemporary life make it of increasing rather than of decreasing importance.

This function of the dog, and other domestic pets, must be considered in relation to the emphasis of certain students of behavior upon the basic need for someone or thing to love, but frequently overlooked in contemporary scientific interpretations of behavior. A number of years ago, Ian Suttie spoke of this omission as "the flight from tenderness." He suggested that, in repudiating theology, modern mental science has reacted too far, and in so doing has deliberately blinded itself to the tender relationships in life so strongly emphasized by Christianity.[5]

No less a psychologist than Gordon W. Allport confesses that a persist-

[3] Dickson Hartwell and Leon F. Whitney, "Dogs Are Big Business," *Collier's,* December 25, 1948, pp. 22, 92.

[4] Cf. James H. S. Bossard, "The Mental Hygiene of Owning a Dog," *Mental Hygiene,* July, 1944, pp. 408–413, for a partial report of the findings. It is reproduced in the main in the pages that follow.

[5] Ian Sutti, *The Origins of Love and Hate,* Kegan Paul, Trench, Trubner and Company, London, 1935.

ent defect of modern psychology is its failure to make a serious study of the affiliative desires and capacities of human beings. Only two theories concerning them have been developed, he says. One was that of the gregarious instinct, the other the Freudian concept which reduced the affiliative motives to sexuality. In general, "the scientist fears that if he looks at affiliative sentiments he may seem sentimental; if he talks about love he may seem emotional; and if he studies personal attachments he may appear personal. Better leave the whole matter to poets, to saints, or to theologians."[6]

Over against these omissions is the emphasis of other students upon the need for the sustaining force of love. Allport, after reviewing modern research in management, personnel relations, military combat units, and the like, concludes that "it behooves us to study far more closely than we have in the past the place of love and hate in human personality."[7] Or there is the declaration of a recent president of the American Psychiatric Association that "all of us need something to sustain us through frustration, loneliness, and suffering that cannot be analyzed in a scientific laboratory . . . Einstein called it 'reverence': devotion to things beyond one's self . . . Freud concluded that 'in the last resort we must learn to love . . . or else fall ill.' "[8] Similar are the implications in recent studies of foster homes and mental health.[9]

2. Moreover, the dog serves each of us according to our respective affectional needs. Not being able to speak or to argue, the dog will not say the wrong thing to dampen our ardor or to spoil the rapport of the moment. Little Jane, out of sorts because her friend Mary will not play her way today, finds solace with her Scottie. Jack hates girls, Mother is busy, and Father gives him no affection, but his Airedale gives to him just what he needs. Mother is spending a long winter evening alone, while Father is entertaining the out-of-town buyer. She overcomes or forgets her doubts because of the friendly collie that lies before her on the living-room rug. Cousin Edna, who is not quite welcome at the relative's home where she is now living, is at least confident of the genuineness of the affection with which the family's energetic Boston pup greets her. Father, returning late at night after a long and discouraging day, is met at the door by a wagging tail and a pair of adoring eyes. Each to his needs, regardless of what they are, no matter how they vary, ready to give, asking nothing even when expecting much, stands the family dog.

Furthermore, there are none of the customary inhibitions to limit or

[6] Gordon W. Allport in Pitirim A. Sorokin (ed.), *Explorations in Altruistic Love and Behavior*, Beacon Press, Boston, 1950, pp. 145–146.

[7] *Ibid.*, p. 149.

[8] Kenneth E. Appel, in a lecture at the University of Pennsylvania, November 30, 1956.

[9] J. Bowlby, *Maternal Health and Mental Health*, World Health Organization, Geneva, Monograph Series, No. 2, 1951; and Howard R. Stanton, "Mother Love in Foster Homes," *Marriage and Family Living*, November, 1956, pp. 301–307.

restrain our affectional relations with the dog. Few of us are wholly free of these inhibitions in our relations with humans; often they operate to some extent even with those who are most close. We leave unsaid the word of endearment or unexpressed the physical signs of our feelings because of the inhibiting shadow of some word or aspect in our relationship. None of this is true with our domestic pets, like the dog. We can love them, we can express our affection, and there are no inhibiting handicaps.

3. There is often a deep and abiding quality about the relationship between a human and a dog. One is struck repeatedly with the mellow tribute of the older person to the canine companions of his youth. Such tributes appear constantly in conversation or in autobiographies. Writes a congressman from Iowa:

After much begging for it, I was given a silver dollar one Saturday morning with which to buy a black collie puppy that I coveted. With the piece of silver clasped tightly in my hand, I ran all the way to town, fearing some other boy might get what I wanted. With the puppy clasped tightly in my arms, I hastened back home. I bestowed the name of Prince on the tiny creature. After that we all made so much ado over that little dog that the old dog on the place . . . died of envy and grief—or was it merely old age?

Prince and I grew up together. We became inseparable companions. I might have taken him to bed with me had my mother been less particular about sheets and pillows. I was very fond of Prince and he was fond of me. He would never play with anyone else or at least not in the same way he played with me. He would growl and snap his teeth at anyone who made so much as a motion of striking me. He must have thought of me as the particular lamb that he had to look after. Every morning I found him waiting for me at the door, and if I did not hasten my steps he would whine and yelp. He always greeted me by jumping almost all over me. One of his favorite tricks was to pick up a stick and dare me to take it away from him. In time I taught him to play many of my games, such as hide-and-seek and ante-over. And he taught me many of his tricks. I am still sure that I learned as much from him as he learned from me. And I am equally certain that if it had not been for Prince, I might have grown up a different kind of boy and even have been a different man.[10]

4. The dog contributes to the development of many a human being the challenge of a continuing responsibility. This matter of a continuing responsibility is one of life's major experiences—sobering, exacting, maturing, character forming. Not all of us have it. Many persons go through life without it; others find it first when parenthood comes to them. This experience may come early in life, to a growing child, when a pet is consigned to his care. Walking the dog each morning and night; feeding him; finding him when lost; looking after his water supply; protecting him from the neighbor's bullying bigger dog; making his bed; if it is a female,

[10] From *I Remember, I Remember,* by Cyrenus Cole, State Historical Society of Iowa, Iowa City, 1936, pp. 20–21.

keeping dogs away when she is in season—in these ways children may profit early in life from a continuing experience with a personal responsibility. Thus the dog may become a very valuable factor in the training and character formation of a growing boy or girl.

5. The dog is an excellent vehicle for parents to use in training children in toilet habits. Josephine, the pup, must be housebroken. Mother, father, brother, sister, are all engaged in the process. They take Josephine out; they chastise her for her making a puddle; there is constant talk about Josey's toilet habits. Small wonder, then, that little Helen presents no problem in her own habits, for she too joins the family circle in the training of Josephine. Here, again, self-discipline evolves as an accessory before the fact of imposing a discipline upon someone else.

6. Again, the dog is a vehicle for parents to use in the sex education of children. First, the external physical differences of sex can be seen, identified, and discussed, without hesitation or inhibition on the part of either parent or child. Then certain habits peculiar to each sex may be discussed, so that sex is a difference not just in physical structure but also in function and in ways of living. If the dog is a female, the alternation of periods has to be faced, and this becomes the medium through which various problems are discussed, including periodicity in the human female. The female may have been spayed or she may be serviced by a male. The ensuing pregnancy and birth of the pups are a demonstration of that which it is perhaps most difficult to teach the younger child. With a dog, they are demonstrated to the eye as they are told to the ear. Such physical demonstration can be made a corrective of a most effective kind of the misinformation on sex that children pick up at various times and places.

7. The dog is a satisfactory victim of personal needs for ego satisfaction and ego gratification. If things have gone wrong, and you feel like kicking someone, there is Waldo, waiting for you. If you have been ordered about by the boss all day, you can go home and order the dog about. If Mother has made you do what you did not want to, you can now work on the dog. Long observation of children's behavior with domestic animals convinces us that this is a very important function. Often the child has been the victim of commands, "directives," shouts, orders, all day long. How soul-satisfying now to take the dog for a walk and order him about! This is a most effective therapeutic procedure.

8. Akin to what has just been said is the fact that the dog satisfies the very human longing or desire for power. The wish to dominate someone seems most fundamental. Wife, husband, child, each finds in the dog an outlet for such conflicting desires. Sometimes this demand for power finds expression in a persistent habit pattern, and the dog, in satisfying it, thereby saves some other member of the family from being its victim. Sometimes it is a sporadic need, growing out of a background of fluctuating experience. At times it is the chronic need of a Casper Milquetoast

who finds only in the dog what he fears to seek in any other human. Here, again, the dog may serve a useful role in the mental hygiene of the child, training the child in the art of command, satisfying the ego in the experience of control, and draining off a resentment at being controlled by some parent or other adult.

9. A dog accustoms one to the idea of the normality of physical processes. We human beings are apt to become so civilized that we forget that we are human; the conventions of life lead us to refrain from certain physical processes when we are in the company of our fellows; reference to some of them is even taboo in conversation. The net result is that there is apt to arise an unconscious conviction that these things are unusual and unnatural. This is particularly true of city folk, who lead an artificial life in many respects, often without contact with other forms of life. To live with domestic animals is to see another animal engage in the same processes you do; the effect upon the observer, and particularly the child, is to gain a net impression of the "naturalness of it all."

10. One phase of this learning process about life is the child's discovery of death, one of the unalterable "facts of life." How can the child best be led to the discovery of death, and yet be protected from needless anxiety and psychological trauma? Several studies have dealt with this question in recent years, with some agreement that for the child it is most helpful if the matter can be talked about openly and without fear.[11] It seems that one excellent approach to so doing could be made on the death of a domestic pet. For many children, this is their first contact with death.

11. A dog serves as an effective social aid. By the time one has walked a dog a few months, one is sure to have increased markedly the range of one's acquaintances, even in the most impersonal city neighborhood. The genial old man stops to chat; the buxom mistress smiles, first at the dog, and then at you; the neighborhood children make friends with the dog and incidentally notice you. Finally, on the dreariest day, when you were least inclined to take him on his outing, fate obliges by having your favorite blonde happen along, and the dog obliges by making up to her, to the end that another "contact" has been made.

The child, again, is the special gainer from all this. He or she makes many contacts in the neighborhood because of the dog. It is a sure way to meet the new children in the block. And you can do them the first favor by letting them hold the leash. You can make that little girl with a turned-up nose jealous because you have a dog. You learn about Mr. Davis; he

---

[11] Sylvia Anthony, *The Child's Discovery of Death*, Kegan Paul, Trench, Trubner and Company, London, 1940; Anna W. M. Wolf, *Helping Your Child to Understand Death*, Child Study Association, New York, 1958; Edgar N. Jackson, *Understanding Grief*, Abingdon Press, Boston, 1957.

is a friendly man and likes dogs. You learn about Mr. Meyers; he barks at you if the dog nears his least favorite shrub. Mrs. Jones feeds a dog, even under war rationing. Mrs. Bird growls at you because she hates "animals of all kinds."

12. An applied social function which the dog may serve was suggested in several of our case studies. These had to do with the use of dogs and other domestic pets in the prevention of juvenile delinquency. A case study will illustrate the suggestion.

Henry, a 14-year-old Negro boy, born out of wedlock, was showing signs of developing a delinquent pattern of behavior. His mother, a domestic, is away from home most days, leaving the boy at loose ends except for an infirm grandmother, with defective vision. At this point, the mother's employer presents the boy with a well-bred Belgian police dog, and a stipend to underwrite the cost of his feeding. To this lonely boy, the dog is a godsend. A deep attachment develops between boy and dog. He readily assumes responsibility for his care. Ownership of the dog gives the boy prestige with other boys. His ownership and care open up a new life for the boy. After five and a half years, during which there have been no further signs of delinquent behavior, Henry leaves home to enter the armed forces. At this time, his mother, grandmother, and Henry agree that the coming of the dog was the turning point in his life.

Is this story a fanciful and sentimental tale? Or does it carry the germ of an idea? What is the possible role of dog ownership in a delinquency-prevention program?

13. Finally, a dog offers companionship. He stays with you when you are alone. He serves as solace when you are lonely. And what excellent company he can be. You can talk to him, you can sing to him. He does not argue concerning the propriety of your remarks or the pertinence of your observations. If you sing, he will not, as a rule, embarrass you with comments on your voice, your enunciation, or the lyrical quality of your performance. A dog is a silent, yet responsive companion, a long-suffering, patient, satisfying, uncritical, seemingly appreciative, constant, faithful companion, more affectionate than you deserve and appreciative far beyond what anyone could expect from a human rival.

A particular form of companionship that is suggested is in the case of persons who are bedfast. Under certain circumstances, a dog, or other pet, can be a boon and constant companion. The comfort and therapeutic value of such companionship may be very great.

To the lonely child and the shy adolescent, to the unhappy wife or the misunderstood husband, to the impatient convalescent and the discouraged paralytic, to men on far-off military locations or on distant construction jobs, innumerable dogs or other domestic animals make their contribution to those aspects of life which cannot be counted, measured, or presented in statistical tables. Without their dogs, the loneliness of count-less people would be unbearable.

Summary

1. The role of domestic animals in family life and child development has been neglected for the most part by serious students, despite their obvious importance.

2. A study of 55 families who kept dogs as household pets shows a variety of functions which they served, and suggests additional possible uses. These include: an outlet for affection, the challenge of a continuing responsibility, a vehicle to use in the training of children, a satisfaction for the ego, a gratification of the desire for power, an education in the nor-mality of physical processes, an effective social aid, and companionship under many varying circumstances.

Chapter 12

Parents' Occupations
and Child Development

One of the first questions people ask about a stranger is: what does he do? The reason for the question is that the answer is so revealing. It tells so much about a person: where he is likely to live, what the regimen of his life is likely to be, with what kind of people he associates, and what his activities and interests are prone to be. Since these are all things which affect the home and family life of the person and his role as a parent, it seems proper to select parental occupations as another facet of family life to be considered in relation to child development. It is to this subject that the present chapter is devoted.

The Social Importance of Occupation

One of the curious facts about the sociological literature in general, and the literature on human behavior in particular, is the variation in the attention given to the occupational factor. Selected sociological texts omit virtually all reference to it; others recognize its importance in general terms; still others refer to specific aspects of its role. Such variation is all the more striking in view of the strong statements of those who stress its importance. "Numerous studies in this field." wrote Sorokin a generation ago, "have made certain the enormous influence of this social condition on man, his behavior, and, through that, on social processes. Neither individual conduct and psychology, nor group behavior and characteristics, nor social antagonisms and solidarity, nor processes of social reconstruction and revolution, nor almost any important social change or irregularity, can be accounted for satisfactorily without the occupational factor. Besides, the studies have disclosed a series of correlations between the nature of occupational groups and their bodily, vital, and mental characteristics."[1]

[1] Pitirim Sorokin, *Contemporary Sociological Theories,* Harper & Brothers, New York, 1928, p. 718.

Somewhat more specific, but equally sweeping, are the same author's comments in his work on social mobility. "Occupation," he wrote, "determines considerably the place and district of our dwelling, its character and type, its furniture and equipment. Occupation determines our budget of income and budget of time: the hours of our working, recreation, getting up, and going to bed. It influences the character of our meals, and recreations, that of our reading and amusements. It fashions our habits, our ethics, our manners, our etiquette. It determines considerably with whom we are associated, whom we meet, with whom we talk and are in contact. All this being taken into consideration makes apparent the enormous influence of occupation on the whole physical, mental, moral, and social nature of man."[2]

The cultural aspect of occupation is stressed by Ogburn and Nimkoff. "Each occupational group likewise," they point out, "has its own special cultural context. There is a distinct set of activities and even vocabulary for each vocation, which results in unique 'vocational attitudes.' "[3] Dawson and Gettys identify occupational as one group of personality types.[4]

A striking illustration from the sociological literature of the importance attached to occupation has been its use as an index of the social status of the individual. The work of W. Lloyd Warner and his associates is most pertinently cited here. In their research work on social class determination, they have utilized two methods for measuring class status. They are the method of Evaluated Participation, combining a number of rating techniques to evaluate the participation of a person as an interacting member of the social system of the community; and the method of Status Characteristics, which measures the socioeconomic levels of the community. This latter method utilizes four status characteristics. Occupation is one of the four, and is accorded prior rank in importance.[5] Such usage, in empirical studies, offers specific confirmation of the general statements on the significance of occupation, previously cited in this chapter.

Another index of its sociological importance is to be found in the periodical literature. Here one finds a considerable number and variety of reports on research studies in recent years. From February, 1936, when the first issue of the *American Sociological Review* appeared, to February, 1952, a total of 60 articles reporting research studies of occupation ap-

[2] Pitirim Sorokin, *Social Mobility*, Harper & Brothers, New York, 1927, p. 322. See also a similar emphasis in the same author's more recent work, *Society, Culture, and Personality*, Harper & Brothers, New York, 1947, pp. 211–215.

[3] William F. Ogburn and Meyer F. Nimkoff, *Sociology*, Houghton Mifflin Company, Boston, 1940, pp. 205–206.

[4] Carl A. Dawson and Warner E. Gettys, *An Introduction to Sociology*, The Ronald Press Company, New York, 1935, p. 781.

[5] W. Lloyd Warner, Marchia Meeker, and Kenneth Eells, *Social Class in America*, Science Research Associates, Chicago, 1949, Chap. 2.

peared in 4 leading sociological journals, namely, the *American Sociological Review*, the *American Journal of Sociology*, *Social Forces*, and *Sociology and Social Research*. Included in these articles are references to 40 other articles and books dealing with sociological aspects of occupation. Tabulation of the articles that appeared in the sociological journals listed above shows that the war lessened markedly the frequency of their appearance. Omitting the war years, the number of research articles in the general field is sufficient to indicate the emergence of the study of occupation as a distinct and new division of sociology.[6]

An analysis of the subject matter of these articles shows a high concentration around three main topics. These are occupational mobility, the prestige and status of occupations, and the cultural characteristics of specific occupations. A lesser number deal with the relation of occupation to birth, marriage, divorce, and mortality rates; intelligence factors and occupational differentials; and the relationship between occupational and certain forms of nonoccupational behavior. Other areas of investigation have been relatively or entirely neglected, and among the latter is the role of occupation in marriage relations and child development. This is a curious omission, particularly in view of what is its obvious operation in the daily life of family and child.

Parents' Occupation and the Child

As an indication of the ways in which occupation may be effective in these areas, three recent studies are summarized at this point.

1. The first of these is an analysis from the psychiatric point of view, growing out of work with emotionally disturbed children. Its main conclusions follow.[7]

a. The authors stress the fact that children tend to view many facts about their parents through the eyes of their own immediate needs. "The occupation of a parent, in particular, assumes personal meaning to the child only as it acquires direct bearing on the child's immediate welfare —whether as the source of livelihood, as the cause of the parent's absence from the home, or as a feature which makes the parent's image more awesome or more powerful. Occupation then expresses for the child such parental reactions as have already been tangibly experienced."[8]

b. Many emotionally disturbed children, when confronted with cultural realities in the world about them, develop persistent magical con-

[6] James H. S. Bossard, *Parent and Child: Studies in Family Behavior*, University of Pennsylvania Press, Philadelphia, 1953, Chap. 11.

[7] Bruno Bettelheim and Emmy Sylvester, "Notes on the Impact of Parental Occupations: Some Cultural Determinants of Symptom Choice in Emotionally Disturbed Children," *American Journal of Orthopsychiatry*, October, 1950, pp. 785–795.

[8] *Ibid.*, p. 786.

cepts concerning these realities and interpret them in terms of their own special needs.

c. Various circumstances about the modern workaday world tend to encourage this tendency. One is the fact that the ways in which many parents earn their livelihood are not readily observable to the child. Once the father enters his office, or the factory door closes behind him, his activities seem shrouded in mystery. This makes magical interpretations and unrealistic elaborations easy for the child.

d. Another factor is the growing division of labor, as a result of which fewer occupations remain meaningful per se, particularly because the child does not have the knowledge to relate the minor task to the larger operation.

e. Added to this is the fact that the complexity of modern employment prevents the child from understanding the ways of adult work. Many adults do not understand this themselves, or deem it important to do so, and the few isolated glimpses which the child obtains, measured in terms of his need to understand, may be of little or no value. Parents may aggravate this by their inability or unwillingness to give the child the necessary information for a realistic approach. As a result, according to the authors, "the child who knows nothing about his parent's occupation (other than the fact that the father spends a certain number of hours outside of the home) may be better off than the child who receives isolated, disconnected and hence meaningless pieces of information which he tries unsuccessfully to synthesize."[9]

f. Some occupations seem to be particularly conducive to the development of magical interpretations by the child. Some of these may be in the professions. If the father is a doctor or a lawyer, it becomes relatively easy for the child to develop magical concepts. Or the father who is a successful investment broker may be thought of as a person who can produce money by the juggling of figures. Resultant attitudes may take distorted forms at times.

g. Particularly dangerous for emotionally disturbed children may be those cases where the father's occupation makes him a source of potential danger, such as the butcher in the stockyards or the surgeon in the hospital; or occupations which give the father special prerogatives or extraordinary powers, such as the presidency of a college, a corporation, or the United States.

h. The impact of the parent's occupation may be complicated by conflicting attitudes toward the occupation by the child's parents. The mother, for example, may not think well of the father's occupation, nor deem it worthy of his abilities. Such attitudes may be conveyed openly and repeatedly, or in highly subtle form.

i. Finally, there is the degree of closeness between parent and child.

[9] *Ibid.,* p. 787.

"Children who are early and extensively damaged do not develop enough closeness to those around them to discern the fine points of parental attitudes. . . . Their evaluation of parental occupation is then chiefly affected by the ups and downs of their variable ambivalence toward the parents and is relatively untouched by the reality of the parent's occupational activities."[10]

2. The second study to be summarized is an exploratory one, made by a sociologist and an anthropologist, of the relationship between the occupational role of the middle-class male and his aims and concerns in the socialization of the child. This study deals almost entirely with fathers and is based on data collected in the course of a research carried out for the Human Relations Service, a group interested in preventive psychiatry, located in a suburb of Boston, and having both clinical and research functions. A total of 20 families were included, with a total of 56 children, of whom 29 were boys and 27 were girls. The families were middle-class according to the Warner Index of Status Characteristics, previously referred to in this chapter. Most of the families were "normal."[11]

The main findings of this study follow.

a. Middle-class father expect their sons to prepare to occupy positions in the middle-class occupational structure.

b. Fathers (more than half of them) accept the possibility of a career for their daughters, but only as a possibility. Most of them want their daughters to marry.

c. Fathers evaluate sons' behavior only in relation to general character traits conducive to success, not specific skills for particular occupations.

d. Recurrent concerns are over obedience, responsibility, initiative, school behavior, insufficiently aggressive or excessively passive behavior, athletic inadequacy, overconformity, excitability, and excessive tearfulness. These traits are stressed more for boys than for girls.

e. Fathers are concerned with the athletic ability of sons, not because they want their boys to grow up to be professional athletes but because failure along these lines symbolizes lack of properly aggressive and competitive abilities.

f. The above traits are emphasized because of their relation to success or failure in middle-class occupational life. This explains why they are stressed more for boys. "If she is a sweet girl, that's enough."

g. Fathers show more concern with a male first-born than a female first-born. Fathers identify with their sons. The latters' failure is considered to reflect on the father as a father.

3. The third study to be summarized was made by the author. It is

[10] *Ibid.*, p. 795.

[11] David F. Aberle and Kaspar D. Naegele, "Middle-Class Fathers' Occupational Role and Attitudes Toward Children," *American Journal of Orthopsychiatry*, April, 1952, pp. 366–378.

based on information gathered from 81 persons, 67 of whom were students in a large urban university and 14 of whom had entered employment following their sixteenth birthday. In age, they ranged from 18 to 30 years at the time that the information was secured; 59 fell in the 18-to-24 age bracket. This age distribution is important because age is an important determinant, not only of occupational choice but of occupational attitudes as well. A recent analysis points out that occupational choice, for example, is not an act of simple decision but rather the result of a developmental process—a kind of progressive commitment, with compromise always as an essential aspect of that process. According to the authors of this study, the young person passes through three stages, beginning with a phantasy stage of occupational interest, then passing into a period of tentative choices, and culminating in a third period of realistic attitudes and choices.[12] The last-named stage covers the years of young adulthood, and it is in this age span that the cases fall. They were at an age of realistic thinking about occupation and yet not too old to have forgotten their earlier attitudes.

The methods utilized in securing the information for this study included free associational writing on a series of stipulated questions, and informal interviews in a selected number of cases. Seventy-six of the 81 cases presented written records; 5 of them preferred to "talk out" their story. Interviews were conducted with 11 persons who had presented written records, by way of supplementing and clarifying their answers. The questions covered the occupations to date of the informant's father; of the mother, if employed; the attitude of the informant toward the parent's occupation; an explanation of the ways it affected the informant's development while growing up, with an estimate of their importance; and the adjustments made by the informant to these factors. About half of the case records were obtained without the director of the research being aware of the identification of the particular informant.

The occupations of the fathers of 80 cases (one father died when the informant was an infant) are distributed as follows:

Occupation	Number	Percent
Proprietor	16	20.0
Executive	4	5.0
University professor or high-school teacher	14	17.5
Other professional	12	15.0
Semiprofessional	6	7.5
Salesman	10	12.5
Clerical	2	2.5
Skilled worker	6	7.5
Semiskilled worker	6	7.5
Farmer	2	2.5
Unemployed	2	2.5

[12] Eli Ginzberg, Sol W. Ginsburg, Sidney Axelrad, and John L. Herma, *Occupational Choice*, Columbia University Press, New York, 1951, Chaps. 7–10.

Obviously, the occupational distribution of the fathers is heavily slanted toward the higher occupational strata, as would be expected among the parents of university students. Thus, 57.5 percent are in the proprietary, executive, and professional classes. On the other hand, more than two-fifths (42.5 percent) are distributed in the lower occupational strata. Twenty-five of the mothers in these families were also employed; 20 to supplement the family income, and 5 as the sole or chief support of the family. Fifteen of these were in professional or proprietary positions; of the remaining 10, 4 were occupied in clerical or sales positions, and 6 in semi- or unskilled occupations.

The main findings of this study follow:[13]

a. Definite attitudes toward fathers' occupations are reported. These group themselves under five heads. Twenty-five (31.2 percent) were proud of their fathers' occupation, declaring this in unequivocal terms, and usually with some enthusiasm. Another 15 (18.7 percent) used the word "respect," rather than any reference to pride. Uppermost in their expressions were statements concerning the worth-whileness of what their fathers were doing. A third group, consisting of 12 cases (15 percent) tended to underscore the idea of acceptance chiefly because their fathers were making a good living (economically) for their families. The word *tolerance* came to one's mind in a number of these cases, as perhaps best indicating the attitude. A fourth group, comprising 17 cases (21 percent) definitely had feelings of shame, as they were growing up, of their fathers' occupation; and the remaining 11, while not using the term *shame*, indicated their low regard for the types of work in which their fathers were engaged, labeling them as uninteresting, unimportant, or "unworthy of my father's abilities." In regard to the 25 mothers who were employed, 12 of the children were proud, and 3 expressed themselves as being satisfied with their mothers' work. The remaining 10, while not pronounced in their attitudes, spoke of their dislike of what their mothers did by way of employment.

b. Just as the attitudes group themselves, so also do the occupations which call forth the various attitudes. Children whose parents are engaged in the traditional professions, or are high-level executives, or proprietors of creative businesses, are proud of them. Occupations "respected" by children range from semiprofessional to the socially useful, like social welfare positions; those "accepted" included proprietors of businesses of little or no prestige or salesmen working on a commission basis. Children were ashamed of jobs from which the parents returned home "dirty" in clothes and body, or where the product handled was not a "nice" one. Finally, there were the routine jobs where feelings of low regard rather than shame were most apparent.

c. How do people in early adulthood think their parents' occupations

[13] For a complete report on this research study, the reader is referred to Bossard, *op. cit.*, Chap. 11.

affected their development as children and as adolescents? This question was asked of the 81 persons included in the study and was emphasized as the major item in the inquiry. The answers given, while showing considerable variation in their concrete expressions, tended to group themselves for the most part under seven main headings. These are stated, together with numbers and percentages, in the accompanying table.

Factor Emphasized	Number of Persons Mentioning	Percent
Resultant home life, other than economic	64	79.0
Social status	57	70.4
Economic aspects	29	35.8
Guests brought to the home	24	29.6
Traits emphasized in the home	19	23.4
Pressures put on children	18	22.2
Selection of child's occupation	16	19.7
Other factors	28	34.5

d. As the accompanying tabular summary indicates, the effect upon the home life and child rearing was mentioned most frequently, and was also the one most stressed for importance.

e. Only a minority of our informants spoke of the occupational factor as a helpful one for family living, in ways other than economic. "Having a long week end," writes one, "my father could spend much time with us. We took many interesting trips together." "My father's leisurely life and his intellectual pursuits," writes another, "made for a rich intellectual atmosphere. We have many interesting table conversations. . . . My father's library of books connected with his work, including some dealing with 'the facts of life' was the source of learning not only for my sister and me but for a good portion of the neighborhood at our age levels. . . . The presence of clear and good books right in the home is a great advantage." What children seem to like is an occupation which allows the parent the time and nervous energy to be a parent. Most of the parents in this study so situated were university professors. Assuredly, this is one of the compensations of this particular profession.

Most of the case records (57 out of the 81) include statements of complaint or plaintive regret because of the ways in which the parents' occupations interfered with family life. "My father was always too busy," was the most common comment. Nineteen of the 81 informants voiced this criticism. Typical statements follow.

We rarely had meals with my father, and had little opportunity to share experiences with him. He was always so busy, working even on Sundays. When he came home from work he was usually too tired to pay much attention to us.

My father's work took him away from the house early in the morning. He would be gone all day. When he came home he was extremely tired, and mother would be tired, too. He rarely played with us or amused us with stories. The most he did for us was occasionally on Sundays he would read the funnies to us.

My father was too busy developing his business to pay any attention to us. He tried to substitute for this by buying our affection.

Because mother worked, we children were left alone a great deal. As the oldest child, I had to take charge of my younger brother and sister and do most of the household tasks since I was 12 years old. When my parents were home, they were too tired to pay much attention to us.

My father was so busy when I was younger that I never developed any affection for him. It was not until in my teens, and later when I saw how much he had accomplished, that I began to respect him. Now it is too late because my father died from the strain of too much work. One of the things I have learned from my father's occupation is that a man should never allow an occupation to take him away from getting to know his family.

Another frequently found criticism was that "father was away from home so much of the time." Ten case records specify this.

My father left home for work early in the morning; he came home after seven at night. He was always very tired when he came home. I saw little of my father during those years.

My father's job was time-consuming, and as a result he spent little time with his children. I felt very shy in his presence and ill at ease with him.

Father's business took him away over long periods of time. When I did see him, it was over week ends. He was never around when I needed him. What home life we had was without him for the most part.

Father away from home too long, father always tired, father too busy: the inevitable result was that the child-rearing process was left largely or wholly to the mother. Seventeen of the cases emphasize this fact, and the situations described in other cases must have led to similar arrangements. The comments concerning the mothers' assumption of control over the children are usually brief and direct. They identify the mother as aggressive (nine use this word) or the father as ineffective. In several cases where the father was too busy or too tired, the mother was ineffective, with results that were unfortunate. Illustrative excerpts follow.

Father was away all day. Mother is an aggressive person.

Mother is an aggressive person and Father is ineffective. Mother just took over.

Because Father was away so much, Mother assumed all the duties of guiding the family's development.

The discipline was left to Mother, but she was ineffective, and we were packed off to boarding schools. Both parents failed us, and we have developed without their guidance. I blame the business for all this.

Where the mother is employed, several distinctly different attitudes appear. There are those cases where, because of family circumstances, the employment of the mother was necessary, and the fact was accepted with little or no comment. Second, there are the cases where the child is proud of the mother for the work she is doing, or the child is interested, or sees distinct advantages to what the mother is doing. Third are the cases with complaints—of the mother's absence over long hours, of the mother's fatigue and irritability, of confusion in the household, or of the mother's inability to share the young child's activities. In analyzing the material bearing on the employment of the mother, one comes to see the play of many factors, including the age of the children, the demands of the job, the health and energy of the mother, the character of the child, and, perhaps most important of all, the extent to which each person involved sees the situation as a whole.

Finally, young people seem to resent any job or business that intrudes upon the home. In seven of the cases, considerable emphasis is given to this. There seems to be in these cases a strong feeling about the privacy of one's home, and that no occupation should be allowed to invade it beyond a certain point. Three cases are presented briefly.

My father is a clergyman. We live in a relatively new home, bought by my father's congregation. We have little or no privacy in our home life. Everyone seems to think they can come to see the "pastor's home" any time they want. Some of the church officials walk in without knocking or ringing the doorbell. Our telephone is ringing from morning to night. We can seldom finish a meal without interruption. People come to our house for all kinds of reasons: to get married, to tell their troubles, to ask for advice, or to complain about another member of the church. Sometimes it takes us several days to finish a conversation. One thing I am sure of, and that is that I'll never marry a minister.

My mother keeps a store that is a part of our house. Business interrupts everything, especially our meals. Often my mother must leave the table to wait on the trade. The fact that I disliked most was that we never closed the door from the store to the home: the customers thus were able to invade our privacy at all times. It was not unusual to see customers' children playing in our living room.

My father is a doctor, with his office at home. In addition to his office, there is a large waiting room. But his patients early took over the living room across the hall. From there, they come upstairs to the bathroom. When they are on the second floor, they walk around, opening doors and looking into the rooms. There is not a square inch of privacy on the first two floors of our home. Often, patients have come filing into the living room and the dining room while we are still at dinner. I have even met patients on the third floor when I come out of my room.

f. Children begin early in life to compare their parents with those of other children. These comparisons early include respective occupations and by the time the teen age arrives, the social rating of what the parents do becomes highly important. Seven out of every 10 of the cases emphasize this factor. Occupation is one of the major factors in determining the status of the family; the child is a member of that family: he identifies himself with it and its status; and other persons tend to accord the family status to the child. Because some children resist such identification, or seek to escape it, or drive themselves to rise above it, this does not minimize in any way the importance of the basic conclusion involved.

g. The economic aspects of parents' occupations were mentioned in 29 (35.8 percent) of the cases. Ten of the 29 emphasized the fact of economic adequacy, pointing out that the father's earnings permitted a good life for the family; 12 stressed economic inadequacy. Others spoke of the irregularity of incomes, otherwise adequate. Fifteen of the 29 spoke about the emphasis upon money, undue in some cases, inevitable in others.

h. Three out of every 10 cases (29.6 percent) noted the guests who came to the home as a result of the parents' occupational life. Most of the comments about guests stressed the cultural contributions which such guests made to the life of the family.

i. A good deal of work has been done in recent years on the identification of occupational types. These studies show that persons in the same occupations tend to have common personality traits or characteristics, due in part to the process which selects persons with certain traits for particular occupations and in part to the fact that occupational demands tend to develop certain patterns of behavior.[14] That the traits emphasized in the parents' occupations are manifest in the home and in the child-rearing process is fully attested in this study. One out of every four (23.4 percent) were conscious of this.

j. Akin to the emphasis upon occupational traits is the pressure upon the child to measure up to the level of the occupational structure attained or sought by the family. Approximately one out of every five cases noted this. The findings here complement the preceding study summarized in this chapter.

k. Other factors noted in the study include the determination of sibling occupation, mobility of residence resulting from the parents' occupational changes, contributions to sex education, and introduction to the field of public service.

l. Finally, it should be pointed out that three-fourths of the persons (60 out of 81, or 74 percent) included in the study rated parents' occupation of the highest importance in their development; 9.9 percent rated it important; 12.3 percent, as of medium importance; and 3.7 percent as of

[14] For illustrative materials, see the January, 1949, issue of the *American Journal of Sociology;* W. F. Cottrell, *The Railroader,* Stanford University Press, Palo Alto, 1940; Logan Wilson, *The Academic Man,* Oxford University Press, New York, 1942; and F. R. Donovan, *The Schoolma'am,* Frederick A. Stokes, New York, 1938.

minor importance. Supplementing the results of this declared rating by the persons included in the study is much additional and incidental information, so that the conclusion is inescapable that the occupation of the parent deserves high rank as a complex in child development.

Constructive Suggestions

The economic structure of modern society is such that many parents are destined to occupy positions at the lower levels of the occupation scale. Many of these occupations are such that interference with the home life and child-rearing processes are inevitable; a large proportion are bound to have a prestige rating lower than their children will like. Our open-class system accentuates dissatisfaction on this score. The question naturally arises: can anything helpful or constructive be done about this, or are embarrassment, frustration, and hurt the inevitable lot of all children who compare their own with other parents?

Two by-products of the author's study just summarized seem to have constructive promise. One is suggested in the case record of one of the families where the father returned from work each night covered with grime and exhausted in body. His only child wrote as follows:

I don't remember much of my preschool attitudes toward the occupation itself. I do remember that much of the dirt and grease he acquired in his job was still with him on his return home, and that I didn't like. When I started going to school, my attitudes changed as I became acquainted with other children and their families. I found that not all fathers worked for the railroad. Some were doctors, lawyers, or businessmen. They arrived home clean, and seemed to be in a different category from my own father. I finally developed the attitude that their occupation was much more desirable than my own father's. This attitude grew with me until I finally wished that he were engaged in something that seemed more important.

As I grew a little older, I became more curious about my father's occupation. Some of my classmates would brag about their fathers' occupations and of how important they were. When they asked me about mine, I tried to put on a brave front, but I didn't have anything to really brag about. Finally I decided to get to the bottom of this business of occupations. I asked both my father and mother about it. They were very obliging, and I was told all about the shops, the particular work my father did, how he had to apprentice when he first worked there, how he was finally promoted to gangleader, and of the many extra things he had to do in connection with this job. My father even took me on a tour of the shops, and showed me where he worked. He let me look in his desk, showed me his tools, and the blueprints he used, and in general gave me a good tour of the entire shop. Although I was too young to actually understand the workings of this huge repair shop, I still remember the feeling of pride I carried around with me. It wasn't every child that had a chance to go through the shops. It was then I began to see my father's occupation in a different light. I realized that he was just as important in what he was doing as some of the other people were in their respective occupations. I was able now to brag as much as any of the other children, and I did, too.

My attitude changed even more when I would listen to my father and some of his friends talk. They all respected him, and often referred to his ability as a machinist. The high point came one day when my father was taking his vacation. The doorbell rang, and there stood one of the men from the shop. We had no phone at the time, and he had been sent to ask my father if he would come to the shop and help them work out a problem that had arisen. Well, that was really something to be proud of. To think that my father was so important that they had to send someone to get him to help them out. From thereon, I regarded my father's occupation from a new perspective. I admitted that he wasn't receiving the salary that others were, but we had as happy a family and had enough of everything. Maybe he did get a little dirty, but he was well liked, and respected, and I had nothing to be ashamed of.

A second suggestion came from a public-school teacher with whom the research project was discussed. Her school was located in a town dominated by one industry. Many of the parents of the children in her school were employed in the shops of this industry. As a project for her class, she described the local industry, its place in the larger industrial situation, the importance of each task in the overall organization of the particular plant and the industry as a whole, all to the end of revealing how important the work of the parents employed in it were in the national economy. Here, again, as in the preceding case, resentment and shame among children of parents employed in the industry gave way to feelings of understanding and pride.

Obviously, children do identify themselves with their parents, with what they do, and where, and how. They do make comparisons with other parents. Life is like that. But apparently, too, understanding can be brought to life situations, to the end that what yesterday was a grievous burden to be borne is today but an incidental fact to be taken in stride.

The Stress of Occupational Requirements

A final approach to the role of parents' occupations in child development may be made in terms of the stresses of occupational requirements, as revealed through analysis of prevailing workaday situations. Such analysis identifies at least four types of situations in our industrial urban culture in which occupational requirements tend to interfere seriously with the child-rearing process.

1. The first is the father's employment away from home. This practice, so commonplace and so taken for granted today, is really a new aspect of family life which did not appear until modern industry removed economic functions from the home. Today, many fathers do not return to their homes for the noonday meal, and spend often considerable time in commuting to and from their jobs. All this takes the father away from home

for a large part of the child's waking hours, with the result that the child is left largely to the care of the mother or of other women. Thus in the period in which the child's dependence on the family is lengthening in point of years and extending in the scope of "administrative" decisions, the decreasing presence of the father makes for the increasing feminization of child rearing. It is true that in many families the minor decisions are left to the mother and the major ones are reserved for the father. One is tempted to speak of the modern "thermostatic father" who "goes on" and functions only when marked changes of "family temperature" occur.[15]

2. The second is the increasing influx of women into gainful occupations away from home. This is far from a wartime development, as much recent discussion would imply. From 1880 to 1940, the percentage of all women 16 years of age and over who were gainfully employed increased from 16.0 to 26.3 percent. Both the First and the Second World Wars stimulated this trend tremendously. At the height of the World War II effort, about 18 million women were employed. In April, 1951, the number stood at 18,602,000, thus indicating that the increase of World War II has remained.

Two aspects of the increasing employment of women are of special importance in the present discussion. One has been the increased spread among the middle and upper classes. Particularly pronounced has been the movement from these two classes into clerical, professional, service, trade, and transportation occupations. The other is the marked increase in the proportion of married women employed outside of the home. In 1900, about 1 out of 20 (5.6 percent) married women were in this group; in 1950, the percentage was 24.8. In 1900, 15.4 percent of all working women were married; in 1950, the percentage was 52.1. The increase has been particularly pronounced since 1940.

From the standpoint of the status of the female sex, these trends are spoken of frequently as indicating the economic emancipation of women and their declining subservience to the male head of the house. Considered in their broader implications, these trends involve the readjustment of family life patterns, including the family's care of the children. One aspect of this is the declining practice of having the older daughters remain at home to aid in the care of younger siblings; another is the absence of mothers, particularly those with younger children, from the home. The latter of these has become particularly prevalent. In 1950, of all women with children under 6 years of age, 25 percent were employed outside of the home during the year. There are many ways in which such

---

[15] An excellent complementary study (with a helpful bibliography) to this part of the chapter is that by Ruth Jacobson Tasch, "The Role of the Father in the Family," *Journal of Experimental Education*, June, 1952, pp. 319–361. See also, O. Spurgeon English and Constance J. Foster, *Fathers Are Parents Too*, G. P. Putnam's Sons, New York, 1951.

situations may be considered. Obviously, the facts of the time and duration of the mother's absence are important. To the extent that the hours of employment are adjusted to domestic requirements, as was done extensively in England during World War II, the effects upon children may be quite different from what would otherwise be the case.[16] Similarly, the effects of the additional income earned by the mother must be weighed against the costs of her absence, as must also the varying nature of the substitute arrangements and the differing personalities of the children and mothers involved.

Certain items in the costs to children of their mothers' employment away from home seem obvious and will be identified briefly. (a) The combined strain of being wife, mother, and outside employee tends to make mothers unduly tired, with consequent feelings of impatience and irritability. The emphasis, in the psychiatric approach to behavior, upon the subtle and many-sided effects of the psychic atmosphere of the home makes this of great importance. Child rearing, it cannot be emphasized too often, is an exacting task, particularly in its demands upon the nervous energy of the parents. (b) There is the loneliness, emotional and otherwise, of the child whose mother is always away from home, or too tired. "My mother is so tired," cries a wartime adolescent, "that she won't even talk to me." (c) There is the child who feels neglected, who is neglected, and who rationalizes that neglect to justify the inevitable consequences of neglect. "They don't care what happens to me, why should I?" (d) Many children seize upon their parents' absence to run riot and to secure greater license than they otherwise could. (e) The working mother is less able to share with the child the impact of his daily adventures. One such adventure is going to school. The impact of the school upon the child, especially if it is a large school, is quite pronounced. The mere fact, especially for the younger child, that there is a mother to go to after the day's school experience is of great importance. Beyond the mere comfort of her presence, there is the need to tell someone of the day's experiences. This has both a therapeutic and an educational value. One of the basic functions of the home is to serve as an assessing station for the child; whether that station functions, and how, determines in large measure the meaning of the day's events for the child. The following case shows how what appeared to a child a serious affront is interpreted by the home as a happy experience:

Karen came home from school in tears. Mary, a classmate, had torn up her bus ticket. Mary, whose parents provided her with no bus tickets, did this so that Karen, who lived near to her, would be compelled to walk home from school. Karen interpreted this as a hurt, and was cross at Mary. Karen's mother, after listening to her patiently, suggested that Mary really must like her very much, and that what she really aimed to do was to have Karen walk home with

---

[16] Women's Bureau, U.S. Department of Labor, *Part-Time Employment of Women in Wartime,* Special Bulletin No. 13, Washington, 1943.

her. Then, suddenly, the mother had a happy thought. "What do you suppose," she said to Karen, "would happen to Daddy if the girls in his office liked him so much that they tore up his bus tickets? Poor Daddy might not come home tonight until long after dark." Karen, who loved her daddy very much, was quite amused at this. The next afternoon, Karen and Mary walked home together to Karen's house and played happily until dinnertime.[17]

f. The mother's employment and absence from home affect her ability to render detailed services which children need—socks to be darned, shoes to be brushed, ribbons ironed, dresses starched, buttons sewed on, etc.—or to stimulate and supervise the child's performance of these services for himself. Many of these services have to do with his appearance, which relates in turn to his conception of himself and to the attitude of other children; yet their nature is such that the working mother and her child may easily neglect them.

Ernestine had a part in her school play. Her working mother rushed there in time to see her daughter appear on the stage displaying an atrocious color combination and stockings with two holes showing. Shortly afterward, the mother withdrew from employment. In her letter to her employer, she wrote that "every growing child needs a mother in the home."[18]

g. Finally, there are the whole series of supervisory and training services which children must obtain, if they do so at all, in their own homes. These have to do with such things as dietary habits, outlets for child energy, the vetoing of selected experiments with objects and persons, and the acquisition of the niceties of social behavior. Just as Sutherland concludes that crime is learned behavior growing out of differential association,[19] so also are courtesy, etiquette, manners, or their opposites. Socially approved behavior, too, is learned behavior, and its teaching is a parental task that no absent or overworked mother can discharge with adequacy. There is, as Marquand puts it, "so little time."[20]

3. Selected occupations of both fathers and mothers tend particularly to interfere with the child-rearing process. Among these are night jobs, with their complement of daytime sleeping. One phase of these jobs combines the late afternoon and early evening; another, the late night and early morning. Long working hours, combined with time-consuming commuting requirements, create another type of situation. Some occupations, even at relatively high income and status levels, involve frequent or continual absence from home in the evening hours. Train crews on transcontinental runs must be away from home for days at a time. Long-distance truck drivers have similarly exacting schedules. Traveling men

[17] From the files of the William T. Carter Foundation.

[18] From the files of the William T. Carter Foundation.

[19] E. H. Sutherland, "White-Collar Criminality," *American Sociological Review,* February, 1940, pp. 1–12.

[20] John P. Marquand, *So Little Time,* Little, Brown and Company, Boston, 1943.

may be away continuously for weeks and months. Common observation will place a long list of jobs in this general category.

The problem-creating aspects of such occupations arise chiefly out of certain facts. First, the hours of employment remove the parents from the home during the hours when the child is not at school or asleep. This means that the ordinary relationships between parent and child have little or no opportunity to develop, and there is the subsequent loss of whatever these relationships might come to mean. Second, the complement of these unusual working hours for the parent is a sleeping schedule which does not fit into the child's life. This may mean that the child cannot play at home, cannot bring other children home, or is constantly restrained and urged to be quiet until all spontaneity is squeezed out of his home life. Third, there are the lengthy absences from home, which in many ways affect the absent parent's relationship with the child and the other parent. Perhaps the primary result is that family life comes to be organized on the basis of the parent's absence. Such a child has, and yet does not have, a parent. This might be termed the problem of intermittent parenthood.

Special mention should be made here of those persons whose occupation or profession involves the care and problems of "other people's children." This group includes teachers, psychologists, pediatricians, social workers, etc. How do such parents react to their own children when they find time for them? Do their occupations drain them dry of the energies which child rearing demands? Do they impose on their own children the hypotheses of their professional practices? Are they too preoccupied with the problems of their workaday children to concern themselves with those in their own homes? We are reminded here of the doctor's wife, cited by Boll,[21] who could get no help with her health problems until she set out to find a good doctor for herself. So weary of illness was her husband that he simply refused to face the possibility of it in his own family. Every complaint was pushed aside by, "You are just imagining it." And there is the university sophomore, the son of a famous surgeon, who had to arrange through his father's secretary for an appointment with his father.

Again, the occupational organization of an entire community may create a pattern of family life with its own distinctive problem of child development. Voss has shown this for the seashore resort family,[22] which is not that of the frolicking vacationists, but the one that remains behind when the gay folk have left.

The most striking characteristic of the seashore community, Ocean City, New Jersey, is its chameleon-like change. In the wintertime it is sparsely populated, with two dwellings to every individual. Its people are almost entirely

[21] James H. S. Bossard and Eleanor S. Boll, *Family Situations,* University of Pennsylvania Press, Philadelphia, 1943, p. 199.

[22] J. Ellis Voss, *Ocean City: An Ecological Analysis of a Satellite Community,* University of Pennsylvania thesis, Philadelphia, 1941.

family people. There is little of the bustle of work. Parents and children have time to be together and to share the communal activities. Suddenly, within a matter almost of days, a maelstrom of activity develops. For every room in Ocean City, there are now two people. Many of the year-round residents move out of their homes and rent them. Most of the others are crowded by boarders. Nearly 39 per cent of the Ocean City mothers are now employed outside of their homes, and in 90 per cent of the families both parents are employed in some way other than the care of their own immediate family. A complete change has taken place in the family set-up and does take place, thus, twice every year. This community "is neither urban nor rural but alternatingly takes on the nature of both." Instead of being a happy medium between the two, this community offers to its families a winter of small-town family relationships and a summer of disorganization, during which the children are relatively free to care for themselves, in the time when festivity is at its height and their parents' work is at its greatest pressure. Crowded out at home, where discipline must be modified to the tastes of the guests, they have the run of the beaches and boardwalks, and the antics of the vacationists to watch and copy. Then, after this taste of freedom, school time comes again. The town quiets down with a great exodus of people, and the frolic is over. Parents now have the leisure winter months to concentrate upon the home, and to make up for the neglect of the summer.[23]

4. Finally, there are the homes in which there is the physical intrusion of the family business or profession. These run a wide gamut—from the small shop which occupies the front room of the downstairs apartment, to the rectory to which everyone feels he has a right to come at any time, to the more imposing residence where the doctor's patients swarm over at least the first two floors.

Such situations have a wide variety of features which affect the social processes of child development. There may be a relative or complete lack of privacy, so that the whole family lives a goldfish-bowl life. The demands of the office or shop may be such that one or more members of the family are always occupied, which means that the family seldom or never functions as a whole. Interruptions of family relations are constant. "I started a conversation with my husband on Tuesday," writes the wife of a doctor, "and we finished it on Friday." The children's problems and needs are particularly likely to be ignored under such circumstances. A 14-year-old boy, faced with a crisis situation in his life, tells of trying for 11 days to talk it over with his father, only to have the telephone ring, to have a patient call, or to be put off with "I can't talk to you now." There was the 22-year-old daughter of a widow realtor, whose office was in their home, who after two weeks despaired of an opportunity to tell her mother of her plans to marry, and resolved her difficulties by a forthright elopement. Nor is it only the actual demands of time and space that interfere; various young children with whom this has been discussed speak of their re-

[23] *Ibid.*, pp. 137–138.

luctance to begin a serious talk with their parents because of the constant imminence of interruption. The following case illustrates what life in the home of a busy physician may mean to the school progress of his son:

Paul was headed for medical school, following the family tradition. He had finished a high-grade preparatory boarding school in the second quintile of his class. He now returned to his home, attending the nearby college as a day student. His father was a general practitioner, with patients "swarming over the first two floors of the house." Twice a week, he performed tonsillectomies and various minor operations in his home. Most of the time two nurses lived in the large rambling house. Paul had his own room on the third floor, but the noise, excitement, and general commotion constantly penetrated into his study. When at times the house quieted down, the very unnaturalness of it came to disturb him. At the end of the first term at college, he was conditioned in two subjects; at the end of the second term, he was dropped for scholastic cause. The father was keenly disappointed and blamed Paul for not applying himself. It was extremely difficult to convince the father to permit Paul, upon his subsequent readmission, to live at the college, but he finally agreed. Paul's college record, from that time on, showed no further academic failure. He is very sure that being at home his first year was the cause of his difficulties, and the college personnel officer agrees with this.

Summary

1. Recognition of the social role of the occupational factor varies considerably in sociological texts and treatises. Those that do refer to it usually accord it very comprehensive and pervasive importance.

2. Research publications in sociological journals in recent years indicate a very marked appreciation of its many-sided significance.

3. Three primary studies of the ways in which the occupation of the parents affects child development, made in recent years, are summarized. These show that whether normal or emotionally disturbed children are considered, the highest importance must be accorded to the occupational factor.

4. By-products of the studies indicate that children often do not understand the nature of their parents' occupations and that efforts by the parents and by teachers in the schools to give adequate information may be very helpful in improving the child's orientation.

5. Four types of occupational situations tend to interfere seriously with the child-rearing process: (a) the father's employment away from home; (b) the increasing employment of women, particularly married women; (c) occupations which run counter to customary routines of family living; and (d) family businesses or professions which intrude physically upon the home.

Part *IV*

Modes of Family Operation

Chapter 13

Family Table Talk

Preceding chapters have emphasized two basic steps in the social development of the child. One is his introduction into the process of living with other persons; the other, his contact with the accumulated modes of living and thinking which constitute the cultural system in which he lives. Both of these are acquired by the child first through his family. These two processes are the essence of child rearing and, on the cultural side, comprise the family's role as the connecting link between successive generations. Much has been written about the importance of what the family does in these respects, but far less attention has been given to the mechanism by which the family achieves these ends. It is to a consideration of this mechanism and some of its more important aspects that this and the succeeding five chapters are devoted.

Formal Instruction Through the Family

The helplessness of the human infant requires a long period of nurture and protection, and it is part of the economy of nature that parents conserve and transmit their experience, knowledge, and understanding to their children during this time. Thus the family is destined by its very nature to be the primary educational agency in the life of the child, and in simpler forms of society a large part of the child's education is obtained from the family. The ancient Jewish household, for example, was the only educational institution for most Jewish folk until the time of Christ, when, for the first time, through the leadership of Rabbi Joshua ben Gamla, schools apart from the home were instituted in the towns and villages of Palestine. Similarly, in colonial American times, both industrial and intellectual training were largely given in the home. It is only as cultural resources and economic means accumulate, and the social organization becomes more differentiated and complex, that specialized educational institutions develop to which the family turns over many of its functions.[1]

Part of this educational process in the family life of more primitive societies, while lacking the formality of present-day schools, was relatively concrete and direct: a projection of the family routine upon the child. To understand the nature and scope of this educational process in earlier times, two facts must be kept in mind. One is the concrete and vocational nature of what the child was taught. The primitive family was engrossed in the all-absorbing task of making a living, and the child was taught as early and as effectively as possible to do his share.[2] The other is the fact that earlier the child was reared in the extended or kinship group form of family in which there were likely to be many more pupils and teachers than in the immediate family of our contemporary urban culture.

The greater part of the family's role in child rearing, however, is achieved through indirection, in ways that are subtle and devious, for the most part unconscious, and as a by-product of family routine. The family might be spoken of as a conditioning agency, and what happens to the child is by way of absorption from the life of the family as a whole. In other words, the family lives its collective life—it eats, talks, laughs, argues, wrangles, its members go about their allotted tasks—and in this life the young child grows and learns to live.

A Methodological Note

It becomes evident at once that the mechanism whereby the family conditions the child must be studied, not from the standpoint of the child merely, but in terms of family operation. It is the process of family life as a whole, not a part of it, which must concern us. This raises a question of methodology. How can this subtle, detailed, comprehensive process be studied? How can the outsider obtain a segment of a family in operation in order to analyze it objectively?

Obviously, the approach must be as casual and indirect as is the family's operation. There is something of the ludicrous in the method of the formal interview, in which the interviewer confronts the person or family to be studied and says, as it were: "Proceed now and go through your routine so that I may study and record it." First and foremost, the family in operation must be studied without its knowledge, otherwise the process will not be natural. The essence of our methodology, then, must be the gathering and recording of data without the family's awareness of the

[1] Cf. Ernest R. Groves, *The Family and Its Social Functions,* J. B. Lippincott Company, Philadelphia, 1940, Chap. 10; also, *Recent Social Trends,* McGraw-Hill Book Company, Inc., New York, 1933, Vol. I, Chap. 13.

[2] Recently the author had the opportunity to observe this in the case of a family living under comparatively simple conditions. The 8-year-old son was given very specific and direct instruction in a series of tasks immediately related to the family's means of livelihood.

fact. Its object must be to hold up a mirror, not for the family or its members to see themselves in, as is the technique of psychoanalysis or of the nondirective interview,[3] but for objective analysis by the student. This, we recall at once, is the method of the drama. People talk, they act, you observe and listen, you understand the role played by the actor, the character he portrays, and the operation of the plot. Similarly, the novelist utilizes this method of portraying his characters by simply permitting them to talk. Sinclair Lewis has utilized this method, with devastating effect.

The recording of a family in operation can best be achieved through the method of first-person reporting. Attention was called to this method for purposes of scientific analysis a number of years ago, and various persons working professionally with problem cases have utilized it over a period of years for its revealing as well as its therapeutic effectiveness. In 1928, Burgess, speaking on how social case records might be made of greater value, suggested that the characters be allowed to speak for themselves. "The first requisite necessary to reveal . . . the person as he really is to himself would be to enter the record in his own language."[4] Such reporting enables us, he continued, to participate in the life history of the individual, in his memories, hopes, attitudes, plans, and philosophy of life.

It was Clifford Shaw, research sociologist at the Institute for Juvenile Research in Chicago, according to Burgess, who first developed consciously the method of first-person reporting and carried it further than anyone else in this country. His book *The Jack-Roller* is a conspicuous illustration of the use of a delinquent boy's own story, as are his subsequent *The Natural History of a Delinquent Career* and *Brothers in Crime*. Not only is his report on the case of Angelus, presented at the meetings of the American Sociological Society held at St. Louis in 1926, a splendid illustration of a case record in which the persons involved are presented in their own words, but his verbatim report of a family conversation in that record is the first utilization of the technique emphasized in this chapter.[5]

In summary, then, it is proposed that family operation, with particular reference to the process of child conditioning, can be studied to advantage through the records of family conversations reported in a form in which each person speaks for himself, and that such records be obtained without the knowledge of the family. To say that these records are difficult to obtain offers, of course, no comment on their value; to point out that they will contain much that is trivial and inconsequential is to con-

[3] Carl R. Rogers, "The Nondirective Method as a Technique for Social Research," *American Journal of Sociology,* January, 1945, pp. 279–284.

[4] Ernest W. Burgess, "What Social Case Records Should Contain to Be Useful for Sociological Interpretation," *Social Forces,* June, 1928, p. 527.

[5] Clifford Shaw, "Case Study Method," *Publications of the American Sociological Society,* 1927, Vol. XXI, pp. 149–157.

fess that bushels of chaff may hide the scattered grain; to contend that they need to be supplemented with other accompanying information is but a recognition of the relative inadequacy of all data. The method here proposed is to be identified as *the family life recording technique.*

The Value of Family Table Talk

Experimental studies made by the William T. Carter Foundation at the University of Pennsylvania suggest the value of transcripts of family table talk for purposes of studying family operation. When this is recorded without the knowledge of the family, one is able to study the family routine much as the scientist observes amoebae swimming about in beef broth.

The significance of the family meal has long been recognized by non-scientific groups. Religion has long recognized its intimate importance. Divine family worship at mealtime has been a common observance and is still continued in the offering of "grace." Christianity immortalizes it in the ceremony of the Last Supper, and renews this recognition endlessly in the continuance of the communion rite. Dramatists stage it with frequent effectiveness. To the novelist it is a constant device for character delineation or plot facilitation. Even the essayists, like Dr. Holmes, build their sage observations around the framework of the breakfast table.

Students of family and child problems may regard family table talk from two main points of view. One is as a form of family interaction. Here the concern is with the relationships between the personalities in the family group, with particular reference to the functioning and formation of personal traits. Also, as far as the children are concerned, there is a good deal of emphasis upon habit formation, such as habits of eating, sitting, speaking, and the like. A second approach sees the family meal as a vehicle for the transmission of the family culture to its younger members. Here the chief point of interest is the role and techniques of family table talk in this continuing process. Before proceeding to the two main points of view just identified, certain general considerations concerning the social nature of the family meal should be noted. Accordingly, the main body of this chapter is presented in three parts: first, the social nature of the family meal; second, its analysis as a form of family interaction; and third, its role in the transmission of the family culture to the younger members.

The Social Nature of the Family Meal

1. The family meal is a distinct aspect of the family's life. Warner and Lunt have recently called attention[6] to the fact that the two rooms in

[6] W. Lloyd Warner and Paul Lunt, *The Social Life of a Modern Community,* Yale University Press, New Haven, 1941, p. 105.

which the family spends most time as a group are the living and the dining rooms. Of the two, the dining room and the family meal are confined, except on definitely recognized occasions, to the intimate participation of the family group. In upper-class families, large and attractive living rooms, and more leisure, tend to emphasize the greater importance of the living room; in lower-class families, the opposite of these facts makes the dining room often the more important or only social center of the household.

2. It is at the dining table, and particularly at dinnertime, that the family is apt to be at its greatest ease, both physically and psychologically. The times when the family is at its best are perhaps most often on the occasion of its more leisured dining, just as the family entertaining at the dining table is the family on exhibition, putting its best foot forward. One is reminded here of the comment of Dr. Holmes that a dinner party of proper intellectual elements "is the last triumph of civilization over barbarism. Nature and art combine to charm the senses; the equatorial zone of the system is soothed by well-studied artifices; the faculties are off duty, and fall into their natural attitudes; you see wisdom in slippers and science in a short jacket."[7]

This more felicitous generalization about the family meal does not, however, mean to overlook the fact that the family meal also at times represents the family in haste, operating with direct bluntness, or the family at war, disturbing the emotions of its members and upsetting the gastric process. The family meal, in short, represents the family in action, focused upon a common interest and a task so absorbing as to let it operate offguard in other important respects.

3. The family meal, especially the main one of the day, holds the members of the family together over an extended period of time. The length of time, and the details of the occasion, naturally vary from one family to another; but, in general, a meal is an extended session of the family personnel, with a relatively high rate of attendance. Mealtime is the family council time, particularly today when under the stress of the differing interests of its various members the family is not likely to get together at any other time. Family prayer time and family councils both are found to a lessening extent in contemporary society.

4. It is significant, in any attempt to appraise the social significance of the family meal, to recall that its role is one of continuing repetition. Many families meet around the table three times a day; most families do so at least once a day. Over a period of years, the simple arithmetic of the situation is enough to emphasize its quantitative effectiveness.

5. Finally, it is obvious that the social significance of the family meal, and the role of table talk, vary from one social class to another. Referring

[7] Oliver Wendell Holmes, *The Autocrat of the Breakfast Table,* James Osgood and Company, Boston, 1878, p. 71.

again to Warner and Lunt, who concerned themselves so largely with class and status systems, we are reminded that

. . . meals in the home have different values which depend upon the social status of the family. The upper-class family, for instance, spends more time over its breakfast and endows this meal with more group significance than do families in other classes.

In upper-class families there are generally servants to perform a large part of the secular household ritual through their daily rounds of tasks and duties which keep the house in order. The mistress of the house ordinarily superintends the activities of her servants, but she does not herself do any of the actual work. However, she and other members of the family perform definite ritual acts which top off the work of their paid employees: arranging flowers; carving at table; lighting the fire; and pouring at tea. Maids serve at the table according to a strictly formalized routine, while the food is prepared by a cook hired especially for that work. Maids are outfitted in uniforms of different types according to the time of day and the specific duties in which they are engaged, their dress symbolizing their subordination to and separation from the family whom they serve. The leisure time accruing to the family that can maintain servants allows more frequent performance of social activities which bring them conspicuously to the attention of the remainder of the community, and the men indulge in a variety of sports, intellectual interests and hobbies, and community activities by means of which they express and constantly reaffirm their social position.

All of the activities which surround the preparation of the table and the serving and eating of the meal are demonstrations of ritual relations between members of the family, the servants, and objects which have esthetic and traditional value in the house. They are also expressions of the meal as a family communion. Non-members of the immediate family—such as collateral kin and clique members—who are invited in to eat at the family table may be said to participate in the "private communion" of the family and household, a secular but highly organized ritual. These ritual elements surrounding the daily life within a household tend to increase in number and intensity of function with the height of the stratification of the family.[8]

Types of Family Meals and Table Talk

Families differ a great deal in their behavior at mealtime. Analyses of recordings of table talk in 200 families reveal at least 5 main types.

First there are the hurried meals, where the members of the family act as though they were engaged in an unavoidable process of refueling. Food tends to be served as though eating were a mere physiological necessity, and gulped down as though the time required was time wasted. Conversation is scant, blunt, and direct. There is a liberal sprinkling of "yes," "no," "uh-huh," "bread," "more," "salt," and the like. Over and over, as one studies these transcripts, there arises the picture of a

[8] Warner and Lunt, *op. cit.*, pp. 105–106.

number of half-snarling dogs cleaning out a trough. In both cases, the gatherings break up with the last morsel of food.

A second type consists of those family meals which are devoted largely to recurrent domestic warfare. Squabbling is a habit, not an episode. Often as high as 80 to 90 percent of all conversation is of this kind in these families. The children are taken to task for past and present misdeeds, parents quarrel with each other, the food is criticized or its preparation is disparaged. Or there may be constant nagging about table manners. Frequently some member of the family leaves the table in tears, anger, or disgrace. Obviously, we have here a family trait, and mealtime offers such families full scope for its expression.

Then there is a third group or type of families whose critical conversation is turned outward. They are "talking about" someone all the time. The Smiths down the block drive a car they can't afford. The neighbor's child is a brat. Mrs. Green's coat looks shoddy. The Brown girl runs around with a fast crowd. Policeman Brady is not honest. The teacher plays favorites. Here we have a family habit of disparagement—"always belittling." We found families in our study whose grist for the conversational mill was almost wholly of this kind. Yet the parents wonder why son Jack has no friends and wants to stop school.

Fourth are the family meals which abound in human-interest talk. Members of the family tell their experiences of the day. Choice bits of news are saved for mealtime. Ellen speaks of a forthcoming basketball trip; Mother talks about the price of meat; and Daddy brings home a funny story he heard at luncheon today. The personal triumphs, disappointments, and pleasantries of the day are related. Public issues may be discussed. One of the most interesting of our case records comes from the home of a well-known public figure who propounded at the beginning of dinner each evening some topic of public interest. The members of the family discussed this topic as the meal progressed until Father summarized, after the coffee was served, the various points that had been brought out. While few families are likely to formalize their mealtime conversation this way, many families in this fourth group do devote some time to public questions of current interest.

Finally, there are the family meals which become occasions for family rituals. These tend to be characterized by order and impressive decorum. Prayers may be said by way of prelude. Candles gleam on the table and the surrounding surfaces. Perhaps everyone stands until Mother is seated. Various other conventions are observed. Coffee in the living room may follow the meal. In these families, mealtime becomes a sort of private tradition for its members. People listen to one another. Such a procedure involves self-discipline, and this bodes well for discipline in other areas of behavior. Self-discipline is a habit which must be acquired, and mealtime ritual may be a helpful beginning.

It is important to add that most families in this study talked habitually in the same way, many invariably, about the same things. Members of these families usually seemed unaware of the habitlike character of their family table talk, nor of its possible importance in the life of the family and the development of the child members. These type differences are particularly significant in the general discussions that follow, and the reader should keep this constantly in mind.

Table Talk as a Form of Family Interaction

The role of the group in the determination of personality is a recognized sociological dictum. The primary character of the family as a group, and its fundamental importance in the development of personal traits, particularly of children, are equally well established. From what has been said concerning the social nature of family table talk, it is obvious that much of the family's interactive process takes place during the family meal. Certain aspects of this process call for special comment.

1. The individual's role in the family group comes to be clearly defined around the table. Since the entire family is together, relationships between individual members are brought out into the open. Feuding members are seated at opposite sides of the table, for example. Covenants secretly arrived at become manifest. Group choices are made—in seating arrangements, in the serving of food, in the assignment of leftovers, in priorities in conversation.

Transcripts of family table talk may reveal with unmistakable clarity the dominating role of one member. The following record, taken from the files of the William T. Carter Foundation, will serve for purposes of illustration.

The Iredell family consists of a father; a mother; a son Bill, aged 9 years; a daughter Helen, aged 20 months; and an unmarried female relative, aged 26 years. The Iredell family is at the dinner table. The family cat has just wandered into the dining room.

RELATIVE: He's fun to watch. (Helen slides from her chair and takes hold of cat.)
    Helen. Helen. Helen.
    I give that cat two weeks to live.
    Oh, look at that. Helen, don't do that. Oh, oh.
    Put a blanket on him. Here is another blanket.
    Look at him. He is so frightened, he's shaking. Oh.
MRS. IREDELL: Let's forget about the cat and go on with our meal.
RELATIVE: Helen, don't. (Looks at Mr. Iredell, who is making a memo on an envelope.)
    I bet five dollars I know what he is doing.
    Helen. Take it out and let it
    Bill is nice with the cat, but Helen

That cat is—

No, let it alone.

MRS. IREDELL (speaking to Helen): Shall we put the cat to sleep?

RELATIVE: Mummie say it's time to put the cat to sleep.

Now look at what she is—

Oh, you are hurting its foot.

Put that box away.

(Relative looks toward Mr. Iredell, who has just made another memo.)

RELATIVE: There he sits, Old Andrew H. Brown. Five Million, ten million.

Listen, Helen, the cat can't breathe.

Don't hold your arm so high.

MRS. IREDELL: Now please, let us forget about the cat and eat.

RELATIVE: Well, she is too rough with it.

Your cat won't live long.

She's mauled it enough for tonight.

Yes, sir, I'll give that cat—

(Mr. Iredell is about to speak for the first time since the meal began.)

RELATIVE: Who was it that I used to put into the big carriage and wheel all around? (Looks coyly at Helen.)

Say, you know the clerks in the stores are the snootiest lot—

Listen, Helen. And you, too, Bill. Do you know that Christmas is only four weeks away. What do you want Santa Claus to bring?

BILL: (who has thus far been avidly stuffing himself with food). I know what I want. Father, you know, too, don't you?

RELATIVE: Does Bill have school tomorrow?

Do you know that blouse I paid Mary three dollars to block?

The trouble with her is that she is too lazy.

Not in my ear. (This to Helen, who evidently is trying to whisper to her.)

The skirt fits me beautifully.

At this point, Mr. Iredell leaves the dining room, with his meal unfinished. The Iredells are described as a quiet, gentle-spoken family, with the exception of the relative. The latter is described as a neurotically talkative bachelor girl who can best be characterized as "perpetual master of ceremonies." She dominates the Iredell household, which thus far has organized its entire life around her conversation, her wishes, and her insistences.

2. The family is an audience for individual performance, chiefly conversational. Through these performances family members reveal their abilities to, and try them out on, each other. One is reminded here again of Dr. Holmes's observation, "There are little-minded people whose thoughts move in such small circles that five minutes of conversation gives you an arc long enough to determine their whole curve." Even silences in table talk are an important part of its art. Again Holmes reminds us that "talking is like playing on the harp; there is as much in laying the hand on the strings to stop their vibrations, as in the twanging them to bring out the music."

3. This table audience, both in the responses which it gives to, and in those which it withholds from, its individual members, carries the greatest weight in the molding of personal traits. Its intimate nature and repetitive force make it often the family's best corrective disciplinarian. Children especially are frank—frequently quite brutally so—in their reactions to one another, and perhaps nowhere are they so with as much self-assurance as under the protective custody of the family meal.

4. One of the distinctive services of family interaction at mealtime is the development of the symbols of expression—again, particularly those of the children. All the members of the family participate in family table talk—from the youngest to the oldest and most erudite. Through this process, the family members enlarge one another's vocabulary. Children in particular acquire symbols to use in learning and in speaking. Much of one's knowledge about the precise meaning of words comes as a by-product to participating in family conversation. In other words, the family meal is a class in oral expression. In a family of any size, meals become "gab-fests." Two or three persons may be talking at the same time. Facility and quickness in expression constitute the price of admittance to the conversation.

5. The family meal represents the family's interaction in its most democratic mood. Now, more than at other times, the younger members get a chance to blossom verbally. Well-fed elders accept with good humor remarks from juveniles which otherwise would not be tolerated. Side conferences prevail also while the main program continues.

6. The family meal is a kind of personality clinic, with both students and clients in attendance. Especially is this true if the family is of any considerable size. Each member comes to be analyzed, dissected, catalogued, and processed by the other members. This is all the more devastating because it takes place before the entire group. Undesirable traits and personal weakness may be particularly identified and castigated.

7. Table talk serves a definite purpose in aiding children to learn the relative roles of the parents and adults in the family. Aunt Minnie jabbers away, does three-fourths of the talking, says little, and tends to be disregarded in family decisions. Mother defers to Daddy as a rule, but takes an emphatic stand at times. Daddy talks very little at the table. Even when they correct the children, Mother and Aunt Minnie turn to him for support. Repeatedly they suggest to him that he take disciplinary measures. Deference to him is constant and repeated. But Father is silent, his face is immobile. His few words to the children at the table, or even a look, suffice. The stereotype of the strong, silent father has been created. Under no other circumstances could the full-length process of this creation be so effectively imprinted upon the child's mind as at mealtime. A family meal, in other words, is like the scene from a drama in which the personalities identify themselves to each other.

Family Table Talk and the Transmission of Culture

Sociologists agree that the family is the chief culture-transmitting agency in our society. The family introduces the child not only to his own particular culture, but also to that of the larger society. In this latter capacity, it not only interprets this larger culture, it creates attitudes toward it. Much of this happens as a by-product of family table talk. In this process the following aspects may be identified.

1. The family meal, particularly dinner, is the clearing house for most of the family's information, news, and experiences. Jack tells about the substitute teacher; Jane about the neighboring girl's new coat; Daddy refers to the fact that Mr. Davis is complaining about the number of government questionnaires, and threatens to go out of business; Mother thinks that Bill is coming down with the grippe. The dining table is like a crossroads through which flows the news of the world as the respective members of the family see it and experience it. Much of this traffic of information and ideas flows swiftly and unobtrusively past, noticed more in its absence than in its presence; but it is there for all to see, hear, and assimilate.

2. The family meal constantly serves as a forum for the discussion of matters of interest and concern to the various members. Questions are asked, answered, or evaded in turn. The range of topics covered may be wide and varied, or monotonous in the recurrence of a few items of interest. Significant for all are the topics meticulously avoided as well as those assiduously discussed. The selection of topics for the family forum is in itself highly indicative.

Considered as a forum, the family meal may take several different forms. First, it may be quite formal. Questions are obviously posed, and discussion is patently stimulated. Second, the mealtime forum may be informal and spontaneous. This is much more frequently the case. Questions arise in the course of the family conversation, and the discussion proceeds out of the fullness of the heart rather than from the prodding of the parent. Topics tend to succeed each other in kaleidoscopic fashion, and the argumentation most often is both brief and direct. Finally, the family forum is often entirely incidental, scarcely recognized as a forum, in which views are expressed by a word, a silence, or a facial expression. Each family tends to have its own words, phrases, idioms, grimaces, signs, gestures, and the like, that are eloquent with meaning for all the members even if somewhat unintelligible to outsiders.

3. The family meal serves constantly as an evaluating conference, especially on the experiences, needs, and interests of the members. There is group discussion. Individual views are expressed, modified, and reconciled often as a family judgment, choice, decision, or attitude emerges.

Whether arrived at experimentally in democratic conference or imposed by an autocratic parent, these evaluations are absorbed on the basis of their emotional relations to the family, so that the line between the two is often indistinct.

As far as the induction of the child into the culture of the family is concerned, this evaluating process in family table talk serves two purposes which Dr. Holmes long ago suggested in his *Autocrat of the Breakfast Table* as requirements for satisfactory conversation. One is agreement upon the ultimate beliefs; the other is agreement upon the secondary questions that depend upon these ultimate beliefs. In other words, table talk not only inducts the child into the fundamental idea patterns and values of the family culture, but also, because of its concrete nature, clarifies the concrete applications which follow therefrom.

4. The family meal often functions as a substitute for classroom instruction. This happens in several ways. First, there are the well-known staged conversations—as a rule, for the benefit of the younger children. Says Mother: "I heard today about a little boy who ran across the railroad tracks"; to which Father replies quite seriously: "I am glad that my children don't do things like that." Or Mother refers to a visit from Mrs. Terry and her daughter, who was very polite. "Oh, yes," says Father, "you can tell that she is going to be quite an attractive young lady."

Again, "lessons" for class instruction may be introduced by one of the children. Helen, aged 12, tells of a neighbor's daughter, a proverbial and perennial scapegoat. Father, who is envious of the neighboring father's business success, expresses himself freely concerning the conduct of his neighbor's daughter. Mother, who dislikes the mother, is equally heated. Without understanding the motives involved, Helen is quite impressed. The neighboring girl's conduct *was* reprehensible.

Finally, many of the lessons learned at family meals are unplanned and spontaneous. "Katie kissed John," pipes up the well-known little brother, and in the wake of this disclosure there may follow either an eloquent silence, or a colorful discussion concerning kissing, John's intentions, John's job, Katie's prospects, and Mother's attitude toward early marriages. Such is perhaps the most common grist in the family round-the-table mill as it grinds, now slowly, now rapidly, but always exceeding fine.

5. Akin to these pedagogical functions are the stimulation and direction of the child's interests. If he has literary or artistic or mechanical interests, family table talk does much to stimulate or dampen their development. One is reminded again of Dr. Holmes: "Writing or printing is like shooting with a rifle; you may hit your reader's mind, or miss it— but talking is like playing at a mark with the pipe of an engine; if it is within reach, and you have time enough, you can't help hitting it."[9]

[9] Holmes, *op. cit.*, p. 30.

In many respects, family table talk may be likened to a university seminar on family culture that continues for a number of semesters. Both are similar in that there are designated reports (at times unscheduled), criticisms which vary with the prestige of the person making them, an exchange of points of view, and boredom for the more sophisticated members of the group. There is teaching, too, and inculcation of point of view; but these follow more from the give-and-take of informal discussion than from formal admonition. As is the case in most seminars, the discussion often rambles; assigned topics are disregarded; the procedure departs from the program which the seminar master (instructor or parent as the case may be) has devised; and seminar members leave the table before the discussion is concluded. Finally, the ultimate effects are, for the most part, subtly devious and intangible.

Common Illustrations of Culture Transmission Through Family Table Talk

1. Much of the family's sense of economic values, and the child's training in them, is indicated in the following sentences that appear repeatedly in the case material in the files of the Carter Foundation.

"Go easy on the butter, it's fifty cents a pound."

"Eggs are sixty cents a dozen now."

"Bill's shoes have to be soled."

"What, again? Why I just paid two dollars for soles three weeks ago."

"I think you ought to be ashamed to waste bread when thousands of Chinese children are starving."

"Mother, Mary soiled her new dress."

"Well, she had better take care of it. We can't buy another until after Christmas."

It is lack of the absorption of values of this kind, so constant in normal family life, which constitutes such a big gap in the training of the child reared in an institution.

2. Political attitudes crystallize early in children's minds as a by-product of table conversations such as the following.

BILL: Mother, Jack made $1.05 playing the machine down at Louey's store.

MOTHER: Jack had better get a job after school instead of playing the machines.

FATHER: Well, Jack comes by that honestly. His old man is a gambler if there ever was one.

OLDER SISTER: There must be money in it. I saw Mrs. Haggerty [Jackie's mother] and she had one of those new fur coats on.

MOTHER: Why don't they raid Louey's place? I saw in the paper about some judge saying they [the machines] were illegal.

FATHER: Guess the police are fixed.

(Bill looks at his father, apparently not wholly clear on what was implied.)

MOTHER: Bill, that shirt has got to go into the wash.

FATHER: Hank O'Brien was telling me yesterday that the police "take" on these machines ran into thousands of dollars a week. He said the lieutenant drove a Cadillac coupe to work, but parked it two blocks away from the station house.

Light seemed to dawn on Bill as he finished his dessert. The boy next door entered the house and Bill rushed from the table.

3. The multiple implications, for a child, of what may seem to the parents merely a routine conversation appears from the following.

FATHER: Well, I'm sorry, but I forgot to bring home some whiskey for the cocktails tomorrow night.

MOTHER: It's all right, I don't think we better serve cocktails.

FATHER: How come?

MOTHER: Well, the Pearsons are coming, and you know him.

SON: Is Dr. Pearson coming, Mother, is he? Is he, Mother?

MOTHER: Yes he is, and Mrs. Pearson is coming too.

DAUGHTER: Why don't we serve cocktails when Dr. Pearson comes?

MOTHER: Well, Dr. Pearson is a doctor, and he thinks cocktails aren't good for people. He says too many people have the cocktail habit.

SON: I like Dr. Pearson.

FATHER: Well, I like him, too. But this means a stupid party. (This to wife.)

MOTHER: I think I'll serve tomato juice. Do you think that will be all right? The red glasses will look nice on that black tray.

FATHER: If Pearson doesn't want to drink that's O.K. with me, but I don't see why that should spoil the party for the rest of us.

MOTHER: Well, I do think out of deference to his views we should have a dry dinner.

SON: I like Dr. Pearson. Is he a good doctor, mother?

This conversation carries these implications for the children: (a) A doctor whom I like does not approve of the social use of alcohol; (b) Father thinks a dry party is dull; (c) Mother sees her obligation as a hostess; (d) a difference of opinion is resolved with deference to a guest, regardless of the wishes of the host and hostess. There is no preaching, no moralizing. All the ideas are transmitted in a matter-of-fact way, incidental to a table conversation, chiefly between the parents, concerning a small dinner party.

Summary

1. It is important to understand the mechanism by which the child is inducted into the life of his family and by the family into the life of the larger society.

2. Part of the family's function in this respect is discharged through formal instruction. This was done more extensively earlier than it is today.

3. The greater part of the family's function is performed through indirection, that is, through a subtle conditioning process. This can best be studied by means of records of family life recorded in the first person.

4. Transcripts of family table talk are particularly valuable for purposes of scientific study.

5. Family table talk is a form of family interaction, important in the identification of personality roles and the development of personality traits.

6. The culture-transmitting function of the family operates with effectiveness during the family meal.

Chapter 14

Family Modes of Expression

Civilization is a verbal complex. The ability to use language and other symbols of communication is what differentiates man from the lower animals because it permits not only the communication of ideas and experience, but also their accumulation, first through memory and then through the recorded word. These symbols of communication are an element in the cultural systems of all societies, and the study of the child's induction into his culture must begin with, and to a large extent center about, their acquisition by him. Accordingly, this chapter is devoted, first, to a brief summary of the role of language in the development of society and the child; second, to the various forms of symbolic communication; and, third, to the role and functioning of family situations in the child's linguistic growth.

The Social Role of Language

Language is a prerequisite for the development of society and its culture. Its role is essentially twofold. First, it is the basis of the interactive relationships which are involved in social organization. As such, it serves many purposes—to give vent to feelings, to gratify the craving for sociability, and to bring about action on the part of others, as well as to convey thought to others. Similarity in modes of expression quickly becomes a bond which holds people together, and perhaps nothing else in the range of human experience is more important in the formation and cohesive strength of social groups. It is operative, not only at the level of national organization, but also in such groups as the family, a college fraternity, a labor union, a social club, and an underworld gang. "They speak the same language" is a common descriptive expression, and it means that within these units of organization there have developed peculiarities of speech which serve to distinguish them from other groups.

The second function of language is to serve as a vehicle for the transmission and preservation of culture. This statement, so fraught with sociological significance, yet fails to tell the whole story. Language is not just a series of objective symbols for the transmission of ideas; it becomes so indelibly associated with these ideas as to be virtually part of them. To express the content of a culture, words must be developed to identify it, and thus the two from the beginning are inextricably associated with each other. In short, words do not just develop parallel to experience; the two interpenetrate—so much so, that among many peoples there develops a virtual identity of the word and the thing which it represents. This is the basis of the magic of spells. Even in our contemporary culture, the line between the two is not sharply drawn. "It is this constant interplay between language and experience," writes Sapir, "which removes language from the cold status of such purely and simply symbolic systems as mathematical symbols of flag signalling."[1] Language is therefore both part and symbol of a culture, reflecting its essence in such a way that another language cannot serve as a substitute. Just as many aspects of a culture cannot be expressed in another language because no words exist to do so, similarly many words can be understood only by explaining them in their cultural setting. In other words, language and all communication are culturally colored.

One other fact concerning the social role of language should be noted, and that is the priority of its development. Because of the nature of its role, it is obvious that language must be the first aspect of the culture to take form, and that its perfection is a prerequisite to the development of the culture as a whole.

The role of language in the development of the child is similar to that in society, for society and the child are but two aspects of the same thing. Language is the key to the child's participation in group life and his introduction to the prevailing culture. In other words, the acquisition of language is necessary to set into motion the two conditioning factors of social interaction and cultural background which mold the personality of the child. With the child, then, as is the case in societal development, the linguistic acquisition comes first and consequently has a pervasive primary significance.

Selected Forms of Communication

The word *language* has been used thus far in a very general sense as though it comprehended the whole range of interhuman communication.

---

[1] Edward Sapir, "Language," *Encyclopaedia of the Social Sciences,* The Macmillan Company, New York, Vol. IX, p. 157. See also in this connection George C. Barker, "The Social Function of Language," *A Review of General Semantics,* Autumn, 1945, pp. 228–234; includes bibliography.

Literally speaking, this is not true, as the following brief description of the forms of communication that are significant in the early life of the child well reveals.

First, communication is not a human monopoly. Dogs bark, horses neigh, snakes hiss, and birds warble. Many of the sounds made by animals express needs, desires, or emotions. Similarly, infants utilize a variety of vocal signals, such as calls for food, gurgles of delight, or cries of discomfort. Chapin speaks of these as laryngeal cries which constitute a "halfway" or "pre-linguistic" stage of communication.[2]

Second are what might be called the nonsymbolic forms of communication, such as gestures, facial expressions, and the like. In part, these are an aspect of preverbal communication, utilized particularly by parents in their relations with children who have not yet acquired speech habits, and they must be regarded largely as physical expressions of emotions and their accompanying demands. There is, of course, a second aspect to these forms of communication, and that is their recognition as physical accompaniments of speech that serve the double purpose of releasing tension for the speaker and adding an expressive overtone for the listener.[3]

Most communication between humans, however, takes the form of articulate speech in which there is what Ogden calls "objective reference."[4] This is a distinctly human achievement, and involves the reduction of experience to familiar terms which come to have general acceptance. This common core of communication symbols constitutes the language of a people, and "phonetic language takes precedence over all other kinds of communicative symbolism, which are by comparison either substitutive, like writing, or merely supplementary, like the gesture accompanying speech."[5]

Family Modes of Expression

Turning now to the more specific aspect of child development, we can note three additional facts in the child's acquisition of his linguistic culture. First is the existence of a family version of the modes of expression. Early in the history of most societies, the total number of symbols and other forms of communication exceeds the needs and capacities of the average person, so that he comes to select from the common storehouse

[2] F. Stuart Chapin, *Cultural Change,* D. Appleton-Century Company, Inc., New York, 1928, pp. 35–36. See also Charles Morris, *Signs, Language and Behavior,* Prentice-Hall, Inc., New York, 1946.

[3] Herbert Blumer, "Social Attitudes and Nonsymbolic Interaction," *Journal of Educational Sociology,* May, 1936, pp. 515–523.

[4] C. K. Ogden, *The Meaning of Psychology,* Harper & Brothers, New York, 1926, p. 150.

[5] Sapir, *op. cit.,* p. 155.

of social forms in developing his own version. Most students of language point out that there is a common or composite, and an individual or family, version of these socially accepted forms of communication. The former consists of the more or less impersonal mass of symbols which reflect the accumulated experiences of society; the latter, of the selections and modifications of this common storehouse made by the individual or family unit which reflect the accumulated experience of the particular individual or family.

Second is the fact that this family version includes all the various forms of communication. In other words, a family not only selects its own words and gives them their distinctive meanings, but supplements them with its own system of gestures, facial expressions, and even laryngeal cries, as Chapin calls them. Moreover, none of these elements in the family version is simple. For example, Sapir, analyzing speech as a personality trait, identified at least five levels at which this form of expressive behavior develops. In addition to vocabulary, there are voice quality; voice dynamics, such as intonation, rhythm, and speed; pronunciation, where again there is an individual and a social pattern; and style, which is a facet of everyday speech just as it is of literature.[6] Similar complexities characterize other aspects of the family version.

Third—and this needs particular emphasis—is the fact that the child first learns the family version of the linguistic culture. This means that he comes to know his world first, and for a number of years, through the symbolic tools which the family gives it. In other words, he identifies things and ideas by means of the words which his family supplies, so that the two are interwoven from the start. This, it should be noted, is both a facilitating and a limiting process, for words not only enable us to grasp ideas but also limit our conception of them. Thus it happens that while the child is learning from his family the mediums of communication through which he comes to know his world, he is learning, too, the limitations and handicaps inherent in this family version. Plant emphasizes in particular the dangers inherent in these limitations. "Our people," he writes, "have learned to manipulate word and number symbols, rather than to understand the relation of these symbols to reality. Anyone who works much with adolescents knows their inability to use meaningfully the symbols which they have so carefully learned by rote."[7]

The child's acquisition of language has been studied in the past chiefly by psychologists and educators, who were interested primarily in the development of the child's verbal competencies, with particular emphasis upon the stages or age levels with regard to the numbers of words

[6] Edward Sapir, "Speech as a Personality Trait," *American Journal of Sociology,* May, 1927, pp. 892–905.
[7] James Plant, "Adolescents in Wartime," *Annals of the American Academy of Political and Social Science,* November, 1944, p. 5.

and the length of sentences used.[8] Our approach here is the situational one, in which the chief concern is with the variations in the situations in which the child acquires his expressive behavior. Studies of such family situations, made under the auspices of the William T. Carter Foundation at the University of Pennsylvania, include 51 case records of family modes of expression, and this material is drawn upon heavily in the remainder of this chapter.

Infant Conditioning Situations

The child's contacts with family modes of expression begin at birth. Particularly important is the mother's response to the child. Observations of the mother's communication behavior with her infant were made in 16 cases, all of them during the first 10 months of the child's life. The observed behavior of the mothers revealed three distinct communication patterns. The first was one chiefly of sounds. This type of mother for the most part coos, gurgles, laughs, talks, and makes other sounds to her baby. Her behavior, as she bathes or "changes" or feeds the infant, is of an outgoing, verbal kind. In the second pattern, the mother's communication behavior is much more one of facial expressions. She catches the child's eye, smiles, frowns, or makes grimaces of one kind or another. There are verbal accompaniments, to be sure; the difference in this re-

[8] The reader who is interested in this approach should consult, among others, the following references, several of which include extended bibliographies: John E. Anderson, "The Development of Spoken Language," *The 38th Yearbook of the National Society for the Study of Education,* The Public School Publishing Co., Bloomington, 1939; E. J. Day, "The Development of Language in Twins: I. A Comparison of Twins and Single Children," *Child Development,* March, 1932, pp. 179–199; M. S. Fisher, *Language Patterns of Preschool Children,* Child Development Monographs, Bureau of Publications, Teachers College, Columbia University, New York, 1934; D. McCarthy, "A Comparison of Children's Language in Different Situations and Its Relation to Personality Traits," *Journal of Genetic Psychology,* December, 1929, pp. 583–591; D. McCarthy, "Language Development," in C. Murchison (ed.), *A Handbook of Child Psychology,* rev. ed., Clark University Press, Worcester, 1933, pp. 329–373; D. McCarthy, *Language Development of the Preschool Child,* University of Minnesota Press, Minneapolis, 1930, No. 4; D. Van Alstyne, *The Environment of Three-Year-Old Children: Factors Related to Intelligence and Vocabulary Tests,* Teachers College, Columbia University, New York, 1929; H. M. Williams, M. L. McFarland, and M. F. Little, *Development of Language and Vocabulary in Young Children,* University of Iowa Press, Iowa City, 1937; E. J. Day, "The Development of Language in Twins: II. The Development of Twins: Their Resemblance and Differences," *Child Development,* March, 1932, pp. 298–316; Ruth Strang, *An Introduction to Child Study,* rev. ed., The Macmillan Company, New York, 1938; M. E. Smith, *An Investigation of the Development of the Sentence and the Extent of the Vocabulary in Young Children,* University of Iowa Press, Iowa City, 1926; Jean Piaget, *The Language and Thought of the Child,* Harcourt, Brace & Company, Inc., New York, 1926; J. R. Grant, "A Child's Vocabulary and Its Growth," *Pedagogical Seminary,* March, 1915, pp. 183–203; Paul H. Furfey, "The Sociological Implications of Substandard English," *American Catholic Sociological Review,* March, 1944; George A. Miller, *Language and Communication,* McGraw-Hill Book Company, Inc., New York, 1951.

spect between the first and second type of mother is wholly one of degree. In the third type, the mother is predominantly active and intent. The face is relatively immobile, action is swift and efficient, and there are fewer sound accompaniments as a rule.

Such are the differences in the earliest situations of expression in which infants find themselves. It is interesting to speculate on the significance of these first conditioning influences. This, however, falls more properly within the province of the psychiatrist; we merely report in the briefest form these first family modes of expression as evidenced in the mothers' linguistic or communication behavior. Our findings here, based on a small number of cases, are presented as highly tentative, and for suggestive purposes only.

Recently Dr. Leo Kanner, child psychiatrist, reported on an unusual type of mental illness affecting children of intelligent parents which may have some relation to the observations just presented. These young patients, nearly half of whom come from families represented in *Who's Who* or *American Men of Science,* or both, seem to live in a strange world of their own, completely without people. Hands that dress and care for them are just hands—objects not belonging to any person. Dr. Kanner raises the question as to whether the gifts of the parents might not have actually contributed to the illness of their children. For the most part, the members of these families are strongly preoccupied with abstractions of a scientific, literary, or artistic nature and are limited with regard to genuine interest in people.[9] This, it is obvious, would particularly characterize the treatment of the young infant.

Preverbal Expression in the Family

Another point to be emphasized is the importance, in the young child's development, of preverbal forms of expression within the family. A good deal of the earliest communication from adult to child consists of facial expressions—smiles, grimaces, frowns, and so on—with some sound accompaniment at times. Until the child has acquired some words, communication with adults must be achieved in this way. Not only moods but ideas and commands are thus transmitted. The parent frowns and utters sharp, staccato sounds; or the mother smiles or gurgles, and food follows. These differing sights and sounds come to define behavior for the child before words are understood. Moreover, this mode of expression is retained after words are used. The child observes the facial expressions of his parents for some years and associates pleasure, anger, happiness, irritation, or annoyance with them. He learns, too, that these are often advance notices of more aggressive behavior on the part of the parent.

[9] Leo Kanner, "Unaware of Others," *Science News Letter,* August 11, 1945, p. 92.

It is doubtful whether the role of facial modes of family expression for the child has been recognized adequately in the study of human behavior. Two of its implications seem particularly important. One is the fact that the child's earliest impressions of the parents are those of visual memory. This suggests that the parent has a "facial personality," and that this is the first personality which the child comes to know. A second implication is that these facial expressions and the accompanying sounds are chiefly expressive forms of emotions. Here, in other words, are to be found early conditioning factors in the child's emotional development, as well as the basis of the emotional accompaniment with conversation. Studies in the beginnings of gesture patterns might be made appropriately at this point.

The Range of Family Semantic Situations

From the time the child learns his first word until he learns to read, the acquisition of words is by ear, that is, by hearing the spoken word. This period covers about six years, and for children who show only slight interest in reading it remains the predominant one. During this period the family is the chief group in which the child acquires words, its relative importance depending upon the extent to which his contacts during the preschool period are confined to the family group. Transcripts of table talk for 35 families in which there were children, gathered through the facilities of the William T. Carter Foundation, permit certain tentative generalizations concerning family linguistic situations. They are presented here in summary form.

1. The amount of conversation per family per unit of time varies tremendously. At one extreme are several families who had almost no talk during a 40-minute dinner. There are long spells of silence. The air is one of marked restraint and formality. Conversation is confined almost wholly to requests for food. The parents are described as "tight-lipped" adults. At the other extreme are records of continuous table talk, often with several members of the family talking at the same time. In other words, the amount of talk to which a child is exposed within the family group varies tremendously.

2. There is a marked difference in the extent of the vocabulary used in the table talk of families. Some families use a very limited number of different words; others reveal what is commonly referred to as an excellent command of language, that is, they utilize a wide variety of words. To a considerable extent, these differences coincide with variations in the subject matter. Many family conversations are confined largely to trite, routine matters, or to personal and kinship affairs. The language here tends to be as drab and limited as the topics discussed. In varying degrees of contrast are the family conversations which cover many subjects. In

table talk records that are equal in the total number of words recorded, there are differences of more than 800 percent in the number of different words used.

3. The process of acquiring a vocabulary is twofold. One involves the learning of new words; the other, the association of meaning with them. Since words do not have a single correct meaning but have what Hayakawa calls "areas of meaning,"[10] the family's role in identifying the meaning of words for children during this early period is particularly important. A careful reading of the case material reveals considerable differences in the meaning given to the same words in different families. Some of these differences have to do with shades of meaning; others are so obviously incorrect that they reveal only the family's ignorance.

There are, however, other factors than knowledge and ignorance. Our material reveals highly significant family attitudes toward words and their meaning. In one of these families, with two children aged 7 and 9 years, there is a continuing attempt on the part of the parents to enlarge the children's semantic grasp. In the course of the family conversation, the children are asked if they understand the words used, or they interrupt to ask, for example, "Daddy what does *emphasize* mean?" Both the father and the mother in this family leave the dinner table to consult the dictionary, with a statement like: "Well, we might as well find out now." In contrast, there is the family where John, aged 13, used the word *preference*, only to have his father curse him and say, "Preference, Preference, I'll Preference you. You with your fancy words. You can't highhat me as long as I pay the bills." Then there is the family in which the child said, "I don't know what that means," to which the parent replied, "If I get the razor strap, you'll understand what I'm saying."

One particular aspect of this family interpretation of words calls for special comment. The child gets from the family not only the meaning of words, but also often a meaning charged with emotion. One semanticist refers to these as *loaded*[11] words. They are words that carry emotions as well as ideas, such as *dago, kike, hunkie, louse, crackpot,* and so on. And there are the words which families use to epitomize a set of conceptions or evaluations and which, transmitted to the child, become barriers to shield them from reality. *Capitalism* is synonymous with *exploitation; Communist* means a wild-eyed, unreasonable person; a *fascist* is a person who disagrees with you; *politics* explains any public or semipublic miscarriages of your ideas of fair play.

4. Family semantic situations vary on the basis of the role permitted to the child. Roughly speaking, families fall into two main types in this respect, differing from each other in degree. There are the child-centered

[10] S. I. Hayakawa, *Language in Action*, Harcourt, Brace & Company, Inc., New York, 1939, p. 71.
[11] *Ibid.*, p. 46.

and the adult-centered table conversations. In the former, the child or children dominate the conversation, or it centers around them. Adults direct the talk toward the children, toward subjects that interest them, and seek to stimulate their participation in the conversation. In contrast are the family conversations that tend characteristically to be adult-centered. Here subjects of adult interest only are discussed, child participation is ridiculed or dismissed as incidental prattle, or the children are admonished to "be quiet and let your elders speak." Differences of this kind presumably have a great deal to do with a child's acquisition of the linguistic culture.

5. One cannot but notice variations in the child's participation in the family table talk on the basis of interruptions by other members of the family group. Family life records show that some children are seldom allowed to finish a sentence. In some families this happens because another person, most often the mother, interrupts to say what the child is trying to say. In other cases, the child's attempts are lost in the general welter of the family's words. In one of these families, a 6-year-old girl was not once allowed to finish a sentence without interruption or verbal help. It is pertinent to raise the question of the relationship of such situations to stammering and other speech defects in the child. Certain kinds of stammer, for example, might well be regarded as a mechanism for holding the floor, conversationally speaking, and having time to think and formulate words. Even savants do this at times, when momentarily at a loss for words.

6. A careful study of family conversations reveals that the mother is the most important factor in the transmission of the child's linguistic culture. This is most apparent when family conversation records other than table talk are considered. In many families, particularly in the lower-income groups where she prepares and serves the meal, the mother often comes to the table after the others are seated, and she may leave it several times during a meal. Records of family table talk in such cases fail to do justice to her importance, especially with the younger children. Considering the situation as a whole in normal homes where the mother devotes herself largely or wholly to the job of homemaker, she converses more with the young child than anyone else. This relative importance of the mother in the child's major scholastic attainment, that is, learning a language, has never been fully assessed. One aspect of it will be discussed in the next chapter. The significance, at home, of the role of the mother who is gainfully employed many hours a day also needs to be examined.

The semantic situations which prevail in different families are presented here as of basic importance in the child's linguistic development. The number of words that a child can use, and use in their accepted meaning, determines in large measure his school progress, especially in the earlier years, and this initial success or failure speedily becomes cumulative in its effects. Again, there are those psychologists who emphasize the role of word equipment in intelligence measurement scores. This again would be particularly true in the earlier years. Finally, words are the mediums through which the child learns about his world. They are avenues by which the world we do not see comes to us. We interpret these reports on the basis of what the words in them mean to us. To the extent that our grasp of words is inadequate, our interpretation of this world is incorrect or incomplete. Moreover, this matter of interpretation is of much greater importance today than it used to be. The colonial child, and adult, could function satisfactorily with much more limited semantic equipment. Today, by contrast, we live in a global setting, mostly in areas of dense population, and with means of communication which deluge us with words. Our lives are filled with words, and to live satisfactorily we must know many words and be able to use them within the framework of social acceptance. Words are therefore a mechanism of social adjustment.

Levels of Language

Students of language often speak of language levels, using the term to indicate that language takes different forms at varying levels or strata in the larger society. Four such sets of language levels may be identified in the records of family conversations.

One of these results from an age-graded use of words in families in which there are children. At least three age levels can easily be distinguished. The first one tends to prevail when the children are quite young; much of the family conversation is at the "baby-talk" level. Later there develops a layer which extends up to the eleventh or twelfth year. During this period, the words customarily used in family conversation, especially by the children, are relatively simple, and are of the kind that seem most easily learned by ear. Still later, as the children progress in school and acquire many words through outside contacts, a third or youth level is obtained. In families where there are no children, another or wholly adult level can be identified.

Two problems suggest themselves in a further analysis of these age levels. One of these concerns the younger children. Such children tend to be ignored in these changes. The family seems to adjust its age level to the older children and to ignore the younger ones, especially if the age differential is not large. Questions about word meanings asked by the younger children are given less consideration, even in our most intelligent families. Apparently this is another example of how family situations differ for individual children in the same family.

A second problem implicit in this material grows out of the differences in children in their capacity to learn by ear. The child's acquisition of words by means of these recurring family conversations is wholly by ear. Some children's apprehension of words is visual: they must see what they hear; in others it is auricular: like Santayana, they must hear what they read.[12] What this means is that children who acquire new words by sight are generally handicapped during this period. One cannot but reflect, too, on the significance of this difference in the many lands and during the long years in which almost all learning took place by ear.

A second set of language levels is based on sex differences. There is a sex-appropriate language for boys and one for girls. The recorded conversations of all the families in which there are children bear witness to these differences and to the family's consciousness of them. "Little girls do not talk that way." "A lady never raises her voice." "He sounds like a boy all right." "Her voice will be a great asset to her." This sex distinction is evident at every turn—in the words used, habits of exclamation, intensity of expression, and stock phrases, as well as the subjects discussed. The child learns early and is reminded constantly that there is prestige in learning the sex-appropriate forms of expression.

The third set of language levels is based on the quality of expression as determined by social usage. It is in this sense that professional students of language usually speak of levels of language, and three such levels are customarily identified. The first is *informal English,* which is most generally encountered in the ordinary life of people of good social standing. "It is the typical language of an educated person going about his everyday business." The second is *formal English,* which is informal English "refined, tidied up," and "shorn of its looseness"; it partakes more of the written language of educated writers. Here one says "presently" instead of "soon," "prematurely" for "too soon," and "it is to be regretted" instead of "it's too bad." Finally, there is *vulgate English,* the everyday speech of less educated people, bristling with "vulgar" words and "bad grammar": "I ain't got none." "I seen it." "You'll see it wrote on the door."[13]

While the main distinctions between these types are quite clear, there exist marked variations from one family to another. There are children in families whose recorded conversation contains few grammatically correct sentences; at the other extreme are the families in which the parents are meticulous regarding the children's good English. These differences are a matter not only of the intelligence and verbal equipment of the parents, but also of their consciousness of and attitude toward the prob-

    [12] George Santayana, *Persons and Places,* Charles Scribner's Sons, New York, 1944, p. 156.

    [13] Leonard Bloomfield, *Language,* rev. ed., Henry Holt & Company, Inc., New York, 1940; Porter G. Perrin, *Writer's Guide and Index to English,* Scott, Foresman & Company, Chicago, 1942; H. L. Mencken, *The American Language,* 4th ed., A. A. Knopf, New York, 1936; Leonard Bloomfield, "Literature and Illiterate Speech," *American Speech,* 1927, pp. 432–439.

lem. Because of a certain informality that characterizes much of our life today, and the contact between children of all classes in the public-school system, many children in language-conscious families bring into their homes the vulgate language of their associates. Some of the comic strips do likewise, and with the prestige of the printed word. The case is similar in regard to slang, which may be regarded as a variety of the vulgate language that grows out of a desire for novelty or vivid emphasis. In our so-called better homes, there are constant efforts in family talk to correct or restrain these lapses. Although the number of our cases does not warrant a generalization, it appears that the higher the family's social level the more standardized its conversation will be at the level of informal or formal language.

Again one cannot but speculate on the significance of these language levels for the child's school progress. The schools use a relatively formalized type of English. The complex ideas and dignified subjects taught necessitate the use of this type; hence the schools naturally lay great emphasis upon proper linguistic behavior. Our records clearly identify the children who are reared in homes in which the language of the school is used, so that no linguistic difference or effort is involved in passing from one to the other. Similarly, one sees the handicap of the child, especially the younger child, who is reared in a family that uses vulgate English and who must constantly pass back and forth from one level to the other in school and at home. Many of these children live a kind of linguistic double life during their school years which cannot but be a handicap to their school progress. Subsequently many of them take jobs where vulgate English will suffice and where any other kind would be conspicuous. How stable the family form of speech may be is indicated by the question of one high-school senior to another: "Is ya done y're Greek yet?"

Language as a Social Index

The more one reads records of family talk, the more he sees language as an index of family social characteristics. Four aspects illustrative of the use of family language as a social index will be presented briefly.

OCCUPATION

Many occupational groups develop distinctive forms of expression. Some of these consist of "shop talk," which includes the lingo of the job, from psychiatry to panhandling; some are figures of speech suggested by the occupational experience. To the extent that an occupational group is isolated from other folks, its members come to use clearly marked varieties of speech. Thus, seafaring men speak their own type of nonstandard English; the hobo has his own speech forms; so do circus people, soldiers in foxholes, and professors who live in ivory towers.

Our records of family conversations are replete with illustrations of the role of the occupational background. This influence may be direct, i.e., through shop talk at home; it may determine the general or nonoccupational topics talked about; or it may dictate the imagery used. People naturally draw on their daily experience for the grist for their conversational mill. Moreover, our limited number of cases suggests that the role of such experience is greater at the lower occupational levels. The professional and executive types of families, many of whom live in suburban communities, make an apparently conscious effort to draw a line, as it were, between the job (office, plant, shop, etc.) and the home. Some parents pride themselves on not "bringing the office" into their family life. In such cases there is less infusion of occupational terminology than there would otherwise be.

RELIGION

It is rather surprising to find the number and variety of religion-identifying references in family conversation records. These are clearest in Roman Catholic and Jewish families. References are either direct, or in the imagery employed, or by implication. Religious holidays, religious observations in everyday life, and relations to other cultural groups are alluded to frequently. In two of our cases words are used that obviously have some religious implication but are meaningless to us. Requests for explanation are evaded. We are reminded here of Bloomfield's observation: "If the special (religious) group is at odds with the rest of the community, it may use its peculiarities of speech as a secret dialect, as do the English-speaking gypsies."[14]

GEOGRAPHICAL AREA

Linguistic diversities based on geographical sections have long been emphasized by students of language. Although most clearly revealed in audible speech, they appear also in written form in the use of identifying words and expressions. Even a person with an excellent mastery of the common language will keep some feature of the "dialect" of his place of origin and "with a certain coquetry flaunt" it before us. However, Jespersen contends that, generally speaking, the more commonplace a person is, the more will his language bear the stamp of the community in which he lives. Obviously, this will also hold true of the family unit.[15] These geographical speech marks appear repeatedly in our records. The family that uses a "lift" and listens to the "wireless" is obviously British. The 13-year-old miss who "is fixing to go" with "you-all" is manifestly not from Vermont. "The potatoes are all" identifies the upstate Pennsylvania Ger-

---

[14] Bloomfield, *Language*, p. 49.
[15] Otto Jespersen, *Language: Its Nature, Origin, and Development*, G. Allen and Unwin, London, 1922, pp. 75, 204.

man. The family who drives to "the end of the cement" came a year ago from the mountainous West. Words and phrases bearing the mark of geographical origin are on almost every page of this material.

SOCIAL CLASS

The phrase *social class* is used to denote general social status as indicated by plane of living, educational attainment, occupational status, and certain additional cultural attainments. Thus conceived, social class is the most striking line of cleavage in our language records. First are the distinctions in the words commonly used. At one level you go to "tea." You "eat supper" in some homes; in others you "are at dinner." At one level, you say, "Oh, I say"; at another you hear "Cheez" every fourth word. A girl may be a "goil," a "moll," a "cutie," a "lassie," or "Miss Helen." In different circles you are invited to "have one," to "have a skittle of suds," or to have a "shot on the run," or a "Scotch and soda."

Again, social classes differ markedly in the use of imagery in conversation, that is, in the degree to which figurative expressions are used. Families at the lower social levels seem much more figurative in their language, less rational, and less logical than other people. Our conclusions here are highly tentative, and reflect chiefly an impression.

We are on somewhat firmer ground with this case material in pointing out a certain class difference in the use of words. Families in the lower social classes show a tendency to slur words, to run them together, so that the combination of words and sounds comes to be the important thing. These families also tend toward the removal of irregularities in language, a process often referred to by language students as leveling. In families in the higher social strata, particularly among intellectual persons, every word tends to be used more in an individual sense. Sentences consist of individual units. They can be taken apart, put together again, and combined in different ways. The distinctions and subtleties in language are emphasized. In other words, as students of language put it, humble folk create language, but the upper classes develop, refine, and systematize it.[16]

Language obviously is a peculiarly revealing form of behavior. It identifies a person more effectively than almost any other form, because it is the result of slow accretion over long periods of time. In its existing version it is the combination of habits that are so deeply ingrained and so unconscious a form of expression as to permit of little consistent dissembling. Language habits not only are singularly persistent; they also reveal life's past content. Language is the verbal aspect of personality, announcing its source and history with every word. Language is behavior; speech, its vocal declaration.

[16] Further references to class differences in language will be made in Chap. 19, "The Child and the Class Structure."

Family Linguistic Systems

Reference to the social determinants of language must not blind us to the fact, so clearly brought out in these studies, that each family has its own linguistic system. The conclusions that follow are based not only on records of conversations but on a large number of supplementary interviews.

1. Each family has its own word peculiarities. These may be words or expressions in common use but with a distinctive family meaning or form, peculiar turns of expression, or words which are not used elsewhere and have meaning only for the family. Karen G., who has an M. A. degree and teaches English in the high school, still says "acrosst" for *across,* as does her entire family. Ruth always says "replentish" for *replenish,* as did her mother and her grandmother. The Powers family used the word *copistatic,* which means to them only: "Well, everything went well today." The Turners use: "We must have gotten that with cigarette coupons," to mean: "I can't understand how that damned thing got into this house (or room, or box)." In other words, each family has a kind of shorthand or dialect which often serves far more effectively than ordinary words to convey meaning, to give praise, or to apply the verbal lash. These word peculiarities are a product of the family history and derive their distinctive meaning from this fact.

2. Each family has its own terms for certain aspects of its life. The most obvious illustrations are the words or phrases that have to do with certain parts of the body, toilet habits, and toilet accessories. As a rule, a family develops these when the children are quite young, and they are retained as a matter of habit. But the list of instances which we have found are far more extensive. They have to do with going out at night, sleeping late on Sunday morning, family chores, social obligations, and many other aspects of life. Several of our families insist that much of this family terminology, especially that dealing with more intimate matters, needs to be studied on the basis of age levels; i.e., children have their own words which they communicate to each other at certain age levels just as adults have their words when they discuss these matters, and this age division coincides with parent-child groupings.[17]

3. Each family has its word taboos or word avoidances. In part, these are reflections of the social patterns, and include words pertaining to certain parts of the body and to certain of its functions; there are also religious taboos upon taking in vain the names of those worshiped or revered; even the names of certain animals may be taboo, usually because

[17] For an intresting case of age (i.e., parent-child) distinction, see Jerre Mangione, *Mount Allegro,* Houghton Mifflin Company, Boston, 1942, pp. 54–55.

of their application to individuals. Among the latter, our families identified such words as *bitch, snake, wolf,* etc.

Within the social pattern is the family pattern of word taboos. Our material emphasizes that these vary a great deal from one family to another, often with no consistency or underlying principle. One family speaks frankly about sex but strictly avoids religious words and names. A family that is openly and habitually profane punishes a younger member for the inadvertent use of the word *whore.* Any reference to bowel movements is labeled as distinctly in bad taste by several of our families who are not otherwise conspicuous for the "cleanliness" of their conversation. The word *bitch* is used normally by Philadelphia suburban families engaged in dog breeding. Another family permits no reference to alcoholic drinks or habits in any form. An adolescent in one family knew only the word *rum.* Beer was rum; whiskey was rum; wine was rum. And one drop of rum defiled. Finally, we cannot avoid mentioning the family in which the word *grandmother* was taboo. In this case, the husband's mother was a tall, statuesque blonde who was not at all willing to be thus reminded that her "salad" days had passed.

It is our observation that a large part of a family's distinctive pattern of word taboos is based on the aversions of the adults or on the marked prejudices of some one member of the family, so that the taboo is maintained as a matter of deference. A family does not use words as a rule which reminds its members of things they do not want to think about. These omissions are significant, then, in that they identify the family avoidances, based chiefly on the past experiences, or lack of experiences, of its adult members. They are usually deeply embedded and show strong emotional association.

Lengthy interviews with a number of families whose modes of expression were studied seem to warrant the following conclusions regarding these taboos. First, the word taboos which prevail in families are an important factor in determining the reaction of the members of the family to other people. We think that persons who violate these taboos are crude, uncouth, ill mannered. Or, at least, their violation arrests our attention in a less than favorable way. Second, children learn these taboos quite early, and by the time adolescence is reached they have become firmly fixed. Our families report various school difficulties growing out of the fact that children from different families observe varying word taboos, and teachers with still other taboo patterns become involved. Third, there arise problems of adjustment between persons who establish intimate and continuing relationships with each other, as in marriage, on the basis of their respective word taboos. "Rapport," one matron pointed out in the course of this study, "is verbal in part. These words taboos are much more important than behavior taboos, because so large a part of our social relationships is verbal." Finally, one is impressed by the fact that word taboos mean subject avoidances. This in turn results in areas of ignorance, at least as far as family instruction or insight is concerned. Betty Smith, the novelist, has reminded us recently that when children ask questions about sex the parents do not know how to answer them because they do not have the words, mutually known and understood, to do so.[18] The program of sex education might well begin with some concern with family modes of expression.

The study of family word taboos leaves one with a profound conviction of the importance of language as a social discipline and culture-transmitting device. Through the processes of word selection and word reaction, the family does much to introduce the child to the social, and, of course, the family, code. This substantiates the conclusions of Groves when he says: "Conventions are in large measure built into the child as attitudes toward words. Some are unseemly, and as a result emotional reactions similar to primitive taboos get tied to certain acts and ideas. Other words are encouraged, and the approval helps establish a favorable disposition toward a different set of behavior and thoughts. Much of this language fellowship of child and parent is carried on without self-consciousness."[19]

Family Patterns of Conversation

In reviewing the material on family conversations, one is impressed by the fact that most families show a specific totality or pattern which is characteristic of that particular family. These are spoken of here as family patterns of conversation, and although a phase of family linguistic systems they are reserved for separate comment. Summary types or classifications, based on a total of 82 cases, are presented briefly.

1. Family conversations may be subjective or objective. By the former are meant those cases in which the conversations are family-centered. That is, the family talks chiefly about itself, its experiences, its achievements, its misfortunes, and its problems. In contrast are those families in which the talk centers largely upon matters outside the family. This group may be divided into two subgroups: (a) those who talk chiefly about other people—friends, enemies, relatives, business or work associates, or public personages; and (b) those who talk about objects—airplanes, tanks, automobiles, books, trucks, and the like.

2. Family conversations may be summarized as analytical or evalu-

---

[18] Betty Smith, *A Tree Grows in Brooklyn*, Harper & Brothers, New York, 1943, p. 223. See also, Cyril Bibby, *Sex Education: A Guide for Parents, Teachers, and Youth Leaders*, Emerson Books, Inc., New York, 1946.

[19] Ernest R. Groves, *The Family and Its Social Functions*, J. B. Lippincott Company, Philadelphia, 1940, p. 152.

ating. The first type consists of conversations in which the general approach is the analysis of a person, object, or event. There are description, analysis, and interpretation. The emphasis is chiefly upon telling about the subject at hand. The contrasting type is concerned with judgment; motives are imputed, purposes and results are evaluated. The conclusions are chiefly (in this study) critical, depreciatory, and denunciatory. These are the families that are "always talking about somebody." In some of the families studied, whose social ambitions were strong, the overwhelming part of the conversation is devoted to the depreciation of the social clique or group they hope to enter.

3. A rather distinctive type of family conversation is the sharp, rapier-like kind. Here the emphasis is upon sharpness and brilliance of execution. It may take the form of making wisecracks, being smart-alecky, or being keenly clever. In any event, the main consideration is fast, sparkling, adroit expression. Further varieties within this type may be identified. In some cases, statements are made as if to attract attention primarily to the speaker. Talk is a kind of exhibitionism or showmanship. It is as though the speaker sought to give a clever performance rather than attempted to convey a thought. He is interested in juggling deftly, no matter whether the balls he juggles are of tinsel or of gold. In some cases there is a sadistic performance. Sometimes a habitual phrase is clearly indicative of a sadistic intent. For example, one adult in the study habitually used the phrase, "So I stuck my knife in there and turned it around to see how they would squirm," to indicate his participation in a discussion. The main purpose is apparently to hurt. Here one finds the cutting speech, the stinging remark. You say something to put someone in his place. In the case of three persons included in this study, more than nine out of every ten remarks recorded for them were of this kind.

4. Family patterns of conversation vary greatly in regard to their general tonal quality. At one extreme are conversations which abound with "snarl words," and much of the talk consists of spasmodically throwing verbal bites at each other as one throws sticks at a dog. There are loud noises, yelling, wrangling, constant interruptions, so that the whole performance partakes of the nature of static on the radio. At the other extreme are the family conversations which suggest, by way of contrast, the Sunday afternoon symphony. A quiet and polite exchange of ideas goes on, "purr words" dominate, there is politeness and consideration when disagreement arises. People are allowed to finish a sentence. Even the children are accorded these courtesies.

The topics of conversation in these 82 families show a rich variety, but the topics discussed by any one family seem as a rule rather limited. In other words, most families talk habitually about a few things. One cannot escape the conviction that the range is determined not so much by the intellectual capacities of the persons involved as by their predilections. For example, some of the highly intelligent families devote their conversational prowess to a very limited number of topics which are discussed both *ad infinitum* and *ad nauseam*. Some families, for example, talk constantly about the neighbors' children; others, about the boss; others, about the movies. It is interesting to note to what extent certain topics of conversation become a matter of habit, a fact which has great meaning for the child and his induction into the culture.

When one notes these and other characteristics of family conversations, he cannot but be impressed with the distinctness of the pattern in any individual family. Family conversation is, from one point of view, a series of habits—in the things that are talked about, how they are discussed, the attitudes which prevail, the kinds of words that are used, and the degree of conversational etiquette reciprocally accorded.

Some Characteristics of Speech

Language is above all a matter of sound. Through the long ages of man's past, most people were illiterate, and to them language was exclusively a vocal form of expression. Today, the recorded form of language is used increasingly; nevertheless, the most frequently used form remains the spoken word. Although this study was concerned chiefly with written records of family conversations, some notes were made regarding certain characteristics of speech which seemed of importance to the child and his induction into the culture.[20]

PRONUNCIATION

Through commonly accepted usage and standard works of reference, society establishes certain forms of word pronunciation. Departures from these accepted forms, more than those due to individual variations in voice timbre, serve to attract attention. These have been noted in this study. They occur constantly, and with marked frequency in certain families. Some of the errors recorded are slight, so that the meaning is still clear; in other cases, families use words which leave one wholly at a loss to understand what is meant. Further observations suggest two conclusions. First, families in which the adults aspire to better speech (and to a higher social position) offend frequently in this respect. Apparently, they see words in print and make an effort to use them; and since they have not been learned by ear, they are mispronounced. The self-educated are particularly apt to mispronounce words. Second, one notes repeatedly a sensitiveness to having one's pronunciation corrected. These records reveal several cases of considerable tension between members of families that resulted from attempted corrections.

[20] See Edward Sapir, "Speech as a Personality Trait," pp. 892–906, for reference to such characteristics.

Considering the mispronunciations noted as a whole, we are impressed with two further facts. First is their significance for children in their educational progress, particularly in its early stages before the school can reorient the use of vocabulary; the second is the significance of these word mistakes in social relationships. Consistent or conspicuous mispronunciation of words identifies the speaker as ignorant or uncouth, or results in his being misunderstood or misunderstanding others. The old saying, "She looked like a lady until she opened her mouth," is at least partially applicable here. The relationship between security in word pronunciation and a sense of personality security is for the psychiatrist to determine.

ACCENT

There is a stress or increased force given to certain syllables in speaking which, together with certain habits of pronunciation, is spoken of here as accent. This is an easily noticeable characteristic of speech in those whose accents differ from that of the observer. Methods for its scientific recording and analysis are rather undeveloped. Although a number of observations were made, the conclusions presented here are highly tentative. It appears that accent is largely a matter of geographical or national origin and of social and educational status, and to a lesser extent a family and individual product. One is particularly impressed by the fact that, in the heterogeneous life of America, with its diverse nationality and linguistic groups, accent is peculiarly indicative of social type. This latter phrase is used to mean the constructs which the group arrives at by selecting and abstracting accentuated forms of conduct displayed by some of its members and having specific connotations in terms of interests, concerns, and dispositions of the group.[21]

GESTURES

This term is used here to mean bodily accompaniments of speech used for purposes of emphasis or explanation. Gestures accompany all speech; in kind and amount they differ with the individual speaker, but to a large extent they are governed by social convention. Students have regarded gesture generally as a culturally patterned development, that is, certain gestures characterize entire groups. Thus Child reports, "Gestures are an important part of the Italian's equipment for communication. They are used a great deal as an accessory to ordinary conversation, especially when speech is excited or emphatic. There are also a number of special gestures which convey a specific meaning by themselves."[22] In our civilization, people of the privileged class gesticulate least.

[21] Samuel Strong, "Social Types in a Minority Group," *American Journal of Sociology*, March, 1943, pp. 563–573.

[22] Irvin L. Child, *Italian or American?* Yale University Press, New Haven, 1943, pp. 22–23.

Observations made in the course of this study suggest that there is also a family pattern of gestures. Our notes indicate repeated instances of some habitual distinctive use of the hands or body by several members of the same family. These similarities occur generally between parent and child and at times are so identical as to be almost uncanny. The use of gestures strikes one in particular as a kind of barometer of nervous output in conversation. Gestures are accompanied usually by a heightened or intensified expression of energy. This multiple form of expression, with its increased demands upon nervous energy, would seem to be of great significance in relation to the other forms of expenditure of energy by the individual.

Summary

1. Language is a distinct form of culture and needs to be considered separately as such.

2. Language is a mechanism or medium for social interaction and for the transmission of all forms of culture. It is a symbolic technique enabling communication between individuals.

3. Modes of expression constitute a distinctive aspect of family situations. Each family has its own words, signs, gestures, pet phrases, humorous references, special words of condemnation, favorite topics, and characteristic forms of expression.

4. Language is behavior, much like manners or dress, whose standards and requirements vary on the basis of class, origin, occupation, activities, and the like.

5. Language, learned early and constantly associated with every other aspect of culture, comes in a peculiar way to serve as a symbol of home, family, class, state, status, and country. This explains why, as Lowie puts it, "Nowhere is the difference between tweedledum and tweedledee a more powerful barrier than in language." Students of behavior, and of international relations, will do well to remember this.

Chapter 15

The Bilingual Child

Bilingualism, or the use of two languages by the same person, is both a very old and a very common phenomenon, existing wherever relationships develop between peoples who speak different languages. The definite form which it takes, however, and the social implications that result, vary a great deal from one country to another; in the United States it emerges as an aftermath of immigration, with the resultant presence of minority groups who, for several generations at least, continue to use their traditional language. As a result, the children learn first the family language, and then later, the use of English. This makes the problem of bilingualism in the United States essentially a phase of the personality development of children, and to it the present chapter is devoted. Attention is directed, first, to the data on bilingualism; second, to a brief summary of the present emphases and current conclusions in the literature on the bilingual child; and, third, to the problems of the bilingual as a person. This last part is based on a study of original case material.

Data on Bilingualism in the United States

Almost one out of every five white persons in the United States grew up in a home in which some language other than English was the principal one spoken during the years of earliest childhood. A total of 21,-996,240 such persons are revealed by the U.S. Census report, *Mother Tongue*, for 1940. This is equal to 18.6 percent of our total white population, to 19.1 percent of the white population who reported mother tongue statistics, and to 16.7 percent of our total population in 1940. Since the overwhelming proportion of these individuals also learned to speak English and use it some extent, the foregoing data serve to identify the approximate extent of bilingualism in the United States. It will be obvious at once that some of the persons included can speak more than two languages; hence the term *bilingual* is not wholly correct. In most cases, however, it is sufficiently accurate to warrant its use for purposes of ordinary discussion.

There are eight linguistic groups which account for 17,646,600, or 80.2 per cent, of all those whose mother tongue was other than English. Table 2 presents these groups, the total for each group, and the percentage this constitutes of the total white population.

TABLE 2. Major Linguistic Groups, by Totals, and Percentage
of Total White Population

Linguistic Group	Total Number	Percentage of Total White Population
German	4,949,780	4.2
Italian	3,766,820	3.2
Polish	2,416,320	2.0
Spanish	1,861,400	1.6
Yiddish	1,751,100	1.5
French	1,412,060	1.2
Swedish	830,900	0.7
Norwegian	658,220	0.6
Total	17,646,600	15.0

The 1940 enumeration of mother tongue statistics is unique in that it includes not only persons of foreign white stock but also native-born whites of native-born white parentage. This complete nativity classification throws some light on the fact of cultural, and particularly linguistic, persistence. Of the 21,996,240 individuals reported as reared in other than English-speaking homes, 8,354,700 were foreign. This is 38 percent of the total bilingual, and 75.2 percent of the foreign-born, population. Another 10,712,480 were native-born of foreign or mixed parents; this is 48.7 percent of the bilinguals and 46.3 percent of this nativity class. Finally, 2,929,060 were native-born whites of native-born white parentage. This is 13.3 percent of the bilinguals and 3.5 per cent of this nativity class in the population. These last data are particularly significant as evidence of cultural persistence, as is also the national origin of the bilinguals in this nativity class. Three linguistic groups account for three-fourths (73.9 percent) of the total. These three are 925,040 of German origin, 718,980 of Spanish origin, and 518,780 descended from French ancestors. As the census authorities point out, these three represent, in the main, the descendants of original settlers in certain areas, such as the Germans in Pennsylvania, the French in Louisiana, and the Spanish in New Mexico.

The bilingual population is concentrated in certain regions in the United States, as are also the predominating linguistic elements. For the South, the percentage is 6.3 of the total white population; in the West, it is 18.3; in the North, it is 23.9. Persons whose mother tongue is Norwegian predominate among bilinguals in the North Central States; the French, in New England and Louisiana; the Italians, in New Jersey and New York; a majority of those whose mother tongue is Yiddish are residents of New York.

Of the total number of bilinguals, a total of 6,250,500 were enumerated as under 25 years of age. This equals more than a quarter (28.4 percent) of the bilingual population, and amounts to approximately one-eighth (12.7 percent) of the total white population who reported language data.

Current Emphases and Conclusions in the Literature on the Bilingual Child

The bilingual child and his problems have been studied for the most part by psychologists and educators, who have concerned themselves chiefly with the relationship of bilingualism to (1) the mental development of the child, (2) his school achievements, (3) the development of speech difficulties, and (4) certain aspects of personality development. Current conclusions on these four points will be presented in summary form.[1]

BILINGUALISM AND MENTAL DEVELOPMENT

The literature on the mental development of the bilingual child is voluminous, and tells chiefly the results of intelligence tests given to comparable groups of bilingual and monoglot children. After examining nearly 100 investigations in this country and abroad, Arsenian draws the following conclusions:

a. Bilingual children as compared with monoglot children of the same age and environment are neither retarded nor accelerated in their mental development. This is particularly evident on the basis of nonlanguage tests of intelligence.

b. When verbal tests are used, bilingual children fall short of their monoglot contemporaries, and the disparity increases as the content of the test becomes more verbal.

c. The older the bilingual child and the higher his level of educational attainment, the smaller is the discrepancy.

d. The verbal intelligence tests show that the apparent retardation of bilingual children varies from place to place and from group to group. Bilingual children in urban areas show less or no retardation.[2]

[1] An excellent summary of the literature on bilingualism is presented by Seth Arsenian under the title, "Bilingualism in the Post-War World," in the *Psychological Bulletin*, February, 1945, pp. 65–86. The article includes a bibliography of 46 selected references.

[2] Arsenian, *op. cit.*, pp. 73–74.

BILINGUALISM AND SCHOOL ACHIEVEMENT

Investigators are almost unanimous in their conclusions regarding the lower school performance of the bilingual child. This deficiency is most apparent in verbal studies, such as reading and history, but tends to disappear in nonverbal subjects, such as arithmetic and science. Also, it decreases with succeeding grades; thus it is most marked at the elementary-school level, at the high-school level the difference is slight, and during the college years it disappears altogether.

BILINGUALISM AND SPEECH DEFECTS

Travis, Johnson, and Shover claim that the chances are 98 to 100 that the bilingual child will stutter more than the monoglot.[3] The Blantons report many bad cases of stuttering which involved bilingualism,[4] but Arsenian thinks that no definite conclusions can be deduced from the studies thus far available.

BILINGUALISM AND PERSONAL ADJUSTMENT

Since the two languages involved in bilingualism are, in the United States, not of equal prestige, the question arises concerning the relation of bilingualism to personal adjustment. Spoerl equated two groups of college freshmen on mental ability, age, sex, and socioeconomic status, and then studied the personal and social adjustment of the two groups; he presents the following findings:

Our conclusion, then, is that the emotional maladjustment of the bilingual student, insofar as it expresses itself in terms of reactions to social frustration, and particularly in terms of family disharmony, is the result of the culture conflict to which the native-born children of immigrants are subjected. But this culture conflict is complicated by the bilingual environment. Thus it is that bilingualism enters into the situation, not in its intrapersonal aspects, but rather as a symbol of one of the environmental factors converging upon the second generation. Most of the emotional maladjustment of the bilingual student is environmentally determined, and is not the result of mental conflict engendered by the complexities of thinking or speaking in two languages. This is true of the social maladjustment, the lack of harmony in the home situation, and the lack of identification with the present environment (coupled with a rejection of the cultural background of the parents), all of which tends to characterize college students who are bilingual.[5]

[3] L. E. Travis, W. Johnson, and J. Shover, "The Relation of Bilingualism to Stuttering," *Journal of Speech Disorders*, 1937, pp. 185–189.
[4] M. G. Blanton and S. Blanton, *Speech Training for Children*, D. Appleton-Century Company, Inc., New York, 1919.
[5] D. T. Spoerl, "Bilinguality and Emotional Adjustment," *Journal of Abnormal and Social Psychology*, January, 1943, pp. 56–57.

The Bilingual as a Person

A careful reading of the literature on bilingualism suggests three further facts. First, its chief significance probably is in the realm of the social development of the person, with particular reference to the emotional reaction of the bilingual and the effect of the "other" language vestiges upon his relations with his fellows. Second, it is when the bilingual is young that the problem is most important, which means also that it is the family situations that are most fraught with significance. Third, it is this relation of bilingualism to personality development, and the nature of the situational approach to the problem, which have been least investigated. As Arsenian puts it, "There are many speculative claims but little experimental evidence."[6] The following inductive study is therefore presented as a possible contribution to this field, and with the hope of suggesting some of the situational aspects which need to be investigated.

METHODOLOGICAL NOTE

This study is based upon 17 case documents. Some of them are self-studies furnished by bilinguals. These individuals are highly intelligent, with some training in personal and social observation, and were selected because they seemed to show evidence of a certain objectivity of insight into their own personality development. A second group of documents was obtained from members of the subjects' families, such as wife, niece, or cousin, who had an opportunity for continued close association with the subjects and who had some training in obtaining and recording social data. A third group of documents was obtained and recorded on the basis of repeated interviews in which, once the project had been explained, the subjects were encouraged to talk along the lines of the nondirective method.[7] Finally, several personal documents, already published, which lent themselves to the purposes of this study, were utilized. This case material was gathered during the years 1941–1945.

Reference should be made to the relative difficulties encountered in obtaining valid case material. There were three groups of adult bilinguals with whom the study was discussed and from whom no satisfactory case material was secured. One group appeared reluctant to give information, at least with any degree of frankness. Feelings of shame or embarrassment were manifest, or a certain degree of impatience, as though the earlier linguistic experience was now forgotten and had better remain so. A second group, quite willing to discuss the study and give information,

[6] Arsenian, *op. cit.*, p. 78.
[7] Carl R. Rogers, "The Nondirective Method as a Technique for Social Research," *American Journal of Sociology*, January, 1945, pp. 279–284.

seemed to reflect an almost aggressive pride in their linguistic background. These were persons who had utilized their bilingual equipment
in an occupational way, and were given to emphasize only the educational and cultural values of facility in more than one language. They
showed little or no interest in the personality problems involved. The
third group, equally willing to offer testimony, reflected an attitude
which can be understood only when viewed in terms of a life span. These
were adults who, early in life, either as immigrants or as their descendants, experienced the immigrant's sense of inferiority about many things
including his language, but who now, after becoming established in life,
had again become conscious, and perhaps proud, of their mother tongue.
None of these individuals is included in the 17 cases utilized in this study,
but their distinguishing attitudes serve to suggest some personality patterns found among bilinguals.

The total number of cases is not large enough to make any statistical
summary or to draw any definite conclusions. This study is meant only to
be suggestive, with the possible hope of stimulating further research in
the general area of investigation.

Two Important Variables

From the material gathered, it is obvious that the nature and importance of the problems identified, as well as of the factors involved, vary
from place to place and from group to group. Two basic variables are
easily apparent. First is the ecological setting of the bilingual. This has to
do principally with the area in which he is considered, and with reference
mainly to the normalcy or unusualness of his bilingualism. For example,
to be bilingual in the heart of the Pennsylvania German belt is to be what
the great bulk of the people are. The bilingual is the normal person, operating with individuals who are also bilingual. The same is true in the
French Acadian settlements in Louisiana and in Spanish settlements in
New Mexico. It is the vogue to be bilingual. This is quite different from
being bilingual in an area which is largely, or almost wholly, unilingual.

A special phase of the ecological setting of the individual, particularly
significant in this connection, obtains in our large urban centers with their
heterogeneous populations. Here there exist, not only large and populous
areas in which one language predominates, but sections in which the
inevitable mixture of linguistic groups results in areas where the particular linguistic situation creates its own norms of expression. For example, in
some areas of our large cities the young people deliberately refrain from
speaking an "unmixed" English lest their "crowd" accuse them of being
"high-hat."

The second basic variable is the social attitude toward the other language. This grows out of the first variable but has in it elements of differ-

ence. The attitude toward a language cannot be separated from the attitude toward the people whose language it is. The upper classes develop the socially accepted medium of speech, so deviations from it appear also as deviations from an upper-class status. What is the social status of the non-English tongue? How are the linguistic differences related to class distinctions? Moreover, the language of minority groups, when they have their own distinctive language, becomes an index of minority group status. In a rapidly status-changing society different phases of the problem become very important.

Impact upon Family Relations

In all these cases, there are references to the differences that developed within the family in the acquisition and use of English. The basic facts are that the different members learned to utilize the second language at differing times and with unequal skills. The pattern of sequence is similar in most cases—the children learn it first, then the father, and last, and at times least, the mother. Some families showed important differences between the siblings, and in at least one case this proved rather troublesome in sibling relationships. Two of the cases, typical of many others, reveal situations in which English-speaking parents of foreign stock taught the "family language" to the child first, and followed this with large doses of English before the school years arrived.

Several of these cases refer to the habit of bilingual conversations in the home, the parent utilizing the non-English language and the child answering in English. At times this seems to have happened with no manifestation of tension, as a concession to the parents; but others emphasize that these two-way conversations involved differences of attitudes toward the languages used, and were attended by feelings of tension, embarrassment, or bitterness.

The significance of these linguistic differences for relationships within the family seems to be much influenced by the parental reactions to them. Where the acquisition of the new language is hailed as a new educational experience in which all the members share, there is far less possibility of tension. But where the parents forbid, discourage, or frown upon the children's efforts, the results are quite different. Mangione describes his mother's reaction to his interest in the non-use of Italian: "My mother took no notice of such childish snobbery. As long as I remained under her jurisdiction she continued to cling to her policy of restricting the family language to Italian. 'I might as well not have my children if I can't talk with them,' she argued. She considered it sinful for relatives to permit their children to speak a language which the entire family could not speak fluently, and claimed that if she were to cast aside Italian, the language of her forebears, it would be like renouncing her own flesh and blood."[8] The attitude of the mother is particularly significant because of her role as the pivotal center of the home, and her constant and continuing contacts with the children.

A careful reading of this case material seems to warrant the following conclusions: (1) In all cases, there is an awareness of the language problem on the part of all members of the family, and a certain preoccupation with it. This is particularly obvious during the period when the children are growing up. (2) Under the most fortunate circumstances, the bilingual situation appears to involve a nervous strain, a certain added effort to shift gears, as it were, from one linguistic level to another. It adds another dimension to family relationships. (3) Children sense that their parents are different from other parents. This precipitates early a certain objectivity in attitude toward the parent, a comparative appraisal, as it were. This was rather clearly revealed in some of our interviews. (4) The effect of the linguistic difference appears to be more marked when family relationships are otherwise intimate and limited and continuing. The size of the family is important: the smaller the family the more significant the linguistic difference. (5) In most cases, the children early developed definite feelings of resentment against the parents because of the latters' inability or unwillingness to keep pace with them in the use of English. At times this takes the form of contempt for the parents' seeming inability, or there is impatience with the slow rate of progress and the parents' lack of interest; often what seems most marked is a general irritation about the situation as a whole. In two of the cases studied, strong feelings of hatred against the parents developed. (6) Several of the cases emphasize that early in life the subjects came to practice an avoidance technique, avoiding conversation with their parents within the home, avoiding their parents away from home, or both. The child who rejects the parental language rejects, as it were, the parent who speaks it. "I remember I used to cross the street to avoid meeting up with my father or mother. Neither had good eyesight, and I would be on the alert whenever I got anywhere near to places where I might see them. Once mother came to school. I saw her in the hallway between classes and ducked out the back door. I had rather a hard time explaining my sudden absence on that day." (7) Almost without exception, the parents and grandparents seem to have no appreciation of the importance of the foreign-language problem to the children, other than its possible effects upon the rate of educational progress. Their own identification with their language is so close that they cannot understand their own child's rejection of it. Especially was this so in two of these cases in which the other language was French. "What do you mean," shouted the regal grandmother, "Jack doesn't want to speak the language which is the standard of culture the

[8] Jerre Mangione, *Mount Allegro*, Houghton Mifflin Company, Boston, 1942, p. 53.

world over?" But Jack's reply was: "The fellows say: 'that's a heck of a language.'"[9]

Bilingualism and Child Development

The acquisition of a language is referred to commonly as the child's outstanding intellectual achievement. The major part of this achievement occurs during the years of early childhood. This is also the period of primary personality development. It seems, then, both inevitable and obvious that the nature of the linguistic development should have meaning for the processes of personality formation. Three aspects of this appeared in the course of this study.

First is the fact of the double linguistic task. The acquisition of two languages and of facility in their use tremendously increases the task imposed upon the child. It is a double task, with the added strain of shifting from one to the other. This the child has to carry when other children with whom he competes face the simpler task of acquiring only one language. Only one of these cases refers explicitly to this, but we sensed it in other subjects in their constant references to their consciousness of the language problem as children; in their reiterated emphasis that it did not interfere with the learning process, "at least not much"; in their repeated allusions to their conscious determination to use one rather than the other language. In other words, the bilingual child has to face a double task, make an extra effort, place himself under a double strain, merely to gain the means of ordinary communication with his fellows. As a rule, this must be done without sympathetic help from his companions and his family— sometimes, without help from his teachers.

Second is the role of bilingualism in the development of confidence in the self. The development of self-confidence is a phase of the process of growing up. It has its time dimension, measured in terms of the first two or three decades of life. In this process, the ability to express oneself adequately and acceptably is of great importance. Here again the bilingual child and youth are apt to experience a handicap. The cases studied indicate this, both by direct statement and through inference. Especially is this true when the "other" language is one that is not socially acceptable. Consciousness of a foreign accent is particularly serious in the adolescent stage, with its strong pull of loyalties to groups other than the family. The bilingual background marks the adolescent as different from other members of these groups. "The difference that pained me most was that of language, probably because I was aware of it most often. Child that I was, I would feel terribly embarrassed whenever my mother called to me in Italian while I was playing on the street, with all

[9] The conclusions presented here may be compared with the point of view presented by Spoerl in *op. cit.*, pp. 35–57.

my playmates there to listen; or when she was buying clothes for me and
would wrangle in broken English with the salesmen about the price."[10]
Awkwardness of expression due to bilingualism, or the audible identification of the accent, imposes additional difficulties in the development of
confidence in the self.

Third, and akin to this, is the social ridicule which children give to the
linguistic variant. Children can be diabolically cruel to each other, and
linguistic differences are often magnified by them to ridicule their companions. "W. Somerset Maugham was born and reared in France. 'He
knew French before he knew English, and when he went to England
after the death of his father to live with a clergyman uncle, the vicar of
Whitstable, he became something of a butt at school because of his frequent mispronunciation of English words. He still remembers the roar of
laughter that greeted him when he read the phrase "unstable as water"
as though "unstable" rhymed with "Dunstable."

"'He had a pronounced stammer, which persists to this day, though in
a far less severe form.'"[11]

The Development of Protective Devices

Most of the persons included in this study refer, in one way or another,
to the development of behavior patterns whose purpose it was to protect
them from the consequences of their bilingualism. These are identified as
protective devices. Four are selected for brief characterization.

RESTRAINED MANNER OF SPEAKING

Robert says that he sensed very early in his school career the social attitude
toward his "other" language. He set himself consciously and persistently to
overcome his accent. He would spend hours reading aloud to himself, and he
would repeat passages, trying all the while to make his voice sound as much as
possible like that of one of his teachers. As time went on, he came to learn that
when he spoke slowly and softly, no or little accent was discernible. It was only
when he became excited, spoke rapidly or angrily, that he betrayed himself.
From his twelfth to his twenty-third year, Robert says that his conscious daily
effort was to speak in a quiet, restrained manner. At that time, he was married.
His wife seems to have been attracted to him in particular because of these
traits.

INCONSPICUOUS BEHAVIOR

When Peter was a boy, there were constant references to his "other" language. Many of these were references of ridicule. Peter was much ashamed of
his lapses into his family language and of his accent. He found that the more
inconspicuous he made himself, the fewer the times when the unwelcome label

[10] Mangione, *op. cit.*, p. 51.
[11] Hamilton Basso, "Profiles," *The New Yorker,* January 6, 1945, p. 28.

was attached to him. Peter says he became quiet and meek, as a result. He remembers that he permitted other boys to impose upon him.

HOME AVOIDANCE

"Another thing I remember," writes John, "is that I brought none of my school friends to my home, because the few times I did, my parents seemed to go out of their way to display their native speech and mannerisms to my friends. What social life I had from my twelfth to my twentieth year was away from home, and most of it was with boys, who were less prone to remind me of my background. During those years, how well do I remember that every friendly relationship I had was manipulated so that I need not bring my companions to my home. One way in which I managed this was to choose all my friends in another part of the city than where I lived."

METICULOUS ENGLISH

All of these cases show a deep consciousness of the importance of language and of the manner of speech. All reveal a compensatory concern with correctness of expression.

Howard tells how, from his first year in school, he steadfastly refused to speak any language but English, even to his foreign-language-speaking family. This involved a series of battles with his family, but after winning out, he turned to the pursuit of perfecting his English. "I lived with a dictionary under my arm. I read avidly, wrote a good deal, and practiced speech when alone. For years, I never spoke without self-consciousness, for fear that the ungrammaticalness of my parents and brothers would creep into my speech. I thought out every word carefully before speaking. At school, I was drawn to my English teachers, who encouraged me and helped me."

For other subjects, this pursuit of "perfect English" dictated occupations, selected friendships, led to withdrawal from kinship groups, and in various other ways influenced the organization of the life pattern, particularly during adolescence, all to the end that an acceptable speech, without foreign trace, might be achieved.

The Linguistic Label

The label is one of the most common devices which people use against each other. It is particularly effective as an instrument of oblique attack or of depreciation. Its constant use by politicians is the best proof of its devastating force. Careful students of social relations await a definitive treatise on the sociology of the label.

Linguistic vestiges which identify one with some particular population group are constantly made the basis of labels. These serve to identify the stereotype. Examples are "The Dutchman," "Hunkie," "Frenchy," "The Swede," and so on. Eight of our subjects refer to the fact that linguistic labels were attached frequently to them, and all but one indicate some resentment of it. In four of the cases the resentment apparently was pronounced.

Bilingual Vestiges: Their Occupational Significance

The ability to express oneself adequately and acceptably is of particular importance in the occupational world, and the higher the occupational level the more important it seems to become. How university graduates in business rate it was revealed clearly in a study made by the author a number of years ago. A total of 1,636 graduates of the Wharton School of Finance and Commerce of the University of Pennsylvania were asked, in the light of their subsequent business experience, to make an appraisal of the importance of the various fields of knowledge covered in their undergraduate days. The outstanding result of these appraisals was the marked emphasis given to "studies and practice in the oral and written use of the English language." More than three-quarters (75.9 percent) of the total number of graduates believed that training in the written and oral use of English was of primary importance. No other field of knowledge was so emphasized.[12]

Four aspects of the occupational significance of bilingual vestiges appear in the case material. One of these emphasizes its professional utilization.

John Wojacks grew up in a foreign-language home. By the time he was graduated from college, he had acquired a good command of the English language, although he spoke it with a pronounced accent, slowly, and occasionally at a loss for the proper word. By the time he acquired the doctorate, he spoke as slowly as ever, but gradually the hesitating and timid manner gave way to a seemingly deliberate ponderous manner, as though he were speaking ex cathedra. After the doctorate was awarded, John went into college teaching, where his progress has been rapid. He speaks today with an accent as pronounced as it was 20 years ago. He still speaks slowly, and with great show of assurance. He does not think a foreign accent is a handicap. He apes the mannerisms of the European scholar, and apparently these have impressed many persons on the staff of his institution. He is spoken of constantly as a great scholar, although his output of scholarly work has been rather meager.

Another case emphasizes the handicap for salesmanship that results from bilingual vestiges.

Benjamin Stern has been a traveling salesman. He was reared in a Yiddish-speaking home, and he speaks English today with a marked Yiddish accent. Benjamin says that this fact handicaps him in selling, particularly in certain areas of the country. He hopes that, when the war is over, his territory will

[12] James H. S. Bossard and J. Frederic Dewhurst, *University Education for Business,* University of Pennsylvania Press, 1931, Chap. 8.

be confined to New York, Philadelphia, and Baltimore, where his accent will be less of a handicap.

A third subject refers to repeated instances in which the "other" language tended to confer professional prestige.

William's background is Greco-Turkish. As a clergyman, he finds that in the eyes of some of his church members this background adds color to his personality and his sermons, and lends authority and prestige to his exegetical study courses or sermons, based upon the Greek texts.

A fourth instance, involving professional discrimination, appears quite incidentally in the case material.

Harry was himself reared in a non-English-speaking home, but has lost most traces of it. In speaking of his referral to a psychiatrist several years ago, he mentioned the fact that this psychiatrist spoke with a pronounced foreign accent. "Imagine sharing your innermost thoughts with a person who cannot talk your language. I did not go back to him again."

The Language of Enemy Nations

Falling into a special group are the cases in which the "other" language is that of a nation with whom the United States is at war. Most important of these is the German. Twice within a generation, persons of German extraction living in the United States have had to face the reactions of their fellows to their own Germanic vestiges. Language and speech are the most "socially visible" of these. In other words, for these people there are, in addition to all the aspects of bilingualism per se, the complications resulting from emotional attitudes toward an enemy, as least from such attitudes as "carry over," consciously and unconsciously, to his language. The case study that follows will serve to indicate not only some of the problems already commented upon but also the implications of an enemy language extending over a life span.

John Rowley is now 52 years old, a rather intelligent man in a semiprofessional occupation. Both of his parents were born in the United States of German stock. He grew up in a town of about 15,000, composed largely of persons of German ancestry. German was commonly spoken in the home and in the community, where it was the language of business and of social relations. Only official records were kept in English, which was also the language of the school, at least so far as the work of the classroom was concerned. John was an only child of lower-middle-class parents. His story follows.

"Until I was four years old, I spoke only German, which was the language of the home and of all our daily relationships. It was when I was about four that an aunt came to visit and told my parents that I ought to learn to speak English, since this was the language I would have to use when I went to school. I have no clear recollection of this visit or of the conversation, I am merely repeating here what I have been told. I can recall learning English words and having their meaning explained in German. Fortunately, an English-speaking family moved next door to us when I was five years old. The daughter, aged eight, took me in hand, taught me some more English and saw to it that I was properly started in my school work.

"From my sixth to my thirteenth year, I was completely bilingual. At home, the language was German; in school, we spoke English; on the playground there was a mixture of both, with English slowly gaining the ascendancy. Although moving constantly from German to English and back again, I felt most at home with the German. German came naturally; English was the result of thought, care and effort. During most of this time, I thought in German, although as I came to read more and more in English books, I began to think about the contents of these books—characters in novels, traits of persons in biographies, qualities of objects and scenes described—in English.

"Concerning the effect of this bilingualism upon my school work, I cannot say that it was any handicap to me during this period whatsoever. Almost all of the children in my class were in the same stage that I was, so that any resultant handicaps were common to all of us. In fact, my ability with the English language was greater than that of many of my classmates, some of whom were handicapped, I am sure, by their awkwardness in the use of English. I remember that the boy at the foot of the class also spoke English quite poorly. We called him that '*Deutscher Dumkopf*' (that German ignoramus).

"My early German-language background was a serious problem in my life for many years, but I cannot say that it ever interfered with the learning process in my school work. The problems it created for me have been wholly social. From about my tenth year on, I began to see that working people and the common classes spoke German, while the educated, refined, and wealthy persons spoke English. Furthermore, I slowly became conscious of something called accent; that some people spoke English as though they had spoken it all of their lives, while others spoke English with a German accent.

"My thoughts about all this came to a focus when, in my fourteenth year, we moved to another town. Here the population was chiefly English and Scotch, and with the Irish as the new immigrant group. My favorite teacher was an English woman who spoke an excellent English. I remember having a crush on a girl in my class with blue eyes, blonde hair, and broad A's.

"My 'Dutch accent,' as it was called, must have been conspicuous. It was noticed and commented upon. Now began a period in my life of definite unhappiness which lasted for about twelve years. In my High School classes, I was ashamed to recite orally; often, when asked a question in class, I would not answer even though I knew what the answer was. I was fearful of comment about my accent. My written work, the teachers all said, was much better than my oral work, and I alone knew the real reason for it. It was because I was ashamed to get up and speak. I can remember, too, making up many excuses to avoid oral recitations—a sore throat, an aching tooth, something in my eye, etc.

"Meanwhile, I was busy trying to do something about it. I began the practice of reading aloud, slowly and distinctly, repeating sentences and phrases to make them sound more English. I insisted that only English be spoken at home. My parents tried to do so, but the linguistic habits of a lifetime are not easy to break. Often they would forget, and then I would become sullen and refuse to answer them. The worst times for me came when my German-speaking relatives arrived for a visit. It was at these times that I was in turn embarrassed, irritated and embittered. I would stay away from home at such times, or, if at home, would speak only when spoken to and then only in monosyllables. Naturally my relatives noticed this. Some were hurt by it, others resented it, while most of them told my parents that I was a badly mannered young man from whom no good could be expected. All of this was embarrassing to my parents, but it left me only the more bitter. I began to hate all Germans—my parents, relatives and friends—because they seemed to personify all my personal problems which grew out of my German ancestry.

"Another thing I remember is that I brought almost none of my school friends to my home, because the few times I did, my parents seemed to go out of their way to display their German speech and mannerisms to my friends. What social life I had was away from my home, and most of it was with boys, who were less prone to remind me of the fact that I was German.

"Just as I was graduating from High School my family moved to the city in which I had been born and where we had lived until I was thirteen. Naturally, my parents were overjoyed to return to their old friends with its preponderance of people of German stock. As for me, I hated it. I kept aloof from my boyhood friends, withdrawing more and more within myself. I found a job and pleaded that I was too busy or too tired to go out. Particularly did I avoid girls, for reasons which I remember today quite distinctly. A Germanized girl I did not want, a non-German, i.e., of English-speaking ancestry, I would be unwilling to bring to my home to meet my German parents. It all seemed very clear to me then that the only safe thing to do was not to allow myself to become deeply interested in any woman. Thus arose my decision to remain unmarried, to which I adhered for a number of years.

"Then came the first World War. The feeling against the Germans in this country was very strong. I was ashamed of my name, of my family and of my ancestry. More and more did I withdraw within myself. I think perhaps the chief effect of my German ancestry upon me during all these years was this —that I never acted naturally. I was always hesitant, afraid, insecure. Later on, I became more and more artificial, playing a part; I became very quiet and reserved. I kept away from my childhood friends and relatives. I was with German folk, lived with them, but was not willing to be of them and to converse freely with them.

"After a short and unexciting war service during which I did not leave this country, I was mustered out with a firm resolution in the back of my mind. I would leave home, go far away, and begin life anew. My continued reading aloud and studied care in speech had enabled me to speak a 'German-less' English. I also made a slight change in my name, much to my parents' disgust.

"All that happened twenty-five years ago. During this time I have not returned once to my boyhood home, save when my mother died. My father has remarried, but I never see him. I have had no contacts during these years with my relatives or my earlier friends. I married when I was thirty-five. My wife knows almost nothing of this earlier part of my life, and I have loved her be-

cause she has asked nothing and never speaks of our lives before we came together. A few times I have met persons from my former world, who knew me as
a boy, but I have never been more than polite.

"Sometimes, especially now that I am getting older, I feel sad about this
complete withdrawing from my earlier life. It is as if I had no real roots. I envy
my friends who do have these things. But now that we are at war with Germany a second time, it is a great relief to live in a community which is not
marked. My wife and I both are active in war work, and the happiness that is
mine now more than repays me for all that I went through when I was a young
man.

"I am 52 years old now and am able to look back over my life and see it in
better perspective. It seems all very clear to me today that my German speech
and my German ancestry have been the key to my whole life and the way in
which it has developed. I cannot think about the first half of my life without
remembering them. It seemed that they were always in my mind, influencing
me, holding me back, embarrassing me, and leading me to do many things to
shield myself from the problems which they created. If I had been willing to
grow up a German, marry a 'Germanized' girl, go around with German-Amer-
ican kinfolk and friends, all might have been well and happy for me. But this I
was never willing to do."

Obviously there are people living in the United States who speak the
language of a one-time national enemy whose reactions are wholly different from the above.

The Refugee as a Bilingual

A phase of the enemy tongue problem, as well as a distinct aspect of
the problem of the bilingual, is the case of the refugee who has come to
the United States within recent years. The problems of these refugees
are numerous and highly complicated, and the reference here is solely
to a specialized aspect of the linguistic factor in these problems. Many
of these refugees in this country acquire English later in life, and as a
phase of the larger adjustment to American ways of life. The acquisition
of English usually comes in connection with the refugee's occupational
readjustment. The result of this, as seen through the eyes of a refugee,
is evident in the case of Karl.

Karl came to the United States when past the thirtieth year. For him this
marked the beginning of a new occupational career, and in a new language.
Karl is an exceedingly able person, with excellent academic training, and with
insight into his own problems. "Waiting in England for my immigration visa,
I felt the first impact of the personality impairment which it means to live in a
country where you know the language only unsatisfactorily. It seemed to me
that I had lost the ability to make use of my personal and professional potentialities because I lacked any adequate facility of communication. I became
convinced that I had to forge for myself a new tool of communication before I

could start to participate again in the game of life. However, for a professional man such a tool has to be of high quality and I soon realized that it would take time to produce it.

"Shortly after my arrival in this country, it was my good fortune to receive guidance which led to my doing graduate work at a college of high standing where I regained control of my ability of communication, but the tool was a new language and this meant that since that time my thinking and living was divided into two different departments dependent on the language I used.

"At home with my wife, in my letters to my parents and European friends, I still express myself and—what is more important—thought in German, but when I closed the apartment door behind me in the morning I stepped into another life which was dominated by English thought and expression. I cannot say that I found it difficult to make this daily transition, but after some time I began to realize that it implied certain limitations for my functioning in either sphere. In the German-language sphere it meant that the whole stock of new professional and life experience had to be retranslated or to be expressed in English which led to a mixed language usage which from the angle of language standards I felt to be regrettable. Similarly I had to translate my former life and professional experience into English if I wanted to use it on the outside in my new life; since here language mixture was unfeasible, this meant a certain handicap and particularly a slowing down of communication which I sometimes felt to be painful.

"At the present time I have enough language facility in English not to experience any handicap in expression, but I am still aware of my foreign accent when I am not carried away by my topic. This awareness again slows me down in speech and makes me appear more deliberate in behaviour than I think I would be on a spontaneity level.

"However, notwithstanding the fact that I am still aware of using a new language tool, I do not feel a professional handicap in this respect. As a matter of fact in my professional life bilingualism has become an asset because of the access which it permits to two spheres of communication complexes with bearing upon each other.

"In my private life, I still am under the impression that the fact that English came into my life so late, implies a certain limitation. In English I can only act as a person of my age, because I have no English child's talk nor adolescent's talk for that matter. If I want to revert to earlier periods in my life I am confined to German thought and expression. On the other hand, if I want to communicate present-day experiences to my relatives and friends it receives a somewhat second-hand character because my respective mental content is English and I have to translate it into German.

"I have tried to check this analysis by an observation of my word associations and have found that my associations are bilingual along the lines indicated. To words or pictures of family life or such matters as food I associate German words, to professional words and visual impressions I associate in English. Looking up from the typewriter in the room where I am typing this report I associated 'books' this very minute, but thinking of going home in the evening I associated 'Nachtmal,' the German word for dinner.

"If I had to bring the result of this analysis on a formula, I should say that bilingualism has decreased the parochialism of my personality which seems to me an asset in personality range but a liability in personality harmony. Bilingualism has formed two compartments in my personality structure, and although they are by no means watertight they are still quite distinct."

At first glance, Karl's case coincides with our concept of the marginal person who lives in two worlds in part and in neither in entirety. This may be the traditional, and dramatic, way of putting it, but one is haunted by the question whether this is wholly and accurately true. Does Karl live in two worlds, and is his, then, a schizoid personality? Or is it the essential fact that he functions at two levels in the same world, playing dual linguistic and cultural roles, his main problem the "wear and tear" of shifting "gears" constantly?

Linguistic Identification with Status

In searching for a key to the various aspects revealed by these 17 cases, as well as the net impressions gained during the study, the concept of *linguistic identification with status* seems to be most fitting to the facts. By this is meant the assignment of status to the individual on the basis of his linguistic behavior measured in terms of the conformity or nonconformity of that behavior to the socially accepted modes of expression. It is proposed here as a fundamental social process, operating within the status system of the prevailing society and in terms of linguistic factors.

It is a further part of the thesis presented here that, although this is a generic process in all societies, it operates in the United States in two dimensions rather than in one. This difference is due to our highly heterogeneous population. In a nation with a homogeneous population, the process operates in one dimension. The socially acceptable form of expression is established in one language on a class basis, and status is determined in terms of adherence to or departure from it. In the United States, as in all countries where there are language minorities, there is for many persons the added dimension of bilingualism operating against a historical background of immigrant sequence and minority group status. In this additional dimension, a second language and its vestiges are bound up with the status of the particular minority group which speaks that language.

How linguistic identification with status operates in the United States may be explained in graphic terms, by means of a right-angle triangle. Let the vertical line be AB, with B at the base. The horizontal line becomes BC. Let B identify the social elite form of expression of the dominant group. Departures from it on a class basis can be marked along the line AB, and bilingual vestiges can be marked along the line BC in terms of the "other" language group status. Consider now the case of individual X. He speaks a low-class or vulgate English, so his place on the perpendicular line AB, marked by X^1, is near A. He is a bilingual whose other language and minority group status, indicated by X^2 on line BC, is quite near point C. The line X, to X^2 is relatively far removed from B; hence his linguistic identification with status is low, measured in both dimensions. Other individuals will vary as either or both points on the status scale differ.

It must be added, by way of conclusion, that linguistic identification with status is not presented here as the whole explanation of the status system, but only as the system is affected by linguistic factors. Obviously, too, the role of these factors will differ from one society to another.

Summary

1. Bilingualism, a phenomenon both common and old, takes different forms in different areas. In countries of immigration, like the United States, it becomes an aspect of minority groups and their status.

2. One out of five white persons in the United States grew up in a home in which some language other than English was the principal one spoken during earliest childhood. Eight linguistic groups account for 17,646,600 such individuals. Most of these people are to be found in the population of foreign-born white stock, but in 1940 there were 2,929,060 cases among the native-born white of native-born white parentage, a significant illustration of cultural persistence.

3. Studies of the effect of bilingualism on child development indicate: (a) some effect upon mental development when verbal tests are given, but this tends to disappear as the level of intellectual attainment rises; (b) a rather general consensus that the school achievement of the bilingual child suffers, especially in the lower grades; (c) that speech defects may be more numerous; and (d) that the chief problems are personal and social adjustment.

4. A study of 17 case histories of bilinguals suggests the nature of the problems of the bilingual as a person, arising chiefly from the fact that the "other" language identifies the child with his minority group status. The concept of linguistic identification with status seems to fit the facts best.

Chapter **16**

Family Rituals
and Child Development

The more one comes to observe and study families at first hand, the more apparent are the existence and operation of certain prescribed forms of group behavior which constitute an important part of family life and the personality formation process of its younger members. These are spoken of as family rituals, and they constitute the final facet of family life to be included in this volume. A more adequate discussion of the meaning of family rituals, their changing nature and extent, the general role of ritualistic behavior, and their significance in family life and child development, constitute the content of this chapter.[1]

The Meaning of Family Ritual

THE TERM RITUAL DEFINED

Ritual is a very old word, but it has been utilized throughout its history mainly by two groups of persons. One of these has consisted of students of religion, who have seen it as the origin of religion, or as a technique of magic or worship, or as a part of the ethical or control system of religion. The other group has comprised anthropologists, who have stressed ritual as one of the obvious and inescapable characteristics of primitive culture, with forms that are highly visible and that pervade every field of human activity. But they, too, have emphasized chiefly its role in the development of religion, so that references to ritual are everywhere interwoven with discussions of magic, taboo, totemism, and the like.

The result of all this has been that ritual is identified, especially at the more popular level, in terms of worship and the ceremonial, with forms

[1] For a more extended discussion of this subject, the reader is referred to James H. S. Bossard and Eleanor S. Boll, *Ritual in Family Living*, University of Pennsylvania Press, Philadelphia, 1950. For a summary of selected aspects, see "Ritual in Family Living," by the same authors, in the *American Sociological Review*, August, 1949, pp. 463–469.

that are imposed by some authority other than that of the lay participants. When the popular notion of ritual carries over into the secular, it usually concerns the rites of fraternal organizations and clubs that are found in a sort of religious twilight zone. Most of these rituals are crises or initiation ceremonies and as such are solemn, spectacular, rigid, and imposed by outside authority. An example of this everyday conception of ritual is found in the 1947 edition of *Webster's Unabridged International Dictionary*, which defines it as "the forms of conducting work, especially as established by tradition or by sacerdotal prescription; religious ceremonial. Ritual is regarded as of paramount importance in primitive and polytheistic religions. . . . Hence, a code or form of ceremonies observed, as by organization or upon any ceremonial occasion, as the *ritual* of the Freemasons."

When one ignores the traditional uses of the term and looks at its basic meaning, there is nothing awesome or mysterious or religious about it. What ritual really is, is a system of procedure, a form or pattern of social interaction, which has three unvarying characteristics. First, it is definitely prescribed. This is the way a thing is to be done. Ritual means exactness and precision in procedure. Second, there is the element of rigidity. The longer the prescribed procedure continues, the more binding its precision becomes. And finally, there is a sense of rightness which emerges from the past history of the process, i.e., the oftener the repetition of the prescribed procedure occurs, the more it comes to be approved. This distinguishes it from mere habit. To deviate from the procedure is wrong, not wholly on utilitarian grounds but also because it breaks the rhythm and the rapport. Ritual is conceived, then, primarily in terms of social process, with definite forms of interaction and a specific cultural content. Thus interpreted, it is not confined to any one field, such as religion, but may develop in any aspect of social life, and especially in one where relatively continuing relationships are maintained.

THE MEANING OF FAMILY RITUAL

Obviously, the family is an aspect of social life in which ritual inevitably develops. It is a social process. It has a definite cultural content. Its relationships are intimate, repetitious, and continue over long periods of time. Many patterns of its behavior come to be prescribed, both for its individual members and for a family as a functioning unit. Routine, habit, rigidity, sense of rightness and wrongness are inevitable accompaniments of these patterns. They also are the essence of much of the life of the family. Just as ritual has been identified as the core of the culture of a people, so it would seem also to be the hard core of family living.

A family ritual may be defined, then, as a prescribed formal procedure, arising out of family interaction, involving a pattern of defined behavior which is directed toward some specific end or purpose and which acquires rigidity and a sense of rightness as a result of its continuing history. Thus defined, ritual develops in connection with many aspects of family life, but clusters particularly about such things as holidays, anniversary days, meals, vacations, religious worship, and collective ways of using leisure time.

Possibly the most effective way of clarifying the concept of family ritual is to cite selected illustrations in briefly summarized form. Four cases, drawn from a large collection of source material gathered under the auspices of the William T. Carter Foundation, are presented here.

1. *The Night Before Christmas Ritual.*   When Kay S. was 3 years old, her father held her on his lap and read to her on Christmas Eve Clement Moore's well-known poem, "The Night Before Christmas." Each Christmas Eve thereafter this has been repeated. When Kay was 5 years old, her sister Jane was born, and during the succeeding years the reading of this poem on Christmas Eve became more and more of a ceremonial event. As the two daughters became older, they would sit on either side of their father on the family sofa, and mother and other relatives would be present. After the reading, refreshments came to be served, and talk would follow about Christmas celebrations of former years. As time went on, the ceremony became more and more elaborate. Candles were lit while other lights were extinguished; the conversational aftermath lengthened. Nothing ever deterred Kay and Jane from being at home on Christmas Eve; dates with boys, even after their engagements had been announced, were not made; once Kay did not accept an invitation to a much-desired trip so that she might be at home for "the reading." After Kay's marriage, she and her husband came to her parents' home on Christmas Eve in order to be present for the event. This practice has been continued down to the present time, both by Kay and her husband and by Jane and her husband. Last year, "father" read to both daughters, their husbands, three grandchildren and grandmother.

2. *The Hair-Washing Ritual.*   Thursday night was always hair-washing night at our house. Religiously, when that night of the week rolled around, mother would march me upstairs and make sure I got into the tub before I had a chance to jump into bed. I usually knew when it was time for this ordeal by listening to the radio. It never failed that when Rudy Vallee would come on the air, Mother would call: "Come on, sister, it's time for your hair washing." To me this was worse than a dose of castor oil. "But all little boys and girls have to have their heads washed," Mother would say. "Look at Daddy and me, we are grown people and we have to wash our hair." "All right," I would say, "but my little girl won't ever have to wash her hair." This would make Mother laugh, but all the same, she would dump me into the tub and start scrubbing away. When the Rudy Vallee program went off the air, I was delighted, for I knew the job was over and I would not have to go through such torture for another week. But now it is many years later, and other radio programs are on the air, but Thursday night is still hair-washing night in my life.

3. *The Saturday Night Egg-Eating Ritual.* I was in my last year in High School when the depression came. Our family was hard hit by it. I succeeded in getting a summer job to help out. The first Saturday I worked, Daddy and I came home at about the same time (ten o'clock) in the evening. I remember that I fried some eggs and made some coffee for us that night. While we ate, we talked about our experiences at work, then we put our weekly wages on the table and, with mother coming in, we planned our expenditures for the week ahead. Thus began a practice which has continued at our house ever since. Every Saturday night, we meet in the kitchen of our home at ten o'clock. Eggs are fried, and coffee or cocoa is served. Then we talk—about our work, experiences of the past week, the family income, our plan for family expenditures, and other matters of family importance. Often these family sessions last until after one o'clock. Six years ago, I was married, but my husband and I have kept our weekly date with Mother and Dad. None of us ever let anything interfere with these Saturday night get-togethers. They surely have become a ritual in the life of our families.

4. *The Saturday Afternoon Gift Ritual.* Saturday afternoons held a very special ritual: the bringing home of the Reading Terminal (a well-known Philadelphia market) package. My father would leave his office at noon, go to the Terminal for his lunch, and then shop. Mother and sister and I waited for him in the den, and he would come straight up and put a huge parcel on Mother's lap. The scissors were ready on the table beside her. There was always a pound of Wilbur Buds for Mother: her favorite candy. There were always two one-half pound boxes of hard candies for sister and me. The other contents varied from week to week, but usually included all sorts of exotic fruits, fresh, candied, and preserved; nuts; dates; and cookies. We all sat still until each package had been opened and exclaimed about, sampling a bit of this and that, and then the party was over until next Saturday. At the end of the party, Daddy handed my sister and me our allowances, and we rushed out as fast as we could to spend them.

The Changing Nature and Extent of Rituals

Family rituals are a product, obviously, of the nature of the family and its collective life: their extent, the result of the importance that its members attach to them, and the time they have to devote to their conduct. A study of rituals in some 400 families, and covering a period of 80 years, has been made as a part of the research program of the William T. Carter Foundation of the University of Pennsylvania. The number of cases, considered by successive decades, seems large enough to suggest some conclusions concerning changes in the nature, and possibly the extent, of family rituals.

First, rituals are revealed as an integral part of the lives of these families during the entire period covered. Those which have taken form within the past few years and centering about some event of contemporary significance are described as intently and viewed as seriously as those which obtained in the 1870's.

Second, ritual in family living has become secularized in large measure. This tendency is clearly revealed, and its recognition is highly important. Once ritual is thought of as a generic process of interaction rather than in terms of some pietistic end, then sherry before dinner may become as much a ritual as family prayer before going to bed; and listening to a Sunday night radio program may become the center of a ritual complex as much as the reading of the Bible.

Third, the question of the changing extent of ritual in family living is a complicated one. The study reported on made no effort to present quantitative evidence on this subject, but records certain impressions. These are that family rituals seem quite clearly to be on the increase, so far as their number is concerned. The reasons for this seem fairly clear. The modern family, and particularly the city family, has more leisure to devote to the refinements of family living, and ritual quite obviously involves the ceremonial use of leisure. Again, the enriched variety of contemporary life offers a greater number of things for families to do together, if they are so minded. Also, there is the pressure of mass advertising, which seeks to build up and exploit the commercial aspects of many rituals, such as gift giving, observance of holidays, and the like.

Fourth is the question whether or not the overall ritualizing of the individual home is increasing. Sufficient data to answer with any degree of assurance are not available at this time. All that can be said is that current rituals are more numerous and more varied, but of shorter duration and apparently of lesser relative importance in the total family configuration.

Finally, there is the question of the relation between family rituals and family size. On this point, the study suggests that the larger the family, the more numerous and rich the rituals, whether the family was large only by number of children or was large by the inclusion of relatives and family servants. This conclusion was particularly buttressed by the autobiographical material. On the other hand, if the material on large urban families at the lower income levels is considered separately, the number and variety of family rituals are relatively small. It would appear that, given education and economic ease, or at least comfort, the larger families had special opportunities for ritual development and took full advantage of it. One even gets the impression that the desire for large families and love for a ritualized home life went hand in hand. The small families, by way of contrast, reported fewer rituals. Younger persons included in the study, reporting a complete or relative lack of family rituals, came mostly from small families, often one-child families. And yet here exceptions must be noted. In the material from one-child families, one discovers a good deal of the formalized, repressive kind of ritual that is deliberately dwelt upon as the hope of the family, as well as the prolonging of rituals of intimate family association, in order to keep the only child from getting away from the family fold. Also, a small immediate family, if in extended contact with a number of kinfolk, may develop considerable ritual.

Class Differentials in Family Rituals

The concept of social class, as representing differences in ways of living, has come to be recognized by contemporary sociologists and will constitute the basis of the next two chapters. Suffice it to say here that the question of class differentials in family rituals rose early in the research study here reported and was set up as a separate phase of the project. A total of 156 families were included, selected from people who lived in neighborhoods, used services, had occupations and belonged to associations that are unequivocally lower, middle, or upper class. Examples of the sources from which these families were recruited included patrons of a social settlement, residents in a community in which most of the women were employed in a domestic service, a public school in a middle-class suburban district, the Junior League and the Social Register.

The overall conclusion was that family rituals increase in number, variety, richness, and willing coöperation by individual family members as one moves upward in the social scale. Also, rituals differ in character from one class to the other. After all, rituals take their shape from the culture in which they arise, and different classes develop cultural levels. Very briefly generalized, the conclusions for each class level are as follows:

1. The lower class is one in which there is little connection with the past. The present is composed of individuals crowded into a space too small for comfort. The religion is predominantly Catholic. The economic situation is not one of affluence. Children see little, if anything, in their families to stimulate a desire to perpetuate what they see. Opportunities for emotional satisfactions in the home are few, even for the adults. The rituals arising from these situations are, for the most part, rituals of expediency to keep the home going and to facilitate escape from home into a more exciting or promising outside world.

2. The middle class is more comfortably situated. There is enough physical space to permit of frequent family interaction, but not enough to allow much isolation of family members. Family finances are such that each member can hope to benefit by close coöperation. The past of the family is in their minds, but usually the present is better and gives challenge for the future. The family tone is one of hopefulness and optimism. There is a scorning, therefore, of habits that might lead in a downward direction, and a pressing forward toward a higher one which tends to

both moral and social carefulness. The rituals here show a coöperative-ness of a desire to reach these goals, as well as a genuine family "to-getherness" in a home where there is need and opportunity for it.

3. The upper class is guarding a way of life which is considered by them, and many others, to be the desirable way of life. They have the time, for the most part the wealth, and the physical surroundings in which they can perpetuate it. The history of their families is something to con-serve and in which to take pride. Their way of life can be preserved by taking seriously the social symbols which are generally acknowledged as standing for it. Their rituals converge around these. They are more formalized than in the other classes, and they are more easily perpetu-ated from generation to generation because of the fortunate circum-stances in their lives.

One further fact must be noted by way of postscript. The chief com-plicating factor in generalizing on these class differentials is the contrari-wise effect of family size. Large families, it has been noted, tend to encourage ritual development, but large families often are found at lower-class levels where the scale of living tends to hamper such development. The play of antithetical forces is nothing new in nature or human society; its importance in this connection must be recognized.

Family Ritual and the Family Cycle

Reference has been made in Chapter 4 to the concept of the family cycle and its significance in the study of family interaction. It is equally important for an understanding of family rituals. Not only do rituals change from one stage in the cycle to another, but the periods of change appear to be times of crisis and heightened emotions over the ritualistic procedures themselves. Sometimes the emotion is excitement and joy: at other times it is irritation or worse. But the change has to occur if the family is to mature normally. Some of these stages and changes will be identified briefly.

1. Marriage is a time for a new deal in family ritual. It involves at least three different processes: (a) a conscious deliberation by each person to be married concerning certain rituals which must be abandoned and others which must be kept; (b) an adjustment of two separate ritual systems between the new husband and wife; and (c) the emergence of new family rituals. Couples devise their own rites consciously, in the excitement of their new freedom, surroundings, and belongings, and find others forming inevitably in the daily process of living together.

2. With the child-bearing stage comes normally a deep sense of a changing role and status of the family. Ritual, among other things, takes on a new meaning. It is no longer a repressive procedure to be freed from, or a practice to promote pleasure and to cement relationships be-

tween married lovers; but it is a means through which the heritage from the past is to be handed down to the future. It is at this time that many religious rituals, holiday customs, and kinship celebrations come into interest for redefining and, where mates do not agree, create new difficulties. Moreover, a wholly different orientation leads new parents to consider rituals appropriate not just to themselves but to the coming generation. The new parents become noticeably more orthodox in their views with the advent of children and tend more toward the traditional, which pleases their kinsfolk; to show off the new baby, the parents re-enter kinsfolk celebrations. All this combines to reassert an emphasis upon the continuity of family patterns.

3. The preschool family period is particularly rich in the formation of many trial-and-error procedures which crystallize into set forms. These are the years when the new two-generation family is learning to live together. Parents and children, siblings and new siblings, are working out a pattern of family life. Disciplinary rituals, in particular, arise, as do many mother-child rites. Many, perhaps most, of these arise as trial-and-error attempts at expediency. Proving their worth, they become rigid and are consciously approved and cultivated.

4. The family with teen-agers comes gradually to revise its rituals. It is now that rites stressing maturity and responsibility appear. The upper-class girl makes her debut. The Jewish boy is feted through the bar mizvah. Boys and girls receive a front door key and a driver's license—all at a definite age. Rites now tend to become sex-divided. Father and mother assume new roles with their grown children. Many rituals come to be on an equality or near-equality basis, often devised to create moments of family intimacy in which to foster child frankness and confidence.

5. Serving as a launching center for the children, either for marriage or a career, brings the family to a stage in its cycle which is prone to be tension-creating and disruptive of family rituals. Parents overeagerly try to perpetuate rituals, and children overzealously try to be free of them. The results are that ritualistic situations are strained and that children often reject what they later redefine and readopt. There is one outstanding exception to this, which appears in cases where children are earning their own money and have a high degree of independence-feeling. In these cases, there is the development of rituals which have the purpose of repaying the parent, usually Mother, of presenting gifts at specific times, of entertaining her on certain days, or of taking over the household to free her once a week.

6. There is a stage which may be called that of the Aging Family, where the children have departed for establishments of their own and the parent couple are left alone. Family rituals now become important because: (a) older people are physically and psychologically disposed

to such regimen; (b) there is an opportunity to return to rituals that enriched married life before the children arrived; and (c) grandparent-grandchild rituals arise to gratify both generations. This is a type of ritual which has been largely overlooked in child development.

The Role of Ritual

It has been pointed out that the study of ritual has been confined through the years to its role in the field of religion. Certainly the abiding religions have been highly ritualistic in character. The Jews, for example, developed early an extensive set of rituals, including the laws of worship, rites of cleanliness, regulation of diets, and the keeping of the Sabbath and various holy days. "There was in the Talmud," writes Durant, "a strong emphasis upon ritual; . . . the ritual was a mark of identity, a bond of unity and continuity."[2] "The laws were given," wrote Abba Areca, a wise Jew, "for the purpose of disciplining and refining men by their observance."[3] The Mohammedans had as extensive a set of rituals as the Jews, and borrowed much from them. Similar is the case of Roman Catholicism. Its rich ritualistic history includes its prayers, hymns, the Mass, ceremonies of religious festivals, and the regulation of many details of the lives of its people. One cannot study religious history without a profound impression of the role of ritual. It seems to satisfy a fundamental desire in the lives of people. It disciplines by its observance, educates through the deposit of its lore, and holds men together by the simple device of having them do things together.

A suggestive conception of the kinds and integrating power of ritual has been presented recently by Erich Fromm. "A ritual, broadly speaking," he writes, "is shared action expressive of common strivings rooted in common values."[4] They cannot be manufactured, he says, for they depend upon the existence of commonly shared values, and only to the extent that such values emerge and become part of human reality can we expect the emergence of meaningful, rational rituals. This would serve to explain why the ritualistic religions have had the strongest hold upon their members; why authoritarian political leaders develop them in the form of politically colored ceremonies; and why fraternal orders have such a wide appeal in a relatively ritual-less democracy.

Fromm differentiates, however, between rational and irrational rituals. Irrational rituals are a form of neurotic compulsion, and have as their purpose the warding off of irrational impulses. An example would be the washing ritual, which is the attempt to rid one's self of a strong sense

[2] Will C. Durant, *The Age of Faith*, Simon and Schuster, New York, 1950, p. 356.
[3] *Ibid.*
[4] Erich Fromm, *Psychoanalysis and Religion*, Yale University Press, New Haven, 1950, p. 108.

of guilt. Rational rituals differ in that they express strivings recognized as values by the individual. Here there is no compulsive drive to perform the procedure: if it is not performed, there is regret but not fear.[5]

Perhaps the most penetrating analysis of the role of ritual in its generic sense is that given by Emile Durkheim, the French sociologist.[6] Rituals, he points out, have a number of social functions which vary with the nature of the particular ceremony being performed, but there are four general functions to which he gives special attention. First is its disciplinary and preparatory function. Ritual prepares an individual for social living by imposing upon him the necessary self-discipline without which society is impossible. Social life is possible only as individuals are able to accept controls, and ritual aids in the development of such controls and does so in a relatively painless kind of way.

Second, and of particular importance, is its adhesive function. Ritual, being a group procedure, serves to bring beings together, to reaffirm their common bonds, and to enhance the social solidarity. Rituals are occasions of social communion and afford the means by which the group reaffirms itself periodically. They are particularly necessary in the modern world because the workaday, private, and personal interests of the individual occupy so large a part of life, and it is only in their joint observance of rituals that their common pool of values is reëstablished.

Third, according to Durkheim, is the vitalizing function of religions. If society is to be kept alive, its members must be made keenly aware of their social heritage: traditions must be renewed, faith must be renewed, values must be transmitted and deeply imbedded. A large number of rituals involve a recalling of the past, in happy and dramatic form, thus serving to recall the social heritage from lapsing into the limbo of the forgotten. Finally, there is the euphoric function of rituals, meaning that they serve to establish a condition or feeling of social well-being. This function takes on a special significance when a group is faced with an actual or threatened crisis. Ritual is very valuable in such a situation because it makes it necessary for people to have and express certain sentiments and to declare them together.

Family Ritual and Family Integration

The foregoing summary serves as an excellent background for the remaining discussion of this chapter, which is devoted specifically to the role of ritual in family living and in child development.

Returning to the study made by the Carter Foundation, there is one thread running through all the material that was gathered, and that is

[5] *Ibid.*, pp. 106–107.
[6] Emile Durkheim, *Les formes élémentaires de la vie religieuse,* Librairie Félix Alcan, Paris, 1912, Book III.

the fact that ritual is a form of regularized personal relationship between members of the family group. This regularization may involve all the members of the family, such as a national holiday or a family anniversary observance. Most family rituals are of this kind, anticipating and ordinarily obtaining the coöperation of all of the members of the family. But rituals also develop between individual members. There are, for example, husband-wife rituals. These begin to develop usually in the newly established family, and especially with the coming of the children, but they may appear at any stage or in any area of the husband-wife relationship. The sex life of married couples appears to be ritualized in many families.

Just as between husband and wife, so the relations between parent and child may be ritualized. Many of our cases are father-daughter or mother-son rituals. These might be a fruitful source of study for the psychoanalytically minded. Here we must content ourselves with the citation of two simple illustrations:

Frank S. lives in a suburb but maintains his office in the nearby city. Every Saturday since his daughter's twelfth birthday, she takes the suburban train and comes to his office by noon. The two then go to a well-known eating place for lunch. After lunch there is a matinee, football game, or other event. This continued for six years until the daughter left to enter a New England college. On these "dates," father and daughter almost never included another person. Most of the problems involving the daughter's school, social, and family life, were talked over by father and daughter on these occasions.

When Richard was married he and his wife began the custom of going to his parents' home every Sunday for dinner. When the dinner was over, Richard and his mother did the dishes. The help of other persons was always rejected. Richard always washed and his mother dried. Each Sunday, he would tease his mother about the same things, pretending to complain about the abundance of dishes and playfully accusing his mother of not having done any dishes since the preceding Sunday. Halfway through the process, his mother heated the coffee and she and Richard sat to sip it, and talk about happenings of the preceding week. When all matters had been discussed, the kitchen chores were finished. Often this task and talk would cover a period of two hours and more. At the end of the period, they would rejoin the others with Richard always telling some fantastic tale of how his mother had exploited him during the interval with work saved up during the preceding week.

Considering the personal relationships described in our case material, what happens in this regularizing of behavior? Four aspects can be identified. First, there is a strong sense of continuity about these relationships. The assumption of the participants is that they will go on and on, being repeated at regular intervals. Second, the relationship becomes standardized, and, like a worn rock, becomes more and more smooth as time goes on. There is the prescribed form and sequence, each step leading to the next with the precision, as it were, of a timetable. Behavior becomes predictable, which makes for ease and comfort in the relationship. Third, the relationship is glamorized. There is the effort to make it attractive, and often to make it impressive. The persons involved seem to say: We like what we are doing, we want to do it well and happily. Finally, the emergence of the ritual and its continuance seem to deepen the relationship. As Dunlap has written recently about the role of ritual: "Faith develops from ritual, rather than ritual from faith. The development of faith from ritual, as an interpretation of ritual, and with further progressive reinterpretations, is obviously consonant with the fact that ritual is a group product."[7]

Rituals, however, are more than patterns of personal relationships. They are procedures which have a purpose: they represent choices and values. They are approved ways of doing and thinking, and this means culture. The more one succeeds in getting on the inside of families, the more one sees them not as mere units of interacting personalities but as having each its own distinctive ways of living. These constitute the family culture, and it would seem that ritual is the one best starting point for the study of family culture patterns, just as it has long been recognized as the best point from which to begin the study of religion. Ritual obviously comprises much of the behavior of which the family is conscious and of which its members definitely approve.

Perhaps the overall conclusion that emerges from the assemblage of the material is that ritual is a relatively reliable index of family integration. What do we mean by family integration? Does it mean absence of discord? Obviously this is an aspect or index of it, even if negative in character. Is it ability to withstand shock or stress or strain? Possibly, but this would seem to be somewhat a matter of accepted values and character traits of the constituent members rather than an interactive product or structural strength. The word *integrate* means to bring together and to make into a whole, and we use the term *family integration* to mean the welding or unification of its diverse elements into a complex whole or harmonious relationship. An integrated family means to us a well-knit family, one bound together with strong and continuing ties and functioning smoothly as a unit.

If one conceives of family integration in generic terms, there are many indexes which may be utilized to identify it. These include the effective meeting of common problems, the ability to resist major crises, smoothness of operation, lack of tension or conflict, evidences of family pride, criteria of family coöperation and continuity, and continuity of family planning. Thinking in terms of process, family integration is unrelated to moral purposes or cultural values. A well-integrated family may evi-

[7] Knight Dunlap, *Religion: Its Functions in Human Life*, McGraw-Hill Book Company, Inc., New York, 1946, pp. vi, vii.

dence its integration in recurrent feuding with another family, in packing boxes for shipment to displaced persons, in periodic outbursts of drunkenness, or long-range planning for the successive education of the children in a large family.

Ritual indicates many things and serves many purposes in the life of a family. The existence of well-established ritual implies, for example, a considerable amount of like-mindedness among the members of a family. Take such a simple yet basic fact as a common interest in family life. The development of a ritual by a family is an index of the common interest of its members in the family as a group. Parents who are conscious of the family as a group, who wish to make a success of family living, who think of their family as a continuing and permanent arrangement, are the ones most likely to initiate and continue the coöperative procedure which yields as a ritual. One can detect, therefore, at the very beginning, a selective process between those family members who develop and utilize ritual, and those who do not. One must be interested in his family, want to make a go of it, and think of it as a permanent relationship, to look forward to the establishment of family rituals and traditions.

Again, rituals are developed coöperatively. This gives and stimulates a sense of group participation, a further sharing of intimacies, and a sense of lively satisfaction. As Adams pointed out years ago, the feelings of satisfaction that accompany the performance of ritual, and the "pause of satisfaction" that follows the achievement of ends in mind, constitute the essence of the aesthetic experience. In other words, the aesthetic experience is a concomitant of successful participation in the ritualistic act.[8] "The rite is performed; control is achieved; the participants rest satisfied."[9]

Third, common participation is a ceremony that carries with it a sense of rightness that makes for family pride. One senses this feeling of pride in almost all of our case records. Even if there was a sort of playful apology or grumbling pose of feminine coyness in the lines of the case record, it was easy to detect the shades of smug satisfaction between the lines which described the family rituals. Apparently family pride makes for ritual; ritual makes for family pride.

Next, many of our rituals involve refinements of living, and adherence to them implies, and stimulates, a common interest in such refinements. Ritual necessitates a certain formality in social relations, and complementary to this are consideration for the rights of others and the discipline of self, all of which makes for good group relations. It is obvious from our material that ritualism and formalism in family relations make

[8] Elizabeth Kemper Adams, *The Aesthetic Experience,* University of Chicago Press, Chicago, 1907.

[9] Frederick G. Henke, *A Study in the Psychology of Ritualism,* University of Chicago Press, Chicago, 1910, p. 84.

for predictability of behavior response, and this tends to reduce strain and disorder.

Family Rituals and Child Development

It has been pointed out that many, perhaps most, family rituals develop with the coming of children. Often the rituals partake of the nature of a family drama, designed to impress the children. Many rituals center about them; usually they participate in them. Naturally, the impression of many family rituals upon the children is very vivid. Proof of this appears constantly in the clarity with which rituals are recalled, the pride shown in pointing out their details and features, by young people with whom the subject is discussed. Similar is the tendency of autobiographers to view their early family life in terms of recurring family rituals.[10]

Again, a large proportion of family rituals have pleasant associations. Often they center about holidays, birthdays, anniversaries, and other happy occasions. Because of the nature of family rituals—their recurrence, the sense of rightness that accompanies them, the pleasurable associations—they groove themselves deeply and pleasantly into the accumulating layers of the youthful mind, which constitute the essence of the unconscious. Considered in more specific terms, this process may be viewed in operation along seven selected lines.

1. *Rituals as group habits.* From the point of view of child and youth development, a significant characteristic of ritual is its habitual character. Rituals are habits, group habits. Moreover, they are the habits of the first, most exclusive and enduring group to which the child belongs, and the one in which emotional ties are deepest. Pressure from such close association is heavy: infraction by members most upsetting. Family ritual, then, assumes power both from its own nature and from its special setting.

The meaning of habit has been well stated by Bogardus. He writes: "Habit means to have. Habit gives possession; it gives permanency to one's experiences. . . . It is strangely true that nothing is well done until it is done by habit. Reliability and thoroughness depend on habit."[11] Obviously, much of the disciplinary role of ritual, of which Durkheim speaks, flows from the repetitive character of its operation, and nowhere is this more manifest than in child rearing.

2. *The standardization of affectional response.* Rituals make for standardized affectional responses between members of the family. This

[10] Bossard and Boll, *Ritual in Family Living*, Chaps. 3 and 4.
[11] Emory S. Bogardus, *Essentials of Social Psychology*, 4th ed., Jesse Ray Miller, Los Angeles, 1923, pp. 45 and 46.

is important because individuals demonstrate affection unequally and differently. Though depth or sincerity of affection may be quite unrelated to any visible display of it, the former, unannounced, is often overlooked completely by a person accustomed to recognizing it by certain overt symbols. This fact is provocative enough of trouble in families to make significant the question: how do we come to be demonstrative or undemonstrative in certain set ways? The study of family rituals contributes an answer to this question. In many families, the expression of affection is a definite, imperative part of their rituals, was performed without question, and came to be, for the children as well as the parents, the accepted mode of behavior.

Three different kinds of demonstration appeared. First, there were the families who ritualized, to them, the high value of physical contact in affection, through kissing or caressing. Such patterns, once established, come to be the *normal* way to behave, and it is the *omission* of the symbol at the proper time which is the conscious act, is noticed, and has a hurtful connotation.

A different kind of affectional demonstration ritualized by certain families is the prescribed thoughtful act to anticipate the comfort of a family member. One such rite, selected from the case material upon which this summary is based, follows:

Each night before Dad would retire, there would be placed on the stand beside his bed a tall glass of orange juice. No one in particular was designated to perform this task, but as each of us came home or went upstairs to bed we would check on this "must." Forgetfulness on our part shamed each of us. The only mention on Dad's part would be a reluctant, "Missed my orange juice last night, everyone must have been tired." That hurt us because we hurt him.

Other such examples were: The preparing of a breakfast in bed for Mother on Sunday mornings; the cocktail made and served to Father by his eldest daughter immediately upon his arrival home from work each evening; the regular brotherly romp with the baby just before bedtime. In some families, this sort of "forethoughtful" rite extended even to the family dog, and required special feeding, a definite play hour, or an automobile ride.

The most frequently mentioned ritual for the expression of affection concerned the giving of presents. In some instances, every holiday or anniversary is a mutual family present-giving event, and sometimes other special occasions were devised regularly for this kind of affectional display:

Rarely did any of us return home from in town, a trip, a holiday, or even from the corner groceries without bringing Mother a remembrance, such as a handkerchief, pastry, and so on. So when at dinnertime, three of us presented her with three different boxes of sweets and cakes, she would smile and thank us. Other than that, such courtesies were taken for granted in our home.

Special forms became connected with this sort of rite: a place to hide the gifts; a game of hunting for them; a way to act upon receiving them. Often the kind of gift became rigidly set. The girls have to receive corsages for Easter, and the men, new ties. Mother would be terribly disappointed if she did not receive a picture for Mother's Day, or a bouquet of flowers for her dressing table each Saturday. And the children, even at college age, were seeing to it that Mother was not disappointed. Sieber and Mueller have described ritual gift giving as being motivated in the primitive by altruism, and in primary and secondary cultures from more practical ends.[12] It would be difficult to be categorical about the motives behind these current gift rituals, since their meaning to students is so obviously both practical and altruistic.

There is no evidence that families which had these rituals were more or less warmly affectionate than other families having no such definite procedures. The significance of them lies in the fact that the symbols used habitually in the home and unconsciously taken for granted come to stand for the thing they express. They may establish habits of expression which mark a certain kind of personality; they may also establish attitudes that make an individual incapable of understanding or finding comfort in a different symbol.

3. *Family etiquette.* Relations between persons, at any above the starkest levels, involve the observance of certain prescribed forms of behavior. These forms or codes vary a great deal and tend to become both more rigid and more important as life becomes more complex and social standards rise. A part of the social development of every person is training in these codes of conventional behavior, and in this the role of the family is fundamental, particularly so through the patterns of family etiquette that are maintained.

An excellent illustration of family etiquette is found in the mealtime rituals that take form. A study of these shows widely differing habits of social graces, table manners, and customs of dress that are distinguishing marks and that have a bearing upon an individual's qualifications for acceptability in particular social spheres. Significant differences are indicated in the two excerpts of case material that follow:

a. Our dinner gong sounds 10 minutes before dinner is ready so that we can finish washing and dressing promptly. . . . If a member of the family is not on time for dinner he is told that breakfast is the next meal. . . . We join hands around the table and say grace, and then sit down all together. Dad sits at the head of the table, Mother is at the foot, and the children are ranged between them according to age. . . . Our dinner table is always set with a white tablecloth and the best china and glassware. The maid passes the plates to each person as Dad carves, and then serves the vegetables from silver dishes. She helps

[12] Sylvester A. Sieber and Franz H. Mueller, *The Social Life of Primitive Man,* B. Herder Book Company, London, 1941, p. 388.

the children who are too young to serve themselves so that they will not stain the cloth. . . . We eat what is put in front of us and no questions asked. We are not allowed to interrupt each other, especially Mother and Dad. We are never allowed to fight or argue during the meal, and the violator is sent to the kitchen to finish the meal. . . . No one can ever get up and leave the table for any reason and come back again. . . . At dinner, we always have four courses, served in order. The first time my brother saw salad served with the main course, he made an embarrassing comment. We could no more think of serving salad with the main course than we could make the mistake of using a salad fork for our meat. Spode service plates are used at dinner, so that the place in front of us is never bare when one course is removed, and the flower on the plate shows up prettily while we wait for the next course. . . . There is no smoking permitted at our table. After we have finished dessert, Mother and Dad look at each other, nod, and we all go into the living room. The maid then brings in the silver service which belonged to Mother's mother, and those of us who are old enough have coffee and cigarettes.

b. Hands are washed after the meal is placed on the table, delaying same. After my mother places desert on the table, she always stops to make tea, thus forcing the rest of us to plumb the depths of impoliteness and begin without her. . . . Father gets the paper first and reads it during breakfast. We are not allowed to touch it until he is finished. I sit there watching him, between sips of coffee, waiting till he is through and wondering when I can get at the funnies. . . . Father does the carving out in the kitchen, because he has had some sad experiences in letting the gravy splash on the table. . . . When we are going to the movies we have our food from the kitchen all on one plate to save dishwashing. . . . We never know when the whole family will arrive, so if they're not all there they eat whenever they come in. . . . When company comes we use our good china and silver. . . . The first one finished is the first one out, but she has to take her own plates into the kitchen and scrape and rinse them. . . . Mother and I always wear a dress for dinner (this is to be distinguished from "dressing for dinner" in that it means one does not appear at dinner in housecoats, jeans, or slacks). . . . The first thing Father does when he comes home for dinner is to take off his shoes and put on his house slippers.[13]

4. *The organization of leisure.* Leisure-time activities constitute a recognized problem in present-day family life. In their experimentation with the problem, many families find patterns of activity so satisfying that they become ritualized. The by-products of these rites are significant in respect to child development.

There are, for example, the reading rituals—of the "funnies," the daily

---

[13] An interesting contrast in mealtime ritual, though it is outside of the present case material, is that practiced in a little community close to where the study was made. Here, in summertime, the practice is for Mother to come to the front door with paper plates in her hand and call to each child, who disposes of his meal without interrupting his play, and throws the plate into the street. In wintertime, these same families eat indoors in relays, because there is neither enough room in the kitchen, nor enough kitchen equipment to feed them all at once.

paper, the weekly issue of *Life*, the Bible, the classics, and selected holiday stories like Dickens' *Christmas Carol*. Another frequently found ritual of family leisure centers around the radio, television, and the victrola. Procedures are strict in many instances, involving the program listened to, the place of seating, who tunes in, and under what circumstances someone else may take over. Other families have definite times and places for the entire family to go to the movies, with set procedures perhaps before and after the show. Still other families approach the rite of the family council in the late evening with an "evening snack": a gathering of the family in the kitchen, around the refrigerator, for pickup eating, with a recapitulation of the day's events. Finally, there are the families in which summer vacations have become a part of the family's ritualistic life.

5. *Religious and holiday observances.* Religious rites are still practiced in many homes, and Sunday[14] and other holidays come to have special significance, even though not always or wholly religious. The observance of Christmas serves as an excellent illustration of a peculiarly important family day;[15] and typical illustrations from families of different national, religious, and racial origins follow:

a. Irish Catholic

Christmas Eve meant more to us than Christmas Day. Coming from a Catholic family, the vigil of Christmas was a day of strict fasting and abstinence until late evening after all preparations were completed, when the immediate family, with each member present, sat down to the traditional meal. This meal consisted of seven varieties of foods, exclusive of meat or fowl. It usually proffered such dishes as imported, dried mushrooms, stewed prunes, a peculiar type of buckwheat pudding, potato pancakes or "bleenies," fried smelts, fruit, cookies, and Mother's special currant bread. Thin, flaky, pastel-colored wafers from church were first broken and divided with each one at the table. Sometimes, in place of the potato pancakes, a potato pudding, or potato sausages were substituted. All foods were prepared from recipes that were transmitted from generation to generation. Grandmother had a record of them from seven previous generations of her maternal ancestors. Dishes of nuts, fruit, cookies, and a plate with the remaining wafers were left on the table and constantly replenished until Twelfth Night. On Christmas Day, another familiar item assumed a place of importance on the table. We have always called it the "French teapot." It was merely Mother's prized electric percolator, in which was brewed a pungent concoction of whiskey, honey, spices, and orange rind, and served hot. A rosy apple stuck on the spout of the percolator still affords much amusement to visitors who are greeted with a glass of the delicious brew.

[14] For a study showing the increasing range of activities open to families for Sunday observances, see Harold Stanley Jacoby, *Remember the Sabboth Day?* University of Pennsylvania dissertation, Philadelphia, 1945.

[15] For a detailed analysis of Christmas ritual, see James H. Barnett, "Christmas in American Culture," *Psychiatry,* February, 1946, pp. 51–65.

b. German Lutheran

Our Christmas is celebrated each year on Christmas Eve. After a sumptuous five o'clock dinner in which some sort of fowl is always included, the family group assembles in the living room. Here everyone exchanges gifts and later on in the evening old friends drop in to join in the fun. Hanging a wreath on our front door is another custom which we observe every year, and never would it be Christmas without the traditional Christmas cookies. Two German varieties called Pfeffernüsse and Springerle are always included among these. Our home would never be without the traditional evergreen tree at this season, and year in and year out it is given a place of honor in our living room. When my Grandfather was alive it was traditional for him to make a type of cake called Pflannen every Christmas.

Our people are famous for cooking. At Christmas time every available crock, jar, and container is filled with home-baked cookies. Not all are kept for our use. But each time we visit a neighbor to see their presents and tree, a bag of cookies is taken along. Likewise when the visit is returned they bring a bag of cookies to us. Great emphasis is placed on turns in visiting. Usually you would not visit the second time unless they had repaid it.

c. Negro

At Christmas time, it is customary to serve candy to friends who come to visit. There are always just three kinds without any variation: chocolate fudge with pecans, caramel with English walnuts, and divinity fudge filled with chopped candied cherries, candied pineapple, and nuts. Special friends are always given a small box of assorted candy to take home with them. The candy is homemade; the children crack the nuts and Mother makes the candy by basketfuls.

Since daughters have become of college age they always give their mother at Christmas something for the table setting since their mother likes to cook and likes a beautiful table arrangement.

d. Anglo-Saxon Protestant

Christmas Eve is always spent in trimming the tree and afterwards going downtown for the midnight service. Immediately after supper, the balls, lights, tinsel, and other ornaments are brought down from the attic while my father is bringing the tree in from outside and setting it in the stand. From then on it is my mother's show. She has to decide where each bauble is to be placed or else she wouldn't think it was just right. After all the bulbs and decorations are fixed so that everybody approves, then the presents are all brought in and arranged under the tree. On completing this, the room is closed and left until the next morning. Everybody gets ready and goes to church to sing carols. On Christmas Day the rest of the tradition unfolds. To my brother and me when we were younger the orders the night before were that my parents were not to be awakened until eight o'clock. Before that time we were allowed to go down to the living room to see what was in our stockings that were hung near the fireplace, but we were not to enter the sunporch where the tree was. At eight everybody went in to the tree together and the presents were opened. The rest of the morning and early afternoon my brother and I would spend comparing our gifts with our buddies around the neighborhood. At two or three our relatives would begin to arrive for the big Christmas meal that was always held at our house. Dinner would last from about four to six and all would stuff themselves with turkey and the trimmings. After dinner the men would go into the living room to smoke while the women cleaned up and washed the dishes. After this was finished we would all sit around and talk until it was time for the relatives to be leaving.

My uncle, ever since my brothers and I received electric trains approximately seven years ago, insists on playing with them and eventually breaking them. During the visit it is customary for my father to mention six or seven times how much his wife's relations eat, how much more they come for a visit than his family, and how much money it costs him. No matter how often repeated, it continually raises a guffaw from my uncle, a sly grin from my aunt, and chuckles from the rest.

To these are added excerpts from the case material concerning the celebration of the Passover:

Passover lasts eight days. The family uses a new set of dishes which have been set aside for the occasion. Bread is forbidden on this holiday. On the first and second day of the holiday, our family has a sedar. The sedar is attended by the family and our close relatives. First a cup of consecration, over which Father, the head of the family, has pronounced a blessing, is drunk. The sedar continues with everyone washing their hands and sitting down for the meal. The meal consists of bitter herbs, raisins, cakes of unleavened bread, a sauce called Haroseth, made from dates, raisins, and horseradish. Father then dips a morsel of unleavened bread into the Haroseth, and eats it. A similar sop is given to everyone present. Afterwards the paschal lamb is eaten, and three sups of wine are drunk at intervals with thanksgiving and singing of the Hallel, Psalms from the book of worship.

An annual ritual of my family is the observance of the Passover service on a designated night early in the spring. Our entire family usually gathers for a festive dinner and the commemoration of the occasion with a proper ceremony of religious readings. The service itself includes several traditions of an unsound basis such as the eating of unleavened bread, eating certain herbs, and the drinking of four glasses of special wine with the meal. The oldest male member at the service, being my father in my family, conducts the religious reading, followed by all others present. The youngest son in the family also has a designated passage which he reads alone. The ceremony is generally one of happiness and relaxation, serving as a means for the entire family to get together and spend a gay and peaceful evening in reunion. The service is not one of deep religious importance, but merely a yearly ritual which the complete family celebrates as a body.[16]

6. *Practice in group adjustment.* All family living is education for group living, but homes vary in the stability of practice situations presented. A highly ritualized home is one in which there is much repetition in the same kinds of situations and group relationships. For family

[16] For one illustration of the celebration of the Passover in its effects upon the members of a family, see Jo Sinclair, *Wasteland*, Harper & Brothers, New York, 1947.

ritual means that the members must be together: at specific times; for certain purposes; to fulfill definite roles and obligations; to perform them in relation to others' roles and obligations. The continuance of the ritual usually means that these conditions are met and performed unfailingly. It would seem from the very nature of ritual that the more family life is formalized by them, the less haphazard would be the socializing process, regardless of whether a family's rites were healthfully socializing or not. The analysis of rituals suggests the molding of many personality traits through repeated practice of obligatory actions which, taken in combinations, tend to habits of social stability and adaptability. It may show one means by which some individuals come to be the ones who are constantly called upon because they are ready and willing to work, are dependable, punctual, and understand their role and status in relation to a group; or why others come to be the ones who are shunned because their performance in all these respects is so perfunctory. Social habits of coöperation, regularity, punctuality, and recognition of the rights of others are offered here as being related to ritualistic procedures. Rights of others come to be ritualized in many families as do, unfortunately, deviations from these.

7. *Family continuity.* The study of family rituals in 400 families emphasizes not only their role in the promotion of family solidarity and in the training of children to patterns of valued behavior, but they serve also to show to the child that his own family circle is but the living link in a chain of generations that composes "the family." This concept of the family is important to the individual not only in respect to his own sense of worth and security, but also in respect to his attitudes toward responsibility for the future of the family.

Three well-defined types of family rituals which are important in this connection will be noted. One is the family reunion, customarily an annual gathering to which every living member of the kinship group is invited, and with formal programs of business and social items. Another is the formalized family gathering, held upon stated holidays, for the purpose of "catching up with each other." Such meetings are less formalized, more restricted in personnel, and more frequent than family reunions. Finally, there are the festive Sunday breakfasts each week, when the married siblings return home with their spouses and children to discuss family affairs and to tell what happened during the week. These Sunday breakfast rites are the most frequent and the least formalized of all. If there is a tribal elder, it is apt to be just "Grandma."

A Final Note on the Role of Family Rituals

As one analyzes the rituals of families, one comes to be impressed with how large a part of the behavior and personality of its individual members is revealed. A thumbnail sketch of a man could be drawn on the basis of his behavior and attitudes toward work, play, leisure, sex, illness, religion, affectional response, etiquette and social graces, responsibility for future generations, and so on. Carrying this consideration one step farther, it can be seen what may be the results to subsequent home life from the combining of two ritual systems. A bride, for instance, who had long looked forward with pride to the time when she could call in her own husband on baking day to "lick the bowl," as the men of her family had always done, was reduced to tears and prolonged resentment when her groom responded "What? That raw stuff!" Superficial as it may appear, this sort of thing, as well as whether to vacation separately or together, to send the children to camp or not, how to celebrate Christmas and Sunday, who does the dishes and the shopping, how one behaves at meals, are not things that are frequently reasoned out before marriage. They are patterns unconsciously *expected* and raise emotional temperatures when observed differently. They become even more important when there are children to be considered, and each parent wants them to perform the "right" way. For these reasons, a careful analysis of family rituals, so individualized and so obscure in the modern family, seems a significant part of the study of that group.

It should be repeated that in this discussion of the influence of family ritual upon children and their development there has been no attempt to suggest sole causation of specific effects. It is all too obvious that a single critical event may completely turn the course of conditioning set by rituals, and further, that rituals themselves are, for the most part, just the channelizing of certain deep-seated desires and attitudes into habitual behavior patterns. The conclusion of this study has been merely that: (1) the ritual is a means of communicating overtly the ways of doing things and the attendant attitudes that a family has found to be most satisfactory for its own use; (2) this ritual behavior is practiced repeatedly, unchanged, and is largely unconsciously performed; (3) it covers many aspects of family life which are inescapable from it, and will continue in the next generation of the family; (4) rituals symbolizing the same phases of life are observed very differently from family to family and are a part of what makes individuals noticeably different from each other; and (5) these individual differences, as crystallized in, and influenced by, rituals are just as significant as comparisons of ritualistic differences from primitive to civilized cultures, or from one national culture to another.

Summary

1. A family ritual is defined as a prescribed form procedure, arising out of family interaction, involving a pattern of defined behavior which is directed toward some specific end or purpose and which acquires

rigidity and a sense of rightness as a result of its continuing history.

2. Ritual develops in connection with many aspects of family life, but clusters particularly about such things as holidays, anniversary days, meals, vacations, religious worship, and collective ways of using leisure time.

3. Family rituals of contemporary origin are viewed as seriously as those which obtained a century ago, but modern rituals have become secularized in large measure.

4. Family rituals vary on a class basis. Those in the lower classes are chiefly rituals of expediency, arising to solve lower-class family problems; those of the middle and upper classes tend more toward the refinements of living and the maintenance of past forms of life.

5. Both the nature and variety of family rituals vary from one stage of the family cycle to another, as do also the attitudes of the family members toward rituals. The coming of children and the years of their early maturing are particularly rich in ritual development.

6. Ritual serves many purposes in social life—disciplinary, adhesive, vitalizing, and euphoric.

7. Ritual is a relatively reliable index of family integration. Its acceptance by family members makes for predictability of behavior response, thus reducing strain and disorder in the family group.

8. Family rituals are particularly important for child development. They serve as group habits, they standardize affectional responses, they become the core of family etiquette, they help to organize leisure time, they give added meaning to religious and holiday observances, they give practice in group adjustment, and they make for family continuity.

Chapter 17

Mothers' Role and Functions

Until quite recently in human history, people were forced to function in rather compact groups in which the relation of the individual to his group was all or nothing. Such was the nature of tribal society in which kinship, real or fictitious, was the bond which held its members together. Later, the feudal system combined land tenure with closely knit personal relationships, only to give way in turn to a form of social structure the ultimate unit of which is the individual. The late Professor Ross used the term *individuation* to designate this process which "pulverized social lumps and released the action of its members."[1] Today, even the immediate family has responded to this liberating process, so that the father and mother tend to function separately in the child-rearing process in addition to those differences which result from the respective status ascribed to each on the basis of their sex.

The present chapter seeks to consider: (1) the changing status of women and its effect upon their roles as mothers; (2) changing functions of the family, especially mothers, for their children; (3) problems of the American mother; and (4) mother-child relationships and some possible effects upon child behavior.

Background Factors in the Changing Status of Women

It is difficult to pinpoint a few factors in changing American life that are responsible for the change in role and function of women, for almost every aspect of life has aided in what is commonly referred to as woman's "emancipation." For instance, it has been claimed that the self-starting automobile freed her from being tied to her home, and that advances in

[1] E. A. Ross, *Principles of Sociology*, The Century Company, New York, 1920, p. 439.

the rubber and synthetics industries freed her from excessive mother-hood. Certainly, the typical suburban mother would agree that the first is true, though she sometimes complains that it has, at the same time, tied her to the family station wagon. The small-family system instituted dur-ing this century is proof enough of the second "freedom." There are liter-ally hundreds of other such influencing factors which might be mentioned here.

However, four conspicuous movements in American life deserve spe-cial attention as they concern changes in the role and function of women —and of mothers.

THE CHANGE FROM THE PRODUCING TO THE CONSUMING FAMILY PATTERN

Fewer than 100 years ago, more than 7 out of every 10 American fam-ilies lived in agricultural areas. Today, nearly 7 out of every 10 live under urban or suburban conditions. This has had a revolutionary effect on the status of women and on the general pattern of family roles and functions. Agricultural life tends to breed patriarchy. The muscularly stronger male becomes the head of the family business, which is the direct production of necessities for family consumption. Women and children are valued workers in such an enterprise, but they are subordinate in position to, and economically dependent upon, the male director of the business. This producing type of family life is self-contained, having relatively little need of contact with, or reliance upon, outsiders. It has the appearance of a "social lump," in which the group and its maintenance is the important value. The individual achieves status in proportion to his or her contribu-tion to the group and not in projecting his talents upon the outside world. A number of sociologists have used the term *familism* to describe the fun-damental attitude about the relationship between individual and group in such a family. A strong we-feeling is developed, and the members are conceived as a team working together in all their life activities. Interde-pendence is stressed, and the welfare of all supersedes the welfare of any individual. As in any well-run business organization, roles and functions are clearly defined. Women are child bearers, child rearers, housekeep-ers, and part-time laborers. They have no function apart from family life.

Urban living has created, for most families, the necessity of the mem-bers leaving the family group to earn a salary. Outside contacts become very important, sometimes to two or more wage-earning members of the same family. They are not working together physically as a team at the most basic function of life—sustenance. The we-feeling weakens; a mem-ber has needs and rights and responsibilities in relation to people outside the family; and the family lump begins to pulverize with the emergence of the individuated lives of family members. In such a situation, attitudes change, too. The importance of the family becomes relative to the particu-lar situation of the individual within it. Who is head of the family no longer depends upon who has the strongest muscles but upon who is able to take command. Thus women need not be subordinate, nor need they have their roles and functions dictated to them. Indeed, at present, it is impossible to state what *is* the proper role and function of a specific woman or mother in the United States. The possibilities are so varied that there is no longer a set pattern and the question of what it *should* be is highly argumentative.

MASS COMPULSORY EDUCATION AND THE GAINFUL EMPLOYMENT OF WOMEN

A very significant factor affecting the varied roles of women is the American emphasis upon educating girls in the same way and according to the same standards that we educate boys. In parts of the world, past and present, where girls are educated only for traditional woman's work, they have little opportunity for job competition with men. In the United States, women can, and have competed successfully in almost every type of employment except in the heaviest type of labor and the Presidency. Added, then, to the present emphasis upon the person, even the woman, as an individual there has come about for her the possibility of partial or complete economic independence from the male. Census statistics indicate the extent to which she has availed herself of this opportunity. In 1950, about 18 million women in the United States were "gainfully employed," and this comprised one-third of all the female population over 15 years of age. Three other facts about women's employment are important here. First, it is generally conceded that before World War I, the large majority of women who worked outside their homes did so because they were obliged to, to maintain their families. This is no longer true. Women, in growing numbers, now seek work as personal careers, or to raise a family level of living which is by no means at a mere subsistence level. Second, since World War I, when *married* women in great numbers first attained employment, the proportion of female workers who are married has been increasing. According to the 1950 Census, one-half of all employed women were married women. Data on gainful employment of women in 1955, showed that nearly 12 million married women were either employed or seeking jobs and that in more than 26 percent of families with husband and wife living together both are in the labor force.[2] Marriage counselors are well aware of the manner in which this has altered the married woman's role with her husband. Once she was totally dependent upon him and, for the most part, fulfilled such functions as he saw fit. Now, if he does not approve of her activities, she can say, "What does it matter what he thinks. I earn my own keep." Third, although the bulk of the female labor force is composed of women without children or with children of school age or older, in 1955, "The proportion of wives with children under six years of age, who have outside employment, is 16 percent."[3]

[2] *Family Life*, February, 1956, p. 5.
[3] *Ibid.*

LABOR-SAVING DEVICES AND SIZE OF HOME

At just about the same time that homes began to shrink in size from the four-story mansion to the ranch house, industry started producing an increasing multitude of devices to make housekeeping less physically draining and time consuming. The results of the captains of industry's altruistic attempts to make life easier for "the little woman" have become big business. Small homes with "standard equipment" now include kitchens with wall ovens so that mother will not have to stoop; mechanical refrigerators which have no ice pans and do not even have to be defrosted; automatic dishwashers to eliminate the perpetual historical chore of women; deep-freeze units to decrease trips to market; disposal units which save many steps outdoors and some very disagreeable cleaning; power washing machines that reduce what was once a full day's work to a few hours—including ironing with the electric mangle and steam iron. The coal range and coal furnace are almost defunct. Vacuum cleaners, electric mixers, not to mention the whole modern production of frozen, half-cooked and ready-to-eat foods, have changed the nature of housekeeping for the average mother. It has been referred to by many people as "push-button housekeeping." As one man put it: "I, who remember my grandmother spending two hours washing the dishes after a family meal, now hear my own daughters arguing about whose turn it is to put them into the dishwasher."

FAMILY SIZE

Partly because of the increased status of woman, the small family system has been instituted during this century. Not only does the average family have fewer children now, but there are fewer relatives welcomed into the household as permanent members. Unmarried daughters and maiden aunties can find employment and support themselves. When social security does not suffice, "convalescent homes" take care of many aged relatives. Indeed, the American family ideal has become a small, nuclear family living alone without "interference from relatives." This, then, has decreased the number of dependents upon Mother's services. Census figures show that the average-sized family has decreased from 5.79 persons in 1790 to 3.51 persons in 1950. This is a decrease of almost three persons per household on the average.

Although it is clear that these different modes of living mean changing patterns of role and function, it is not quite so clear what the patterns are and what this means concretely to the society, the family institution, and the future children of the United States. The pertinent question in this chapter is: what do mothers actually *do* in their altered situation? Have they taken advantage of their "emancipation" to slough off family duties? To what extent has Mother become individuated from her husband and children?

Functions of the Modern American Family

The subject of family functions has received much attention from sociologists during the past 25 years and has become an almost standard inclusion in textbooks on the family. Current thinking on this subject is the larger background for attitudes as to how mothers are functioning at the present time.

In 1929,[4] and again in 1933,[5] Ogburn spoke of the *declining* functions of the family. He and his followers have maintained that most of the historic functions of the family are no longer performed by that group, but by other institutions and agencies. Production, recreation, protection in illness and dependency and danger are taken over by industry, big business, commercialized amusement, the doctors, hospitals, police, and so on. Education is now the province of the schools, colleges, and universities. According to Drs. Truxall and Merrill, even the important family function of conferring status upon the child is no longer a significant part of family life. In a time of such great family mobility, they feel, no one knows enough about family backgrounds to confer status on that basis, and each individual earns his status for himself. A textbook by Drs. Burgess and Locke, entitled *The Family: From Institution to Companionship*, indicates the extent to which the institutional aspects of family life are considered to have slipped away from it, changing it to a companionship group whose definition is "A unity of interacting personalities." The three basic functions remaining to the family are those of procreation, affection, and socialization. It is pointed out that even the biological function of giving birth is not fulfilled quantitatively as it once was, since families are smaller. The affectional function, however, is assumed to be more important than ever in a time of mobile and rather anonymous living. The few stable affectional relationships a child has, become extremely significant. Since no other institution has ever been found to socialize the child as the family does, that important function, too, remains with the family.[6]

These conclusions concerning family functions are based largely on statistical indices of actual and possible activities outside the home (such as employment of married women with children, enrollment of children in schools and other agencies for education, child care, and recreation)

[4] William F. Ogburn, "The Changing Family," *Publications of the American Sociological Society*, Vol. XXIII, 1929, pp. 114–133.

[5] William F. Ogburn, *Recent Social Trends in the United States*, McGraw-Hill Book Company, New York, 1933, Vol. I, p. 661.

[6] Representative of the views of many authors on the subject of family functions are the following books: Ernest W. Burgess and Harvey J. Locke, *The Family: From Institution to Companionship*, American Book Company, New York, 1953, pp. 462–479; Andrew G. Truxall and Francis E. Merrill, *Marriage and the Family in American Culture*, Prentice-Hall, Inc., New York, 1953, pp. 312–354; Robert F. Winch, *The Modern Family*, Henry Holt and Company, New York, 1952, pp. 50–176; William F. Ogburn and Meyer F. Nimkoff, *Technology and the Changing Family*, Houghton Mifflin Company, Boston, 1955.

and on estimates of the decreased time necessary for homemaking because of the growing use of labor-saving devices in the home. Goods produced for sale and services to the family rather than by the family is another source of evidence. The results paint a picture of little interdependence and extreme individuation in the current American family. The *decline* of functions is clearly emphasized.

In 1934, Bossard suggested that family functions were in a state of *change,* that the historic ones were not so much lost to the family and taken over wholly by other groups as that the family's part in them has had to change with changing times.[7]

The voices of professional women who are themselves mothers have recently been raised, emphasizing this interpretation of what is happening to Mother and her functions.[8] A summary of the comments runs something like this. Though the family does not produce most of the goods for its own consumption, someone has to produce the wherewithal to buy the goods—or go on relief. Fortunately, it is still the minority of American families which resort to that. Furthermore, consuming patterns have become so increasingly complicated with the addition of new brands and new products that wise selection becomes an important family function. For example, when the first women's college was instituted in the United States, there were no closets, but only three hooks on the walls of the students' rooms. One was for the Sunday dress; one for the nightdress, and one for the school dress. Most of these were painstakingly made at home. Now, in late August and early September, women's clothing stores are bombarded by entering college girls and their mothers, spending hours in careful selection of this year's college wardrobe. In much the same way, the earlier family menu was the result of choice from what had been grown on the farm and whatever meat, fish, and poultry were available. Now, it would seem that in order to make the best nutritional choice for one's family, one should have at least a course in Elementary Physics, Chemistry, and Home Economics.

Dr. Margaret Mead writes of the modern mother:

She shops, she markets, she chooses, she transports, she integrates, she coordinates, she fits little bits of time together so as "to get through the week," and her proudest boast often has to be "it was a good week. Nothing went wrong."

The average young American woman is very cheerful over these tasks. They are a drain on her nervous energy rather than on her physical strength, time-consuming rather than back breaking. . . .[9]

[7] James H. S. Bossard, *Social Change and Social Problems,* Harper & Brothers, New York, 1938, pp. 606 ff.

[8] Among others representing this point of view are Margaret Mead, Sidonie Matsner Gruenberg, Evelyn Millis Duvall, Dorothy Barclay, and Dorothy Thompson.

[9] Margaret Mead, *Male and Female,* William Morrow & Company, Inc., New York, 1949, p. 330.

Dr. Nimkoff, summarizing a survey made at Bryn Mawr College, shows that "push-button housekeeping" may give rise to misleading ideas. Women with more labor-saving devices were found to spend more time, not less, on housework. The typical farm mother spends 60.55 hours a week in housework; the typical mother in cities under 100,000 spends 78.35 hours a week in such work; and the mother in cities over 100,000 spends 80.57 hours. Dr. Nimkoff adds:

> The reason seems to be that the farm woman has more varied household and out-of-the-home duties and therefore devotes less time to any particular duty. . . . Perhaps the fact is that the household labor-saving devices make it possible for the modern housewife to be a better housekeeper than her predecessor, with fewer economic functions to perform, and with efficient machines at her disposal for cleaning, cooking and washing, the modern housewife can perform her domestic duties in less time and with less energy and is therefore in a position to perform them more often. The availability of the labor-saving devices invites their use as does the ease of operation. The result is that the modern wife who has a vacuum cleaner probably cleans her house more often, and the one who has a washing machine does the wash more often. The effect of the household appliances is, then, to make it possible for the housewife to do a more thorough job of housekeeping *as well as* to provide her with more leisure for out-of-the-home pursuits.[10]

Dorothy Thompson, after making a survey of products bought by the American family, comes to the conclusion that modern technology is leading to greater self-sufficiency within the family unit. The question, she insists, is what people *do* with the time technology has handed back to them. Her answer is:

> In the conventional picture they sit at television sets, go to movies, play canasta, and that is about all. In reality they also paint pictures, set out gardens, decorate and even build their own houses. . . .
> The Singer Sewing Machine Co. recently reported that today 30 million American women make at least some of their own and their children's clothes. Last year home dressmakers bought a half billion dollars' worth of yard goods. In 1950, the last year for which figures are available, they bought over 100 million dress patterns. Women not only sew to get more for their money. They sew to get clothes that are "different."
> Of the billion and a half dollars' worth of paint sold last year, 65 per cent was put on walls by housewives or their husbands—at a fifth of the cost of hiring someone to do it. . . .
> The net effect of the division of labor and the enormous efficiency resulting from the gadgets we have developed is to return man to himself and to his home, to increase his self-sufficiency and range of activities.[11]

---

[10] Meyer F. Nimkoff, "What Do Modern Inventions Do to Family Life?" *Annals of the American Academy of Political and Social Science*, November, 1950, p. 56.

[11] Dorothy Thompson, "Our Gadgets Set Us Free," *Ladies' Home Journal*, May, 1953.

As for the educational function, much of this is done at home, for better or for worse, throughout the life of the child. Not only is socialization a part of the educational process, but a great deal of formal education takes place at home both before and after the child goes to school. Every time (as has already been suggested in former chapters) a child's question is answered, every time a child is told what to do, every time a child "observes" something that happens in his own family circle, he is being educated. In recreation and in protection a great deal of guidance is the family's function. Does Mary attend burlesque or opera? At what age may she begin to date? What does she do about speaking to strangers on the street? Who decides whether she should go to school with that cold? Does she have the operation that the school doctor recommends or does she not? What church, what school does Mary attend, and how often? All of these matters and literally thousands of others are, in the last analysis, in the hands of the family. Either the family gives the guidance and makes the decisions or no one does, until Mary is old enough to make them for herself.

Also, at least two students of the family have pointed out that the small-family system does not necessarily add to the leisure time of the mother. One writes:

In small families the parents are called upon to do for their children, especially when they are young, what in the old-fashioned family the other children of various ages and other adults did casually and incidentally. Parents have to double as friends and playmates while remaining fathers and mothers. They have to find sibling and cousin substitutes as well as aunt or grandmother substitutes. Where children in the past somehow picked up their companions and formed their own play groups casually and informally, parents today have to proceed deliberately. They have to find a day nursery or nursery school, or even find neighbors who will join to start one where there never has been any before. The anomaly reaches a climax in that new social phenomenon known as the sitter. In a large family there was always somebody who could "mind" the baby while going on with other business about the house or yard. The sitter, however, is a special functionary engaged to be around chiefly as an emergency resource, and has only minimal concern with the infant in question.

The need for parents to make special plans to be able to go out of an evening or to have a safe place in which the child can play of a morning or to find the child suitable companions or to do any of the things that took care of themselves automatically in a large family, seems to reflect upon their competence. Outsiders, with old-fashioned notions of the family and its workings, openly reproach these parents for "shifting their responsibilities" to others. Yet it is the most conscientious parents who do such planning, who make the special effort to provide for their children what they need beyond the constant companionship of the mother.[12]

[12] Sidonie Matsner Gruenberg, "Changing Conceptions of the Family," *Annals of the American Academy of Political and Social Science*, May, 1947, p. 130.

To which Dr. Mead adds:

Each home has been reduced to the bare essentials—to barer essentials than most primitive people would consider possible. Only one woman's hands to feed the baby, answer the telephone, turn off the gas under the pot that is boiling over, soothe the older child who has broken a toy, and open both doors at once.[13]

So, according to this line of thought, though there are at present other agencies which aid the family in its more extensive job, the successful mother still has these functions to perform and in many ways they are more difficult and complex than ever before.

There is more to these differing points of view than mere pedantic quibbling. As far as the future functioning of the family institution is concerned two different types of service are implied. If the family now serves only to give birth, to love, and to socialize its children, then services of the government, the church, the school, welfare agencies, and so on, must continue to be increased, strengthened, and supported in order to take over the rest of child rearing. If, on the other hand, there are families which function well with the type of assistance already available (and it is obvious that there are such families) then a program of education is implied—the education of families in the manner of performance that is successful in the twentieth century.

A Study of Mothers' Functions

In order to get some picture of what modern American mothers really do from hour to hour and day to day, one of the authors attempted a small-scale study. No effort was made to find a representative sample of the entire population. Rather, mothers were selected who were not marked as conspicuous failures, but who were of varying economic status, with different-sized families and ages of children.

METHODOLOGY

A preliminary study was devised through the use of two types of questionnaires.[14] One was a directed schedule on which only a Yes, No, a check mark, or a time interval was required. It consisted of four mimeographed pages (8½ by 14 inches), down the length of which were listed every possible activity of mothers which could be conceived of by the planners of the schedule. Across the top the days of the week were indicated. The participant then had only to find the activities in which they did engage during the day and mark the time duration in the appropriate space.

[13] Mead, *op. cit.*, p. 334.
[14] The author is indebted to Mr. Jay Ripka for assistance with this part of the study.

There was also arranged an open schedule composed of two mimeographed sheets (8½ by 14 inches) for each day of the week. Time intervals only were listed down the length of the page. The participants then had the chore of writing into the appropriate spaces exactly what they had done during every hour of each day. Although the schedules were distributed in equal numbers (25), 15 of the directed and 22 of the open schedules were returned. Upon analysis of them, the conclusion was that the open schedule was more productive for such a purpose. Some of the reasons were as follows:

1. Of the 15 who filled out the directed schedule, 7 appended notes. Their frustration was obvious. What mothers do, as conceived by someone else, cramped them to such an extent that they felt they had been unable to describe their actual activities and they wanted it to be known.

2. Eight of the participants (two with open schedules and six with directed ones) pointed out that there had not been any provision for explaining unusual circumstances which had changed the usual pattern of their functions during that week. They mentioned pregnancy, the absence of the father on business trips, the illness of a relative who had to be taken care of in the home.

3. The open schedule, in spite of its greater length and the respondents' handwriting, was more satisfactory to use in analysis of the data. The activities of a day could be seen as a unit. Day-to-day comparisons could be easily made. The rhythm and nature of the individual pattern was shown in a continuous sequence. In order to obtain such a picture from the directed schedules, the entire material had to be rewritten and rearranged in sequence.

General impressions gained from the comparison of schedules were these: First, although both types of schedule have their advantage, the open schedule should precede the directed when it is the matter of a quest for family living patterns. Social change creates new patterns which can be found only from the source of them and not from asking questions based upon stereotyped academic concepts. Second, the directed schedule appeared to lead to less honest recording. Mothers, confronted with impressive lists of functions (bathing children, vacuuming, making the beds, etc.), apparently helped themselves to the reputation of punctual performance every day of the week. It is difficult to believe that the mothers who filled out the directed questionnaires just happened to be more rigid and compulsive than the other mothers—particularly since all of them were presented with one or the other schedule and given no choice between the two. A third impression was that there is a tendency to underestimate the extent to which the family public will give of free time and effort and conscientiousness if they are captured by the possible value of a study of family life. At various economic levels the people filling out our schedules were so much interested in the project that they complained about our limiting methods and went to a great deal of trouble to explain those limitations.

This attempt led to the belief that more insight into the actual performance of mothers could be gained by having fewer of them record in diary fashion exactly what they did throughout their waking hours for two weeks. Twenty-one mothers were paid for this service.[15] They were given notebooks and a two-sheet questionnaire on which were such items as age, address, nationality, race, religion, occupation, salary and income, family make-up, domestic help, and hobbies and extrafamily activities of all members of the family. In the notebook, they recorded descriptively the entire two-week activity, with precise timing noted in the margin. All 21 notebooks were returned, completed, within the time allotted; and after an examination of them, there was every indication that these schedules had been filled in with seriousness and conscientiousness. In the author's opinion, this part of the study was of much greater reality value than the former part, and should be the base from which any meaningful questionnaire is devised in order to study a much larger number of mothers.

THE POPULATION

Employment status of the families was as follows. Sixteen husbands and five wives in these families were regular salary earners. In three cases, both had regular earned salaries. One of the mothers had just given up full-time employment because of the problems it created for her young son. Three more of the wives, whose husbands were employed, had incomes of their own from investments. Two mothers were the sole family support. In one case the mother was on public relief with some help from a relative, and in another a college-student husband, who earned very little, received ample support from his parents. The following table shows the occupations of the major breadwinners in the nuclear families.

TABLE 3.

Occupation	Number of Cases
Professional	4
Proprietor, manager or official	4
Clerk and kindred worker	3
Skilled workman and foreman	3
Semiskilled workman	1
Unskilled	3
Unclassifiable	1
None	2
Total	21

[15] This part of the study was financed by a grant to Dr. Boll from the Committee on the Advancement of Research, University of Pennsylvania.

Salaries and incomes combined for the families were as follows:

TABLE 4.

Salary and Income	Number of Cases
Over $10,000	7
$6,000– 7,999	3
$5,000– 6,999	4
$3,000– 4,999	2
$1,000– 1,999	3
Under 1,000	2
Total	21

The data on income and occupation indicate that these families are above the national average (as they are, also, in education). This is a difficulty usually found in the type of study in which lengthy written records are required and means that the results of it cannot be projected upon the total population of modern American mothers. However, this does not deny the fact that valuable depth records are received, individually, from persons ranking very high and very low in the income-occupation scale. These give basic leads for further investigation of larger and more representative samples.[16]

The ages of the mothers in the study ranged from 54 to 21 and of the fathers from 60 to 23. In terms of marital status, 18 mothers were married, 1 separated, 1 widowed, and 1 divorced. This is a slightly lower rate of broken families than is found in the general population as viewed cross-sectionally by the United States Census. Numbers of children, their ages, and their current activity are shown in the following charts.

TABLE 5.

Number of Children	Number of Families
1	6
2	9
3	4
4	2
Total	21

TABLE 6.

Age Range of Children	Number of Children
Under 6	9
6–12	11
12–18	13
18–21	6
Over 21	5
Total	44

[16] For more detailed observations upon this method of research see: James H. S. Bossard and Eleanor S. Boll, *Ritual in Family Living*, University of Pennsylvania Press, Philadelphia, 1950, pp. 208 ff.

TABLE 7.

Activity of Children	Number of Children
Preschool	9
School	25
College	5
Employed	4
Adult dependent	1
Total	44

A large majority of these mothers, then, are involved with school and preschool children though other cases included serve to reveal the continuing functions of motherhood at later stages of the family cycle.

THE MOTHERS' SCHEDULES

The average waking day of the mothers ranged from 17 hours and 24 minutes to 13 hours and 54 minutes. These hours were divided into the following categories:

1. Work directly concerned with service to family and home.

2. Socializing with family (this included mealtimes spent together).

3. Personal service, rest and recreation for the mother herself (this included activities of an exceedingly wide range, from a manicure, to reading the daily paper, to napping, to bathing and dressing).

4. Social recreation with other than family but sometimes including family members.

5. Community work.

6. Services to friends and kinsfolk.

7. Mother's hobby.

8. Religious activities.

9. Mother's education (student mothers).

10. Employment.

Average numbers of hours per day spent in the above activities gave no picture of the actual role of any one mother—as if often true of averages. Their patterns of activity varied greatly and it was the organization and values inherent in the individual patterns that were significant.

Some highlights of the findings, of which there were too many to include all in this chapter, are summarized as follows:

1. Time spent on homemaking functions was closely related to family needs, organization, and values. Only one mother spent as little as 2 hours and 54 minutes per day on work directly concerned with service to family and home.

Mrs. A. had one child, a teen-aged boy. Her husband had just bought a store and had started in business for himself. Since he had no other employees, she spent four and a half hours every day working in the store while the boy was at school. This was her "employment," for which she was paid only in terms of family income from the business. In return for this sorely needed help, her husband had hired domestic help twice a week to do all housework except marketing and cooking. This family placed high value upon being together and upon socializing with friends. This they accomplished during the evenings and week ends, so that the daily average spent on these activities was over three and a half hours each. This left the mother less than two hours per day for any activity by herself and for all personal service for herself. Community and religious organizations and service for friends and relatives were cut from Mrs. A's schedule during this particular time of family life.

The patterns of the two mothers with the highest daily average of home and family service hours show an interesting contrast.

Mrs. B., 24 years of age, had twin sons 15 months old and a 3-month-old daughter. Her husband's salary was $1,700. She spent nearly 9¾ hours per day in direct service to her family, "played" with them for 4¼ hours more, found 1¾ hours for her own personal needs, a half hour apiece during the two weeks for social and religious activities, and managed to get rest by spending nearly 10-hour nights with intermittent rises to feed and change babies. Her life was almost entirely contained within her own home.

Mrs. C. was a registered nurse who had recently given up employment to be with her 8-year-old son. Her interfaith marriage was not an entirely happy one, and her desire was to have her son identified with her own side of the family. This, and her hospital training, resulted in a program of a 10-hour and 54-minute daily "home service" routine. The house was kept in an almost sterilized condition as were the occupants, their clothing, and their dog. Her 1¾ hour daily period of socializing with her family involved only eating well-balanced meals and watching TV. The 24-minute average of socializing with others meant taking the boy to visit his maternal grandmother; the only other activity was the 1¾ hours per day kept for herself, primarily taking short rests after a series of household chores.

Twelve of the 21 mothers had no help at all, either from domestic servants or relatives. Of these, 8 spent more than an 8-hour day on home services, and none spent fewer than 4¾ hours.

2. The amount of time spent in relaxed socializing with family bore no relation to age of family, number of children, income, or even hours of housework. The mothers who enjoyed such periods found time for them. One might say, more correctly, that they planned so as to make the time for them. These mothers apparently created an atmosphere that made other family members also enjoy such periods. There was a marked contrast, here, with other families, in that weekday dinners and most weekend meals were prolonged and social. Two other observations were made. The families that socialized together most did so least by means of watching TV programs. Also, those among them who had higher incomes, help, and older children found more time than other families for socializing with friends and relatives. It seemed that the family trait of "liking people" included both family members and others.

3. The amount of time that the mothers spent for their own personal needs and for those quiet solo moments of "restoring one's soul" was appallingly little. Especially so since this category included such a wide range of "personal services." Only three mothers had as much as three hours a day to bathe, dress, repair their clothes, have a midday snack, nap, relax, read, watch TV, and so on. Two of these mothers had only adult children, and the other had domestic help and two teen-agers who were active in school organizations. For mothers of young children, with or without help, such moments were rare and not often consecutive. One mother of three boys in the strenuous years of age, who also had a strong sense of social, religious, and community responsibility, managed to account for an average of 36 minutes per day to take care of her own needs.

4. Daily averages of time spent socializing with friends and relatives ranged from 12 minutes to 4 hours and 6 minutes. Several distinct patterns were seen. The young mothers with preschool children, with low incomes and no help did not find much time for such activity. They talked with the neighbor over the fence, or a friend dropped in for a cup of coffee, and that comprised their "social life." Mothers in the same circumstances but in medium-income brackets lived in neighborhoods composed of other families like them. Here, after the household chores were done, several young mothers would meet together in one home with all of their children, thus pooling child care and taking advantage of adult companionship, for averages of from an hour to two and a half hours per day. Mothers of preadolescent school children found time for socializing while their youngsters were in school. For those whose children did not come home to eat in the middle of the day, "lunch with friends" was a popular activity. Evening socializing, however, was rare. In fact, there were almost no social engagements for husband and wife together in the evenings in families with preadolescent children. One exception was in the case of a woman with three of them, but with a high income, a reliable babysitter, and a strong sense of social obligation. There was rarely a dinner in the home without guests and she was also able to accept evening engagements, so that she averaged over four hours a day of "social life" (this added to nearly six hours of service to home and family, and more than two socializing with family members alone). With the adolescence of children, the rate of socializing with others increased for all income brackets. In some families most of it included the children, but in all cases the husband and wife found occasions to "escape" alone with their own friends.

5. Nine of the cases performed no community service during the two-week period. Three of these women were employed outside the home, two had very recently moved into new neighborhoods and were not yet "at home," one was living on public assistance with an "emotionally disturbed" daughter, two more had very small babies, and one of these moth-

ers was also a college student. The last was the former registered nurse, whose situation has already been described. All of the others performed some community service, ranging from 3 minutes to 1 hour and 18 minutes per day. A general pattern emerged here, too. The mothers of younger children served by making telephone calls, baking cakes for charity sales, and other chores which could be done at home in the course of their regular routine. The other mothers were much more active outside the home as chauffeurs, PTA and Scout workers, Red Cross aides, and so on. The mother with the most hours of community service had two grown sons. After over five hours of housework a day, she still had more time than any others for service to others, her own personal services, and her hobby.

6. Fifteen of the cases found some time during the two weeks to perform some service (other than social) for friends or relatives. The nature of the help was quite varied, but most of it went to relatives. Elderly parents and grandchildren were the most time-consuming recipients. One mother spent an average of 1 hour and 10 minutes a day doing "good deeds" for other than immediate family members. She was a woman who had grown up in the same community in which she now lived, knew many people in it, and had many elderly relatives living nearby. At the moment, immediate family demands upon her were decreasing in time. She thus increased her hours of aid to others and to her community.

7. Only five mothers stated that they had no hobbies. Of the other 16, only 6 of them mentioned any hobbies which would take them outside their own home. The hobbies of the other 10 were of two sorts: those that added to the attractiveness of their homes, such as sewing, crocheting, painting, interior decorating, gardening, and flower arranging; and those that could be enjoyed during short intervals of quiet and relaxation, such as piano playing, reading, taking pictures of the children, listening to hi-fi recordings, making family scrapbooks, and raising African violets. In spite of their reports of having such hobbies, however, only three mothers had any time to spend on them during the recorded weeks. A woman with two small children spent an average of 18 minutes every evening crocheting after the youngsters were in bed. Another, with school-age children, found half an hour a day to hook a rug. The third, with older children, was readying her garden for the winter and spent half an hour a day on it. Thirteen mothers found no time for such indulgence.

8. Religious activities were reported by 10 of the mothers. All of these attended Sunday morning church services with the father and/or the children. Three more mothers drove the children to Sunday School and back. Two others commented that the family usually went to church together on Sundays but did not during these two weeks for specified reasons. One was a family emergency and the other, the week-end visit of friends. The other six made no mention of church attendance and none

of the mothers reported any during weekdays. Seven of the mothers, however, supervised the saying of bedtime prayers by the children daily.

9. Only two of the mothers were pursuing formalized education. Their life patterns were quite different.

Mrs. D., 22 years old, was married to a medical student. They had an 11½ month old son. She was finishing her senior year at college under circumstances unusually fortunate in such a situation. Though her husband earned only $682 a year, the D.'s lived with his parents, where they gave "partial help" including a nursemaid for the child, and a cleaning woman who also did the ironing. Mrs. D. had the shortest waking day of all the cases, was second lowest in hours spent on service to home and family, spent over 4 hours a day socializing with friends and family, and 4 hours, and 24 minutes a day in the classroom and in studying. Religious, community and other service activities were not on her schedule.

In contrast was the second case.

Mrs. E. was a registered nurse with one son, 15. Gainful employment accounted for 4 hours and 24 minutes a day and "homework" the same amount of time. Another 2 hours and 48 minutes were spent in the classroom and in studying for a master's degree in nursing. Mrs. E. also spent nearly 4 hours daily socializing with family and friends, and managed a few minutes of community and other service daily. Only 3 other mothers had a longer waking day than did Mrs. E.

10. Of the five mothers who were gainfully employed, only one spent appreciably less time on "homework" than on the job, and she had more domestic help than any of the others. Four of these five mothers had waking days of slightly over or under 17 hours. In these cases there seemed to be an emphasis upon "making up to the family" for the hours spent in employment, for all of them recorded more hours socializing with family than was average for the whole group of mothers. The reasons for employment of the women were these. One was filling in, in a family emergency; two, a widow and a divorcee, were the supporting heads of their families; another had resumed her "career" upon the adolescence of her only child; and the last took a chauffeuring job to supplement her husband's $5,000 income, which seemed to them insufficient for a family of four.

SUMMARY

The mothers in this study represent the kinds of parents who are *not* contributing to juvenile delinquency in their children. What functions such mothers perform, how they distribute their time, and what their values are concerning the relative merits of their various activities may indicate some successful patterns of functioning in America at the present time.

Certain few generalizations may be made about the group as a whole.

1. Except in one case, where the mother was very young, new to motherhood, and still a student, these people were primarily family-oriented and adjusted their time with that prime value in mind. In the exceptional case, it was obvious that the "in-laws" were still maintaining the role of parents during temporary emergency. This, too, is a parental function.

2. Wherever the needs of the family were greatest (young children, low finances, current family problems, lack of other help, etc.) the mothers spent least time for and by themselves. Except where the pressures were extreme, they did not necessarily curtail social life with family and others. Employed mothers, and ones with very demanding preschool children, went out of their way to find time for such activities, though the latter could not spend as much with friends as the former. It was also apparent that the social life of husband and wife together suffered with the presence of young children and became more active as the children grew in independence. It would seem that a second value of the mothers was relaxed socializing with "people," including family members. This implies an attempt at family "togetherness," a sharing of family recreation, and a community of friendship with others which, among other things, is a means of social control. It may also imply that mothers feel they can be better mothers if they can manage such periods of recreation. Their days were long; their functions varied; their lives complex, often hectic. Perhaps the conscientious modern American mother needs to seek relaxation from nervous strain more than an earlier type of mother did from heavier physical work in a more placid world.

3. These parents were community-conscious. Those who performed no such services during the two weeks had very clear family reasons for not doing so. For the others there was a very clear pattern. Service to the community increased as family demands decreased. The fact is, however, that only one mother gave over an hour a day to the community, and most of them measured such service in minutes. This points to a current question asked by many parents whose communities make many demands upon them and who feel somewhat shamed by not being more civic-minded. They wonder what they should do. The mothers in this study have answered the question for themselves. They give for the community what they can after family needs and recreation are taken care of. To the community this might indicate that the soliciting of such services might be, successfully, adjusted to specific families, in terms of types of service and amount of time requested. Ordinarily, it is the mothers of school-age children upon whom the greatest demands are made by the community. There may be other kinds of women and mothers who could serve more and as well.

4. The mothers in this study did not seek employment or higher education "in spite of" their families. In every case in which the mother worked or went to school there were very adequate provisions made for the chil-

dren, and in most cases the employment was either necessary or thought of as benefiting the family. In no case were young children left alone, and with the exception of time spent normally in school, none of them had to be accommodated by any other agency while their parent was at work. This might, perhaps, serve as a guide to the many women college students who want a categorical answer to the question "Should we continue school or work after our children arrive?"

5. After examining the 21 schedules in the light of discussions on the waning functions of the family, one thing would seem clear. If the only remaining functions are biological, affectional, and socializing, the term *socializing* covers a multitude of activities not usually considered under that heading. The most time-consuming function of the mothers, "Service to home and family," includes not merely the routine housekeeping chores of shopping, cooking, washing, cleaning, mending, and so on, but also many hours of chauffeuring, conferring with teachers, overseeing homework, taking children to doctors and dentists, attending sick children, patching up wounds, disciplining and so on *ad infinitum*.

6. The average time for all mothers spent on counseling children was three hours a week, in spite of the fact that our sample included babies and adult children. Some of this counseling concerned discipline. It is quicker to spank, but these mothers "talked it over" instead. One mother described such an hour spent with her son in this way: "He is apt to be rather grumpy around home, especially if things don't go the way *he* wants them to go. It means a more tactful approach on so many things, and if things are presented right there isn't a better little worker. But his personality definitely requires more patience on our part." Most of the maternal counseling, however, illustrated the kind of guidance needed by children living in a complex and individuated society. Many hours were spent trying to weigh the values of a desired activity, type of recreation or education, the best way for a child to spend money he earned, difficulties with playmates, dating behavior. This sort of guidance was not confined to the younger children. Married ones brought their problems to parents for discussion, and one mother wrote, "My husband and I spent the whole evening talking over the complications of the latest love affair with the 20-year-old son." It seemed clear that both modern theories of child rearing and the nature of our society have increased the importance of the parental function of guidance.

Some Problems of the Modern American Mother

Although the role of the good homemaker has become more complex and demanding of nervous energy, her status in that role has not been rated high by the society. The term "only a housewife" is a familiar one. A penalty that women have had to pay for their "emancipation" is that if they do not use it they are often considered to be shirking an important responsibility. One mother, for instance, had been working for two years on the problem of getting her twin sons into college. Along with the usual routine of caring for a family of six, she had seen to it that the twins got a remedial reading course, she sent for and examined dozens of catalogues, filled in as many application blanks, drove the boys hundreds of miles to visit various colleges and the deans of admission. Finally, the boys were accepted into a college of their choice. While checking upon a questionnaire which was sent to them, their mother noted that both boys had written "Mother's Occupation—Nothing."

At the same time the society's expectations of her role have become greater in at least two ways. The first has been very aptly described by Dr. Margaret Mead who feels that through the pressure of advertising the housekeeper is expected to keep up to standards never thought of before.

> She doesn't give the sort of party where she is admired because of the heaps of food that she has ostentatiously prepared, but instead she is admired just in proportion to the way she "looks as if it had taken her no time at all." As our factories move towards the ideal of eliminating human labour, our home ideals have paralleled them; the successful home-maker to-day should always look as if she had neither done any work nor would have to do any; she should produce a finished effect effortlessly, even if she has to spend all day Saturday rehearsing the way in which she will serve an effortless Sunday-morning breakfast. The creativity that is expected of her is a creativity of management of an assembly-line, not of materials lovingly fashioned into food and clothes for children. She shops, she markets, she chooses, she transports, she integrates, she co-ordinates, she fits little bits of time together so as "to get through the week," and her proudest boast often has to be "It was a good week. Nothing went wrong."[17]

To the extent that she is successful in this respect, the effort that she puts into it is apt to be underestimated by others. The second heightened expectation is one that she shares with school teachers, who have been complaining recently that their role is now supposed to include that of psychologist, psychiatrist, policeman, health officer, crime-prevention officer, referee, educational theorist, sociologist, and so on. The same is true of the mother, and perhaps to a greater extent.

Added to this, there is evidence that education for women in the recent past has not been designed so as to ameliorate these problems. College-graduated women have themselves expressed the opinion that college gave them "culture" but did not prepare them, in skills or in attitudes, for the parent role which has become their life's work.[18] They graduate ex-

[17] Margaret Mead, *Male and Female*, William Morrow & Company, Inc., New York, 1949, p. 333.
[18] John Willig, "Class of '34 (Female) Fifteen Years Later," *New York Times Magazine*, June 12, 1949, pp. 10 ff.; and Mirra Komarovsky, *Women in the Modern World: Their Education and Their Dilemmas*, Little, Brown and Company, Boston, 1953.

pecting to be "outstanding women" and find themselves "bogged down" in motherhood.

The combination of these facts causes resentment, uncertainty, or a sense of unworthiness and failure in many mothers, none of which feelings are aids to healthful child rearing. In some mothers, it produces a confusion of values that results in neglect of children. One such case is Mrs. Adams, a civic worker *par excellence* who always knows the latest in current events, literature, science, and the opera, but has two petty-thieving, unhappy, and undernourished children. Other mothers, who know Mrs. Adams' family only casually, admire her greatly and wonder why they cannot organize their lives as she does.

Mother-Child Relationships and Child Rearing

There is little question that as production has been removed from the home Mother has assumed a more dominant role in it. She is the one who is on hand during most of the child-rearing process, and being there, she must make all the hundreds of quick decisions that are required during this process. Eddie Cantor illustrated how this operates when he said "I make all the major decisions for my family, and my wife makes all the minor ones; but there hasn't been a major decision in the past 20 years."

This means that in many families the mother becomes the authoritarian parent, and not the buffer between the children and the patriarch as pictured in Clarence Day's *Life with Father*. That this is a general trend in our society is suggested by Dr. Campisi's study of the Italian family, in which patriarchy is a strong tradition.[19] His conclusions are that after two generations in the United States there is only a slight survival of the once supreme dominance of the Italian father. The results of this change in respect to mother-child relations is not entirely clear, but there are some indications that it increases conflict and hostility between them. Psychiatric literature has supported this notion for some time, but more recently two sociological studies have indicated that same thing. One showed that "a much higher percentage of parents who are more dominant than their spouse is reported to have conflict relationships with their children. . . ."[20] The other, a study of college girls' conflicts with their parents, revealed that father-child difficulties centered around choice of date and mate; but mother-child conflict covered so many life areas that it seemed like a general unrest in relationship.[21] This may be another price the American

[19] Paul J. Campisi, "Ethnic Family Patterns: The Italian Family in the United States," *American Sociological Review,* May, 1948, pp. 444–445.

[20] Yi-Chuang Lu, "Parental Role and Parent Child Relationship," *Marriage and Family Living,* November, 1952, p. 294.

[21] Margaret S. Wilson, *Conformity and Nonconformity of College Girls to the Standards of Their Parents,* University of Pennsylvania dissertation, 1952.

woman must pay for her increased status, particularly in a society whose traditional philosophy is to rebel against authority.

One other aspect of mother-child relationship may be mentioned here. With the father away and with few children, it tends to be intense and rather exclusive in terms of rearing. One hears rather too often the remarks of mothers who resent the "interference" of their husbands in child discipline. This leads to a feminization of child rearing, and, in the case of boys, much has been written about the ill effects of it.[22] Although the undesirability of raising a generation of "sissy" boys is well recognized, much less attention has been given to the fact that the behavior and attitudes of girls, too, may be shaped in a less healthy direction if they do not have the complementing functions of the male and female parent in their upbringing.

Summary

1. Whereas the basic unit of function used to be the compact group, through a process of individuation mothers and fathers have come to function more separately in their roles as parents.

2. The changed status of women during the past century has affected the role she plays and the functions she fulfills. Some of the factors influencing her new status have been: (a) a change from the producing family to the consuming family pattern; (b) mass compulsory education and gainful employment of women; (c) the increase in labor-saving devices and decrease in size of homes; and (d) the small-family system.

3. As the society has changed, so has the nature of the historical functions of the family become altered. Some of them, such as the recreational, educational, and protective, have been partly assumed by other agencies. Others, like the affectional and socializing, have achieved greater importance. The functions of counseling and guidance have assumed great significance and are increasingly complex and difficult.

4. A study of the total activity of 21 "successful" mothers for a period of two weeks illustrates the manner in which these women are adjusting their roles and functions to present-day family life.

5. Problems are created for the mother as a parent because, though the title of "homemaker" carries low status, more is expected of her in that role than formerly. Not only are standards of housekeeping higher, but the mother is expected to be a director of human relations and an expert in child development. Her education, up to the present, has not been oriented toward helping her fulfill these roles.

6. The dominance of the mother in an individuated home can lead to two difficulties: (a) mother-child conflict; and (b) the feminization of child rearing.

[22] See Edward A. Strecker, M.D., *Their Mothers' Sons,* J. B. Lippincott Company, Philadelphia, 1946.

Chapter 18

Fathers' Role and Functions

Roles of mother and father have always been regarded as serving complementary functions in the family. The roles, however, have not been the same at all times nor in all societies, as has been indicated in the previous chapter in respect to the mother's role. Although the mother, as the key person in the family, has been the subject of much interest for students of the family, the father has received less attention. It is true, nevertheless, that his role, too, changes as a society changes; that he has been affected also by the individuating process; and that as the mother's behavior in family life alters, so must the father's if the complementary relationship is to be maintained. In this chapter consideration will be given to: (1) the status of the father; (2) his primary function as seen by the society; (3) changes in the role and functions of the father; (4) certain aspects of father-child relationships; (5) increasing expectations of the father role; and (6) parental roles and social change.

Father, the Forgotten Man

One of the most striking changes for the American father as the traditional family has changed in form is the way in which society as a whole regards his place in family life. Once he was the most significant figure in the family, the head of the household in all important matters. Roman law gave him control over his wife and children. In the event of crises or problems, he was the decision maker. If conflict arose between a family member and the society, the father was the person called upon as responsible for the behavior. Though the legal power of the "paterfamilias" over his family members weakened in time, the tradition of the father as authority was passed down from the Romans to the British, and hence became part of early American life.

Today, his situation is much altered. Every aspect of social change (discussed in Chapter 17) has tended to produce a less obvious and less potent position in the family for the male parent. As women have assumed a stronger and more active role, the man's has seemed to decline correspondingly as concerns family life.

This has had considerable effect on the way in which the society regards the father. Advertisers, appreciating that it is women who do most of the buying for their homes, carefully attempt to catch the female eye and interest in the area of household purchases. "Women's magazines" crowd the newsstands. Their content covers all aspects of homemaking, child rearing, and family relationships. For men, magazines deal chiefly in sports, science, and do-it-yourself projects. If a child gets into trouble at school, it is rarely that the father is called upon by the school authorities. The mother has become the important contact to the extent that if she does not care to inform her husband of the problem he may remain entirely ignorant of it. Parent-teacher associations and other family-community organizations have been largely populated by mothers and until recently have made little attempt to draw the attendance of fathers. Child-guidance clinics, particularly those operating through the concepts of psychiatric therapy, have dealt almost exclusively with the mother and child and have done the father and the family great injustice by considering him and his relation to his family only as it has been reported by his wife and child. Though there is a plethora of scientific and pseudo-scientific books intended to educate women for their roles as wives and mothers, there is a lack of such materials for husbands and fathers. Except in the books on sex techniques and methods of infant care which are written for both sexes, the male has been largely ignored. Such a glaring omission was noted by the psychiatrist Dr. O. Spurgeon English and Constance J. Foster in 1951, when they published a book entitled *Fathers Are Parents, Too*.[1] Even before then World War II served to remind students of the family that fathers were an important part of the group relationship. Suddenly, so many men were taken away from their families. Hundreds of boys became fathers, precipitately. Not a few had children born whom they never saw for a year or more while the men were overseas. Father's presence had been rather taken for granted, but his absence and subsequent return to his family were noted with interest.[2] From that time on there has been a slowly growing attention given to fathers in both scientific and popular literature. As is the case with mother, the current opinions vary widely as to what is happening to the role and functions of

[1] O. Spurgeon English, M.D., and Constance J. Foster, *Fathers Are Parents, Too*, G. P. Putnam's Sons, New York, 1951.

[2] See: Virginia Van Meter Underwood, "Student Fathers with Their Children," *Marriage and Family Living*, Summer, 1949, p. 101; Rex A. Skidmore, Therese L. Smith, and Delbert L. Nye, "Characteristics of Married Veterans," *Marriage and Family Living*, Summer, 1949, pp. 102–104; Lois Meek Stolz, *Father Relations of War-Born Children*, Stanford University Press, Stanford, California, 1954.

the father, and as to the results of the changes to him, to his wife, to their children, and to the society. The picture is confused, but Father at least has a place in it.

Father's Function—Breadwinner

Available evidence points to the fact that the prime duty of a father is regarded to be the support of his family financially. Various studies have indicated that the male parent, the family members, and the society in general concur in this feeling. Dr. Evelyn Millis Duvall writes: "Now as always, a man is expected to be the primary breadwinner and set up his little family in the style to which he wants them to become accustomed."[3] In a study of 416 adolescent boys who were questioned as to whether they expected their future wives to work, over three-fourths of the answers were an unqualified "No." Only one in eight responded in the affirmative.[4] Another investigation of 85 fathers by depth interview concluded that "the concept of the father as one who makes material provision for his family appears to be basic to thinking about what the father's role is. . . . It ranked first in discussion of 'concept' and second in discussion of father's own performance and in his advice to future fathers." In relating the findings of the study to other literature on this subject, the author wrote:

At first glance, the reiteration of this function by so many fathers of this study might seem to identify it as one common only to modern urbanized man, reinforced as it is by the writings of modern authors. Among others, Parsons . . . writes that the kinship system of modern industrial society is characterized by the "relatively isolated conjugal family" in which wife and children depend upon the occupational status of husband and father for their own status and income. Social status itself hinges on "earning a living" in "an approved occupational role." . . . Failure to have an adequate job, "earn a living," and thus to provide for the family, may have consequences that go beyond loss of status. In view of the "alteration in basic masculine role in the direction of occupation," . . . the husband and father does not measure up to our accepted notion of what a man should be when he fails in this "fundamental" function. . . . Thus, Parsons observes that to be an economic provider is "virtually the only way to be a real man in our society.". . . Such a man is thought of as "real," "normal," . . . and more matured and experienced than his wife. . . . Hollingworth expresses a similar view when he writes that "in the course of time a man tends to become his occupation.". . .

Yet, students of social organization among human and animal communities assure us that "nurturing behavior" was unique to the human male as long ago

---

[3] Evelyn Millis Duvall, *Family Development*, J. B. Lippincott Company, Philadelphia, 1957, p. 197.

[4] Raymond Payne, "Adolescents' Attitudes Toward the Working Wife," *Marriage and Family Living*, November, 1956, pp. 345–348.

as the dawn of human history. They take special pains to point out that such behavior is distinctively "human.". . .

Thus, when the fathers of this study placed emphasis on the function of economic provider, they were not merely giving expression to the approved stereotype of the "basic masculine role" in modern urban industrial society, but to a historical function that is peculiar to the human male.[5]

Deeply rooted social tradition as well as the exigencies of present-day life, then, seem to make the idea of the "adequate husband and father" also that of "the main family provider."

The majority of American fathers are fulfilling this function. There are the others, however, who do not; and their number cannot be easily estimated for they are of many types. The department of public assistance in just one state reported a one-month payment of two and a half million dollars for families whose fathers had deserted them. The courts often find it difficult to do more than "order" support from divorced fathers. Some men cannot find gainful employment; others will not and much prefer to depend upon the salary or income of wife and children. Then, too, there is a growing number of young marriages in which one of two things happens. The couple is supported by their own families, or the husband is "treated" to an education by his young wife. If it is true that social tradition about fathers' function is still strong, then these fathers are to some extent seen by themselves and others as failures.

Father's Domestic Role

There are two different conceptions at the present time as to what the father's role actually should be in respect to domestic duties while he is not at his place of gainful employment. The traditional conception is that of a definite division of labor between male and female. The man must not be expected to do what is considered as "woman's work." The companionate conception is quite different. The man and wife are to be helpmates to each other in all areas of life. Responsibilities should be shared not on a sex-delineated basis but according to the most efficient, healthy, and pleasurable organization of the family's life.

The first concept, the traditional, is a heritage from the past. It was strong when father was head of the family business, when families were

[5] Ruth Jacobson Tasch, "The Role of the Father in the Family," *Journal of Experimental Education*, June, 1952, p. 348. The author's quotations are from: Talcott Parsons, "Age and Sex in the Social Structure of the U.S.," *American Sociological Review*, October, 1942, pp. 604–616; "The Social Structure of the Family," in R. N. Anshen (ed.), *The Family: Its Function and Destiny*, Harper & Brothers, New York, 1949, pp. 173–201; H. L. Hollingworth, in C. M. Morgan, *The Attitudes and Adjustment of Recipients of Old Age Assistance in Upstate and Metropolitan New York*, Archives of Psychology, No. 214, Columbia University Press, New York, 1937; and S. Zuckerman, *Functional Affinities of Man, Monkeys and Apes*, Harcourt, Brace & Company, Inc., New York, 1933.

large, and domestic servants available. Under such circumstances there were a number of females available (older daughters, female relatives, hired help) so that the mother need not ask the men and older boys to help very much with household chores and routine child care. Their job was the work that supported the family.

Now, the traditional concept is being questioned by many who see the emergence of the companionate role in the family. Not only does this make for closer relationships and better understanding in the home, they say, but the more complex role of the mother outside of the home requires assistance from her husband at a time when other sources of help have decreased. The depression of the 30's and World War II both made their effects felt in the changing attitudes of some men about household chores. With incomes depressed, many fathers considered it quite manly to help their wives at home. War veterans who had learned to peel potatoes, darn socks, and do their own wash under circumstances in which they were considered heroes, often felt no hesitation about continuing these duties at home—and some were interested enough to learn and teach their wives new short cuts in housekeeping. A noted family-life consultant writes:

Now that men have a reasonably short working week (as compared with 60 or more hours in the nineteenth-century work week), they have more time at home. Household tasks in the modern home, with its electrified equipment and packaged goods, are less arduous, more fun, and require less technical knowledge. Any man who wants to can whip up a tasty meal in today's kitchen. And many of them do. Now with wives out of the home carrying the variety of roles characteristic of modern women, husbands are finding a new place for themselves in the family.[6]

There is not 100 percent agreement as to whether this change in father's role is desirable or healthy. One example of remonstrance against it in popular literature is an article entitled "Husbands: The New Servant Class," in which the author states the results of three polls as follows:

Crosley says that more than a third of the husbands in several of our northeastern states do the dishes, clean house and look after the children, and more than half of them do a lot of the shopping. The Gallup poll insists that 62 per cent of American husbands are intimate with dishwater and about 40 per cent help with the cooking. Kenneth Fink, director of the Princeton Research Service, has discovered that in New York 87 per cent of the young men from 21 to 29 help with the housework, but there seems to be some slight advantage in growing older—only 70 per cent of men over 45 are part-time women.[7]

The attitude of the writer is one of frank disapproval of "the man in the apron." He believes this a weakness, of man's own making, but taken

[6] Duvall, *op. cit.*, p. 164.
[7] Russell Lynes, *Look*, December 14, 1954.

advantage of by women who demand "a husband and also a part-time wife." Attitudes of students of family life have been summarized by Dorothy Barclay, New York *Times* columnist.[8] One group decries the demasculinizing of the father, believes that the pattern will be passed on to their sons, and feels it creates a confusion of sex roles in children. The other group see these changing roles (of both husband and wife) as complementary adjustments to modern civilization which should not be judged on the basis of what was "right" in a different sort of world. Children, they say, are bound to reflect these changes as they grow up, not only because of the model but because of the kind of life they will be living. The attitudes of several hundred college students (male and female) about this role of their father have been found in their written family case records.[9] They complain mildly about the father who is a good provider but will not lift his hand to any housework, and about the "lazy" mother who expects her husband to do her work when he comes home, tired, from his own. The real tirades against father, however, are reserved for the men who do not give enough economic support to afford any help for their wives, and still insist upon playing the part of the patriarch who sits and is served by his womenfolk. In the minds of these particular young men and women, this behavior is not only passé, but arbitrary and unjust. In general they look with approval upon the parents who work as a team, each helping the other as much as possible. They see this as a sign that their parents are devoted to, and happy with, each other. In the minds of these college students, such behavior also makes for good family organization and they express their intention of establishing such a pattern in their own homes when they marry.

To don the apron or not, however, is only one aspect of the father's domestic role. Another is his part in infant and child care. Here, again, the traditional conception has been that this is women's responsibility—though there have always been individual fathers who enjoyed this role and were well fitted to it. In general, though, feeding, bathing, and diapering babies had not been considered a manly art. It was also assumed that the mother should rear the young children in such a way that the disciplining, which was father's realm, would not often be necessary. Apparently, many of the forces which have changed some men's attitudes toward housework have led them to think differently about the child-rearing function. In the Tasch study,[10] 77 of the 85 fathers reported active participation in child-rearing duties; and in their advice to future fathers they indicated their attitude that this was part of the requirement of the

[8] Dorothy Barclay, "Trousered Mothers and Dishwashing Dads," *New York Times Magazine*, April 28, 1957, p. 48.
[9] Materials being gathered for a research project by the authors under the sponsorship of the William T. Carter Foundation for Child Development.
[10] Tasch, *op. cit.*, p. 352.

father role. Added to this, their image of the father as guide and teacher of his children was mentioned more frequently than any other aspect of his role.[11] Representative of the findings in the studies of World War II veteran fathers are those in the Underwood sample.[12] The 20 fathers, with one child each between the ages of 2 and 5, spent a mean time of 1 hour and 11 minutes per day with their children, and 17 of them stated that they thought of their relationship with the child as guide and teacher. It was also noted that problems over child care caused these fathers their greatest "headaches." They did not read the books—which are written largely for women—and resorted to their own "experience" or that of their fathers. Better education for a generation of fathers involved in child care was clearly implied.

In the materials collected for a study of family ritual,[13] veteran student fathers of young children expressed delight in the period they set aside from their work each day at a special time in order to take over the care of their offspring. Some of them indicated that war experience had done something to their value system—that "society" came to be thought of not in terms of "things" but in good and intimate relationships with one's family. Here are some actual comments from World War II veterans concerning the effects of their service on attitudes toward the family:

"I realize more what the family means and what the children mean in my life." "I was father to so many young kids in service that I feel I was educated to help adolescents." "I used to think I didn't want the responsibility of my family any more, but after seeing German kids wanting to eat scraps from my mess kit, I decided that I should accept the responsibility for my own family." "I saw things that I didn't want to have happen to my family; it stabilized what I want and made me more sensible."[14]

Perhaps the coming of the atomic age has had the effect of continuing this attitude in the postwar generation. Educated young people not only *say* they want more children than has been the average national pattern, but they *do* have more. J. M. Mogey of Oxford University has this comment to make:

All the evidence available points to an increase in the participation of fathers in the activities of the household over the past two decades. . . . This newer father behavior is best described as participation, the re-integration of fathers into the conspicuous consumption as well as the child rearing sides of family life. And in a family unit where, over and above marital and mother-child rela-

---

[11] *Ibid.*, p. 349.

[12] Underwood, *op. cit.*

[13] James H. S. Bossard and Eleanor S. Boll, *Ritual in Family Living*, University of Pennsylvania Press, Philadelphia, 1950.

[14] Rachel Ann Elder, "Traditional and Developmental Conceptions of Fatherhood," *Marriage and Family Living*, Summer, 1949, p. 106.

tions, there also exists harmonious father-child relations, stability should en-sue.[15]

He adds that the continuing baby boom is largely concentrated among the educated, urban, white-collar workers in the United States, and that such births must be desired by both partners since these people are most sophisticated about contraceptives. He feels that "A change in the posi-tion of the husband from a rigorous insistence on responsibility with its concomitant of social distance to a more active participation in domestic routines helps to explain these new developments."[16] He also foresees a cont nued drop in the divorce rate with this new definition of the father role.

What happens about Father's participation in child rearing as the child grows to school age and older? This question deserves much more empiri-cal study than has been devoted to it for the answer is important. There is some slight indication that Father's involvement decreases. Philip Wylie, the famous social critic, looks with a stern eye at the American father and writes: "There are 168 hours in a week. The average man spends about 40 of them at work. Allow another 15 hours for commuting time, lunch, overtime, etc. Then set aside 56 hours, eight each night, for sleep. That adds up to 111 hours—leaving Dad 57 hours for eating, relax-ing, or whatever he wants to do. Surely in those 57 hours he could find time to be a father to his children."[17] To indicate that Dad does not, he cites an experiment by Gordon Schroeder. Three hundred seventh- and eighth-grade boys kept an accurate record for two weeks of the time spent together by father and son. The average time was found to be seven and a half minutes per week.

If this picture of the decline of the child-rearing function as children grow is a true one, there may be two reasons for it. First, it has been said that it is not the initial cost of a baby but the upkeep that is expensive. Young fathers, with enthusiasm about having babies rather than things, come to discover in later years that children do require many things. One does not have to look far to see the obviously overworked father, strug-gling to keep up with the financial demands of his maturing family. He has little time and less physical and nervous energy for "fathering" them. Secondly, wholesale participation by Dad in child rearing is rather new. Methods of child rearing are more intricate than they used to be because of "scientific insistence." Children themselves become increasingly com-plicated mechanisms as they age. A father then, who enjoys, and feels competent in, the care of a cuddly and relatively uncomplicated young

[15] J. M. Mogey, "A Century of Declining Parental Authority," *Marriage and Family Living*, August, 1957, p. 238.

[16] *Ibid.*, p. 239.

[17] Philip Wylie, "American Men Are Lousy Fathers," *The American Weekly*, November 27, 1955.

child, may be completely unable to cope with the guide and teacher function later. Since many mothers express a growing sense of inadequacy in this respect, it is understandable if the same is true of their husbands whose training has not been so heavily directed toward parenthood as has their wives'.

Father-Child Relationships

Although the amount of time given to a personal relationship is meaningful, the quality of it is much more important. It simply cannot be said that the father who has the most time to spend with his family becomes, automatically, the best father. The kinds of relationships existing between father and child have undergone a number of changes and what the relationships *ought to be* is currently a subject of much discussion. Several of these changes and current attitudes about their results will be presented here.

AUTHORITY AND DISCIPLINE

As has been suggested in the previous chapter, the mother has had to take a great deal of the authority over, and disciplining of, children that was formerly the father's role, and simply because most fathers are away from home during the greater part of the day. This decline in authority is especially true in the home with young children since so much of decision making for them requires prompt action. One cannot wait till father comes home to decide whether the toddler may go out in the snow-storm, to play with the neighbor's children, or what to do about the ink bottle that is poised over the living-room rug. One acts, immediately. The rearing of small children is composed of thousands of such details that require authority and discipline. Such being the case, the mother who is there attends to such details in the way that she sees fit, and through much experience may become, or fancy herself, as an expert in this respect. Some very good mothers and loving wives have fitted so well into this role of decision maker and discipline dispenser that they come to regard their husbands as "interfering" when they take a hand in such matters. As one mother put it:

I guess I got used to being boss when the kids were little. Now that they are older I just keep on helping them decide, or telling them, what they can or cannot do. After all, I'm with them much more than Dave is and they naturally come to me. The children and I talk things over during the day, then Dave comes home for dinner and disagrees with some plan they've made. It annoys the children, because he doesn't know all the pros and cons that we talked over, and we have to go all through it again. I must admit it annoys me sometimes, too. I wish he would just trust my judgment. But then, a father really ought to have *some* say in what his children can do.

Apparently, fathers feel they should, too. In the Tasch study "the traditional concept of the father as 'head of the house,' the person in whom authority resides, the law-giver, arbiter, and disciplinarian, was given a good deal of support . . ."[18] Certain doctors, clergymen, and social scientists agree that paternal authority should be maintained to a considerable extent for the health of the family relationships and the development of the children. Dr. Strecker's book on "Momism" is a case in point.[19] Too much mother domination is creating a group of weaklings among the lads in America. Little recognition has been given to the fact that there may be serious effects for daughters, too; but the authors feel that the influence of male authority is exceedingly important for girls in respect, among other things, to dating, marriage choice, and marital and occupational adjustment. Male authority may be discounted at present in some homes, but it certainly cannot be in the outer society. Rabbi Robert L. Katz expresses with strength his opinion on the subject of fathers' authority.

The power of the father has been broken. But we ourselves must still learn how to be fathers and to fulfill many of the functions traditionally assigned to the father. We have so long protested the abuses of fatherly authority and we are so imbued with the traumas of the father-son relationship that we have been all too prone to neglect its creative and necessary side. In psychiatric literature, too . . . the fatherly role has been greatly overshadowed by the motherly role and the stress on the emotional security of good mother-child relationships. . . . A religious view holds out the possibility of the father's combining authority and love. It emphasizes his role in helping the child to achieve a sense of integrity and individuality at the same time that he learns to participate in the community. There is no irreconcilable conflict between these two goals. The good father is the symbol, the embodiment of this type of personality. He gives to his son an example to follow, he is the father and the teacher. . . ."[20]

A word, perhaps, should be added here on a special problem of the authority relationship with children as it pertains to the United States. Can a parent combine authority and love—or lack of hostility in children? Two studies already cited, suggest that as mother gains more power she also creates more conflict,[21] and that as the patriarchal authority becomes more democratic he is less feared and more loved.[22] A third study, of parent-child conflict-attachment relations, gives the following conclusions. A sample of such relationships in the United States shows that the more authoritarian parent elicits more hostility from children. This does not

[18] Tasch, *op. cit.*, p. 350.

[19] Edward A. Strecker, M.D., *Their Mothers' Sons*, J. B. Lippincott Company, Philadelphia, 1946.

[20] Rabbi Robert L. Katz, "The Role of the Father," *Mental Hygiene Quarterly*, October, 1957, pp. 519–520.

[21] Margaret S. Wilson, *Conformity and Nonconformity of College Girls to the Standards of Their Parents*, University of Pennsylvania dissertation, 1952.

[22] Paul J. Campisi, "Ethnic Family Patterns: The Italian Family in the United States," *American Sociological Review*, May, 1948, pp. 444–445.

hold merely on the Freudian principle of mother-daughter and father-son hostility, but in any combination (father-daughter and mother-son, also). The author of this study comments that this would result in a society like ours because of our attitudes about authority itself, whereas it might not in such a situation as the traditional Chinese family where a great respect for, and subservience to authority, is a strong tradition.[23] The problem of authority without conflict and rebellion, then, may be a particularly difficult one for the American family with its traditions of individualism, permissiveness, and "democracy" in human relations.

One analysis of hundreds of family case records has revealed certain authority patterns as they actually exist in families at the present time. In one, the mother attempts to maintain the father's authority by saving the disciplining of children for him whenever he is at home. According to the children's reactions, the plan is not too healthy. Their comments range from "I was always scared for Dad to come home," to "I didn't have much respect for him. Mother told him what to do and he did. But he didn't know what it was all about." In patterns where one parent or the other clearly dominated, children seemed, for the most part, resentful of the one parent and sorry for, or scornful of, the other. There was an exception to this attitude if one parent took over the authority because the other was actually incapable of it. There, children seemed to sense that some authority was needed, and they had some appreciation for it, especially if the father was taking over because of an ineffectual mother. Very much resented was the arbitrary, autocratic father who insisted upon being the head of the household whether he was fitted for it or not. Finally, children reacted most agreeably in cases where they felt that both parents shared equally in the command of the home.

THE COMPANION RELATIONSHIP

Quite apart from the authority relationship between father and child, there is a level upon which their relationship operates. One might say that in an earlier era the level was usually man to dependent child, growing as the child grew, into man to man. For some time now, however, the American father has been urged to be a "pal" to his children—and particularly to his sons—in other words, to develop a different level, child-to-child. Active participation in the energetic interests of children is not always easy for their fathers, but many have struggled hard and become "pals."

Recently, some voices have been raised in protest over this role. Dr. Otto Pollak questions whether the child needs a pal as much as a father figure, and if the pal role may not interfere with normal Oedipal de-

[23] Yi-Chuang Lu, "Parental Role and Parent-Child Relationship," *Marriage and Family Living*, November, 1952, pp. 294–297.

velopment.[24] Rabbi Katz writes: "At best, dad or pop is the captain of the team. Sometimes he is cast in the role of a gray-haired sibling. Less jealous for the authority and responsibility of his office than for the freedom and self-expression of his children, the modern father chafes under the burden of his increasing years, envies the youth of his children, and struggles to remain their peer."[25]

The attitudes of children toward the pal role seem to be that though they enjoy "romping with Dad" when they are small, the thing can be overdone. Adolescent children prefer to look upon their father as a man rather than as a perennial boy scout and often feel shamed by the antics of the latter. Continuing companionship they do enjoy, but not as a pal; nor are they always agreeable to much "participation" with teen-age activities. Yet, a pattern has been set which may be difficult for Dad to change. A common complaint of such fathers is that their children seem to be growing away from them—when their children are wishing that Dad would grow up. Boys mention a special problem they have in this respect. The father who is used to "sharing" everything tends to share too much of his son's best girl. The "pal" is then looked upon as somewhat of a rival.

Dorothy Barclay, in writing of the high-pressured city father whose "pal" activities with children almost must be artificially produced, says: "A father needn't be expected to play baseball with "the gang" every Saturday to prove his belief in the value of vigorous action. The way he meets a request for a new ball or glove, for a tennis racket or a book of tickets to a nearby pool, will reflect his real valuation of children's sports activities."[26] And a college student comments: "I think this business of parents being pals came up because kids need someone to play with and there are so few playmates around. I think it would be better if parents had more babies and saw to it that the kids had nice children next door. Then the parents could relax and just be parents."

PATERNAL EXAMPLE

William M. Cooper, discussing education for responsible husbandhood, writes that whether fathers like it or not they are acting as examples for their children, and their duty is to make this example as helpful as possible.[27] Source of the difficulties in this respect for the modern father is suggested in a most thought-provoking book written by a journalist, Frederic F. van De Waters. It is an autobiographical account of a relation-

[24] Otto Pollak, *Social Science and Psychotherapy for Children,* Russell Sage Foundation, New York, 1952.

[25] Katz, *op. cit.,* p. 518.

[26] Dorothy Barclay, *Understanding the City Child,* Franklin Watts, Inc., New York, 1959, p. 131.

[27] William M. Cooper, "Education for Responsible Husbandhood," *Marriage and Family Living,* Summer, 1949, p. 97.

ship of father and son from the birth of the boy until the attaining of his majority.[28] The description of the author's role as example shows a contrast with that of fathers in a different type of family. Once fathers and sons not only lived together but also worked together. Father was an example, for good or bad, of a whole man. Now, with the lives of family members individuated, this is not always the case. Especially is the work life of the father apt to be separate from his children. One sees, in the picture painted by Mr. van De Waters that during the time a father is at home, his example to his children may be largely in the area of manners, etiquette, and moral philosophy. The first two pose a problem because home is where Father would like to relax from them. The last may be difficult particularly for the most educated and sophisticated fathers. Education in the United States has been largely aimed at questioning, at scientific probing, at skepticism rather than at the unqualified acceptance of traditional values. Because of this, many fathers, able to accept doubt or disbelief for themselves as adults find it hard to answer their own children's questions and sometimes feel like hypocrites when they do. Says Mr. van De Waters: "I have lied to you after due thought and with the best intentions in the world. . . . It isn't much fun to imitate the Voice from Sinai, particularly when you doubt the validity of some of the Ten Commandments. It is even less entertaining to answer questions when your sympathy is wholly with the questioner and his doubts."[29]

The Society and Fathers' Role

Although less attention has been paid to fathers' role than to mothers' it is nevertheless true that increasing demands are being made upon him just as they are upon her. The ideal of the good father includes the good businessman, the good family man, and the good community man.

An article on "The New Burdens of Masculinity"[30] points out a change in expectations of father as a breadwinner. He still carries burdens surviving from the past but also has new ones created by a modern age, through emphases on occupational mobility, the importance of education, vocational adjustment, and new traits such as "politicking" which are required for high-level positions. At the same time, "men are now expected to demonstrate the manipulative skill in interpersonal relations formerly reserved for women under the headings of intuition, charm, tact, coquetry, womanly wiles, etc. They are asked to bring patience, understanding, gentleness to their human dealings. Yet, with regard to women

[28] Frederic F. van De Waters, *Fathers Are Funny*, John Day Company, New York, 1939.
[29] *Ibid.*, pp. 97–98.
[30] Helen Mayer Hacker, "The New Burdens of Masculinity," *Marriage and Family Living*, August, 1957, pp. 227–233.

they must still be steady oaks."[31] They are also supposed to honor the new position of their wives without "castrating" themselves, and be heads of their families by democratic means.

At the same time, the community which has become so demanding of mothers is reaching out increasingly for fathers, too. One hears comments that men are endangering their society when they leave the community largely in the hands of women. It becomes a community scandal when no father is found willing to be leader of the local Boy Scout troop or organizer for the Little League.

The expectations of our society are high in respect to mothers, schoolteachers, and fathers.

Changing Roles and Functions of Parents—A Social Adjustment

Because of the apparently growing rate of juvenile delinquency and general disorganization in this country for several decades, many tirades have been voiced against modern American parents. "They are not what they used to be." This is true. "They ought to be put in reformatories, instead of their children." It would probably be helpful if some were. However, it is a superficial view that indicts modern parenthood for all the evils of the age.

The fact is that the behavior changes which have been discussed in this chapter and the previous one have come about because of a process of general social change which has not only been constant but also has been quickening in its rate for generations. A change in one part of a culture necessitates adjustment in others. Given time, and if the situation stabilizes, groups usually find a satisfactory way to adapt to new ways. Recent history, however, has afforded neither the American family nor the so-called "experts" any level plateau which could be considered "what the situation now is." That of one generation has not been that of the succeeding one, nor will it be that of the next.

Under such circumstances, to suggest that parental roles be reinstituted as they were when the family seemed more successful is to overlook a basic sociological principle. In order for a society to be well organized, its various parts must adjust to each other, or become "synchronized." The family does not "cause" the society as it is. The family is but a part of the society which it influences and to which it must adjust.

A serious problem of parents as to their roles and functions at present is that there are no 100 percent positive answers as to what these should be in order to be most effective. Once roles were simpler and much more clearly delineated. Right or wrong, most parents felt they knew how the "good mother" and the "good father" performed. Now they are, in a sense, pioneers. There are few guideposts, and those that exist are often

[31] *Ibid.,* p. 229.

conflicting. Essentially, each family is experimenting in a pattern of group living in an unknown land. During this process, many of them fail completely and add to the disequilibrium of the complex and changing society. At the other extreme are the notable successes, developing behavior patterns in family life which are satisfactory adjustments to the present and to social change itself. The ways these families have found are, probably, the best answers to "what are the roles and functions of modern American parents."

Summary

1. As a society changes, so must the role of the father, in order to adjust to new family needs, and also to retain the complementariness of function with the mother.

2. For some time the importance of the father role has been overshadowed by that of the mother. This is true in respect to the community as well as to those concerned with the study of, and therapy in, the family and behavior. Quite recently, there has been a growing interest in total group interaction, which has aided increasing interest in fathers' role and functions.

3. Attitudes toward the domestic role of the father have been changing, not only in respect to sharing of household chores but also as concerns early and late child rearing. Opinions vary as to the effects on children of the so-called "demasculinizing" of the male parent. The changes that have come about, however, seem to have arisen as new family situations have developed.

4. The aspects of father-child relationships emerging from role change which have been most stressed in the literature are: (a) the authority relationship, which is weakening; (b) the companion relationship, which is growing; and (c) the paternal example which consists in more of what father is like after work and at home than what he is as a whole person.

5. The roles and functions of both mothers and fathers are in a process of adjustment to the constant social change that is characteristic of their society. They cannot remain as they were and operate successfully. There are no set answers for the most effective behavior. Parents are, in a sense, pioneering in the quest for satisfactory family patterns.

Part *V*

Class and Status Differentials

Chapter 19

The Child and the Class Structure

Thus far, the family background of child development has been analyzed in general terms with only slight reference to those major differentiations, known as social classes, which exist in all but perhaps the most primitive societies. It is the purpose of this chapter, first, to survey briefly the nature of these differentiations in our contemporary society, and then to consider, somewhat more at length, their meaning for child development.

The Concept of Social Class

EARLIER ECONOMIC EMPHASIS

The concept of class came into the literature of sociology from economic sources and until recently has been considered chiefly in its economic implications. The differences between classes were expressed largely in terms of wealth and income, and what these have been able to command by way of goods and services. In line with this emphasis, the processes of social stratification were identified in terms of economic competition and conflict, until a considerable number of students of society, following the lead of Marx and Engels, interpreted the whole social process in terms of the class struggle. "The history of all hitherto existing society," they wrote in the *Communist Manifesto,* "is the history of the class struggle."

Because of the common assumption that social classes are primarily economic in origin and character, the findings of Landtman are significant. After examining a vast amount of anthropological material, he emphasizes rather the fundamental importance of such original factors as age, sex, and differences in personal endowments. Through the maze of ceremony and customs of various societies, he traces the rise of certain elements in the population to positions of superiority, showing how differences in personal traits break down the utopian equalities of primitive culture. Differences in wealth are of subsequent importance (1) in enabling certain classes to acquire various prestige symbols which become identifying characteristics, (2) in the acquisition of advantages which can be turned into sources of new distinction, and (3) in the transmission of class advantages from one generation to another. Wealth, in other words, tends to reinforce and to perpetuate inequalities which result from the operation of other factors.[1]

CLASS IN TERMS OF STATUS

Contemporary sociologists have defined social classes primarily in terms of status. Although historically distinct, the combination of the ideas of class and status systems is easy to understand since they exist side by side and frequently overlap. A social class, thus defined, is an aggregate of persons having approximately the same social status in a given society. Status is utilized as a generalized concept implying the arrangement of groups of people on a comparative scale, in terms of social distance and prestige as well as of reciprocal rights and duties. Reference has already been made to the Warner method of determining social status on the basis of evaluating the participation of an individual in the life of the community, and utilizing an index of four status characteristics: occupation, income, house type, and dwelling area.[2]

The conception of social classes in terms of status, so emphasized by current sociologists and applied particularly to the status systems of modern urban communities, involves primarily a sociopsychological approach. Its criteria are not so much functional and objective as they are subjective, emphasizing primarily how people regard themselves and each other. Such an emphasis is likely to prevail in a society where class distinctions are in process of rapidly developing into relatively fixed formalities.

CLASS AS A CULTURE CONCEPT

There is another possible way to approach the study of social classes and that is to conceive of them as selective cultural groupings, each with its identifying mode of living and habits of thought. Such a conception takes the direction of Max Weber's unfinished definition of class in which he includes the possession of economic means, an external standard of living, cultural and recreational facilities, and the possibilities of communal action.[3] It tends to coincide with Werner Sombart's emphases upon common interests, ideology, consciousness of cohesion, and particularly ways of thinking which are representative of particular systems of eco-

[1] Gunnar Landtman, *The Origin of the Inequality of the Social Classes,* University of Chicago Press, Chicago, 1938.

[2] W. Lloyd Warner, Marchia Meeker, and Kenneth Eells, *Social Class in America,* Science Research Associates, Chicago, 1949.

[3] C. W. Mills and H. H. Gerth, in *Politics,* October, 1944, pp. 271–278.

nomic organization.[4] It embodies Ginsberg's definition of a social class as a group of individuals who, through common consent and similarity of occupation, wealth, and education, have come to have a similar mode of life and a similar stock of ideas, feelings, attitudes, and forms of behavior and who, on any or all of these grounds, meet one another on equal terms and regard themselves, although with varying degrees of explicitness, as belonging to one group.[5] Or, put more pithily, it makes a social class "the largest group of persons whose members have intimate access to each other."[6]

A social class, properly understood, is a cultural reality. Approached scientifically, its identification is not an academic exercise in snobbery or a subjective evaluation, but a recognition of the fact that people live and work and play and think at different levels. The differences between classes are not merely financial or ostentatious; they encompass the entire range of social behavior—occupation, consumption habits, education, manner of speaking, mode of dress, philosophy of life, recreational pursuits, associational activity, social attitudes, family life, and the like. Once social classes and class differences are thus conceived in terms of relatively fixed patterns of behavior, the whole subject of class is opened for objective study.

How distinct and fixed class patterns are varies a good deal from place to place and time to time. Some of the more important factors affecting this process, as identified by Cooley years ago,[7] are: (1) marked differences in the constituent parts of the population; (2) little communication and enlightenment; and (3) a slow rate of social change. Others include differences in wealth, increasing division of labor, and size of community. Generally speaking, the more a social class is segregated and isolated, the more definitely do its members tend to develop their own distinctive activities and interests. In other words, the more social classes become distinct and fixed, the more do their respective members reveal a fixity and predictability of class behavior.

The Contemporary Class Pattern

Common usage has long recognized three social classes—upper, middle, and lower. This tripartite system roughly classifies the rich, the poor, and those who are in between. Recently, Warner and his associates,[8]

---

[4] Werner Sombart, *Der moderne Kapitalismus*, Munich, 1924–1927.

[5] Morris Ginsberg, "Class Consciousness," in the *Encyclopaedia of the Social Sciences*, Vol. III, p. 536.

[6] Allison Davis, B. B. Gardner, and Mary R. Gardner, *Deep South*, University of Chicago Press, Chicago, 1941, p. 59.

[7] Charles H. Cooley, *Social Organization*, Charles Scribner's Sons, New York, 1922, pp. 217 ff.

[8] W. Lloyd Warner and Paul S. Lunt, *The Social Life of a Modern Community*, Yale University Press, New Haven, 1941. Cf. also Davis, Gardner, and Gardner, *op. cit.*

accepting this basic division, have subdivided each into an upper and a lower group thus resulting in a sixfold classification of upper upper, lower upper, upper middle, lower middle, upper lower, and lower lower. Whatever else may be said concerning this classification, it has the double merit for our purposes of allowing a relatively sufficient number of social levels for generalized study, and also of being the result of inductive identification. Obviously, the number and relative size of social classes vary markedly from one social area to another.

Four other distinguishing features of the American class system should be noted briefly. One is its ethnic coloring. In certain parts of the country, particularly the North and East where the immigrant stream of past decades largely congregated, social stratification coincides with, and is reinforced by, ethnic differences. Two recent studies throw light on this relationship. The first is Warner and Lunt's summary for "Yankee City." Although half of its population in 1930 was of foreign white stock, the upper upper class is wholly of Yankee origin, and the lower upper class admits only a few older Irish families. To the two middle classes some French, Jewish, Italians, and Armenians are admitted; there is a small sprinkling of Greeks, and almost no Poles and Russians. More than half of the Greeks, and about three-quarters of the Russians, nine-tenths of the Poles, and all the Negroes are in the lower lower class.[9] The second study is of Burlington, Vermont, made by Anderson.[10] This work shows a fine appreciation of the role of ethnic differences in the class system and of how deeply rooted these differences are, continuing past the second and third generation. Particularly significant is it that the social and religious life of these people, as well as the marriages, are confined largely to their own ethnic group.

Another characteristic of the American class system is the extent to which class and ethnic distinctions are reinforced by religious differences. The United States has been historically a Protestant country, the overwhelming proportion of its earlier settlers being of that persuasion. Since 1880, however, a very large proportion of the immigrant stream has been Roman Catholic, and to a lesser extent, Jewish and of other religious beliefs. As a result, the newer ethnic groups and the less economically established elements particularly in certain sections of the country belong to non-Protestant groups. What gives added significance to this fact is that the deepest roots of religion are cultural rather than theological. Not infrequently, therefore, the religious organization expresses the integrity of a group and its distinctiveness from another group, as, for example, in the case of the Irish whose Catholicism is a symbol of their separateness from the English.

A third characteristic of the American social class system is its relative

---

[9] Warner and Lunt, *op. cit.*, Chap. 9.

[10] Elin L. Anderson, *We Americans,* Harvard University Press, Cambridge, 1938.

mobility, i.e., the extent to which there is movement up and down the social ladder. Although the majority of individuals in this country remain in the class into which they are born,[11] there is general agreement that class lines are less sharply drawn and changes in class status are more frequently achieved here than in most other countries. This is due to a number of historical factors—the relative youth of the country, its democratic traditions, the existence of free or cheap land, the rapid development of capitalistic business enterprise, and the continuing influence of the frontier with its attendant renewal of pioneer culture. There is considerable evidence to warrant the judgment that, with advancing national maturity, class lines in the United States are destined to become both more obvious and more rigid. This seems to be happening, not only in the older and urban parts of the country, but also in the prairie states.[12]

Finally, the American class system includes a caste, which may be thought of in general terms as a class which has become hereditary and occupies a relatively fixed place in the social structure. Specific features of a caste system include: (1) an entrenched arrangement whereby the privileges, duties, and obligations are distributed unequally between an upper and lower group; (2) the lack of opportunity to change from one caste to another; and (3) the complete absence of any social sanction of marriage between persons from different castes. This identification of a caste as a part of the class system of the United States has been made by sociologists in recent years, with particular reference to the Southern states, and with color and certain supplementary physical traits as the criteria of caste identification.

Class Differentials in Child Development

The chief interest of this volume in class differentials lies in their significance for child development. It must be obvious that this significance is great, and for at least three reasons. First, the conception of classes in terms of cultural levels means that class differences are both fundamental and comprehensive. Thinking of a social class as a mode of life and of thought means that it pervades every aspect of life. Second, such cultural levels express themselves, then, nowhere more clearly than in the intimate, everyday details of family life, from which it follows that the family becomes the chief vehicle in the transmission of the class culture. This means, third, that class differences enter the child-rearing process from the beginning of the child's life, and continue as operating factors as long as the child has any relationship with his family. In other words, just as the child is inducted by his family into the ethos or national

[11] P. A. Sorokin, *Social Mobility*, Harper & Brothers, New York, 1927.
[12] John Useem, Pierre Tangent, and Ruth Useem, "Stratification in a Prairie Town," *American Sociological Review*, June, 1942, pp. 331–342.

culture and into a regional culture, so he is also inducted into a class culture. The remainder of this chapter is devoted to a discussion of some of the more important aspects of family-child relationships with reference to the operation of class differentials.

Survival and Health

It seems proper to begin this analysis of class differentials in family life by considering their relationship to the child's chances of survival. Being a child is a dangerous occupation. Despite recent reductions in infant mortality rates, the death rate of children in the earlier age groups is relatively high. These early life hazards, however, are not evenly divided. They vary in part on the basis of class differences. Recent studies have emphasized the social class patterning in child-rearing practices. These include methods of infant feeding, time of weaning, age of bowel and bladder training, age and extent of helping at home, time of going to bed, and frequency of movie attendance, as well as other aspects of socialization, such as aggression control, techniques of discipline, agents of discipline, father-child relations, and the like. Some of these studies, like the Davis-Havighurst studies in Chicago, showed significant differences on a class basis, both for white and Negro children. Other studies, like the Harvard-Newton one and the Littman-Moore-Pierce-Jones one, differ in their findings. It might be concluded that, because of these differences, social class is not significant as a factor in socialization practices in child rearing. On the other hand, inadequacies of sampling may explain some of the differences in conclusions, as may differences in interpretation of the base material. Nor dare differences in subculture areas be ignored. Chicago (Illinois), Newton (Massachusetts), and Eugene (Oregon) are three quite different places, each with a culture complex of its own.[13]

[13] Allison Davis and Robert J. Havighurst, "Social Class and Color Differences in Child-Rearing," *American Sociological Review*, December, 1946, pp. 698–710; Robert J. Havighurst and Allison Davis, "A Comparison of the Chicago and Harvard Studies of Social Class Differences in Child Rearing," *ibid.*, August, 1955, pp. 438–442; Eleanor E. Maccoby, Patricia K. Gibbs, and others, "Methods of Child Rearing in Two Social Classes," in William E. Martin and Celia B. Stendler (eds.), *Readings in Child Development*, Harcourt, Brace & Company, Inc., New York, 1954; Richard A. Littman, Robert C. A. Moore, and John Pierce-Jones, "Social Class Differences in Child Rearing: A Third Community for Comparison with Chicago and Newton," *American Sociological Review*, December, 1957, pp. 694–704; and Martha Sturm White, "Social Class, Child Rearing Practices, and Child Behavior," *ibid.*, pp. 704–712. For critical analyses of the significance of differences in early child rearing, see William H. Sewell, "Infant Training and the Personality of the Child," *American Journal of Sociology*, September, 1952, pp. 150–159; William H. Sewell and Paul H. Mussen, "The Effects of Feeding, Weaning, and Scheduling Procedures on Childhood Adjustment and the Formation of Oral Symptoms," *Child Development*, September, 1952, pp. 185–191; and William H. Sewell, Paul H. Mussen, and Chester W. Harris, "Relationships Among Child Training Practices," *American Sociological Review*, April, 1955, pp. 137–148.

Whatever the role of differences in these respects may be, it has been established that sickness rates and other health aspects of child life vary on a class basis. Persons in the lower classes are sick more frequently; their sicknesses are of longer duration and tend to be more disabling; the adequacy of medical attention may be less, so that the sequelae of the major sicknesses at least are also more frequent and more serious. With these differences go other class differentials. The nature of the family insight into the child's health problems and their implications for his daily life; the availability of resources, other than medical, for dealing with these problems; the possibilities of working out satisfactory life adjustments—all of these tend to vary on a class basis, so that some children tend to enter adolescent and adult life much better equipped in a physical way than others.

Class Variations in Family Structure

One of the most clearly established facts in contemporary population data is the variation in the size of the family of procreation from one social group to another. To some considerable extent, these variations occur on a class basis. This is probably most true when the broader threefold division into upper, middle, and lower classes is utilized, and with particular reference to the economic basis of the class structure. What differences obtain when a sixfold class structure like that of Warner and Lunt is utilized, and when broadly cultural rather than specific economic factors are emphasized, we cannot say with precision. This is a research task for the future. By way of general summary, however, there is substantial reason to conclude that as one moves from the lower lower to the upper upper class, he finds increasingly that children live as part of a small-family system. This means, basically, that there is a class differential in the size of the child's most intimate socializing group. The Law of Family Interaction, presented in Chapter 7, permits a more concise consideration of this fact.

A second aspect of the family structure that seems to vary on a class basis is the composition of the family household unit. Are children in the upper classes reared prevailingly in homes occupied only by the family of procreation? Is the family of orientation more prevalent among the lower classes? Does the larger kinship group appear in the same household more frequently in the lower classes? Here again it is impossible to write with satisfactory precision; but on the basis of economic differences as well as of ethnic factors, all these questions can be answered in the affirmative. Speaking generally, the immediate family and the procreative form of it tend to prevail in the upper classes because financial circumstances permit, and in the middle classes, in large measure, because ambition dictates; in the lower classes, however, larger families, lower incomes, and shorter working-life spans necessitate in greater measure the inclusion of kinsfolk in the household unit. These differences, combined with differentials in space per person within the home, have great meaning in the child-rearing process.

The Setting of Family Life

The phrase, the setting of family life, has reference to certain conditions and circumstances in the living quarters of families which have particular significance in the operation of everyday family life. Those bearing more directly upon child development will be described briefly.

There is, to begin with, the physical appearance of the home; that is, how it looks and compares with other homes, both inside and out. This really involves a dual comparison: first, with homes of other families within the person's class, and second, with homes in general. Such comparisons are related to the conception which members of a family have of themselves and of their relations to others. How early this factor operates in child development is debatable. As this volume is being written, an 11-year-old boy volunteers the observation, in answer to a neighbor's comment that his home is attractive: "Yes, it's a nice feeling to live here."

Second, there are the number and size of rooms in the home, particularly in relation to the number of members in the family. Does each person have his own room? If not, how many share a bedroom? Its drawer space? The living room? It is significant to note the extent to which the members of the family, particularly the children, have an opportunity within the home to be by themselves, to have their own bedroom, bed, drawer space, room to study, room to listen to their own choice of radio program, and to what extent these must be shared constantly with others.

Does the family own its home? Are the words *my* or *our* applied constantly, even if unconsciously, to the place in which the child grows up? Or are his relationship to his home, and the behavior of the adults which he observes, those of the renter? It is commonly understood, among persons competent to make the comparison, that the behavior patterns of home-owning families differ in many respects from those of renters, particularly in their treatment of the home in which they live, and that in many instances the differences are marked. "Acting like a renter" is a common expression in certain parts of the country.

Home ownership is related closely to duration of occupancy, and both must be thought of as having particular importance, not only for the feeling (or lack) of permanence of family life, but also for the degree of the child's sense of security. The study of feelings of security or their lack might well begin with the mobility of families which have young children. Growing up in physical surroundings which remain relatively unchanged may be a basic factor in the development of the child's sense of having a place of his own in the larger scheme of things.

Again, there are what are here called the *facilitating aids* in home life. This term is used to indicate the range of material equipment and services whose presence or absence affects the atmosphere and tempo of home life, particularly the processes of child development. These include servants in the home; mechanical appliances of a labor-saving nature; specialized rooms, such as game rooms, study nooks, space for a laboratory set or a hobby; the number of radios and victrolas; and home recreational facilities. Factors of this kind determine not only the child's activities within the home but also, often, the whole nature of parent-child relationships.

Just as there are facilitating aids, so there are special handicaps which hamper normal family life. Many families live in a physical setting which presents particular difficulties for children—cramped apartments, lack of play space, a home dominated by adult activities, fastidious concern with household furnishings, and the like.

Another special phase of the setting of family life is the degree to which purely family relations and parent-child relations are isolated from other activities of the members. There are families, as in some suburbs of large cities, in which the family life of their members is cut off almost entirely from other activities. Business or "the office" is not brought home, even on the telephone. In other cases, by contrast, storerooms, professional offices, candy shops, display rooms, etc., are operated in the home and their activities constantly intrude, on both a time and a space basis, upon the family's life. The writer recently observed the home of a physician; there were patients in all the downstairs rooms save the kitchen; they were using the upstairs toilet room, and peeping occasionally into other rooms on the second floor. Both of the adolescent children in this family present special scholastic problems.

Finally, there is the spatial relation of the home in relation to other homes. How near in terms of distance do other families live? How near in terms of sound? How much separateness and distinctness of family life are possible, measured in terms of the physical setting of the home? These and other aspects of the physical setting of home life vary a great deal from one social class to another, with the result that family and child life flourish under significantly different conditions.

In the upper classes, children tend to be reared in families which, in their physical setting, give them "a nice feeling to live here." Homes or apartment buildings are attractive on the outside, and are well furnished inside. Many of them have "an air" about them. They are not just houses, they are homes. The children have their own rooms, each child usually having his own bedroom, clothes closet, drawer space, and toys. This is true from infancy on, and must be related to the development of the child's sense of possession. It means, too, that the child can be by himself at least part of each day, and that there is an opportunity to develop a sense of personal inviolability. The percentage of home ownership is high.

Often, especially in the case of the upper upper class, the home may be the ancestral home. Or, if not, it is one with a history, and a status in the eyes of the community. Families tend to remain settled, although in recent years a migratory executive group, well salaried and living on upper-class levels, has appeared in many urban areas. For the most part, however, there is a relative continuity of the home background during the child's life. Servants are present to assume responsibility for many of the chores of housekeeping, which means that there is leisure for family life and for parent-child relationships of an even, unhurried sort. There is time for the amenities of life and for social entertainment. Parents have more time and greater reserves of nervous energy to aid their children in meeting specific problems. There is more opportunity for the parents to help them in properly assessing their experiences. There are other facilitating aids. Specialized rooms for different activities are available for the child and his friends. As a result, upper-class children organize a large part of their activities in terms of their own and their friends' homes. The relative isolation of their home life from the intrusion of adults and from the homes of neighbors also facilitates this. The sleep of upper-class children tends to be less disturbed by home and neighborhood noises; in fact, one of the striking facts to be noted here is that many routine phases of child rearing can be better provided in upper-class homes because of the absence of competing disturbances.

Middle-class home life and child rearing share many of the advantages found among the upper classes. Especially is this true of the upper middle class. To cover the situation as a whole, it may be said these advantages are present in the upper middle class, but less often, and with the more frequent intrusion of complicating factors. Middle-class homes are smaller, with fewer rooms, often less attractive to the eye, and furnished with less elegance if not in poorer taste. The percentage of home ownership is smaller, particularly so in the lower middle class; the duration of occupancy is correspondingly shorter. The physical background of the middle-class child tends to be less stable, which perhaps leads to a resultant lessened sense of security. Professional and business activities of the adult members of the family are more likely to be brought into the range of home activities. Middle-class children are less insulated from the competing activities of their fellows, on the basis of both the physical setting of their homes and the social barriers of their class. In regard to the conditions of middle-class family and child life, there is this fundamental generalization to be made, that members of the upper middle class tend to approximate the upper classes, and members of the lower middle class, the lower classes of the Warner and Lunt classification.

Anything that may be said concerning family and child culture at the lower-class levels must recognize the ethnic inclusions of these classes, particularly in the North and East, and the heavy Negro representation in other areas where they seem to constitute a class rather than a separate caste. Both our more recent immigrant groups and the northern Negroes are at a stage in their historical development in which most of them have a lower class status. Speaking generally, these classes have the least attractive home settings as a rule. Most of the homes are small dwellings or apartments; the rooms are smaller in size and fewer in number, and the families are larger. As a result, the members of these families live much more "on top of each other," "get into each other's way" a great deal more, are compelled from the beginning of their life to share much more than children in other classes. Lower-class homes do not permit the "atomistic" existence that is so readily possible in upper-class homes. Again, lower-class homes are less often in good functioning order, and these deficiencies have a way of intruding into the range of family living. The child is much less able to organize his activities in the home; his home often is not attractive enough to invite his friends, even if other facilities permitted. The percentage of home ownership is low; the duration of occupancy, relatively brief; the behavior patterns of the renter, often manifest. Frequent changes of residence require corresponding adjustments—making new friends, finding a place in a new neighborhood, fighting your way in a new school. Finally, lower-class homes are not insulated, or isolated—the street is outside the window, the neighbors are on the other side of thin walls, neighborhood feuds are common, there is less quiet and relaxation.

The Bond of Kinship

The term bond of kinship is used here to cover the nature and role of intrakinship relations and attitudes, with particular reference to the child. Three aspects will be emphasized: (1) the family's attitude toward the child; (2) the relations between the immediate family and the larger kinship group; and (3) the sense of family solidarity. In each of these, significant class differentials are apparent.

THE FAMILY'S ATTITUDE TOWARD THE CHILD

1. The attitude of upper-class families toward the child is characteristically one of possessive pride and hope. This is a product in large measure of two factors. The first is family pride, pride of present achievements or past histories or both; the second is the economic means enabling one to luxuriate in the satisfactions of parenthood. Children therefore tend to be wanted in specific numbers to guarantee and fortify the family position, but to be limited to the number in keeping with the family's capacity for child rearing on its class plane. The child is regarded, commonly and consciously, as the carrier of the family name, its traditions, heritage, and status. Fathers who have established businesses, for ex-

ample, expect or hope their sons to carry on; mothers with an assured social position are concerned as a rule that both sons and daughters will maintain it, if not better it.

This fundamental attitude toward the child, coupled with the relative ability to carry the costs of child rearing and the facilitating aids in the home, all combine to work for a pleasant home life and for high standards of child care. The child receives the best that the family knows of, his development is closely watched, and he is received early on a basis of equality. Coupled with this care and interest is a strong sense of group pressure in the child's development. Upper-class children are expected to measure up to the class culture and to the traditional performance at the level of their particular family. In fact, as the child grows into maturity, he is given to understand that he must not merely retain the family place but, if a male, he must retain or regain the material resources required, and, if a female, "marry them." Four further facts may be noted about these family pressures. First, the selective factor which operates most strongly is social prestige; there is much less concern about the moral aspects of behavior. Second, the higher up one moves on the social scale, the stronger these family pressures become. Similarly, as the child grows older, the stronger the pressure becomes. Finally, there is the important fact that at the upper-class level these pressures derive not only from the immediate family but from the whole range of kinsfolk. In many cases, this includes kinsfolk who are dead. "What would your Grandmother Elson say?"

Many of the problems peculiar to upper-class children are the result, directly and indirectly, of these pressures. Children may not have the ability to measure up to the level of their family's performance. After all, the next generation has a biological heritage of abilities and disabilities partially different from that of the parent. Or the children may not possess the health or energy needed to function at the family level. There may not be the interest or inclination to do so. Again, parents and other kinsfolk may fail to realize that situations have changed and that what they expect is both difficult and futile. Persons familiar with the problems of students in universities and professional schools know the number, variety, and often the tragic role of these family pressures.

2. Family attitudes toward the child in the lower classes are in sharp contrast in many respects. To begin with, lower-class parents, while not lacking in love and affection for their children, tend to regard them as a sort of inevitable price which fate exacts in payment for sex relations. This is acceptable up to a certain point, when the chief concern comes to center upon their number. With incomes and housing facilities sharply limited, each additional child, after a given point is reached (and it is reached early in the family's life), takes on elements of a crisis. At these class levels, particularly the lowest one, there is little knowledge of

satisfactory contraceptives or of the means of securing them, and often little interest in their use. Coupled with this is the strong emphasis upon the sex side of marital life. Out of this combination grows in large measure not only the multitude of tragic family problems which plague lower-class families but also the prevailing attitudes toward and treatment of their children.

Furthermore, the whole nature and role of the family structure is different among the lower classes. There naturally is less family pride, less concern for the continuance of family status and traditions. More than that, the family is a less permanent structure. The rate of disorganization is much higher. There is more divorce, more desertion, and a far larger number of transitory illegal unions. The changing of sex mates, with or without benefit of clergy, is far more frequent in the lower classes.

The natural result of this is what one also finds in the more primitive cultures: the prevalence of the mother-centered child. The lower-class child is largely reared by the mother, even if punished chiefly by the father. Through the changing vicissitudes of family relationships, the children tend to go with the mother, and to stay with her in case of remarriage or a new union of a less conventional kind. Because of this, as well as of the higher death rates among parents in the lower classes, the relative number of cases of stepchildren and child dependents is high at these levels. In case of the mother's remarriage or new alliance, the children become the responsibility of the new father, with no help as a rule from the natural father. Since the economic means of the mother and of the acquired "father" are both limited, the children of earlier unions tend to be a source of constant irritation and conflict, with a resulting disordering of their personalities. Family situations of this kind are the source of many of the personality problems which prevail in the lower classes.

The chief emphasis in lower-class child rearing is upon not being an annoyance or a nuisance. Children must keep quiet and not disturb the adults in the home or the neighbors nearby. The reasons for this emphasis are obvious. Houses or apartments are small, families are large, walls are thin, neighbors are close. Many people must live within a small area, the adults are occupied with the pressure of making a living, and the children must be trained to adjust to the requirements of these conditions. What this really means for the child has been well stated by Davis and the Gardners: "In a sense, there is no 'child's world' in the lower classes; children are expected to behave as adults at an early age. Fewer concessions are made to immaturity, and the child's pattern of behavior differs from the adult pattern less than in other class groups."[14]

Such emphases and purposes in child rearing naturally lead to a considerable premium upon obedience and on the further virtue of promptness. The well-brought-up child is the one who "stops what he is doing,"

[14] Davis, Gardner, and Gardner, *op. cit.,* p. 129.

and at once. In securing this promptness and obedience, the chief reliance is upon physical punishment. Since often this is administered by the male head of the family, and since the number of stepchildren in these classes is relatively high, the effect upon "father"-child relations is again obvious.

A second emphasis in lower-class child rearing is upon being helpful. Children are taught early to run errands, to do chores, and to assume responsibility for the care of the home and the other children. Lower-class daughters become "little mothers" early in life; where circumstances permit, boys are expected to go with the father and help him. Here, again, necessity is crowned as a virtue. Children are reared, not with an eye to the development of their capacities, but to meet the dictates of the family's need. It is at this point that lower-class family standards and the requirements of child labor and compulsory school attendance laws conflict.

3. The attitudes of middle-class families toward the child range between the two already noted, with some marked distinctions between the upper and lower divisions. Here, as in other cases, the upper middle class tends more in the direction of the upper classes, and the lower middle class approximates the attitudes and values of the lower classes.

The child in middle-class families is wanted, perhaps, chiefly as a form of marriage fulfillment. There is, however—especially in the upper middle class—marked interest in planned parenthood through the use of contraceptives. Family limitation is desired, not generally as a matter of sheer economic necessity as in the lower classes, but as an aspect of family planning. The number of persons to plan for is the basic criterion of the planning process.

But there is a second aspect of the middle-class family's attitude: the fact that the child is seen as the possibility of the fulfillment of hopes. Reference has been made to this in an earlier chapter; it is pointed out here that such cases are probably most prevalent in the middle-class groups. This fact has a particular bearing upon family conceptions of child rearing.

The chief emphasis in child rearing in the middle classes grows out of their place in the class configuration. Above them is the appraising challenge of the upper classes; below, the enticing envy of the lower classes. The former stand ready to reject them; the latter threaten to engulf them. The natural result is a marked emphasis upon "appearances," upon "what people will say" and "how things will look." The middle-class code thus becomes one of rigidly controlled behavior, with a strong insistence that children conform to the formalized patterns of behavior.

Obviously, this cannot be brought about by physical punishment alone. Children at this class level are more likely to be reasoned with, the values of such conduct are pointed out, self-interest is appealed to, nonphysical forms of discipline are invoked. Although child rearing in the middle classes is of necessity carried on largely by the mother, there is considerable coöperation from the father. There are family consultations, definite programs are initiated, outside help may be solicited. Here are the parents who take children to clinics, who go to hear lectures, who want to read books on "child psychology." Many of these parents become confused and others become skeptical in their effort to substitute these newer methods for the old-time disciplines; unfortunately some, in their despair, reduce their efforts to a minimum.

THE RELATIONSHIP BETWEEN THE IMMEDIATE FAMILY AND THE LARGER KINSHIP GROUP

The immediate family's relationship with the kinship group is a fundamental factor in the family background of the child, and it varies considerably on a class basis.

1. The upper-class pattern, particularly of the upper division, is quite definite. The kinship group rather than the immediate family tends to be the focal point and the ultimate consideration in the life of its members. Pride in the family name stems from the history of the larger group; individuals and immediate family units bask and share in its reflected glory; to it rather than the immediate family is given prior loyalty. It is within the kinship group that a general pattern of behavior develops which sets the norms for its constituent members; to it the immediate family unit is subordinate.

This type of relationship is perhaps most strongly developed in the area of the old South, and its nature and social significance can best be studied there. Its clarity and frequency in other parts of the country vary a good deal, depending upon the age of the region and the horizontal mobility of the upper-class population, as well as its vertical mobility. Its relative importance also is probably less in the lower upper class, since the families at this level are more recent arrivals in the social sense, and have less of an idealized past in terms of family history to utilize and exploit.

Some of the significant implications of this dominance of the kinship group will be stated briefly. First, it involves pressure upon the immediate family to conform to the general kinship behavior patterns, with particular reference to the field of child rearing. Second, it follows that relatives share to some extent in the process of child rearing. The role of grandparents is considerable, especially of those who are the particular personification of the family glory or the holder of the family fortunes. Third, there is much emphasis upon respect for older relatives, which comes to be generalized into respect for one's elders. Fourth, the "family's" influence in the choice of matrimonial mates is great, as it is also in the choice of professional or business careers. Fifth, close relations with the circle of kinsfolk are common after marriage. Sixth, as the younger members of the family grow up, there is emphasis upon the examples set by earlier members in regard to community, political, military, and other forms of public service. This emphasis, so marked in older cultures where vestiges of feudal life and the responsibilities of the liege lord prevail, is perhaps less operative in American life. It may develop as a phase of the democratic way of life in this country as time goes on.

2. The middle classes put more emphasis upon the immediate family, although there is a considerable variation between the extreme ends of this social span. In general it may be said that as we go from the top of the upper middle class toward the lower classes, the immediate family grows in importance as the focal unit in the life of its members.

Two basic factors possibly account for its relative position in the middle classes. The first is the individualizing aspect of middle-class life, with its emphasis upon individual effort, achievement, and acceptance of responsibility in the democracy of the home. The particularizing of relationships with kinsfolk is thus only another phase of the same tendency. Second is the fact that middle-class families are socially mobile; many of them have "arrived" recently, and many hope to move higher. This means that collateral branches of the same kinship group have acquired a differing status. Families living in the city have "country" relatives; prosperous families have poor relatives; "newly elegant" families have crude cousins. This tends to be particularly true of members of ethnic groups who have recently acquired middle-class status. The combined effect of these two factors is to make for a rather highly selective process in the relations between the middle-class immediate family and its wider circle of kinsfolk.

The implications for child development follow correspondingly. The middle-class child is reared by his parents; relatives are not expected to interfere. His attitude toward relatives is individual, not general and inevitable. Choices involving the child's training and career and his matrimonial mate are made within the immediate family. Relations between generations after his marriage are dictated more by mutual respect than by "family" duty.

3. In the lower classes, too, the focal point is the immediate family; its relative lack of permanence has been referred to previously in this chapter. What importance attaches to the larger circle of kinsfolk is called forth by the needs of its members, and not as a rule by their sharing in an idealized past. The form taken by this relationship beyond the immediate family is most frequently a close association between brothers and sisters, who after marriage may live near each other and share their common problems and experiences.

There are, however, notable exceptions to what has just been said. These are found chiefly in the ethnic groups in our larger cities, where the lower-class status coincides with Old World vestiges of kinship family structures. Reference to this will be made in subsequent chapters dealing with culture conflict situations. But even in these families, the secondary group life prevalent in contemporary urban centers has tended to dissolve the cohesive bonds of these extended family structures, so that the younger generation tends to ignore them even as their elders seek tragically to maintain them.

THE SENSE OF FAMILY SOLIDARITY

Family solidarity is an intangible thing, however tangible its manifestations may be from time to time. On the positive side it may be defined as a consolidation or union of interest of the members of a family; on the negative side it involves chiefly the rendering of aid in time of crisis. Thus conceived, some sense of solidarity prevails in every family; the chief concern here is with significant variations in its nature or extent from one class to another.

1. In the upper classes, family solidarity is a product primarily of the self-interest of its members. Three factors in its production readily suggest themselves. First, there often exists in upper-class families common participation in business or other projects; second, there are often family fortunes to conserve; and, third, there is the family honor or good name which must be preserved. In time of crisis, the family prestige must be preserved; in good times, it must be enhanced. The family name is a stock in trade whose value must be protected; this is the common interest of the upper-class family. What the family does for its children, and what is expected of the younger generation, is dominated by considerations of this kind.

2. Family solidarity in the middle classes is more voluntary, social, and selective. It seems more like the friendly participation of independent persons, rather than the common effort of the crew of a smart yacht. Possibly economic considerations are effective here. Middle-class families are concentrated largely in the stabilized occupations. They are members of the professional and salaried groups. There is a relative security, even if not an imposing amount, of family income. Middle-class families tend to participate with relative adequacy in the insurance features of modern life; there is as a rule some surplus to draw on. The result of all this is that crisis situations are less prone to arise in the middle classes, and no class pattern develops in this respect.

3. Family solidarity in the lower classes is characterized chiefly by three facts. First, it concerns itself for the most part with crisis situations. These are common in lower-class families. Needs are urgent and have to do often with the essentials of life—food, shelter, and refuge in case of illness. Furthermore, these families are large in size. Responsibility for aid in time of crisis is expected and generally accepted. Second, family solidarity tends to be matrilinear. This is the result of what has already

been said concerning the relative role of the mother. Not only is she a more constant factor in the family's life, but she is also more often the basic person involved in the need situation. Reciprocal demands between mother and child, and the demands of the sister upon her brother, are more common. Third, there is again the pattern of family solidarity in lower-class ethnic groups where there is the relative subordination of the individual, particularly the individual child, to the family group, and the ideal of economic security for family members through family solidarity.

The Educational Pattern[15]

In discussing the educational process as an aspect of child development, something broader than classroom instruction is implied. The term *educational pattern* is used to identify this broader concept, and include such elements as the linguistic equipment which the child obtains in the home, the family attitude toward education, the nature of the school curriculum, the length of the school experience, the child's social status in the school world, and the values emphasized in the course of school life. Variations in these and other elements on a class basis are obvious in the educational pattern, and serve both as an expression of the social stratification in the adult world and also as the mechanism for its perpetuation.

1. Reference has been made in a preceding chapter to class differentials in the linguistic culture. Upper-class children come to school with a language equipment which both adequately serves their school progress and promptly identifies their social background. The words used, the habits of expression, the shades of meaning, the subtleties of expression, the range of topics discussed, all reveal the upper-class home training. The importance of education is taken for granted. It is the thing to do. Going to college is looked forward to, not only in preparing for a vocation but also in equipping one with the interests and standards of his class. Curriculums are selected and shaped toward this end. Upper-class children for the most part go to private schools—boys to private preparatory schools and girls to finishing schools that have preparatory and collegiate features. Throughout this school process, the child is indoctrinated with the attitudes, manners, rituals, and routines of his class. Upper-class children usually do not work while going to school. Financial allowances tend to be adequate, although as a rule they are more conspicuously generous in the lower upper class.

A problem in parent-child relationships frequently results from the fact

[15] For an excellent discussion of education as a sorting and selecting agency, cf. Robert J. Havighurst and Bernice L. Neugarten, *Society and Education*, Allyn and Bacon, Inc., Boston, 1957, Chap. 10. For a study suggesting how early attitudes of parents toward education become effective, cf. Celia Burns Stendler, "Social Class Differences in Parental Attitude Toward School at Grade 1 Level," *Child Development*, March, 1951, pp. 37–46.

that children from the upper upper and the lower upper classes go to the same private schools and mingle together. Somewhere en route in their school experience, the lower upper-class children come to sense that their parents are not socially acceptable on the same plane as the upper upper-class parents, or even the children in the latter class. This often leads to a situation in which lower upper-class children develop attitudes of condescension or resentment toward their parents. This is apt to develop wherever children attain a status beyond that of their parents, but it tends to be more conspicuous in the upper class, by way of comparison with the subordination and respect shown by upper upper-class children toward their parents.

2. In most communities the American public-school system is a middle-class product. Its teachers are drawn chiefly from this group, the language it utilizes in its instruction and the values it emphasizes are representative of the middle class. Its directive control is middle class. When the middle-class child goes to public school he goes into a typical middle-class institution. The linguistic equipment he brings from home fits into the school life, and without attracting attention to itself. Middle-class pupils and middle-class teachers speak the same language. Especially is this true when the children come from professional, semiprofessional, and junior executive homes. There is more than a friendly attitude toward education; it shades into a marked emphasis upon its value, not as a social grace but as a tool with which to rise in the world, particularly in an economic or professional way. Middle-class children go to high school. They tend to elect classical and scientific courses; many plan to go to college. Where state universities, scholarships, and stipends of various sorts are available, the percentage who go to college is high. The incidental values emphasized during their school experience, simply stated, are these: Behave yourself, do well in your studies, be a go-getter, search out all the facilitating aids that society offers for higher training, and you will get along in the world, i.e., raise your status.

There is a marked distinction between upper and lower middle-class children. Here again the upper division approximates the upper-class child, whereas the lower division has more in common with the lower-class child. Upper middle-class children ape those in the upper class and often tend to outgrow sympathetic relations with their parents; lower-class children incline to give up the race, indulging in cryptic references to upper middle-class children as "thinking they are somebody" or "thinking they are too good for us." Lower middle-class children are more handicapped in their educational progress. Many of them work after school and on Saturdays. Home conditions are less favorable for study. Family difficulties tend more frequently to intrude. In the ethnic groups, bilingualism and cultural conflicts are present as complicating factors. A number of the children go to parochial schools and hence may be outside the public-school pattern in many ways.

3. Lower-class children have handicaps in their educational process from the very beginning. Their linguistic equipment is not that of the school. Words, grammar, forms of expression must be relearned. They identify themselves as lower class to teachers and pupils. Their home background tends to make them critical of or unsympathetic to the idea of education. Their milieu furnishes few incentives to the learning process which are not direct and obvious. The courses selected therefore are those designed for immediate and practical use. A large number of these children work during the school term, often to the point of interfering with their school work. Attendance is less regular than that of children in the other classes. The incidence of disturbances in the family background is high. Changes in schools attended are frequent. Retardation is more common. Economic pressure and lack of sympathy lead to an early withdrawal from school. The school's emphasis on "getting on in the world" is twisted into bitter cynicism. Lacking the middle-class graces, these children rationalize the situation by depreciating their importance. Delinquent behavior and contacts with "the law" on the part of either their parents or themselves are common.

Reference has been made to the parochial school in this discussion. Since the Roman Catholic Church has its greatest following in the ethnic groups who have mostly lower-class and lower middle-class status, its role is largely confined to these class levels;[16] and that role is inevitably one of maintaining the cultural persistence of its clientele. It is the purpose of the parochial schools to keep alive the educational pattern of its religio-ethnic groups. Since this pattern is largely a variant culture-class pattern, its inculcation by these schools makes for the retention of the social distance between these groups and the remainder of the population, thus insuring the continuance of the former's lower-class status.[17]

Social Activities and Participation

Class differences, so evident in the family and school life of the child, are fully maintained throughout the range of out-of-the-home activities.

1. The social activities of upper-class children tend to be full and varied. A wide range of choices is open to them, as a result of the economic position of their families, the relative leisure of the members of this class, and their ability to contact the necessary sources of information about interesting things to do. Sports are much emphasized, for sports' sake. There is concern with playing the game and, whatever else may betide, playing it well.

[16] Stanley Chapman, "Church Schools," *Journal of Educational Sociology*, February, 1945, pp. 340–351; Betty Smith, *A Tree Grows in Brooklyn*, Harper & Brothers, New York, 1943, p. 60; André Siegfried, *America Comes of Age*, Harcourt, Brace & Company, Inc., New York, 1927, p. 23.

[17] W. Lloyd Warner and Leo Srole, *The Social Systems of American Ethnic Groups*, Yale University Press, New Haven, 1945, particularly Chap. 8.

One of the distinctive features about the social activities of upper-class children is their relative exclusiveness. For them, social participation, no matter how full and varied, tends to be segregated. In their recreational pursuits, they go or are taken to areas, resorts, hotels, summer camps, etc., patronized by their own class. Although they mingle freely, it is with their own kind. Part of this aloofness, no doubt, is consciously created and maintained, but in large part it is the result of a sorting process carried out by like-minded and like-financed people. Common interests, common traditions, and common capacities make for a way of socializing which is exclusive.

By way of generalization, it may be said that the higher one goes in the social scale, the more social distance is reinforced by geographical separation. Upper-class children tend to live in large houses with adequate surrounding space, in sections where they are in contact chiefly with children of their own class. Their whole manner of life is such as to insulate them, as it were, from contacts outside their class. Going to private schools, being driven to and from school by a chauffeur, a general lack, in normal times, of the need to use public conveyances, vacationing in exclusive summer camps or resorts—all are parts of the same pattern. It is essentially insulation against the rawness and rough edges of life.

2. If the social participations of upper-class children are exclusive, those of the middle class tend to be selective. Middle-class families on the whole do not have the resources to maintain the foregoing features of aloofness in the lives of their children, but they tend rigorously to impose standards of selection. In upper-class families, relative isolation accomplishes rather unconsciously what middle-class parents must achieve consciously, that is, sorting out and selecting the proper associates and activities for their children; hence the superficial student may conclude that social snobbery is primarily a middle-class weapon.

Middle-class children utilize public (as opposed to private) facilities, although there is care to select suitable ones. The distinction between the upper and lower middle classes becomes noticeable here, as in the whole range of social activities. Upper middle-class families tend to be much more discriminatory, calculating, and ambitious in the pressures which they exert upon their children, with the result that the children's activities are more purposive and have more of an air of strain and effort rather than sheer enjoyment.

Special mention should be made of the scientific interests and pursuits of many middle-class children, especially those in the upper middle class. This is clearly manifested in the high-school courses chosen by middle-class children, and is echoed in the hobbies and avocations of the adolescent stage. The reasons for this are fairly obvious. A rapidly changing and developing science is replete with the opportunities which are the basis of the middle-class hope of a rise in status.

3. The social participations of lower-class children may be characterized as residual. These children do chiefly what is available for them, which often is meager enough. Parents have neither the time, the leisure, nor the knowledge to be of much help; they are too preoccupied with their own problems and insecurities. True, there are selective factors at work here, but they operate within the confines of their class configuration. Ethnic considerations weigh heavily. Welfare projects, whose opportunities were once regarded with scant skepticism, are now considered a public service. Athletic and other recreational activities are particularly emphasized, both as a means of achieving individual status and also as an escape from the drab routine of lower-class existence. For lower-class children there is no insulation against the rawness and rough edges of life, only the immunity which comes from constant exposure.

Family Rank Order

For purposes of a generalized summary, it has been somewhat assumed thus far that all the families in the same social class enjoy the same status. Actually, this is far from true. Each family tends to have a rank order in its class, and this order determines not only the extent to which the family is representative of its class culture but also its attitude toward other social classes and other families in its own class. Everyone with social experience can identify the family that fawns upon the families that obviously outrank them in their own class and treat with derisive scorn those in the class immediately below them. Lower-ranking families in the upper classes are under considerable pressure as a rule, feelings of insecurity manifest themselves in many ways, and the whole atmosphere of the home becomes one of extreme tension. In contrast are the middle-class families who are firmly established in the higher rank orders and who maintain their position with comfort and confidence, secure in the prestige of their relative rank order. The home atmosphere here may be one of ease and contentment. Finally, we may identify the upper lower-class immigrant family, hard-working, living carefully, realizing its class status for the time being but hopefully anticipating the future. Here is a family obviously on the up.

The family's rank order in its class is of the highest importance in the creation of the psychic atmosphere of the home which psychiatrists are wont to emphasize in their study of juvenile behavior disorders.

The Child and His Class Nurture

Two basic premises are inherent in the relationship between the child and his class setting. The first is that child rearing is the social mechanism in the maintenance of the class structure; the second, that child rearing is utilized as the chief social device for attaining a rise in class status. Each of these has great social significance.

CHILD REARING AS THE SOCIAL MECHANISM IN THE MAINTENANCE OF THE CLASS STRUCTURE

Social classes live in different worlds, and families reflect the world of their class. This world, or class culture, they transmit to their children from the beginning of the child's life. From infancy on, children are conditioned to certain modes of behavior, so that by the time they reach adulthood they have the techniques for living at their class level. Two further facts need emphasis. One is that this behavior includes relations not only with one's own class, but also with persons in other classes—or out-groups, as the sociologists term them. Second, this class culture includes ways of thinking as well as ways of doing. The child is reared in the mental world of his class; thus he absorbs, as from the air he breathes, the beliefs, prejudices, attitudes, and values which characterize his class.

An appreciation of this process explains the pervasive persistence of the class culture. So deeply ingrained and so strongly emotionalized is it that its hold upon the individual often exceeds the force of other cultural pressures. History is replete with examples where the class hold has been stronger than that of the ethos. One such illustration comes from the history of France. There is much reason to believe that that country's debacle, and the development of Pétainism, resulted from the convictions of the dominant classes in France that coming to terms with the historic foe from across the Rhine was preferable to a rapport with Frenchmen of other classes. Similarly, in the United States there is the Communist type for whom Soviet Russia can do no wrong.

CHILD REARING AS THE SOCIAL DEVICE FOR ATTAINING A RISE IN CLASS STATUS

To most parents, children personify another chance at life achievement. From this it follows that the key to much parental effort in a country with a high rate of vertical mobility is a desire to secure for the child opportunities denied to the parents; and the driving force in parental pressure upon the child, to achieve a status the parent never attained. It is a definite feature of the American social class system that the child becomes the spearhead of parental ambition.

This creates many problems for American children, problems permeated by a series of cruel dilemmas. For the child who succeeds in attaining a status higher than his parent's, there is the problem of parent-child relationships. What inevitably follows is that successive generations find their lateral associates at different social levels. The continuity of family life is broken. The price of vertical mobility is the disorganization of parent-child relationships. For the child who fails, there are frustration and the aftermath of isolation or bitterness, or both. Some of the failures reject their parents' class and the class to which they aspire rejects them, with the resultant loneliness of a social no-man's land. Others, dropping back to their original status, develop strong feelings of class bitterness. This ambition to utilize children to achieve a higher social status leads to much unhappiness, and for many children.

Summary

1. The concept of class came into sociology from economic fields. Contemporary sociologists define class primarily in terms of status. It can also be thought of in terms of cultural levels.

2. Three social classes—upper, middle, and lower—are usually recognized. Recent studies have divided each into an upper and a lower division, and show a distribution that does not wholly conform to the figure of a truncated pyramid.

3. The American class system is characterized by (a) a decided ethnic coloring; (b) a background of religious differentials; (c) its relative mobility; and (d) the inclusion of a caste system.

4. Class differentials are both obvious and important in child development. They are manifest in (a) the child's chances of survival and health; (b) the family structure; (c) the setting of family life; (d) the bond of kinship, including the family's attitude toward the child, the relations between the immediate and the kinship group families, and the sense of family solidarity; (e) the educational pattern; and (f) social activities and participation.

5. The child's family not only is a member of a given class, but also has a rank order in that class, which has an effect upon the family life, particularly its psychic life.

6. Two basic processes inhere in the relationship between the child and his class setting. One is that child rearing serves as the social mechanism for the maintenance of the class structure; the other, that child rearing is utilized as the chief social device for attaining a rise in class status.

Chapter **20**

The Individual Child and His Status

The concept of status, implicit throughout the entire preceding chapter, has its individual as well as its group and class aspects, and it is to a consideration of the status system of society in relation to the individual child that the present chapter is devoted. Three main topics will be considered: first, the meaning and types of status; second, factors and problems in the ascription of status; and third, status achievement in contemporary American society.[1]

The Meaning and Types of Status

The simplest way to define individual status is to say that it means a person's relative social position, assumed by him and acknowledged by his fellows in their reciprocal relationships. Another way of expressing it, from the standpoint of formalized behavior, is to say that it means one's polar position in the patterns of reciprocal behavior in a functioning society; from the individual's standpoint, it is a collection of rights and duties; and from a neutral point of view, it may be described as a specific social position which carries with it definite privileges and obligations.

Considered specifically, a person has many statuses, as many as there are groups with whom he has relations. For example, John Smith as a practicing attorney has a status as a lawyer among the fellow members of his guild; as a deacon in the Methodist Church, he has a status among

---

[1] For an excellent summary, in readable form, of features included in this discussion, the reader is referred to Ralph Linton, *The Study of Man,* D. Appleton-Century Company, Inc., New York, 1936, Chap. 8; Kingsley Davis, "The Child and the Social Structure," *Journal of Educational Sociology,* December, 1940, pp. 217–230; Allison Davis, "American Status Systems and the Socialization of the Child," *American Sociological Review,* June, 1941, pp. 345 ff.; Ralph Linton, "Age and Sex Categories," *ibid.,* October, 1942, pp. 589–603; Talcott Parsons, "Age and Sex in the Social Structure of the United States," *ibid.,* pp. 604–616; Leonard S. Cottrell, Jr., "The Adjustment of the Individual to His Age and Sex Roles," *ibid.,* pp. 617–620.

churchgoers, especially among Methodists; as a Knight Templar, he has a status in the fraternal world; and as the burgess of his borough, he has a status in his suburban neighborhood. In addition to these particularized statuses, he has also a composite or general status, which is the emergent total of all the particular statuses and which represents his polar position in the generalized life of society.

It is generally assumed that the latter is the significant status, and under certain conditions this is so. However, in the specialized secondary group life of our larger urban centers, the particularized status is often the only one that is known within the group; hence to its members, it, rather than the general status, is the important one. It might be added here that one of the problems of the individual in contemporary secondary group society grows out of the rather complete distinctness between the various groups of which he is a member and within each of which he has a separate status. Many people have to make sharp adjustments as they pass from one group to another in which they hold widely differing statuses.

Another and basically important distinction is that between the ascribed and the achieved statuses. The ascribed statuses are those which are assigned to individuals on the basis of certain facts about them other than indicated ability. Some of these facts exist from birth; others follow in a more or less prescribed sequence during individual development. The importance of this, for child development, is that they can be predicted and trained for from birth. The achieved statuses, as the term implies, are those which must be earned. They are not assigned as a matter of course, but are left open to be attained through competitive individual effort.

Factors and Problems in the Ascription of Status

In organizing the outstanding factors in the ascription of status, we see that they seem to fall into two main groups. In the first are those which ascribe status to the individual child because of his membership in certain population groups. These factors may be thought of, for purposes of contrast, as operating along vertical lines, as ascribing a relative status to an entire population group. The factors of color, ethnic origin, and class readily suggest themselves. The second series may be thought of as operating horizontally, that is, within each of the vertical categories. These include sex, age, age relationship, order of birth, plural birth, and the like. Membership in a given kinship group runs through and serves as a connecting link between all of them.

THE COLOR COMPLEX

For one who takes a realistic view of life, color is one of the two factors which fix permanently, from the beginning of life, and in more ways than one, the status of the child. Associated with color are certain other physical traits which combine to constitute the essence of social visibility. These may be spoken of as the color complex. Here is a factor which determines the child's status as a world citizen, i.e., not only in relation to other color groups distributed throughout the world, but also in relation to well-defined color complex groups within the United States. Since the predominant color group here is white, this factor has particular meaning for children who are born into nonwhite groups.

The basis for the ascription of status to these nonwhite groups is a product in large measure of their history in this country. All the numerically important groups were brought here either as slaves or as less-skilled laborers. As a result, a definite status was assigned to them, with resultant attitudes on the part of the dominant group. In the course of time these attitudes hardened, became emotionalized and persistent. Since deeply rooted attitudes in the dominant culture change slowly, they are operative today to a marked degree.

ETHNIC ORIGIN

The ethnic factor operates along the lines of the color complex, except that it is neither so definite nor so pronounced. In the United States, the status significance of ethnic groups differs considerably from one group to another, and for the same group from place to place. Students of minority groups tend at times to overlook these variables in an apparent oversimplification of their problems. The status of the Irish as a group differs from that of the Poles, and that of the French Canadian may be quite different in Quebec from what it is in Connecticut. Here again one sees the role of historical development, as well as the divergence of the culture of the particular ethnic group from that of the dominant element. There is an extensive literature on minority group relations, and there is no thought here of summarizing it; the one point of emphasis is that the individual child has ascribed to him the status of his ethnic group at any particular time and place.

CLASS

The factor of class has been discussed in the preceding chapter; it is mentioned here only to complete the threefold linkage of the factors which operate on a vertical basis, each involving large segments of the population.

SEX

Sex is in many ways the simplest and most universally used of the reference points in the ascription of status. Sex is apparent from birth, it remains fixed for life, and all societies prescribe the various attitudes and roles on a sex basis. The age at which this differentiation begins, how-

ever, and the extent to which it develops vary from one culture to another. Parsons concludes that in this country the distinction develops relatively late and to a lesser degree than in many cultures, and that this is
particularly true of sex privileges and responsibilities.[2] Whatever the time
and degree, there is from the beginning of life an association, in the minds
of the responsible members of society, of the two sexes with different
functions, training, and responsibilities. The entire, even if intangible,
weight of family and other group expectancies differs on a sex basis.

This sex typing of behavior and privileges is not only rigid and lasting
but covers an extensive range. In most societies, the male is typed and
trained for the superordinate role; the female, for the subordinate role,
but with social allowances for certain forms of devious aggression against,
or sabotage of, the male role. Modes of expressing fear and affection, as
well as aggression, are socially typed for each sex. There are sex-appropriate language, clothes, gait, intonation of voice, play, recreation, and
occupation. There is a noticeable difference in the control of the sex life,
or events leading up to sex experience, girls being much more rigidly
supervised in this respect. In this country, and probably in most societies,
the crucial definition of the sex-appropriate role is formulated at adolescence, and it occurs earlier for girls than for boys.

It is, then, one of the essentials in the social development of the child
that the social personality of each one shall match his sex in the biological
sense; that is, boys must be boys and have masculine habits, and girls
must have girls' habits. This typed behavior is largely a social creation.
Earlier there was a good deal of rationalization to the effect that these
different social roles were assigned on the basis of physiological differences, but their changing character from place to place and time to time
can only mean that they are culturally determined. Similarly, they are
socially enforced. The system of rewards for sex-appropriate and punishments for sex-inappropriate behavior constitutes a large part of the social
code of any society. It operates with relative severity, begins early in the
family's treatment of the child, and is reinforced later by the controls of
the school, the gang, the social clique, and the adult world. For the child,
particularly the female child, the road to prestige is paved with the rewards of observing the sex-appropriate code, especially as one moves
from the lower to the higher social classes.

Reference has been made to the fact that the more crucial definitions
of appropriate sex behavior are formulated earlier for girls than for boys.
Perhaps this is due to the earlier maturing of girls, perhaps to a greater
concern on the part of parents with the behavior of girls. At any rate it is
at this stage that girls often withdraw from their easy camaraderie with
boys of their own age and become interested in boys several years older.
This creates a situation for the boys in the younger age group, which is

[2] Parsons, *op. cit.*, pp. 604–605.

aggravated by school systems that compel them and girls to attend the same classes. The boys are left "up in the air," as it were. Outraged male pride does its best—with attention-getting behavior, some so irritating and some so ludicrous to their elders, particularly their teachers. Keeping the two sexes together in the same classroom during these years probably creates and intensifies behavior problems for the teachers. The problem period usually extends from the seventh to the tenth grade, and in some cases beyond. "Perhaps sometime," writes Plant, "the schools which so loudly proclaim their interest in 'the whole child' will make at least a perfunctory bow to the marked biological difference in their groups at this age."[3]

AGE

Another obvious, highly visible fact about the child is his age; and its use as a reference point in the ascription of status is as old and universal as that of sex. Unlike sex, it is a constantly changing condition and as a result cannot give rise to permanent lifetime statuses. Age works on a developmental basis, with each person passing through a series of positions and pressures on an age basis.

Age grading is much emphasized in primitive societies. The age grades consititute distinct groups whose members are especially identified. Definite ceremonial rites mark the entrance into and exit from each group. Behavior appropriate to the members of each group is defined and often ritualized, and each group is organized into a hierarchy. In this country, age grading is obviously present, but it is characterized by a certain informality and lack of ceremonial observance which, however, in no way detract from its reality and effectiveness. Much of the learning process of the contemporary American child comes through his experience in conforming to the requirements of his age group,[4] for each group has its own pattern of expected behavior, privileges, and opportunities. In brief, each age group has its own status.

To achieve conformity of behavior in the specific age category, a system of rewards and punishments is used. Ridicule or ostracism, particularly by the members of one's age group, is usually employed for not "acting your age." Similarly, there are rewards by way of increased authority, privileges, and opportunities for a prompt advance to the next age category.

Society utilizes all sorts of prestige symbols which operate on an age basis. A child's hair is cut differently from that of the adolescent and adult. A very young child sits at the table on a high chair; later he has

---

[3] James S. Plant, "Social Significance of War Impact on Adolescents," *Annals of the American Academy of Political and Social Science,* November, 1944, p. 4.

[4] John Dollard and Neal E. Miller, *Social Learning and Imitation,* Yale University Press, New Haven, 1941, pp. 184–188.

an adult chair but sits on the side of the table. Upper-class homes may have a special dining room for children up to a certain age. Certain words and phrases are forbidden to children before they reach a certain age. The time for retiring at night, crossing the street alone, going out after dark, having your own door key—these are but a few of the many privileges which vary on an age basis.

Both home and school emphasize age as a reference point for behavior. Much of the competition among children for the parents' favor, and the parents' emphasis on child behavior, operates through a system of age privileges. To beat customary age privileges is to gain from the parents more recognition or responsibility than one's age accords. But the present-day school is our most thoroughly age-graded insitution. With compulsory promotion now operating widely, there results a form of automatic age grading which has few parallels, even in primitive societies. In the social life of many elementary- and secondary-school children, there is wide variation in rank and clique behavior among children separated by only one-year age grades.

Certain problems of child behavior which grow out of the operation of the age factor in the ascription of status may be noted briefly. First, children differ markedly in their adaptation to the age hierarchy prevalent in the family's life, as well as in that of the larger society. Some children accept the customary age roles and move along with changes in them. Others strive desperately for the privileges of a higher age group. Still others retreat to the demands of a lower level. There is considerable reason to believe that the second group is the most likely to develop behavior problems, particularly during the adolescent period.

A second problem is the relative abruptness of change from one age category to another. This varies greatly from one society to another. In some it is very gradual, with no clear lines of demarcation from one to another. In others, "it is more nearly comparable to a string of beads, each period being set off sharply from those that precede and follow it."[5] In this country there are certain of the latter type of change. One is the sudden change for many children at the age of 6 from living entirely at home to going to school full time. The gradual transition through nursery school and kindergarten would seem to be much easier and more satisfactory. Even more abrupt is the change from a full-time school status, at ages 16 to 18, to full-time employment in the world of industry. This happens with particular frequency among upper middle-class urban children. Rural children usually have no such difficulties.

A third problem grows out of the difference between the physical passage from childhood to maturity and the social transfer of the child to the status of adult. This problem does not arise in primitive societies which observe rites to signalize the outstanding landmarks in the life of

[5] Linton, "Age and Sex Categories," p. 602.

the individual. In our society, the lack of such rites, combined with the high standards of compulsory school attendance and social protection, results in a situation in which grown young people retain the legal status of children long after they have become adults in other respects.

AGE RELATIONSHIP

If age operates on a developmental basis with but temporary status, the age relationship between given persons remains fixed and carries with it the implications of a permanent status. "Will I always be two years younger than Betty?" wails a 4-year-old. "Yes, always," replies the mother to her disconsolate daughter.

This age relationship is a status-fixing factor of tremendous significance in the relationship between closely associated persons. It has, for example, a very definite role in the kinship group structure. From birth on, each child has a fixed relationship, based on the age differential, with every other person in the prescribed kinship circle. This relationship covers a constant and comprehensive series of the detailed aspects of the life of the individual child, and of the adult as well. In the child's school life, this age relationship, reinforced by class affiliations and numerals, becomes the basis of much of the social life of students. Among the most frequent comments by one student about another are such as these: "Oh, she is in ninth grade," "He was a sophomore when I was a freshman," "She graduated the year before I did," "I was a grade ahead of her." How significant these comments are can be seen from the fact that they may be made in old age in reference to early school associates. It might be added that age relationship is a constant basis of status also in academic and professional circles.

ORDER OF BIRTH

Order of birth is in large measure only another name for age relationship, except that at times it has significance because of the particular order of birth in the family or social configuration as a whole. The middle child, and also the oldest and the youngest, may be said to have a status resulting from that fact, not covered wholly by the fact of age relationship. This was discussed in Chapter 5.

PRIMOGENITURE

Particular mention should be made of the special status, both legal and social, of the eldest child over the centuries. The source of this goes back far in human history, probably to religious conceptions of the special value or virtue of first fruits. Its social importance has been considerable, and in a variety of ways. First, it has been utilized as the general method of monarchial succession. Second, it has served the great landowning families in maintaining their position, through the inheritance both of titles and of landed estates. For many centuries, especially during the feudal stage of history, this maintenance of unity in family estates served as a prop for the stability of the social and economic order. Third, its operation has made for family unity during long periods of time when lack of the principle and its resultant family unity could only have resulted in social disintegration. Fourth, it has tended within the family group to fix the occupation of the oldest male, as well as his range of responsibilities toward other members. Its importance has declined greatly in recent decades, in large measure because of the greater degree of security afforded by the larger society.

PLURAL BIRTH

The birth of more than one child at a time is rare enough mathematically and unique enough socially to result in the ascription of a special status for all multiple-birth children. This practice has been common throughout human history. In many primitive societies, the custom of putting twins and other multiple-birth infants to death is common and widespread. The reasons given for doing so are many and varied. They include the difficulty of rearing more than one infant at a time, and the belief that they are an evidence of the mother's unfaithfulness, the progeny of a dead person, a punishment for an offense committed by a clan member, or that they will keep the rain from falling. The idea that twin children possess extraordinary powers over nature, especially over rain and the weather, is particularly common. On the other hand, some primitive peoples consider multiple-birth children a happy omen, with the result that their coming is welcomed and they are regarded with reverence and respect. The basic idea seems to be that multiple births, being abnormal, have a special significance that is interpreted as malefic by some and as omens of good fortune by others.[6]

In our contemporary culture, most of these age-old interpretations have disappeared, except perhaps the common (but incorrect) belief that multiple births are due to successive copulations at the time of conception. The general significance attached to multiple birth today is wholly social —the assignment of a special social status. On the one side, this status involves an almost complete lack of individual identity. A twin is never just John Smith or Mary Jones, but always one of the Smith or Jones twins. Similar, but more so, is the case with triplets, quadruplets, and quintuplets. On the more positive side, plural birth confers an attention-getting or publicity status which in certain cases is exploited by the parents or some other interested agency.

[6] Hutton Webster, *Taboo: A Sociological Study*, Stanford University Press, Stanford University, 1942, pp. 61–67, 101; Sir James G. Frazer, *The Golden Bough*, abr. ed., The Macmillan Company, New York, 1940.

ADOPTION

Adoption is a legal fiction by which an individual, usually a young child, who belongs by birth to one kinship group acquires an equivalent status in another one. It was very common in the earlier stages of cultural development, often occurring on almost a mass scale. This was due undoubtedly to such factors as a high death rate among younger parents, large families, and generally unsettled conditions of life which created large numbers of orphaned children. To meet this problem, large-scale rationalization developed the institution of adoption as a family duty and a social virtue. In other instances, as among the Romans, the prevailing emphasis upon family continuity emphasized the desirability of adoption for those cases where the barrenness of the wife meant the lack of a natural heir.

Adoption in this country seems to have been on the increase ever since the First World War. The details have been brought more and more under the regulation of the law and the surveillance of public authorities, to the end of safeguarding the dual process of conferring the privileges of parenthood upon the childless and securing a satisfactory home for the parentless. Thus protected, the status of the adopted child is one that has certain intangible social implications. These are indicated by such statements as the following: "Fred is one of the Smith boys. He is the adopted one." "The Browns have two children. You know, they are both adopted." "Mother, who really am I? What were my people like?" Such statements, and their significance, possibly vary considerably on a class basis.

ILLEGITIMACY

Illegitimacy of birth affects the status of the child in many ways. Suffice it here to refer to the general conclusions of anthropological research that one of the universal social rules is that no child, if he is to have full legal and social status, shall be brought into the world save within the limits of socially approved arrangements. The history of childhood furnishes the complement to this, for it indicates how throughout human history the child born outside of these socially approved limitations has had a special status as a social pariah. One of the most unpleasant aspects of man's inhumanity to man is the way in which the established order has vented its disapproval of the offending parents upon their helpless child.

KINSHIP UNIT

Membership in the kinship unit is the initial factor through which the entire system of ascribed statuses operates. Not only is it the oldest, it is also the most universally accepted determinant of status. Originally, man obtains his status through his personal traits and exploits. Frequently, and in time, these come to be extended to his family, and then to his descendants. In a manner like the inheritance of biological traits and accumulated possessions, status is transmitted from one generation to another.

The ascription of status through membership in a kinship unit operates in several ways. First, the child has ascribed to him at birth a status within his kinship group. This involves the socialized pattern of his relations to his parents, brothers, sisters, and relatives to a certain degree of kinship. This is particularly significant because it involves his relationship with a whole series of persons with whom he will have, for a number of years, his most constant and intimate relations. These prescribed patterns are both positive, indicating how he is to act toward certain people, and negative and prohibitive, including what he may not do. In all societies the initial status of every normal individual, according to Parsons, is the child's status in a given kinship unit.[7]

Second, membership in the kinship unit determines the status ascribed to the child in relation to other kinship groups. In this way, the family serves as the vehicle through which ascriptions of the bases of the color complex, ethnic origin, and class are made, as well as the rank order in each of these categories.

GENERAL IMPORTANCE OF THE ASCRIBED STATUSES

An amazingly large part of the ordinary business of living is included in the operation of these ascribed statuses, particularly those of age, sex, and membership in the kinship unit. The relative importance of the ascribed statuses is not the same, however, in all societies. It seems evident that in small and comparatively stable groups they are emphasized a great deal. In such societies, social habits are fixed, and the reciprocal patterns of behavior are so clearly defined that they are readily imposed upon the young child. His induction into his culture takes the form of his acceptance of the age, sex, and other subordinations which are involved. But in a large and rapidly changing society, reliance upon the ascribed statuses is more difficult. Old statuses become specialized and new ones appear; hence the family's initial role in introducing the child to the status system both is more complicated and comes to be shared with other agencies whose conceptions and emphases may also be different.

In addition to the customary differences in social complexity and rates of social change, a society sometimes passes through an age of iconoclasm when the status systems, among various other aspects of the social structure, are destroyed or recast. There may be a deliberate mass urge to let girls behave as boys do; young men are placed in authority over old ones, members of subject races are raised to pinnacles of power, and the common man is glorified to the exclusion of all others. These developments seem to take the form of outbursts so impulsive and irrational as to

[7] Parsons, *op. cit.*, p. 604.

suggest that they are a therapeutic mass drainage of resentment against conditions far removed from their manifestations.

The problems involved in the socialization of the child, which is only another term to identify the adjustment processes of the individual, vary directly with the rate of change and the clarity with which the requirements of the ascribed statuses are defined. This clarity is increased by similarity between what a child is told and what he sees in practice, by lack of contact with other culture groups which maintain different ascribed status requirements, and by uniform conformity with the status pattern on the part of the adult members of the child's social world. In other words, if a child grows up in a society in which the patterns of reciprocal behavior are clearly defined and universally practiced, his socialization is relatively simple. The reverse of these conditions naturally increases the difficulties.[8]

Achieved Statuses and Their Attainment

Every society has a number of statuses which are open to individual achievement. Their number and the difficulty of attainment vary a great deal, as does their importance in the functioning of any particular society. Linton insists that most of the statuses open to achievement do not touch the business of living very deeply and that, although satisfying to the persons who achieve them, they are designed, from the standpoint of society, chiefly "to serve as bait for socially acceptable behavior or as escapes for the individual."[9] Such a judgment seems to run counter to the great emphasis on status achievement in this country, where the more recently arrived ethnic groups have been particularly concerned that the road to this end be kept open and that the status-achieving devices be made available to them. This makes all the more striking the relative absence, in the literature on status systems, of a consideration of the achieved statuses and the devices utilized to attain them. The subject has amazing ramifications and requires a vast amount of study and research. By way of a move in this direction, some status-achieving devices significant for the younger age groups are presented briefly.

ATHLETIC SKILL

Activities of an athletic nature play a large part in American life. This is true particularly in the segment of the population which is under 25 years of age. Much of the life of American youth is organized around scholastic and collegiate athletic programs, from which it follows that a considerable part of the comparative rating which takes place in the child's and youth's world is based on athletic achievement. Naturally this

[8] Cottrell, *op. cit.*, pp. 617–620.
[9] Linton, *The Study of Man,* p. 128.

is more marked among boys than girls, and it is rather more significant in the lower than in the upper classes. This does not mean that there is less participation in sports among upper-class boys, for often the reverse is true. Reference is intended rather to the variations in the interpretation and exploitation of success in athletic competitions among the different classes. Thus upper-class children tend to engage in sports for sport's sake; lower-class boys, to achieve status, i.e., honors, social recognition, and prestige.

ARTISTIC ACHIEVEMENT

Achievement in the arts operates somewhat along the lines of athletic ability, but is more significant for girls than for boys, and seems in many ways to be more effective as a status-achieving device. Warner has written about one aspect of this.

One of the usual methods by which the children of members of the lower groups raise themselves is to exercise various semi-artistic talents. So-called schools of dancing, music, and elocution are attended by such children where they learn how to tap dance, play a saxophone, or recite pieces. Such trained talents are utilized by the various associations, clubs, and lodges for their entertainment, and the growing youth comes to their notice and frequently to membership. He thus climbs out of his lower status to a higher group and stabilizes his rise by becoming a member of an association in a higher group. This method of rising is, of course, not confined to the lower groups. The middle and lower upper classes also use their occasional talents as equipment for raising their class participation. The wealthy son or daughter of a "recently arrived" textile manufacturer, after completing his or her training at one of the older colleges with its higher social prestige, goes to an art school in Paris, or trains his or her voice "on the continent," or goes to New York to learn to write. If such attempts succeed in launching a generally recognized artistic career, his status is raised and his sphere of behavior enlarged in the field of upper-class activity. If he fails, he frequently becomes emotionally unstable and in some cases develops psychoneurotic behavior.[10]

Success on the stage has been, for a long time, a short cut for many young girls to the achievement of a higher social status. In recent decades, radio and the movies have offered similar opportunities, and on an extensive scale. How effective artistic achievement of a high order may be as a status-achieving device is indicated by the fact that in "café society," so-called, the Social Registerite accepts only the equality of the artist.

EDUCATIONAL ATTAINMENT

"Go to school, study your lessons, and you won't have to work as I do"— so speaks the ambitious lower-class parent to his child. "Be an outstand-

[10] W. Lloyd Warner, "Formal Education and the Social Structure," *Journal of Educational Sociology*, May, 1936, p. 520.

ing student, and you'll find your way to the top"—this is the advice of the middle-class parent. "Why, of course, Bill's going to the university," for both child and parent in the upper classes assume that this is the thing to do. These statements, at differing levels, express the American attitude toward education. Education everywhere is an outstanding agency chiefly to raise status and, incidentally, to prevent loss of it. It is part of the American creed and intellect and talent can be educated and therefore improved, that people doing so should be rewarded, that the rewards should include prestige and money, which can be transformed into social status.[11]

In the united States, all of this becomes particularly significant because of the mass migrations into this country. Education has been utilized, on the one hand, by us to assimilate the masses of European children, and on the other by these children and their parents to raise their own status. In other words, for them our system of public instruction ceases to be a vehicle for transmitting the accumulated traditions and skills of the group, and serves instead to develop new cultural values, new loyalties, and in many cases a status higher than that of the parents. This is most marked in the field of higher education, which is being profoundly influenced and possibly even transformed in certain areas under the impact of larger numbers of second-generation American students. The application of these students is unusual, in selected aspects of the higher education pattern; their hopes are particularly forward-looking; their expectation is specific. There is particular concern with the prestige symbols in education, such as grades, honors, and degrees. The doctor's degree is especially esteemed; and colleges of pharmacy and the like, in which its attainment has been relatively easy, have proved particularly attractive, as enrollment data clearly indicate.

It should be emphasized, however, that this interest in education as a status-achieving or -maintaining device is not confined to any nativity group in the population. A large proportion of the students in the American educational system, as well as their parents, regard a school or college as a place to go to make advantageous contacts, to gain the proper entree, to get in with the right people, and ultimately to secure the right of identifying themselves with a particular institution, as one of its accredited representatives. Many educators do not like to face these implications.

GROUP MEMBERSHIP

The joiner is a product of an open class system, and this device is utilized early in the child's life, when membership in certain groups is sought in order to raise his status. This may begin early with enrollment in a given Sunday School, or later with confirmation in a given church.

[11] W. Lloyd Warner, *Environment and Education,* Supplementary Educational Monograph No. 59, University of Chicago Press, Chicago, 1942, pp. 16–28.

Later, there are selected dancing classes, private schools or particular public schools, social clubs, high-school and college fraternities, and cliques. This aspect of the child's socialization will be discussed in a subsequent chapter; the reference here is solely to their utilization as status-achieving devices.

PLACE OF RESIDENCE

Early in life, status comes to be assigned on the basis of place of residence. The right and wrong sides of the railroad track are identified for children almost from the time they enter school; the comparative status of selected areas in large cities and suburbs becomes known to most children as a by-product of competitive school athletics, as well as of their mixture in centrally located high schools. All of this is, of course, an extension into the early age period of what obtains among adults. An example of its operation in the nation's capital follows:

> Like any other socially ambitious newcomer, Mrs. Toy would like to move immediately into the embassy circle and pass from there into the more powerful Cabinet group. To accomplish these aims she must know the right people, and the right people are found, of course, only in the right places. Washington's most correct residential districts are Massachusetts Avenue, where most of the embassies are; Arlington across the bridge; or Georgetown, the one-time Negro colony whose old brick houses are now occupied by such celebrities as the Harry Hopkinses, the James B. Forrestals, the Francis Biddles, and Mrs. Edward B. McLean. The newcomer whose husband can afford it (and if he can't, she'd better stay home) can rent a small furnished house in Georgetown for about four hundred dollars a month.[12]

STATUS-CROSSING ROMANCES

The role of marriage as a status-achieving device has been emphasized recently in sociological literature.[13] Obviously, in this respect marriage is only one step in a process which begins before marriage and does not culminate with it. The whole range of romantic relations may be considered from the standpoint of their role in the status systems of society. This process begins with courtship. To become the favored one of a member of the opposite sex who belongs to a higher prestige group is an effective and frequently successful way of moving across a class line. The method of operation is somewhat as follows: The boy or girl of higher status inter-

---

[12] Margaret Case Harriman, "How to Woo Washington," *Harper's Magazine*, August, 1944, pp. 227–228. See also Walter Firey, "Sentiment and Symbolism as Ecological Variables," *American Sociological Review*, April, 1945, pp. 140–149.

[13] James H. S. Bossard, "Marriage as a Status Achieving Device," *Sociology and Social Research*, September–October, 1944, pp. 3–10. For a more complete analysis of marriage as a status-achieving device and its significance for marriage and child development, see James H. S. Bossard and Eleanor S. Boll, *Why Marriages Go Wrong*, The Ronald Press Company, New York, 1958, Chap. 8.

cedes with his or her crowd in behalf of the chosen one. Tolerance of the chosen one may follow. Subsequently, there are invitations from the higher-status crowd. Such invitations create a special opportunity. If the neophyte measures up to requirements, group acceptance may follow, and the newly arrived one becomes a member of the clique, especially in the eyes of outside observers.

There are various specific aspects of such class-crossing romances. One consists of the cases where relationships are with or between minority groups. As in marriage, so in premarital romantic attachments there is often the opportunity for escape from an ascribed status. Another aspect involves premarital sex relationships. Studies of sex delinquency among girls reveal how frequently the girl of lower status seeks to "put herself across" with a higher-status boy on the basis of sex relationships. The relative status of the mothers and fathers of children born out of wedlock is an illustration in point. Similar in implication are Whyte's studies of Italian attitudes. He writes: "In the social and ethnic group category, the most desirable woman for non-marital sex relations is the girl of old American stock background, preferably blonde, who has a higher status than the corner-boy."[14]

Relative Emphases in Status Systems

One of the continuing problems in every society, of special significance for those in the lower age groups, is the proper relative emphasis upon the ascribed and the achieved statuses. The foregoing analysis should have made it clear that a great deal of the business of living is taken care of by the ascribed statuses, that the behavior involved in these roles is socially typed, and that the child can be trained for it. Clarity and definiteness in group expectancies, and habit in behavior patterns, seem necessary for survival and desirable for the development of stable personalities. The individual child does need a cultural ledge sufficiently broad and stable to permit satisfactory performance and adequate security.

On the other hand, too much limitation in the achieved status is a curb on the ambitions and development of the child. A curb on the former makes for feelings of frustration; limitation of the latter entails a loss of social efficiency and leadership. In younger societies, and where conditions are changing constantly, this may prove particularly serious. As a society matures, and the adjustive relationships between groups and between the society and its physical environment come into being, such limitations may be considered of less importance.

[14] William F. Whyte, "A Slum Sex Code," *American Journal of Sociology*, July, 1943, p. 28.

Summary

1. Status may be defined as relative social position. Thus conceived, it has its individual as well as its group and class aspects.

2. There are two main groups of statuses: the ascribed and the achieved.

3. The factors underlying the ascription of status include the color complex, ethnic origin, social class, sex, age, age relationship, order of birth, primogeniture, plural birth, adoption, illegitimacy, and membership in a kinship unit.

4. A large part of the ordinary business of living is included in the operation of the ascribed statuses. Their relative importance is greatest in small and relatively stable societies.

5. Every society includes a number of achieved statuses which are open to competitive achievement. Some of the status-achieving devices which are particularly significant in child and youth development are athletic skill, artistic achievement, educational attainment, group membership, place of residence, and class-crossing romances.

6. The proper relative emphasis upon the ascribed and achieved statuses is a continuing problem in every society. The essential requirement is balance, and this point seems to change with the development of the particular society.

Part *VI*

Some Problem Families

Chapter 21

Parents with Problem Attitudes

Thus far, the approach to the sociology of child development has been through the analysis of family situations, with reference to their significance for children. The effort has been to show how the family operates to mold the personality of the child, how the family inducts him into the prevailing culture, what differentials in this process occur from one class to another, and how behavior requirements and stimuli are typed at different status levels. Speaking generally, these discussions reflect the changes in child study from the earlier emphasis on problems of social misconduct and economic need to the contemporary stress on the processes of child rearing, and from a primary concern with socially disadvantaged children to concern with those at all cultural levels.

Some emphasis should be given, however, to the problem approach; and this chapter, together with the next two, will be devoted to family situations which have been identified as of the problem-creating kind. One group of these situations is caused by the attitudes of parents toward their children, and an analysis of these constitutes the major part of the present chapter. The following two chapters are devoted to homes with conflict situations and to families under stress, chiefly in the latter case because of the impact of external factors upon family life. Following the basic approach in this volume, it seems proper to think of these as problem homes with children, rather than of homes with problem children.

The Range of Family Situations

Before proceeding to a discussion of these selected groups of family problems, we should say something about the range of family situations. How extensive this range is can be gathered from the preceding chapters, in which some of the chief aspects or dimensions of family life and of family-life relationships have been identified. If each such dimension is thought of as a straight line running from zero to 100, it will be evident that any given family may be at any point on this line. If, now, several of these so-called dimensions are combined, some idea of the individuality and variety of family situations will become apparent. The range of specific family situations is endless.

The study of family situations began with an analysis of the more conspicuous problem-creating cases. At first, these were considered chiefly from the standpoint of the good of the child, with emphasis upon broad moral factors. Gradually, however, other factors which could be easily detected as well as tested and measured, such as health, education, and economic status, were included. The procedure for studying the family developed into an examination of the situations of individuals with specific behavior irregularities, in order to find which of these measurable factors were most constant in the homes of these individuals.

Although many types of family situations in terms of these factors were identified, two discoveries led to the formation of a new approach. The first was the realization that selected unhealthy factors do not inevitably produce unhealthy home situations; the second was the development of newer insights into the processes and significance of personality formation, especially through family interaction. The result has been the emergence in recent years of an approach to the study of family situations as groups of interacting persons influenced by special sets of circumstances, to which the family reacts in specific ways.

The very number of these studies has led, still more recently, to attempts to systematize and classify family situations. These attempts have been reviewed by Boll,[1] who considers this movement in the social sciences in relation to similar developments in the other older sciences. Particularly helpful and suggestive are the classificatory schemes proposed by Weill[2] and Symonds.[3] Mrs. Boll's classification is reproduced in Table 8 as an inductive summary of the literature covering the years 1926 to 1940.

Parents Who Reject Their Children

Reference was made in Chapter 4 to the role of parental attitudes toward parenthood and children, and to the chief sources of these attitudes. From that discussion, it follows that many parents tend to reject their children, with obvious consequences for the development of the child.

---

[1] James H. S. Bossard and Eleanor S. Boll, *Family Situations,* University of Pennsylvania Press, Philadelphia, 1943, Chaps. 4–8.

[2] Blanche Weill, *Behavior of Young Children in the Same Family,* Harvard University Press, Cambridge, 1928.

[3] Percival M. Symonds, *The Psychology of Parent-Child Relationships,* D. Appleton-Century Company, Inc., New York, 1939.

TABLE 8. A Classification of Family Situations[4]

Intrafamily Relationships

I. Affectional relationships

A. Excess of affection
1. The possessive home
2. The oversolicitous home
3. The overindulgent home

B. Normal affection
1. The companionable home

C. Discrimination in affection
1. The divided home
2. The favored-child home
3. The "impartial" home

D. Inconsistency of affection
1. The bickering home
2. The unreliable home

E. Displacement of affection
1. The home with a new member

F. Lack of affection
1. The nagging home
2. The frigid home
3. The neglectful home

G. Frank rejection
1. The home of the unwanted child

II. Subjectual relationships

A. Repression
1. The mother-controlled home
2. The father-dominated home
3. The overly demanding home

B. Anarchy
1. The child-dictated home

C. Confusion
1. The home with too many bosses

D. Approaching balance
1. The democratic home

Family Patterns

A. Size
1. The large family
2. The one-child family

B. Organization
1. The coöperative family
2. The independent family
3. The incomplete family

C. Activity
1. The nomadic family
2. The "joiner" family
3. The family of the intelligentsia
4. The "cliff-dweller" family
5. The community-benefactor family

D. Values and goals
1. The social-climber family
2. The materialistic family
3. The overly religious family
4. The scientific family
5. The superstitious family
6. The conventional family

External Factors

A. Socioeconomic status
1. The inadequately financed home
2. The suddenly wealthy home
3. The large-inheritance home
4. The mother-supported family
5. The family marked by peculiar occupational characteristics

[4] Bossard and Boll, op. cit., pp. 111–112.

TABLE 8—(*Continued*)

External Factors—(Continued)

	6. The home of culture conflict 7. The disgraced home 8. The family in the public eye
B. Neighborhood	1. The farm family 2. The small-town family 3. The city family 4. The summer resort family 5. The misfit-in-the-neighborhood family 6. The family in a substandard neighborhood
C. Health	1. The home of the invalid 2. The home of the defective

---

This is the first of the problems of family personnel to be considered in this chapter.

This type of problem home first came to the attention of students of social relations because of the resultant behavior of the children involved. After reviewing the literature on the subject, Symonds concluded that when either or both parents reject a child, he is likely to be characterized as aggressive, annoying in school, attention-getting, hostile, hyperactive, jealous, or rebellious; and that he may commit such delinquencies as truancy, thieving, or lying.[5] There is every evidence that such children are driven abnormally by two quests: one, to attract attention, i.e., to gain group acceptance; the other, to see their teachers and parents upset about them. Obviously, both of these are compensatory.[6]

More recently, the subject of child rejection has been emphasized in the literature on planned parenthood. Because of the lack of knowledge, or the unavailability, of reliable contraceptives, it is pointed out that many unplanned pregnancies ensue, with the subsequent birth of children who are not wanted by their parents. The facts on abortion bear eloquent testimony to the urgent desperation of such parents.

The chief concern here is with the nature of the family situation in child rejection. This, we contend, needs considerably more careful analysis than has been given to it. Parental rejection of the child has been referred to generally as though it were relatively simple, effective from birth throughout the child's life, and involved similar attitudes for both parents. Obviously, this represents an oversimplification of the facts. While such situations do exist, they are only a minor part of a much larger situation. It may help, therefore, to conceive of rejection situations as having at

---

[5] Symonds, *op. cit.*, p. 45.

[6] For an excellent study of parental acceptance and rejection, see *ibid.*, Chap. 2, and Hilde Bruch, *Don't Be Afraid of Your Child*, Farrar, Straus and Young, New York, 1952, Chap. 5.

least three dimensions. First, there is the number of persons in the family group who reject the child, for the attitudes of all are involved in the family situation. It may be the mother, father, sibling, grandparent, or whoever are members of the child's family of orientation, singly, or in any possible combination.

The Black family illustrates rejection by the father and acceptance by the mother.

Mr. and Mrs. Black were married when they were 26 and 22 years of age, respectively. They lived in a three-room apartment in a large city. Mr. Black earned a relatively high salary. Mrs. Black stayed at home and kept house. Their relations, including their sex life, were mutually satisfactory. But Mrs. Black became lonely after a time, and "tricked" her husband, as she put it, into parenthood. From the beginning of her pregnancy, he was not interested in the coming of the child, apparently indicating a resentment against it for breaking into a happy, carefree relationship with his wife. After the child was born, he lost interest in her, and finally, when the child was seven months old, deserted. Some time afterwards, he began living with another woman. For a time, he made occasional payments in support of his wife and child. Mrs. Black seems devoted to her child, and does an excellent job of mothering it. Recently, after her divorce, she has remarried. There have been no children with the second husband, who seems somewhat lukewarm toward his stepchild.

During the war period, many children were reared in the homes of their grandparents. The case of the Carstairs illustrates what may happen.

Helen Carstairs married an army lieutenant before Pearl Harbor. By the time she discovered she was pregnant, her husband was out of the country. She lived with her parents when her child was born. The parents were not happy over the marriage of their daughter, they did not consider the son-in-law worthy of the daughter, and were secretly rather displeased over the coming of the new grandchild. There is an apparent difference in their attitude toward this one and their other grandchildren. Mrs. Carstairs is already conscious of this difference, sensing the elements of rejection in their attitude. She seems to be unusually solicitous about her son's welfare, as if to compensate for the grandparents.

A child may be rejected by the other siblings in the family. This sometimes happens in the case of a child born late in life, after the other children in the family are full grown or nearly so.

John Lott was born when his mother was 44 years old. His parents had four other children, ranging from 17 to 24 years. The Lotts live in a small town, and there has been a good deal of bantering comment about the late arrival. The other children have had to take a lot of teasing about the new brother. The attitude of the parents is tinged with feelings of shame, and three of the four siblings look upon the newcomer with mingled feelings in which there are ridicule and feelings of rejection. Only one of the siblings is receptive, markedly so, which appears in striking contrast to the attitudes of the others. John early displayed marked signs of aggressive behavior, as though he would compel you to notice him, whether you would or no.

The most obvious cases of families' division in regard to acceptance of a child appear in remarriages when one or both mates have children. Remarriage, as pointed out in Chapter 8, occurs with considerable frequency. About one out of every five marriages is a remarriage for one or both parties; in one out of fourteen cases, it is a remarriage for both.[7] Smith[8] has recently summarized the literature on the stepchild, and much of the material available can be viewed from the standpoint of child acceptance and rejection. In addition to remarriage there is the informal shifting of mates, so prevalent in the lower classes. Here, too, the problem of rejection looms large, with added implications for the child because of his knowledge of the extramarital relationship. The reconstruction of a home, whether through remarriage of the parent or not, often means that the child is "bounced here and there like a ball" and does not know to whom he can go or where he belongs.[9]

In summary, the basic fact in regard to this first so-called dimension is that family attitudes toward a child involve the attitude of all the members of the family of orientation. While the mother's acceptance-rejection response is in many ways of primary importance, the response of the other members is also significant, both in its meaning for the child and also in the effect which rejection by one member has upon the other members.

A second dimension of rejection situations involves their time aspect. The rejection of a child may be permanent or temporary. Here, as elsewhere, there is the possibility of an honest change of attitude. This seems to be illustrated in the following case:

Mrs. King did not want to have a child. This attitude may have been created largely by her mother, who repeatedly had expressed the hope that her daughter would not "have to have a child." When Mrs. King became pregnant, she was both frightened and resentful, and her mother continued to express her hope that "something" might happen. However, the child was born after a rather difficult delivery. After the birth, Mrs. King gave clear evidence of her rejection of her child, and turned rather frigid toward her husband. About two years later, while taking her child to a public park one day, she met two other young mothers, both of whom were quite proud of their motherhood. The three speedily became quite friendly, and gradually Mrs. King began to absorb the attitude of her two friends. Gradually, she seems to have relaxed and her attitude toward her husband changed. Meanwhile, her child was developing into a very attractive young person. At this time, Mrs. King had a prolonged

    [7] James H. S. Bossard, *Parent and Child,* University of Pennsylvania Press, Philadelphia, 1953, Chap. 8.
    [8] William C. Smith, "The Stepchild," *American Sociological Review,* April, 1945, pp. 237–242.
    [9] *Ibid.,* p. 241.

illness, and during her convalescence she did some serious thinking. Something in the nature of a complete change toward life seems to have occurred. She freed herself from her mother's influence. A year and a half later, she had a second, and planned, child. She says that the coming of these two children, and especially the first, were the turning point in her life.

A third dimension of rejection situations concerns the form or nature which the rejection takes. This is in part a matter of degree, but is much more a form of expression. For example, rejection may be physical, involving the child himself, as in the case of abandoned children. Ordinarily, physical rejection occurs with illegitimate children and may take the form of abandoning the child on a doorstep or a dump pile or along a country road; or it may involve surrendering him to an agency or relative or adopting family. In some instances, however, married couples turn their child over at birth or soon afterward to a relative or some other person "to raise." Rejection later in the child's life may involve placement in an institution, reform school, boarding school, convent, or military school. Again, it may express itself chiefly in economic ways, in a failure to provide adequately—lack of toys, inadequate clothing, no personal allowance, and the like. The mink-coated mother and the daughter in the frayed dress tell their own story. In other cases, the rejection is of an educational nature, chiefly omission. There is a lack of guidance, supervision, or educational facilities. The parents have other interests, and delegate the training of their children to servants, nurses, or relatives. Finally, rejection may be emotional in character; this is by far the most emphasized form in recent years. Contemporary students seem to think that emotional rejection of the child has more serious consequences than any other parental fault.[10] What it means above all else is that the child's basic craving for intimate response, his desire to be loved, is not satisfied. It is this that hurts most, and gives meaning to other forms of rejection. In other words, there is a spiritual inadequacy in such homes, and the child's payment for it is a basic lack of security.

There are reasons why this emotional rejection is particularly serious today. One is the predominance of the immediate form of family; a second, the small-family system. Combined, these two mean, as was pointed out in Chapter 4, that the child views the world from a very narrow psychosocial ledge, as it were, and when this narrow ledge is uncertain or unfriendly, the result can only be great insecurity. Along with these factors is the marked vertical mobility of many families. This was particularly operative during and immediately after the war years. Millions of families have been away from their kinsfolk, and not integrated in the life of the new community. The children in these families naturally have felt iso-

[10] For an excellent example, see Jessie Taft, "The Effect of an Unsatisfactory Mother-Daughter Relationship upon the Development of a Personality," *The Family,* March, 1926, pp. 10–17.

lated, often pathetically so. When, in addition, they feel rejected by their own parents, the result can only be marked feelings of loneliness and insecurity, and a starving for affection and attention. In this emotional dilemma, some children turn to their teachers or the opposite sex, or identify themselves with some mass explosive movement like that of the Sinatra bobbysocksers.

A final word should be said about parents who reject their children. Not all are heartless and selfish, as is often assumed. Many young people who become parents and reject their children are themselves the victims of maladjustment;[11] hence they are only the transmitters of what was done to them. Some of these parents may appreciate their own inaptitudes, so their fundamental unwillingness to be parents represents a reasoned judgment rather than a selfish whim. Again, some young people are high-pressured into being parents, and their resentment against this pressure may find expression in their attitudes toward their children. Such pressure may be exerted within the circle of kinsfolk, as in the case of upper-class families which put marked emphasis upon family continuity. Or it may be community pressure, such as one finds in small towns, where persons are paired off, married, and become parents, under the innuendoes and suggestions of their friends. Again, a parent's rejection of a particular child may grow out of that child's relation to the sex balance within the family. A couple with four girls may be none too pleased when the fifth child is a girl. Five boys and a husband may give a wife strong feelings of resentment against a sixth son. Finally, rejection of a child may symbolize the parents' deep-seated rejection of the world. To many thoughtful people, the world today is not a happy or pleasing prospect to give the bearer of a new life. To reject a child may only express resentment at one's cosmic destiny. Perhaps all that has been said suggests that parental rejection of a child is not a simple factor, operating alone, but is a phase of a larger pattern of attitudes and values. Parents who reject their children need understanding, too. Moreover, parental rejection is often partial, and is modified by misgivings of various kinds. This is a highly significant fact, for it means that the rejection of a child leads to feelings of guilt which express themselves in a marked solicitousness concerning the child. Such a combination results in a family situation which combines the evils of rejection and of oversolicitousness. It is to the latter type of situation that we turn next.

Parents Who Magnify Their Responsibilities

A second group of problem parents stands in direct contrast to those who reject their children. In part, these parents reveal a tendency to over-accept their children, but the group envisaged here involves a somewhat

[11] Symonds, *op. cit.*, pp. 94 ff.

broader and perhaps more significant concept. In going through the literature on child behavior problems, one finds a number of family situations in which the common element is the tendency on the part of parents to magnify their parental responsibilities in one or more ways. As a group, these parents take themselves too seriously. Obviously, this is again a matter of degree, with a cultural determination of the point at which it is considered a problem. The concrete expressions of such situations, as well as their particular emphases, come to attention in a variety of ways, the more important and common of which will be identified briefly.

1. First are the parents who overprotect their children.[12] This may be the father, mother, grandparent, sibling, or other family member, singly or in combination. The mother, however, is the most common offender, and it is usually a son whom she overprotects. When a father overprotects, a daughter is most often the object. Overprotection, in its milder forms, is quite prevalent. Frequently, too, it is temporary, ceasing with the birth of another child or with the advancing maturity of the parents. Probably the most serious type, and certainly the most frequent clinical type, is maternal overprotection which masks or is compensatory for a strong rejection of a child.

Maternal overprotection, which is synonymous with the mother's excessive care of her children, manifests itself usually in three ways. First, there is excessive contact—"the mother is always there." This involves continuous companionship between mother and child, prolonged nursing care, excessive fondling, and sleeping with the mother long past infancy. Second is infantilization, which means prolonging infancy by rendering services to the child far beyond the customary age. Illustrative of such services are breast feeding, bathing, feeding, punishing, and the like. In short, what these cases involve is an undue prolongation of the "waiting-on" period. Third is the prevention of social maturity—"she won't let him grow up." Here one finds an active prevention of the child's growth in the direction of self-reliance. Within the home, there is no emphasis upon family chores, self-care, or the care of rooms or personal possessions; outside the home, there is prevention of experiences which make for growth in social adaptation, which lead to meeting one's own problems and fighting one's own way.

Two specific problems, frequently encountered, may be noted here. One relates to the child's school experience. The overprotecting mother coaches the child, may prepare his lessons, makes frequent visits to the school, conflicts with the teacher, and at times becomes an interfering nuisance. In the more extreme forms, she tries to set the child against the

[12] In the voluminous literature on this type of parent, Levy's analysis is a model of insight and clarity of presentation, and his findings are heavily drawn upon in the next few paragraphs. Cf. David M. Levy, *Maternal Overprotection*, Columbia University Press, New York, 1943.

teacher. It is as though she resented the school and the teacher, seeing in them a threat to her monopolistic control of her child. The second problem results from the child's formation of friendships. Here again, the overprotecting mother tends to reach out as if to combat the process, or at least to direct and control it to her child's advantage. Many parents apparently seek to narrow the social contacts of their children.

2. A distinct form of overprotection is often found among the parents of children who present health or physical disability problems. That such children should evoke more parental care and concern than healthy ones warrants no explanation in terms of neuroses. Levy does not think that illnesses per se are productive of maternal overprotection, but he concludes that they may intensify a tendency to overprotect that is already present; i.e., illness gives an added push to an attitude present before the appearance of the illness. Also, one should recognize the difference between serious illnesses and others, between illnesses which require prolonged nursing and those which do not. Moreover, certain mothers may have been "sensitized" by experience with other very serious illnesses.

In the case of deformed or defective children parental attitudes and behavior seem much more pronounced. "In the mental and emotional attitudes of parents toward the physically defective child in the family," writes Laura Hood, "there were characteristics so constant that they might fairly be considered as representing a 'psychology of parents of a crippled child.' To have a little child paralyzed or otherwise physically defective is an experience probably more devastating to mind and spirit than to suffer grave physical impairment one's self, and the psychological adjustments required may be more complex."[13]

In many of these cases, parents are filled with a sense of hopelessness that finds expression in an emotional pattern based on pity. When these disabilities occur in families which have no conception of the possibilities of modern orthopedic work, these patterns take a permanent form. Often, too, the parental reactions are complicated by feelings of guilt over an imagined responsibility or proof of a family taint. From this complex of circumstances there result family situations which not only impair the possibilities for any constructive program dealing with the child's condition or defect, but also create serious difficulties for his personal and social development.

3. Some parents magnify their responsibilities because of their own life experiences. These are persons who may have gained some degree of success in life, but at considerable cost. They have come through, but in the hard way. Their experiences have been such as to leave psychic scars which, even though they have healed, are always visible by way of reminder. Such parents develop at times an almost neurotic susceptibility to

[13] Laura Hood, "On Interviewing Parents of Crippled Children," *Social Service Review,* March, 1928, pp. 62–63.

human competition. Some of them tend to withdraw from it to lead an isolated life; others seek to project such a pattern upon their children. They seek to insulate their children against the raw edges of life, as it were. "I never want my child to go through what I did."

A special aspect of this problem is found often among individuals who become parents late in life. Social workers who are concerned with the selection of homes for child placement know the problems which overage parents present. Coupled with the financial ability of such parents is frequently the tendency to overprotect the children in their care.

4. Akin to overprotecting parents are those who interfere too much with the lives of their growing children. They want always to know what the children are doing, where they are going, with whom, who said what and to whom. Here is a form of parental aggressiveness which may take many forms and stem from various roots. There may be elements of jealousy and resentfulness, a desire to put the children on the defensive for stepping outside the range of family activities. It may derive from an overly active imagination or glandular system. At times it may be the expression of a personality trait, a tendency to take oneself too seriously. Such parents extend the range of their concern over too wide an area of their children's lives. This frequently leads to parent-child conflicts during adolescence, for it is then that the child's own area of operation broadens, and the tendency to exclude adults from this area begins to manifest itself. Most students of behavior problems in children have regarded this as the effort of parents to extend the period of infantile dependence; the emphasis here is on a somewhat different situation, in which parents face the growing-up process of their children but insist on sharing their experience, actually or vicariously, while doing so.

5. Finally, there are the parents who work too hard at the craft of parenthood. Looming large among these are those who are always reading books or attending lectures on "child psychology," are always rejoicing in the "latest theory" of "psychoanalysis," and applying it to their own children. The particular "theory" seldom remains the same over any considerable period of time; but while it is in favor, its acceptance is exclusive and complete. It is to be understood, of course, that there is intended here no reference to the efforts of serious-minded parents who seek to equip themselves for obligations whose importance they recognize. Rather the problem involves a sort of dilettantism, or pseudoscientific faddism, which reminds one at best of the truth of the statement, "A little learning is a dangerous thing."

SOME SOURCES OF TENDENCIES TO MAGNIFY PARENTAL RESPONSIBILITIES

In addition to the foregoing suggestions, some of the factors which may lead parents to magnify their responsibilities will be noted briefly. First are the parents who have a child after a long period of sterility or a series of miscarriages or stillbirths. There may be the continuing fear that no other pregnancy will ensue. Naturally, such circumstances tend to give a heightened evaluation of the child, and may be coupled with unduly apprehensive and protective reactions. Similar is the case where there has been a difficult confinement, with the fear or expectation that it will be the last one. Second is the emphasis upon compensatory pressures. Hostile feelings toward pregnancy are common in our culture; and from one point of view, as Levy suggests, maternal overprotection can be regarded as compensatory to unconscious hostility. Third are unhappy marriages, particularly for the women. Just as a wife devoted to her husband cannot be exclusively a mother, so the child bears the brunt of his mother's unsatisfied or unsatisfactory love life. The sexually frustrated mother naturally drains off the libido energy by oversolicitude for her child. Something should be said in this connection about, fourth, the thwarted ambitions of parents. As pointed out in an earlier chapter, the child gives the parent an opportunity to relive his life, with the result that thwarted parental ambitions are projected upon the child. This is often spoken of as the desire of parents to give their children what they themselves were denied. In many cases, this takes the normal form of having strong ambitions for the child, but in others, it develops to a pathological degree which creates problems for the child.

In addition to the foregoing, there are three other factors in contemporary society which suggest that the parents who magnify their responsibility are on the increase. One is the increasing prevalence of the small-family system which, coupled with early marriage, means that the period of childbearing is over relatively early in the life of the mother. Another factor is the increased longevity of the mother, together with the general rise in standards of positive health and vitality in the middle and older age brackets. At the same time, the separation of home and occupation means that the husband is away from home the greater part of the day. In combination, this means that for many present-day mothers the period of childbearing, and even of child rearing, is over while life is still at the flood tide for them. Confronted with this situation, an increasing number of mothers are finding an outlet in employment or in public service careers. There are those, however, who can find no form of satisfactory adjustment save in an intensification of their parental duties. It is here that danger lurks for the child.

BASIC ASPECTS OF FAMILIES WHO MAGNIFY THEIR RESPONSIBILITIES

A final word should be said concerning the basic aspects of the group of families under discussion. Three such aspects stand out clearly, both from a descriptive analysis of family situations in general and from the literature on behavior problems as it deals with the products of such situations. The first of these is a life situation or configuration which is weighted unduly in the child's favor. To put it another way, there is a lack of balance in the pattern of personal relationships. The child receives more than a properly proportionate share of attention, affection, and service. The cards of personal relationships are stacked in his favor. When early developed and long continued, this results in the creation of the egocentric psychopath who wants to be the beloved tyrant in every situation.[14] When this feeling is of lesser degree or shorter duration, there appears the demanding type of person who expects and anticipates all kinds of special attentions and services, or the aggressive, bullying, resentful type who seeks to compel special consideration. A second basic aspect is the interference with the growing-up process. The child is not allowed to develop responsibility, to stand on his own feet, and above all, to experiment with life. Growing up to be an adult is a hard, long, slow process, which is best done the hard way. Hence when parents magnify their responsibilities, they either do the experimenting themselves or interfere with the child's learning-from-experience process by interposing themselves into it. The incidental but serious effect for the child is the maintenance of infantile or subage responses. A third and quite obvious aspect is the impediments placed in the child's relations with his friends. The children in the group of families under consideration reveal a general difficulty in making friends, for the obvious reasons that their parents keep them away from the necessary experimental contacts, or interfere in the process, or have built up in them a dependence on their parents and other adults which precludes friendships with their own age group.

Parents Who Disregard the Personalities of Their Children

A third main group of problem parents are those who tend to disregard the personalities of their children. These are the parents who cannot see their children as separate and distinct personalities but at best see them as vest-pocket editions of themselves. As conceived here, this group involves in part the dominance-submission dimension emphasized in the child behavior literature of the past generation, but our attempt is to present a broader and possibly a more fundamental concept. To look at parent-child relations from the dominance-submission point of view is to see them through adult eyes; to speak of a disregard of personalities is to think in terms of child development. Perhaps the broader aspects of this concept will become clear from an examination of some of the family situations and parental types involved.

First are the families dominated by acquisitive-minded parents who have a strong sense of the "mine and thine" aspects of life. For them, objects and people fall into two groups: those that belong to them and those

---

[14] Cf. Levy, *op. cit.*, Chap. 8. Consult also Alfred Adler, *The Pattern of Life,* Cosmopolitan Book Co., New York, 1930.

that do not. The latter are rather strictly abjured; they do not register except incidentally in the orbit of their attention. But the things which belong to them are completely and wholly theirs. It is *my* car, *my* house, *my* wife, *my* child. Life is a series of possessive relationships, of which they are the center, from which it follows that the relationships are to be shaped in accordance with this fact.

There are two interpretative approaches to such parents. First, they may be driven by an unconscious need to "possess" and manage someone in order to gain assurance of their own importance; there has been a good deal of emphasis upon this kind of explanation. Somewhat less has been said about the successful parent who has a rather conscious assurance of his own abilities and who discharges his parental duties with the same aggressive vigor that distinguishes him in his occupational relationships. Consider, for example, a certain type of successful executive. His breakfast is served at his order. Then he confers with his gardener and gives instructions for the tasks of the day. A chauffeur drives him to his office, where a touch of a button summons people all day long. Today he "handles" a dozen difficult situations involving many persons, and does so exceedingly well. Returning home, a problem concerning his child is presented to him. He acts promptly, feeling very confident of his judgment, his insight into life, and his knowledge of life's values. There is not only his confidence, but also his assumption of the dominant role in every situation. There are those persons who carry as their sole responsibility the complete range of life, and who think of everything—perpetual masters of ceremonies. Obviously, here one is confronted with a character complex rather than a neurotic pattern. Such individuals manage their children because they are the type of people who always manage.

Second are the family situations dominated by parents who have strong ideas, convictions, or philosophies. They may be successful executives who generalize their experience, they may be academic introverts who have arrived at a theory, they may be "crackpots" who have absorbed some singular notion; their common condition is their exclusive devotion to an idea. Such ideas may be of any type. Two types are of particular significance here: those which relate to child rearing, and those which relate to careers.

The field of child rearing is the peculiarly happy hunting ground for faddists with their momentary theories of human development. "What children need is—" is their positive cry, although their agreement ends with this unfinished sentence. One such theory and what it means in a child's life may be ascertained from the following case:

Frank Pierce is vice-president of a bank. He has risen to his present position from the ranks. He is devoted to his job, his church, and his family. For some time now, he has been friendly with a colonel in the infantry during World War II. What children need, he and the colonel keep on telling each other, is discipline—strict, severe, rigorous. Children should be taught to obey, promptly and completely. The way the father applies this theory is illustrated by the following incident. His 3-year-old child is engrossed in play on the floor. The father watches for the moment when he is completely absorbed in his play, to say: "Junior, get Daddy a drink of water." For failure to obey at once, Junior is punished.

The second type of fixed ideas which prevail among parents concerns the careers of children. These are the parents who, from the day the children are born or from early infancy, have "plans" for them. They are to go to this school, college, and professional school; they are to engage in this particular sport or acquire that selected skill; they are to go into a certain occupation or make a certain kind of marriage. Such positive ideas or plans spring from various sources. At the upper-class levels, where the incidence of such situations is high, they often derive from family pride and a wish for the continuance of traditional performance at the family level. The longer such traditions have prevailed, the greater the pressure upon the child may be. At times it is not only the pressure of the living members of the family; the influence of the deceased members still remains. At slightly lower social levels, the parents may be social climbers who bear down upon their children to complete an unfinished program of class ascent. At the lowest class levels it is perhaps more often in regard to the selection of an occupation that an ambitious parent, perhaps the mother, seeks to exert undue influence. Throughout this entire range of situations, the unfulfilled wishes of the parents come to be projected in many cases upon the children; i.e., the parents seek to relive their lives in those of their children.

A third variety of family situation in which the children's personalities tend to be disregarded are those in which the children are utilized to satisfy the emotional needs of the parents or other adults in the family. This includes the well-known "silver cord" cases, where a parent, most often the mother, binds the children to her to satisfy a thwarted emotion. Strecker has discussed these situations in relation to the problems of military service. Silver cords, he writes, come in varying lengths. Sometimes they are very short, but much more often they are very long, often extremely long. Seldom is a silver cord an obviously binding tie. It appears in many guises. There is the oversolicitous mother whose gentle, sacrificing manner hides a dominance that is hard and arbitrary; and the frail, weak little mother who, after giving her health and strength to "the children," wants at least one to find happiness in never leaving her side; and the artificially "happy" home where everyone loves each other too much to quarrel.[15] In addition, there is the mother who is so unhappy that only the devotion of her children "keeps her going"; the unmarried aunt who "devotes herself" to a niece or nephew; and the father who, denied recognition in his adult world, emphasizes over and again the respect and

[15] Edward A. Strecker, "Psychiatry Speaks to Democracy," *Mental Hygiene,* October, 1945, pp. 591–605.

obedience that are a father's due. Parental disregard of the personalities of children may take the form of stark dominance, harsh and cold and exacting against the canvas of family life; but much more often it is a soft and loving tyranny, the satisfaction of parental demands as a debit due for services rendered. The variety of family situations under discussion here are chiefly of this kind.

Finally, there are the parents of today who are still steeped in the authoritarian lore of the past. Here we find not a pose, or an occupational habit, or of necessity a disguised emotional need, but a traditional conviction. Children must obey; it is the responsibility of the parents to compel it. "You do this because I say so. I am your father." This, it is well to remember, was the prevailing principle of child rearing in the family of past centuries. The dominating authoritarian father was only part of a larger pattern of family life which included the exercise of paternal authority over all the members, rigorous discipline, and the subordination of the individual to the family group, all to the end of family solidarity. Such powers on the part of the father were recognized in the law and hallowed by the church.[16]

The carry-over of authoritarian-minded parents into today is found chiefly in two groups. The first is the first-generation Americans who have brought to this country the heritage of their past. These are chiefly European immigrants, often with a rural background, who believe in the patterns of the past and cannot adjust to new ideas and methods of parenthood. Second are the native American families who still cling to the ideas of the past. These are congregated chiefly in certain rural areas where changes in such ideas have occurred much more slowly than in our urban centers.

When these families move to the city, as has happened in millions of cases in recent decades, and come into contact with new forms of parent-child relationships, several reactions occur. Often the parents become confused, and in their confusion grow weak and inefficient between severe authoritarian outbursts. In other cases, they become aroused, stubborn, and, at times, even more confirmed in their convictions. In either event, the very contrast between their behavior and the prevailing pattern makes their procedure all the more startling, and the problem for the children all the more serious. It is only another of the social costs of the mobility of the population.

Summary

1. The range in family situations is extensive. There are a number of dimensions by which these situations may be measured, and any particular family may be placed at any point in the line of each dimension.

---

[16] For studies of authoritarianism, consult T. W. Adorno, and others, *The Authoritarian Personality*, Harper & Brothers, New York, 1950.

2. The accumulation of analyses of differing family situations has led to attempts to classify such situations. These classificatory schemes have become constantly more comprehensive. The Bossard-Boll classification is presented by way of example.

3. Among the problem family situations, three types are discussed. The first includes the parents who reject their children. Rejection situations are very complex. The rejecting person may be any member of the family group, and the attitude is subject to change at any time, often extremely so. Rejection may be physical, economic, or emotional in character. The latter type is particularly emphasized today.

4. A second type includes parents who magnify their responsibilities. This may take the form of overprotecting the child, usually on the part of the mother. Overprotection takes a distinct form in the case of children with health or disability problems. Parents take their parental duties too seriously, sometimes because of their own bitter experiences and sometimes because they have too aggressive an interest in their children's affairs.

5. The third main type includes parents who disregard the personalities of their children. These may be acquisitive-minded parents, with an overly developed sense of possession; they may be parents with very strong ideas, convictions, or philosophies which involve child development; the parents may have strong emotional needs, to satisfy which the children are exploited; and, finally, there is the authoritarian-minded parent who still insists upon being the master of his family.

Homes with Conflict Situations

The family is a miniature society, it has been pointed out, that is unique for the continuing intimacy and the naked incisiveness of the interrelations between its members. From this it follows that one of the most important groups of family problems has to do with the harmonious adjustment of these interrelations. These problems, in turn, may be considered from the point of view of husband-wife relationships, or of their bearing upon the processes of child development. This chapter is devoted to homes with conflict situations, with particular reference to child development. Three separate groups of such situations are selected because of their importance for children: first, excessive quarreling between members of the family; second, culture conflicts between the parents; and, third, homes which become disorganized to the point where their unity is gone. Intergeneration conflicts are reserved for a subsequent chapter.

Parents Who Quarrel

RELATIVE NEGLECT IN CHILD STUDY

The literature on family problems gives due emphasis to the problems of personality adjustment within the family and to the fact that, as marriage becomes more and more a romantic, personal affair rather than a socially controlled institution, these problems grow increasingly important. Most of this emphasis, however, is devoted to the relationship between the marital partners. Family discord and conflicts are thus considered as a form of interaction between the adults in the family, with reference chiefly to the durability of the marriage and the personality development of the conflicting parties, and only incidental mention of any significance for child development.

Summary reports of cases brought to behavior clinics show remarkably little mention of children from homes with quarreling parents. This is, perhaps, another evidence of the selective nature of clinic cases, resulting chiefly from the fact that it is parents and not children who decide upon clinic contacts. Obviously, quarreling parents do not bring their children nearly so often as overprotective parents or those who show feelings of guilt over rejecting their child.

Similarly sparse are the references to quarreling homes in juvenile-delinquency studies. A notable exception is to be found in Healy and Bronner's summary of 4,000 cases, presented over 30 years ago. "Excessive quarreling in the home," they wrote, "is one of the conditions that has been cited both by delinquents and relatives as making directly for bad conduct. We have come to know that in 12 per cent of our total 4000 cases there was excessive quarreling at home. Without any means of gauging in what percentage of families among our general population good temper gives way to quarreling in excess, we nevertheless feel that the proportion in our group must be unduly large."[1] Ten years later, Healy emphasized that in many cases of delinquency only the more superficial factors are stressed, that among the deeper causes are the emotional experiences of the delinquents, and that one of the most common of these is intense feelings of discomfort about family disharmony.[2]

QUARRELING AN INTERACTIVE PROCESS

Conflict is a process, and quarreling is a form of conflict. Quarreling must be studied, therefore, as an interaction concept, which means, as Folsom points out, that we are concerned not with the behavior of the individuals who quarrel but with their interrelations. Their behavior may take any given form, and may differ from one person to another. The essential fact is that each person directly and intentionally opposes the other.[3] Thus conceived, quarreling must be recognized as a normal process in family life. Students of the family no longer think of the happy family as one in which there is no discord. Conflict within limitations is a process whereby problems are faced and frequently resolved. As with so many other things, it is the degree or extent of the process that is pathological.

This conception of quarreling is inherent in the interesting distinction between destructive and productive quarreling made by Duvall and Hill.[4] Destructive quarrels are those which concentrate on the ego of the other, tending to destroy the illusions and fictions by which people live.

[1] William Healy and Augusta F. Bronner, *Delinquents and Criminals: Their Making and Unmaking*, The Macmillan Company, New York, 1926, p. 126.

[2] William Healy and Augusta F. Bronner, *New Light on Delinquency and Its Treatment*, Yale University Press, New Haven, 1936, Chaps. 6, 14.

[3] Joseph K. Folsom, *The Family and Democratic Society*, John Wiley & Sons, Inc., New York, 1943, p. 42.

[4] Evelyn M. Duvall and Reuben Hill, *When You Marry*, D. C. Heath & Company, Boston, 1945, pp. 188–190.

Productive quarrels, on the other hand, are concerned with issues and problems; they involve redefinitions of situations; they relax the strain of emotional intimacies of the honeymoon period of marriage; and they often reveal the underlying strength of relationships between quarreling family members. Jersild develops somewhat the same concept of children's fights and quarrels.[5]

Insight into the nature and processes of marital discord can be found in the works of Burgess, Folsom, Groves, the Mowrers, and others. Two terms, conflict and tension, have customarily been used in their discussions, each with its own distinctive meaning. Burgess and Locke have written recently of the difference between them. Conflicts are fights which arise in families over all possible kinds of differences, but which tend to be solved or to terminate; tensions may be defined as unsolved conflicts which may find open expression or be repressed, with accumulating emotional force.[6] Both of these terms represent social realities; the latter seems particularly pertinent in the analysis of marital relations, and the former conforms to the pattern of thought presented in this chapter.

As a process of interaction, family conflicts may be *acute* or *chronic*. Acute conflict is characterized by a sudden outbreak, often taking a violent form and, when it results in a settlement, leaving no emotional scar. In chronic conflict, the conflict becomes constant, often at a certain level. Families in chronic conflict are in what the poet calls a "constant state of warfaring condition." Folsom speaks of *habituated* conflict as a form of conflict which reaches a certain level and continues there indefinitely. He also uses the term *progressive conflict* for conflict that "grows worse and worse."[7]

Quarreling as a process may be considered also in terms of the precipitating agents or circumstances. It may result from the presence in the family of a disorganized personality who cannot meet the trivial annoyances of the day, or the faultfinding of a shrew who distills her chief joy in life from continually reminding her husband and children of some neglect of duty. It may be the work of a crass nagger, or of an ego that makes extremely stringent demands upon other members of the household. At times it is a daughter who reacts with automatic negativism to every effort to help her, or an adolescent who is trying to make her family over. Similar in kind is the wife who pinpricks her husband incessantly about minor points of etiquette so that she need not feel ashamed of him in their "crowd." Not infrequently older brothers and sisters, who ought to be

[5] Arthur T. Jersild, *Child Psychology,* rev. ed., Prentice-Hall, Inc., New York, 1942, pp. 175 ff.

[6] Ernest W. Burgess and Harvey J. Locke, *The Family,* American Book Company, New York, 1945, p. 560.

[7] Ernest Groves and William Ogburn, *American Marriage and Family Relationships,* Henry Holt & Company, Inc., New York, 1928, Chap. 6; Folsom, *op. cit.,* pp. 445–446.

leaving home to establish their own families, stay and raise the family pot
to the boiling point. Much of the significance of family quarrels for children stems from the nature of those who precipitate and stage the quarrels.

FAMILY QUARRELING AND THE CHILD

From the standpoint of the child, there are at least five aspects of family quarreling which merit special consideration. First is the scope of the
quarrel. How many members of the family are involved? Is it one parent
indulging in his daily habit? Do both parents actively participate? Are the
children drawn into the quarrels, and to what extent? Are other adult
members of the family involved? How large is the family, and how many
of its members are engaged, and to what extent? Second is the stage setting of the quarrel. Do the parents quarrel in "the secrecy of their bou-
doir," or is the scene staged at the dinner table? Many families do their
quarreling at mealtime, with the result, in addition to other consequences,
that nutrition and the digestive process are interfered with. Studies of the
effects of fear, anger, and other emotional states upon the chemistry of the
body are highly pertinent here. Another important fact about the staging
of family quarrels is the extent to which the neighbors can hear them.
This is particularly pertinent in the thin-walled houses and apartments
in congested areas, for it means that the child's sense of shame is involved,
and shame is a social factor as significant as it has been ignored in the
literature of behavior. Third, there is the nature of the quarreling. The
various forms of quarreling remain to be explored. They include half-
irritated wrangling; a series of venomous, sharp-tongued exchanges; an
icy repartee; a succession of sly thrusts; the fury of high anger; a cre-
scendo of threats; and, finally, the climax of physical violence. Perhaps
the basic dimension of parental quarreling, as far as its meaning for children is concerned, is its emotion-provoking character. A fourth significant
aspect of family quarrels is the extent to which they consume the attention, time, and energy of the parents. The child-rearing process is highly
exacting, and the essential problem of many children grows out of the
fact that the best efforts and energy of their parents go into fighting with
each other, leaving only the husks of a spent passion for the children.
Akin to this are the cases in which the emotion aroused in the quarreling
parent is projected upon the child. Taking one's spite out on the children
is very common, as is the habit of many parents of showing their disdain
for each other by neglecting or being cruel to their children. It is quite
clear that many cases of cruel treatment of children by their parents are
only distorted expressions of hatred between the parents. The mother who
has been beaten by her husband *can* in turn beat her child who is the
image of the offending father. On the milder side, quarreling parents lose
the sense of calmness, judgment, and insight necessary for normal and

helpful relations with children. They are too occupied with their own emotions and problems to be of help to the children with theirs. Finally, there is the child's evaluation of parental quarrels. There may be a vague, uncritical acceptance of it all as the way of life. Santayana speaks of this in his own case in these words:

After they [my mother and sisters] left, my uncle Santiago, with his wife Maria Josefa and his daughter Antonita, came to live with us, and a new and distinct chapter begins in my experience. The scene, the persons, the events are still present with me most vividly. I didn't feel deeply or understand what was going on, but somehow the force of it impressed my young mind and established there a sort of criterion or standard of reality. That crowded, strained, disunited, and tragic family life remains for me the type of what life really is: something confused, hideous and useless. I do not hate it or rebel against it, as people do who think they have been wronged. It caused me no suffering: I was a child carried along as in a baby-carriage through the crowd of strangers: I was neither much bothered nor seriously neglected: and my eyes and ears become accustomed to the unvarnished truth of the world, neither selected for my instruction nor hidden from me for my benefit.[8]

Similar to this is the child's acceptance of quarreling as a habitual form of interaction. Quarreling parents make quarreling children who grow up to be quarreling mates—this is but a restatement of some of the findings on adjustment in marriage.[9] Other children lose respect for their quarreling parents, or confidence in their ability. Often the parental bickering comes at the very time that the child has a problem and needs help, or has had an experience which needs to be evaluated in the light of calm adult insight. Particularly difficult is the situation for an older child, perhaps most often a son, who sees a mother beaten or threatened. He may be physically too small to interfere but mature enough to feel highly frustrated. He may be perplexed as to his duty, torn by internal conflict. He may interfere, only to aggravate the whole sorry situation. These are the children who become hard, bitter, calculating, revengeful, full of hate for a parent or an entire family group.

Finally, it should be emphasized that both the process of quarreling as a form of family interaction and the assessment of its meaning for child development must be approached in terms of class differentials. At lower class levels, quarreling is much more likely to involve physical violence. The physical mistreatment of mates and children is more common. In fact, a frequent justification for living with a man without benefit of clergy is that he is less given to physical violence when a lover than when he has the status of husband. In the upper classes, the more verbal forms of quarreling predominate, perhaps in large measure because

---

[8] George Santayana, *Persons and Places*, Charles Scribner's Sons, New York, 1944, p. 119.

[9] Ernest W. Burgess and Leonard S. Cottrell, Jr., *Predicting Success or Failure in Marriage*, Prentice-Hall, Inc., New York, 1939, Chap. 7.

an adequate linguistic equipment is available for quarreling purposes. The sharp slur or the stinging sentence takes the place of a poke in the eye. Similarly, there are class differentials in the extent to which children and neighbors are drawn into or become aware of the quarreling. These depend in part on the size of the home and its physical isolation or nearness in relation to other homes and families. A rereading of Chapter 19 will suggest various other points of class differences.

Culture Conflicts Between Parents

No two persons ever have exactly the same cultural background; hence every marriage represents, in the strictest sense of the word, the union of two personality types between whom there are instances of culture conflict. Many of these, however, are minor in character and can be adjusted with a modicum of difficulty; some are more serious and rend the family life in twain. How serious these may be for marital relationships has been shown in studies made by Burgess and Cottrell and others.[10] Our present concern is with the more serious of such culture conflicts between parents, with reference to the processes of child development. Three kinds of these conflicts will be considered briefly.

RELIGIOUS DIFFERENCES IN MARRIAGE

Most persons have some religious affiliation, either by formal membership, family heritage, or other form of acceptance. A federal census, as of March, 1957, reveals that, of all persons 14 years of age and over, 96 percent reported a religious affiliation or preference, with 3 percent indicating no religion and 1 percent making no report.[11] While religious adherents are divided commonly into three main groups (Protestants, Roman Catholics, and Jews), actually the situation is much more complex. Because of the diverse origins of the American people and the complete freedom of religious worship, a great variety of organized religious groups exist in the United States. In 1951, there were in the continental United States a total of 265 different religious bodies. Seventy of these had memberships of more than 50,000 each, and 19 had a membership of a million or more. In view of this general situation and the emphasis upon the role of individual choice in marriage in this country, it is evident, first, that a large number of interfaith marriages will occur, and second, that all kinds of possible combinations will result.[12]

Some idea of the extent of interfaith marriages can be formed on the basis of the 1957 census report alluded to above. "Among all married

---

[10] *Ibid.*

[11] U.S. Bureau of the Census, *Current Population Reports,* Series P-20, No. 79, Release February 2, 1958, pp. 1–2.

[12] James H. S. Bossard and Eleanor S. Boll, *One Marriage, Two Faiths,* The Ronald Press Company, New York, 1957, Chap. 1.

couples in which one partner was reported as Protestant, Roman Catholic or Jewish, in 94 percent of the cases the other partner was reported in the same religious group. If marriages occurred at random in respect to religion, this proportion would have been 56 per cent."[13]

Tabulated by main religious groups, the above report reveals that "among married couples in which the husband or wife were reported as Roman Catholic, 22 per cent of the husbands or wives reported that they were Protestant or Jewish. For couples in which one spouse was reported as Protestant, 9 per cent of the husbands or wives were reported as Roman Catholic or Jewish. For couples in which one spouse was reported as Jewish, 7 per cent of the husbands or wives were reported as Protestant or Roman Catholic."[14]

Data on the children in these marriages are also given. "About 44,397,-000 children under 14 years of age were in families in which both the head and his wife reported the same major religious group, or in which the head but no spouse was present. About 4,148,000 children under 14 years old were in families in which the family head and his wife were not both reported in the same major religious group."[15]

Helpful as these data on a national scale are, they must be recognized as understatements of the facts, and for two obvious reasons. First, as the census report acknowledges, it does not distinguish those cases in which one of the partners changed his religion to conform to that of the other; and second, it does not allow for marriages between different Protestant denominations, some of which differ greatly from each other.

Supplementary light on these data can be found in two specialized studies. One, by Father John L. Thomas, a Roman Catholic sociologist, and based on annual listings in *The Official Catholic Directory*, concludes that during the last two decades mixed marriages—as marriages between different religious faiths are usually called—account for from one-fourth to one-third of all valid Roman Catholic marriages, "valid marriages" meaning those performed in compliance with the requirements laid down by the church and sanctioned by it. To this proportion must be added those mixed marriages which the Roman Catholic church terms invalid because they are not performed in accordance with the requirements of the church. Studies show that each year between 15 and 25 percent of all marriages involving Roman Catholics are invalid. Combining these two sets of figures, it seems safe to conclude that now, each year, close to one-half of all Roman Catholics marrying find their mates outside of their church.[16]

[13] *Current Population Reports*, p. 2.
[14] *Ibid.*
[15] *Ibid.*
[16] John L. Thomas, *The American Catholic Family*, Prentice-Hall, Inc., Englewood Cliffs, N.J., 1956, Chap. 6.

A second source of information on a comprehensive scale is to be found in a nationwide study of marriages of members of the United Lutheran Church in America. This study secured information for 382 Lutheran congregations, scattered throughout 28 states, the District of Columbia, 5 provinces in Canada, and the Virgin Islands. It showed that, for the five-year period 1946–1950, of the Lutherans in these congregations who married, 58 percent found their mates outside of the Lutheran church. Of all the Lutherans who married outside their church, one out of five (20.5 percent) married Roman Catholics; close to another one-fifth (18.8 percent) married nonchurch members; and almost three-fifths married members of other Protestant churches. The percentage that married Jews and other non-Protestants was very small.[17]

Church attitudes and mixed marriages. Injunctions against intermarriage between religious groups are age-old and well-nigh universal. All of the principal religious groups in the United States have declared their opposition to mixed marriages. Only the degree of opposition varies. Most positive and clear-cut is that of the Roman Catholic church. Because of its conception of marriage as a sacrament and of the church as the divinely appointed custodian of all sacraments, the Roman Catholic church cannot accept the principle of state control and regulation of marriage, and has imposed its own requirements upon its members. The existing policy is based on the revised code of the canon law of 1918 which, while it reiterates opposition to mixed marriages, permits them under the following conditions: first, that the Catholic partner be allowed free exercise of his religion; second, that all the offspring be baptized and reared as Catholics; third, that the Catholic partner promise to do all he can to convert the non-Catholic; fourth, that the non-Catholic make his promises in writing; and fifth, that the marriage take place in the presence of an accredited priest and two witnesses.[18]

The union of gentile and Jew has been frowned upon from the beginning, as witness Deuteronomy vii, 1–3: "When the Lord thy God shall bring thee into the land whither thou goest to possess it, and hath cast out many nations before thee, . . . thou shalt make no covenant with them, . . . Neither shalt thou make marriages with them; thy daughter thou shalt not give unto his son, nor his daughter shalt thou take unto thy son." These prohibitions were repeated with equal directness by the later prophets, such as Ezra and Nehemiah, and established the policies laid

---

[17] James H. S. Bossard and Harold C. Letts, "Mixed Marriages Involving Lutherans —A Research Report," *Marriage and Family Living*, November, 1956, pp. 308–310.

[18] Clement S. Mihanovich, Gerald J. Schnepp, and John L. Thomas, *Marriage and the Family*, Bruce Publishing Co., Milwaukee, 1952; John J. Kane, *Marriage and the Family*, The Dryden Press, New York, 1952; and the Ave Maria Report, "What You Should Know About Mixed Marriage," *The Ave Maria* (Catholic Home Weekly, Notre Dame, Indiana), November 24, 1956, pp. 8–13.

down by rabbinical authorities since. While the degree of opposition has varied from the rabbis who followed the more lenient German Reformed movement to the more strict attitude of Orthodox and Conservative rabbis, there is no doubt concerning the fundamental opposition of Judaism to marriages outside of the faith.

American Protestantism had no definite policy toward mixed marriages for many years, chiefly because of the Protestant emphasis upon the role of the individual conscience and the American tradition of civil control of marriage. In recent years, however, the opposition of many Protestant clergymen has been succeeded by formal declarations of attitudes. Chief among these are those of the Presbyterian, Methodist, United Lutheran, Protestant Episcopal, Northern Baptist, Southern Baptist, Disciples of Christ, and the Evangelical and Reformed churches.[19]

The social significance of religious differences. To appreciate the significance of such marriages, it is necessary to recall the social significance of religious differences. In all religions, there is an interpenetration of religion into the other aspects of social life and organization. This is particularly true in regard to family life and the mores of behavior, both of which are areas which organized religion considers as fields for its special authority. This interrelationship is most marked in a country like India, where religion is identified with the caste system and involves the whole range of social life. In the United States, the interrelationship, while less marked, is still of great importance. In some cases, religion is identified with group history and class status; in others, it is intertwined with ethnic origin, and in still others, with the general paucity of compensations of life, the church involving a large part of the organized life of the group. How important even the smaller sect may be in this connection has been pointed out recently by Clark in his analysis of Canadian experience. Sects, he says, arise usually as revolutionary forces in social as well as in religious life, they are often dominated by a personnel recruited from one class, and not infrequently they are forced into politics, so that, in the course of its history, the sect becomes a culture complex of religious, social, and political ideas.[20]

What all this comes to is that the religious labels which men use are symbolic of fundamental cultural differences. Roman Catholicism, sociologically considered, is not merely a theological system or a traditional ritual; it is a culture complex. Methodism is not just a form of worship; it is a way of living and thinking. The name Quaker or Friend serves to identify more than simplicity in church architecture; it is a demeanor, a way of dealing with life situations, a set of values. These

---

[19] For a full statement of these, see Bossard and Boll, *op. cit.*, Chap. 5.

[20] S. D. Clark, "The Religious Sect in Canadian Politics," *American Journal of Sociology*, November, 1945, pp. 207–217.

larger aspects of religion, intertwined with the minutiae of living, are centered particularly in the intimate, familial aspects of life, an area which organized religious groups invariably reserve as their own special field of dominance. In other words, a marriage between members of different religious groups is not merely a union between two persons who happen to "go to different churches," to be resolved with no more effort than a casual broad-mindedness about a place and form of worship; it represents a supposedly permanent relationship between people who have been reared with fundamental differences in ways of living and thinking.

Significance for the child.[21] It has been pointed out that religious differences are cultural in character, that they are pervasive in scope, that they find expression in the minutiae of daily living, and that they center chiefly in family life. To the extent that the personalities of the parents have been molded by their religious culture, and to the degree with which they identify themselves with their religious groups, religious differences between the parents become significant, both for marital relations and for child development. From the standpoint of the child, it means that the family's cultural background is divided, with inevitable conflicts in family life.

These conflicts come to a focus more sharply in the rearing of children than in any other aspect of the family's life, for child rearing, as pointed out in an earlier chapter, is essentially a series of decisions by the parents. Two periods of the child's life in particular are involved: one is early childhood; the other, adolescence. In both periods, crucial decisions have to be made; both periods are emphasized as of outstanding importance in the process of personality formation. The problems at issue may begin with the practice of birth control and the child's coming; they include the religious rites of infancy, such as baptism; the selection of a name, a Sunday School, a school, a church, social contacts; and patterns of behavior and moral teachings of all kinds.

The conflict between the parents may take many forms. Most frequently, perhaps, it is a struggle to control the child's development; often, too, the undertones indicate that the parents are trying to dominate each other through their child. Since these conflict situations are often accompanied by the separation of the parents, the conflict frequently takes the form of a struggle for the possession of the child, in which the larger kinship group may join. Sometimes this struggle takes the form of seeking to select, on the basis of religious affiliation, the child-caring agency to

[21] For a further discussion of mixed marriages, see John L. Thomas, "The Factor of Religion in the Selection of Marriage Mates," *American Sociological Review*, August, 1951, pp. 487–491; Judson T. Landis, "Marriages of Mixed and Non-Mixed Religious Faith," *ibid.*, June, 1949, pp. 401–407; Milton L. Barron, *People Who Intermarry*, Syracuse University Press, Syracuse, 1946; Murray H. Leiffer, *The Christian Century*, January 19 and 26, 1949; and Bossard and Boll, *op. cit.*, Chaps, 3, 6, 7, and 8.

which the child is to be committed. In many cases the conflict expresses itself in less overt form. One parent may submit, ostensibly, to the demands of the other but seek to undermine the latter's hold over the child. In still other cases, one parent acquiesces, but with an obvious air of defeatism which may not be lost or without effects on the child. There are the families of toleration, so-called, in which both sets of demands are accepted. The child goes to mass at the Roman Catholic Church in the morning, and to the Methodist Sunday school in the afternoon. One Sunday the family plays cards and drinks beer with one set of relatives; the next Sunday the Sabbath is observed with meticulous correctness in the company of another group. To younger children especially, all this may be highly confusing. There are also tolerant families in which nothing is settled, nothing accepted. There is the tolerance of a neutral indifference. Finally, we must include those apparently unsatisfactory arrangements in families whereby all the children of one sex follow the religion of one parent, and those of the other sex, that of the other parent.

MARRIAGES BETWEEN ETHNIC GROUPS

A second group of family conflict situations grows out of the intermarriage of ethnic groups in the United States. This is another result of the heterogeneity of our population. Such marriages are largely intercultural, although the degree of cultural differences varies considerably with the groups involved.

Extent of ethnic intermarriages. The extent of ethnic intermarriages varies naturally with the composition of the population, the persistence of ethnic communities in which the continuance of the Old World cultures is fostered and a sentiment against intermarriage is cultivated, and the predominating nativity class. Studies made in New York City, New Haven, Conn., New York State other than New York City, and elsewhere warrant the following conclusions: (1) the rate of ethnic intermarriage has been increasing; (2) about one-third of all marriages in heterogeneous urban centers in recent years have been interethnic; (3) when internativity marriages are included, the proportion approximates one-half; (4) the percentages vary considerably from one ethnic group to another, being relatively low for Jews, Italians, Irish, Poles, and British Americans, and higher for some of the northern and northwestern European groups. It was pointed out earlier that ethnic intermarriages are largely channeled by religious barriers.[22]

[22] Julius Drachsler, *Democracy and Assimilation*, The Macmillan Company, New York, 1920, pp. 146–147; Ruby Jo Reeves Kennedy, "Single or Triple Melting-Pot?" *American Journal of Sociology*, January, 1944, p. 339; James H. S. Bossard, *Marriage and the Child*, University of Pennsylvania Press, Philadelphia, 1940, Chap. 5; J. V. DePorte, "Marriages in the State of New York, with Special Reference to Nativity," *Human Biology*, Vol. III, 1931, pp. 376–396; and Edmund de S. Brunner, *Immigrant Farmers and Their Children*, Garden City Pub. Co., Inc., New York, 1929.

An idea of the extent of international marriages on a state-wide basis before the outbreak of the Second World War can be gathered from an analysis of the 1939 report of the Bureau of Vital Statistics of the Department of Health of New York State. Of a total of 3,421 foreign-born residents of New York outside of New York City, who married during the year, 1,007, or 29 percent, married women who were native-born white of native-born white parents; 532, or 15.5 percent, married brides who were native-born of foreign-born or mixed parents of a national origin other than that of the groom; and 231, or almost 7 percent, married foreign-born brides of a national origin other than their own. In other words, a total of 1,770, or slightly more than half, married into another national origin group, or into a nativity group at least two generations removed from their own. Similarly, of 10,384 native-born grooms of foreign or mixed parentage, 5,311, or 51 percent, married into the native-born nativity group, or into national origin groups other than their own.[23]

Recent developments. Two recent developments in regard to inter-ethnic marriages call for special comment. One comprises the international marriages which have resulted from the Second World War. Since 1941, millions of American soldiers have gone to the ends of the world in pursuit of the war effort, and as yet uncounted thousands of them have married wives in the countries to which they were assigned. Marriages with English, Irish, and Australian women loom particularly large in number, but the range is far more extensive. Most of these marriages were consummated against the background of the romantic reaction of youth to the psychology of war, without knowledge of the "civilian nature" of the grooms, and often with a rather distorted conception of the nature of American life on the part of the brides. These unions pose a problem of marital relations, but their implications for child rearing may be as great, if not greater. Many of these women are facing the responsibilities of motherhood, as well as wifehood, in a strange country to which they have been transported suddenly, and without knowledge of much of the information, detailed and otherwise, that effective motherhood entails.

A second, and specialized, development of this is seen when the marriages are between American men (or women) in the services and mates who derive from enemy countries. Here the complications are similar in kind but likely to be exaggerated in degree and scope. Cultural differences tend to be exaggerated, as well as considered against an emotionally tinged background that only a relatively few can consider with complete objectivity. Moreover, child development in these families must be viewed in a longer perspective. Will the gulf between the coun-

[23] Department of Health of New York State, Division of Vital Statistics, *Sixtieth Annual Report,* 1939, Vol. II, pp. 220–225.

tries involved be maintained, narrowed, or widened? Will crisis relations be renewed in another generation?[24] Many children of marriages consummated a generation or so ago between British and Germans and Americans and Germans had to face during the Second World War the complications of their familial heritage. War, it must be remembered, aggravates feelings of nationality, makes us more aware of national differences, and recalls national origins even when they go back several generations.

MARRIAGES BETWEEN SOCIAL CLASSES

Recognition of the reality of social classes, as well as of their cultural significance, has been rather recent in the United States, and is still only partial in degree. The result is that relatively little is known about interclass marriages, their extent, and their meaning for marital relations and for child development. Enough is known, however, to indicate the fruitfulness of this area for research studies. Some of the problems which need to be considered will be mentioned here. To what extent are class lines crossed in marriage? What is the social distance between the classes united? For example, in any particular case does upper upper mate with upper lower, or is it lower upper with lower middle, or merely upper upper with lower upper? What are the cultural elements which differ? For example, the religious element may be the same but the linguistic and artistic elements may differ widely. Obviously, too, differing elements in the culture have differing significance for family life. The sex pattern, for instance, will be highly significant. Studies now being made reveal the most striking differences in the forms of sex behavior at various class levels. The sex mores differ, as do the concept of the sex role in marriage, the requirements of sex adjustment in marriage, the aspects of sex relationships which are considered important, sex experience in marriage, the use of contraceptives, and many other points. Culture differentials in the rearing of children have been indicated in Chapter 19 and will serve to suggest how numerous may be the points of issue in interclass marriages in the field of child development.[25]

GENERAL OBSERVATIONS ON BICULTURAL FAMILIES

Highly important as the crossing of the cultural line in marriage is, whether religion or class or nationality, the resultant family situations are not easy to study, especially in their deeper meaning for the personality development of the members. Three complicating factors seem to be of

[24] Cf. Henrietta Leslie, *Mrs. Fischer's War*, Houghton Mifflin Company, Boston, 1931, for a life-span study of the son of a British-German marriage prior to the First World War.

[25] For further discussion see James H. S. Bossard, *Parent and Child: Studies in Family Behavior*, University of Pennsylvania Press, Philadelphia, 1953, Chap. 9.

primary importance. First, such marriages usually are at first based on a good deal of love and affection, strong enough to overcome the resistance of cultural differences. Common observation suggests that often a strong physical attraction is involved in such unions. As a result, many inter-cultural marriages begin with certain added elements of attraction, especially significant in the earlier years when physical and romantic bonds in marriage are relatively more important. Second, another unusual bond in these unions is the pride of the partners, equivalent in many cases to stubbornness. This arises from the fact that these marriages have usually been consummated in the face of contrary advice from friends and relatives. If this pressure is strong enough, the partners may proceed to marry in a spirit akin to defiance. Subsequently, unwillingness to admit that a mistake has been made may keep these marriages from disruption or may hold them together longer than might otherwise be the case.

The third complicating factor has to do with the personalities of those who consummate mixed marriages. Is there a selective process in such marriages? Are they confined largely to certain personality types? The truth is that we know less about this than is essential, but Slotkin's study of intermarriage between gentiles and Jews is highly suggestive. On the basis of 183 such intermarriages, he identifies eight types of persons: demoralized, promiscuous, adventurous, detached, rebellious, marginal, acculturated, and emancipated. Of the 289 persons marrying who were classified by personality type, 142 or almost half were classified as emancipated. If to these are added the rebellious, marginal, detached, and acculturated individuals, the total is 190, or 65 percent of all those classified. The combined total of the demoralized, promiscuous, and adventurous accounts for 99, or 35 percent of the total.[26] This latter summary tabulation suggests that two-thirds of the mates were persons who tended to reject the mores of their own group; the other group may have been actuated largely by motives of sex attraction and adventure.

Bicultural families are perhaps more likely to have "in-law" troubles than other families, for it is among the two kinship groups that the cultural differences appear without the softening or restraining influence of romance. In many cases the kinsfolk of one or both mates may have tried to prevent the marriage, or at least counseled against it, a fact which is not forgotten after the marriage has taken place. In those cases where the relationship between one mate and his own kinsfolk is close, the latter's opposition to the marriage is correspondingly meaningful. Even when he rejects his kinship group along with their mores, strong in-group feelings may drive the kinsfolk to seek to regain the errant one.

Again, bicultural marriages as a rule involve the union of groups with differing statuses. What is the status of the new family? Does it have a

[26] J. S. Slotkin, "Jewish-Gentile Intermarriage in Chicago," *American Sociological Review*, February, 1942, pp. 34–39.

marginal position, occupying a sort of social "no man's land?" It is rejected by the superior and accepted by the inferior cultural group? How uncertain is the situation in the eyes of friends and relatives? Is their attitude aloofness, hesitance, or condescension? Is one member accepted and the other rejected? What status is ascribed to the children? How does each mate react to the attitude toward himself and the other? To what extent are cultural differences seized upon, by friends, relatives, and the couple themselves, as pretexts to disguise other differences? Cultural differences are seldom unrelated to other aspects of family life. What seems to happen in many bicultural families is a continuing disagreement, coupled with a determined effort to stay together. There is attraction between the parents, and they could be happy if it were not for these irreconcilable differences. They cannot agree to agree, nor can they agree to disagree.

All these differences, cultural and personal, within both the immediate family and the kinship group, come to a focus on the children. They become particularly pronounced in relation to specific decisions which tend to fix the relatively permanent status of the children. Such decisions become involved with the self-respect of the parents and the pride of the respective kinship groups, as well as their deepest cultural values. Behind the crisis periods thus precipitated, the "feel" of the conflict situation is ever present. This has been expressed poignantly by one who was reared in a bicultural family. "There never was a time in my life," he writes, "when I first became conscious of religion. Like the concept of 'mother,' it seemed always to have been present as a great and awful question upon which adults did not agree, and upon which they would brook no discussion."[27]

The conflicts may focus upon one cultural element, as in the case of religion, or they may comprehend the entire ethos. They may express themselves in a continuing tug of war, with overt recognition of the points at issue; or they may reach a compromise in ways and degrees which vary with the intricate complexities of human situations. The significant fact here is that the children come to personify the problems at issue, and their personalities reflect the conflicts, compromises, and adjustments that are made. To restate somewhat the fundamental principle of this volume, the personality of the child is the reflection of the family culture, of its conflicts and tensions and differences, as well as of its agreements and harmonies.

Broken Families

The third group of family situations with which this chapter deals comprises those in which the personal or culture conflicts, or both types, between the parents have led to a termination, for the time being, of

[27] From the files of the William T. Carter Foundation.

the family relationship. The termination may be permanent, as in annulment or divorce; it may be uncertain and unsettled, as in desertion or separation.

EXTENT OF THE PROBLEM

The number of women reported annually as separated, in *Current Population Reports* of the federal Bureau of the Census, for the 1950's varies from a million to a million and a half. This category includes women "legally separated from their husbands, those living apart with the intention of securing a divorce," and those "permanently or temporarily estranged from their spouses because of marital discord." These figures may be taken, then, as one index of marital conflict, as evidenced by separation. How many children are involved in these cases is not known, but census tabulations for the 1,042,440 women reported as separated in that year show that 27 percent had no children, 45 percent had one or two, and 28 percent had three or more.[28]

The reader will realize: (1) these enumerations admittedly are incomplete, (2) they represent the facts only as of a single year, and (3) they do not include other forms of marital separation, such as desertion and prolonged absences of spouse under pretexts of one kind or another without having reached tacit agreement for separation and divorce. With these facts in mind, it must be obvious that the number of children in broken homes is very large.

BROKEN FAMILIES AND CHILD DEVELOPMENT

A great deal has been written about the relationship of broken homes to such problems as juvenile delinquency and child dependency. Particularly have the effects of divorce been emphasized, both in the literature on child problems[29] and in modern novels and the drama.[30] Somewhat less, however, has been said about its meaning for the processes of child development. Thus considered, some of the facts which stand out will be briefly summarized.

To understand what the breakup of a home means to a child, one must

---

[28] U.S. Census of Population, 1950, *Duration of Current Marital Status,* Government Printing Office, Washington, 1955, Tables 16, 18, 21, 23.

[29] Leon C. Marshall and Geoffrey May, *The Divorce Court,* Johns Hopkins Press, Baltimore, Vol. I (Maryland), 1932, p. 79, Vol. II (Ohio), 1933, p. 112; T. Earl Sullenger, *Social Determinants in Juvenile Delinquency,* John Wiley & Sons, Inc., New York, 1936.

[30] Among the novels are Wilson, *The Kenworthys,* 1925; Johnson, *Children of Divorce,* 1927; Wharton, *The Children,* 1928; Sedgwick, *Philippa,* 1930; Spencer, *The Incompetents,* 1933; Savage, *Summer Hail,* 1936; Eliot, *Angel's Mirth,* 1936; and Pope, *The Sentence of Youth,* 1936. Among the plays are Crothers, *Susan and God,* 1937; Ford, *What Imagination Will Do,* 1928; and Atlas, *Wednesday's Child,* 1934. For a fuller discussion of these and other literary discussions, the reader should consult James Barnett, *Divorce and the American Divorce Novel, 1858–1937,* 1939; and Donald Nelson Koster, *The Theme of Divorce in American Drama, 1871–1939,* 1942, both of which are University of Pennsylvania thesis publications.

go back to the fundamental functioning and values of the monogamous family. These grow out of a relatively permanent union between a father and a mother, each of whom plays a basic role in the culture-transmitting and personality-forming processes of family life. Not only does each parent bring his heritage, but each also colors on a sex basis what is transmitted. That is to say, the father brings a male, the mother a female, culture. Thus each parent is not only an addition but also a complement to the other in the child-rearing process. When a family breaks up, this normal process is interfered with, to an extent and with a significance which vary on the basis of the particular circumstances involved.

SEQUENCES TO FAMILY DISRUPTION

Three general sets of such circumstances are of basic importance. First are the new family relations which the parents establish. Four types of these relations most commonly appear. Both parents may live apart, neither one remarrying. This is perhaps the least frequent. Or one parent may remarry, and the other not, and the new couple may or may not have children. Again, both parents may remarry, with the alternate possibilities of other children, past and future. Finally, either or both parents may establish a new romantic relationship without benefit of clergy. Such illicit unions are found with particular frequency, as already noted, at the lower class levels.

A second set of circumstances of basic importance involves the disposal that is made of the children in the broken family. There are a number of possibilities. The child or children may live with one parent, by agreement of all concerned. Such an agreement may be observed with varying degrees of good faith. Second, there may be an agreement for the children to be shared, with a shifting from one parent to the other, such agreements again varying in fidelity of observance by either parent. Third, there may be a struggle, acute, chronic, or intermittent, for the custody and control of the child's development. The struggle may take place between the parents, or it may be between the opposing groups of kinsfolk. Fourth, the child may be placed in an institution or a foster home, such cases constituting a large proportion of dependent children thus cared for. Finally, the court may award custody of the child. In many cases, decrees for maintenance and custody are necessary; they are often followed by appeals, modifications, and extensive litigation. The courts supposedly award custody on the basis of the welfare of the child, but the decision as to what this means depends on the judgment of the court. No uniform standards exist to guide such decisions, so in actual practice they depend on the judge's special knowledge and experience, his knowledge of the family, the number of cases handled, the time available for each case, and the general attitude of the community. One principle usually observed is that custody goes to the so-called innocent party. This status of "innocence" grows out of the American legal principle that a divorce must be granted not on the basis of mutual consent, but as an award to an innocent or aggrieved party. Obviously such "innocence" has nothing to do with the security and best interests of the child.[31]

The third and possibly the most important set of circumstances involves the attitudes and behavior of separated or divorced parents toward their children. A number of well-defined patterns can be discerned. There are the parents who compete for the affection (and perhaps custody) of the child. This competition is prone to take unwise forms—an undue playing up to the child, overindulgence, displays of extravagance, and the like. Again, in many cases, the parents continue to fight each other through their children. Either or both parents, in part as an expression of personal animus and in part as a compensation for marital unhappiness, seek consolation, revenge, release, prestige, or security through their children. The result is that the child becomes the special victim of parental interference. As the only remaining link between former mates, he becomes the agency through which they can express their resentment toward life and each other. Such exploitation of a child takes many specific forms— he may be utilized to spy on a parent, the mother may incite the child to make all sorts of expensive demands on the father, or the child may be utilized to bear tidings of one parent's new-found happiness with another mate. Third, the parent may utilize the breakup of the family as the occasion to reject physically a child who was never wanted. It is particularly true that the child who is rejected is identified with the marital partner who is rejected. Finally, it must be emphasized that the experience of passing through marital crises is enough to lessen the parental effectiveness of many persons. In places where a stigma attaches to divorce, the parent must face and adjust to this. In any event, there is for the parents a continuing awareness or consciousness of their crises. Under the stress of all this, the child and his problem may be forgotten or neglected. Parental absorption in their own crises poses many a child problem. At times, the child not only sees his problems neglected, but is further utilized to bolster a faltering ego; that is, his loyalty is sought to atone for the self-condemnation of the marital failure.

FAMILY DISRUPTION FROM THE STANDPOINT OF THE CHILD

Finally it is essential to consider all these marital and family situations from the standpoint of the child. The aspects which appear most generally in these cases will be summarized briefly.

1. Perhaps the basic situation which a broken home creates for a child is internal conflict. A child ordinarily has some emotional attachment to

[31] For a detailed analysis of the legal aspects of such cases, the reader is referred to Kingsley Davis, "Children of Divorced Parents, Sociological and Statistical Analysis," *Law and Contemporary Problems,* Summer, 1944, pp. 713–714.

both parents. This feeling is independent of what other persons think of the parents, and of the parents' relations with each other. In many cases, people, including parents, do not understand this. When the family is broken and the parents separate, the child is called upon to make a decision which he finds difficult to make, which he is unwilling and often unprepared to make. Yet the very fact of his parents' separation necessitates it. Often the parents further complicate the situation by demanding that the decision be made. The problems thus created may be particularly difficult for older children who have an insight into the merits of the case and are also aware of their own economic necessities or personal advantages.

2. In many cases, the child goes from a broken home to a home in which he is a stepchild. What this involves has been referred to in an earlier chapter. In the case of a home broken by divorce, however, there are particular difficulties. The child must adjust to a stepparent while the real parent of that sex is alive. He may resemble the parent that is being replaced—a constant reminder of an earlier, unpleasant experience. Other children, born to the new union, compete and naturally have a better hold upon the parents. The child may resent the parent with which circumstances force him to live. He may resent the inferior position assigned to the parent with whom he does not live.

3. The child who is shifted back and forth between two parents must adjust to two different domestic milieus, and possibly to two stepchild situations. The two homes will differ, and in various ways. They may operate on different economic levels. The religious background may be different. Social differentiation may be present, perhaps in marked degree. Thus the child must learn to live at two domestic levels. A wide range of personal habits may have to be altered in going from one family to the other.

4. The foregoing suggests the problem of the restraints that are placed upon the child, on his conversational habits and other social relationships. Care must be taken not to speak of the other parent; reference to the past may be taboo. How should the new parent be addressed? How should he be described to friends? Is it advisable to bring friends home? How much should be told about the past? What comments are in order as one goes from one parent to the other? These are questions which merit the insight and restraint of an adult; for a child they must be both difficult and confusing.

5. The child with a broken-home background cannot but make comparisons with the home life of other children. When contacts with other children show that they have parents who live happily together, feelings of inferiority, self-pity, disappointment, or resentment may prevail. The average child is not a philosopher, nor is it of any comfort to know the statistical probabilities for a child to live in a complete and happy home.

6. The child, like the parent, carries the burden of a continuing awareness of his problems. There may be a vivid consciousness of the events which led to the separation of the parents, there may have been an emotional or dramatic high point in the separation, there may be the burning recollection of publicity and court procedures, there may be a gnawing awareness of being regarded always as a problem. The sense of disturbance that comes from being part of a record, written in unknown words and kept at some vague place, is something that makers of case records all too frequently overlook. Again, a child comes at an early age to sense the attitudes of kinsfolk, friends, and the community. The child from a broken home quickly becomes aware of furtive glances, incompleted sentences, crude innuendoes, and tactless remarks from persons preoccupied, thoughtless, or vicious, as the case may be. The moral condemnation of divorce attaches to him and makes his position more difficult than it would be otherwise.

7. One must not overlook the fact that the child develops attitudes toward the parents which become an integral part of the situation. Not understanding the purposes of the parents' interference or their attempts to use him to maintain a guerrilla warfare with the other parent, the child may become confused; understand them, there may develop disappointment and bitterness. Or he may develop a panicky terror over the prospects of a new parental alliance. Not a few children from broken homes come sooner or later to reject one or both of their parents with the callous air of "a plague on both your houses." This may subsequently take the form of a critical attitude toward the institution of marriage, or at least a critical awareness of it. Mowrer, for example, thinks that in this way divorce is often passed on from one generation to another.[32]

It requires no complete psychoanalytic equipment to understand that in some cases the child will identify himself with one of the estranged parents. This identification usually involves the parent of the opposite sex and, in early childhood, operates chiefly at the unconscious level. That is to say, the child's unconscious is identified with the unconscious of the parent. Because of this principle of psychological identification, the disturbing forces which lie below the level of conscious adult life are absorbed by the child. It is in this connection that the feelings of guilt, failure, apprehension, defeatism, bitterness, and the like, which many divorced or separated mates develop, become so insidiously important in the development of their children.

There is the added complication that the attitudes of child to parent and of parent to child change from time to time. The mother who is divorced by her husband when he has found a new attraction, clings to her child by way of comfort. She stimulates him to become a foe of his

[32] Ernest R. Mowrer, "Divorce and Readjustment," *Annals of the American Academy of Political and Social Science,* March, 1932, pp. 191–196.

other parent. Later, when she finds a new romantic interest, she discovers that her child is a handicap. Or he may be critical of the new spouse-to-be. Thus the child may find himself at odds with, or rejected by, both parents. Or the father, established in his new happiness, may become reconciled with the child, who now leaves his mother. These shifting loyalties complicate the child's attitudes, as well as increase his general insecurity.

8. Finally, what cannot be emphasized too much is that the disruption of a child's home life breaks the continuity of his emotional and intellectual development. After all, what is involved is a crisis situation in the most intimate and sensitive aspect of his life, and the reverberations that follow extend into every phase of his life. The continuity of his school life, and certainly the quality of his school work, are disturbed. Old friends may be lost, new ones must be gained. Life, with its demands and values, may have to be faced at a new level. Economic circumstances as a rule are disturbed, demanding curtailments of many kinds.

THE OTHER SIDE OF FAMILY DISRUPTION

Not all family disruptions are attended with bitterness or followed by aggravated personal problems for those involved. There are couples who are divorced with a minimum of ill feeling. Both parents may act like mature adults, frankly facing a mutual mistake and cooperating in the adjustment of their respective problems. There are divorces in which there is a substantial carry-over of good will, respect, and even affection. It would be an interesting research problem to determine how frequently the semblance of a natural family continues after the legal family has been dissolved.

Fred Blank divorced his wife 26 years ago, the mother retaining the custody of their son. Three years later, he married again. This second marriage apparently has been quite happy, and two children have been born to this union. The first wife has not remarried. She says she is still in love with her former husband, and both acknowledge that they have had sex relations a number of times since their divorce. The first wife visits him at his office from time to time, and he has continued to act as her business adviser, as well as contributing to the support of their son. Recently, the son has entered the army, and father, mother and son had a number of visits together. The second Mrs. Blank apparently knows nothing of all this, and Mr. Blank insists that it has not affected his relations with her.

Finally, whatever one's theories about separation or divorce may be, the fact remains that some marriages are a tribulation for all concerned. The child is apt to be the special scapegoat in these cases. The termination of such families, and possibly the new deal of another family setting, may mean only the stimulus of better conditions and new opportunities for the child and possibly the parents too. Divorce not infrequently is a solution which closes a whole chapter of family turmoil.

FAMILY CONFLICT AND THE CHILD IN CONTEMPORARY CULTURE

It seems not amiss to recall, by way of concluding this chapter, certain features of family culture in contemporary American society which make family conflict situations of such great importance in child development.

Four features stand out with impressing clarity. First is the prevailing emphasis upon, and the relative independence of, the immediate family as the unit of family relationships; second, and complementary to the first, is the secondary importance and lessened responsibility of the kinship group; third is the resultant high emotional concentration within the immediate family; and fourth is the equalitarian principle in regard to the child.[33] Taken together—and in many ways they are but so many aspects of the same process—they carry great meaning for children in homes with conflict situations. Three results are noted as of primary importance. The first is that the development of the child's personality, the satisfaction of his deepest personal and emotional needs, as well as responsibility for his economic and social maintenance, rest upon the small immediate family of modern times. Second, when this unit falters or fails, there is no larger kinship group to take charge, to which parent and child can turn to assume responsibility. Third, there is no accepted principle on the basis of which responsibility for the child is guaranteed by parents, except the uncertain personal opinions of legally trained jurists. As pointed out in the third chapter, the contemporary child in the American small-family system views the world from a very narrow ledge. When that ledge is wobbly, insecurity is as pronounced as it is inevitable.

Summary

1. Many families are characterized by a lack of harmony among their members in personal relations or cultural patterns, or both. These situations, which have been considered chiefly in their bearing upon husband-wife relationships, are also significant for child development.

2. Quarreling is one form of conflict. It prevails to some extent in virtually every family. In a more exaggerated degree, it takes many forms of expression, each of which has its own meaning for child development. Parents who quarrel excessively create many problems for their children.

3. A second group of conflict situations grows out of cultural differences between the parents. These may focus upon some one cultural element, such as religion, or they may comprehend the range of a class or the entire ethos. They may express themselves in a continuing tug of war,

[33] For a suggestive discussion of these factors, see Kingsley Davis, *op. cit.*, pp. 700–710.

or shade into the more subtle strains of compromise. In each and all events, these cultural conflicts express themselves in the personalities of the child members of these families.

4. The third group of conflict situations are those in which the unity of the family has disappeared, as in desertion, divorce, and the like. An enormous number of children are thus affected. Among the problems which such children face are basic internal conflicts; life in stepparent situations; frequent shifts from one family milieu to another; usually restraints upon behavior and conversation; feelings of inferiority, self-pity, resentment, or disappointment; continuing preoccupation with personal problems; the development of critical attitudes toward parents; and breaks in the continuity of emotional and intellectual development.

5. There is sometimes another side to the termination of a family. It may mean a solution of unhappy situations and the opportunity of a new chance. This may be particularly fortunate and promising in the case of younger children.

6. The problems for children in conflict family situations are particularly important in our contemporary culture because of (a) the prevailing emphasis upon the immediate family, (b) the lessened responsibility of the kinship group, (c) a high emotional concentration within the immediate family, and (d) the equalitarian principle in regard to child care.

Chapter

Families Under Stress

There are two distinct approaches to the study of the family and its problems. One is to consider it, relatively speaking, as a unity in itself, with emphasis upon the family situations of its members—their interaction with each other and their cultural relatedness. It is from this point of view that the preceding chapters have been written, with reference primarily to the development of the child. The other approach sees the family as part and parcel of the larger society, stressing the continuing interrelations between the two, and giving particular emphasis to the ways in which the family reflects and reacts to changes and forces in the social organization as a whole. A number of the current sociological books on the family are written, wholly or in large part, from this point of view.

Whatever the relative emphasis or approach, it is clear that family situations cannot be considered without reference to the impact of external forces; and obviously, the section on problem families would not be complete without recognition of the large number of families in which problems of internal relations arise from the stress of outside influences. Such problem situations result most clearly from major social crises, such as war or widespread economic depression, but the principle involved has a broader and more constantly recurring application. This chapter seeks to describe selected problem families in which serious difficulties in internal relationships result from the impact of external factors. For purpose of convenience, the discussion is organized around the factors considered, and these are grouped under six heads: (1) the physical basis of home life; (2) the impact of residential mobility; (3) economic pressures; (4) the time-energy requirement of parenthood; (5) the stress of shame; and (6) family crises.[1]

[1] For an analysis, with illustrative case material, of external factors in relation to family situations, see James H. S. Bossard and Eleanor S. Boll, *Family Situations,* University of Pennsylvania Press, Philadelphia, 1943, Chap. 8.

Physical Basis of Home Life

Family life has a physical setting, a material structure within which the family functions; and the character of this structure affects in many ways the nature of the functioning process. Perhaps no aspect of family life is exempt from its conditioning influence. This is the real essence of the housing problem. There are, to be sure, relationships between specific aspects of housing, such as the number of persons per room of prescribed size and the morbidity or mortality rates of the inhabitants, and often statistical evidence can be produced to establish such relationships; but the broader problem of housing concerns its adequacy for the maintenance of a normal family life. There is a sociology as well as an architecture of home planning. A house or apartment has too long and too largely been considered as a physical shelter to which the family must adjust its life. There is much more to be said with propriety about the adaptation of a physical structure to the life of its occupants. Just as we have come to emphasize the family as the matrix out of which develop the personalities of its members, so must housing be conceived as the means of providing facilities adequate for the family to function in these respects.

Thus considered, and viewed more particularly from the standpoint of the child, many aspects of the family's physical setting fall into their proper perspective—the possibility of a room of his own, with space for clothes, toys, and books; the nature of the sleeping arrangements; quietness for rest; sleep unbroken by household, adult, and neighborhood noises; separation of adults and child; a place to prepare his school work; a place, amid proper surroundings, to bring his friends; a place for all the members of the family to live their own lives, both as members of a family group and as individuals. Each of these items, and many others, could be separated for more complete analysis; they are both the minutiae and the substance of family life and of child development.

It is one of the tragic realities of life that many families live under the stress of housing inadequacies, and that these bear with particular heaviness upon the life of the children in these families. Included here is the home where privacy is unknown; where crowding imperils health and prevents comfort; where activity must be subdued because of the immediate presence of others; where the sick, aged, or irritable cannot be segregated; where the child must prepare his school work in the only room available for the entire family group; and where the entertainment of friends, and even courtship, must be carried on in a room shared by the parents or next to their sleeping quarters. Both the size and the arrangement of living space are important.

Similarly important, particularly for the child, is the outside appearance of the home. This advertises the family's status to all who pass by or come to call. Children comment at an early age on the appearance of their friends' homes, and the attitudes of adults are revealed by studies of family budgets which show that in the lower-income groups preference is given to housing over food. To young and old alike, but especially to adolescents preoccupied with desires for social recognition and prestige, the appearance of the home flaunts their identification to all who have eyes to see. The key to the behavior problems of many adolescents is a home-avoidance technique; they select their friends, conduct their courtships, and organize their lives in general so as not to bring their friends home.

Mention should be made, too, of certain groups of families who live under the stress of unusual housing arrangements. One of these groups is the families who live in trailers. Cowgill has studied trailer life[2] with revealing insight into the trailer family. Two-fifths of the 128 families he studied had child members, and some of his observations are particularly pertinent for child development. There is the obvious factor of overcrowding. This is clearly associated with the problem of privacy. He writes: "Privacy is an important factor in the development and maintenance of individual integrity. The French sociologist, Durkheim, expresses the opinion that satisfactory mental health, hence personality integration, is dependent upon achieving a balance between group life and individual life. One type of suicide results from too much individuation, and another from the opposite extreme of submergence of the individual in the group and his complete submission to collective representations. In trailer life we have a situation somewhat akin to the latter situation."[3] There are times in everyone's life when he needs to be alone. This need does not fit into the trailer scheme of life. Furthermore, the taboo against bodily exposure becomes difficult, if not impossible, to uphold in a trailer. Family quarrels are open to all; on the other hand, because of their isolation and the lack of a stable community life, trailer families commonly act together in many phases of life.

Similarly abnormal in physical setting for the family is hotel life. Hayner,[4] who has studied this problem, emphasizes its disorganizing effects upon family life, with particular reference to the failure of family ties to form in the depersonalized hotel atmosphere and the likelihood of previously established families disintegrating because of the lack of a common life to hold the members together. On the other hand, Burgess and Locke[5] question this in part, pointing out that hotel life makes for a social

[2] Donald O. Cowgill, *Mobile Homes: A Study in Trailer Life*, American Council on Public Affairs, Washington, 1941.

[3] Ibid., p. 35.

[4] Norman Hayner, *Hotel Life*, University of North Carolina Press, Chapel Hill, 1936.

[5] Ernest W. Burgess and Harvey J. Locke, *The Family*, American Book Company, New York, 1945, p. 549.

isolation of the family similar to the physical isolation of the farm family, so that the family is thrown more upon its own resources than in a well-integrated neighborhood environment. Unfortunately, these studies are concerned more with marital relations than child development. Obviously, the child reared in an apartment hotel lives an unusual life, and in many ways. He is unusually dependent upon his family. There is likely to be no immediately available play group. There is no neighborhood group. Most of the other families have no children. The majority of the adults are in the older age brackets. This makes for restraint in behavior. Much of his life is of the "goldfish in the bowl" variety. Spontaneity becomes curiously out of place. For the child, hotel life is likely to be lived under the stress of restraint.

A SPATIAL INDEX FOR FAMILY INTERACTION

Recently, there has been proposed a spatial index for family interaction, which seems pertinent to the foregoing discussion. This index is based upon, and is an extension of, the Law of Family Interaction set forth in Chapter 7. It combines with this law the data on the physical area of the home (i.e., floor space) within which the family functions, expressed in terms of square feet. For the determination of the index, three groups of facts are necessary: (1) the number of persons within the household or family group, (2) the resultant number of interrelationships, and (3) the number of square feet of floor space in the living quarters. The index is obtained by dividing the second number into the third of these variables.

For example, the Brown family consists of 6 members. Applying the formula of the Law of Family Interaction, it is found that there are $\frac{36-6}{2}$ or 15 sets of personal interrelationships. Measurement of the living quarters of the Brown family reveals a total of 1,380 square feet. With 15 sets of personal interrelationships, our interaction space index then is 92, or an average of 92 square feet for each personal interrelationship within the family group. The Black family, on the other hand, with 4 members and 6 sets of personal interrelationships, living in an apartment of the same size, has an interaction space index of 230. The Jones family, with 3 members and 3 sets of personal interrelationships, shows an index of 460 in a domicile of equal space.

This index is a quantitative expression of the spatial setting of intragroup relations. It is, in other words, an index of the pressure of the physical nearness of persons who are interacting, or, better still, a quantitative indication of the degree to which the home space may be presumed to place pressure upon the family members in their relations with each other. It is presented as an advance over the commonly used ratio of the number of persons per room in a household. The sociologist's primary concern, and especially that of the student of family living, is not so much with the number of persons per room, as with the number and complexity of interrelationships within a given space. The two differ, and increasingly so, with the addition of each person to the group.

There are, of course, other than interindividual relationships within a group, and these must be considered too in this connection. In Chapter 7, it was pointed out that the total number of potential relationships within a group is always mathematically determinable within a given formula. Applying this formula results in a much larger number than if only interindividual relationships are considered. In a family of 4, for example, there are 25 potential relationships; in a family of 5, the total is 90.

The fundamental implication of this index is forecast in Emile Durkheim's *De la division du travail social* (1893), where he points out that increase in the number of contacts multiplies the occasions when people find themselves interrelated, when problems arise necessitating adjustment, and when life has to be lived in conformity with rules and regulations.[6] This implies rather clearly the basic importance of the spatial setting of social interaction.

More specifically, the thesis advanced here is that the spatial dimensions of living quarters are related to the stresses, strains, and frustrations of family living. This does not imply that family members are necessarily aware of this factor, although material on family quarreling, gathered under the auspices of the William T. Carter Foundation, reveals a considerable number of references to "nothing but four walls to look at," and other expressions implying the cramped quarters in which the family lives. It is as a background factor that the spatial index, with its quantitative expression, becomes a measurable tool for research in the problems of family living. It is particularly germane in a situational approach to the study of family behavior.

The Impact of Residential Mobility

The term *residential mobility* is used here to mean changes in family location or residence. Such changes occur in some degree at all times and among all peoples; the American family is peculiar in the extent and intricacies of its mobility. A few statistical summaries will indicate the general proportions. Every year, before World War II, more than a million American farmers changed farms. More than four million persons migrated annually across state lines in pursuit of industrial employment. More than one-fifth of all native-born Americans lived in states other than those in which they were born. Thompson's analysis of reciprocal popula-

[6] Cf. George Simpson, *Emile Durkheim on the Division of Labor in Society*, The Macmillan Company, New York, 1933, Book II.

tion movements between city and country during the years 1920 to 1935 shows a total population change or turnover of 46,330,000.[7] Data from the federal Census Bureau show that in 1940 a total of 12 percent of the population lived in counties other than those in which they lived on April 1, 1935.[8] With the advent of World War II, the mobility of the population was greatly increased, and it is estimated that more than 30 million Americans changed their residence during the war years. By mid-century, the federal Census Bureau places the number of mobile persons at about 19 percent of the total population 1 year old and over.[9] Since 1950, annual reports indicate that approximately one-fifth of the population changes residence each year, about 1 out of 15 moves outside of the county each year, and in excess of 3 percent cross a state line in their moves. In 1950, one-quarter (25.6 percent) of the native-born population was living in a state other than the one in which they were born. Wide variations, however, existed between the states. In California, 58 percent of the residents were born in some other state; in South Carolina, only 11 percent.

Residential mobility obviously has great meaning for family life. A change in residence for a family is like transplanting a tree or plant; for both plant and family it involves a separation from the matrix, a disturbance of the root system and consequently of the functioning of the organism, followed by the problems of adjusting to a new setting. In both cases, too, the specific consequences depend on various factors—the extent to which the plant or family has developed and spread out its root system, the skill with which the transfer is made, the similarity or dissimilarity of the new soil (in the case of the plant) or culture (for the family), and the frequency with which such transfers occur. The culture differential involved in residential mobility is of the highest importance; it is the key to the relative significance of such movements as those from one farm or one city street to another nearby, from one region to another, from farm or village to metropolitan center, and from one country to another.

For mobile families, the common problems may be summarized as follows: (1) maintenance of social participation in the new community, (2) continuance of subjection to community controls of behavior, (3) retention of social status, (4) readjustment of traditional attitudes toward the demands of new cultural situations, and (5) maintenance of family solidarity in the readjustment process. A large number of American fami-

---

[7] Warren S. Thompson, *Research Memorandum on Internal Migration in the Depression*, Publications of the Social Science Research Council, New York, 1937, pp. 19 ff.

[8] *Internal Migration, 1935–1940*, Government Printing Office, Washington, 1943.

[9] Current Population Reports, *Population Characteristics*, Series P-20, No. 36, December 9, 1951, p. 1. Cf. also Newton Edwards, "Population Change in the United States," *Annals of the American Academy of Political and Social Science*, September, 1949, pp. 80–91.

lies, with a history of repeated changes of residence, have not worked out the foregoing problems satisfactorily, and the existence of these problems and the resultant characteristics of such failure constitute one of the basic problems in contemporary society.

One additional effect of mobility upon the family which requires special comment is the inevitable separation of the immediate family from the larger kinship group. Much as one hears of the interference of inlaws, there is a reverse side to this. For many younger families in particular, the presence of kinsfolk nearby confers many beneficial advantages. In case of need, there is someone to advise, to aid, to comfort, to encourage, to admonish, or to restrain. The young couple from New Jersey who marry and move to Oregon a year later may glow with a sense of independence, but their background ledge in case of any disturbance in their pattern of life is narrow indeed.

RESIDENTIAL MOBILITY AND CHILD DEVELOPMENT

Turning to the role of residential mobility in the development of the child, one finds at least six aspects that seem to be of primary significance.

1. Change of residence breaks the continuity of life as expressed in the tangible tokens of family possession. This has its meaning for all the members of the family, but one who understands the concreteness of child thinking and feeling will quickly sense that the physical symbols of family unity and continuity mean more to him than to any but the very old members of the family. Adults are far too prone to overlook this fact, with glib references to the "adaptability of the child." The house and street where one lives are symbols, too, of stability. Their unchanging continuance simplifies life, and the child, especially when younger, is not fitted to grapple with complexity. Moreover, it is not simply the continuance of his routine but the child's conception of himself and his family and the integration of personality and situation which are involved in the persistence or nonpersistence of these symbols. These, to be sure, are of the intangibles of life, but because they defy the naïveté of a statistical table, one must not underrate their importance.

2. Residential mobility generally means a change of school for the child. This is apt to precipitate many problems, considering for the moment only the scholastic aspects of the situation. Involved are adjustment problems to new courses, tasks, methods, and teachers. Some work may have to be repeated; in other cases subjects, either in whole or in part, will never be covered. In such subjects as mathematics and languages, this lack of sequence may be serious for the child's progress. A grade may be lost or gained, with varying consequences for his attitude toward his studies. His rank order in his class may be changed, upward or downward. Furthermore, many changes in school enrollment are made during,

instead of at the beginning of, the year, and in such cases the danger is particularly great that the child's school work may be disturbed and tend to become fragmentary and disconnected.

3. The child neither lives nor studies in a vacuum. Change of residence means also change in friendships, social contacts, and social acceptances. First, there is the break with old friends. To try to hold on to them may impede the child's adjustment to new situations; to terminate the contact may constitute a real loss. "All my life," writes Sheila, who moved eight times with her family before she was 17, "I have felt emptiness because certain people I liked passed out of my life." These losses, comments a teacher of wide experience, seem less important for the younger child, but become increasingly serious after the eleventh or twelfth year.

Second, there is the immediate problem of social contacts and acceptance in the community and school system the child enters. For the boy, this may mean a series of fights to try out the newcomer, with the resultant assignment of status. For the girl, the struggle may be less physical but by no means less stark and cruel. The assignment of the newcomer to the proper pecking order is not confined to barnyard society. Here again one comes to appreciate the fact that the child from a small family who enters a large school system is in a far different position than the child of a century ago when conditions were reversed. Dr. Plant, who has called attention to the frequency with which mobile children come to the attention of the psychiatrist, describes the situation as follows:

As we see the situation in clinical practice, constant moving may affect the child in at least two ways. The demands of new adjustments are hard for many youngsters. Each one must find a new place for himself, must establish a new vantage-point of struggle for acceptance and importance, usually in a milieu in which the child culture pattern is already considerably crystallized. There is a difference between this moving and the placement of a child in camp or private school, where the child recognizes that a large share of the others are quite as new to the affair as is he. There is the added difficulty in our area that often the racial or cultural background of the immigrant family is not relished by its new neighbors. As a means of establishing the family, the child is exhorted at home to play with the neighboring children, who in turn show with a consistent and open cruelty that they do not care for the interloper. Caught between two fires the child finds his struggles to establish himself all the more intensified. We have seen evidences in children that one such change in address involves inadequacy (or inferiority) very much more than insecurity, but that repeated situations of this sort very definitely begin to give the picture of insecurity in the child.[10]

4. In this process of finding his social place in a new community, the problems of the mobile child must be considered against the background of his family. His family, too, is mobile. One result of this may be

[10] James S. Plant, *Personality and the Cultural Pattern*, Commonwealth Fund, New York, 1937, p. 107.

that the family can be of little or no help to the child. The parents do not "know the ropes," or "the right people." They may be preoccupied with their own problems. The family may be mobile because the father is dead, or the parents quarrel or are shiftless or have separated or been divorced. The mobile child may have been shifted from the home of one relative to another, or from kinsfolk to institution and back again, or from one foster home to another. Human problems have a way of becoming interwoven in the fabric of family life.

Perhaps most significant for the mobile child is his family's status, or lack of it. A subsequent chapter dealing with school situations will discuss this more fully. To be emphasized here is the point brought out so well by Plant, that security and status for the child are to a great extent a family affair. Writing of the security aspect of this, Plant says: "The development of security is to a great extent a family affair—some sense of belongingness that the psycho-motor tensions of the parents transmit to the child. The resulting satisfaction is so basic a sentiment that it is only the most serious or prolonged series of threats that disturb it. The child who has not achieved this sense of security, the child who has not ever had a feeling that he has an unassailable place because of who he is regardless of what he is or what he does, shows a rather typical picture of anxiety and panic."[11]

One large-scale aspect of this family angle developed during the recent war. Written while the war was in progress, the following words are a fitting description:

Migrant war workers, or "defense workers" as they are generally called, have a rather distinctive status in the communities to which they have come. They tend to be spoken of as "those families who are here on defense jobs," with an implication that they are fly-by-night sort of folks. In many areas they are resented because they overtax living, schooling, and recreational facilities already strained. In other places they are crowded in trailer camps that may come to be regarded as a menace to the community. In some cities, like Detroit, they particularly accentuate housing conditions already quite bad. In other cases their status is complicated by the fact that they represent minority groups. Rather generally, older residents resent their use of community facilities to whose maintenance they have not contributed through taxation; they particularly resent their special privileges as defense workers in securing new automobiles and extra gasoline allotments. On the whole, and to a considerable extent, migrant war-working families live in war communities as strangers, objects of a rather pervasive social isolation.[12]

5. Residential mobility often involves a change from one cultural setting to another for the child and his family. The significance of this has

---

[11] *Ibid.*, p. 204.

[12] James H. S. Bossard, "Family Backgrounds of Wartime Adolescents," *Annals of the American Academy of Political and Social Science,* November, 1944, p. 41.

been emphasized thus far chiefly in regard to migrations from Europe to America. However, with the increasing identification by sociologists and anthropologists of, and emphasis upon, subcultural areas, it becomes evident that changes of residence within the United States, at times within the same state, may be a more radical procedure than has commonly been supposed. Certainly one would not depreciate the problems of a North Carolina Methodist farm boy who comes to live in an Irish Catholic urban area.

6. "Don't forget the cumulative aspect of this problem of moving from place to place," writes a young wife who herself moved more than a dozen times before graduation from high school.[13] The point is well taken. It is to be remembered that we have been considering not the effects of a change of residence, but of their recurrence. Whatever the meaning to the child of any particular change of residence, whatever the similarity or difference may be, the significant fact is that both these experiences and his definition of them accumulate. "There comes to be," writes the above young woman, "a vagueness about places where you have lived, of apartments and neighborhoods you didn't know well, or had come to dislike. Perhaps there were some you had liked. But after a time there comes to be an unreality about them, so that sometimes you are not quite sure whether this is something you have known in life or only in dreams." Obviously, the results of residential mobility are not all undesirable. Landis has pointed out general aspects of the reverse side.[14] The mobile child learns to be alert, adaptable, resourceful, democratic. Change of situation may stimulate to the point of becoming a pressure. "Mobility has its advantages," again to quote the case history just cited, "but I wouldn't wish them on anyone."

Economic Pressures

Most families are under economic pressure of one sort or another; we are concerned here with a degree of pressure which has a considerable meaning for child-family relationships. Such pressures are conceived here as being of two kinds: first, those which arise from economic inadequacy, and second, those deriving from sudden economic changes and dislocations.

ECONOMIC INADEQUACY

The concept of economic inadequacy includes many different kinds of concrete situations—the inadequately financed home,[15] the mother-supported home,[16] the home with heavy drains upon its financial resources,

---

[13] From the files of the William T. Carter Foundation.
[14] Paul Landis, "The Case for Mobility," *The Survey*, March, 1943, pp. 74–76.
[15] Bossard and Boll. *op. cit.*, pp. 185–188.
[16] *Ibid.*, pp. 194–197.

the family with many young children, the family with unemployment,[17] the family on relief,[18] the white-collar poor, the improvident family, and the family whose spending routine is a complete pattern of unwise expenditures. It is well to warn the reader here against one of the common faults in so much of the recent socioeconomical writing, which assumes that economic inadequacy is wholly or primarily a matter of insufficient wages for industrial workers. Inadequate income does exist, but unwise outgo and general financial ineffectiveness are both prevalent and productive of similar results. Moreover, ineffective management of finances is not simply a factor, but also a symbol of various character traits of the parents. Similarly, it should be recalled that economic inadequacy is a relative term, and as far as family planes of living are concerned it can be measured by the yardstick of ordinary working-class patterns (i.e., how one's friends and associates do live) and by the foot rule of need as established by scientific investigation (i.e., how scientists think they ought to live).

ECONOMIC CHANGES

One specific aspect of the problem of economic inadequacy results from the rapidity of changes in the price and wage levels. A few statistical facts will serve to illustrate the general situation. The wholesale price index for all commodities, month of January, shows a rise from 50.0 in 1939 to 116.9 in 1957 (1947–1949 = 100). The purchasing power of the dollar for consumer goods, with the same base (1947–1949 = 100), fell from 168.4 in 1940 to 86.1 in 1956. True, wages and personal and family incomes have risen during these years, but such changes have been far from evenly distributed.

It has long been the contention of economists that there is no particular merit or demerit in either high or low prices, but that the change from one price level to another always involves serious consequences. Much the same can be said about the economic status of the family; sudden changes are highly significant, and in proportion to the extent and speed of their occurrence. Here the suddenly wealthy family is one with the suddenly poor. Both types of change have been the fate of a relatively large number of American families. One of the results of the churning waves of social change that have surged back and forth over this country

[17] Ernest W. Burgess, "Unemployment and the Family," *Marriage and Family Living*, Autumn, 1945, p. 87; also James H. S. Bossard, *Social Change and Social Problems*, rev. ed., Harper & Brothers, New York, 1938, Chap. 12.

[18] Ruth S. Cavan and Katherine Ranck, *The Family and the Depression*, University of Chicago Press, Chicago, 1938; Bessie H. McClenahan, "The Child of the Relief Agency," *Social Forces*, May, 1935, pp. 560–567; James H. S. Bossard (ed.), "Children in a Depression Decade," *Annals of the American Academy of Political and Social Science*, November, 1940; Horst Mendershausen, *Changes in Income Distribution During the Great Depression*, National Bureau of Economic Research, Inc., New York, 1946.

during its history is the sudden rise and fall in economic status of individual families. The fortune-making periods of American history in particular furnish their full quota of this kind of family. The history of the immigrant stream is replete with illustrations, particularly of families by whom the path from Old World peasant status to urban mansion has been traversed in a relatively few years. In more recent years, the sequence of two World Wars and a world-wide depression has continued these rapid turns of the economical wheel.[19]

The effects of economic inadequacy, with particular reference to the physical appointments of family living, have been emphasized with considerable insistence in recent years, and many problems of child development go back to the lack of the necessary bases for normal family life. Chapters 19 and 20 offered many concrete illustrations of this fact.[20] On the other hand, perhaps less than sufficient attention has been paid to the effects of economic pressures of this kind upon the attitudes and conceptions of the child. The economic status of the family does much to influence the ideological development of its younger members. The child in a low-income home sees himself as such in comparison with other children and homes. Economic inadequacy expresses itself in concrete deficiencies whose values are largely social, i.e., comparative. Out of these comparisons grow the child's conceptions of himself and his attitude toward others, including his family. We are reminded here of Samuel Johnson's dictum, "Poor people's children never respect them."[21] Meltzer has thrown light in the same direction with his study of children's attitudes toward their parents, and his conclusion that children living at the lowest economic level had the least pleasantly toned attitudes toward their parents.[22]

"So Little Time"[23]

There is a dimension of family life which has to do with the time and energy, nervous and physical, that the maintenance of satisfactory family relations requires. Students of the family tend quite generally to ignore this dimension, although its basic importance is obvious. It is a particularly necessary requisite today for wise and effective parenthood because of the nature of child rearing in our contemporary culture. Not only is our

---

[19] For a convincing study, in novel form, of the adverse effects of a sudden change of fortune upon a family, the reader is referred to William Dean Howells, *A Hazard of New Fortunes*, Harper & Brothers, New York, 1889.

[20] For a discussion of income as a factor in well-being, consult Bossard, *Social Change and Social Problems*, Chap. 8.

[21] Joseph Wood Krutch, *Samuel Johnson*, Henry Holt & Company, Inc., New York, 1944, p. 4.

[22] H. Meltzer, "Economic Security and Children's Attitudes to Parents," *American Journal of Orthopsychiatry*, October, 1936, pp. 590–608.

[23] John P. Marquand, *So Little Time*, Little, Brown and Company, Boston, 1943.

culture, especially our urban culture, a highly complicated one, presenting many opportunities and problems to the child, but the role of parenthood has changed with the development of numerous specialized child-
serving agencies and institutions. Confronted with the realities of the
present child culture, the parent is cast more and more into an administrative role in which he becomes adviser, assessor, interpreter, and se-
lector of the child's experiences and opportunities. Elsewhere, in analyzing the changing protective functions of the modern family, it has been
pointed out that "instead of the overt dangers of two centuries ago, those
of our contemporary society are more subtle and insidious, and thus inevitably call for new protective methods. Now, instead of physical force,
there is needed keen judgment; instead of brute strength, there must be
wise counsel; instead of regulation, the demand is for instruction; and suggestion must replace compulsion."[24]

In other words, the contention here is that parenthood in the modern
family, calling for the tactful management of the children in relation to
the diverse opportunities and range of contacts of all kinds now open to
them, needs considerable time and energy if it is to function effectively;
for these are tasks which require investigation, analysis, judgment, planning, decision—and none of them can be hurried or performed effectively
with tired nerves.

It would be an avoidance of reality to overlook the many aspects of contemporary life which tend to reduce the time-energy dimensions of parenthood below the normal requirement. Moreover, it is in the upper social, economic, and often educational brackets that one must begin the
identification of these aspects. William Healy, philosophizing after a lifetime of studying child behavior problems, points out how the pressure of
business and of social affairs greatly outweighs concern about structuring
the personalities of children. "As I interview parents," he writes, "I find
that comparatively few of those who are on the quick upgrade financially
are in any measure alive to what they may be doing to their children."[25]
Nor are the fathers who are putting themselves under pressure to amass a
fortune or to attain professional or political leadership the sole offenders
in this respect. In many such families, the mothers, seeking to complement the ambitious design for the family, devote their time and energy to
projects of public service or social prestige or even child welfare, all the
time neglecting their own maternal responsibilities and permitting their
children to run wild or handing them over to the care of domestic servants, at times not of a high order.

The war period witnessed the development of many aspects of life
which made serious inroads upon the time and energy of parents. For

[24] Bossard, *Social Change and Social Problems*, p. 609.
[25] William Healy, *Personality in Formation and Action*, W. W. Norton & Company,
Inc., New York, 1938, p. 145.

millions of mothers, housekeeping had become a far more exacting task. Rationing, shortages requiring shopping at several stores or on successive days, long lines in stores because of shortage of help, curtailment of delivery services—all these and other wartime developments increased not only the time but also the nervous energy involved in what was considered routine housework. Lack of servants had thrown homemaking duties on members of the family not accustomed to, and perhaps not qualified for, such tasks. Community and civic groups related to war work made additional demands of all kinds. Many fathers and mothers had taken on additional jobs in order to meet the rising tide of taxes and living costs. Many of these conditions continued in the postwar period.

Disgraced Families: The Stress of Shame

The role of shame in human relationships is far more important than contemporary students have recognized. Both the psychology and the sociology of shame have yet to be written. Its significance in the development of the child, especially in the adolescent stage, is particularly great. The disgraced family, to employ the phrase utilized by Boll,[26] must be given major emphasis, therefore, in any consideration of families under stress.

A disgraced family is one which experiences a decline of status because of an adverse attitude on the part of the community toward the behavior of some one or more of its members. Since these attitudes involve the mores of the specific group which reacts to this behavior, it follows that the type of behavior condemned, and the degree of social disapproval expressed, vary a good deal from one social class to another, as well as from region to region. However, for purposes of general discussion, the following types of behavior commonly tend to affect unfavorably the social status of families: crime, especially major penal offenses; imprisonment; illegitimacy; drug addiction; chronic drunkenness; mental illness; and suicide. The number of families thus affected is large, as any inclusive index of these forms of behavior would show. Moreover, one must think in terms of the proportion of families which go through such experiences, not merely the number to be found at any one moment. Human problems are cumulative, not merely cross sectional.

Many factors determine the meaning of family disgrace for child development. First, there is the family's definition of its own behavior. Data on the family backgrounds of delinquent children show that a large proportion come from homes in which criminal behavior is a more or less accepted pattern.[27] Often, too, families of this kind tend to live near each other, so the neighborhood pattern may coincide with that of the family.

---

[26] Bossard and Boll, *op. cit.*, p. 202.
[27] Edwin H. Sutherland, *Principles of Criminology*, J. B. Lippincott Company, Philadelphia, 1939, Chap. 9.

This means that neither in the family nor in the neighborhood is there any critical sensitivity to a criminal record. "Marie is such a good girl," her mother tells the probation officer; "she always brings home everything she steals." Second, there is the degree of unity and emotional interdependence which exists between family members, particularly the degree of attachment between parents and children.[28] Third, loss of status resulting from family disgrace becomes more serious as one moves upward in the social scale—"the higher they come, the harder they fall." Fourth, the size and anonymity of the community are significant. Family disgrace in a stable, rural, primary-group community tends to be much more serious than in a mobile, urban, secondary-group area. Fifth, the age of the child is important. Family status means more in the adolescent than in any other age span.

Obviously, disgraced families and their significance for the child are a highly individual matter, but again certain common aspects may be identified. First, one would expect a loss of self-assurance, both for the child and for the other members of the family. Status is inextricably associated with self-confidence and self-respect, so the loss of the former cannot but involve modifications of the latter. As time goes on, accompanying feelings ranging from vague frustration to bitter resentment may develop. At an early age, the child of normal insight cannot help sensing that he is paying the price for the misdeeds of others. Second is an inevitable preoccupation with one's problems. For the child this may range from mere abstraction to worry, to obsessive reveries. One result of this in turn may be a lack of social or scholastic effectiveness, which brings further problems and complications in its wake. Parents and other older members of the family, too, are likely to be preoccupied, so they fail the child at a time when he most needs reliance on their comfort and help. Third is the effect upon relationships within the family. These may take several different forms. There is, for example, the situation in which the members form a conspiracy to conceal the family skeleton, trying to hide the act, the offender, or the knowledge of what has occurred. Or the situation may resolve itself into a conflict between the erring one and the rest of the family, with the possibility of all kinds of complications. Also present frequently may be feelings of sorrow. These prevail most often in families with strong affectional ties. Foremost in its meaning for the child in such cases might be the disappointment in the parent, the feeling of disillusionment that comes with the shattering of the childhood ideal of the parent or other offending kin.

Perhaps the most generally observed consequence of family disgrace is the social isolation of the family. Such isolation often is self-imposed. The child or the entire family may withdraw from normal contacts. There

---

[28] Burgess and Locke, *op. cit.*, p. 601.

is a conscious effort to avoid former associates and friends. A great variety of avoidance techniques are developed to meet such situations. Or the isolation may be imposed by the group. Particularly does this happen in the case of children. The child from the disgraced family may be avoided, or snubbed by friends, or dropped by the clique, or disbarred from the playground. Such isolation may take a positive form or the negativism of the silent treatment. Anyone who observes juvenile behavior cannot but see that children often are very cruel to each other, especially at a time in life when the wish for social recognition is very strong. Frequently, the isolation is imposed upon the child before he is of an age to have developed the spiritual resources which could enable him to cope with such situations.

Complementary to this isolation from the group, there often develops the tendency to form new social contacts at a lower status level. Actually this is a ready adjustment to an existing situation. Since the community has changed the person's status, the thing to do is to form compensatory contacts at a lower level. How this may set up a chain of circumstances which extend over a long period of time is illustrated in the following case document:

Richard was a senior in college when his father for the third time brought disgrace upon his family, only this time the precipitating behavior was more reprehensible than on the former occasions. Richard had fought to retain his individual status, following his father's earlier episodes, and through the help of stalwart friends, had succeeded in large measure in doing so. The third blow, coming after years of a determined effort to "keep his chin up," apparently broke Richard's spirit. Although his college clique had had upper social class status, soon after leaving college he began to go around with girls from the "other side of the railroad tracks." According to his own statement, he had developed the fixed idea that no "nice" girl would marry him because of his father, and that if he wished to marry, he must find his mate on a social level so low that she and her family would not object to his father. Some time later, he settled down to a girl of upper lower-class status, and relatively soon, sex relations between them became a part of the courtship routine. After an engagement extending over a year and a half, they were married. During this entire period, Richard was in a state of constant inner conflict. He avoided his earlier upper-class contacts. His attitude toward his fiancée alternated between an awareness of her social shortcomings and his relative satisfaction with her as a sexual mate, with a strong overtone of his duty to her because of the relationship which had developed between them. Although a virile physical type, he fainted four times during the two-week period before his marriage. Furthermore, he stated that he did not sleep a wink for forty-eight hours before the ceremony. The marriage lasted four years, during which time two children were born. Divorce ultimately loosened the bond, but the inner conflict was not resolved until some 15 years later. The psychological scars of the experience still remain, of course, and Richard is quietly but consistently bitter toward his father. He says that his father has ruined his life and that of his two children.

Unfortunately, the element of disgrace does not operate alone as a rule. Most often disgrace is an expression, in "the public relations" of the family, of a whole complex of disorganizing circumstances. Consider the obvious case of the imprisonment of a parent. In addition to the stress of shame, the results commonly found include dependence upon relatives or social agencies for support; the separation of children from their mothers or from brothers and sisters; the employment of the mother; the employment of the children; the interruption of the children's schooling; the loss of property through forced sales or the inability to continue payments; and the mother's assumption of illegal relationships.[29]

Another illustrative study is that by Treudley, showing how mental illness interferes with family routines.[30] In addition to withdrawal from social participation because of feelings of shame, the following additional complications may arise: (1) The family income and plane of living may be lowered. (2) Different members of the family adjust or react differently to the arrangements necessitated by the illness. (3) The mentally ill member projects his discomfort, illness, or complaint on the rest of the household. (4) The public peace of the neighborhood may be disturbed by the ill person. (5) If the mother is ill, the management of the appearance and functions of the home may deteriorate. (6) Eating and other dining-room routines are broken or upset, with subsequent effects upon the digestion of the children. (7) There is unpredictability of household routines. Meals are served at irregular times, for example. (8) Tensions develop between family members over these irregularities. (9) The mentally ill person becomes notional about food, clothing, bed, etc. (10) The mentally ill individual may become sadistic, deliberately seeking to destroy the family pleasure. (11) The sleep of the members of the family is broken. (12) The children are not disciplined or supervised. (13) There is no coöperation between home and school. The children may miss school, be late, or be unable to study. (14) The children's play life and other forms of spontaneity may be interfered with seriously. (15) The pet notions, aversions, prejudices, etc., of the mentally ill member may interfere with the normal lives, friendships, and activities of the children. (16) Feelings of nervous strain are inevitable. (17) The behavior of the mentally ill member either is not predictable or is unpleasantly predictable.

Other Family Crises

This survey of families under stress would not be complete without reference to cases where chronic illness, bereavement, unemployment,

[29] Ruth Bloodgood, *Welfare of Prisoners' Families in Kentucky,* U. S. Children's Bureau Publication No. 182, 1928, p. 21.

[30] Mary B. Treudley, "Mental Illness and Family Routines," *Mental Hygiene,* April, 1946, pp. 235–249.

war, and other crucial situations afflict the family and its members. Adequate discussion of these lies outside the physical limitations of this volume and the scope of its conception. There is a considerable literature on each of these crises and each has its special meanings for family relations and child development.[31]

These crisis situations are essentially disruptive in their effects, tending to disorganize or terminate the processes and relationships in the normal development of children, such as are stressed in this volume. Also, they may operate to reverse processes that have been described. Consider, for example, the Laws of Family Interaction cited in Chapter 7. The reader will recall how an increase in family size from 4 to 5 members means an increase of from 6 to 10 sets of personal interrelationships, and an increase of from 25 to 90 in the total number of possible interactive relationships. Reversing the process now, the loss of a single member means corresponding decreases in these totals. This is emphasized in a letter to the author, written by a widow with three children.

The adjustment to Blank's [her husband] passing has been somewhat rugged. The main difficulty has been in the family interaction pattern. If you revise your book, you should add that subtracting relationships can be just as complicating as adding to them. That is, by reducing the number of interacting personalities in the family and thus reducing the number of interacting patterns, a lot of things are made to happen to the remaining patterns. For example, my daughter used to own her father, which left me for the little boy. Each had a parent and there was a fair equilibrium. With Blank's passing, my little girl has turned to me, which seemed to the boy like horning in on his preserves. The competition for my time and attention became extremely intense and spread to all their other relationships. For a while, they woke up quarreling and went on quarreling all day. This is beginning to subside somewhat now. But we have by no means achieved serenity in the household. There is the baby and there is competition for him, too. All in all, it is a fairly complex business.[32]

Of great value in this connection are the studies by Hill of families under stress, showing that common factors are involved in all family crises,

---

[31] James H. S. Bossard, "War and the Family," *American Sociological Review*, June, 1941, pp. 330–344; "The Family in Past Wars," *Annals of the American Academy of Political and Social Science*, September, 1943, pp. 1–10; "Family Backgrounds of Wartime Adolescents," *ibid.*, November, 1944, pp. 33–42; and "Family Problems in Wartime," *Psychiatry*, February, 1944, pp. 65–72. See also Howard Becker and Reuben Hill, *Family, Marriage and Parenthood*, D. C. Heath & Company, Boston, 1948; Reuben Hill, *Families Under Stress*, Harper & Brothers, New York, 1949; E. L. Koos, *Families in Trouble*, King's Crown Press, New York, 1946; R. C. Angell, *The Family Encounters the Depression*, Charles Scribner's Sons, New York, 1936; James H. S. Bossard (ed.), "Toward Family Stability," *Annals of the American Academy of Political and Social Science*, November, 1950, article by Elise Boulding, pp. 59–67; Ruth Cavan and Katherine Ranck, *The Family and the Depression*, University of Chicago Press, Chicago, 1938; and Mirra Komarovsky, *The Unemployed Man and His Family*, The Dryden Press, New York, 1940.

[32] From the files of the William T. Carter Foundation.

as well as in the varying reactions and adjustment patterns involved. "The majority of generalizations from ten studies concerning the dynamics of family adjustment and recovery in the crises of impoverishment, bereavement, divorce, and other critical troubles, were confirmed as applying also to the war-born crisis situations of separation and reunion."[33]

Particularly significant are his conclusions concerning the factors making for successful adjustment. "Success in dealing with family problems," he writes, "and in getting along with others is probably learned largely within the parental family of the spouses, but it can also be learned elsewhere in friend-friend relationships, or in the successful families of acquaintances, or even . . . through trial and error in the process of early marriage adjustment. . . . It was not the form of the family, but its processes and substance of living that determined its success as a family . . . we found the ingredients of family success in a wide variety of family organizations. These ingredients appear to be: the recognition of interdependence of all members upon one another, the satisfaction of playing one's roles in the family whatever they are, the sharing of home management duties among all members, the flexibility of the family when facing new situations, the adequacy of intrafamily communication, and the opportunities for growth and development in the family milieu."[34]

Two Functions of the Home

The more one studies the problems of children in families under stress, the more one comes to consider and evaluate the child's home from two different but complementary points of view: First, the home is the place from which the child goes to participate in the larger social life; and, second, it is the place to which he returns after his social experience. This suggests the basic importance of two functions of the family in the child's development: the family's role, first, as a status-defining agency, and second, as an experience-defining agency. It seems appropriate to conclude the part of this volume devoted to the analysis of family situations in child development with a brief consideration of these two functions.

THE HOME AS A STATUS-DEFINING AGENCY

When the child begins making social contacts outside his family, he is identified at first largely in terms of the home from which he comes and to which he brings his friends. The home serves therefore as a very important factor in the process of his social identification and the ascription of his status. This factor operates in the social development of all children, and at all social levels; but it is particularly important for girls, for they must operate, socially speaking, more in terms of the home basis

[33] Hill, *Families Under Stress*, p. 333.
[34] *Ibid.*, pp. 319–322.

than must boys. This is especially true during the adolescent stage, when the drive for social recognition is strongest.

Once the universality of the foregoing process is recognized, one is in a position to understand a number of things about child behavior. It explains, for example, that oft-noted critical attitude which adolescents, particularly adolescent girls, manifest toward their parents—their efforts to "bring up father," to make over the family and the home. Similarly, too, it enables one to assess the stresses and strains of family life which have been described in the preceding pages. The essential tragedy of so many of the young people in these homes is that their families are a social handicap, or are believed to be so, during those years when the children's chief interest is their social acceptance outside the home. It is our considered judgment that the behavior problems of many adolescents should be reinterpreted and restudied as attempts to work out an adjustment to the social isolation or discrimination which they experience because of their family origins. This would be particularly true, and keen, in a country with traditions of social democracy and with a large population of recent immigrant origin. More will be said about this in a later chapter.

THE HOME AS AN EXPERIENCE-DEFINING AGENCY

Complementary to the role of the family as a status-defining agency is its function in defining the experiences of its members. Much has been written recently of the importance of the home as a cushioned retreat for husband and wife; obviously the larger aspects of such use have great meaning in child development. Home is the place the child comes back to, with his experiences. It is the lair to which he retreats to lick his wounds; the stage to which he returns to parade the glory of his achievements; the refuge he finds in which to brood over his ill treatment, real and fancied. Home, in other words, is the place to which one brings the everyday run of social experiences, to sift, to evaluate, to appraise, to understand, or to be twisted, to fester, to be magnified, or ignored, as the case may be. Here again one sees a universal process in child development, with families under stress often scoring their most signal failures in this respect. Such families are families in which the parents are preoccupied with problems other than those arising in the social development of their children. From this it follows that parental failures in these families most often take the form of "sins of omission." Child rearing, let it be emphasized again, is for the parents a teaching process, and teachers under stress do not make good teachers.

Summary

1. Family situations cannot be considered without reference to the impact of external forces. In many families, problems of internal relations result from the stress of outside influences.

2. The physical setting of family life affects its functioning processes. Many families live under the stress of housing inadequacies, which often bear with particular heaviness upon the life of the child. Postwar housing shortages, trailer camps, and hotel life represent special aspects of this problem.

3. Residential mobility affects the child in many ways. It breaks the continuity of life; and involves a change of school, adjustment to new social contacts, lessened family help and guidance, and, at times, marked changes in cultural contacts.

4. Economic pressures on family life include both economic inadequacy and the impact of sudden changes and dislocations.

5. Satisfactory parent-child relationships require adequate time and energy. Many families, especially at the upper economic and social levels, are under stresses which result in inadequacies in this respect.

6. The role of shame is very important in child development. Disgraced families are a serious handicap to their child members, particularly in their social contacts. Outstanding illustrations of such families are those in which imprisonment, illegitimacy, drug addiction, chronic drunkenness, and so on, occur.

7. Families with crisis situations represent another category of families under stress. These include cases of chronic illness, bereavement, unemployment, war, and the like.

8. The problems of children in families under stress must be considered in the light of two basic functions of the home for the child: (a) the home as a status-defining agency, and (b) the home as an experience-defining agency.

Part *VII*

Child Development and Nonfamily Groups

Chapter 24

Growing Out of the Family

Personality is a product of slow and gradual growth. Students of child behavior who analyze the emergence and early growth of behavior patterns place great emphasis upon the concept of development. This concept has been elaborated in particular by students of the physical and mental aspects of child life, and its philosophy has been made the lodestone of their constructive efforts. "Child guidance is growth guidance," write Gesell and his collaborators. "The refinements of the psychological care of normal and deviate child alike depend upon a developmental philosophy. A genetic approach is more important than rule of thumb and clever modes of discipline. A developmental outlook permits us to see the total tide of development in perspective. This gives a constructive forward reference to our methods and a more tolerant understanding of the difficulties of immaturity."[1]

Similar emphases appear today in the studies of the social behavior of the child. From the moment that life begins, the child is a social being. Even before birth, he has a profound effect upon those about him. At first, his role in social relationships is rather passive; but with continued growth, his responses become more active and aggressive. From one point of view, these changes in behavior involve his individualization, that is, his emergence as an independent and relatively self-sufficient person; from the other, this is merely the story of his socialization, of his integration into group life and his acquisiton of values which have a social orientation.[2]

This chapter is concerned with certain situational changes which underlie this process of the child's socialization, involving principally his

---

[1] Arnold Gesell, Frances L. Ilg, and others, *Infant and Child in the Culture of Today*, Harper & Brothers, New York, 1943, p. 5.

[2] Arthur T. Jersild, *Child Psychology*, rev. ed., Prentice-Hall, Inc., New York, 1942, pp. 156–157.

growth beyond the world of his family into that of the larger society. The main emphases, following reference to selected aspects of these situational changes, will be upon the problems which they tend to create for the child and his family.

The Social Development of the Child[3]

Obviously, the child's first social world is that of his family. In it the biological tasks of birth, protection, and feeding take place; within it develop those first and intimate associations with persons of different ages and sexes which form the basis of his personality development; from it are learned the manifold items which constitute its culture. It is a world in itself, in which the child learns to live, to move, and to have his being; and for a number of years his immaturity keeps him within the limits of its confines.

Early in life, however, the child begins to make forays into the other world outside. Gesell fixes the age for this at 18 months. "When a child reaches the age of 18 months, his behavior extends beyond the confines of his home. He goes abroad. He may attend a nursery school. His behavior has an enlarged cultural significance."[4] Certainly by the age of 2, instances of coöperative give-and-take, even if only of short duration, begin to appear. From this time on, response to the demands of other children and interest in the social world outside the family progress at a continuous even if irregular rate. Psychologists, observing manifestations of child behavior from year to year, tend to identify a sequence of relatively well-defined stages in this process of social development.[5] Five such stages will be identified briefly.

FIVE STAGES OF CHILDHOOD

1. First is the period of infancy, extending from birth to about the end of the second year. This is the period of the beginnings of social behavior: the child learns to distinguish between persons and objects; shows selective attention to the human face, recognizing familiar persons; attempts speech; shows reactions to persons of the same age; imitates those about him; and manifests some degree of rivalry in play with other children.

---

[3] For an interesting and suggestive analysis of the social development of the child in spatial terms, cf. Robert J. Havighurst and Bernice L. Neugarten, *Society and Education*, Allyn and Bacon, Inc., Boston, 1957, Chap. 7.

[4] Gesell, Ilg, and others, *op. cit.*, p. 3.

[5] For a good brief summary, the reader is referred to Elizabeth B. Hurlock, *Child Development*, McGraw-Hill Book Company, Inc., New York, 1942, Chap. 9; Gesell, Ilg, and others, *op. cit.*; Arnold Gesell and Frances L. Ilg, *The Child from Five to Ten*, Harper & Brothers, New York, 1946; and L. Joseph Stone and Joseph Church, *Childhood and Adolescence*, Random House, New York, 1957.

2. Second are the years from 2 to 6, usually referred to as the preschool years, and sometimes as the pregang stage. During these years children progress from being relatively nonsocial to being distinctly socialized. Among observable changes are an increase in the size of the coöperating group, in the length of duration of coöperative activity, in capacity to identify oneself with a club or team, in ability to follow the complex rules of a game, in perception of social relationships, in awareness of status compared with that of others, in capacity for self-criticism with reference to the standards set by others, and in capacity to formulate in words the traits and characteristics of others which they like and dislike.

3. Third is the gang period or stage, which begins at about the age of 6, when most children enter school; it extends to about the twelfth year. During these years the child shifts his interests more and more from the social world of his family to the group life of his peers. Social consciousness develops rapidly, the chief interest is in group activities, group loyalty becomes highly important, sportsmanship is emphasized, there is growing susceptibility to social approval and disapproval, social discrimination begins to make its appearance, and there is a growing revolt against adult domination. Significant differences in these respects between boys and girls appear now, as a result chiefly of cultural determinants.

4. Just before the onset of puberty, from 11 to 13 in girls and from 13 to 15 in boys, the child passes through a stage which has aptly been called the negative phase.[6] Among its characteristics are various manifestations of antisocial behavior, with a definite backward trend in social adjustments. There is a critical attitude toward home, parents, society, and so on, coupled with a desire to withdraw from former friends and associates. Fortunately this phase is of short duration.

5. With puberty comes the beginning of adolescence. This stage customarily extends from the twelfth to the twentieth year. It is the transition stage from childhood to maturity, during which new patterns of behavior have to develop to meet the demands both of the larger and more diversified life of his peers, and of the adult society which he begins to enter. More will be said later about this stage.

THE SOCIAL CRISIS OF CHILDHOOD

Obviously, there is a considerable variation from one child to another, not only as to the age when these successive stages occur, but also in the exact nature of their manifestations. Throughout this entire process of development, two changes continue to take place. First, the child spends less and less time with his family and derives less enjoyment from their

---

[6] Charlotte Bühler, *From Birth to Maturity*, Kegan Paul, London, 1935.

company; and second, there is a corresponding increase in his association with children of his own age. At first, the separations from his family are relatively brief and incidental—short trips or excursions, like fledglings darting from the nest to a nearby branch and then hopping back to the protective nest again. But as time goes on, these separations increase not only in frequency and length of time, but also in their psychosocial implications. What comes basically to be involved is a shift in the center of the child's social orientation from his family to his peer group. Gradually and imperceptibly his loyalties to and his interests in his peer group grow until they equal, and finally tend to surpass, those he has for his family. To speak in situational terms, this transfer is a major social process in child development, precipitating what is for many persons life's first major social crisis. What actually happens during these years is that the child continues to live in the social world of his family, to whose requirements he must submit himself, while he is busy transferring his activities and allegiances to the social world of his peers, whose approvals and disapprovals come to have paramount importance for him. It is to the phases, factors, and problems associated with this process that we turn next.

Toward the Peerage of One's Age

The transfer from the social world of one's family to that of one's peers in childhood has been identified as a social process extending over a period of years. Although it begins very early in life in the form of casual excursions from the family fold, it is when the child starts attending school regularly that the process gets fully under way.

Going to school involves for the child a revolution in his situational setting. First, familiar objects and places are left behind. The child enters a new physical environment, different from his home. This difference may be quite pronounced, in the direction of either increased comfort and attractiveness or the reverse. Second, the population of this new world is much larger than that of his home. Perhaps the number is very large. Accordingly, freedom has to be curtailed. Contacts are multiplied, there are more rivals, more adjustments to other persons are necessary. This competition with other children takes one form in the schoolroom, another on the school playground, and often still another on the way to and from school. There are children who have to fight their way to school and back home again. Third, a new authority emerges in the child's life—that of the teacher, who now takes the place of the parent and in certain respects seems to supersede the parent. Furthermore, new responses to this person of authority are necessary. Instead of the shared intimacy with the parental authority, there is the more impersonal, ofttimes entirely impersonal, authority of the teacher. Truly, for the child this is a new world, with new criteria, new rules, new requirements. Viewed from his standpoint, the change must be revolutionary, and one cannot but speculate about its crucial meaning for the child and about two further questions involving social policy. First, how early in life may children be submitted safely to such a revolutionary transfer of social worlds; and second, what other obligations are more important than the mother's presence in the home in helping the child assimilate this experience?

SOME PROBLEM ASPECTS OF THE TRANSFER

Entrance into the school-peer-group world creates two sets of problems for the child: first, he has to learn to live in this new world; and second, he must learn to live in two worlds, for he continues also to live in his family world. In this continuing transfer from one world to another, many difficulties arise, some of which are selected for brief analysis. Throughout this entire discussion of the transfer process, its problems, and the child's responses to them, the children discussed are primarily below the age of 12.

1. First is the passage from protected to unprotected competition. This constitutes in large measure the early socialization of the child. Children gathered together in school or other groups in the earliest years come mostly from homes in which they have enjoyed protected competition, i.e., in which situations have been devised and manipulated to show them off, to let them win, and so on. When such children gather in groups, their first reaction is to play by themselves, without much reference to the presence of others, and to deal with each other only when conflicts arise. Subsequently, playing with each other begins, on the basis of unprotected or free competition. This is a most significant situational change that opens up an entirely new world, in which the child must gain status without benefit of adult manipulations. Parents and other adults are prone to encourage child competition during this period, and in a form more stark and unrestricted than they employ in their adult relations. Viewed through the eyes of the child, this is a hard world, in which the contestants often are extremely cruel to each other.

2. A second set of problems involves the child's experience with patterns of response to his peers and to other persons as well. In the family world, he sees and learns to use certain ways of approaching people and responding to them. These may be patterns of friendliness, resentment, rebellion, submission, excessive volubility, or sullen silence. "The examples set for the child by his parents, older persons and associates operate from birth onward," writes Anderson. "Older persons transmit a variety of techniques and attitudes. . . . Thus the child observes his parents greeting neighbors or friends, hears the comments made by his parents on individuals, organizations, and activities, and is given examples of

either good or poor sportsmanship when he plays with his parents. . . . If parents quarrel frequently in the presence of the child, he not only acquires quarreling as a mode of approach to others but may react with uneasiness and frustration."[7]

Much of the child's early socialization is a trying out of these techniques or modes of approach. However they work at home, the peer world renders its own verdict. Some elicit favorable, others unfavorable, reactions. "A boy sent to a clinic because of his unpopularity was socially isolated among his fellows because of his many caustic comments and criticisms. It was found that his father was known throughout his community for similar behavior. Here what seemed abnormal in the boy had been learned in the normal manner directly from a parent."[8] On the basis of this experience with the peer group, there goes on in the child a continuous selection and valuation of responses, with a continuance of some and a modification or elimination of others.

Children differ markedly in the opportunities which they have to gain social experience of this kind. Some children have contacts during these early years with many other children, both at home and in peer groups outside the home. The ages of the children in these peer groups may be the appropriate ones to stimulate the socializing process. On the other hand, there are children who are the only children in the family group and who have very limited contacts, over a period of years, with other children of their own age. Parents often fail to consider situations of this kind in selecting the home and neighborhood in which they live, yet they are of basic importance in the child's social development. Washburn and Hilgard have shown that the persistence of poor social techniques in many children is due to inexperience rather than to inability to acquire the techniques if appropriate experiences are given.[9] Updegraff and Herbst have found that social behavior varies with the type of play equipment;[10] and Cockrell found that an environment rich in play materials produced the most social contacts and those of the highest order. Where little or no equipment was available, undesirable social behavior seemed to result.[11]

[7] John E. Anderson, "The Development of Social Behavior," *American Journal of Sociology*, May, 1939, p. 849.

[8] *Ibid.*, p. 849.

[9] Ruth W. Washburn and Josephine R. Hilgard, "A Quantitative Clinical Method of Recording the Social Behavior of Young Children," *Journal of Genetic Psychology*, December, 1934, pp. 390–405.

[10] Ruth Updegraff and Esther K. Herbst, "An Experimental Study of the Social Behavior Stimulated in Young Children by Certain Play Materials," *ibid.*, June, 1933, pp. 372–391.

[11] D. L. Cockrell, "A Study of the Play of Children of Preschool Age by an Unobserved Observer," *Genetic Psychological Monographs*, December, 1935, pp. 377–469.

In the course of this learning process, many a child comes to discover that there is a fundamental difference between the response patterns emphasized to him in the family world and those prescribed for him in the peer world. In the former, he is told by parents and teachers, and is shown by the examples of other children, to be obedient and submissive. He is to accept leadership and direction. Mother knows best, and it is not for him to question. But in the peer world the prescribed responses are apt to be those of self-assertion. There the chief virtue is domination; the most important qualities are those of leadership. In fact, there is much evidence to show that the more dominating the parent is in his relations with his child and the more submissive he expects the child to be toward him, the more self-assertive he wants the child to be in his relations with other children.

3. A third group of problems for children arises from the differences between the culture of the family and that of the peer world. Such differences are very prevalent, and at times quite marked, in a country like ours, with its rich variety of cultural groups, its sectional traditions, its regional differences, and its class distinctions. Furthermore, the high rate of residential mobility of our population, with its changing contacts, increases the incidence of contacts between cultural groups. Thus the North Carolina small-town Protestant family comes to live among the Irish Catholic in Boston; the Polish Catholic family migrates to a Protestant German area; the Vermont couple, with their 7-year-old son, are transferred to a job in Georgia; the intellectually overstimulated son of a university professor lives on the edge of a changing urban neighborhood that is rapidly being taken over by Negroes; the child of wealthy parents, keenly alive to the social amenities, finds his peer contacts with a host of upper lower and lower middle-class children whose interests are for the most part considerably different from his own.

If we remember that the term *culture* includes ways of thinking and believing as well as material artifacts, the significance of cultural differences between family and peer worlds will be evident. From the family standpoint, the culturally different peer world stands for habits, ideas, and values which the family seeks to avoid in rearing its child; to the peers, the child's family appears as peculiar, old-fashioned, or unreasonable. From the standpoint of the child, the situation is both difficult and confusing. In his home world he is being trained, to the point of coercion perhaps, to certain cultural values, and his peers in the child world emphasize another set; he must live in both worlds, and at a time when he lacks insight into the peculiarities of life, his parents, and his peers. Sometimes these cultural differences are minor, and cause only a passing wonder in his mind; in other cases, they are broad or deep, or both, resulting in the direct conflicts between the two worlds in which he must live. This is perhaps the place to point out the possible role of the private school, if properly selected, in bringing children of relatively similar cultural backgrounds together.

4. A fourth group of problems has to do with the reactions of the parents to this early socializing process of the child. Of the more commonly found parental attitudes, four, which tend to hamper the child's social development, will be identified briefly. There are the parents, for example, who brook no competition. They tend to ignore or to reject the claims of the child or his peer world. They fail to realize its meaning to him or its role in his development. Second, there are the parents who seek to lure their child away from contacts with other children and try to restrict him to contacts within the family. "We and our children do everything together," say many parents with pride in their own exclusive parenthood. Again, some parents place themselves as a shield between the child and his social experiences with other children. Early in his life, they arbitrarily take him out of situations before he can learn to accommodate to them. This keeps the natural socializing process from functioning. It narrows the child's opportunity to develop the techniques of getting along with his peers. One of the major problems of parenthood is to learn one's proper place in this social learning process involving the child and his relations to other children. In a fourth type of situation the child is overpraised for even his more minor achievements, the obvious effect of which is to prevent him from learning the satisfactions of real achievement. In other words, the parent becomes a soft pillow between the child and the realities of life, and there is a resultant development of attitudes in the child which often continue into adult life. One can readily detect the persons in the adult world who expect praise and even outright flattery for doing only the more ordinary tasks.

In summary, how the child transfers from the world of family life to that of childhood, and later to adulthood, depends to a large extent on the parents, how they have functioned and what they have sought to achieve. Have they contrived to make the child independent and capable of dealing with his problems, have they sheltered him, has their major objective been to instill obedience, or have they kept him in ignorance of the realities of life? These parental attitudes toward the child's social experiences in his own world, and the child's responses to them, constitute an integral chapter in human development.

Child Responses to Transfer Problems

Child responses to these transfer problems are considered usually in terms of the rate and consequent age at which the transfer is made, and children are grouped as developing socially at (1) a normal, (2) an accelerated, or (3) a retarded rate of growth. This approach is important, particularly when related to measurements of other aspects of child development. Emphasis here, however, will be upon the type of response, in terms of social interaction, which children make to these transfer problems. To understand these responses, it seems pertinent again to recall the dual nature of the child's life. He is expected to learn to live with other children; he is compelled to live with his family. His problems are therefore basically twofold, centering in (1) his relations with his parents or his family world and (2) his relations with his peers in the child world; his responses are accordingly grouped under these two headings.

RESPONSES IN RELATION TO PARENTS

The ways of doing and thinking followed by the child or his peer world often do not meet the approval of the parent and the adult world. Most often this disapproval is mild, the peer world being regarded with amused tolerance as among the vagaries of childhood; at times, however, the disapproval may be so marked that his conduct is spoken of as "delinquent behavior." In making their judgments, parents tend to overlook the criterion by which the child is judging, in his desire for social recognition. The essential fact which parents are so prone to forget is that the child whom other children like and seek as a companion is succeeding in building up desirable habits of social behavior. From the adults' point of view his habits and attitudes may not appear satisfactory, but his own group has placed its approval on his manner of working and playing with them and from that standpoint his behavior may be called adequate and efficient. Hence a significant criterion in appraising the social behavior of growing children is the amount of recognition received from the group with whom the children are in daily contact under a variety of circumstances.[12]

It is in the difference between these two criteria that many of the conflicts between child and parent begin; confronted with these conflicts, the following types of response are characteristic of many children:

1. Responses of hostility and resentment are both frequent and inevitable. Karen Horney, the psychoanalyst, emphasizes this type of response and its significance. "The more difficult are his experiences in the family, the more will a child be inclined to develop not only a reaction of hatred toward the parents and other children but a distrustful or spiteful attitude toward everyone. . . . The more a child covers up his grudge against his family, as for instance by conforming with his parents' attitudes, the more he projects his anxiety to the outside world. . . . The general anxiety concerning the 'world' may also develop or increase

---

[12] For a study of this kind, the reader is referred to Martha C. Hardy, "Social Recognition at the Elementary School Age," *Journal of Social Psychology*, August, 1937, pp. 365–384.

rapidly."[13] The basic response perhaps is rebellion against the parents, leading to open and direct opposition, to efforts at circumvention, or to compliance but with a sullen smoldering resentment. If deeply enough established, such attitudes naturally will be retained and carried over to the adult world.

2. Withdrawal from the child world, coupled with devotion to the teacher rather than the parent, occurs at times. These are the children who seek to become exemplary students in school; their behavior conforms to the teacher's demands; they develop the customary "bag of tricks" to draw attention to their own behavior as well as to the nonconforming behavior of other children. They are the adroit "apple polishers" of the school world.

3. In some cases, however, the withdrawing child centers his allegiance upon the parent. Such children reject the peer world and remain loyal to the family world. Coupled with this, there is often a clever play upon parental generosity or sympathy. There may be hints to the parents about the discrimination of "other children"; and when the "other children" are of different cultural groups, the possibilities for the development of trouble are many and varied. Suggestions may be made to the parents to buy things so that the children may impress other children. Apparently, the opportunities in these situations for parents and children to exploit each other are numerous and tempting.

4. There are many cases in which the differing claims of the family and the peer worlds create conflicts which become crucial, and at times insoluble. Such children are early torn between loyalty to their families and the very human desire for social recognition in the world of other children. It is conflicts of this type which seem to relate themselves to the anxieties which Horney emphasizes as that "insidiously increasing all-pervading feeling of being lonely and helpless in a hostile world."[14]

5. There is, of course, always the possibility of dissociation as a response. This consists in keeping the peer world and the family world apart. Just as the adult learns to organize his Sundays about his duties as a pillar of the church and his Mondays about the realities of the business world, so children adjust early to conflicting situations by compartmentalizing their lives. It is amazing to discover how many children learn to lead double lives; the one, with their peers, and the other, in their families, straddling in one leap the differences between them and contriving steadily to keep one out of sight of the other.

RESPONSES IN RELATION TO PEERS

Because responses in relation to peers will be dealt with in subsequent chapters, reference to them here will be brief. It will suffice only to point

---

[13] Karen Horney, *The Neurotic Personality of Our Time*, W. W. Norton & Company, Inc., New York, 1937, pp. 88–89.

[14] *Ibid.*, p. 89.

out that the normal child tends to give priority to the peer world over the family world in his deep desire to gain social recognition, and that when he does so, many a modern parent becomes alarmed and rushes him to a clinic or to "the psychologist" to find out what is the matter with him. We cannot help recalling here the story of the distraught mother of such a child who rushed to a noted psychiatrist and asked where she could find a good psychiatric clinic. The psychiatrist gravely told her and added this terse bit of advice: "And while you are there, be sure you get a good examination."

Less than ordinary success for the child in his peer world often leads to other types of response, and these will be considered briefly.

1. The child may seek another child world in which special privileges will be given to him. He will search for playmates who will grant protected competition. It may be the neighboring child who has no one else to play with, or a smaller child, or a child of another color, or a child of lower status. Such responses, made by the child or suggested by the parent, are symptomatic and should receive early attention.

2. Some children seek to buy special favors, immunities, or recognition in the peer world. Out of such situations arise those inordinate demands for money which are often encountered in children. In some cases, these demands are met by the parent; in others, the child early seeks ways of earning the money; in still others, he makes theft the solution. Petty thieving among school children is very common and is, for the most part, overlooked or dealt with in a casual manner; it is usually only when large amounts of money or material are involved that a "hue and cry" is raised. There is little doubt but that much of the stealing by children who are old enough to distinguish between mine and thine results from their search for the means of achieving social success.

3. Children withdraw from the child world without transferring their allegiance to teacher or parent. They withdraw now in order to recapture it later. Here one finds the child who practices something in which there is for the time being no competition. This is the child who takes private lessons, usually in activities in which there is a possibility of individual achievement and subsequent success. Often such children are actuated by a strong driving force which seems to say, "I'll show them, I will." We find these children with particular frequence in certain ethnic groups who have peculiar problems in regard to social recognition. It is out of situations of this kind that the artist arises early, with his paradoxical combination of withdrawing from his fellows to achieve levels of performance which will enable him to gain their subsequent acclaim. The spiritual home of the artist has ever been on the terraced slopes of a social no man's land.

4. At times, the child who fails with his peers withdraws only from competition with his own sex, transferring his activities to the opposite sex. This group includes the girl who "hates" other girls. She likes to play

only with boys, among whom she finds protected competition. A little later, to enable her to retain her position with the boys, she may permit them special privileges. Some of these may be sexual in nature. One thus comes naturally to understand why sex delinquency and illegitimacy come to be spoken of as forms of compensatory behavior. There is the boy who wants to play only with girls. The other boys are too rough, he says, or uncouth, or uninteresting. To retain his position with the girls, he soon realizes his need for money, and theft may, in time, be his definition of the situation.

5. A great many children who fail or meet with inadequate success in the social life of their peer world seek early to compensate with success in their school work. School success serves many purposes for a child. Through it, he is proving to himself that he is no failure, he is showing other children that there is something in which he can surpass them, he is impressing his parents and other adults who regard such success as a virtue. Solutions of this kind are particularly feasible among middle-class persons, but it is not too much to say that among all classes very high levels of scholastic performance are a product of the withdrawing technique. This serves to explain also the widespread reluctance of many "bright" children to be too conspicuous in their school performance. Developments of this kind are, however, most frequent in the adolescent years.[15]

The Process of Social Weaning

As the child grows older, the relative importance which he attaches to his peer and his family worlds gradually changes. At first, as has been noted, the family world is of primary importance to him, and the peer world is incidental. But by the time that the ordinary boy and girl reach their twelfth year, the peer world definitely surpasses the family world in its importance to them. From the twelfth to the twentieth year, the young person reorganizes his personality on an increasingly independent basis. Obviously, this entails the establishment of a new relationship between child and family, involving a modification of family attitudes and ties to meet the child's demands for self-affirmation. The child is growing away from the family, it is commonly said. There is an emotional detachment from the family, and a reorganization of habit patterns away from obedience and dependence to a relative independence permitting the young person to face the world "without turning back." For this growing-away process, the term *social weaning* seems appropriate.

To avoid possible misunderstanding, it should be pointed out that social weaning does not mean necessarily leaving the parental roof, al-

[15] Annie G. Beck, "School Success as a Withdrawal Mechanism in Two Adolescents," *Journal of Abnormal and Social Psychology*, April–June, 1935, pp. 87–94.

though this is often involved; or defiance of the parents' legitimate authority, although this may have to be reinterpreted; or the manifestation of insolent or disorderly behavior, although this appears at times as a by-product. Social weaning means a reorganization of the child-parent relationship in recognition of the child's growing maturity. It is this aspect which is fundamental and needs to be emphasized.

Although this process is most obvious between the twelfth and twentieth years, a recent study suggests that its beginnings often are to be found earlier in life, as a by-product of childhood visiting. Such visiting seems to follow a somewhat regular pattern, first to near relatives, such as grandparents, uncles, and aunts, and then to more distant kinsfolk and nonrelatives. At first these visits are for short distances and periods of time, like the hopping of fledglings away from nests to neighboring friendly spots, and then gradually extending in both duration and space. Invariably they are a major social experience for the child: a definite phase of growing up, an awareness of other people and places than those found at home. They involve a gradual conquest of distance, a sense of freedom from parental control, an insight into life in other families, a comparison of their own with other parents. The process of being weaned socially from the parents involves a continuing accumulation of the minutiae of experience in living. Visiting away from home involves some of the child's first social steps.[16]

Social weaning is neither easy nor simple, being characterized often by a series of relative crises in parent-child relationships. Certain aspects of contemporary life are prone to complicate it. The role of the small-family system, early marriage and childbirth, and the increased health and longevity of parents have already been referred to as tending to create the possessive parent, i.e., the parent who will not let go. Another factor, generally overlooked, is the modern prolongation of childhood resulting from advanced standards of public education and child labor. Not only do these present-day standards postpone the child's entrance into the workaday world and, economically speaking, into the world of self-maintenance, but they also correspondingly prolong the period as well as the completeness of his dependence upon his parents. This situation is seen in its more exaggerated form among students at the collegiate and professional school level. A large proportion of young people have been going to college in recent years. To a large extent, this development has been assessed in terms of the intellectual sharpening of the younger generation. Two additional aspects may, however, be considered. One is the whole personality development of collegiate youth. Is their development balanced, or does the intellectual run beyond the emotional and the social? Does growth in the world of ideas too far ex-

[16] James H. S. Bossard, "Process in Social Weaning: A Study of Childhood Visiting," *Child Development*, September, 1951, pp. 211–220.

ceed acquaintance with the world of reality? Questions of this kind, however important they are per se, are somewhat incidental to our main query here: what does this prolongation of dependence upon their parents do to young people? Does it tend to create a dependent, exacting, taking but not giving type of person—the abused citizen in a world of historically unparalleled luxury? How does a youth of 20 to 22, for example, define to himself his dependence upon his parents? Is it true that he develops often unconsciously a deep and intense emotional resentment against his parents? Is it inevitable that because he owes them so much which it would be so difficult to repay, he tends to rationalize the situation so as to excuse himself from his obligations: (1) his parents are unreasonable in their demands, (2) they do not understand him and are crippling the development of his personality, or (3) they are really much more blessed with this world's goods than they seem and can well afford the expenditures which they have made?

SOME SYMPTOMS OF AN UNWEANED CONDITION

Social weaning, however, is unlike physical weaning in one marked respect—the fact that frequently it does not happen, wholly or at least in part. In everyday life, one constantly meets the people who have failed at being socially weaned, who have never learned or been allowed to let go of their dependence upon their parents, and who because of the characteristic symptoms that ensue are incapacitated for the activities of adult life. Two illustrations will suffice.

1. In the workaday world, the unweaned person is likely to be constantly expecting or asking for special consideration from his employer. The employer, being the person in authority, is expected to act as the parent did. When this is refused, the employee may indulge in temper tantrums, talk to himself, develop a persecution complex, act like a long-suffering hero, or resign in a huff. Many such persons become intolerable nuisances in the world of business and the professions. Undoubtedly, many a life spent in occupational drifting or failure results from the characteristics of social unweaning.

2. Many a matrimonial failure, too, goes back to a lack of social weaning. The unweaned individual expects his mate to act the way the parent did, to display the attitudes and to assume the roles of the parent in his earlier home life. "Better not marry a man who is tied to his mother's apron strings" is a very old adage which the very new insights are still revealing. "Sometimes," wrote the late Dr. Hollingworth, "the unweaned adult will even refuse to leave the parental home at marriage, and thus subjects the mate to what is likely to be a very restricted life under the roof of parents-in-law. In milder cases, the unweaned mate does not find it necessary to live actually in the parents' house after marriage, but still refuses to leave the town or vicinity where they reside.

Perhaps it is stipulated that the mate must live next door, or on the same street with the parental house. In this way a wife may, and often does, ruin the career of her husband by restriction; and a husband may ruin the happiness of his wife by compelling her to live under the direction of his parents."[17]

One particular matrimonial manifestation of an unweaned condition is the choice of a much older person as a marriage partner. A young man still dominated by his mother is especially likely to marry a woman much older than himself. Statistics on the age of marriage reveal that in 10 to 15 percent of all marriages the bride is older than the groom.

A Sociological Theory of Adolescence[18]

Adolescence is one of the most discussed periods of the life span. Whatever conceptions and interpretations of it are presented, there is general agreement that it is a period of stress and strain for the maturing individual. Obviously, adolescence involves many things—complex changes in body structure and functions, accompanying changes in mental expansion and emotional maturing, developing self-consciousness, crystallization of life's values and plans, continuing experiments in social adjustment, and many other things. It is the purpose of the present discussion, not to develop or appraise any of these, but to advance a conception of adolescence in terms of its basic social situations.

The essential fact about this part of the life span is that a rapidly growing and not yet mature person is living, not in one, or two, but in three social worlds. One of these continues to be his family world. True, it is said that the child has been growing out of this world for some time, but there is still the stubborn fact that he remains in it. Moreover, as has been emphasized, the contemporary boy and girl who complete high school, customarily at the age of 18, are obliged to live in, and to be subject to—at least in many respects—their family world. Whatever the individual variations of the situation may be, the basic facts are that the adolescent lives at home, is dependent upon his parents economically and otherwise, and continues to be subject to at least some of the rules and requirements of the family world. Moreover, the intangible bonds of family loyalty continue to hold him. To this family world the adolescent must adjust, at least in one large segment of his life.

The second world in which the adolescent lives is his peer world, i.e., the world of other adolescents. These are the years when the desire

---

[17] Leta Hollingworth, *The Psychology of the Adolescent*, D. Appleton-Century Company, Inc., New York, 1928, pp. 52–53.

[18] For survey of various conceptions of adolescence and phases of its development, see the *Forty-Third Yearbook of the National Society for the Study of Education,* Part I, Nelson B. Henry (ed.), University of Chicago Press, Chicago, 1944.

for social approval is stronger than perhaps at any other time of life, and there is the added fact of a shift to the adolescent world of the opposite sex. With this shift a whole new world opens, in which one must achieve status and recognition and to which one must adjust. It is as if the peer world had added another dimension.

Third, there is the adult nonfamily world, which has been creeping slowly over the horizon and has gradually been making itself known to the adolescent. Early contacts with this world are sporadic and incidental—through kinsfolk, in books, as a phase of neighborhood relationships, through the radio and daily press, perhaps in the realities of part-time employment, and finally in the prospects of and plans for future employment. Somewhere, sometime, in this adolescent period comes the realization, at times quite suddenly, of the stark reality of this adult world, its inevitability, its serious and exacting nature, its distinctive code and requirements.

Sometimes, however, the shift from the peer to the adult nonfamily world is very abrupt. This is particularly true in the case of many college and university folk. Four years of a happy and relatively carefree life in the peer world and the transfer into the adult world may occur within the twinkling of a week. The late William Percy has written about this with understanding. "Probably there is no nostalgia so long-lived and hopeless," he says, "as that of the college graduate returning to his native town. He is a stranger though he is at home. He is sick for a communal life that was and can never be again, a life merry with youth, and unshadowed by responsibilities. He is hungry for the easy intimacies which competitive anxious living does not provide. He is unproved when proof is demanded on every side. In this alien environment, the only one he may now call his own, he is unknown, even to himself."[19]

This, then, is the perennial sociological problem of the adolescent, that he must live in three worlds, each distinct in many respects from the others, each changing with the passage of time, and each changing in its meaning and importance to him. However intriguing, however romantically expectant, this is not an easy stage in the life span.

The modern age brings its own complexities. In olden times, in primitive societies, in sacred cultures, these three worlds are not too dissimilar. The ways of doing and saying tend to be much alike, and there is considerable overlapping of personnel. The peer world consists of siblings and kinsfolk, and the adult world is but an enlarged family. Today, the cultural patterns and pressures of these three worlds are often wholly or largely unlike each other, with little or no duplication of personnel. It is in the caldron of the modern American community that these conflicting values and colliding behavior patterns are thrown together and, heated

[19] William Alexander Percy, *Lanterns on the Levee,* Alfred A. Knopf, New York, 1941, p. 125.

by the fires of adolescence, attain at times an explosive force. This is the contemporary sociological problem of adolescence.

Rites of Passage

The social development of the individual, in all societies, involves a series of well-defined stages, each of which is characterized by its own pattern of obligations, privileges, and types of relationships with his fellows. We are concerned here with these stages in the earlier part of the life cycle. In terms of the frame of reference employed in this chapter, these changes mean the transfer from one world of childhood to another. Other recent discussions speak of the transfer from one age category to another;[20] although it uses a different classificatory device, this is similar in meaning.

When these changes are so marked and comprehensive as to involve the individual's whole habitual interaction system, the term *crises* is applied to them. For example, when a person comes to puberty, gets married, or is initiated into some important new association, his relations to large numbers of other individuals are changed. To restore equilibrium after such crises, many peoples develop ceremonial rites which may be thought of as social techniques to restore equilibrium among the affected person on a new basis. When these rites are associated with the crises in the social development of the individual, they are spoken of as *rites of passage,* a term first introduced by van Gennep.[21] Several types of such rites will be described briefly.

1. Rites marking the transfer from infant to child or from the family to the child world are not found very frequently. When they do occur, they tend to be simple in character and limited in scope of observation to the family circle. "However, in societies in which children are used as an excuse for ostentation in connection with competitions for prestige they may become elaborate public affairs. Also, in societies having strong patterns of primogeniture, the early category transfers of an eldest child may be accompanied by elaborate rituals while those of younger children receive little or no attention."[22] In contemporary American society there is little of this character except the child's formal enrollment in school, or the children's social gatherings to signalize the beginning of the school career.

2. Much more frequent are the ceremonial rites marking the transfer from childhood to the adolescent stage. Many societies commemorate this in a rather spectacular way, by means of the well-known puberty

---

[20] Ralph Linton, "Age and Sex Categories," *American Sociological Review,* October, 1942, pp. 589–604.

[21] A. van Gennep, *Les rites de passage,* Nourry, Paris, 1909.

[22] Linton, *op. cit.,* pp. 598–599.

rites. The implications of these rites, in their exactions from the novitiate, are often severe, particularly for boys.[23] The custom of mutilating or marking the candidate is quite frequent. The scarification of boys by knocking out their front teeth, circumcision, subincision, and tattooing are common steps in these ceremonies, serving as symbols of membership and the new relationships being entered. Among many peoples, too, the puberty rite serves as a period of instruction, the accompanying physiological activities functioning to impress the novitiate with the importance of the lessons he is learning.

In our contemporary culture, there are certain observances which have a somewhat similar significance in this transitional process. Among these may be enrollment in a dancing class, the privilege of entertaining the opposite sex, entrance to high school, confirmation, or a little later, for girls in the upper classes, a formal coming-out party.

3. Marriage is the most universally observed and the most strongly emphasized of all the crises rites. It also serves the most functions. Among these are: (a) the founding of a new conjugal family unit, (b) the establishment of new relationships between the two kinship groups, and (c) the transfer of the participants to the adult stage. This third function operates much more frequently for the male than for the female. "Except in the case of child marriage," Linton writes, "a first wedding always promotes a man to full adult status, but there are a number of societies in which women are promoted only with the birth of a first child."[24] The importance of this function is proved by the frequency with which remarriages receive slight or even no ceremonial accompaniment.

This reference to function serves to call attention to the basic purpose in all these rites. Van Gennep, who first recognized the significance of this type of ceremony, pointed out that in all such rites there were three consecutive parts, always occurring in the same order. These he termed *separation, marge,* and *aggregation,* which may be restated as *separation, transition,* and *incorporation.* These steps suggest what the crises rites really do. They call attention, in a formal and solemn manner, to the fact that the person is leaving one stage, group, age category, or social world, and entering another. This transfer is impressed upon the group that is left (separation), and the group that is entered (incorporation). Besides serving the ends of beauty and the nonrational needs of human beings, the ceremony indicates in a definitely precise manner what is happening, emphasizes the exceptional importance of the occasion, and makes it more impressive, just as the prestige of the law is enhanced by the cere-

[23] For an interesting illustration of the puberty rite, the reader is referred to A. R. Brown, *The Andaman Islanders,* University Press, Cambridge, 1922; Raymond Firth, *We, the Tikopia,* American Book Company, New York, 1936, Chap. 13; and John W. M. Whiting, *Becoming a Kwoma,* Yale University Press, New Haven, 1941.
[24] Linton, *op. cit.,* p. 598.

mony of court procedure, or the majesty of the king by his coronation in church.

THE CONTEMPORARY STATUS OF RITES OF PASSAGE

Recent centuries have witnessed a definite trend away from ceremonialism in our Western culture. Many factors have combined to bring this about. One goes back to the rise of Protestantism. An inevitable phase of this religious revolt was a rebellion against the elaborate ritual of the Roman Catholic Church, and its subsequent development of the barren and austere meeting house in New England and the general meagerness of the Protestant ritual. Second has been the increase of other forms of aesthetic satisfaction, for ceremony undoubtedly is often set up as an end in itself to satisfy the aesthetic needs of people. Similarly, education and individual judgment have come to be emphasized as ways of meeting crises, in preference to the prescribed routine of the ceremonial rite. Finally, the spread of the democratic cult, with its matter-of-fact tonal quality, has broken the hold of the conventional and traditional way of doing a thing. Obviously, it is in the United States that these factors have developed historically in very strong form, so that, coupled with the newness of the country and the sparsity of its cultural past, the lack of the ceremonial has come, in many ways, to be raised to the proportions of a national virtue.

It cannot be denied that puberty ceremonials have declined most rapidly of all the rites of passage. Puberty has little significance among us today, and involves little change in the culturally patterned behavior of the individual. One finds almost no reference to it in everyday life except for certain periodic problems which girls have with the start of the menstrual flow. The child and the adolescent world constitute distinct stages, but for parents and other adults the lines between them fade out in the continuation of school attendance. Among parents who assume financial responsibility for their children as they continue their training from the sixth or an earlier year to the eighteenth or twenty-second, or, in the case of professional school students, to the twenty-fifth or twenty-seventh, there is an understandable tendency to ignore the successive stages in their children's development. The same thing is true of other adults. The neighbor's son remains a schoolboy, even though he is a second-year medical-school student aged 24. Ceremonials emphasizing the stages in this school training, in the form of commencement exercises, seem entirely proper; rites commemorating stages of advancing maturity of other kinds come to be regarded as out of place.

This relative absence of rites of passage in the lives of modern American youth would seem to have great significance. To neither nonrelated adult, parent, nor child is there brought in a formal and impressive way a clear consciousness of the changes which the young person is really undergoing. Because the school career continues, because the financial dependence upon the parents remains unchanged, adult society continues to regard these young people as children, insists that they retain the submissive role of childhood, and, what is most significant, demands that they follow the behavior patterns of childhood. These adult attitudes focus most sharply upon sex, and during the very period of the young person's sexual awakening and biological preparation for sex experimentation. One of the strongest taboos in our culture is on a child's sexual activity; in most states, he is not allowed to marry without the consent of his parents. Everywhere there is a taboo, supported by law, religion, and popular sanctions, against sexual relations between persons who are not married. In some circles, these restrictions are so strong that the subject of sex is not even supposed to be mentioned.[25]

This decline of ceremonialism is manifest even in so solemn and beautiful a crisis as marriage. A recent writer has called attention to the "dreary, dingy room," far less inviting than "the visitors' section of a jail," in which New York City issued its 93,085 marriage licenses in 1941. "Cigar and cigarette butts littered the floor. The benches and chairs were battered, and the tables were covered by filthy, ink-stained blotters."[26] Further reference is made to the prevalence of civil ceremonies, especially during the war years; the pitiful, garish marriage parlors, open day and night; the short ceremony, taking only 30 seconds; and the marrying justices who specialize in this type of matrimonial arrangements. Public concern with the rising tide of divorce and other family problems might do well to focus attention upon the ceremonial setting of this crisis rite.

Summary

1. The child's social development involves his gradual growth from complete dependence upon his family to his emergence as a relatively self-sufficient person.

2. Five well-defined stages are customarily identified in this process. They are: (a) the period of infancy, (b) the pregang stage, (c) the gang stage, (d) the negative phase, and (e) adolescence.

3. Transfer from the family world to the school and gang or peer world involves revolutionary changes and major problems for the child, such as: (a) the passage from protected to unprotected competition, (b) the changed responses expected, (c) differences between the culture of the family and that of the peer world, and (d) conflicts with parental attitudes.

[25] John Dollard, Leonard W. Doob, and others, *Frustration and Aggression*, Yale University Press, New Haven, 1939.

[26] Dorothy Walworth, "Just Married—And How," *Kiwanis Magazine*, October, 1942.

4. In answer to these transfer problems, children develop a variety of responses toward their parents and the peer world, ranging from intense conflict to marked compensatory loyalty.

5. The concept of social weaning is applied to the process whereby the child grows away from his family and learns to reorganize his personality on an increasingly independent basis. Modern culture often makes this an exceedingly difficult process.

6. Some children are never weaned socially from their parents. The resultant symptoms often incapacitate them for the activities of adult life, especially in the occupational and matrimonial spheres of life.

7. Adolescence, conceived in situational terms, is a peculiarly difficult period, involving the combined problems of living in three social worlds: the family world, that of one's peers, and the adult nonfamily world. Often the demands and pressures of the three worlds are in disagreement.

8. Among many peoples, these crises changes are commemorated by ceremonial rites which serve to call the attention of all interested persons to the stages which are left behind and those which are being entered.

9. There is a definite trend away from ceremonialism in contemporary American culture. Current emphases are upon education and individual judgment as methods of meeting life's crises.

Chapter **25**

Children Who Reject Their Parents

It is the common fate of all of us to grow from a stage of complete dependence upon our families to one of relative independence as an individual. In this process, stresses and strains appear as the inevitable price of life's growth. In most cases, fortunately, these conflicts are resolved without serious damage to the personalities of those involved. There is, however, a substantial proportion of cases in which the resultant problems are more serious and the forms of attitudes and behavior patterns that ensue deviate from the socially accepted norms. It is to this phase of the process of growing out of the family that the present chapter is devoted.

The proportion of such cases in this country is unduly large. The reasons for this seem to arise principally from the fact that so many young people are growing up in, and adjusting to, a peer and a nonfamily adult culture which differs materially from the culture of their family world. Such culture differentials are of many kinds and degrees, and are present to some extent in the situational background of most children; but there are at least three groups of children in which the incidence of marked differentials is relatively high. They are: (1) children growing up in foreign-culture homes, (2) urban-dwelling children of rural-reared parents, and (3) cases in which the general currents of cultural change have been accepted in very unequal degrees by the members of the family world. An analysis of these three groups, their problems, and characteristic responses, constitutes the subject of this chapter.

American Children in Foreign-Culture Homes

The rearing of American-born children in foreign-culture homes has been the perennial result of the stream of immigration flowing into this country. In fact, its dimensions identify it as a deluge rather than a stream. From 1820 to 1956, inclusive, the total number of legally admitted immigrants into the United States was 40,734,745. Emphasis is given to the fact that these were *legal* admissions, for it is well known that the smuggling of immigrants into this country has been a time-honored form of law violation. Historically, this inflow of people is as old as our national history; statistically, the major portion of it took place within a generation. A few strokes of the mathematical brush will outline the picture. In 1890, the population of the United States was, in round numbers, 63,000,000. From 1890 to 1924, a period of 34 years, 22,500,000 immigrants were admitted legally—a mass movement with few if any parallels in human history. Obviously we have here, as a background fact, one of the outstanding facts of history.

It is clear that a mass movement of such proportions will give rise to many problems, and the literature dealing with immigration and its aftermath has given consideration to many of them. Some of the problems emphasized have dealt with the effects of this large-scale impact upon the country and its institutional life; others have concerned the nature and range of the changes resulting among the newcomers themselves. In considering this latter group of effects, there has been a tendency to include only the changes in the first generation, and to deal only with the more tangible evidences of their adjustment, such as conformity to American dress, learning the English language, naturalization, and other similar forms of behavior. Only gradually did there develop any appreciation of the meaning of this migration for the second and third generations, and how it would evidence itself, not in regard to the externals of living, but in the more subtle aspects of attitudes, values, compensatory philosophies, family patterns, and intergeneration conflicts. It is with these subsequent and, in a sense, secondary effects upon the second and third generations that we are concerned in this chapter.

SOME STATISTICAL HIGHLIGHTS[1]

The second generation is a definite population element to use as a working basis in this connection. In its nativity classification, the United States Census Bureau identifies this generation as the native-born white population of foreign-born or mixed parentage. The total number of such persons is given by the 1950 census reports as 23,589,485, or 15.6 percent of the total population. This compares with 23,157,580, or 17.5 percent of the 1940 population, and 25,902,383, or 21.1 percent in 1930.

It is customary in discussions of this kind to add the foreign-born white

---

[1] For an analysis of the statistical trends for the years 1850–1950 concerning the children of immigrants, see Edward P. Hutchinson, *Immigrants and Their Children, 1850–1950,* John Wiley & Sons, Inc., New York, 1956.

population to the above nativity class. The term *foreign white stock* is used to indicate these two nativity classes. In the 1950 census reports, there were 33,750,653 persons in this category, comprising 22.4 percent of the total population. This compares with 34,576,718, or 26.1 percent of the 1940 population, and 39,885,788, or 32.5 percent in 1930.

The concentration of these population elements in a relatively small part of the nation is also significant. More than three out of every five (61.7 percent) native-born whites of foreign-born or mixed white parentage were located at the time of the census of 1950 in seven states (California, Illinois, Massachusetts, Michigan, New Jersey, New York, and Pennsylvania). Almost seven of every ten (68.8 percent) of the foreign-born whites resided in these states. In fact, half of the foreign-born whites are in four states (California, Illinois, New York, and Pennsylvania), and more than two out of every five (43.5 percent) native born of foreign and mixed parentage resided in these four states. Moreover, it is chiefly in the large cities in these states (New York, Chicago, Los Angeles, and Philadelphia) that these population elements are found. More than one-quarter of the foreign-born white and about one-fifth of the second generation were located in these four cities.

The composition of the foreign white stock in terms of national origin is particularly important in the present discussion, in that it reveals its cultural diversity. Of the 10,161,168 foreign-born whites in 1950, roughly one out of five (22.9 percent) was of northwestern European origin; 29.0 percent hailed from central Europe; 12.5 percent from eastern Europe; 16.7 percent from southern Europe; 15.4 percent from America (Canada, Mexico, etc.); 1.8 percent from Asia; and 1.4 percent from other areas. Of the 23,589,485 native-born whites of foreign or mixed parentage, 27.5 percent hailed from northwestern Europe (Ireland, Great Britain, Sweden, Norway, etc.); 33.3 percent from central Europe, chiefly Germany and Poland; 9.3 percent from eastern Europe, mainly Russia; 14.9 percent from southern Europe, principally from Italy; 12.6 percent from America, chiefly Canada and Mexico; and 2.2 percent from other areas. Comparing the percentages of 1950 with those of 1920, the proportion in both of the foregoing nativity classes who hail from northwestern Europe has been declining, as has that from central Europe. Proportions from eastern and southern Europe, on the other hand, as that of America, have been increasing. Particularly striking in the case of the last-named area are the increases of Mexicans and French Canadians.

Some idea of the cultural diversity of the foreign white stock may be obtained by a look at the totals by principal countries of origin. There are 23 countries that have contributed more than 200,000 of this population element; 10, more than a million each; 7, more than two million; and 2, more than four million each (Italy and Germany). Nor does this summary include such groups as the Puerto Ricans, whose number in New

York City alone was placed at 550,000 on January 1, 1957, by the City Planning Commission.

Many Americans are prone to think of immigration as something that terminated a number of years ago as a result of restrictive legislation. It is pertinent, therefore, to point out that 4,635,640 immigrants were admitted to the United States during the years 1921–1940, and that by the end of 1956 the total was 7,079,942.

Data on the mother tongue spoken in the homes of the American people, as gathered in the 1940 census enumeration, are particularly important in this connection, and the reader is urged to reëxamine the summary of these figures presented in Chapter 15. To appreciate their significance fully, the sociological role of language should be recalled. First, language is part of the culture of a people comparable to its family system, its economic life, or its religious institutions. Second, it is also a mechanism which transmits the remainder of the cultural system. Because of this function, it comes to be peculiarly interrelated with the details and spirit of the entire culture. Language is therefore both part and symbol of a culture, reflecting its essence in such a way that another language cannot serve as a substitute. Just as many aspects of a culture cannot be expressed in another language because there are no words to do so, similarly many words can be understood only by explaining them in their cultural setting. Words represent not things but our behavior with regard to things. It is through words that we organize our thoughts about things. Speech, which may be thought of as the active, individual expression of language, is the vocal aspect of personality. It is particularly revealing, first because it is vocal, and second because, being learned early in life and thoroughly ingrained from constant use, it betrays, as almost nothing else does, the origin and background of the person. The linguistic culture is, then, a peculiarly pervasive aspect of the entire cultural background of the personality.

An examination of mother-tongue data for the United States suggests, among other things, two facts which are very pertinent to the present discussion. First, the persistence of languages of Old World origin may be taken as an indication of the persistence of other parts of the cultural configuration, presumably of those parts that have an important bearing upon behavior. So much has been said about cultural changes and conformity to the American pattern on the part of various immigrant groups that it is well to recognize the other side of this process, that is, the dogged persistence among them of many cultural elements. From this follows the second fact, namely, that the problems to be identified in this chapter are not confined necessarily to second-generation families. The data on the persistence of foreign-language homes where both parents are native-born of native-born parentage furnish ample evidence on this point.

SOME PROBLEMS THAT ARISE[2]

The person and the family who come to this country as immigrants are the product of the culture in which they were reared. Naturally they bring that culture with them, and on the basis of it begin life in the New World. From the very beginning, however, modifications must be made, particularly in what might be called the externals of life—clothing, housing, domestic equipment, occupations, and the like. On the other hand, ways of thinking, attitudes, ideas, values, especially as they express themselves in matters of religion, family life, and parent-child relationships, are modified very slowly, if at all.

For the children in these families the situation is considerably different. Being young, their integration into the parents' culture is not so complete and fixed, to begin with. Moreover, their contacts are chiefly with the school and other peer agencies in the new culture which are concerned with the world of ideas, attitudes, values, philosophies, and patterns of parent-child relationships. In short, the cultural pressures in America upon the children of immigrants differ materially from those exerted upon their parents, being strongest for the children in the elements of the culture in which they are weakest for the parents.

Two other sets of cultural pressures show similar generational differences. One consists of the standardizing pressures of the contemporary world, such as the daily press, the cinema, the radio, and modern methods of transportation, which make increasingly difficult, if not impossible, the maintenance of cultural pockets in which selected groups can isolate themselves socially to follow their own cultural patterns. The other set of pressures are sociopsychological in character and consist of the drive for conformity, the desire to belong, the longing to be accepted by one's peer group. Obviously, both sets operate much more strongly in childhood and the adolescent years.

What happens inevitably, as a result of these pressures, is that the younger generation grow away from their more conservative and culturally persistent elders, so that, as time goes on, they come more and more to live in different cultural worlds. But for the younger generation there is the added complication that they are forced, to the extent that they are subject to the control of their elders, to live in both worlds.

This situation has been considered by a number of sociological students. Some of them, following Thomas[3] and Park and Miller,[4] have

---

[2] The literature on the problems of the second generation is too extensive to be listed here. For an excellent summary, together with bibliography, the reader is referred to William Carlson Smith's excellent work, *Americans in the Making*, D. Appleton-Century Company, Inc., New York, 1939.

[3] W. I. Thomas and Florian Znaniecki, *The Polish Peasant*, Richard G. Badger, Boston, 1919.

[4] Robert E. Park and Herbert A. Miller, *Old World Traits Transplanted*, Harper & Brothers, New York, 1921.

viewed it primarily as a transitional process in which the immigrant slowly learns to adjust to his new social heritage. These earlier treatises are particularly valuable in showing how extensive and pervasive are the necessary changes—from one set of values to another, from a primary-group form of living to one consisting largely or wholly of secondary-group contacts, from the extended kinship group to the immediate form of family, from tradition to education as a regulating principle of behavior, and from communal to individual habits of life, all of these expressing themselves not in the form of broad principles but rather in the minutiae of everyday living.[5]

The problems of culture conflict. Most of the more recent students, however, have viewed the process in terms of conflict between successive generations. Writing of his own experience, Mangione says: "The more aware I became of the great differences between their [the parents'] Latin world and the Anglo-Saxon world, the more disturbed I was; nor was I the only child of Sicilian parents who was disturbed. We sensed the conflict between the two worlds in almost everything our parents did or said. Yet we had to adjust ourselves to their world if we wanted any peace."[6] One of Pauline Young's cases speaks similarly: "You see, we young people live in two worlds, and learn the ways of both worlds—the ways of our parents and the ways of the big world. Sometimes we get mixed up and we fight. . . . Many times I get mad, and then I leave the house. You see, I don't want to hurt my parents and still I want to live like I see is right—that is, right according to American ways. They can't see it my way, and I can't see it theirs."[7] To epitomize the process just described, a number of sociologists have utilized the concept of culture conflict, which may be said to be compounded out of the sociological emphasis upon culture and its role in the determination of personality, the idea of conflict as a social process, and the psychiatric emphasis upon mental conflict as developed by Healy[8] and others. This concept has been used particularly as a tool in the analysis of behavior problems of children of the second generation.[9] Its essential idea is a conflict between successive generations so comprehensive and pervasive in character as to warrant the use of the term cultural.

[5] For an excellent illustration of how seemingly unimportant differences even in material culture may have far-reaching implications, see K. Shridharani, *My India, My America*, Duell, Sloan & Pearce, Inc., New York, 1941, Chap. 5.

[6] Jerre Mangione, *Mount Allegro*, Houghton Mifflin Company, Boston, 1942, p. 228.

[7] Pauline V. Young, *The Pilgrims of Russian Town*, University of Chicago Press, Chicago, 1932, pp. 114–115.

[8] William Healy, *Mental Conflict and Misconduct*, Little, Brown & Company, Boston, 1917.

[9] Louis Wirth, "Culture Conflict and Misconduct," *Social Forces*, June, 1931, pp. 484–492. Consult also Maurice Price, "The Concept 'Culture Conflict,'" *ibid.*, December, 1930, pp. 164–167.

The problem of parental inadequacy. The more one studies these family situations, however, the more he is impressed with the fact that there are problems other than those of culture conflict. What of the capacity of these elders in their role as parents? The rearing and guidance of children in modern America, particularly in the larger cities in which so many families of foreign stock have congregated, include a great many things—the satisfaction of their physical needs, the selection of clothing and other essentials in a socially acceptable form, the choice of a school, supervision of school progress, guidance in selecting school and other peer companions, appreciation of recreational needs and their proper selection in an urban setting, and judgment of surrounding influences and of both overt and insidious dangers to be avoided. Adequate parenthood has become a complex and difficult challenge in all families, requiring knowledge not only of the intricacies of the world in which the child lives, but also of its social resources and how to use them effectively. This knowledge the foreign-born parent, or even the second-generation parent, often does not have. This is especially true of the mothers in these families, upon whom so large a part of the responsibility in the child's earlier years must of necessity rest. Such mothers are apt to labor under two particular difficulties. One is the fact that, as a rule, they make so little progress in mastering the English language; the other results from the traditions of their culture, which frown upon their development of out-of-home contacts. As a result, in many of these families there ia a relative, and often a complete, lack of parental capacity. What happens all too often is a reversal of the process: it is the child who comes to the aid of the parents, the child who acts as interpreter, the child who becomes the intermediary between parent and landlord, the child who learns where the parent can find a job. Thus, whereas all children pass through the stage where they think they know more than their parents, these children *know* that they know more. This may be one of the basic factors in the subsequent development of their personalities.

One of the most perplexing problems for parents of more recent foreign extraction has to do with the techniques of parenthood. The idea is widespread in this country that a child should not be trained and disciplined to be subservient to the parent, but should be helped to develop his own personality. This involves a democratic-experimental approach to child rearing, a greater respect for the child's intelligence and his capacity for self-discipline. These ideas are, to be sure, of comparatively new formulation, many of them dating from recent developments in the sciences of human behavior. They are still understood by a relatively small proportion of the community, but they are acted upon in general by a much larger part of the population. The problems which this changing philosophy of child rearing creates are not easy for intelligent American parents who are capable emotionally of accepting the ideas involved; they are particularly difficult for many parents who are still dominated by ideas of another and older sort. The majority of the immigrants who have come into this country since 1900 hail from countries whose culture was not imbued with democratic family ideals, where standards of behavior were more fixed and exacting, and where rigorous training during youth was supplemented by the practices and traditions of compulsory military training. Their American-born and -reared children, going to American schools in which these newer ideals and techniques were applied, and mingling with other children reared in such an atmosphere, have looked to their parents for similar treatment. Their parents, on the other hand, informed poorly if at all about the new, naturally cling to the traditions of a lengthy past in which they have been reared, and which to them seem as natural and inevitable as the rising and setting of the sun. Not that the issues on this score were ever fought out on the grounds of abstract principles and philosophies. In the families under consideration they give rise to concrete wrangles over the age at which the child will go to work, the control of his earnings, expenditures for clothing and recreation, and other vital realities in everyday family life. Bewildered parents attempt to enforce Old World ideas with Old World methods; restive children respond with anger and ridicule.

The problem of undue social pressure. Not all families of recent immigrant origin stick resolutely to the old. Many of them hasten with undue speed and aggressiveness to reach for the new. They reject the old before they understand or attain the new. At times, the path from the steerage on the immigrant ship to the gilded mansion and to aspiration to membership in the exclusive social club has been traversed within a single generation; more often, it has been done within only two. The problems of children in such families arise primarily from a too rapid adjustment to American culture and a too intense climbing of the social ladder. As emphasized in an earlier chapter, it is the child who in this driving process becomes the spearhead of the family's ambitions; it is upon him that the resistance, and perhaps resentment, of the older and established groups focus. Thus the child in these families is caught in a cross fire of pressures, one from his kinsfolk, urging him to "make it"; the other from the groups to which he aspires, rejecting his aspirations.

Cultural mobility and family disorganization. Considering the situation of families of foreign stock as a whole, the basic process seems to be one of cultural mobility; and the basic resulting problems, those of family and individual disorganization. In the transfer from the Old World culture to that of the New, different members of the family progress at unequal rates. To speak in general terms, the children tend to move more rapidly than the parents; examined more specifically, what occurs most often is that the father moves more rapidly than the mother, and the younger children more easily and rapidly than the older ones. Under the individualizing influences of American life, every member of the family moves at his particular rate. The inevitable result is the disorganization of the family and the development of conflict situations based on the difference not merely in personality traits but also in cultural allegiances.

SOME PATTERNS OF RESPONSE

It is impossible within the confines of a few pages to assess the response patterns of millions of children to crises of cultural mobility such as have been described in families of foreign white stock. Life is too complex and richly varied to do this. We can at best attempt only to identify some of the more apparent of their responses under the following five headings:

The child's rejection of his parents. Perhaps the basic reaction in the field of parent-child relationships that runs like a recurrent theme through the responses of so many of these children is rejection of their parents. Much has been said about the fact that many parents reject their children; here the process is in reverse. Just as the parents' rejection of the child takes many forms, so the child's rejection of his parents expresses itself in a variety of ways. In some cases, there is refusal to tolerate the parent's presence or to remain under the parental roof. This is the child who runs away from home, who engages in delinquencies which promise or express his independence, or who merely drop out of sight. More often, however, the rejection is partial and symbolic. For example, the child changes his name. Giovanni is transmuted to Grant, Cohen becomes Gaylord, and Rudyzpka is eased into Smith. To be sure, such changes are rationalized in various ways, but rejection of the parent is the substance which casts the rationalizing shadows. Or the child rejects the parental religion. Literally thousands of younger Jews in this country in recent years have cut adrift from their biological and cultural destiny by their rejection of their family's religious rituals. Most frequent of all, and in many ways as serious as any, is rejection of the parents' authority. A combination of facts tends to precipitate this response. First, the child grows beyond his parents in his understanding of life situations and resources. He knows more about many things than they do, and has better insight into what the situation demands. Second, the parents, feeling insecure, become defensive and stubbornly insist on their authoritarian rights as transmitted through their cultural heritage. In the inevitable conflict that follows, the child rebels against their authority. Because the conflict is usually chronic, rebellion against authority becomes a habit of response. Once formed and exercised against the first embodiment of authority that the child knows, the transfer of these habits to subsequent forms of authority—in the school room, the workshop, and one's own home—frequently follows. Thus, the second-generation child often develops into the type of social rebel that is clearly identifiable in contemporary society by an unfailing willingness to rebel against anything, once it is recognized as part of the established order of things.

The marginal man. The child's rejection of his family, whether partial or complete, substantial or symbolic, is but part of the larger transition process from immigrant to American status and culture. In the course of this process, which is generally slow and often painful, there is characteristically an intermediate stage in which the immigrant, or his child or even his grandchild, lets go of the old culture, but not wholeheartedly, and takes on the new, but not completely. The result is the emergence of a person who lives and shares the cultural life of two peoples without being entirely identified with either one. To designate this type, Robert E. Park coined the phrase *marginal man*, and it has found widespread acceptance. As defined by Park, a marginal person is "a cultural hybrid, a man living and sharing in the cultural life and traditions of two distinct peoples; never quite willing to break, even if he were permitted to do so, with his past and his tradition, and not quite accepted . . . in the new society in which he now seeks a place."[10] In other words, he is in a marginal position between two cultures that have not fused and that may be in conflict with each other.

A great deal of the autobiographical material that has been left by immigrants and their descendants fits into and illustrates this basic concept. Its essential meaning for the individual, as revealed by this material, has been well stated by Stonequist when he spoke of the marginal man as "one who is poised in psychological uncertainty between two (or more) social worlds, reflecting in his soul the discords and harmonies, repulsions and attractions of these worlds, one of which is often 'dominant' over the other; within which membership is implicitly if not explicitly based upon birth or ancestry (race or nationality); and where exclusion removes the individual from a system of group relations."[11] Equally penetrating is the identification of this poised psychological uncertainty by a nonsociologist, the late Colonel T. E. Lawrence, in referring to his attempts to become an Arab.

In my case, the effort for these years to live in the dress of Arabs, and to imitate their mental foundation, quitted me of my English self, and let me look at the West and its conventions with new eyes; they destroyed it all for me. At the same time, I could not sincerely take on the Arab skin; it was an affectation only. Easily was a man made an infidel, but hardly might he be made a convert to another faith. I had dropped one form and not taken on the other, and was become like Mohammed's coffin in our legend, with a resultant feeling

[10] Robert E. Park, "Human Migration and the Marginal Man," *American Journal of Sociology*, May, 1928, p. 892.

[11] Everett V. Stonequist, *The Marginal Man: A Study in Personality and Culture Conflict*, Charles Scribner's Sons, New York, 1937, p. 8.

of intense loneliness in life, and a contempt, not for other men, but for what they do. Such detachment came at times to a man exhausted by prolonged physical effort and isolation. His body plodded on mechanically, while his reasonable mind left him, and from without looked down critically on him, wondering what that futile lumber did and why. Sometimes these selves would converse in the void: and then madness was very near, as I believe it would be near the man who could see things through the veils at once of two customs, two educations, two environments.[12]

Similarly apt is Roucek's remark about living in a spiritual vacuum.[13]

Two further developments of the concept of the marginal man, presented by Stonequist, are of value and will be discussed briefly. The first involves the existence of two general types of situation: one where the cultural difference also includes a racial (biological) difference, as is the case with the mulatto, the Eurasian, and the Jew; the second, where the difference is purely cultural. Each of these obviously can be further subdivided, with significant differences.

The second development of the concept involves its examination in terms of the life cycle of the individual. Stonequist refers to three stages. The first is the stage of preparation, when the individual is being introduced into the two cultures. Usually this stage is confined to early childhood, and the person involved may not be conscious of a personality problem. The second is the crisis stage, when an awareness of the conflict appears and the individual's life organization may become seriously disturbed. The third stage covers the period when the enduring responses of the individual to the situation are made. Some of the forms which these responses may take will appear in succeeding sections of this chapter.

Frustration and aggression. The marginal position is ordinarily not only confusing but also distressing. Movement away from it tends to be slow and difficult. Often there is opposition from the dominant culture and group. The inevitable result is that marginal persons develop strong feelings of frustration, and it is out of these feelings that certain characteristic response patterns develop.[14]

One of the common responses to continued frustration is the development of an oppression psychosis. This manifests itself characteristically in marked hypersensitivity. Such a person or group reveals a complete incapacity to view himself or his problems objectively. Miller illustrates this in the case of women who through long history have belonged to an oppressed group; their prevailing psychosis is shown by the reply of the woman whose husband said to her, "The trouble with women is that they

---

[12] T. E. Lawrence, *Seven Pillars of Wisdom,* Jonathan Cape, London, 1935, pp. 31–32.

[13] J. S. Roucek, "The Problem of Becoming Americanized," *Sociology and Social Research,* January–February, 1933, p. 243.

[14] John Dollard, Leonard W. Doob, and others, *Frustration and Aggression,* Yale University Press, New Haven, 1939.

take everything personally." "That isn't so," she said heatedly, "I don't." Whatever one's reaction to this illustration, its underlying nature can easily be identified in the contemporary generation of the immigrant stream whose aspirations are still being balked by time, their own inadequacies, or the opposition of the dominant group.[15]

Perhaps the inevitable consequence of frustration is aggression, a lack of which can certainly not be attributed as a rule to the second- and third-generation stock. Aggressive behavior takes a variety of forms. At times, it shows itself in a tendency to be rather grasping. It is as though the afflicted person must obtain more than his share, often considerably more, to be convinced that he is merely obtaining his minimum due. One who knows frustrated groups will realize at once how common this trait is. Not always understood, it arouses further antagonism in those dealing with such individuals, so that, like most pathological behavior, it defeats its own basic purposes.

At other times, aggression takes the form of conspicuous behavior. There is a straining effort to attract attention, to do the exceptional or unusual or striking thing. It is as though the frustrated person were saying: "You are not noticing me the way I want to be noticed. See what I am doing. Don't you think it is striking? Am I not a most unusual person, who ought therefore to be singled out for adequate social recognition?" Unfortunately, this "showing-off" process frequently passes beyond the conventional bounds. Then it expresses itself in behavior that departs from good taste, that becomes illicitly unconventional or turns into delinquency. The relatively higher rate of juvenile delinquency among second-generation immigrant children is one of the accepted conclusions in the literature on criminology.

In many cases, there is an aggressive philosophy or set of attitudes which may accompany or take the place of aggressive behavior. Of these, one of the most common forms is the tendency to depreciate the success of the dominant group or, even more frequently, to become critical of the entire social system. Thus, we find large proportions of young Jews among our foreign white stock who, despite the Jew's traditional drive for individual economic success, blossom forth into aggressive Communists. This incongruous combination is, however, by no means confined to the Jewish group, for it includes the widespread type of American who reveals the curious paradox of developing ideological cults which compensate for his lower-class origins but which completely belie his upper-class aspirations. This paradox seems to be the key to the behavior of many young Americans.

Finally, reference should be made to other compensatory values which frustrated groups in this country have developed. Undoubtedly, the Jews'

[15] Herbert A. Miller, "The Oppression Psychosis and the Immigrant," *Annals of the American Academy of Political and Social Science,* January, 1921, p. 141.

drive for financial success has been a compensatory development. The Irish, whose history in the old country has for centuries been one of continued frustration, become the policemen of the New World, alert to direct and control the activities of their fellow Americans. Sometimes the compensatory value may take the form of racial or religious solidarity. Here we are again reminded of the Irish whose Catholicism is an obvious symbol of a united front against the Protestant English.

Leaving the marginal status. The marginal position is not ordinarily a stationary one. Most such persons, especially those in the younger age groups, tend to move in one direction or another. The direction and speed of this movement have considerable bearing as a rule upon the behavior pattern of the individual, so a brief summary of the prevailing situations is next in order.

Most marginal persons, both children and parents, tend to move toward the dominant group and its culture until relative or complete acceptance is obtained. This happens, of course, most frequently where there is no biological barrier. Movement in this direction is often accompanied by a change in names, at times by a renunciation of nationality identification with increasing frequency of marriage into the dominant group, and by other aspects of emancipation from the traditional group. There is some reason to think that this transfer to the dominant group occurs most frequently in the upper and lower classes, and least often at the middle-class level, and that its occurrence among the lower classes often involves a merging with the cheapest and worst aspects of American life.

Movement from the marginal position may be in the opposite direction, involving a withdrawal from earlier aspirations and a return to one's own group. These are the second-generation Greeks, Italians, and so on, who are more Greek or Italian than their parents. Disappointment and defeat lead to a strong compensatory allegiance to their original culture and group, and its expression may take several different forms. Some become leaders of their national culture groups, serving as teachers, editors, lawyers, clergymen, or labor leaders. They act as spokesmen for their people and fight for an improvement in their condition and status. Commonly there is a commercialization of the compensatory drive which they have developed. Others turn hard and bitter, utilizing their influence to rebel against the dominant group and its culture. Such people often develop into aggressive nationalists or revolutionists in the class struggle. Since the dominant group has generally a higher class status, the marginal rebel focuses the resentment he has built up upon the existing class structure.[16]

[16] Herbert A. Miller, *Races, Nations and Classes*, J. B. Lippincott Company, Philadelphia, 1924.

A third possible movement is away from both groups and culture. Here one finds the lonely, isolated person who organizes his life in the solitude of a social no man's land. Sometimes such individuals harness all their energy to some occupational goal, devoting themselves with a zeal akin to genius to the achievement of some task, finding in its completion the satisfactions that life otherwise denies. Second-generation immigrant children often become excellent students in school in just this way. But the isolated person does not always turn to constructive achievement. Here again is the other fork of the road, with its inevitable accompaniments of delinquency, suicide, alcoholism, occupational drifting, and the like.

Cultural and mental conflict. Some years ago (1917), William Healy introduced the term *mental conflict* into general usage among students of behavior. He defined it as "a conflict between elements of mental life, and [it] occurs when two elements or systems of elements are out of harmony with each other."[17] The concept *cultural conflict* which social scientists have developed in recent years is similar in nature; and their principle that personality is the subjective aspect of culture makes mental and cultural conflict two aspects of the same fundamental situation. Obviously, then, the cultural conflicts which have been shown to characterize so many children of foreign white stock are a fruitful source of mental conflicts.

Healy found mental conflict an important factor in the production of juvenile delinquency, and he became increasingly impressed with its relative significance as his work with delinquents continued. Sutherland and others, making their approach from the social side, conclude that culture conflicts are the "stuff" out of which much misconduct develops, and that "the conflict of cultures is . . . the fundamental principle in the explanation of crime."[18] Thus we return again, on the basis of both approaches, to the relatively high rate of delinquency in the second-generation group.

But mental conflicts produce other patterns of response. Here one enters the field of the neuroses and psychoses which are the special province of the psychiatrist. However, the mental symptoms which they identify have significance for sociologists, too. The individual who is neurotically exhausted by the inner conflict of his divided cultural loyalties is a socially uneffective person; mental conflicts are often resolved by rash and

[17] Healy, *op. cit.*
[18] Edwin H. Sutherland, *Principles of Criminology,* J. B. Lippincott Company, Philadelphia, 1939, p. 52. See also Thorsten Sellin, "Culture Conflict and Crime," Bulletin, Social Science Research Council, New York, 1938; Louis Wirth, "Culture Conflict and Delinquency," *Social Forces,* June, 1931, pp. 484–492; Eleanor Glueck, "Culture Conflict and Delinquency," *Mental Hygiene,* January, 1937, pp. 46–66.

impulsive forms of escape which deviate from the commonly accepted social norms.

Not all culture conflicts lead to misconduct, nor are the majority of children of foreign white stock to be thought of as problem children. The effort in the foregoing pages has been to analyze a life process involving a large number of Americans, that is basically important in its implications yet is usually given only limited and superficial attention. One cannot but recall here the words of Santayana: "Fixity of tradition, of custom, of language, is perhaps a prerequisite to a complete harmony in life and mind. Variety in these matters is a lesson to the philosopher and drives him into the cold arms of reason: but it confuses the poet and the saint, and embitters society."[19]

Urban-Dwelling Children of Rural-Reared Parents

THE URBAN TREND

Similar in many respects to the immigration stream has been the migration of millions of persons from farms and villages to American cities. A few statistical summaries will reveal the scope of this movement in the United States. In 1880, approximately a quarter (28.2 percent) of the American people lived in cities of 2,500 or more inhabitants; by 1950, the percentage was 59. Redefining the term *urban* in the 1950 tabulation to include areas not incorporated but urban in character, this percentage is revised to 64. Moreover, much of the urban influx from the rural areas goes into the larger cities and metropolitan areas. According to the last census, 3 out of every 10 persons in the United States (29.4 percent) lived in cities of 100,000 and over, one-fifth of the total population (19.5 percent) lived in the 5 largest metropolitan areas, and more than one-fourth (26.1 per cent) lived in the 10 largest metropolitan districts.

One distinct phase of this movement has been from the rural South to the urban North, principally Southern rural Negroes migrating to Northern cities. From 1910 to 1940, the Negro population of New York City increased from 97,721 to 468,444; of Chicago, from 46,226 to 277,731; of Philadelphia, from 85,637 to 250,880; and of Detroit, from 5,840 to 149,119. Totals for nonwhite populations in 1950 now available show 775,529 for New York, 509,437 for Chicago, 378,968 for Philadelphia, and 303,721 for Detroit. The last census shows the nonwhite population of New York City at 9.8 percent of the total (for Manhattan Borough, it was 20.6 percent); of Chicago, 14.1 percent; of Philadelphia, 18.3 percent; of Detroit, 16.4 percent; and of Baltimore, 18.3 percent.

The social significance. Most students who have concerned themselves with the data on rural-urban migration have emphasized some one

[19] George Santayana, *Persons and Places,* Charles Scribner's Sons, New York, 1944, p. 103.

or more specialized aspects of this trend, such as new patterns of population distribution, residential mobility, changes in the labor market, the disturbance of political voting strength, or the creation of housing crises. Somewhat less has been said about what would seem to be the basic change involved: the transplanting of millions of individuals and families from one culture to another. For rural life is a cultural system, as is urban life. The differences between them are numerous, fundamental, and pervasive, as Sorokin, Zimmerman, and Galpin, and Burgess, Wirth, and others have shown.[20]

Rural life develops primarily around one occupational complex, agriculture. Cities are industrial and commercial, and thus also more diverse in their occupational range. Rural life involves continuing contacts with nature and knowledge of her gifts and forces, as well as of the limitations she imposes; the urban environment is artificial, with technological progress interjecting ever more artificial layers between man and nature. The rural community is smaller, particularly since the advent of the metropolitan area. The density of population, with its attendant proximity of contacts and multiplication of problems of human relations, differs materially between country and city, as does the homogeneity of the population. Cities are made up, much more largely than the country, of diverse races, nationalities, and religions. Social differentiation and stratification vary widely, too, the country not knowing the diversity of roles and social distinctions that are the inevitable accompaniment of city life. Urban life, again, is more mobile, both in point of space and in pursuit of occupation. When rural folks migrate within the rural setting, the movement usually is from one farm to another. Particularly different are the contrasting systems of social interaction. Country people have fewer contacts, they function mostly in primary groups, and there is emphasis upon personalization and continuity of relations, as well as upon a relative informality. City people have more but less durable contacts and they function largely through secondary groups, with the result that their social contacts are more impersonal, more transitory, superficial, conventionalized, and formalized.

---

[20] P. A. Sorokin, Carle C. Zimmerman, and Charles J. Galpin, *A Systematic Source Book in Rural Sociology,* University of Minnesota Press, Minneapolis, 1930, Vol. I, Chap. 4; Ernest W. Burgess, "Environment and Education," *Supplementary Educational Monographs,* No. 54, University of Chicago Press, Chicago, March, 1942, pp. 1–15; Louis Wirth, "Urbanism as a Way of Life," *American Journal of Sociology,* July, 1938, pp. 1–24; Arnold W. Green, "The Middle Class Male Child and Neurosis," *American Sociological Review,* February, 1946, pp. 31–41; Robert C. Jones, "Mexican Youth in the United States," *The American Teacher,* March, 1944, pp. 11–15; Carle C. Zimmerman and Richard E. Du Wors, *Graphic Regional Sociology,* The Phillips Book Store, Cambridge, Mass., 1952; Marvin B. Sussman, "Family Continuity: Selective Factors Which Affect Relationships Between Families at Generational Levels," *Marriage and Family Living,* May, 1954, pp. 112–120; S. N. Eisenstadt, *From Generation to Generation,* Free Press, Glencoe, Ill., 1956.

It is clear that country and city people live in two quite different environments. The urban environment is highly mechanized, rational, mobile, impersonal, commercialized, cynical, and heterogeneous; the rural environment involves more physical but less nervous effort, there is a closer adjustment to nature, relationships are personalized, there is more stability and informality. These differing environments call forth different ways of living, different sets of values, different personality traits and types. The urban type is identified as intellectual, mercenary, calculating, reserved, sophisticated, and precocious, in contrast to the rural personification of the opposite of these qualities.

Resultant problems of child development. The transfer from a rural to an urban culture is a momentous change, involving virtually every aspect of life. In many respects it is similar to the experience of the European immigrant who comes to America. True, there are not the language difficulties that there are in the case of the immigrant; but the very fact that the migration is within the same country, perhaps the same region, with no legal or linguistic barriers, disarms both rural migrants and the urban areas they enter from a proper appreciation of what is actually happening. Certainly, the problems of adjustment faced by rural Negroes who are catapulted overnight into our large Northern cities are no less in number and seriousness than those which confronted the immigrant family of a generation ago. On the other hand, many families who migrate to the city from rural areas adjacent to and under the domination of the city find the transfer less difficult in many ways. In this process of adjusting to an urban culture, different members of the family have different problems. We are concerned here with those common to the children, and three will be considered briefly.

First, there are the problems of the country child's adjustment to the city schools. Dependent upon his capacities and previous training, this may be a relatively simple task. Often, however, this is not the case, especially for children who come from backward rural areas with inadequate schools and teachers, and low scholastic standards. Such children find themselves thrown into trying, conspicuous positions, either as members of a class with much younger and, what is more important, smaller children, or as incompetent students in a class of their own age. Situations of this kind may be very painful, especially to a sensitive child. Considered in scholastic terms, their real significance is to be found in their effect upon the attitudes and behavior of the children involved.

Second, and more important than the challenge of the classroom, there is the country child's adjustment to the social life of his city peers. As was pointed out in an earlier chapter, the newcomer must be tried out. Among boys, this trying-out process involves physical combat. The question whether country or city boys are better fighters is perennial in many school yards, and is resettled with the advent of each new country boy. In this process of social adjustment, the country child again is in a conspicuous position. Social visibility here may be a matter of clothes, speech, or palpable ignorance of city ways; and, as always, it is the bully and the less successful city child who seizes upon this less adjusted member as a vent for the hurt of his own inadequacies. The country boy whose identification as such affords a Roman holiday for his urban tormentors may "pass" in another year or two, but the memory of his experience leaves scars which, though they heal, remain as a permanent testimonial. By way of illustration, a university professor, now in his middle forties, offers these comments from his own experience:

I was a raw, inexperienced, naïve country boy of 15 when my family moved to a large Midwestern city. I must have been an impossible lad in those days. Sometimes, when I lie awake at night, I squirm at the memories of those earlier years. I think I received in those crucial adolescent years a basic insecurity which I have never been able to overcome. Even today, when I stand at the window of my office and see the students flock to my classroom, I am almost overcome at times by my feelings of inferiority. It is as though my subconscious mind were saying: "If these young people knew how impossible you were as a lad, they wouldn't come to your classes." At times like that, I must struggle with myself to go to face my class.

Third, there are the problems of parent-child relationships. These are often similar to those arising in immigrant homes. The children live in a world which their parents do not understand, or only partly so, with the result that many of them are caught between an emotional allegiance to their families and an intellectual conclusion that their parents cannot help and do not understand. The conflicts that arise involve a variety of things—school needs, especially for extracurricular activities; clothing requirements, particularly for girls; social amenities, often over matters which to other families might seem highly trivial. If the parents are alert to the new cultural demands and are socially aggressive, the child may be "used" by the parents or be put under pressure to serve as a spearhead for the family's ambitions, or both. In other cases, country-reared parents tend to retain their rural conceptions, particularly in such matters as child rearing and their idea of what constitutes proper behavior norms for the children. Such parents are not haunted, as is so often the case with immigrant parents, by the idea that they are living in a new world and that they ought to modify their concepts by way of adjustment. American parents who move to cities stay in their own country, they insist that they know what its ways and needs are, and they often adhere stubbornly to their traditional views.

It should be realized, however, that the first-generation city child often presents special behavior problems. These arise basically from the anonymity that life in the city, particularly the big city, affords. To many such children, and at times to their parents, this anonymity seems like an invitation to run riot. Nobody knows and nobody seems to care. The restraining influences of the rural primary-group neighborhood are gone. All the facilities of communication combine to shift attention from the neighborhood to the larger, less choate, less exacting society. Reinforcing the effects of urban anonymity are the cynicism and tolerance that city life breeds. Urbanites tend to have few illusions, and the resultant sinister sophistication is particularly evident to persons when they first come to know the city and before they understand its deeper values. When such cynicism is combined with an open-handed tolerance which seems to indicate a lack of standards rather than of mutual understanding, the isolated individual and family is likely to emerge, standing alone and thrown back upon the organic impulse of the individual. One obvious form of expression of this is pleasure seeking; and perhaps the clearest evidence of its prevalence is to be found in the rapid growth of commercialized amusements, in the excessive consumption of alcohol, and in other quests for stimulation and organic satisfactions which Sorokin characterizes as sensate culture. It is against this background that we must seek to understand the behavior problems of large groups of juveniles in such American cities as Detroit, for example, for it is in such cities that we find large groups of first-generation city children who have sloughed off their primary-group controls but have not yet developed substitute restraints.

Cultural Change and Parent-Child Relations

A third basic factor in the creation of marked cultural differentials between successive generations is to be found in the rapidity of cultural change which has characterized recent decades. Since this factor operates in all but a few isolated cultural pockets in this country, its significance is general, differing perhaps only in degree from one family to another.

The comprehensive and pervasive character of contemporary cultural change is so well established in sociological literature that no further emphasis or exposition is necessary here. We may proceed, therefore, to assess its specific meaning for the relationship between successive generations.

First, cultural change increases the cultural distance between successive generations. Since the time interval between generations is relatively fixed at about 30 years, the difference between the cultural milieus in which their personalities are formed depends wholly upon the rapidity with which cultural change occurs. Other things being equal, the more rapid the processes of cultural change, the greater the cultural distance between generations.

The significance of this for parent-child relations has been well stated by Davis.

Extremely rapid change in modern civilization, in contrast to most societies, tends to increase parent-youth conflict, for within a fast changing social order the time-interval between generations, ordinarily but a mere moment in the life of a social system, becomes historically significant, thereby creating a hiatus between one generation and the next. Inevitably, under such a condition, youth is reared in a milieu different from that of the parents; hence the parents become old-fashioned, youth rebellious, and clashes occur which, in the closely confined circle of the immediate family, generate sharp emotion. . . . Our rapid social change has crowded historical meaning into the family time span, has thereby given the offspring a different social context from that which the child acquired, and consequently has added to the already existent intrinsic differences between parent and youth, a set of extrinsic ones which double the chance of alienation. Moreover, our great social complexity, our evident cultural conflict, and our emphasis upon open competition for socioeconomic status have all added to this initial effect. . . . They have disorganized the improper relation of parental authority by confusing the goals of child control, setting up competing authorities, creating a small family system, making necessary certain significant choices at the time of adolescence, and leading to an absence of definite institutional mechanisms to symbolize and enforce the progressively changing stages of parental power.[21]

Another approach to the significance of cultural change in parent-youth relations is to consider its effect upon the respective roles in society of the old and the young. An interview given by the late Henry Ford at the time the Ford Motor Company shifted production from the old Model T Fords to a gearshift car offers an appropriate illustration of the point. When one makes radical and revolutionary changes in a plant, he said, old and experienced employees lose their value to the employer. Rather is it true that they prove to be a handicap, for old and experienced employees have set ideas and ways of doing things, which means that new, untried, and inexperienced workers can learn the newly devised ways much better and more quickly.

Cultural change, in other words, tends to depreciate the value of experience. It discredits precedents, traditional ideas, and techniques. The older person is at a disadvantage by reason both of what he must unlearn and of what he may not yet have mastered. The emphasis is upon experimentation, and a premium is put upon youth as being more versatile and adaptable. Old-fogeyism becomes a popular cry. Especially must current ideologies be revised by the young; and when, as in Nazi

[21] Kingsley Davis, "The Sociology of Parent-Youth Conflict," *American Sociological Review*, August, 1940, pp. 523–535.

Germany, Soviet Russia, and possibly other countries, the power and prestige of the state are placed behind these revisions, parents are to be obeyed only as long as they have the "correct" ideas.[22]

The experience of China through centuries of her history offers striking evidence of the foregoing in reverse. Lang has pointed out recently how the dependence upon agriculture, the importance of the public official, and the static nature of Chinese civilization all combined to strengthen the position of the elders. "The old man represented an accumulation of wisdom. The young man wanted to imitate him, not to fight him. For hundreds and thousands of years there was no conflict of generations in China."[23]

The current dislocation and reversal of the roles of old and young naturally come to a focus in family life. Children as always question their parents' understanding, only more so; what is particularly significant is the extent to which modern parents question their own capacities and judgments. In most societies, parents bring up their children in their own way of life, and the task is reasonably clear. But the contemporary parent succumbs not only to the confusion of rapid change but also to what might be called the great American fear of being naïve. This is a current dread of upholding an old virtue or point of view or method of doing a thing, lest it imply that one does not know the new one; and large numbers of parents permit this to become an inferiority complex of the first magnitude. Living in a small immediate family, free from the domination of the elder kinsfolk, lacking authoritative sources of information other than the radio or the attractive young doctor down the street, looking askance and sidewise at the neighbors who are similarly confused, many a present-day parent feels nothing as much as uncertainty, a feeling which his children may sense before he is aware of it.

There are, of course, other families in which the situation takes a different turn. Here the parents adhere resolutely to old ways and values and seek to impose them upon their resistant offspring. At times, the very insecurity of the parents in a changing world leads to their compensatory devotion to the old, and then the conflicts are even more bitter. In many of these families, the cultural conflicts become involved with questions of family loyalty, the parents demanding loyalty not only to themselves on the basis of family affection, but also to the attitudes, ideas, and values which they set up as part of the family pattern. Such situations often become painful and disturbing, especially to the children, and they result in internal conflicts between emotional loyalty and intellectual judgment. The further complications which may arise from the influence

[22] Sigmund Neumann, "The Conflict of Generations in Contemporary Europe from Versailles to Munich," *Vital Speeches of the Day*, August 1, 1939, pp. 623-628.

[23] Olga Lang, *Chinese Family and Society*, Yale University Press, New Haven, 1946, p. 10.

of the school and other formal educational agencies are obvious here but will be discussed in a subsequent chapter.

A final word should be said about the stabilizing role of the family in a period of rapid cultural change. It is easy, and it has been customary in certain quarters, to criticize parents for being old-fashioned and too resistant to new ideas in the school and youth culture of their children. Such an indictment, whatever its merit in any individual case, must be weighed against the family's responsibility as a conservator of old values and as a stabilizing force in a world in which so little remains true to itself through the space of a decade. After all, the mortality rate of new attitudes, ideas, and values is relatively high, perhaps as high as that of inventions in other fields; and a certain sheer resistance to change, quite apart from critical evaluation, seems both wholesome and essential. Moreover, there are things that are permanent. Courtship customs may be revolutionized by the automobile, and in turn by the airplane, but the way of a man with a maid has about it certain unchanging aspects. "There are values," Groves reminded us, "aside from those that come from human adjustment to mechanical processes or even to social organization. We sometimes call these spiritual values. The important thing is to recognize that they are basic in any program for human satisfaction. . . . In times of social flux the family becomes more than ever the final refuge for those who can find little sense of security elsewhere."[24]

Child Development and National Characteristics

There is an extensive literature today, cutting across the fields of psychiatry and sociology, which emphasizes the neurotic quality of our culture.[25] The substance of this literature is that our culture is conflict-ridden and conflict-laden, that the source of these conflicts is to be found in cultural contradictions in society, and that these take expression in the form of mental conflicts in the individual.

In the various analyses of the nature and sources of these cultural conflicts that have been presented, relatively little attention has been paid to culture conflicts in the personality development of children, and to the social forces which create these culture conflict situations on a large scale. The three factors emphasized in this chapter—(1) migration from an alien culture outside of the country in which one or one's parents lived,

[24] Ernest R. Groves, *The Family and Its Social Functions,* J. B. Lippincott Company, Philadelphia, 1940, pp. 450–453.

[25] Karen Horney, *The Neurotic Personality of Our Time,* W. W. Norton & Company, Inc., New York, 1937; George Devereux, "Maladjustment and Social Neurosis," *American Sociological Review,* December, 1939, pp. 844–851; Read Bain, "Our Schizoid Culture," *Sociology and Social Research,* March, 1934, pp. 267–276; Lawrence Frank, "Society as the Patient," *American Journal of Sociology,* November, 1936, pp. 335–345.

(2) migration from a different culture within a nation of continental proportions, and (3) constant cultural migration from one time span to another—would seem to affect the overwhelming proportion of people who have grown to maturity in the United States in recent years. In short, the cultural situations identified are operating on a large enough scale to produce characteristics national in scope. Similarly, the elements which produce neuroses are present in the situation described: cultural conflicts in early personality development, conflicts with family members over basic issues, opposing pulls of deep-seated loyalties, recurring frustration, and habitual response patterns of insecurity or rebellion or both.

Looming behind the whole process is the necessity for crucial choices by children whose deepest developmental interests deviate from those of their parents, choices whose inevitable solution involves the rejection, actual or symbolic, of their own nearest of kind. It is this which Margaret Mead implies in her phrase "the purposeful forgetting of ancestry," and in her insistence that Americans as a people are third-generation folk, that is, newly arrived.[26] Perhaps this explains much about America and Americans—the outward glow of material and social achievement and the inward sense of loss that comes when the continuity of life is broken, for life seems to flourish best when its fundamental meaning is passed on through the subtle intangibles from one generation to another.

Summary

1. A large proportion of children in the United States have grown up in homes in which there are marked cultural differences between parents and children.

2. One group is the second-generation children in homes of immigrants. They constitute a large proportion of the child population and are congregated particularly in large cities. The cultural world in which they grow up differs materially from that of their Old World parents, giving rise to the resultant problems of culture conflict, parental inadequacy, undue social pressure, and family disorganization. Common response patterns include the child's rejection of his parents, the appearance of the marginal man, frustration coupled with aggressive behavior, and the crystallization of mental conflicts.

3. A second group consists of the large number of children who are being brought up in cities by parents reared in rural situations. The differences in background are cultural in nature and comprehensive in scope. The problems of many such children are similar in many respects to those of the second-generation immigrant group, except for the element of language differences.

[26] Margaret Mead, *And Keep Your Powder Dry,* William Morrow & Company, Inc., New York, 1943.

4. Rapid cultural change tends to affect all families by lengthening the cultural distance between successive generations, thus creating problems of cultural differentials for additional groups of children, as well as intensifying those of the groups already mentioned.

5. These three groups of children tend to have similar problems of parent-child relationships, and naturally they tend to develop similar patterns of response. These apparently exist on a scale numerically large enough to affect prevailing national characteristics.

The Peer Group—Preschool Playmates

Reference has been made in preceding chapters to the fact that, at a given time in his development, the interests of the child begin to shift from his family to the group life of children of approximately his own age. On the negative side, this expresses itself in a growing revolt against parental control and often in a critical attitude toward home and parents; on the positive side, in the increase of interests in group activities and group loyalties. In Chapter 24, this process was analyzed in terms of a growth away from home; in Chapter 25, in terms of a rebellion which is particularly pronounced in certain elements in the child population. The purpose of the present chapter is to discuss: (1) the meaning and range of these contemporary age groupings among children, and (2) the nature and role of their development among preschool children. The succeeding chapter will analyze the nature and role of later age groups.

Peer Groups: Their Meaning and Range

A peer in the common social sense of the word is a person whom one meets on terms of approximate equality, a companion or fellow. For a child, a peer, negatively considered, is a nonadult, a nonparent, a nonteacher; on the positive side, it means another child, relatively of the same age, in certain instances of the same sex, with whom he can associate on terms of equal status, at least so far as his elders are concerned. It is important that this dual nature of the peer concept be recognized, for the peer group is often more than an association of equals whose concern is with each other; it is, in a certain specific sense, also a grouping in which the adult is excluded. The peer group is the child's own social world, with its own language, its own mode of interaction, its own values and acceptable forms of behavior, many of which grownups cannot understand. It is a world in which the child has equal and even at times superior status with others, and not the subordinate status that he has invariably with parents and other adults.[1]

Chronologically, peer groups take form early in the child's life. The exact time varies, both with the nature of the family situation and the availability of age-mates. However, the process of moving away from the small world of the family to the engrossing world of one's fellows is usually under way before the fourth year. In the earlier years, these peer groups are relatively informal and transitory, adapted quickly to changing circumstances in the child's situation. Examples are the play group, the clique, and many gangs. Later come the more formally organized groups, such as clubs, fraternities, fighting gangs, and the like. Perhaps we should include here such character-building agencies as the Boy Scouts, Campfire Girls, and so forth. However, since the latter are not constituted and operated entirely as peer groups, they are omitted from consideration, although this is not to be interpreted as a lack of recognition of their very great importance.

The Play Group

The play group is the most informal of the peer groupings and also the earliest in the child's life to develop. Conceived as a group, it is essentially an association of equals to share in a common play experience, with emphasis upon common rules and an understanding of the limitations which group activity places upon the individual. As most frequently used, the term is applied to groups of children in the lower age brackets. Gesell and Ilg,[2] as well as Hurlock[3] and others, have shown that from somewhere between the third and fourth year children prefer to play in groups, that the size of the group depends on the age of the children, and that the size increases with their age. Periods of preference for solitary play intervene from time to time, but gradually these begin to disappear, interest in organized play activities arises, and boys and girls begin to play separately. These play groupings tend to be temporary in character and limited in scope to some particular kind of play or the use of some common play space or equipment. In many cases, their origin is voluntary and spontaneous; in other instances, particularly at the lower age levels, they are engineered in large part by adult intervention as an adjunct to some other activity, such as that of a school, settlement house, or

[1] Robert J. Havighurst and Bernice L. Neugarten, *Society and Education,* Allyn and Bacon, Inc., Boston, 1957, pp. 107–108.

[2] Arnold Gesell and Frances Ilg, *The Child from Five to Ten,* Harper & Brothers, New York, 1946, pp. 359–373.

[3] Elizabeth B. Hurlock, *Child Development,* McGraw-Hill Book Company, Inc., New York, 1942, p. 226.

hospital. Play groups operate chiefly in schools and at neighborhood centers, and from the fourth to the twelfth year. They may be thought of as cliques and gangs in embryo.

The Preschool Play Group

The major emphasis in studies of child development has been upon early family environment. Lately, there has been an increasing interest in the role of school situations in a child's continuing personality growth and behavior patterns. Organized preschool groups, such as nursery schools and kindergartens, have also received some attention. There has, however, with a few exceptions mentioned later in this chapter, been an almost complete ignoring of the fact that the average child spends a considerable part of his time after infancy and before entering school with his playmates.

Play groups of children that form before school days have at least two characteristics which set them apart from later play groups. In the first place, the choice of playmates is relatively restricted, in kind and in number. Once in school, a child may select from many, and have ever-increasing power of locomotion to play away from his own neighborhood. This is not true of the preschool child, who must accept or reject whoever happens to be available in his immediate area. Secondly, the preschool play group is his *first* introduction to a group which assesses him as a child from a child's point of view, and teaches him the rules of behavior from the same point of view. That these are different from adult assessments and rules is generally acknowledged. The neat, obedient, and rather prissy youngster may be a joy to his parents, but usually has a few new lessons to learn before he can fit in with his peers. In similar vein, the "spoiled brat" may have to discover that peers can be more strong-minded than parents. Also, Jean Piaget has described not only how children's rules are different from adults' rules but that they are considered differently by children. The former are arbitrarily imposed, and to be broken as pleases. The latter have the strength of federal law. An adult teaching youngsters to play a game can expect them to evade and argue about his rules. Left alone, the children will make up their own, and woe betide the peer who defies them.

These two characteristics of the preschool play group signify that the child is entering a new, different, and very powerful world when he joins the group, and that the composition of the immediate neighborhood has importance in his development. The matter of who is available and what he is like was considered by many parents long before sociologists became interested in the subject. One mother says: "Since Betty is destined to be an only child, I am glad we live where there are other nice boys and girls of her own age." Another complains: "We are looking for a new home in another community because we do not want to have to forbid our children to play with the little roughnecks in this one." Thus parents have manipulated, for their own purposes, their children's play-group environments, recognizing what may be said here in more "scientific" terms.

The play group is a social situation and has, as does any other group, its own specific structure, interactive process, and cultural content. The plasticity of the young child, so much stressed in the study of early family influences, still exists during the years of preschool play. It seems rather obvious, then, that the play group must have some importance in directing his development and behavior.

A child, however, is not merely a product of the play group but also of the rest of his environment which, before school days, is, for the most part, his family. Therefore, it is the interplay between these two groups which has real meaning for the child. The study which is reported below is an attempt to discover the effects on children of their particular play groups as related to their own family situations.

Methodology

Case-method studies of childhood playmates have been approached in two ways. One is to question young children. By this method, memory need not be relied upon, nor is there the risk of the embroidering of sad and happy events as they may be seen years later. The reporting, though, is temporally cross-sectional both as to the friends known and as to the group's effects upon development. Another method is to question adults about the past. Here the element of memory has to be considered. However, a positive value seems to lie in perspective, depth, and a better opportunity for evaluating influences over a long period of time.

Detailed case records of 50 persons ranging in age from 18 to 54 form the source materials for this analysis. Most of them were in their teens or early twenties. Thirty-four of the cases were female and 16 were male. Both whites and Negroes were represented. Social status was predominantly middle class, with a few cases of upper and upper-lower included. The persons were asked to describe their family structure, interaction, and culture during preschool days; the structure, interaction, and culture of their play group; and their own opinions as to how the combination of the two had affected them, if at all. The foregoing terms were explained carefully to all those participating. Every effort was made to effect informal and clear communication between researcher and cases. In the analysis of the data, more reliance was placed upon the stated facts than upon the interpretations, though in most cases the interpretations seemed to follow very logically from the situations as they were described.

Family and Play Group Structure

One of the hypotheses on which this study was based was that the relationships between (a) numbers of siblings and numbers of playmates, and (b) sex of siblings and sex of playmates, might have a bearing upon socialization, sex identification, and ability to understand members of the same, or opposite, sex.

THE FACTOR OF SIZE

Table 9 shows the composition of our sample in respect to number of siblings, and indicates that the cases are very predominantly members of

TABLE 9.   Family Size

Number of Siblings	Male	Female	Total
0	7	11	18
1	7	12	19
2	1	7	8
3	0	1	1
4	1	1	2
5	0	1	1
6	0	1	1
Total	16	34	50

the small-family system. Ninety percent of the respondents came from families with three children or less. Census data for 1950 show the corresponding figure for the general population to be 79.3 percent. The fact that our sample is a college-attending group very probably accounts for the higher ratio. It is clear, then, that the following analyses are descriptive, chiefly, of the role of the preschool play group for children in the small-family system.

Because the cases who had no siblings at all most strikingly illustrate the relationship between number of siblings and number of playmates, their situations will be considered below. In Table 10, the size of their play groups is tabulated. It indicates a wide numerical range and suggests many varieties of resulting situations, a few of which follow.

Jack, an only child, lived in a neighborhood composed mostly of foundry workers of foreign extraction, though his own family was not of this group. He was not permitted to associate with the children of the workers, and when he ran off to do so on several occasions he was brought home and spanked. There was just one approved playmate within his distance of free locomotion—a girl a year older than he. He admitted that he did not much care to play with her and felt she did not care to play with him, but she was the only available person. His one other playmate was the son of friends of his parents, three years

TABLE 10. Size of Play Group of Only Children

Number of Playmates	Male	Female	Total
1	0	1	1
2	1	1	2
3	2	2	4
4	0	0	0
5	0	1	1
6	0	3	3
7	1	0	1
8	0	0	0
9	2	0	2
10	1	0	1
"a group"	0	3	3
Total	7	11	18

older than he, who lived on the other side of town. Every time they played together they had to be taken and brought home by parents. This was unsatisfactory, as was the difference in their ages.

Another only child, Bill, lived in a neighborhood which consisted almost wholly of young family people and of college-educated parents. Most of the fathers were professional men, the major portion being college and high school teachers. There was a great deal of socializing among the parents who had many common interests. Quite naturally, their children grew up together. This boy had no difficulty in finding a continuous play group, easily accessible, from among nine children of both sexes and within one year of his own age.

Horace, a little Negro boy, whose father died when the child was 4 years old, moved at that time from his home where there had been no playmates available, to live with his mother who was 23; an aunt, 33; and two boarders (a married couple), 24 and 27. Formerly, he had been pampered as an only child and was *the* center of his parents' attention. With the move, he became the lone child "against" four adults, three of whom "took authority" because his mother taught school during the day. He wrote: "Limitations and frustrations began to pile up." He was aware that this could have been a very unhappy situation for him. However, the new neighborhood, by its constitution, enabled this lad to have a supremely happy preschool existence. The community was white middle-class, with just five Negro families of college-educated backgrounds and good economic status. There was no race conflict whatsoever, but a mutual agreement not to mix socially. The five Negro families had a total of 10 children, within 3 years in age of the boy. Their social segregation made them stick together almost clannishly. The boy's need to get out from under adult domination made this group of children exceedingly important to him. He spent most of his day out "with the other kids, learning how to get along with other people." One cannot help but add here how much difference it could have made to the boy had there been no other children of his own race, age, and class status available to take a hand in his preschool development of behavior patterns and conceptions of himself as a person.

In three cases of only children, there were other children living in the family. In one, a girl's male cousin one year older than she; in another, a girl's two male cousins, one and three years younger; and in the third, a boy's two cousins, a male cousin four years older and a female cousin three years younger. In the first two of these cases, the roles of the cousins were more like those of real siblings, with the result that there was no feeling of being an only child. Playmates were found together and shared together and there were a number of both sexes. In the third case, the boy was very conscious of being an only child. There was decided rivalry between him and his older boy cousin, because the older boy was permitted to "do things first," and yet was not the real son of the household. The little girl cousin was just a baby and of no use as a playmate. In this case, there was no joining of forces. The lad had to make his own associations, with the result that he found one girl, his own age, to whom he referred as his "sweetheart," and two boys of the same age who never seemed like "real people" to him and of whom he no longer has any distinct recollection.

It was not just the only children who attributed their ease, or lack, of early socialization to the presence or absence of neighborhood playmates. The same sort of comment was made frequently in larger families in cases where the siblings were widely separated in age and/or of different sexes. Here, too, they directly related their own withdrawnness to an isolation from age peers, or spoke with gratitude of the playmates who reversed this tendency in them.

A study of social isolation and mental illness, made by Dr. Herman R. Lantz,[4] reveals an even more critical relation between numbers of friends and mental hygiene. Though cause and effect are not clear, the fact is that cases having no mental disease ranked high in reporting many childhood friends, and low in reporting few or none. The ranking of the psychotics was exactly reversed.

THE SEX FACTOR

The sex composition of the two- and three-child families is shown in Tables 11 and 12, and they indicate that 63 percent of those children were reared with siblings of the opposite sex. All of the larger families in the sample included children of both sexes.

Table 13 shows the sex composition of the play groups. Sixty-two percent of them included children of both sexes, a percentage remarkably close to that for the family sex composition.

Careful analysis of the nine cases in which siblings were all of the same sex revealed that in six of them the preschool play group afforded

[4] Herman R. Lantz, "Number of Childhood Friends as Reported in the Life Histories of a Psychiatrically Diagnosed Group of 1,000," *Marriage and Family Living*, May, 1956, pp. 107–108.

TABLE 11. Sex Composition of Two-Child Families

Sex of Siblings	Male	Female	Total
Same sex	3	3	6
Opposite sex	4	9	13
Total	7	12	19

TABLE 12. Sex Composition of Three-Child Families

Sex of Siblings	Male	Female	Total
Both male	1	1	2
Both female	0	2	2
Both sexes	0	4	4
Total	1	7	8

first association with children of the opposite sex, and three had no such associations before they entered school. A few comments from the individuals involved throw some light on the meaning, to them, of these structures in their interrelationships.

TABLE 13. Sex Composition of Play Group

Sex of Playmates	Male	Female	Total
Both sexes	12	19	31
Opposite sex only	0	4	4
Same sex only	2	9	11
No playmates	2	2	4
Total	16	34	50

Ours was a very feminine household, and Mother was dedicated to making little ladies out of us. My older sister and I were even sent to private girls' academies until high school age. My sister had never played with anyone but girls up to that time and when, at the age of 14½, she started at a coeducational school, she got into various sorts of troubles. She was fascinated by suddenly being surrounded by boys who were quite ready to date her. But she didn't know anything about boys, really, nor their rules of the game, nor how to behave with them. The results were that first she got a badly turned head, then she got into trouble with the principal and finally she got her heart broken. She was "off men" for several years. It was so different with me. I went to the same schools at the same ages, but I grew up with a gang of boys and girls from the tender age of three. We were together constantly and a little bit of Mother's "femininity training" was rubbed off me even before I went to the academy. Since my friendships with these same playmates continued for many years, I hadn't the slightest trouble in changing to the high school. Boys were "old hat" to me. I had had *their* ideas about proper girls' behavior pounded into me thoroughly and I had also learned a good deal about *them*.

I was the third daughter born to a man who desperately wanted a son. As chance would have it, the only children on my street were a number of young boys. Thus, while other little girls, I suppose, were busy playing with dolls or cutouts, I was out in the street tossing a soft-ball or climbing lampposts. The boys accepted me as one of them and I was happy. The "rub" came when I entered grammar school and found myself face to face with the problem of learning, under social pressure, How to Act Like a Young Lady. This was indeed quite a problem. It seemed I had to learn, often by painful experience, the behavior patterns which were second nature to other girls. I had to learn what seemed at the time a whole new vocabulary, a whole new manner of dress, a whole new set of interests. It was not easy. I had to learn these things not only to fit in with the other girls, but I discovered, to my pain, that boys perfer tomboy girls only up to a certain age.

A boy whose only brother was three and a half years younger than he, and who had only one, and a very close and continuing, male playmate, wrote of being "terrified" by being in a classroom with girls, that he never made friends of them, and even at present is much more comfortable with men than with women. One sentence from his case record is of special interest. After describing the lifelong association with his friend, he wrote: "We were more like brother and *sister*."

THE AGE FACTOR

Another hypothesis, arrived at during the process of this study, was that the age structure of the play group is also meaningful in terms of child development. It has already been suggested that the fact of age composition of family and available playmates has some importance where siblings are spaced so far apart as almost to preclude common interests, and that in some such cases playmates have proved a satisfactory substitute in sharing, competing, and teaching. There are, however, other facets of the significance of age composition.

First, it seems proper to emphasize that slight age differences between very young children seem much greater than they do between adults. It is a common experience that age gaps increasingly diminish in significance as one grows older. In the case of very young children, the facts of maturation and muscular development and control add further highlights to age differences. Even four or six months, when one is 3, can make a great difference in actual ability, let alone in interests and in what Mother permits one to do. And a year or two makes a whole world of difference. For these reasons, the age composition of the play group in itself has been noted as important in our records.

A lad with a sister three and a half years older than he, and a group of eight playmates from seven to nine years older than he, wrote the following:

Being younger, and with sister more or less of a boss, I became a follower and a cry-baby when I couldn't keep up with the older kids and when they made fun of me. I even developed stuttering, but, thanks to my mother who didn't sympathize with me, I got over it. She convinced me there was nothing organically wrong with me, that I could stop it if I wanted to. I did try hard, and it worked (although under extremely tense situations I feel it coming back, but I always suppress it). When my sister was in high school, my parents and she always insisted I go wherever my sister and her friends went (swimming, movies, to other girls' houses). I always felt out of place and not really wanted although everyone said I was very foolish to think such a thing.

A girl with a brother eight years older and a sister four and a half years younger tells this story:

The only children in the block were about six boys all exactly my brother's age. As a result, there was no one for me to play with. But my brother's friends played with me, not regularly, but I was treated to bicycle rides, swings, etc., when they were in the mood. As a result . . . I never had a "till death us do part" bosom pal. I have a hard time talking to other people about things that are important. I enjoy being with myself. Reading is a favorite sport. And I sometimes wonder if the fact that I have always gotten along (on a dating basis) with fellows quite a bit older than I isn't caused by the earlier associations with my brother's friends.

Two other cases (not tabulated in this study) show interesting contrasts to the above. A young lady who is remarkably competent at everything she undertakes, and for the simple reason that she studies each new problem carefully and keeps practicing until she is satisfied with the results, had the following experience. She was the youngest of seven playmates, the next closest in age being six months older. Apparently the greater motor abilities of the others challenged her. When she was just old enough to dress herself, she was found sneaking out into the yard one morning at six o'clock. When observed and questioned, her explanation was that she was going to "pwactice yumpin'." "Practicing jumping" has been characteristic of her behavior ever since. Finally, an extremely successful businessman, who has made his way by starting a number of times on jobs quite below his ability and economic value and then working himself upward, attributed his willingness to do this to attitudes formed in his earliest training. He had a sister five years his senior. The only other children in the neighborhood were girls of her age, and the little boy who tagged along was an abomination to them. He was very lonely and discovered that the only way he could "get in" was to offer to do the "dirty work" and "play the most menial roles." When he did this, he was not only accepted, but achieved success in his goal for companionship.

Further light on the relation between age and sex of siblings and play groups has been shed in a recent study.[5] Children actually expressed a preference for playmates of their own sex, but a preference for those of the opposite sex was higher among children who had a sibling of the opposite sex. This decreased as the age between the siblings widened. It would seem, then, that those children who were not exposed to peers of the opposite sex in their families, and who might profit by playing with them outside the home, were the ones who would not seek them out by preference.

Finally, a 20-year-old girl with a brother two years her senior commented upon her good fortune in the healthy age and sex make-up of her family and play group as it had affected her up to the present day, and of how different could have been the results had her and her brother's birth orders been reversed. As it was, the girl knew, played with, and became accustomed to boys a little older than she, grew up with them, and at dating age was "all set." Her brother had a similar experience, having learned to get along with girls of an age relationship from which he would normally choose a wife. Had the birth orders in this family been different, the girl felt that both she and her brother would have had to find new friends during adolescence and would have gone their separate ways. Instead of that, a continuing and comradely relationship had endured between them and with all their friends, promising, she hoped, close family ties and a sharing of social life in the future.

Family and Play Group Interactive Processes

In situational analysis, the separation of a group into structure, process, and content is a necessary technique but a highly superficial one. It is necessary because it is impossible by word of mouth or in writing to analyze a situation in its total configuration. It is superficial because structure, process, and content are so completely interrelated that in a real life situation no one of them stands alone as a determining influence. Already, in the analysis of structure, there has been much reference to both interaction and cultural content. This is inescapable. However, as structure has been the chief emphasis in the preceding section, and content will be in the following one, so interaction is stressed here. Three aspects of it will be illustrated.

THE PLAY GROUP INTERACTIVE PATTERN

The general patterns of play group interaction in our case records provided interesting contrasts. There were the very congenial ones in which even the parents sometimes helpfully participated when they were re-

[5] Helen L. Koch, "The Relation in Young Children Between Characteristics of Their Playmates and Certain Attributes of Their Siblings," *Child Development,* June, 1957, pp. 175–202.

quired, in which statuses and roles were clearly defined and agreeable to all the children, so that little or no friction resulted in the groups even during competitive play. "We all got along swell" is the tone of comments about such groups. At the other extreme were the play groups that battled incessantly, sticking together, but with a continuous jockeying for statuses and roles. In the records of such groups, the usual comment is something like, "I learned how to stand up for myself. I had to." Between these two polar extremes there were many-shaded mixtures of such interaction. Furthermore, there was one other distinct type: the close-knit group that achieved its closeness from an effort to protect itself against, or take it out upon, a second close-knit neighborhood play group. Interestingly enough, the respondents, both male and female, who recorded this type of interaction, spoke of their groups as "gangs." The process described within them was very similar to that described in Thrasher's classic study of gangs,[6] here pushed back in time to preschool play.

INDIVIDUAL PLAYMATES AND THE EMPATHIC COMPLEX

Many studies in child development which are psychologically or psychoanalytically oriented stress that early psychic experience in family interaction may result in patterning a child's behavior and attitudes toward all other people and throughout life. For example, the family-rejected child may feel rejected by everyone else and even when he becomes an adult. Such cases do occur, and frequently come to light in clinics. Thus it is almost natural to attribute the results to family rejection. There are also, though, many obviously family-rejected children who do not react throughout life in this way. They do not usually show up in clinics (at least, not for rejection symptoms) and it is therefore very difficult to discover why their reactions have been so different.

A sociological, or situational, analysis of the total interactive group experience, rather than of just early family interaction, may shed light on possible answers to this question, and for the following reasons. For some people, the *realities* of their experiences throughout life correspond to, and reinforce, the influences of their intrafamily experiences. For others, this is not so; and at times quite abrupt reversals of behavior and attitudes result from new experiences. Our case records give indications that this does happen.

One very persistent story running through the records has to do with the ability, or lack of ability, to form close, intimate relationships with other people, to talk oneself out freely, to give confidences. In every case where a child had felt no such closeness with a family member, because of a variety of circumstances, and the play group offered no person of similar age and/or interests, the individual remarked upon a

[6] Frederic M. Thrasher, *The Gang*, 2nd rev. ed., University of Chicago Press, Chicago, 1936.

continuation of his "apartness" during school days and a lingering bit of difficulty in this respect up to the present. On the other hand, when the family situation was similar, but close pals had been found in the pre-school period, the writer spoke of this as the beginning of learning to share himself with another.

The story, however, is broader than it appears on the basis of these comments. The authors have used the concept of "the empathic complex" to describe one of the ways in which personalities take form. The term *empathic complex* means "the particular emotional linkage between a child and the significant persons in his environment."[7] A child does not respond to all the people in his environment with equal emotionality. Some, he loves because they fulfill his emotional and/or physical needs; others, he dislikes because they do not; still others seem neutral persons to him. Regardless of the actual social value of the behavior of these people, a child tends to react in two ways. First, he tends to adopt the behavior patterns of those he loves, and to avoid those of the ones he dislikes; second, he tends to develop a certain type of behavior pattern of his own which is appropriate to the relationship between him and the specific person. He is selective about this in his own family, and our cases indicate that he is equally selective among his own playmates. For example:

George had a circle of little friends whom he saw most frequently at birthday parties and Sunday school. Most of them were "neutrals" to him, and he rarely sought out their company. Jean, a girl one and a half years older than he, definitely appealed to him, however, and he spent most of his time with her. She was "likable," came from a "nice middle-class family of the same religious background," and "generally set a good example as to her character." Not only was she a "character example" to George, but he felt his association with her carried over into his later life. He prefers the kind of girl Jean was, now that he is at the dating age, and he thinks of girls as friends, and not just as "mere objects of sexual attraction." George had a strong emotional feeling about one other playmate, Harry. Harry was six months older but a "coward and not too intelligent." His character was "a little shoddy," he always told his parents lies and seldom got away with it. Through Harry, George discovered that "crime does not pay," and he felt that Harry influenced him negatively almost as much as Jean did positively—not because of the actual moral values represented, but just because George happened to like the one very much and despise the other.

In Grace's play group, Mary Louise was her favorite friend. Mary Louise was a year younger, and Grace always felt that she was "taking care" of the younger girl. The relationship was so pleasant and happy for both that when Mary Louise had a baby sister Grace extended her protective attitude to include the baby. Grace says that she loves young children, likes to work with them, and wants four of her own.

[7] James H. S. Bossard and Eleanor S. Boll, "Child Behavior and the Empathic Complex," *Child Development*, March, 1957, p. 37.

A very similar case record involves a girl whose closest friend was a cripple. They spent a very happy childhood together; the recorder never lost her interest in people with physical incapacities and became a nurse, specializing in orthopedics. This case was in striking contrast to the statement of still a third girl whose next-door neighbor was a victim of paralysis of the right arm. She wrote that she was forced to play with this boy and that his nasty disposition and vicious temper developed through frustration had made her steer very clear of anyone who had any kind of deformity.

RELATION BETWEEN FAMILY AND PLAY GROUP INTERACTION

Finally, the combination of interactive processes within the home and those encountered outside have their own specific effects.

Gloria writes that she was born when her parents were 39 and 41. Their first baby died at the age of 3. They had long since given up any hopes of parenthood before Gloria arrived. When she did, she was the apple of her parents' and kinsfolk's eyes, and very severely overprotected. She describes herself as "sensitive, isolated, and hesitant." The children in her neighborhood ran around in a "pack," and were boisterous and active. She wished so much for some one or few quiet children like herself to play with; but she could not become a member of the "pack" and she had no other resources than "imaginary playmates." She wrote: "Now that I have grown up, I realize the advantages of group play. Play is a great builder, not just of bodies and minds, but also of social awareness, for in play a child must take other children into consideration. He learns many valuable lessons in adjusting himself to the demands and ideals of his group as he will later have to adjust himself to the demands and ideals of his community."

Robert, an only child who lived on a large farm, contributed the following record:

I was quite lonely as a child, in fact, very lonely. My mother was not a talkative woman, and my father was a busy man. There were two groups of children available for me to play with and I was eager to play with them. One was a large family of about eight children. My parents did not think much of the family. The father was irregularly employed. One girl had had an illegitimate child. One boy had been in some kind of trouble. My mother thought they were trash, but she also had insight into the loneliness of a little boy. In addition to the social barrier between us . . . I early had to face certain problems. They cheated at play. They depreciated my superior toys but used them often and broke them. When I got a tricycle, they wanted to ride it all the time but yet it was not a good tricycle. They knew people who had better ones. Also, I envied them. They were a large family. They had a good time, it seemed. There was always somebody to do something with. These children did some petty thieving . . . I remember much talk about it in our home. My father wanted to go to the mat with them, but my mother said she didn't want trouble with them since they were, after all, our nearest neighbors and were the only children usually available for me to play with. About this time, the boy two years older than me began picking on me. My father told me the next time it happened to punch him. I did. I struck him and piled him up on the mud. This made a tremendous and lasting impression on me. He was older, he was a head bigger, yet I learned that fight can overcome what seemed like insurmountable obstacles. I don't think I was ever afraid after that of anyone, at least not for many years. The other thing I remember. These older children gave me my first introduction to sex. The girls as well as the boys joined in. I worried about this for years. The other children that I played with—and always separately from the first family—were my two cousins, a girl and a boy. The girl was a few months younger than I and the boy about a year and a half. The girl and I have always hit it off well together and we ganged up just a bit on the boy. We made him sort of fetch and carry for us. She and I always sort of understood each other and respected each other. Our parents liked each other and there were many happy days when her mother and she came to stay at our house. Then, she and I, and sometimes the boy cousin, ranged all over the place and the fields and played nicely and happily together. The psychoanalysts might well find in my happy play hours with her the development of a deep-seated need which it took many years to fill again. I think that my dual conception of women came from this far back. At six, I was fully aware that there were two kinds, with two different statuses.

Culture of Family and Play Group

Two different aspects of the cultural content of family and play group seemed to affect significantly the writers of our case records. One was the similarity or dissimilarity of family culture and play group culture, so far as nativity, religion, race, and socioeconomic status were concerned. The other was the actual content of play activities within the play groups themselves. This section will be devoted to a brief consideration of each.

THE RELATIONSHIPS BETWEEN FAMILY CULTURE AND
PLAY GROUP CULTURE

Three patterns emerged in the reports on group cultures.

One was that of a child living in a very homogeneous neighborhood in which the values, attitudes, interests, and general way of life of all the families coincided. The children attended the same school and, with their parents, the same church. Family, school, and church all reinforced each other in the acculturation of the children, and in the same manner. It almost goes without saying that the content of the play group was a close reflection of unicultural upbringing. There was, of course, some conflict between family and play group, based on "misbehavior" as interpreted by parents. There was little resentment against parents because of this, however, since the children all *knew* what was the approved way to behave and play. They broke the rules sometimes, and they expected to be punished for it. As adults, they commented on "the comfort of cultural consistency." "We always knew where we stood, what we shouldn't do, and what would happen if we did. There was no confusion in our minds." "It was not as if we were children *against* parents or children *against* each other. We all pulled together, amicably, and once in a while us kids would have a spat or decide to kick over the traces." The case of Bill, cited earlier, is an excellent illustration of such a pattern. The whole neighborhood was young, family-minded, social, college-oriented, of similar socioeconomic status. Bill, as a college student, still has as his closest friends some of his preschool playmates. Two are classmates at the same university. One is to be best man at his wedding after graduation. Bill is a conscientious, relaxed, self-assured young man, who says, in his own words, that he believes something about the continuities in his group experiences has resulted in making him comfortable and happy.

A second pattern was that in which the neighborhood was culturally divided into at least two distinct groups. Here the children were "told" with whom they could and could not play. Sometimes they were told by their own parents; at other times, they were rejected by the parents of the children with whom they wanted to play; and again, by those children themselves. The meaning of these divisions to children seemed to depend upon the specific group to which they belonged (high or low status, and majority or minority group) and the availability of playmates whom they liked within their own group. Striking contrasts appeared. Horace, for instance (the little Negro boy who was mentioned formerly), was of minority-group status in a sharply divided neighborhood; but he had his own social resources and cultural homogeneity within his own group. Now that he attends a university that is of heterogeneous make-up and liberal attitude, Horace preserves his social separatism of his own accord, with no resentment, and with self-confidence. A Catholic girl, however, who was the only child of her faith and age in a neighborhood divided between Catholics and strong anti-Catholics, did not have such a relatively easy adjustment. Under pressure of their parents, the other children rejected her from their play group. She was alone and lonely until her parents finally sent her to a parochial school. There she found that, though her religion was accepted, her person was not. She did not know how to get along with children—only with adults. She favored the Sisters and the Sisters favored her. This strengthened the notion of the other students that she was a "square." She relates that it took her years to find friends of her own age and to get over her hatred of Protestants. Then there was also the girl, in a divided neighborhood, who was a member of the minority group. This group, however, was superior in socioeconomic and educational status to the majority group. Her parents would not let her play with the children in the latter group; but the children in her own seemed "stuffy and cold" to her. She was intrigued by the adventuresome play of the others, and was determined to avail herself of it whenever possible. This resulted in constant intrafamily conflict and, during adolescence especially, a very rebellious girl. She is attracted only by peers of whom her parents do not approve, and is happy to be living away from home so that she can "get out from under."

The third pattern existed in "neighborhoods" which should not accurately be called by that name. They were found chiefly in urban areas of dense population whose make-up was so heterogeneous that there were few, sometimes no, cultural ties between the individual families. It was as if each family lived on its own cultural island. The play groups consisted of some rather exotic cultural combinations. Parents exerted little or no pressure. The children sorted themselves out. It was under such circumstances that the aforementioned "gangs" emerged even in preschool years. They ranged from the gangs that played tricks on each other, through the ones that vied for play localities and equipment, to several gangs that were surprisingly rough and vicious for children so young. It was in these situations that writers commented variously: "I learned that you had to be rough to make your own way," "It didn't pay to be alone, you needed some pal with you," "I think my fear of tough people stems from those gangs. I always avoid anyone who looks tough," and "My feeling has always been that if you aren't sharp you'll be outsmarted."

ACTIVITIES WITHIN THE PLAY GROUP

All of life is a learning process in which each new experience adds to the individual's cultural acquisitions. This is a selective process, however, and each individual learns only certain specific elements, or levels, of the wealth of cultural accumulations in his society. The specific selection is limited by the actual life experience of each person. In the family, the child learns his own family's version of the culture. In the play group, he is immersed in the content of children's activities.

Children's play is a direct reflection of the behavior and knowledge of the adult society. In a simple society, such as a fishing or agricultural tribe, one can fairly easily predict the forms that play will take—there are so few roles, behavior patterns, and forms of activity. In a complex society, this is not so; and the learning process, through play, is much more varied.

This proved to be so with our cases. In group activities, the children learned very different modes of behavior during their preschool years. The variations were so many that only a few are selected to illustrate some points on the gamut.

Andy, the five-year-old son of an urban minister, was set upon by the local "gang"—first- and second-grade boys. They had thought the "minister's kid" would be an easy mark. Andy, however, was wiry and strong, fought back, and took his beating bravely. Instead of becoming a scapegoat, he achieved high status among this band of youngsters whose sole activity was composed of devising ways to throw stones at automobiles and through windows without getting caught. Aided by an older gang, some members of which had already become acquainted with the Juvenile Court, the play group taught the minister's son a great deal about the law and its evasion, and the excitement of "getting away with it." Andy says that he is the "black sheep" of his family. In school, he perpetually got into trouble for cheating. He said, "I knew it was wrong, but it's like a game and I get away with it more often than not. Even in college, I was up before the executive committee; but they don't do much to a minister's son."

In contrast:

Bill, who lived in an education-minded community, reported that most of his preschool play was "intellectual in nature." All the parents stimulated all the children, educationally. In their play, they taught each other the ABC's; how to count; the fundamentals of reading and spelling. When this group started to school together, they were well advanced over the rest of the students. They were soon set apart as the leading student group—academically speaking. They remained so through elementary and secondary school. Bill recognized, as time went on, that he was not exactly a brilliant student. The work became increasingly hard for him. He applied himself very conscientiously, however, because he could not lose his status nor let his clique down. At present, with two members of his preschool group still in his own class, he is devoting all his energies to making "at least a B average," and is quite confident that he can do it.

One girl writes:

I spent all my days, before I went to school, playing house with my friends. We had dolls, and paper dolls, and kittens and puppies for the babies. We had all kinds of tiny housekeeping equipment—even a real electric stove on which we cooked real food, and a little hand sewing machine with which we made clothes for our dolls. We bathed our babies, took them for walks in their coaches, fed them (I had a hollow doll that had to be broken open once to remove the decayed food!), and I nursed them when they were sick.

And finally, another girl describes her preschool play in this way:

We did *everything*. We went "bird watching" in the woods and on nature hunts, and we drew what we had seen and collected specimens in albums. We gave our own little block parties, and sold lemonade in hot weather. We grew plants in eggshells, and in the winter we sledded, built snowmen, and knitted little wool square for blankets for the Red Cross. We even tried to sell War Bonds, but we weren't very successful at that.

Added Observations

Up to this point, this study has attempted to describe some of the general aspects of child development as influenced by the structure, process, and content of the preschool play-group situation. It seems pertinent to comment further on two observations made during analysis of the materials.

SCHOOL ADJUSTMENT

Without having been asked to report on school adjustment, 36 out of the 50 cases did so. To them, their school adjustment clearly related to absence or presence of a play group and to the make-up and content of it. Since this has already been suggested in excerpts from case records, a very brief summary of what they reported will suffice here.

1. When the respondent was older than his playmates and the leader of them, and had only younger siblings, he had to cope with the problem of his "bossiness" in social relations at school.

2. When he was the baby of his play group, and was babied at home, his problems were those of establishing relations of equality among his age peers at school and of not being overly dependent upon classmates and teachers.

3. The child who had played, in family and neighborhood group, only with children of his own sex found some difficulties in adjusting to schoolmates of the opposite sex.

4. In the case of a child without siblings or playmates, entering a classroom with a number of other children was usually "terrifying."

5. The child who was used to playing with others of his own age and of both sexes found the transition to the classroom to be quite easy, as a rule.

6. Finally, the activity content of the play group, as it prepared the child, or did not prepare him, for participation in school learning, affected his interest, his status, and his adjustment in the school situation.

CHANGES IN PRESCHOOL PLAY GROUP

Twelve of our cases changed their play-group situations with a change of residence during their preschool days. These cases gave added conviction of the meaning of such groups to young children, for all of them mentioned the change as a real life crisis.

In seven of the cases, the move was a great relief. There had been no playmates available, or only wholly unsuitable ones. Here the move was spoken of as the beginning of better times or better adjustment. In four cases, the writers thought that their parents had made the move with this specific purpose in mind.

The other five cases were not so fortunate. They were "torn up by the roots" from their best friends and constant companions, to find loneliness, bad influences, or, at best, very poor substitutes for what they once had. All five of these mentioned that they could not find satisfactory associations until some time after they started school and got into some kind of amiable group once more.

Summary

1. The term *peer* is used in this chapter to mean another child, that is, a nonadult. The peer group is an association of children or youth that operates in the child-youth world, and the chief concern of its members is with each other.

2. The preschool play group, the subject of this chapter, is the first peer group of a child. It is informal, relatively free from adult supervision, and is unique in that it is made up for the most part of whatever number and kind of children are available in the immediate neighborhood.

3. The play group, like any social situation, is composed of a specific structure, interactive process, and cultural content. The meaning of these to the development of any particular child is related to his experiences in his own home, that is, to his family situation.

4. The following factors seem to be significant for the development of personality and behavior patterns: (a) size of family and size of play group; (b) sex of siblings and of play-group members; (c) age of sibling and available playmates; (d) the relationship of patterns of interaction, and of cultural content, between family and play group; and (e) the specific activities content within the play group.

5. There are indications that a child's school adjustment may be related to the combined natures of his family and his preschool peer group.

Chapter *27*

Later Age Peer Groups

The child's introduction into the social world outside the family begins early in life, as pointed out in the preceding chapter. Moreover, it is customarily a gradual process, involving informal and temporary association, usually for play purposes, with other children. By the time the child reaches a certain age, however, varying from the eighth to the twelfth year, these peer groups become more definite, more stable, and, for the child, more important. It is the purpose of the present chapter to survey: (1) some examples of such later age groups; (2) selected characteristics of peer groups; (3) their role in child development; and (4) differentials in the child's experience with peer groups.

Some Later Age Groups

THE CLIQUE

After the twelfth year, when social distinctions begin to manifest themselves in the child's life, references appear with increasing frequency to "our crowd," "our set," and so on. In recent years, the term *clique* has been used in sociological literature to designate this type of peer group.

A clique may be defined as a small, intimate social participation group consisting of persons of the same social status and in agreement concerning the exclusion of other individuals from the group. Some students of the clique, like Davis and the Gardners,[1] differentiate between the small or clique proper and the extended clique, the latter including a somewhat larger group with whom one is willing to participate, whose opinions matter, but with whom association is not intimate.

A clique has a definite membership which may vary in number from 2 to as many as 30. It may or may not be age-graded, and it may be uni-

[1] Allison Davis, B. B. Gardner, and Mary R. Gardner, *Deep South,* University of Chicago Press, Chicago, 1941, p. 138.

sexual or bisexual. Its organization is informal. It has no explicit rules of entrance or exit. The bond which holds it together is intimacy of interaction among the members, a strong sense of solidarity, and a common behavior pattern. Its significance for its members on the emotional side is very great. This expresses itself principally in two ways. First, as between members, it involves strong feelings of friendship and of responsibility to render mutal assistance in case of need; second, in regard to other groups and outside demands, the clique is given preference, even over the families of its members.

The clique operates primarily as an instrument of the class structure. It is essentially a prestige device to achieve, maintain, or confirm class status. It is most important at the upper-class levels, where it functions informally and intimately. In the middle classes, cliques are more formal, restrained, and conventional. Members participate in many ways, but to a more limited degree than at the upper-class levels. Middle-class cliques are more casual and are often formally organized. Lower-class boys and girls, it is significant to note, do not participate in cliques as a rule, having neither the time, leisure, social graces, social interests, nor home opportunities. This variation of clique operation is highly significant because it confirms the role of the clique in class functioning. Cliques operate constantly in school, athletic, and social activities. They are particularly favored by social climbers, who seek to utilize them to gain constant identification with a higher status group. The life of the clique, however, is generally not of long duration.

THE GANG

The concept of the gang, as it has been developed in sociological literature, is based upon conflict. This has been true throughout the period of its serious study. Almost a half century ago, McCormick wrote of the gang as a conflict group: "A gang can never thrive without another gang to fight with."[2] Similarly, Puffer, writing in 1905, defined a gang in terms of "the conflict test."[3] It is in the work of Thrasher, foremost among modern students of the gang, that this conflict concept is most definitely emphasized. Thrasher defines a gang as "an interstitial group originally formed spontaneously, and then integrated through conflict" (p. 57). "When it becomes a conflict group it becomes a gang" (p. 30). "To become a true gang the group as a whole must move through space (linear action) and eventually . . . must meet some hostile element which precipitates conflict" (p. 54).[4]

[2] William McCormick, *The Boy and His Clubs,* Fleming H. Revell Company, New York, 1912.
[3] J. Adams Puffer, "Boy's Gangs," *Pedagogical Seminary,* June, 1905, p. 175.
[4] Frederic M. Thrasher, *The Gang,* 2nd rev. ed., University of Chicago Press, Chicago, 1936.

Current analyses identify the gang as a more integrated and, in a sense, a more formal group than the clique. It tends to have a longer life, and as a result of its greater experience it develops more in the way of tradition and morale. The bond of solidarity is often strong, but membership is less exclusive and more capable of being earned than in the clique. Its objectives tend more in the direction of activity, even if socially not acceptable, than is the case with the clique. Its greater concreteness tends to express itself through formal symbols, such as names, slogans, passwords, grips, uniforms, and so on.

The term *gang* is the victim of guilt by association. It is used most often in connection with crime and various forms of delinquent behavior. There are at least four reasons for this. First has been the constant reference in the daily press to gangs and their criminal activities, with the result that the term *gangster* has become synonymous in the public mind with criminal. Second was the conclusion of various scientific studies of crime, which showed that it is so largely a gang operation. Solitary individuals do commit crime, but by far the greater part of it is a companionship affair. Third was the fact that the gang was viewed as a leisure-time phenomenon during a period when leisure time was increasing and was being studied primarily from the standpoint of cleansing it from the "stain" of antisocial behavior. Finally, there has been the growth of the school of Gestalt psychology, with its insistence upon seeing the delinquent or other behavior case in his configurational setting. The result of these and other factors was the crystallization of a general attitude that a gang is a group whose membership is to be identified, whose behavior is to be controlled, and whose existence is to be terminated.

In the last few years, the larger and more normal aspects of these peer groups have come to be recognized by students of social behavior. It is now realized that there are other peer groups than antisocial gangs, and their function in the lives of growing boys and girls is both natural and important. In other words, these peer groups take form for the most part naturally, even if at times riotously like weeds, in the area between the family group and such later adult institutions as the state, industry, or the church.

Selected Characteristics of Peer Groups

Peer groups, like the boys and girls who compose them, are singularly individual in many respects. Each is a separate sociological phenomenon; each is, in some way or other, unique. From the study of individual cases, however, certain generalizations concerning the development of these groups may be made, and these are noted briefly.

PEER GROUPS ARE A SOCIAL PRODUCT

Earlier, there was considerable emphasis on explaining peer groups in terms of innate traits and tendencies in the individual, such as the existence of a gang instinct; but contemporary scholarship, in both psychology and sociology, no longer accepts this point of view. Peer groups are now seen as a function of specific social situations. They seem to develop in definite and predictable ways, as a result of specific sociological factors and processes. As a social product and social situation, the peer group is a proper and important object of sociological analysis.

PEER GROUPS ARISE TO SATISFY VERY DEFINITE NEEDS

Peer groups represent the efforts of boys and girls to create a society for themselves. In part, this involves, as already pointed out, a negative impulse—to escape the supervision and domination of their elders; in part, it results from a positive effort to function with like-minded persons. "It fills a gap and affords an escape."[5] In both aspects there inheres the satisfaction, and thrill, of functioning on one's own and of participating in forms of activity which one's peers rather than their elders select. It is highly important to recognize these facts, for they mean that peer groups serve a legitimate function in the development and socialization of the child. They represent his efforts to create his own world, an experimental and practice world, to fill in the transition from family domination to adult independence. It is in this age span that peer groups function; it is for these purposes that they arise.[6]

THE DEVELOPMENT OF PEER GROUPS FOLLOWS THE CHARACTER OF THE NEED

The relation between the nature of the peer group and the type of need is shown partly in the adaptation of such groups to the age hierarchy, but much more in their adjustment to the prevailing cultural situations in which they arise and flourish. In an age span and in a cultural setting where social stratification is emphasized, the clique appears as the most important peer group. When children are younger and play is uppermost among their needs, the play group is the prevailing one. But it is in the studies of the gang that this relation is most evident. Most of the studies of the gang have emphasized it as a conflict group, emerging as a symptom of certain forms of community life. Ecologically, they have been shown to "congregate in interstitial areas, that is, in areas which

---

[5] *Ibid.*, p. 38.
[6] William E. Martin and Celia B. Stendler, *Child Development*, Harcourt, Brace & Company, Inc., New York, 1953, pp. 444 ff.

represent fissures and breaks in the social organization, and in which all kinds of debris and foreign matter tend to congregate."[7]

We have thought of these gangland areas as urban industrial frontier conditions. The gang as a conflict group is a manifestation of frontier conditions. This fact serves to explain the widespread prevalence of adult gangs in American history as growing out of the unsettled grouping of diverse elements, inadequate social controls, and the ease of escape from authority and settled community life which characterized frontier life. As the American frontier moved westward, it witnessed the recurrent development of a great variety of lawless gangs. Frontiers in Australia, China, Mexico, and Russia have similarly been the habitat of lawless gangs.[8]

RACE, NATIONAL ORGIN, AND RELIGIOUS ASPECTS

Contemporary urban conditions, suggestive of the unsettled frontier conditions of an earlier era, can be found in many cities today. These arise out of the conglomeration of races, national origin, and religious groups which live side by side in our American cities, with many points of contact, invasion, resistance, and withdrawal. Distinctions and preferences between these elements manifest themselves early in life—in the play groups and cliques formed to include some and exclude others. It is in the gang, however, as a conflict group, that cleavages of this kind are most clearly revealed.

At least four significant generalizations may be made concerning the role of such factors in gang development. First, being found most frequently in first- and second-generation immigrant areas, gangs appear more often among the Polish, Italian, Irish, etc., than among such older groups as the Swedish and the Germans. Second, gang formation and rivalry often result from the carry-over of Old World antagonisms to the New World. The bitter enmity between Jews and Poles in Europe is transplanted to our cities, and when anti-Semitism flares in Europe its echoes become increasingly clear here. Even the animosities in the Orient, between Syrian and Assyrian Persians, are brought to Chicago, according to Thrasher.[9] Third, territorial clashes between nationality groups that have become segregated into relatively homogeneous groups often flare forth and at times develop into traditional feuds which are continued on a territorial basis after the originally antagonistic elements have lost their distinctive identity. Fourth, race riots, growing out of the expansion of Black Belts in various northern cities, have gang reverber-

---

[7] Frederic M. Thrasher, "The Gang as a Symptom of Community Disorganization," *Journal of Applied Sociology,* January, 1926, pp. 3–21.

[8] Frederic M. Thrasher, "Gangs," *Encyclopaedia of the Social Sciences,* Vol. VI, p. 564.

[9] Thrasher, *The Gang,* p. 197.

ations. According to Bradford Chambers, who has investigated juvenile gangs in New York, Boston, Philadelphia, and other cities:

Today gang wars are based to a large extent on racial and religious hatreds and frustrations. It is in the borderline districts of diverse racial and religious groupings and within racially segregated areas that the gangs glory in battle; it is in these neighborhoods that adolescents are being killed. In Manhattan, gang warfare takes place almost exclusively in uptown areas, where the over-crowded Harlem Negroes and Puerto Ricans are pushing their way into better housing areas. Recently these groups have been moving into the Bronx, and strife has broken out there too. In 1939, when jobs became abundant, Man-hattan Negroes began to acquire the income necessary to move out of the re-stricted slum districts. As the war brought higher wages and a fresh wave of migration from the South, the Negro influx into white areas was accelerated. It was about then that the conflict gangs came into being. Before that time, street corner clubs in upper Manhattan had served mainly as outlets for athletic ac-tivity, as the groups farther downtown still do. When the traditional colored districts began to expand, however, the white boys' clubs, led by the Hancocks, the Rainbows and the Irish Dukes, turned to conflict.[10]

PEER GROUPS HAVE NATURAL HISTORIES

The conditions which call peer groups forth, the experiences they undergo, the leadership which evolves, the treatment given them by out-side agencies, the opposition they encounter, all combine to determine the specific course which their histories will take.

Peer groups arise spontaneously in most cases. That is to say, they are not consciously planned, but take form as children happen to gather at certain places and, because of certain common interests and needs, begin to function collectively. In many instances, their life is short; often the group bond is very loose; there is a continuous ebb and flow in the mem-bership; conflicting personalities and contrasting diversions arise and break up whatever unity may previously have developed. For many children, and in various areas, the very conditions which create a strong need for peer groups make their strong and relatively long-lived develop-ment impossible. Here we must note the importance of such factors as the high degree of mobility of many children and their families, the fact that children are subject to various interfering pressures and restraints from their families and other adult groups, and the fact that childhood interests are short-lived and often change with considerable rapidity.

On the other hand, the reverse of all this may happen. Play groups are usually thought of as rather transitory, yet the author is familiar with one such group that developed in a stable neighborhood among children of the same approximate age and has persisted for 13 years at the present writing. Under favorable conditions for the development of peer groups,

[10] Bradford Chambers, "The Juvenile Gangs of New York," *American Mercury*, April, 1946, pp. 480–481.

a strong we-feeling may appear, leadership may emerge, satisfactory common interests may be found, a strongly integrated organization may take form, and a heritage of memories and tradition may accumulate.

Thrasher has shown these contrasting courses of development in the natural history of the gang. In many instances, only a diffuse type of gang appears, with little solidarity and group loyalty, and a short life in point of time; in a lesser number of cases, a solidified type appears, with a longer history, a stronger morale, and a higher degree of integration. Either type, but more especially the latter, may in turn take a variety of forms; it may either veer in the direction of the more conventional club whose activities are socially approved and whose life is incorporated into the structure of the community, or it may become an integrated fighting machine, specializing in some one or several forms of delinquent behavior.

This concept of a natural history of peer groups has significant implications, particularly with reference to their treatment by family and community forces. The customary method of approach has been the direct frontal attack, which sees the peer group as a problem per se, and its breakup or elimination as the major end to be achieved. Obviously, the proper approach must be the indirect or flank approach, which recognizes it as arising to meet definite needs and developing on the basis of conditioning factors. Such an approach offers the possibilities of conscious and constructive direction of the peer group, to the end that its socially legitimate purposes may be served.

Peer Groups and Child Development[11]

Many other features about the development, structure, life, and activities of peer groups have been investigated, and their complete analysis constitutes interesting chapters. The chief concern here, however, is with the more outstanding ways in which these groups operate in the field of child development.

RECOGNITION OF THE RIGHTS OF OTHERS

Perhaps the first and most difficult step in the socialization of the child is the recognition of the rights of others. This involves a process of social education, more particularly in the lower age brackets and principally through the medium of experience. This process begins, of course, with the child's life with his family, as a number of the earlier chapters have

[11] Complementary discussions of the influence of the peer group can be found in Martin and Stendler, *op. cit.*, pp. 450–482; Robert J. Havighurst and Bernice L. Neugarten, *Society and Education*, Allyn and Bacon, Inc., Boston, 1957, Chap. 5; Albert K. Cohen, *Delinquent Boys*, Free Press, Glencoe, Ill., 1955; and L. Joseph Stone and Joseph Church, *Childhood and Adolescence*, Random House, New York, 1957, pp. 214–222.

shown. But the family, from one standpoint, is often an unnatural or inadequate socializing group. Frequently it is too small, especially the contemporary family; its personnel is too largely adult; and all its members tend to be emotionally disposed toward a type of relationship which differs from that prevailing in society as a whole. The peer group differs in these important respects from the family group: it consists of equals, that is, persons of the same approximate age and stage of development, and there is no emotional bond of the kind that is found in the family. The peer group involves association on a normal basis with equals who are equally bent on their own interests and self-expression. It is from experience in such groups, more particularly the earlier play groups, that the child gains an understanding of the limitations which group life places upon the individual. This is the first lesson learned in living with others, and it can best, and perhaps only, be learned through experience.

Early in this experience, common rules based on common experience begin to develop. These rules are requisite conditions for the existence of the group; the mere fact of group existence and action calls them forth. In part they are inventions of the group members, devised to meet a specific situation or problem; in part they are borrowed from other groups of children, usually older ones; in part they are obtained from or imposed by adults.

The acceptance of these rules, as in play groups, is characteristically slow and sporadic. For some years, usually between the third and the seventh year, the child partly accepts them and partly does not. Thus one sees children of this age playing, now in groups and in observance of the rules; now, off by themselves. Sometime after the seventh year, Piaget identifies a stage of *incipient coöperation,* in which "all begin to concern themselves with the question of mutual control and of unification of the rules."[12] Although some degree of agreement is reached, the rules remain rather vague and it is not until the eleventh or twelfth year that the codification of rules is made. Then, too, comes their acceptance by mutual consent. A child must respect the rules of the peer group if he wishes to belong. "This is the way we play the game." Coöperative teamwork develops, and the requirements for participation are now socialized.

Utilizing the terminology of morals, Piaget develops an interesting contrast between the morality of constraint and that of coöperation. Morality of constraint consists of a series of objective duties based on respect for persons in authority. It is imposed upon the child from above, and is accepted because of the prestige and power of its source. Acceptance is much like that of language, as one of the realities imposed by the adult world. Morality is a duty. The right thing to do is to obey the will of the parent; the wrong thing is to have a will of one's own. Morality of co-

[12] Jean Piaget, *The Moral Judgment of the Child,* Kegan Paul, London, 1932, p. 17.

operation rests upon mutual understanding between equals. It involves autonomy of conformity. Free from adult supervision, the child inspires his own rules. "As soon as the individual escapes from the domination of age, he tends toward coöperation as the normal form of social equilibrium."[13] These rules are accepted because the child realizes that they are necessary for the continuance of group life. As a result, he imposes these rules upon himself. Consciousness of a sense of justice now appears, and this sense of justice "requires nothing more for its development than the mutual respect and solidarity which holds among children themselves."[14]

THE PEER GROUP AS AN AGENCY OF CONTROL

Complementary to what has just been said is the fact that the peer group has great importance as an agency in controlling the behavior of its members. To be accepted, members must conform to the standards of the group. The peer group is a primary group among equals, its relationships are intimate in character, there is relative familiarity, and the members are closely identified with each other. As a result, they become very sensitive to each other's approval and disapproval, which means that group pressure upon the individual is great. Ogburn and Nimkoff point out two principles regarding the primary group in this connection: first, that the group frequently exerts a more effective control over the conduct of its members than can an outside individual charged with special authority; and second, that the most efficient regulator of all is a group of persons of the same age and interests.[15] These are commonplace facts in the sociology of primary group life; what happens is that most parents, and sometimes students of child development, fail to appreciate that primary groups among children operate in the same way as they do among adults. Several aspects of their operation will be noted briefly.

The peer group imposes its own rules or codes, that is, those which center around its activities and purposes. Piaget has shown this process in the play group, as has Murphy in her excellent study of a nursery-school group.[16] In fact, a large part of the purpose and success of the present-day nursery school lies in its power to control effectively the behavior of its young members. Davis and the Gardners[17] have emphasized this in particular about the clique. Each clique has a common behavior pattern (p. 168). The behavior of its members is controlled, in their relations both with each other and with other persons (p. 169). Being an instrument of the class structure, the clique determines with what members of

---

[13] *Ibid.*, p. 99.

[14] *Ibid.*, pp. 195–196.

[15] W. F. Ogburn and Meyer Nimkoff, *Sociology*, Houghton Mifflin Company, Boston, 1940, p. 266.

[16] Lois Barclay Murphy, *Social Behavior and Child Personality*, Columbia University Press, New York, 1937.

[17] Davis, Gardner, and Gardner, *op. cit.*, Chaps. 7 and 9.

other cliques the member may have occasional informal and formal participation. The more stable the clique, the more marked is its control over the activities and associations of its members (pp. 169–170). Similarly, Thrasher has emphasized group control in the gang.[18] The gang, he says, is a unit which enforces its code upon its members in a variety of ways. Some of these are consciously and definitely directed, and others operate at the unconscious and unreflective level; but in virtually all cases there are emphases upon the common primary group virtues and the particular attitudes which focus about the group. Finally, we might include as examples of group control the various developments of the honor system, as in student examinations or in boys' reformatories.

Special mention should be made of the peer group's control over the attitude and behavior of its members toward persons outside the group. This has been most clearly emphasized in the case of the clique, but it is prevalent in all peer groups. Particularly evident is the control of attitudes toward adults with whom members of the peer groups come most often or most closely in contact, such as teachers, parents, and policemen. Since one purpose of many such groups is to ascribe the status of alien to adults with whom they are concerned, the next step often is to identify these adults as enemies, until at times a comprehensive pattern of behavior toward some adult may become the heart of the group's *esprit de corps*. Most persons can find ready illustrations of this in their own school experiences, usually in the junior or senior high school period. Proprietors of small shops in the neighborhood of a school—their importance in the social development of young boys and girls has never been adequately appreciated or studied—often play a significant role in the development of the attitudinal patterns of peer groups. This is well illustrated in the following case:

The "Union Avenue Crowd" had as their hangout a candy and tobacco store at Third and Union Avenue, which was two blocks away from the senior high school. Because of its nearness to the school, it was a convenient place to gather until the last minute before school time, as well as after sessions. Early in October, 19—, talk among the "crowd" that gathered there began to focus upon a new physics teacher. Apparently without experience as a teacher or facility as a disciplinarian, trouble developed between him and several members of the crowd. The proprietor of the shop was a former circus performer and small bit actor, with some special ability in mimicry. Having seen the new physics teacher, he was quick to seize upon several of his mannerisms as affording a special outlet for his powers of mimicry. This greatly delighted the crowd, and suggested a pattern of mimicry of the new teacher which was carried subtly and surreptitiously into the classroom by the more adept performers among the boys. The teacher's further disciplinary attempts only aggravated matters. The proprietor, because of his role as original imitator, was drawn increasingly, and

---

[18] Thrasher, *The Gang*, Chap. 15.

as an active agent, into the tension between the teacher and the crowd. The matter subsequently passed from the control of the physics teacher to the school's administrative heads who, ignorant of the role of the shopkeeper and the existence of a definitely unified peer group, meted out disciplinary measures upon a few of the boys in the class.

Again, the peer group serves to correct extremes or deviations of behavior among its members, thus illustrating the well-known sociological principle that the primary group exerts a conservative influence on behavior. Among peer groups, these deviations are generally the ones that are out of line with the age, sex, or class range of its members. We might speak of them as the usual run of adolescent vagaries. For the boy who is a noisy braggart, nothing more subduing can be devised than close association with other boys, equally braggart if possible. The girl whose endless poses before the mirror are "a trial and affliction" to her parents can be cured, if at all, by several healthy young male extroverts. The lad who always insists on having his own way needs to run with the pack. Even more complex problems can be handled most effectively by the peer group, as Bill's case illustrates.

Bill was a late adolescent who began to run around with a girl who not only lived on the other side of the railroad tracks, but who had most of the traits associated with that oft-used phrase. Bill's family was upper class, Bill was personally most attractive, and his mother knew the power of a peer group. Calling Bill to her, she explained with disarming friendliness that she had heard of his new girl and wanted to meet her. Wouldn't he bring her to the house, and to make it less formal, she would invite a few of his favorite friends. Upon securing Bill's wondering and semireluctant consent, the mother proceeded to promote, secretly, a gala event, to which she invited all of Bill's extended clique. Bill's relations with the new girl just barely survived until the end of the party.

One final fact about the peer group as an agency of control over its members requires emphasis, and this is the priority it has in the mind of the child. Careful students of child development have emphasized repeatedly that it exercises a greater degree of control than the family. "An adolescent member of a boys' or girls' clique," write Warner and Lunt,[19] "will sometimes defy his or her family to maintain the respect of clique mates, should the interests of the two groups run counter to each other." Davis and the Gardners conclude that the clique is a more powerful mechanism for controlling behavior than the family because they too find that, when confronted by conflicts between their families and their cliques, adolescents respond positively to the demands of their cliques and repudiate those of their families. Obviously, this is even truer in the case of a more integrated peer group such as a gang. Parents often fail to

[19] W. Lloyd Warner and Paul Lunt, *The Social Life of a Modern Community*, Yale University Press, New Haven, 1941, p. 351.

understand the logic of this, and berate the child as disobedient, incorrigible, or ungrateful. The problem becomes particularly keen when the family's culture differs from that of the peer group, as happens so continually and inevitably as a by-product of cultural change and residential mobility. Viewed objectively, the child's prior rating of his peer group is entirely normal and natural. Like calls unto like the world over.

THE PEER GROUP AS A SECURITY DEVICE

The hold of the peer group upon its members is further strengthened in many cases by the very distinctive role which it plays in the modern urban area. By this we refer to the sense of safety and security which it gives the child. To understand the meaning and import of this, certain facts concerning the modern urban community and family need to be brought together here for brief recapitulation. The modern urban center tends to be large. The 1950 Census shows that almost 3 out of every 10 persons in the United States live in the 14 metropolitan areas with populations in excess of one million. School buildings and school populations tend to be large. The old-fashioned primary-group community has largely disappeared. Urban life tends to be impersonal. The families of children who go to school together often do not know one another. Populations are mobile, which means that families and their children are coming and going constantly. Among other things, this involves constant dislocations and readjustments of personal relationships among school children. In certain areas and among selected groups, the percentage of population turnover is particularly high. This is true usually of families whose children have, as a whole, more than their share of other problems and difficulties. Combined with all these is the further fact, previously referred to, that the present-day child comes from a small family, which means few if any siblings upon whom to rely.

One result of all this is that the peer group, in one form or other, becomes very important to the child because it gives security to its members. An obvious illustration is the necessity in many areas for white, Negro, gentile, and Jewish children each to form groups, both for physical safety and for psychological assurance. But there are selective forces other than those which are racial or religious, and the child who stands out because of other characteristics has his problems, too. Moreover, the racketeering practices rife among adults in the past generation have seeped down into the lower age brackets. There are organized gangs in schools which levy taxes for "protection," systematically "invite" other children to "share" their lunches or lunch money, "borrow" written work, and engage in various other similar practices. Against threats and violations of this kind the isolated child is helpless; the peer group offers something, even for those with no immediate problems, that is both important and comforting. Considerations of this kind are often in the background when the child, forced into the cruel dilemma of choice, stands by his peer group against the dictates of his school or home, or both.

The Peer Group as a Cultural Entity

Each peer group tends to have a culture which is distinctly its own. More specifically, this means that every such group has its own range of activities, its own interests, its own values and choices, which unite to form the social pattern of the group. The development of this cultural identity begins early in the child's life, with the formation of the play group. The composition of the play group and the content of the play indicate the first steps in this direction; the clique, the gang, and other groups merely carry on at a subsequent level.

The culture of the peer group is in large measure a reflection of the culture of its members and the community from which they come. "The play patterns of the children," writes Murphy in her study of a nursery-school group, "are a mirror of the culture which surrounds them, and this culture provides the raw material for their activity and fantasy."[20] Continuing, she points out that "if we look at these play patterns of the children as an indication of what the children are assimilating from their culture, we find a few outstanding interests predominating over a variety of miscellaneous ones." She groups these in the following way:

1. Domestic patterns, including playing house, furnishing a house, cooking, eating, and having tea parties, taking care of babies, and being fathers and mothers.
2. Selling and buying.
3. Activities connected with transportation, riding in automobiles or trains, being engineers, putting in gas or air, sailing boats.
4. Punishing, playing policeman, and gun play in general.
5. Burning and playing fireman.
6. Killing and dying.
7. Playing the part of legendary persons, Santa Claus, Cinderella, and above all the Big Bad Wolf.[21]

In general, then, the play of children tends to follow the adult patterns. One can readily grasp the national aspects of this. In Spain, children play at bullfighting; in Fascist countries, at war games; in England, at cricket; in America, at baseball. The principle is similar for occupational, class, and community patterns. When 8-year-old Mildred plays at making a call and says to her playmate: "Are you following the hounds this fall?" or "Does your husband still spend all his pay envelope on drink?" we know a great deal of the cultural background of the particular group involved. It is this basic fact that has led psychiatrists to utilize the play

[20] Murphy, *op. cit.*, p. 60.
[21] *Ibid.*, p. 63.

technique in their analysis of children with behavior problems. The child brings into the peer group the culture of his family and community as clearly as he brings in the mud on his shoes.

Certain types of children are particularly important in fixing the cultural pattern of their peer groups. In studying the spread of a specific culture trait in a group, Murphy concludes that personalities "unusually intelligent and sensitive to the patterns of adults and aggressive in their social responses, were pivotal points in what might be seen as a process of cultural diffusion."[22] Similarly, the role of the child in the group is highly significant.

Recognition of the role of the peer group's cultural background in determining its pattern of social behavior enables one to understand the role of the gang in criminal behavior. Gangs, it has been pointed out, are characteristic of interstitial areas, of intramural frontiers. They arise from the more or less spontaneous effort of boys to create a society for themselves in age spans and social areas where no others adequate to their needs exist. In developing their gangs, boys cannot go beyond their experiences and the observations and activities of their families and other elders, "and hence their codes and chosen activities must be studied with reference to the moral codes and activities they meet in the communities where they live."[23] In other words, just as the gang as a conflict peer group is a symptom of community disorganization, so it is a reflection of the culture of these disorganized areas.

The adult patterns of behavior in the areas in which most delinquent gangs arise and operate are dominated by or literally sprinkled with crime and vice. Many adults are connected with or interested in various forms of racketeering or "easy-money" pursuits of one form or another. Gambling is prevalent, as are stealing, the receipt of stolen goods, begging, panhandling, and the like. These areas will be considered more fully in the next chapter. Reference here is confined to the fact that in so many of these gang-breeding sections not only the overt activities but the argot, the current terminology, the subjects discussed, and all the forms and forces of community conditioning are likely to center around matters which the larger society labels as anti- or non-social.

Furthermore, these areas are isolated from the culture of other areas. The gang member does not have access to the cultural heritages of the dominant social order. The reasons for this are obvious but are often disregarded. In part they are ethnic, the interstitial areas in which gangs flourish being for the most part first- and second-generation immigrant ones, or areas of first entrance for native migrating groups, such as the Negro, Oriental, Mexican, and so on. In part, also, there are class factors, for most of the population of these areas represents a segregation of

[22] *Ibid.*, p. 132.
[23] Thrasher, *The Gang*, p. 255.

lower-class persons. Finally, the reasons are developmental in part, for these gangs consist of individuals who are merely in the lower stages of a process of urbanization and social achievement through which other elements in the population have passed successfully. But for the time being, the social isolation and the socially deviant behavior of these sections and their inhabitants combine to call forth philosophies which seek to justify their present social patterns, and these, too, come to be absorbed by the younger boy and girl. Delinquent gangs, then, are a natural product of the social education process in areas where the prevailing patterns are antisocial.

A suggestive illustration of the foregoing is the concept of the socialized delinquency behavior syndrome pattern advanced by Hewitt and Jenkins. Three ideas are basic to this concept. One is the fact that the individual children in many delinquent gangs are well socialized in the sense that they get along well with other children of their own type. Second, the group patterns of behavior to which they are loyal are directed, not against specific persons per se, but against formal property rights and conduct codes established by the larger society. Third, this group pattern is the product of the environment of the gang. In this environment many social deviation pressures are exerted. The homes of these children are located in deteriorated neighborhoods where traditions of delinquency and disrespect for the law are most likely to flourish. Their families offer little in the way of training in conforming to the rules of the larger society.[24] This antisocial group pattern explains the difficulty of dealing with gangs of this kind, as noted by Chambers in his study of New York gangs. According to him:

> Juvenile conflict gangs are non-conformist groups. They shy away from supervision. They shun organized agency programs. In fact, they thrive on independence from all outside discipline and authority. Settlement houses, big boys' clubs, and other youth-serving agencies naturally find it difficult to compete with the wild, carefree life of gangs. In the case of those gangs that are enticed into agency buildings, the agencies complain that they disrupt programs and that they have a destructive influence on the more conformist members already within the agencies' fold. Moreover, a significant finding of the research is that case work techniques, probation and reform school treatment are unable to get far with the gangs, mainly because they cannot deal effectively with the gang member without first controlling his gang and without at the same time working to change the destructive influences and conditions within the gang boys' environment. Gang controls and attractions are strong, and one fundamental conclusion of the study is that the only way to deal with the individual gang boy is first to reach the whole gang.[25]

[24] Lester E. Hewitt and Richard L. Jenkins, *Fundamental Patterns of Maladjustment: The Dynamics of Their Origin,* printed by authority of the State of Illinois, 1946, pp. 28, 29, 43, 44.

[25] Bradford Chambers, in report on Grant No. 845 to the American Philosophical Society. Made available to the author through the kindness of Mr. Chambers.

Recently Cohen has spelled out the foregoing summary in clear detail in the area of delinquent behavior. Juvenile delinquents, he points out, are the products of a persistent subculture that is traditional in certain neighborhoods, usually of lower-class status. This subculture has its definite characteristics—malice, negativism, short-run hedonism, intolerance of restraint, and the like. This subculture envelops and conditions the development of its young, just as do other class and community subcultures.[26]

One final comment is necessary by way of warning against oversimplification in this connection. The social pattern of each peer group represents its own distinctive combinations of the culture of its members and their communities.

For many years there have been those students who have been impressed by a "novelty of behavior arising from the specific interaction or organization of a number of elements, whether inorganic, organic or mental, which thereby constitute a whole, as distinguished from their mere sum, or 'resultant.'" The simplest illustration of this idea is that of water—a combination of hydrogen and oxygen, in certain definite proportions, and under well-defined conditions, to form a liquid emergent, which exhibits very different properties, i.e., behavior, than either of its gaseous components. The existence and importance of this factor of special relatedness has been recognized by a number of thinkers of the nineteenth century, such as John Stuart Mill, Lester F. Ward, Spaulding, Wundt, and others, and various terms such as "heteropathic causation," "creative synthesis," "evolutionary naturalism," "holism," "organicism," have been used to designate it. Mr. C. L. Morgan's term "emergent evolution" has apparently found most favor among the contemporary philosophers, biologists, sociologists, and the like, who utilize the concept.[27]

For the understanding and successful control of any peer group, this distinctive nonadditive character of its cultural pattern must be recognized. For the adult who is called upon to deal with a peer group, access to this distinctive pattern is not an easy matter, for its development is in part an effort to create a life to which the adult is an alien. One of the perennial traditions in most peer groups is the unassimilable alien character of the adult. Yet what the members of the peer group tell each other about subjects which are important to them, such as sex, their teachers, their studies, and so on, often constitutes the core of the problem they present to adult society.

THE INDIVIDUAL'S ROLE IN THE PEER GROUP

Thus far the peer group has been considered as a group; it is necessary next to analyze the interactive process within the group, with special reference to the emergence of the individualized roles of its members.

---

[26] Cohen, *op. cit.*

[27] James H. S. Bossard, "Robert Ellis Thompson—Pioneer Professor in Social Science," *American Journal of Sociology*, September, 1929, pp. 246–247.

In any group containing more than two persons, distinctions and divisions arise, since the members are not equal in nature or ability, nor do they have the same relationships to all the others. Just as the child's behavior cannot be understood without knowing his particular position in the family group, so also is it necessary to know his place in the informal social grouping which he forms with other children.

Three aspects of the process by which the individual role emerges within the peer group can be noted. First, common enterprise entails division of labor. Each peer group exists for certain purposes, and the more important and enduring the group, the more specific and clearly defined these ends will be. In order to bring about their achievement, organization and leadership are necessary, as is specialization of function. Second, the members of the peer group each have their own particular traits, interests, aptitudes, and skills, on the basis of which competition among them for these specialized functions develops. The peer group is a small society, and life within it, as in all societies, is competitive. Third, in the collective experience of the group, individual assignments of roles and functions come to be assessed. A consensus or generalized conception of individual members crystallizes, on the basis of which individual roles are definitely assumed and assigned, to be conformed to or revised on the basis of still further experience. The more complex and varied its activities, the more highly organized and integrated the peer group becomes, and the more distinct and individualized these roles become, until in many such groups every member has his place, his job, and his niche in the group's life.

The status or role gained by the individual member of a peer group may be ascribed by the group on the basis of age, sex, physical appearance, physical prowess, or physical disability, in accordance with the analysis in Chapter 20. In many peer groups, however, there are a democracy of operation and a play of competition which make for a number of achieved statuses or roles. Thrasher has identified some of the better known of these specialized roles in the gang, and to a considerable extent these are typical of most peer groups.[28] Every group has its leader or leaders. If it is a play group under adult supervision, the leader may be the child who is unusually intelligent and sensitive to adult direction. If it is a social clique, the leader may be the suave and clever member who is well versed in class distinctions and traditions. If it is a fighting gang, leadership is achieved on the basis of size, strength, courage, foresight—good fighting. Most peer groups, especially at the older age levels, develop one reliable member who can be trusted to look after the details of peer activity. Here is the embryo secretary-treasurer of later organizations. Peer groups have their jealous custodians of group membership.

[28] Thrasher, *The Gang*, Chap. 17.

This is particularly noticeable in cliques. Often the custodians are members who have themselves just "shaved in," and who rather quickly become zealous keepers of the keys. Most peer groups have their "funny boys" whose behavior and, at times irresponsibility, are tolerated because of the humor they contribute or may be expected to in the future. Few such groups are without their gossips, whose special role it is to gather, dress up in interesting fashion, and distribute the latest information about persons in whom the gang is interested. The gossip columnists of today are merely an adult commercialization of this role, originally developed in peer-group experience, usually to compensate for failure in performance. Often there is a "sissy" member of the peer group, who may be assigned this status for a variety of reasons. How undesirable it is can be gathered from the rather extreme lengths to which many boys and girls will go to avoid this role. "The other kids would think me a sissy" is the key to much behavior, of both commission and omission, at certain age levels. Virtually every peer group has its loud-mouthed member, the show-off, the braggart, whose account of anything comes to be discounted by the group. Akin to this member is the aggressive member. This one is an ambitious imperialist, always reaching out for more territory, always willing to engage in a fight, but with the others doing the fighting. "Let's fight them, fellows. I'll hold your coats." Every gang, according to Thrasher—and probably most other peer groups—have their "goats." These are the boys of lower intelligence, slow of wit, and not infrequently combining some special peculiarity of manner, speech, or appearance with their subnormalities. These are the members who invariably get caught, who are often sacrificed or used as a decoy or cat's-paw by the group.

Incidentally, this same specialization of personality role in the group was illustrated in striking manner in our study of the large family system, reference to which was made in Chapter 3. When 64 groups of siblings were imposed upon each other, and analyzed for personality roles, it was found that 8 general types tended to appear, often in a relatively given order. There was the responsible one, often the first-born; the popular, sociable one, not infrequently the second-born; the socially ambitious one, usually females, third, fourth, or fifth in the order of birth; the studious one; the self-centered isolate; the irresponsible one; the chronically ill or hypochondriacal; and the "spoiled brat" or babied type.[29]

That some of these specialized roles do not seem to adults to have any particular prestige does not mean that they are so regarded by either the peer group or the individual possessors of these roles. All studies of peer groups emphasize two facts that it is important to note. First, individual

[29] James H. S. Bossard and Eleanor S. Boll, *The Large Family System,* University of Pennsylvania Press, Philadelphia, 1956, Chap. 10.

status within such a group is for most members a very real and highly important matter, bringing often keen and vivid satisfaction. Not only are these statuses achieved, but they have been gained in the child's own world. They involve recognition by his peers; and many a young boy or girl finds greater satisfaction in being the doorkeeper or errand boy for the gang than to receive the approval of adults. This role in the peer group becomes a powerful determinant in the formation of the child's conception of himself. It is for reasons of this kind, again, that an understanding of these roles is so important for parents, teachers, school attendance officers, probation officers, policemen, and others who deal habitually with children. The second fact is that peer-group status has special significance for children whose opportunities otherwise are relatively limited. The boy and girl who have not succeeded in gaining a satisfactory status within their family; whose family is nonexistent, inadequate, or in perennial conflict; whose relations with their parents and other older people at home involve a constant struggle against domination or neglect; whose school achievements are nil or unsatisfactory; whose opportunities to engage in other community activities are scant at best—all these and many other types of frustrated and underprivileged children can find in peer groups, especially conflict gangs, the opportunity for individual achievement otherwise denied. As a general rule, the less rewarding and the more drab the child's life outside of the peer group is, the more does a role within the group mean to him. Peer roles are often compensatory achievements affording great satisfaction to boys and girls.

Differentials in the Child's Experience with Peer Groups

In assessing the nature and role of peer-group situations in the process of child development, it is necessary to recognize the differences which prevail in the child's use of and experience with these groups. Two types of factors are particularly important in determining these differences.

First, there are wide variations in the number of years during which the child gives allegiance to peer groups. Keeping in mind the fact that they are transitional groups in the growing-up process, dominating the period between his social emancipation from his family and his integration into adult society, we see clearly that two variables are active in determining this time span. One is the age of emancipation from the family; the other, that of arrival at adulthood. All kinds of combinations exist, and we can readily identify from common observation types like the following. There is, for example, the child whose emancipation from the family occurs late but whose integration into the adult world takes place at the normal time. Here the period of peer-group life is relatively short. By way of contrast is the child for whom the former comes early and the latter is late. Emmy Lou, whose story is recorded in the files of the Carter Foundation, was withdrawn from family life at the age of 3, because of the death of her father. She was placed in an institution and remained there in several capacities until her twenty-sixth year, after which she made a slow and rather painful adjustment to adult life. On the whole, in analyzing the available cases, it appears that class differentials also prevail here. The lower the class status, the earlier the social emancipation from the family, and the earlier the entrance into adult life.

Second, the relative social need for peer-group activities varies to a considerable extent, and this naturally affects the child's utilization of these groups. Many details and circumstances are involved here, and these, too, seem to vary a good deal on a class basis. There are, for example, such factors as the pressure upon the child to acquire individual skills, involving music lessons, dancing lessons, art instruction, and so on, and the resultant time spent in practice; the scope and variety of family activities; and the extent to which community resources are available to the individual child. It will be recalled here that students of peer groups persistently emphasize their development as the result of children's efforts to meet needs not otherwise met. In short, the principle which operates here may be stated something like this: the number, appeal, and utilization of peer groups varies with the appeal and diversity of such competing groups as the family and the community.

If we think of the child's development in terms of process, it is evident that life in the peer group during the growing-up period is, for most children, one of life's major experiences, and that these peer-group experiences constitute one of the basic factors in the determination of the adult personality. A selected few phases of this process will be identified briefly.

To begin with, there are the children who have had no, or very little, peer-group experience. Perhaps the parents did not permit it, perhaps the circumstances of life did not, perhaps the child's traits led him to avoid it. Such children are often referred to as having had no childhood. What they have not had is experience in living and competing with and being disciplined by equals; growing up, they become adults who associate themselves first with persons much older than themselves, and subsequently, with those much younger. Having been inadequately socialized, they often are rather "difficult" individuals.

Some children make unsuccessful or painful adjustments to their peer groups so that memories of their experiences rankle and smart; but, because they do, there is often a spur to a much greater and more effective effort in the adult world. These are the persons who not infrequently turn out well, to the wonder of their adolescent friends. "I never expected him to turn out the way he did." "I didn't think he had it in him."

At times a lack of success in peer-group adjustments is found among children who mature relatively early in life, or who prematurely gain unusual insight into life situations and come to sense the serious imminence of the adult world. The adult world shines through the papier-mâché of the peer-group world. These are the young people who are impatient with adolescence. They will not take it in their stride. For this reason they become men before they learn to be boys. To become a man too soon may mean that one becomes a small man.

There are cases, of course, in which life presses hard upon youth. These are the young people who must go to work early in life, who are sobered prematurely by adult responsibilities. Perhaps they rationalize the appeal of the peer group, perhaps they actually are out of sympathy with it, perhaps they cast longing glances at it but are washed past it. When such persons attain financial success as adults, they often leave endowments or make contributions to youth activities in the community.

There are the children whose relations with peer groups are complicated unduly by their parents. The parents may be hard and unsympathetic to these groups; they may seek to keep the child away, tethering him with a silver cord; they may embarrass him whenever other children are about; they may disgrace the family name, or the home may be such that the child will not bring his associates there. Such children tend to marry early, often unwisely, or to affiliate themselves with peer groups which operate surreptitiously.

Finally, there are the children who adjust so well to peer-group life, who find so much personal satisfaction therein, that membership in them is continued unduly. Because they find in the peer group what life otherwise denies or makes too difficult for them to obtain, they cling to it. In the gang category and at the antisocial level, such persons perpetuate their gangs, shifting into various "easy-money" activities. Thus emerges the postadolescent and adult gangster. On the more conventional side, there are the people who grow up to be the joiners, the clubsters, the active organization men. Among college alumni, these are the old grads who never grow up and who insist at times on living at the "house" years after their classmates have vanished into maturity. The world is amazingly full of individuals who have not grown beyond the gang or peer-group stage.

Summary

1. The term *peer* is used in this chapter to mean another child, that is, a nonadult. The peer group is an association of children or youths that operates in the child-youth world, and the chief concern of its members is with each other.

2. Peer groups have been studied too largely in terms of one form, that

is, the gang, and in relation to antisocial behavior. This has created the idea that peer groups are vehicles of crime and delinquency. Recently their larger and more normal aspects have been recognized.

3. The peer groups chiefly discussed are the play group, which is an association, usually of younger children, with common play interests; the clique, a small, intimate social participation group, operating as an instrument of the class structure; and the gang, developed thus far in the literature chiefly as a conflict group, and the product of an interstitial setting.

4. Peer groups are singularly individual. Each is a separate sociological phenomenon. To generalize their development, it is evident that (a) they are social products, (b) they take form on the basis of age gradations, (c) they arise to meet definite needs, (d) their development follows the character of these needs, (e) they have natural histories, and (f) they often reflect racial, national, and religious distinctions of the larger society.

5. Peer groups play an important role in child development (a) through their emphasis upon the rights of others, (b) as agencies controlling their members, (c) as a security device, (d) as a cultural entity, and (e) as a determinant of personality roles.

6. The child's use of and experience with peer groups varies considerably on the basis of (a) the number of years he belongs and (b) his relative need for peer-group activities.

7. The child's life in his peer groups is one of life's major experiences, and such experience constitutes one of the basic factors in determining the adult personality.

School Situations
and Child Development

It is customary to think of the school primarily as an agency in the formal education of the child, with the emphasis chiefly upon problems of curriculum, equipment, and pedagogy. Consideration of the child and the role of the school in his social development is, from this point of view, somewhat secondary and incidental to the main objectives of effectiveness in instruction. The purpose of this chapter is to emphasize the school as a complex of social situations in which children live, compete, perform, develop attitudes, form response patterns, fail and succeed in the process of getting along in the world. Such an approach has been neglected, relatively. In the study of behavior during the past generation, overwhelming importance has been attached to home situations; yet, at an early age the child is legally required to leave his home and, for as many as 12 years, is under a legal obligation of spending the major part of his waking hours in the world of school life. Moreover, this school world is for a large proportion of today's children quite different from their family world; it is a world which the parents may not understand and with which they often are in conflict.

More specifically, two aspects of the school world are to be emphasized. First, school life consists of a series of performance situations. More prosaically put, the school is a work place to which the child goes. He is paid to do so, both by the public treasury through its expenditures for school purposes, and by his parents through their maintenance of him. These payments, both direct and indirect, may be more than a subsequent employer will pay for some years. In this workaday world the child develops work behavior patterns; certain educators, particularly in foreign systems of education, have stressed this as the most important part of the educational process. In other words, it is not so important what he studies, as it is with what attitudes and effectiveness the student learns to approach and execute his task.

In the second place, the school world is where much of the child's social life centers. Writing of Middletown, for example, the Lynds said: "The high school, with its athletics, clubs, sororities, fraternities, dances, parties and other 'extracurricular activities' is a fairly complete social cosmos in itself, and about this city within a city the social life of the intermediate generation centers. Here the social sifting devices of their elders—money, clothes, personal attractiveness, male physical prowess, exclusive clubs, elections to positions of leadership—are all for the first time set going."[1] In other words, school is where the child gains experience in social living for a number of years, learns to compete and to cooperate with his fellows, and develops habitual modes of response. Again, there are those who emphasize this aspect of the educational process, claiming that the child's social adjustment is of prior importance.

Obviously, there are many types of schools—day schools and boarding schools, public and private schools, grade schools and colleges, commercial and professional schools, each with its own characteristics. Waller, who has studied these differences, finds five characteristics which are common and which set schools apart as social unities. These are as follows: (1) They have a definite population; (2) they have a clearly defined social structure, arising from the mode of social interaction peculiar to the school; (3) they represent a compact network of social relationships; (4) they are pervaded by a we-feeling; and (5) they have a culture which is definitely their own.[2]

The main body of this chapter is devoted to a consideration of specific aspects or problems arising from these common characteristics. The topics to be discussed include: (1) the role of school life, particularly as suggested by autobiographical material; (2) problems of teacher personnel, including reference to the age, sex, marital status, mental hygiene, behavior emphases, and personality make-up; (3) characteristic factors in pupil relationships, such as the size, mobility, age composition, sex make-up, class distinctions, and cultural origins, in the school world; and (4) the nature of cultural differences between school and home.

School Life in Retrospect[3]

Recollections of school days found in 21 autobiographies highlight the crucial aspects of school to children who grew up to record its significance

---

[1] Robert and Helen Lynd, *Middletown*, Harcourt, Brace & Company, Inc., New York, 1929, p. 211.
[2] Willard W. Waller, *The Sociology of Teaching*, John Wiley & Sons, Inc., New York, 1932, Chap. 2.
[3] The school situations presented are taken from randomly selected autobiographies constituting part of a study of family life being made by Dr. Eleanor S. Boll, who is the author of this section.

for themselves. One generalization is brought into clear focus by these records: although school was a place of lessons and grades and, more important, of teachers of varying personalities, it was, above all else, a place where these children had to live for long periods of time in a position of considerable and unprotected intimacy with their peers. The separate situations evolving from this aspect of school formed a significant portion of the autobiographers' memories of school days. Five of these situations will be discussed briefly.

1. To the writers, the most spectacular situation was first beginning school or changing to a new school. Though the circumstances of each situation varied, the common elements were these: (a) each one entered alone and unknown an unfamiliar group of children who looked at him objectively and estimatingly and put upon him the burden of gaining acceptance, a role, and a status; and (b) this was their first introduction to gaining these recognitions on their own merits and outside the family circle.

They found the following differences in rules and values that prepared them for participation in subsequent secondary groups. First, there was no such strong incentive to accepting a new classmate as there was to accepting a new family member. One could just as easily leave him alone. Augustus Long speaks of such treatment given to a classmate of his, a boy who was branded as rough and uncouth, but whose loneliness was what remained to haunt Long. He wrote that few things in life had shamed him as much, in remembering them, as his treatment of that boy.[4] Second, there was no such gratuitous conferring of roles as frequently occurs in family life. At school, the roles were earned realistically from observable behavior. Charles Sherrill, one-time ambassador to Turkey, for instance, still wore kilts and long curls when he started school. This, of course, made him a "sissy." He offered to fight to prove that he was a man, but fighting did not happen to be the way to prestige in his class. A man was one who kissed girls at recess time. Sherrill recognized that the rules for his success were new, laid down by his classmates. He had never kissed a girl, but he did so and thus became a man among men, though he had his mouth washed out by the teacher.[5] Third, once having a recognized role, one's status depended upon the value of that role in the eyes of the class, and this was often strikingly different from values previously taken for granted at home. When Marianne Oswald started school, she had a very deep voice, cultivated because her parents had wanted her to be a boy. Naturally, the girl was proud of her tomboy qualities. Nevertheless she learned through pinches and name calling that the boys in her class had no high opinion of deep-voiced, competi-

---

[4] Augustus White Long, *Son of Carolina*, Duke University Press, Durham, 1939, pp. 93–95.

[5] Charles Hitchcock Sherrill, *My Story Book*, privately published, 1937, pp. 9–10.

tive tomboys. What they liked was shrill and frail femininity. The role with which she strove for success at home was destined to make her a social failure at school.[6] This status value of a certain role in a certain school was especially problem-creating among children who were half-grown and changed from one school to another. Some of them found the change so great that they *could* not fit into a role that would satisfy their former estimate of themselves. Lady Eleanor Smith describes her complete unhappiness at a school where she, an intellectual of a freely unconventional type, found herself in a group of pious little prigs. She never could win a worthy status for herself at that school because she would not be a prig. Relief from her plight came only when she changed to another school where she did not have to be convention-bound in order to be a proper person.[7] Brander Matthews mentioned this same problem in a school where only a fighting bully could achieve recognition. He did not rebel as did Lady Eleanor. He did a great deal of fighting in order to gain prestige, but the role was abhorrent to him, and he finally left the school.[8]

One further difficulty in gaining a place was that in many cases it had to be acquired in the face of organized bullying. For the boys this was chiefly physical; for the girls, psychological. For both it required great tenacity to escape humiliation.

This process of surviving and fitting in had to be carried on concurrently with learning the three R's, and was of far greater importance to the children. Under compulsory education a child cannot retreat from this situation except psychologically; nor under the public school system can it be solved by a free choice of schools. On the other hand, our present-day mobility forces many children to face this particular situation many times during their individual school careers.

2. A second school situation in the autobiographies emerged when in the process of the children's living together at school, certain differences in background became apparent. One's classmates then began to be known as children of their parents. Carl Schleich wrote that at school he was reputed to be one of a gang of roughnecks. But there was a certain "zone of inviolable respect" between him and his schoolmasters because most of them were entertained at his parents' parties. At these same events, his friends were permitted to be present and to watch them. Roughneck or not, Carl was obviously someone to command respect.[9] Lady Eleanor knew that her behavior at a school would have forced her

---

[6] Marianne Oswald, *One Small Voice*, McGraw-Hill Book Company, Inc., New York, 1945, pp. 12–15.

[7] Lady Eleanor Smith, *Life's a Circus*, Doubleday, Doran & Company, Inc., New York, 1940, pp. 72–81.

[8] Brander Matthews, *These Many Years*, Charles Scribner's Sons, New York, 1917, pp. 55–57.

[9] Carl Ludwig Schleich, *Those Were Good Days!* translated by Bernard Miall, W. W. Norton & Company, Inc., New York, 1936, p. 76.

expulsion had not her father been Lord Chancellor.[10] At the other extreme, Marianne Oswald, who went through kindergarten with Kiki, the daughter of the family washwoman, as her best friend, found that Kiki could not go to private school with her even if the tuition was paid.[11] Henry Sedgwick told of pranks played upon a classmate whose family standards of changing his linen were very different from those of most of the class. The date would be secretly marked in pencil upon the boy's collar. The class would then watch to see how many days he wore that collar.[12]

Race and color were also part of this situation. Because Vambéry was a Jewish boy, his teacher mocked him and advised him to stop school because he would be better off as a kosher butcher. This, Vambéry said, was the prevailing tone at his school.[13] John Franklin Carter revealed a similar situation from the other side of the window. He wrote that in his school there were a few Negro and Jewish children and that no one thought anything about it. But he added: "Father and Mother let us play with them all, regardless, but never encouraged us to invite them into the house."[14] This was no doubt a satisfactory solution for the little Carters, but the uninvited had their problems to solve. It is reasonable to suppose that the increased size of modern schools and the mixed population of most school districts have added to the number and, perhaps, the intensity of such situations.

3. A third situation of significance in the autobiographies was that of the immigrant boy entering an American school. The new element here was the immigrant's very real lack of the techniques with which to find his way into the group. John Cournos, telling of his own experience, mentioned his three chief handicaps. His inexperience with the language set him back several grades; his "sylvan past" incapacitated him in the presence of crowds of children; his lack of familiarity with the play customs of his classmates and his desire to adopt them got him into trouble. He frankly did not know such things as under what conditions it was comradely to call a boy a son-of-a-bitch and when it was insulting.[15] This lack of techniques must characterize the school situations not only of immigrant children, but also of second- and third-generation youngsters who have lived within their parents' culture circles and then been sent to a big city school.

[10] Smith, *op. cit.*

[11] Oswald, *op. cit.*

[12] Henry Dwight Sedgwick, *Memoirs of an Epicurean,* Bobbs-Merrill Company, Indianapolis, 1942, p. 54.

[13] Arminius Vambéry, *The Story of My Struggles,* E. P. Dutton & Co., Inc., New York, 1904, pp. 47–48.

[14] John Franklin Carter, *The Rectory Family,* Coward-McCann, Inc., New York, 1937, pp. 154–156.

[15] John Cournos, *Autobiography,* G. P. Putnam's Sons, New York, 1935, pp. 69–71.

4. Another situation brought out in the life histories was that of the protectively reared and rather sensitive child being awakened to certain crudities of life as they will appear in school. Edgar Lee Masters loathed his first days at school. He wrote: "The schoolroom had no proper ventilation, the air that we breathed was full of offense. The toilets were foul beyond description; the first day at school I learned all the obscene words that were then current."[16] John Carter's sensibilities were attacked in the same way. "The school," he said, "was, physically, a dreadfully depressing place. The sanitary arrangements were neglected and the boys' room was distinguished by a large pool in the center of the asphalt floor while the traditional method of attending to the needs of nature was to stand on the seat and contribute to the little lake. There was a certain amount of competition in this line and altogether it was a liberal education in the ways of the world to boys who had been reared to open plumbing."[17] Cournos was appalled at the ribaldry of the boys when speaking of girls. It was beyond his nature and experience even to speak aloud of a girl as having fine legs.[18] Masters' and Carter's descriptions may sound to the uninitiated like conditions predating modern public-school buildings and corrected in them. That this is not always the case many a schoolteacher can testify. Ribaldry, it is common knowledge, runs riot among certain groups in most schools. Avoidance of or adjustment to this situation must be an issue for children who are "protected" and fastidious but who want to be "one of the gang." To all of them it is an "education."

5. A final situation described by the writers was the classroom as a little world of romance. Most of these schools were coeducational, but romance flourished even in those where the sexes were separated in classes. All sorts of individual results followed these young but intense affairs. Cournos adored the fair sex, but was unable to court girls and felt quite frustrated. The very presence of a girl made him speechless. Yet, when he fell in love with a young teacher who could unembarrass him, he discovered that the eternal feminine "had its practical as well as spiritual uses." He found pleasure in his work and did it properly.[19] Masters improved his spelling because of the affection between him and a teacher. At the same time he developed a kind of "amorous madness" for a schoolmate.[20] More complicated relationships of love and rivalry were described. Leonard Feeney was caught in the current of one of these when Alicia, the class belle, broke a bottle of ink on the floor. A brave boy told the teacher he had done it, and before the whole class he took Alicia's punishment. Leonard watched in misery—if he had thought of it, he

[16] Edgar Lee Masters, *Across Spoon River*, Farrar & Rinehart, Inc., New York, 1936, pp. 26–27.
[17] Carter, *op. cit.*, p. 154.
[18] Cournos, *op. cit.*
[19] *Ibid.*
[20] Masters, *op. cit.*

could have done this brave thing. He had learned a lesson in chivalry, but he was afraid there might be no "next time."[21] Love complications existed among the girls too. Marianne Oswald had looked with favor on André even before she came to school. But André preferred Yvonne and was insulting to Marianne. She was humbled—until Roger began championing her. Roger had been reared in *Paris* and was no ordinary mortal. Thus Marianne's unrequited love found consolation and her stock in herself went up in value.[22] This is the complicated world of classroom romance at the kindergarten level, where success, or the lack of it, can be just as important to children, for the moment, as more mature affairs are to adults.

In summation, these writers pictured themselves as confronted in school with a number of social problem situations which were serious, important, and some of them momentarily all-absorbing. Their happiness in their school life depended largely upon their individual adjustment to these situations. Furthermore, success or the lack of it correlated with their adjustment to academic learning. The stories showed that unhappiness in school relationships went hand in hand with failure or with the overcompensation of retreat into precocious academic attainments; satisfaction seemed for some to facilitate success in schoolwork, and for others it helped to place academic honors in a position of relative value. Finally, these school experiences in social relationships were an early training for the similar experiences which all adults meet. These children were experimenting early, and under classroom conditions, with the techniques which they might use as permanent tools in all their social relationships.

Teacher Personnel in School Situations

Teachers constitute a small but important part of the school population. They represent the institutional type of leadership functioning in the school situation.[23] They have a directive and supervisory responsibility. In the performance aspects of the school world, they set the tasks and direct their execution. In addition, they play various roles in the social life of the school. Often a personalized relationship develops between an individual teacher and child. In short, the teacher not only is concerned with the intellectual life of the child, but often carries a major

[21] Leonard Feeney, *Survival Till Seventeen,* Sheed & Ward, Inc., New York, 1941, pp. 75–77.

[22] Oswald, *op. cit.*

[23] For an excellent analysis of the teacher in the school situation, see Robert J. Havighurst and Bernice L. Neugarten, *Society and Education,* Allyn and Bacon, Inc., Boston, 1957, Chaps. 16, 17, 18, and 19; Lindley J. Stiles (ed.), *The Teacher's Role in American Society,* John Dewey Society, Fourteenth Yearbook, 1957; Joseph S. Roucek, and others, *Sociological Foundations of Education,* The Thomas Y. Crowell Company, New York, 1942; and Lloyd A. and Elaine F. Cook, *A Sociological Approach to Education,* McGraw-Hill Book Company, Inc., 1950.

responsibility in his socialization, playing the role of disciplinarian, counselor, confidant, and friend. To say that the teacher is often identified as a foe by the child is to comment upon the tone but not the roles of the teacher-child relationship. It is apparent, therefore, that a number of facts about teachers in addition to their scholastic equipment and pedagogical effectiveness become significant in the school world, especially from the standpoint of the child.

1. First is the age of the teacher, the significance of which is difficult to assess, because both of the variables which must be considered and of the intangible nature of the evidence that is available. Obviously, the teacher's age is more than a chronological measurement; it involves more particularly poise, social experience, the maturing of understanding and judgment, the attitude toward children, and the manner in which one has adjusted to his age. The behavior of young teachers who grow beards and act stilted, and of those past 50 who insist on gamboling on the green, constitutes part of the age complex.

Perhaps the age of the teacher has meaning primarily when compared with that of his pupils, the age differential being an index of the personality-cultural distance between the two. This distance seems a highly significant factor, both in pupil-teacher relationships, and in determining the particular role played by the teacher in the school situation. When he is relatively near his students in age, he has the advantage of understanding better their cultural world and its problems, but he runs the danger of becoming too vitally interested in their activities and longing too intensely to participate in them. This frequently creates two types of problems. First, in becoming too friendly and perhaps familiar with his students, he is confronted with the problem of reconciling friendship with authority, and he often ends up by losing both. Second, if frustrated in his longing to participate actively in student life, the compensatory developments may take the form of "hard marking," a "tough attitude," or other unsympathetic manifestations.

Older teachers, by way of contrast, often have more difficulty in putting themselves in the place of students, and in sympathizing with the vagaries of behavior characteristic of the earlier years. On the other hand, older teachers seem more able to sublimate their own interests and ambitions in the development of their pupils, and to secure more easily their subordination because their students accept the teacher as a parent-substitute. The combination of these two sets of results creates the paradoxical problem peculiar to the teacher whose age separates him too far from his students: he has authority but little or no influence. The student's reaction to this situation is that he accepts the former fact while concealing the latter. The most effective age differential, according to Waller, exists when the teacher is a young adult, sufficiently past adolescence to have solved its problems, yet still near enough to be understanding and tolerant of its challenge for others; old enough not to see the student as a rival but young enough to speak his language; old enough to be identified as an adult but not so old as to cease to have, for the student, the status of being a person.[24]

2. Similarly significant is the sex of the teacher. Mention of this factor precipitates a whole series of questions: How does the almost exclusive dominance of teaching below the high-school level by women affect the behavior of girl students? Of boy students? How does it influence the performance levels which are established? How does it affect the students' attitude toward the school process? What is its meaning for teacher-pupil relationships? How do men and women teachers differ in their conceptions of what constitute disciplinary problems and how they should be handled? The answers to these questions go both to the heart of child, and subsequently of national, development; the scientific evidence bearing upon them is sparse indeed, as have been efforts to find evidence of this nature.

The significance of the teacher's sex for teacher-pupil relationships is perhaps the most obvious aspect. Rapport between pupil and teacher, based on cross-sex attraction, is both frequent and normal. Perhaps most often this is a one-way process: the high-school girl is secretly in love with her history teacher, or the spinster teacher develops a "special relationship" with one of "her boys." Since the mores of the scholastic world frown upon any affectional interchange between teachers and students, such tendencies are usually suppressed or disguised. Surface manifestations take various oblique forms. The girl student tries to "work" her male teacher for high grades, extra privileges, special tutoring, or conferences concerning her personal problems; an interested teacher may show off before the love object, lean over backward with extra harsh treatment, or express his affection in more pathological forms. Problems of homosexuality also arise, precipitating a patent silliness of behavior which destroys the teacher's effectiveness as both teacher and person, leads to a favoritism which is destructive of school discipline, or stimulates among students a diversion of normal trends into unwholesome channels. In summary, it is not too much to say that the atmosphere of many a schoolroom is charged with undercurrents of a sex attraction between teacher and pupils, sometimes with the resultant zest of added charm and interest, in other cases with the disruptive force of a vague unrest.

The sex of the teacher takes on added importance at times in view of the nationality background of the student population. Women teachers, for example, often have additional disciplinary problems with male students who come, as do the Italians for instance, from homes where the

[24] *Ibid.*, p. 216.

tradition of male dominance is very strong. Among such groups there is usually the complementary tradition that the mother is to be loved but not necessarily obeyed. It is the father who is to be feared and obeyed. The projection of early family-conditioned attitudes on to the teacher has been noted by many students of behavior, and the point emphasized here is merely a further elaboration of that fact. Perhaps the basic principle which should be stressed is that every distinct cultural group has its traditional conception of the respective roles of the father and the mother as disciplinarians, and that when these are transferred to the school world they become significant when related to the sex of the teacher.

Possibly the most important problem involving the teacher's sex is the effect of the relative dominance of the educational process by women during the child's early and presumably the significantly formative years. There is widespread belief that this country has been experiencing a feminization of its culture in recent years, and that a very specific phase of this has been the feminization of child training.[25] Three factors may be identified in this connection. First is the fact that the modern father is away from home a large part of the child's waking day, thus leaving the responsibility for rearing him to his mother, or a woman substitute. Second is women's monopolization of the teaching process, especially below the high-school level. Third is the fact that many of the functions performed earlier by the family, in which the father presumably had some share, are now delegated to social agencies of various kinds, staffed chiefly by women. In combination, these factors are interpreted to mean that women's dominance of the child-conditioning process is constant and pervasive—in the home, in the school, in many child and youth activities —and that, as a result, women determine not only the child's ways but also his attitudes, ideals, values, and, by indirection, his conception of what it is to be masculine.

3. The marital status of the teacher has significance for the present discussion in a variety of ways. To begin with, it determines his status in the school world, particularly among students who have reached the adolescent stage. The teacher who is married, particularly if a woman, is one who has "made it"; the unmarried one has failed. To girl students, the latter personifies what is to be avoided; for school boys, the unmarried woman teacher retains some elements of intrigue only up to a certain age. From the teacher's status it is only a short step to the attitude toward what he teaches.

Reinforcing his status in the school world is the teacher's status in the adult (parent, community, etc.) world. Here, too, marital status is important. "Old-maid schoolteacher" has long been used by parents as a special weapon with which to disparage a teacher and thus dispose of what

[25] Roy Helton, "The Inner Threat: Our Own Softness," *Harper's Magazine*, September, 1940, pp. 337–343.

the child is expected to do in school or bring to it. Teachers have unusually difficult problems in many communities in acquiring a normal status, and the marital status may easily tip the scale in either direction.[26]

Fortunately, there is increasing diversity in the marital status of teachers. As a part of the influx of married women into gainful occupations outside of the home, the opposition to married women as teachers is rapidly disappearing, and more married women are teaching. Particularly noteworthy is the return of mothers who are going back to teaching after an interval of some years, during which they have reared their own children to school age.

On the other hand, marriage, especially for women teachers, presents its own handicaps. These arise chiefly from the extra responsibilities which marriage involves. Many a married woman teacher, in addition to being a full-time teacher, is trying to manage a home, be a wife, and possibly rear children of her own. To say that she may fail in one or more of these tasks, or may age prematurely, is merely to allude to the inevitable. Furthermore, if she fails with her own children or her husband or her household management, she may lose prestige in the school world or in the community, or in both.

The teacher's marital status is related, too, to the sex problems of the school world. The married teacher may be less actively involved in the cross-sex attractions of the classroom; he may show a less vicarious interest in the romantic activities of the students, a greater tolerance toward the "puppy love" stage, and a better understanding of the students' sex problems. The Kinsey data showing the differing ages of sex development and experience between younger men and women pose some challenging problems of still another sort, for they indicate that adolescent boys tend to have had more awareness and maturity in this area of life than unmarried women teachers 10 years older.[27] Here, as in other respects, marital status is one of many facts bearing upon the teacher's role in the school world.

4. The mental hygiene of the teacher has received considerable stress in the mental hygiene literature of recent years, with reference primarily to the importance of the teacher's mental adjustment as a factor in determining the mental health of the pupil.[28] Two phases of these discussions will be summarized briefly.

First, frequent reference is made to the large number of teachers who

---

[26] James H. S. Bossard, "Marriage as a Status-Achieving Device," *Sociology and Social Research*, September–October, 1944, pp. 3–10.

[27] Alfred C. Kinsey, Wardell B. Pomeroy, and Clyde E. Martin, *Sexual Behavior in the Human Male*, W. B. Saunders Company, Philadelphia, 1948, and Alfred C. Kinsey, Wardell B. Pomeroy, Clyde E. Martin, and Paul H. Gebhard, *Sexual Behavior in the Human Female*, W. B. Saunders Company, Philadelphia, 1953.

[28] Fritz Redl and William Wattenberg, *Mental Hygiene in Teaching*, Harcourt, Brace & Company, Inc., New York, 1951.

are not in good mental health and who give ample evidence of the fact in their relations with their students. To account for this, some of the motives are mentioned which lead people to enter the teaching profession, such as an escape (for women) from unpleasant home conditions, a refuge from the rigors of other occupations, the desire to dominate situations (made possible by working with younger persons), or a form of sublimation of a desire for children; but due recognition is given to the repressive pressures which society tends to exert upon the teacher. He is expected all too often to be a repressed person, a paragon of virtues, by a community that is seeking freedom from its own unconscious guilt. Nothing is said about the role of nervous fatigue in a profession in which the emphasis is upon the output of nervous energy but where the length of the working day is still measured in terms of ordinary manual labor.

Second, there is the role of the teacher in creating the mental attitudes of the students. Teachers dominate the child's work requirements, and thus may become a major factor in determining whether the child develops ennui over set tasks, boredom with meaningless content, intellectual satiety, and a distaste for thinking, or vitalizing drives exactly opposite in character. It is significant to note how frequently students with fine records of achievement, both in school and afterward, attribute their records to the motivation given by an outstanding teacher.

Perhaps more pervasive and important are the subtle and intangible mental hygiene characteristics of the teacher which affect the atmosphere of the school. These include his morale, feelings of anxiety, worries, demeanor, voice, poise, tension, feelings of security, and relations with other teachers. Mental hygiene may be as airborne as are certain communicable diseases. Certainly the atmosphere of the home has been much emphasized in psychiatric literature; it seems equally important as an attribute of the school.[29]

5. Since no other professional group comes into close touch with children so frequently and for so long a time as does the teacher, what he identifies as behavior problems, and how those problems are handled by teachers, become of the highest importance.

The teacher's conception of behavior problems, in special contrast to that of mental hygienists, was the subject of a widely publicized study a number of years ago. Teachers in several large elementary public-school systems were asked: (a) to list the behavior problems they had encountered in their experience, (b) to check the frequency of the problems listed, (c) to rate the total behavior adjustment of each child, and (d) to rate the relative seriousness of the various problems.[30] According to this

[29] Garry C. Myers, "The Present Crisis and the Mental Health of the School Child, *Mental Hygiene*, April, 1934, pp. 294–298.
[30] E. K. Wickman, *Children's Behavior and Teachers' Attitudes*, 6th printing, Commonwealth Fund, New York, 1937.

study: (a) Teachers tended to stress behavior disturbances that threatened their standard of morality, obedience, orderliness, and application to schoolwork. On the whole, they seemed to be mostly concerned with the stubborn, disorderly, irresponsible, untruthful, and disobedient child. (b) The problems reported most frequently were those involving violations of specific classroom rules and the children's failure to meet prescribed standards of schoolwork. (c) The problem child, as identified by them, was antagonistic to authority, did not conform to classroom order and routine, did not make the expected application to prescribed school tasks, and violated standards of integrity. On the other hand, the purely personal problems of children which did not frustrate the immediate purposes of teaching were not regarded as symptomatic of significant maladjustment. (d) The ratings of the relative seriousness of behavior problems, by the teachers and the mental hygienists, were strikingly different. Teachers ranked as most serious the problems relating to sex, dishonesty, and disobedience, and at least serious such traits as shyness, sensitiveness, unsocialness, fearfulness, and dreaminess. This latter group, together with unhappiness, depression, resentfulness, cowardliness, and overcriticalness, was at the top of the mental hygienists' list. The items describing defiance to authority appear to teachers to be very serious; they are near the bottom of the psychiatric rating. Problems designating the failure of pupils to uphold classroom discipline were emphasized by teachers but greatly discounted by the psychiatrists, who rated them as the least serious of all. In short, teachers react mostly to the attacking, frustrating forms of behavior problems, counterattacking in turn; their response to the withdrawing forms of behavior is sympathy and protective feelings aroused by the dependence and inadequacy of the pupils.

This study has been utilized widely to discredit teacher handling of behavior problems. Granted certain assumptions implicit in the study, this may seem justifiable. A counter line of argument, however, might be presented. Obviously, psychiatrists as well as teachers present a rating which is the product of *their* experience. This may be the larger fact revealed. Each group tends to emphasize the traits which seem important to its respective professional approach. Each is dealing with the realities of its task. Furthermore, what assurance is there for the independent student that the frustrated, attacking type of behavior, identified by the teacher, is less significant in the complex life of the modern industrial-urban order, than the retiring, withdrawing type? The point is at least debatable.

Teachers naturally vary a great deal in the ways in which they deal with behavior problems, and certain aspects of the differing approaches are particularly important. Close attention to the comments of children concerning their teachers indicates that fairness and reasonableness are emphasized more than most aspects, some teachers being constantly criticized on this score, and others seldom if at all. The following three short case documents illustrate teachers' methods of dealing with behavior:[31]

I sat very quietly at my table while the children came to me for morning inspection. The last pupil in line was Dorothy, a Negro girl. As she was a new student, I had to inquire into her social and health background. During the interview, she gave vent to the hurts and heart burnings that had been swelling up within her since her enrollment at our school. I made no attempt to check her as she denounced the unfairness of everyone at the school. Finally, she turned on me and said with a depth of feeling that we rarely see in children, "And how would you feel if they called you nigger, even if you was one?"

I was stirred at the unnecessary burdens that she had been bearing. I was sure the woman for whom Dorothy's mother worked knew nothing of the race problem that she had unfortunately created. However, I suppose Dorothy had to be sent to school, and ours was the nearest and most convenient for her to reach. Dorothy stood watching me closely; so I humbly assured her that I was humiliated that any of our children talked that way to anyone. Triumphantly she said, "That's the way everybody here talks."

I was distressed. I knew she was mistaken, but how could I get her to see the real attitude of the majority?

"I am sorry. I had thought that Mary Alice was always nice to everyone," I said quietly.

"Well, I live at Mary Alice's house, and she is a lady. She always treats me well."

I gathered hope. I asked how others treated her. She admitted that Mary Alice was not the only one who treated her well. We began to make lists of those who treated her well and those who did not. I asked her to count the names on each list. The number of those who had been nice to her was greater than the number of those who had not. Then, I remembered her statement that some of the children were not nice to me, refusing to do what I asked them at the morning inspection. So, we made out lists of those who were coöperative with me.

Then, I had a real inspiration. I suggested to her that some children were more coöperative than others. We compared all the lists we had made. The appreciative ones in my list tallied with hers.

The scowl disappeared from her dark face. Gone was the hostile feeling that made her stand at the other side of the room. Instead, there was a happy smile as she stood by my chair and scanned the lists we had prepared.

Then she added a bit of philosophy that many a member of a minority race has had to assume, "Miss Smith, some folks is just trash, ain't they?"

I knew I hadn't solved her problem, but that she had a lifetime of adjusting and accepting ahead of her because she was a member of a minority group. But I hope I helped her somewhat to face the many problems she will meet.

Marian (aged 12) says that Donald is the worst boy in school. But this is not really his fault. When he was 4, his mother died. He loved her very much. After

[31] From the files of the William T. Carter Foundation, University of Pennsylvania.

she died, Donald had no one to wash him and dress him properly to come to school. The other children say that he was dirty, and not neat, and that he smells. So they said nasty things to him and he said nasty things back to them. Now Donald's father has married again. He hates his stepmother. And she hates him, too. She fights with him in the morning before he comes to school, so Donald is cross when he comes, and he says ugly things to us, and then we say them back.

Donald is very good in science, and a man wrote a letter to the teacher when Donald was in seventh grade saying that he might be a great scientist one day. Then Mr. Hart said that greatness was only slightly different from insanity and laughed. This afternoon, I found Donald sitting alone in school, crying. He said he was worried because he was afraid that he would be crazy when he was older, and that the teacher had said that he would. I don't think that Mr. Hart showed good sense. So Jane and I have decided Donald needs a friend and that we will be nice to him.

Katherine, now 35 years of age, still recalls vividly her first days in the sixth grade of a fashionable private school. She says: My first uncomfortable day at school was the one on which I entered Lower Knollcrest School in the sixth grade. Although there was actually no headmistress of the Lower School, the French teacher, Mademoiselle Jeanne, had taken that role upon herself and ruled the school like a dictator.

Mademoiselle Jeanne was angry with me to begin with. I had had to take placement examinations upon entering the school, and she had found my French so faulty that she felt I should be retarded two grades. My mother refused to enter me if that was done. All my other grades were satisfactory and she felt that French was not so important that I could not get ahead with it if I worked hard. In the face of Mother's intransigence, Mademoiselle ungracefully gave in and retarded me but one grade.

At the opening, however, of my first French class, Mademoiselle immediately called my name and asked me to stand in front of the class and read a passage from a French novel. I did so, thinking I was pretty smart because I had had French since first grade. In the middle of the passage, she literally snatched the book out of my hand, told me to remain where I was, and called upon a girl named Martha Toland to come and read the passage. The beautifully flowing French that rolled off Martha's tongue sounded like a new language to me. I had never heard French like that before. As Martha finished reading, Mademoiselle said, "*That* is the way we read French at *Knollcrest*." We took our seats and during the rest of the period girls were called to the front of the room, one after another, to read aloud, the performance of each of them being equal to Martha's. I felt quite desperate. I did not see how I could ever make my tongue conform to that kind of French and felt doomed to failure for the first time in my life.

At recess time Martha Toland and Grace Pepper drew me aside. They explained to me that this was an initiation ceremony visited upon many newcomers by Mademoiselle. Every girl who had been called upon to read, except me, had been raised from infancy by a French governess and had grown up as a true bilingual. There were many girls in the school, they said, whose French pronunciation was not even so good as mine.

Hope revived. I had always been good friends with my teachers, and considered on equal terms with my classmates, and I intended to stay that way. I determined to work hard enough to justify my existence in Mademoiselle's eyes. I was still completely ignorant that her prejudice against me was based upon something much more fundamental than my pronunciation of French.

I got my first understanding of the real situation in this way. Certain periods of each week were devoted entirely to French grammar. We had written quizzes, marked our neighbor's paper, counted errors, and then were lined up in order of the number of our errors, so that we, and everyone else, might see just where we stood in relation to each other. It so happened that the girls who spoke French fluently were very intolerant of the rules of grammar in its most spectacular subjunctive phases. They could speak French—so what? I, on the other hand, dug into my grammar to save my life and reputation. I crept up steadily in the grammar line, unnoticed, until one day I found myself, triumphant, ahead of Martha Toland. Mademoiselle found me there, too. Her reaction shocked me speechless. In a very real French temper, she delivered a tirade upon Martha—for letting a Jones get ahead of a Toland! That put into very direct words what the battle was all about and I saw that it was not one to be waged by being a good girl and studying one's lessons.

6. Much of the preceding discussion is related to the problem of the personality make-up of the teacher. Undoubtedly, this is as basic a factor in his success as is his professional equipment. Granted this, however, the personality traits necessary for successful teaching and teacher-pupil relationships have as yet not been wholly determined.[32] Perhaps agreement on the following points might be generally obtained: (a) professional zeal and confidence, (b) a sense of self-assurance and self-confidence, (c) ability to accept criticism and opposition, (d) ability to treat students calmly and impartially, (e) a sense of humor sufficient to prevent taking oneself too seriously, (f) some objective understanding of oneself and others, and (g) an adequate adjustment to the realities of life. "The teacher," says Orgel, "must be so stabilized that she will not suffer a nervous collapse when she finds some obscene note a student has written. She must appreciate the fact that stealing, lying, truancy, and other asocial types of conduct are not evidences of moral degradation; they are symptoms that occur in the life of many children."[33]

Perhaps as significant as any factor is the objectivity of the teacher's attitude toward the pupil. This has been well stated by Glueck:

One of the outstanding conditions which determine success or failure in child-teacher relationships has to do with the question of objectivity of attitude

[32] Harry M. Rivlin, "The Personality Problems of Teachers," *Mental Hygiene,* July, 1939, pp. 12–24.
[33] Samuel Z. Orgel, "Bringing Up Children," *Mental Hygiene,* July, 1937, pp. 438–439.

and behavior. Ordinarily, we are apt to be more rational in our relations with our fellows, the more successful we are in maintaining an attitude of objectivity. By this attitude we simply mean the ability to see things as they actually are, and to deal with them on that basis. The opposite of this is the tendency to color and distort events and things in accordance with the particular bias we may be entertaining at the time by projecting onto them our personal feelings.[34]

Such distortions come not only from the emotional bias of an unstable personality; they may be the result of devotion to a pedagogical cult which worships the theory of some noted educator, or be the unconscious product of a religious creed. An illustration of the latter is found in Fred's case:

Fred is 10 years old. He has had a serious attack of pneumonia. The effects of the illness, and of the high-powered medicines used by the doctors, have left him very nervous and given to semihysterical outbreaks at home. After four weeks, his parents decide he should return to the small Friends School where he is a student. The day before he returns, the parents visit the school and explain the situation to the teacher, carefully avoiding, however, any request for special treatment of Fred. The teacher, a member of the Society of Friends, interprets her religion to mean that all persons are equal, and all children are to be treated equally. Upon Fred's return to school, the teacher makes it a point to require, not only all that is expected of the other children, but a trifle more, lest anyone think that Fred is not treated as is every other child.

Pupil Relationships in the School World

Turning to the school world as it exists and operates primarily among the pupil personnel, the reader is asked to recall that this school world is a social world relatively complete in itself, with its own population, social structure, network of social relationships, culture, and group consciousness. Out of these characteristics arise a variety of factors which affect this social world as a milieu for child development. A selected number of these factors will receive brief consideration.

1. The size of the school world, both the pupil's class and the student body as a whole, is important in a number of ways, for it involves the impact of numbers upon the individual. The present-day problem is one chiefly of very large classes and schools. One result of this is that teachers and administrators become increasingly concerned with problems of discipline instead of teaching. Large numbers multiply contacts and thus problems of relationships, as well as create vague fears that situations may get out of hand. Many teachers in large schools seem haunted by an almost neurotic fear of student disturbances. The effect of large groups upon the social development of an individual member is a problem which has not been adequately studied or, may it be added, recognized as a

[34] Quoted in *ibid.*, p. 439.

problem. Common observation reveals many difficulties among individual students who are lost in the maze of the mass. It is far from easy for a 12-year-old to develop poise, self-assurance, and self-esteem when he finds himself identified as the eighth boy in the ninth row in Section 29 in a junior high school with a total of 1,300 students. The establishment of intimate personal relationships with students or teacher presents special difficulties. Moreover, the size of the school world takes on added significance when compared with the size of the child's family world. Whereas formerly a child came from a large family group, along with a number of other siblings, and entered a small school, the contemporary child tends to come from a small family, often alone, and to enter a very large school world. This change in the background of millions of children may prove, in retrospect, to be of revolutionary significance.

Older students constantly emphasize to the author the role of an alphabetical seating order in connection with large classes. The child sitting in the front row is relatively conspicuous. The teacher comes to know him, and other students see him. There are additional stimuli for him to be attentive, since he expects to be called upon to recite more frequently. In contrast, the child in the last row is inclined to take a chance; possibly he cannot hear as well; what the teacher is doing and saying is less vivid. If he can be inconspicuous enough, he may be called upon less often to recite. The significance of seating order, whatever it may be proved to be in the school world, may be contrasted with its role in a military training camp. The rookie in the front row is spotted by the sergeant who learns the rookie's name, and life may be anything but a bed of roses for him from then on.

2. The mobility of the school population has been referred to in general terms in Chapter 23. Obviously, its effects intensify many of the problems appearing in large, impersonal school systems, as well as create additional ones. The following, written by a Negro teacher in a Negro school in a large city, reveals vividly some of the implications of student mobility.

In the early days of my teaching experience, I gave no thought to the problems of student mobility. Rather, I could never understand why I became a referee from the time I entered school until the time I left. And believe you me—in those days they were real fights. I had one boy in particular that I remember. One hundred and eighty pounds, six feet tall, a former inmate of a corrective institution, a veteran discharged from the Great Lakes Training center because of his tender years, and an amateur prize fighter of some note in an outstanding Athletic club in ————————.

The same 8B class included the captain, lieutenant and several privates of the Safety Patrol. They kept fighting in the school yard down to a minimum and kept the late lines passing orderly—even if they did add a little vice to this legitimate business. By the way, the vice connected with the Safety Patrol business was a system of protection from anyone who wishes to fight you—just pay the captain or his trustees 5 to 50¢ per week, and they would fight all your battles for you. And believe it or not, the pupils engaged in this business, once we had come to understand each other, were actually most lovable chaps. Even now when I see them occasionally, they tip their hats, wave to me at a distance, and periodically drop in school to let me know how they are getting along.

The girls in this class presented the same problem. They were always bickering among themselves. A newcomer whether male or female was always cause for a new battle, and as newcomers were frequent, this new teacher, meaning myself, usually slept from 6 P.M. straight through until 7 A.M. for the first month of service at this school.

To aid further in this quest for understanding my pupils, I began to consider this problem: Do children coming into a new school situation adjust readily? Most adults are of the opinion that children fit in anywhere with great ease. My general experience in the classroom is that when a new student enters, the pupil is usually the object of much curiosity, teasing, and maltreatment. If the new pupil reacts like a spineless jellyfish to this treatment, which includes physical abuse that may be slight or intense depending upon the emotions of the class, there is no serious difficulty other than convincing the members of the class that they are being cruel to this tearful, unhappy child. But if the new pupil reacts like the normal child an argument follows which is usually ensued by a fight. The fight may take place inside or outside of the school. In any case it is usually referred back again to the school for a solution.

These fights may range from the classroom bout, where both parties will stop upon request of the teacher, or the parties may be so angered that they literally must be taken away from each other. At this stage any dangerous weapon may be used. This usually happens at the urgings of an onlooker, or onlookers, to the losing party. These weapons may even be passed to the losing party as most parents do not allow their children to carry anything dangerous upon their person. Outside fights are apt to be more tragic, since onlooking grownups do not seem to stop fights until they are actually sure that someone will be hurt.

New students do not precipitate in all school systems an invitation to physical combat. Student interaction is a form of social interaction which is learned, and this differs from one school population to another. Perhaps the fundamental fact to be stressed is that mobility multiplies and intensifies the problems of adjustment of individual pupils to their school world. How change from one school to another operates at an upper-class level may be seen in the case of Virginia, as summarized by a trained student of personality problems who shared much of Virginia's life.

Virginia went to the Ames School for Girls from her first through her eighth grades, at which time the headmistress who was admired by the entire community retired, and a new and modern regime took over the school. Virginia was then shifted, at the beginning of her high school career, to Bates School.

There were at least four differences between these two schools that helped to produce an entirely new social situation for Virginia. First, the Bates School was much larger than Ames. Supervision of individual students was almost nil compared with the watchfulness of Miss Bently at Ames, where the small size of the student body and of the physical limits of the school made it almost impossible for a student to be unobserved by a teacher at any moment. Ames was like a large family with Mother ever-present. Bates was like a small city in comparison. Virginia was thus presented for the first time with the responsibility for her own behavior in school, and the possibility of "getting away with something." The second difference was that the academic standard at Bates was much higher than at Ames. At the latter school, learning to be a lady was the prime requisite, and the winds of academic symbols were gently tempered on the report cards of little ladies of lightweight intellect. At Bates one stood or fell by the letters on one's quiz books. Virginia, who had early learned the outward trappings of ladyhood, was always on the "Honor Roll" at Ames. That was the status she was used to and the picture she had of herself—a well-mannered little lady who was always on the "Honor Roll." At Bates she trailed the class, and the pathos of that lay in the fact that though it hurt her pride and she tried to work hard, she had to face for the first time the reality that, academically, she could not keep pace, and could never again be a member of the "Honor Roll Elite" to which group she was accustomed to belonging. A third difference in the schools was in the teaching staff. About 50 percent of the teachers at Bates were men. Virginia had never had a man teacher before. She had no men in her home. She was terrified of the men teachers and did not know how to converse or behave with them. In their classes she could not function even at her own best level and she got a reputation from them as a stupid, silly sort of little girl who could not answer questions and did not care. And the fourth difference was boys. In all her life, Virginia had never been within tickling distance of a boy of her own age. At Bates School her classes were full of them. Furthermore, she was the "new" girl. The boys' eyes were upon her, and they found her fair. She was light-hearted, light-headed, fifteen, and extremely pretty.

The combination of these changes in Virginia's school life had results which nearly ended in her being asked to leave the school, and which put her sister's name in an immovable last place on the waiting list for entrance. The more she was called upon to account for her grades, and the more she became aware that she could not better them, the more she came to defend her status by discounting the value of grades in comparison with the value of popularity. She "showed them" by becoming one of the most sought-after members of a clique of the prettiest and most heedless and reckless girls in the school, who were aided and abetted in their pranks by 90 percent of the boys. To Virginia, high school became a social whirl definitely restricted to this select group. Strictly outside the pale were the earnest students, who were "greasy grinds"; the teachers, who were "people you can't have any fun with"; and books, which were "something to be burned on graduation day." No institution of higher learning ever subsequently got its clutches on Virginia.

There was a very real change in Virginia, from Ames personality to Bates personality, a change which her family summed up as a certain deliberate giddiness to cover humiliation, and a certain bitterness toward the kinds of people who made that humiliation possible. It seems extremely doubtful that Virginia would have acquired these specific behavior patterns, attitudes, and reactions had she continued in a school atmosphere where her confidence in her academic ability was not so quickly and rudely deflated, where she had not the experience at the same time of terror in facing men teachers, where there was no new, exciting presence of boys giving a possibility of compensation, nor where relative independence from supervision gave her ample opportunity to pursue the compensations.

3. The age composition of the school population is important in a number of ways, varying in significance from one age group to another. Reference has already been made to the extent and rigidity of age grading and the ascription of status on an age basis. Age composition is a factor, then, in the social structure of the school and in the relationship of students with one another. Many concrete results follow from this—leadership on an age basis; the time necessary to reach the top grade, as for instance in a school with two grades in contrast with one with six; and the prevalence of "crushes" on older students.

A teacher of experience and keen insight suggests that the system of junior and senior high schools in vogue in many areas has a certain unsteadying effect upon youngsters because of the way in which it changes their statuses quickly and repeatedly. The "big fellows" come up from elementary school and become freshmen in junior high. Within a space of two years, they are the "big fellows" again. They are seniors in junior high, are allowed privileges that are not given the others, and are permitted activities that are actually way beyond them merely because they are the oldest students in the school. The next year they go to senior high and become the babies of the school again. Two years later they are once more, and this time real, seniors and receive all the school's admiration and privileges. They do not have time to get their feet steadied in any one status position. Of course, this can be carried one step further, into college and university.

Another significant aspect of age composition in the school world is seen in the experience levels which it brings together. Chronological age is roughly an index of experience in life, and one phase of the process of normal social development is the timing of the child's experience, i.e., so that he learns and experiences things at the proper time and sequence. Considerable harm results at times from learning a thing too soon and out of the proper sequence, and the age spread of the school world becomes an important factor in the timing of selected aspects of the learning process, particularly those that are confined to pupil contacts. One simple illustration will suffice. The presence of a 12-year-old girl in a class of 9- and 10-year-olds projects the experience of menstruation into the attention and knowledge of the class before its younger members are prepared to receive it.

4. The significance of the sex make-up of a class or a school is an old

topic, perennially considered in open debate or involved in the determination of scholastic policies. Less importance has been attached to its role in the earlier years, but its effects upon the conditioning of sex attitudes during these years may be more significant than is commonly supposed. In the stage when girls begin to reject boys their own age in favor of those two or three years older, the combination of boys and girls of approximately the same age in the same class may be the genesis of many of the disciplinary problems that perplex the junior high-school teacher. The situation here is one of conflict between the two sexes, in which the boys seek to regain their standing with the girls, often experimenting with behavior which neither the school authorities nor adult society labels as socially desirable. Other questions arise later. Can the educational process proceed normally on a coeducational basis? The present tendency in most educational systems is to ignore the sex line, this attitude being as extreme as that of an earlier age which favored the exact opposite. Interested observers tend to agree that the passing of sex lines in American education has been a change of great importance, but evidence regarding the specific results is vague and episodic.

5. The age at which class distinctions manifest themselves in the school world varies somewhat, but with many children they appear around the twelfth year. The distinctions and the sifting and selective forces which appear then derive principally from the families of the pupils. How these operate has been shown by several recent studies, three of which will be summarized briefly.

First are the studies made by Warner and his associates.[35] These show how selective forces operate in the child's scholastic life. There is, to begin with, the separation of public- and private-school students. Next, there is the factor of ecological distribution among the elementary schools within a city—for example, lower-class children largely attending one school, and middle-class children going to the school in their local area. At the high-school level, distribution among the differing curricula becomes largely a class distribution. Close analysis of the child's school life from the standpoint of these factors indicates that by the end of the first or second year in high school, the class structure of the school world and the approximate distribution of the school population, on the basis of both social and geographic distance, has taken form.

A recent study by Neugarten throws light on the ways in which the social status of the family affects the social development of children. This study includes data on 380 children in a Midwestern town, where the population is about 90 percent native-born whites, with no Negroes or Orientals, and only two small ethnic groups. Five social classes exist with some distinctness. The children were asked to indicate who were their

[35] W. Lloyd Warner and Paul Lunt, *The Social Life of a Modern Community,* Yale University Press, New Haven, 1941. See particularly Chap. 17.

best friends, whom they did not want to play with, whom their mothers wanted them to play or not to play with, and whom they would choose for a friend if they could choose anyone they wanted. Also, they were asked to give short descriptions and characterizations of the reputations of other children.[36] Significant among the findings of this study are the following:

1. With the exception of the lowest status group, children tend to select as friends, first, children of a status higher than their own, and second, children of their own status level.

2. The child from a family of upper status occupies an enviable position; many of his classmates consider him their friend or would choose him for a friend, or mention him as their parents' choice. Few of his classmates mention him as a person they would not want for a friend.

3. The child from the family of lower status faces the opposite situation. He is seldom mentioned as a friend, and then only by children of his own status, but he is mentioned often as a person whom his classmates do not like and whom parents do not want their children to play with.

4. The lower-class child has the reputation of being poorly dressed, not good-looking, unpopular, aggressive; of not liking school; of being dirty and bad-mannered; of not having a good time; and of not playing fair. These opinions tend to be held even by members of his own status group.

5. The child of a family of upper status enjoys a reputation almost exactly the opposite—he is considered well dressed, good-looking, popular; as liking school; as being clean and well mannered; as always having a good time; and as playing fair.

6. It is clear that by the time the child reaches the fifth grade, the lower-class child faces a very different problem of adjustment in his school life than do the middle- and upper-class child.

7. By the time adolescence has arrived, boys and girls of upper status are conspicuous among their classmates, irrespective of their personal attributes; some enjoy desirable and others undesirable reputations. Adolescents of high status find themselves in the limelight, and both attractive and unattractive characteristics are revealed. Those of middle and lower status, being less conspicuous, have less well-differentiated reputations.

8. Lowest-status boys and girls, to judge by the data on both friendship and reputation, are, as a group, socially isolated and ignored by the other children.

9. As regards reputation, social class seems to operate at two age levels

[36] For details of the methodology, consult Bernice L. Neugarten, "Social Class and Friendship Among School Children," *American Journal of Sociology,* January, 1946, pp. 305–313.

somewhat in the following manner. At the fifth- and sixth-grade levels, membership in an upper-class group carries with it a kind of insurance that one's reputation will be favorable. Membership in a lower class is almost certain to result in an unfavorable reputation among one's peers. At the high-school level, upper status is a sure indication that the adolescent will be the object of attention in his group, whether his reputation is favorable or not. On the other hand, as the lower-class child grows older, he drops out of school or, by taking on the behavior or values of his middle-class associates, he tends to lose his distinguishing lower-class characteristics.

10. The fact that social class differences in friendship and reputation are so well established by the time children reach the fifth grade seems of considerable significance. The child of 11 or 12 soon becomes aware of his reputation and desirability as a friend, and he must make his adjustment in the light of what others think of him. It may well be that one of the reasons why the lower-class child is so often a behavior problem in school is that he finds himself rejected by his classmates and has an unenviable reputation. This may also be one of the reasons why such a child often welcomes the first opportunity to leave school altogether.[37]

Highly significant are the findings of Hollingshead in his Elmtown study of the impact of the social structure upon 752 boys and girls of high school age. Five social classes, identified by symbols I, II, III, IV, and V, are distinguished. Of these, three (I, II, III) "rate" socially, in varying degrees; the other two (IV and V) do not. Among many suggestive findings are the following:

1. Policies of the Board of Education, the administration of the schools, the sensitivity of school officials, the ways that discipline is administered —all reflect class interests and distinctions.

2. The curricula (college preparatory, general, and commercial) are significantly related to class position, the prestige bias being particularly clear among the girls.

3. The principal ambition of many of the children in classes IV and V, and especially the latter, is to escape from the authority of teachers, as well as of parents.

4. Parents and children in classes IV and V tend to be indifferent or hostile to high school, considering it a drain on family finances, and are cynical of the school and teachers' fairness.

5. Children in classes IV and V do not rate socially for dates and clique membership, and participate little in extracurricular and social activities.

Distinctions of other kinds project themselves into the school world. Educators report that children living in federal housing projects in large

[37] *Ibid.*, pp. 310–313.

cities are identified as such in school, and definitely lose caste as a result. During World War II, a similar situation prevailed in regard to "defense workers" and their families.[38]

Significance is often attached by the school world to distinctions between pupils living in the school area and commuters from the outside. Many school districts, especially suburbs, are too small to maintain adequate high-school facilities, and hence arrange for such pupils to go to school in a larger, neighboring district. This may be a feasible and often necessary arrangement, but it has reverberations in these children's social development which have been overlooked. These "outsiders" are generally spotted as such, and tend to be discriminated against in various ways, such as election to class and school offices, membership in fraternal and social clubs, and so on. Discussion of this experience with persons who have gone through it indicates that, even after 20 or more years, memories of these discriminations are often vivid and emotionally colored. Similar distinctions prevail at certain boarding schools between the boarding and the day students.

6. No school world can be understood without recognizing the existence of a separate culture in it. This fact needs to be considered from two points of view. First, the school culture is an entity, separate from the adult culture which the children share. This school culture is in part an unconscious accumulation growing out of the past life of the school; in part, it is a conscious creation, designed for the purpose of shutting out the adult, whether teacher, parent, or other. In the school culture, the adult has the status of an alien.

The second approach to the school culture is in terms of the elements that compose it. First, there are the many cultural backgrounds from which the children come. The heterogeneity of the American population is reflected in the cultural diversity of its schoolrooms. This has been emphasized by a number of students,[39] and we quote briefly from Thrasher.

A complicating factor for all educational programs is the number and variety of different social backgrounds which give conflicting definitions of social values. Among preliterate peoples and in simple European peasant communities cultural diffusion is largely absent. There is a consistent series of social definitions which govern all human activities. In the American city, on the contrary, we find a kaleidoscopic variety of natural areas representing many diverse cultural and nationality backgrounds which do not mutually support each other in the social definitions which they are accustomed to impart to their children.

[38] Cf. James H. S. Bossard, "Family Backgrounds of Wartime Adolescents," *Annals of the American Academy of Political and Social Science*, November, 1944, p. 41.

[39] Waller, *op. cit.*; Havighurst and Neugarten, *op. cit.*, Parts III and IV; Hilda Taba, *School Culture*, American Council on Education, Washington, D.C., 1955; and Janet Agnes Kelley, *College Life and the Mores*, Bureau of Publications, Teachers College, New York, 1949.

A further confusion is brought about by the concurrence of many different social worlds, not ecologically defined necessarily, but existing more or less independently in the same community. These social worlds, although of many types, often take on the character of racial or nationality groupings. Of importance also are the occupational groupings, such as those of the artist, the working classes represented by various labor organizations, the teachers, lawyers, the underworld, the Bohemians, and so on. . . . Little Italy, Chinatown, and the Ghetto, which may be taken as illustrative of these numerous and contrasting social backgrounds, each have their own social values, brought to America from other lands and places and expressed in widely divergent attitudes and customs. Even within a single nationality grouping one finds wide differences in language, traditions, customs and philosophies of life. These divergencies are well illustrated within the Italian and Jewish groups.[40]

The teaching profession, too, reflects the cultural diversity of America. This has its social class aspects, with large infusions from the lower classes. C. Wright Mills has written of the strong plebeian strain in modern college professors, recruited from the lower-middle class, who have acquired, as Logan Wilson put it, the intellectual rather than the social graces.[41] More Roman Catholics and Jews are entering the teaching profession, more members of minority ethnic and racial groups, more married and divorced women. Teachers increasingly reflect all social types.

Finally, there is the specific combination of these groups and their interrelations, which constitutes a separate and unique entity, and which gives any particular place or school its distinctive character or flavor. It is in these specific situations that the current problems of intergroup conflict are found. These are problems which seem destined to plague our educational system for many years.

Cultural Differences Between School and Home

Cultural differences, particularly of an ideological nature, inevitably develop between the school and the family world. Many of these are minor in character or degree of difference, but some become so serious as to create major difficulties in either parent-child or school-child relationships, or both. Selected aspects of these differences will be considered briefly.

1. The school, as the formal and official instrumentality of American culture, runs counter to the culture of various immigrant groups. The differences that exist may cover the range of language, mores, family life, political traditions, conceptions of the universe, philosophy of man's role, and many other social values. In school, through formal instruction and

---

[40] Frederic M. Thrasher, "Social Background and Informal Education," *Journal of Educational Sociology*, April, 1944, pp. 471 and 479.

[41] C. Wright Mills, *White Collar*, Oxford University Press, New York, 1951, pp. 129–130.

informal contacts, the children learn to live in a world which is alien to their parents. Many, having learned the American way of life, tend to set themselves off from the parental group. Teachers in the school at times reflect the attitude that whatever is foreign is inferior. They attempt to Americanize the children as rapidly as possible. Frequently they put pressure upon the children to turn away from everything resembling the culture of the parents. Influenced by this attitude, the children begin to despise the customs and culture of their forbears. The school thus stimulates the child to reject his parents and their culture.

How fundamental and far reaching these ideological differences may be is suggested in a contrast pointed out by Mangione.[42] The Sicilians, he says, lay everything on the doorstep of destiny. *E U Destino*—this single phrase explains everything. For centuries this has been the comforting philosophy of the Sicilians. Priests talked about it. Teachers emphasized it. But in America, children come home from school with the philosophy that every man is the architect of his own fortune, that anyone who works hard and has plenty of ambition can achieve anything he wants. When children talk about this at home, their parents only complain that the teachers teach them fairy tales.

2. The school as a nonpartisan, nonsectarian culture-transmitting agency naturally runs counter to the ideological patterns of many families. Some of these conflicts are open and avowed, but others arise by way of implication. In groups where religious affiliation is taken so seriously as to dominate the life and thought of the members, the resultant conflicts may be irreconcilable. Obvious illustrations include religious cults that forbid children to participate in patriotic exercises at school, such as flag-raising ceremonies; the observance of holidays other than those on the public-school calendar; and interpretations of and conclusions about life problems, imposed by a religious body and at variance with those developed in the school's regular courses of instruction. Most often, however, the differences which arise between the school's nonpartisan and nonsectarian approach and the insistences of specific groups do not take the form of overt conflict, but resolve themselves into a subtle game of cultural pressures and diplomatic avoidances and resistances, as in the case of the Roman Catholic opposition to the public-school program for sex instruction. The development of church schools, like parochial and other denominational schools, is an obvious device of the groups which seek to perpetuate their own culture in contrast to that of the public school.

An illustration of a culture conflict like the foregoing, but somewhat in reverse, is given by Malinowski and concerns the establishment of mission schools in Africa. Here a school system, based on elements de-

---

[42] Jerre Mangione, *Mount Allegro,* Houghton Mifflin Company, Boston, 1942, p. 83.

rived from a highly mechanized, capitalistic, and sophisticated culture, is established by Christian missionaries, whereas the life of the people operates on a tribal basis. The results, as described by Malinowski, are rather unfortunate, involving the loss for the African of much of his cultural heritage, without a corresponding gain or acquisition of the new culture.[43]

3. There are social class pressures which differ from those of the public school. As pointed out in the chapter on class differentials, the public school tends everywhere to be a middle-class institution, directed by middle-class officials and administrators, taught by middle-class teachers, and maintaining middle-class norms of behavior. Lower-class children tend not to fit in, and another of the reasons why they present behavior problems at times is the antagonisms to the school culture which are aroused in them by their parents. Many lower-class homes are in conflict with the schools, and the conflict is usually resolved by having the children withdraw from school as early as possible. Similarly, the cultural pressures of upper-class homes differ from those of the public school, but the conflict here is resolved in many cases by transferring the child to an upper-class private school. Such schools serve several purposes: they add geographic to social distance, they make possible the segregation of relatively homogeneous cultural groups, and they facilitate the transmission of the class culture. Upper-class children who continue in public school, on the other hand, often become the victims of the cultural conflict to which reference has been made.

4. One of the chief points of culture conflict between many homes and schools involves the patterns of child training. Obviously, this is basic to the parents' as well as the teachers' relations with the child. In many parts of the world, there are now and have been no problems in this connection, since both home and school agree on aims and methodology. But in contemporary America, the situation in home and school is in flux. In terms of the home, widely differing emphases prevail. In some homes, the fundamental purpose of child rearing is to train the child to conform; in others, it is to rear him so as to stimulate his development. Perhaps another way of bringing out the contrast is to ask if the child is parent-dominated, one on whom the parent imposes patterns of behavior; or whether the family is a democratic one in which the children have some leeway in developing their own patterns in response to their specific needs. The difference is basic, coloring many of the minutiae of family life.

There are similar differences in regard to the role of the school. Should the school impose upon the child a set of behavior patterns and a curriculum, so as to implement readily his induction into the prevailing culture,

---

[43] Bronislaw Malinowski, "The Pan African Problem of Culture Contact," *American Journal of Sociology*, May, 1943, pp. 649–666.

or should the child be encouraged to utilize the school to work out his own answers to the problems confronting him? This, in rather general terms, may be thought of as the contrast between conventional and progressive methods in education.

The development of many children is complicated by the fact that the systems of child rearing utilized at home and in school differ materially. Children from democratic homes go to conventional schools; the products of autocratic homes are sent to progressive schools. All kinds of combinations are possible, and the following case illustrates one of them:

Blankville is an upper-class residential community. Homes average in cost in normal times from $25,000 to $50,000. Parents are considerably above the average in intellectual interests and in their demand for the best for their children. In most homes, the emphasis is upon the strict training of children to accept the behavior patterns of their upper-class status, i.e., to conform to the prevailing code. On the other hand, the intellectual interest of the community expressed itself in a demand for a public school system "second to none." In pursuance of this interest, noted progressive educators were invited to Blankville to set up "an up-to-date" school system, and this was done for the first eight grades. The high school span was not included, and retained its traditional emphases. The result of all this, from the standpoint of the children of Blankville, has been somewhat as follows. From a home in which the training is directed toward conformity the child moves to a school system in which the emphasis for eight years is upon a progressive stimulation of the child's self-development, necessitating that he shuttle back and forth each day from one world to another. Then, having been trained in school by progressive methods for eight years, the child now proceeds to the high school in which the old conventional emphases are reasserted.

5. A final cultural conflict between school and home arises from their contrasting interpretations of life and the universe. The significant fact here is that much of our thinking and many of our modes of interpretation have been revolutionized within the span of a generation or two. Utilizing the Comtean terminology, the shift has been from a theological to a scientific interpretation of life. The result of this sudden and relatively complete shift has been that large numbers of parents and elder kinsfolk still think in theological terms, whereas the children have acquired a scientific approach and mode of interpretation. Here is a significant cultural conflict coinciding with the difference between generations. Its seriousness varies from one part of the country to another, but seems to be more marked in the South and parts of the West. In some cases, when families send their children to the universities, often at considerable financial sacrifice, only to find them returning with this "new nonsense," the problem becomes particularly keen. At times, parents or children or both personalize the issue, and then the deeper loyalties of family life become involved.

6. Whatever one's personal loyalties to the cause of education, the fact remains that, in our contemporary society, the school is often the creator of cultural conflicts for the child. At a very tender age, a child is taken away from his home to enter this specialized institution, which develops its own dual culture: that of the classroom and that of a more purely social world. Development of conflict between the schematized teaching of the school and the pervasive influences of the home is but the more obvious aspect of a much larger conflict situation. Some of this larger culture conflict is due to the cultural diversity of our population, some of it to the rapidity with which our culture undergoes change and the relative place of successive generations in that change. It is much aggravated when the school undertakes, as some educators insist that it shall do, to educate for cultural discontinuities rather than for cultural continuity.

The problems involved are not simple. Parents are voters and taxpayers, they have sired the children and are maintaining them. They have at least the prestige of maturity and the passing rights of trusteeship. Educators are trained to perform a specialized function in society, they are supposed to have superior knowledge and insight, and they are expected to prepare children for living in what today is a rapidly changing world, confident of its ability to remake itself in the interests of a better and more abundant life. Educators, in other words, have their responsibilities. Children are young. They owe allegiance to their parents, but they need preparation for life. They too have their needs and their rights. The problem of adjusting these conflicting interests becomes particularly keen and may reach pathological forms when totalitarian nations, backed by the resources of the state, take their children in hand to mold them into specific types of personalities, to the end that they may become an interchangeable cog or part in a vast human machine which is subject to the party in power. Such processes—and dangers, it should be added—are not confined to Fascist cultures alone.

Summary

1. A school is a complex of social situations in which children live. In part, it is a workaday world in which they perform; in part, it is a social world in which the life of the intermediate generation centers.

2. Teachers constitute a small but important part of the school population. Many facts about teachers, in addition to their professional preparation, are important in this connection, such as their age, sex, marital status, mental hygiene, conception of behavior problems, ways of handling them, and personality make-up.

3. There is a pupil world separate from the teacher personnel. The factors which affect this world as a milieu for child development include the size of the school world, the mobility of the school population, its age

and sex composition, the appearance of class distinctions, and the distinctness of the school culture.

4. Cultural differences between the school and the home are inevitable and often serious. The culture of the school may run counter to that of specific cultural groups; its nonpartisan and nonsectarian role may differ from the ideological patterns of political, religious, and other groups; class cultural pressures may differ from those of the public school; systems of child rearing may show marked contrasts; contrasting interpretations of life and the universe may be accepted by home and school, respectively.

5. The problems of this cultural rift between school and home are difficult, and, in a sense, insoluble. Parents, educators, and children each have their own respective needs and rights and, because of rapidly changing ideologies, they tend to remain apart. The resultant conflicts and differences are imposed upon the child, another link in the chain of social causation which makes doubt and uncertainty such characteristic aspects of the philosophy of contemporary man.

Part *VIII*

The Larger Social Setting
for Child Development

Chapter 29

Children as a Population Element

Preceding chapters of this book have been devoted to an analysis of the role of group interaction and the cultural milieu in child development. The emphasis has been upon the individual child and the situational factors in his rearing. There is, however, another phase of the whole process of child development which needs to be considered. This is the relationship of children as an age group to other age groups in the population. Basically this may be defined as the problem of the status of children as a population element, and it is to this phase of the sociology of child development that the remaining chapters of this volume are devoted. Included in the discussions of this phase are historical changes in the status of children, with particular reference to their present social position; social movements directed to further changes in directions which are considered desirable; and some basic problems of culture correlations which are involved. First, however, it is necessary to consider the age structure of the population, the factors which determine its form in any society, some indication of the forms it takes in various parts of this country, the nature of functional age groupings, the social significance of the age structure, and child status conceived in terms of social process. These constitute the substance of this chapter.

The Age Structure of the Population[1]

One of the basic facts about any given society is its age structure. This means the relative size and arrangement of the successive age layers that are represented in the population. At the bottom of the structure are the lower age groups. Arranged by years, the first layer consists of people

[1] For a summary and analysis of the population and other data on the child element in the population, the reader is referred to Eleanor H. Bernert, *America's Children,* John Wiley & Sons, Inc., New York, 1958.

under 1, next are those between 1 and 2, and so on through the length of life. For convenience in statistical tables and graphic representation, these ages are usually combined into five-year groups.

In a normally growing society, with no in- or out-migration and with conditions of life relatively stable and persistent, these age groups or layers take the form of an elongated isosceles triangle, and, because of annual depletions through death, each succeeding layer grows narrower. As the ages advance, there are fewer and fewer individuals in the respective groups, so the figure tapers off to a thin line after 65. The graphic representation of this is called a population pyramid.

In actual practice this population pyramid takes diverse forms in different populations, depending upon the relative operation of the factors which determine it. There are three such fundamental factors. The first is the birth rate. When the birth rate increases, the lower age groups broaden in relation to the rest of the pyramid; when it declines over a period of years, their relative width decreases. Obviously, either modification changes the shape of the pyramid as a whole. Second is the death rate, differentiated on an age basis. If a relatively large number of persons in the lower age groups die, the base of the pyramid contracts correspondingly; similarly, a low death rate in the upper age groups causes that part of the pyramid to bulge. The third factor is migration, with special reference to the age characteristics of those migrating. The migration of any particular age group from one area into another obviously creates a corresponding contraction and expansion, respectively, of the population pyramid at the age level involved.

Each society or social area, then, has its own distinctive population figure, a product of the operation of these three factors at the particular time and place involved. In the contemporary United States, the population pyramid of the South has a relatively broad base and a relatively narrow spread in the working age groups. In the Northeast, these facts are reversed. Rural areas show an excess of persons under 20; urban areas, of people between 20 and 45. In villages, many more persons are in the upper age groups, whereas suburban areas often contain an unusually large number of young couples and children. Pioneer communities have a preponderance of younger middle-class males. The foreign-born in the United States have an unusually small ratio of children.[2]

Just as each social area has its own distinctive age structure, so variations occur from one era to another in the same society. Changing birth, death, and migration rates over a period of several decades can bring about striking changes. Such a change has occurred in the United States in recent years and is generally referred to as the aging of our population.

[2] For an extended discussion of these variations, the reader is referred to Edward P. Hutchinson, *Immigrants and Their Children, 1850–1950*, John Wiley & Sons, Inc., New York, 1956.

The operating factors which produced this change may be summarized as follows: First, during the generation after the Civil War, the birth rate tended to remain high. Second, from 1880 to 1914, there was a large-scale immigration of younger age groups into this country. These two factors in combination meant a relatively large population in the advanced age groups in recent years. Third, the death rate declined, particularly after 1900. Included here was the fact that many people in the older age brackets lived longer. Finally, since 1910, and most noticeably since 1920, the birth rate declined. In combination, these factors made for a marked contraction of the population pyramid in the lower age groups and its relative expansion at the upper age levels. These changes are sometimes simplified and expressed in terms of the changing median age of the population, which shows an increase from 16 years in 1800, to 21.4 in 1890, and to 30.1 in 1950. More specifically, these changes are revealed in the data in Table 14.

TABLE 14. Five-Year Age Groups, by Percentage, U.S. Population 1880–1950

Age Group	1950	1940	1930	1920	1910	1900	1890	1880
Under 5	10.8	8.0	9.3	10.9	11.6	12.1	12.2	13.8
5–9	8.8	8.1	10.3	10.8	10.6	11.7	12.1	12.9
10–14	7.5	8.9	9.8	10.1	9.9	10.6	11.2	11.4
15–19	7.1	9.4	9.4	8.9	9.9	9.9	10.5	10.0
20–24	7.5	8.8	8.9	8.8	9.8	9.7	9.9	10.1
25–29	8.0	8.4	8.0	8.6	8.9	8.6	8.3	8.1
30–34	7.7	7.8	7.4	7.6	7.6	7.3	7.3	6.7
35–39	7.4	7.2	7.5	7.4	7.0	6.5	6.2	6.0
40–44	6.7	6.7	6.5	6.0	5.7	5.6	5.1	4.9
45–49	6.0	6.3	5.7	5.5	4.9	4.5	4.4	4.2
50–54	5.5	5.5	4.9	4.5	4.2	3.9	3.7	3.7
55–59	5.5	4.4	3.8	3.4	3.0	2.9	2.7	2.5
60–64	4.8	3.6	3.1	2.8	2.5	2.4	2.3	2.2
65–69	3.9	2.9	2.3	2.0	1.8	1.7	1.6	1.4
70–74	2.3	2.0	1.6	1.3	1.2	1.2	1.1	1.0
75–	2.5	2.0	1.6	1.4	1.2	1.2	1.1	1.0

Functional and Status Groupings Within the Age Structure

Statistical summaries and graphic representations of the age structure are presented usually in terms of one- or five-year classifications. In the organization of the life of society, however, chronological ages are grouped on the basis of function and status. Reference was made in Chapter 17 to the universal practice of age grading, and Linton asserts that age and sex categories are more important for an understanding of the operation of most societies than are family systems.[3]

[3] Ralph Linton, "A Neglected Aspect of Social Organization," *American Journal of Sociology*, May, 1940, p. 872.

All societies recognize at least three age groups: child, adult, and elder. This corresponds roughly to a threefold functional classification on the basis of economic production and consumption. The child group is economically dependent, not yet part of the productive system. As a group, it is in process of preparation for subsequent usefulness. In financial terms, it is a liability at the moment but is considered as an investment in future values. The adult is the producing group; it carries the burden of maintaining the society, which includes the maintenance of the two dependent groups. The elders are the second dependent group, having reverted to this status after a span of usefulness, and being maintained now as an obligation for past contributions.

Each of these main classes may be divided in any given society into various subgroupings. Linton points out how in certain African tribes the entire male population is divided into units composed of those born in the same year or within two- or three-year intervals.[4] The Inca of Peru distinguished 10 age groupings for males alone.[5] Our interest is centered upon the divisions recognized in the lower age groups in our contemporary culture. There are today four such divisions: infant, preschool child, child, and youth. The term *infant* is used customarily to mean a child under the age of 1. The preschool years cover the ages of 2 to 5, inclusive. The word *child* tends to be used in the literature in two ways, one general and the other specific. As a general term, the word means a young person ranging in age from birth to an upper level not exactly determined, but approximately the fifteenth to the sixteenth year. Specifically, the term *child* is used for children from 6 to 14 years, inclusive. In recent years, the word *youth* has been used with the somewhat expansive interpretative range of 15 to 24, inclusive.

MODERN LEGISLATORS DEFINE CHILDHOOD

The drawing of precise lines identifying certain age groups and assigning them a legal status or function has become increasingly frequent in modern culture, chiefly because of various types of social legislation based on age distinctions. A large part of this legislation is aimed at the protection of childhood against certain social hazards; other laws are permissive in character, such as those having to do with the operation of motor vehicles, voting, enlistment for military service, and the like. Legislation of such kinds requires the designation of some age limit above or below which a particular law, function, or responsibility does not apply.

The more common attempts of legislators to define childhood have centered in recent years about such matters as age of adoption, rape,

[4] Ralph Linton, *The Study of Man*, D. Appleton-Century Company, Inc., New York, 1936, p. 118.

[5] Ralph Linton, "Age and Sex Categories," *American Sociological Review*, October, 1942, p. 593.

marriage, compulsory school attendance, employment, juvenile court jurisdiction, and dependency. Most of these laws in the United States have been enacted on a state basis and passed over a period of years, so that naturally considerable variation exists. Only certain general summaries will be made here. (1) Most laws requiring consent for adoption specify 12 to 14 years. (2) Legislation specifying rape mentions chiefly 16 or 18 years. (3) For marriage, the parents' consent is required for girls in most states up to 18 years, and for boys up to 21 years. (4) Compulsory school attendance is required in most states to age 16, with some recent advances to 17 and 18 years. (5) Age limitations on employment tend naturally to coincide with those on compulsory school attendance. (6) Federal legislation fixing the maximum age for aid to dependent children followed the school and employment ages commonly designated by the states, that is, 16 to 18 years. (7) The most frequently established age for juvenile court jurisdiction is now 18 years, having been advanced from 16 years in the more recent acts. In short, child protective legislation covers, with few exceptions, the first 15 years of life; the more recent legislation has advanced the ages by one or more years to protect children from being treated as adults too soon.[6]

The Social Significance of the Age Structure

Once the fact is grasped that age groups have differing functional roles in society, the fundamental importance of the age structure becomes apparent. Obviously, the structure sets the pattern of the human resources and social responsibilities of a society at any given time. Changes in this pattern over a period of time in the same society involve basic readjustments. Differentials between social areas in the same country, or between one country and another, may change not only the status of any particular age group, but also affect the relative position of the country as a whole. Some of the specific ways in which the age structure is of social importance will be considered briefly.

1. The age structure is one of the determinants of the productive capacity of a population. This is true for the very obvious reason that the economic maintenance of any society rests upon a designated middle age span, from which it follows that changes in the relative proportion of this age span result in corresponding changes in the labor potential. Levin has attempted to calculate in statistical terms the earning capacity in terms of age.[7] His conclusion is that the maximum working capacity occurs at

---

[6] Isabel Gordon Carter, "Legislators Define Childhood," *Annals of the American Academy of Political and Social Science*, November, 1940, pp. 38–41.

[7] N. P. Levin, "Statistical Study of the Economic and Sociological Significance of Population Age," *Journal of the American Statistical Association*, March, 1938, pp. 41 ff.

40 years of age. Using this maximum point as 100 in his index, he rates age 15 at 50 and age 74 at 42, with the intervening years distributed up and down from his 40-year maximum.

It is clear that a more precise rating would have to be worked out with reference to each occupational group. The high point of efficiency for unskilled labor would naturally be at a much lower age than for such professions as the law, medicine, and teaching. A considerable literature has grown up around the question of how old is old, and when; but such discussions after all involve only the details in the calculation which Levin attempted, and however these details are determined, the basic fact remains that the age make-up has great importance for national efficiency and productivity.

2. Similarly, the age structure affects the consumption pattern of a society. Each age group has its own distinctive needs for commodities and services, and as these needs are expressed in the democracy of the market, the entire economic structure is affected thereby. Particularly is this evident when the larger age groups are compared, such as children with the aged. Children need baby carriages, baby clothes, milk, toys, scooters, sleds, express wagons, footballs, and ballet slippers. There is scant market for these goods among people past 50, just as children do not consume canes, whiskey, false teeth, wheel chairs, pipes, and bifocal eyeglasses. Baker has shown, for example, that children consume almost twice as much milk per capita as adults;[8] this makes differentials in the age structure an important fact for the dairy industry. Similar analyses for many other products, with more detailed references to the changes from one age period to another, could be of great service to American business.

3. The age structure, together with the sex ratio, is a determinant of the reproductive capacity of a society. First there is the conventional age of marriage; hence the mathematics of the population for these periods are important. Normally, in this country, about 95 percent of reproduction takes place within the marriage bond. Second, reproduction is a physical function confined to a certain age span in the life of women, a period equivalent in our culture to about one-third of the life span. Specifically, therefore, the crude birth rate depends in large measure upon the proportion of married women in the population between 18 and 45 years of age. Other factors which determine the birth rate are significant only as they affect married couples in this age group. Another possibility, suggested by Landis,[9] is that a large grandparent quota (the group above 50) in proportion to the parent quota may have an effect on the birth rate, since

---

[8] O. E. Baker, "The Future Need for Farm Land," mimeographed, Bureau of Agricultural Economics, Washington, 1934, p. 8.

[9] Paul Landis, *Population Problems,* American Book Company, New York, 1943, pp. 290–291.

many families with an increasing number of aged people to care for will reduce the number of their offspring.

4. The age structure is related to various social problems. The health needs and problems of a population of elders differ from those when there is a preponderance of children and younger married couples. Changes in the age structure are particularly important in their implications for problems of institutional care. The population in old folks' homes and institutions for the aged sick is expected to increase in the coming years.

Similarly, recreational needs differ. Each age group has its own recreational preferences, and these differentials express themselves in terms of equipment, space, activities, and nature of commercial facilities and programs offered. It has been suggested, for example, that the aging of the population in the United States will result in an increased sale of radios, as well as affect the type of program put on the air. Melvin has pointed out that in villages where age dominates, recreational life is institutionalized, routinized, formal, and patronizing.[10] It is not unlikely that the problems of juvenile delinquency which have perplexed many areas in recent years have arisen chiefly from sudden, large-scale changes in the age structure, involving the influx of many teen-agers into communities whose recreational life was adapted to, and dominated by, much older age groups.

5. The age structure determines the ratio of aged persons to the potential productive population. In contemporary analyses, persons 65 years of age and over are identified as the aged; those from 20 to 64, inclusive, are thought of as the economically supporting base of the population. While not all persons 65 and over are dependent and not all of those 20 to 64 are economically productive, the ratio between the two is an approximate index of the "old age" problem which society is called upon to carry.

Two facts about this index should be noted here. One is its changing nature. The percentage of the population 65 and over has been increasing rapidly. A glance at Table 14 shows that in 1880, 3.4 percent fell into that group, whereas in 1950 it was 8.2 percent. Meanwhile, the percentage in the 20 to 64 age span has increased from 48.4 to 57.5. While this, too, is a marked increase, it is less than proportionate to the relative increase in the proportion of elders.

The second fact is the variation in these percentages and their relationship from one part of the country to another. Such variations have existed for many years. Edwards, analyzing the census data for 1930, pointed out a variation in the ratio of persons 65 and over per 1000 sup-

---

[10] Bruce Melvin, *Age and Sex Distribution in Relation to Rural Behavior*, Publications of the American Sociological Society, 1929, pp. 93–100.

porting males, by regions, from 76 in the Southwest (Oklahoma, Texas, New Mexico, and Arizona) to 160 in Maine, New Hampshire, and Vermont.[11] Preliminary data from the 1950 census are shown in Table 15, and reveal similar variations by regions.

The aged population poses many social and economic problems.[12] Their increasing seriousness can be seen in the field of political developments in recent decades. Two aspects will be noted briefly. One is the emergence of an old age element as a pressure group. Constituting a substantial and increasing part of the electorate in this country, with leisure to devote to politics, they have given evidence of marked susceptibility to demagogues who have promised them utopia in exchange for votes. The formation of a political group on the basis of a rapidly growing age group in our population presents new and possibly difficult problems in the democratic process.[13] The second aspect is the threat of such demands upon the public treasury in relation to other kinds of welfare activities, particularly those concerned with education and other child welfare projects. This presents the unique situation of an age group with voting status competing with an age group that must rely upon other appeals.

6. Finally, the age structure determines the extent of the child-rearing responsibilities which a society must assume, according to the standards which it accepts. This, together with complementary facts, has much to do with the status of childhood.

Four sets of related data need to be considered in this connection.

a. First are the overall changes that have occurred in recent decades in the percentages of the population in the lower age brackets. Here again Table 14 tells the story. In 1880, of the total population, 38.1 percent was under 15 years of age, and 48.1 percent was under 20. By 1950, those percentages, despite the large baby crop of the war and the postwar years, were 27.1 and 34.2, respectively. Translating those changes into actual numbers of children means a tremendous decrease in the quantitative aspects of our child development responsibilities. One example will suffice. In 1950, a total of 51,658,000 persons in the United States were under 20 years of age. If the proportion of 1880 still prevailed, the number would be almost 72,500,000. This involves a relative decline of about a third in familial, infant, preschool, and school responsibilities from 1880 to 1950. Obviously, the society of 1950 should do more for, and accord a higher status to, its children than the society of 70 years ago.

The changes must be related, however, to those of the potential pro-

[11] Newton Edwards, "Youth as a Population Element," *Annals of the American Academy of Political and Social Science*, November, 1937, p. 9.

[12] Cf. First National Conference on Aging, *Man and His Years*, Health Publications Institute, Inc., Raleigh, N.C., 1951; and Clark Tibbitts (ed.), "Social Contribution by the Aging," *Annals of the American Academy of Political and Social Science*, January, 1952.

[13] Landis, *op. cit.*, pp. 294–295.

ductive population, 20 to 64 years, and the aged, that is, those 65 and over. Table 14 indicates these changes, showing that between 1880 and 1950, while the percentage of the population under 20 declined from 48.1 to 34.2, the percentage in the 20 to 64 age brackets increased, as has been noted previously, from 48.4 to 57.5. In other words, the declining percentage of persons under 20, and the increasing proportion of the adult (20 to 64) population, have combined to make possible a higher status for children, in spite of the increase of elders, previously noted.

b. A second group of related facts concern the variations in the age structure from one part of the country to another. Some areas have a relatively high proportion of children, with a corresponding low proportion of persons in the economically productive years; in others, the reverse is true. Edwards, in his analysis of the 1930 census data, pointed out the following facts:

The task of the supporting adult group, 20 to 64, in caring for its young dependents of elementary school age is 80 per cent greater in the Southeast than in the Far West, and about 44 per cent greater than in either the Middle States or the Northeast. State variations in the burden of child nurture and education are even more marked. For one group of states the ratios of children 5 to 13 to adults are as follows: South Carolina, 523; North Carolina, 491; Alabama, 441; New Mexico, 445; Utah, 438; and West Virginia, 438. In another group of states, at the other end of the scale, the ratios are strikingly lower: Ohio, 296; Massachusetts, 283; Illinois, 270; New York, 254; and California, 225.[14]

Similar variations obtained in 1940. In the Pacific Coast States in that year, 28.3 percent of the population was under 20 and 62.5 percent was between 20 and 64; whereas in the East South Central States the percentages were 41.5 and 52.7, respectively.

Table 15 reveals these variations for 1950, as indicated in preliminary tabulations. These variations appear to be less pronounced than in 1930 and 1940, but are still large enough to be highly significant.

TABLE 15. Percentage Distribution, by Urban, Rural Non-Farm, Rural Farm, by Regions, and by Three Age Groupings

Age Grouping	Urban	Rural Non-Farm	Rural Farm	North-east	North Central	South	West
0–19 years	31.0	38.4	42.6	30.7	33.2	38.7	33.2
20–64 years	60.8	53.3	49.9	60.4	57.7	54.5	58.7
65 years and over	8.3	8.3	7.5	8.9	9.2	6.7	8.0

c. The relative proportions of the child element of the population that must be reared by the adult productive population must also be related to the general economic status of the particular area under consideration.

[14] Edwards, *op. cit.*, pp. 8–10.

In this connection, the data on family incomes obtained in the 1950 census enumeration are particularly valuable. Tabulation of this information by regions, comparable with those utilized in Table 15, is presented in Table 16.

TABLE 16.   Family Incomes, by Income Class, by Regions, 1950[a]

Income Class	United States	North-east	North Central	South	West
Under $2500	39.5	30.5	34.4	55.1	31.9
$2500–4999	40.7	46.1	44.4	31.3	44.7
$5000 and over	19.8	23.4	21.2	13.6	23.6

[a] Information from Bureau of the Census, *Employment and Income in the United States, by Regions: 1950*, Preliminary Reports, Series PC-7, No. 2, April 11, 1951.

Similar variations in age structure and family income distribution are shown in the census data for 1950 for standard metropolitan areas. This information is arranged for selected areas in Table 17.

d. A final group of facts which affects the situation in a comparison of one area with another is that of the nature and extent of their migration experience. Internal migration is thought of ordinarily as a means of

TABLE 17.   Age Groupings and Family Income Distribution, by Standard
Metropolitan Areas, 1950[a]

	Age Groupings			Income by Families		
Area	Under 15	15–64	65 and Over	Less than $2000	$2000 to $4999	$5000 and Over
Akron, Ohio	27	67	7	15	62	23
Boston, Mass.	23	66	10	16	59	26
Chicago, Ill.	23	70	8	14	52	34
Los Angeles, Cal.	24	66	9	21	53	26
Memphis, Tenn.	26	67	6	33	50	17
New York, N.Y.	22	70	7	18	52	30
Philadelphia, Pa.	24	69	8	21	52	27
San Antonio, Tex.	31	63	6	36	52	12
St. Louis, Mo.	22	67	10	22	57	21
Tampa, Fla.	22	64	13	40	47	13
Wilkes Barre, Pa.	25	68	8	24	57	18

[a] Information from Bureau of the Census, *Summary of Characteristics of the Population of Standard Metropolitan Areas: April 1, 1950*, Preliminary Reports, Series PC-7, No. 4, November 20, 1951.

maintaining something of a balance between people and resources. People tend to move from areas in which the pressure of population on resources is great to areas of less intense pressure. We are concerned here with the implications of such movements as reflected in their age make-up. Persons who migrate from one area to another are usually the youth or early maturity age brackets, or the more advanced years of complete or partial economic retirement. This means that certain areas which serve as reservoirs of population are bearing the economic responsibility of rearing the younger migrants, only to lose them when, or soon after, they reach the productive period of life. The South, for example, lost approximately 2,800,000 from 1940 to 1947, while the West gained through migration almost as many. Similarly, areas to which the aged move carry unusual burdens. When such migratory movements occur on a large scale and over a period of years, the economic drain involved is great.

In summary, the more one ponders the national scene, studying the variations in the age structure of its population from one area to another, the economic differentials which obtain between them, and the internal movements of their peoples, the more it is apparent that variations in the status of childhood, as reflected in school, work, and child-care standards of all kinds, represent in large measure the relative size of the nonproductive and the productive groups, and the capacities of the latter to service the former.

Child Status in Terms of Social Process

Underlying the entire discussion in this chapter is the concept of a social process. This process is one of conflict, involving shifting balances between functional age groupings. Many social scientists have come to emphasize this as a fundamental social process. More than a quarter of a century ago, Lowie wrote: "The conception of society as a structure segmented into age-layers . . . reveals genuine insight into sociological dynamics. . . . Its importance must be acknowledged as overwhelming." It is "too deeply rooted in human nature not to loom largely amidst all the flux of cultural variation, though the class of greatest prominence will vary, as will the ideals of the age classes."[15] More recent is the implied emphasis upon the age conflict process in the study of the ascription of status by Linton and others. Similarly, Ross identifies it as one of the basic conflict processes.[16] This process may go on between any particular age groups and it may take a variety of forms; we are concerned here with the relationship between the three groupings of dependent children, productive adults, and dependent elders as defined in this chapter. For purposes of clarity in discussion, they may be thought of in terms of a seesaw, the two dependent groups occupying the opposite ends of the board, the board resting upon the middle trestle, which is the adult producing group. This trestle is the supporting base of the social process; and its characteristics, such as size, virility, and strength, determine both

[15] Robert H. Lowie, *Primitive Society*, Boni & Liveright, New York, 1920, pp. 314–315.

[16] E. A. Ross, *Principles of Sociology*, D. Appleton-Century Company, Inc., New York, 1929, Chap. 18.

the size of the dependent groups that can be supported and the stability of the process as a whole. Similarly, changes in any one of the three groups affect correspondingly the status of the other two.

It is this larger conception of the process as a whole that needs to be grasped by the reader. The status of childhood is not an independent development, capable of modification at will and without regard to the size and status of all the elements in the population. The status of children in any society and at any particular time is a phase or a product of the larger process of the interaction between the age groupings of the entire society. This is basic to an understanding of the remaining chapters in this volume. Not that child status is entirely a matter of the arithmetic of population; the role of other factors, ideological, traditional, sociopsychological, and cultural must be recognized. An appreciation of all these factors, as well as a sense of the larger social process involved, will, it is hoped, appear in the succeeding chapters.

Summary

1. Each society has its characteristic age structure that reveals the relative size of the varying age groups in its population.

2. The age structure is the product of three factors: the birth rate, the death rate, and migration. Changes in any or all of these factors produce different age structures at different times and places.

3. Age classes are grouped on the basis of function and status. These vary from one society to another, but all societies recognize at least three: child, adult, and elder. This division is based largely on economic considerations, the adult being the producing and the other two the dependent consuming groups.

4. The drawing of precise lines at certain ages and the assigning of legal status on the basis of these lines have become increasingly frequent in modern culture. Attempts by legislators to define childhood have centered in recent years around such matters as adoption, rape, marriage, school attendance, employment, and juvenile court jurisdiction.

5. The age structure is socially significant because it helps to determine (a) the productive capacity; (b) the consumption pattern; (c) the reproductive capacity; (d) the nature of many social problems, such as health and recreation; (e) the ratio of aged dependents to supporting adults; (f) the extent of the child-rearing problem.

6. Child status is the result of the social process of the conflict between age groups in the population.

Chapter 30

The Historical Status of Childhood

Childhood is humanity in its first and formative stage. Its history, therefore, coincides with that of the human race; its challenge is its inevitable continuity. If, then, there is any subject which ought to be approached historically, it is childhood.

Unfortunately, the history of childhood has never been written, and there is some doubt whether it ever can be written. Such a project would encounter two sets of difficulties. One is the wide scope of such an undertaking. Just as the history of childhood coincides with that of the human race in point of time, so it tends to do likewise in regard to subject matter. Child life is so inextricably bound up with every other aspect of life that its history would necessarily have to cover much of the range of the human past. The second and quite specific difficulty is the dearth of historical data bearing on childhood. The student of original sources of history finds relatively few references to children, and those he finds are comparatively lacking in quality. The ancients made virtually no records of the life of young children; classic Rome, for example, furnishes almost no data for child study. Legal codes, so fruitful a source of light on many historical topics, have seemed for centuries to recognize children chiefly as channels for the transmission of property. Even medical writings, dealing with problems in which children inevitably occupy a large part, are conspicuous for the relative lack of emphasis they give to children's diseases and the problems of their specific physical welfare.

Although there are wide gaps in our knowledge about the life of children in past ages, there is information on certain specific points that is helpful in our efforts to gain a historical perspective for our modern studies. One such specific topic is the status of childhood, by which is meant the position of children in relation to their parents and the larger social group of which they are a part. Possibly it is because the question of their status, rather than the children themselves, touched the interests of their elders that relatively more information is available on this subject. Fortunately, it is a topic of outstanding importance to the material in this volume, and to it this chapter is devoted.

The Child in Primitive Societies

Children were numerically a larger portion of primitive society than they are today. Studies by Krzywicki[1] tend to show that "amongst primitive peoples who have not been led out of their ancient way of life," children constituted nearly one-half of the population rather than the one-third which prevails in contemporary societies. Both a higher birth rate and a shorter span of adult life accounted for this fact.

THE DESIRE FOR CHILDREN

There is every reason to believe that children were desired by primitive folk. The position of women in many groups turned on their ability to have children. The barren woman was despised. The childless husband appeared ridiculous. So fervent was the wish for offspring that it at times eclipsed the fact of legitimacy. To meet the problem of childlessness, the social fiction of adoption was developed as a restorative of the lapsed prestige of parenthood. With the domestication of animals, and as their other duties waned, women became much more important as bearers of valued property. Brides began to be bought. The barren wife was returned to the seller. Marriage became a durable bond for the protection of the young, and adultery was considered as a species of theft.

Children are a practical asset to primitive peoples; their value lies in the contribution they can make to the all-consuming struggle for existence. Besides these more utilitarian considerations, a large family carries with it a sense of dignity, a feeling of prestige, so that vanity reinforces the motive of gain. Supernatural advantages reinforce those of a more material kind, for children often become the caretakers of the parental spirits. Children spell not only comfort in this world but security in the next, and the relative value of boys and girls takes form early as they function in these respective ways to the advantage of their parents.

From the standpoint of the larger social group, the child assumes importance as the main instrument in the perpetuation of culture. Where there is no written language, it is only through the child that continuity of culture is assured. Then again, primitive society is based on kinship. The blood bond runs like an obsession through these simple forms of social life. It is, one might say, the organizing thread in primitive society. This bond is most obvious in the case of mother and child. It is a relationship easy to grasp, and obviously much was made of it in very early times.

[1] Ludwik Krzywicki, *Primitive Society and Its Vital Statistics*, Macmillan & Co., Ltd., London, 1934, pp. 243 ff.

In keeping with the foregoing picture is the fact that primitive elders seem only seldom to resort to corporal punishment of children. Lowie[2] cites some interesting cases. A trader in Samoa was nearly lynched because he whipped his own child. An Australian native beat his wife because she struck their child. Lowie quotes Dr. George B. Grinnell, who studied the Plains Indians for decades, as follows: "Indians never whip their children. . . . Sometimes a mother, irritated by the resistance of a yelling child, will give it an impatient shake by one arm as she drags it along, but I have never witnessed anything in the nature of a punishment of a child by a parent."[3] On the basis of a good deal of evidence, there seems to be a rather direct ratio between the crudeness of culture and gentleness with children, thus suggesting that as culture accumulates and comes to be taken more seriously, the pressure exerted on the child by the parent to compel conformity becomes correspondingly greater.

ABORTION

The picture of primitive childhood, however, is not entirely, or even perhaps largely, one of sweetness and light. Quite different practices, revealing other attitudes, appear constantly in the studies of primitive cultures. Abortion, for example, occurs early and with varying degrees of social acceptance. Many primitive groups looked upon it without disapproval. The Code of Hammurabi and the Mosaic law did not condemn it. The later Judaic law regarded the fetus as merely a part of the mother, without independent existence. One seeks in vain in Egyptian lore for the prohibition of abortion.

INFANTICIDE

Infanticide, including exposure and abandonment, is common. Studies of primitive cultures are replete with references to it, indicating not only its frequency but also its variety of motivation. We can identify, perhaps, four phases of its development among primitive people. The first phase involves its use as an individual act of self-defense against such dangers as famine or disease. In his earliest stages, primitive man has no population policy, so his reactions to the problem presented by the newly born baby are individual, irregular, and in direct answer to insistent needs. This explains no doubt the intermittent character of infanticide at certain times and places. Somewhat later there appears a second phase, in which the practice becomes habitual, extensive, and standardized—"a keen-bladed knife that trims off the threatened excess of child population." At times as many as half or two-thirds of the children are thus sacrificed. The practice is now regarded with varying degrees of social approval. On the whole, there is not much objection because the infant child in these

---

[2] Robert H. Lowie, *Are We Civilized?* Harcourt, Brace & Company, Inc., New York, 1929, pp. 167 ff.
[3] *Ibid.*, p. 167.

cultures is not considered as having any status in the group, so there is nothing strange or strained in the parental exercise of discretion in accepting or rejecting him. In the third phase of its development, infanticide becomes selective, with some implications of a eugenic nature. There is the question not simply whether the newborn baby shall be allowed to live or not, but what sort of infant he is. Curious indeed are some of the earliest bases of selection. In addition to the obvious rejection of the physically defective or babies who seem destined to be weak, there are cases where twins, one of twins, or the quieter of twins, were not allowed to live. Finally, in its fourth phase, there crystallizes resentment against infanticide. This seems to arise at about the time when plants and animals are being domesticated, when recognition of the economic value of the male as their domesticator, and of the female as the bearer of such males, makes its appearance. Gradually the mores now come to be reshaped, and the right of rejecting the child at birth, although not necessarily denied, is now confined to the prerogatives of the husband and father.

CHILD SPACING

Child spacing, now so much emphasized in discussions on birth control, was achieved through the limitation of sexual intercourse between parents for a given period after the birth of a child. The length of this period might be two years, as long as four years, until the child was weaned or until he was running about. This practice seems to have grown up in the wake of an understanding of paternity; and as experience proved its effectiveness, it became part of the mores of the group, made effective both by ghost fear and by fear of the ridicule of neighboring kin.

It will be helpful to remember throughout this discussion that in earlier cultures the individual family was often a rather unstable unit. Although there is no such institution as "the primitive family," but rather a large variety of diverse forms of family organization, there are many primitive societies which have to rely upon other types of social groups for a permanent form because the husband-wife relationship is too unstable and discontinuous, and in which the biological family is obliterated by a much larger group, so that the child is required to adjust himself to a group of some 15 or 20 persons.[4]

SHORTNESS OF INFANCY

Another of the basic facts in the lives of primitive children is the short period of infancy. Just as the comparative study of animal life shows the shortest period of infancy among the simplest forms, so apparently at the human level the earlier the stage of social development, the shorter

---

[4] Margaret Mead, "The Primitive Family," in *Encyclopaedia of the Social Sciences*, The Macmillan Company, New York, 1931, Vol. VI, pp. 65–67.

the period of infancy. During these years, the life of the child is much like that of young animals. The practices of many groups indicate a concept of young children as a sort of undifferentiated mass of humanity. The aim of the parents during this period is not to train the child, but to cleanse him and purify him of the ghostly influences of his prenatal life. It is significant that the child is not given a name until his seventh or eighth year, for it is then, but then only, that he is believed to assume a separate and distinct individuality.

EARLY LABOR OF CHILDREN

The complement to brevity of immaturity is the early labor of children. The child in primitive societies must learn early to do his share of the work. Getting food is a communal effort of the kinship group, and the child is hardly weaned before he takes on his proportionate burdens. These tasks include stirring soup, kneading dough, hulling rice, washing roots, watching cattle, milking the goat, cleaning the cooking utensils, carrying water, and toting the inevitable younger child around. The primitive child, in other words, discovers reality before he has learned to play. The carefree, joyous child seems to be confined to the imagination of poets and the realities of these later days.

The early education of the primitive child contains few ideas of an ordered, purposeful instruction; rather it is a haphazard, uncontrolled, vague sort of training which can be bared in outline no more than can the growth of a puppy. What there is of more formalized instruction seems directed toward the dual purpose of emphasizing the uniqueness of his people and accepting the psychological domination of his elders. It is considered especially important that he develop the proper attitudes and disposition parallel in point of time with his physical and economic maturing. The force of religion supplements the influence of such education. "The whole terrifying threat of the malignancy of the spirit world is let loose upon those who tend to dispute the power and threaten the interests of the predominant sex, class, or group. Those who stray from the beaten path of custom become tainted with moral iniquity."[5]

From what has been said, it is clear that the child has but little status in primitive societies. Both the lighter and the more rigorous aspects of the picture point to this conclusion. The absence of corporal punishment, the prevalence of infanticide, and early child labor all agree in their fundamental meaning that the young child is of little or no importance. He must fit into the scheme of primitive life early; he has no rights of his own; his status turns wholly upon the convenience of the group rather than any rights of the child himself. It is the welfare of the group, not of the child, that is the determining factor in his position.

[5] Nathan Miller, *The Child in Primitive Society*, Brentano's, New York, 1928, pp 33, 34.

The Child in Early Civilizations

With social development comes differentiation of social structure, function, and value, all of which have to do with the way in which children are regarded and treated. The minutiae of child life would be quite different, for example, in caste-colored India than among the monotheistic Israelites or the sun-bathing Greeks. We must guard, therefore, against the danger of generalizing too much with facts which of necessity vary a great deal; on the other hand, there are certain similarities in the fundamental outlines of the picture, and it is these which we shall consider briefly here.

Children in the early civilizations of Greece, Rome, India, China, Persia, and so on, were customarily welcomed at birth. Generally speaking, they were desired, even if there were limitations to the number that were genuinely welcomed. Thus feeling varied, as to both place and time, on the basis of socioeconomic circumstances; it was greater usually in the case of the birth of a male child. Available glimpses of parent-child relationships in those days, the games children played, the nature of the disciplinary controls customarily employed, indicate that child life had its happy and compensating features. On the other hand, there were darker practices involving children which, both in their direct effects and in their implications, are significant in their bearing upon our central theme, the status of children.

INFANTICIDE

Infanticide was one of the customary ways in which earlier civilizations limited the number of their children. Only among those peoples for whom the bounties of nature or the existing sparsity of the population necessitated no such limitations does one note its absence. The practice was particularly common with baby girls, as in India and China. Ordinarily such discrimination against females at birth was associated with institutionalized social arrangements which resulted in women having less value in the economic scale, such as a status of relative idleness for women at the higher social levels, the necessity of finding a dowry for a daughter, or the woman leaving her own clan at marriage for that of her husband.

In some of the early civilizations, infanticide was practiced under direction of the state, with conscious eugenic intent, as in ancient Sparta, or among the Romans, whose Twelve Tables forbade the rearing of deformed children; or at the discretion of the parents, as among the Athenians. In either event, the practice flourished with legal approval in actual enactments, like those of Lycurgus and Solon or in the ideal legislative proposals of Plato and Aristotle.

ABANDONMENT AND EXPOSURE

The usual method of infanticide was by suffocation or drowning, but these more direct and unequivocal forms gave way early, in many cases, to abandonment and exposure. This was a definite step forward, since it allowed the possibility, and encouraged the hope, that the infant would not actually die but would be picked up and reared by strangers. This is clearly implied in the fact that infants were exposed so often where they could be seen—and saved: at the entrance to the temples, in the sacred grottoes, the hippodromes, the open highways, in vegetable gardens, on the banks of rivers or the seashore where bathers were wont to congregate. This practice of placing a child in a basket or earthen vessel and leaving it in a temple or some other public and accessible place was known among the Greeks as "potting the child." In Rome, costly ornaments were often put on the exposed infant in order to induce people to take him.

Particularly frequent are the references to abandonment and exposure in the records of classic Greece. Wherever one finds a Greek colony, says Payne, he finds also the popular tradition of a notable human or a mythical deity who began his history as an exposed infant.[6] In the plays of the fourth century B.C., a favorite theme for comedy, and for tragedy too, was the child who had been exposed and saved, and subsequently found by his parents. Later, Terrence and Plautus exploited this theme for the Romans.

A reading of the religious and literary myths of the classic civilizations indicates that a number of exposed children were saved. Sometimes they were saved by courtesans or wives, who sought, by pretending that these rescued children were their own, to prod the waning ardor of a lover or husband; sometimes they were rescued by slaves or persons of menial status, who saw in them opportunities for future exploitation, such as rearing them as slaves or maiming and blinding them for use in the profession of begging. Not infrequently the tales of the times tell how goats or wolves or some other wild animal suckled and kept alive an exposed child, the purpose of such stories apparently being to make people ashamed that animals, and not they, rescued these children. The story of Romulus and Remus is well known.

Significant in a number of ways are the measures taken against infanticide and its substitutes. Consider the situation in Rome. The first attempt to check the practice came apparently from Romulus, who, bent on the development of a powerful fighting machine, pledged his people to bring up all males except those who were lame or monstrous from birth, and at least the first-born female child. More constructive, even if in-

[6] George Henry Payne, *The Child in Human Progress*, G. P. Putnam's Sons, New York, 1916, p. 191.

direct, was the order of Augustus, emperor at the time of Christ, to set aside a reward of 2,000 sesterces (about $40.00) for the person who would rear an orphan. About a century later, 97 A.D., came Nerva's order that assistance be given parents who found themselves without the means of bringing up their children. (By 100 A.D., there were 5,000 such cases.) The fourth century witnessed a series of notable advances, possibly under the growing influence of the Christian religion. In 315 A.D., Constantine the Great issued an edict directing magistrates to give immediate and adequate aid to all parents who produced children which they were too poor to rear. An edict of 331 A.D. gave title to those who rescued an exposed child, against any subsequent claims of his parents. In 374, Emperor Valentinian definitely forbade, under stringent punishment, the exposure of infants.

Paralleling these secular measures and reinforcing their effect were the actions taken by the general Councils of the Church. Beginning in the fourth century, and for several centuries thereafter, these Council actions both denounced and ordered ecclesiastical punishments of varying severity for parents who killed or exposed their offspring. At the same time, the Church became active in the establishment of institutions for foundlings, which amounted in a sense to an attack upon the practice through the indirect approach of offering a substitute. The Xanodocheion, or village asylums, ordered by the Council of Nicaea in 325 were the first systematic step in this direction, and the development of a substitute approach to the problem had the sanction of the Church for more than a thousand years. This offer of an asylum for abandoned children was a wise policy on the part of the Church, both because it provided an effective answer to the problem and because it tended to identify the Church with mother love in the minds of many people.

Church and state united in the movement for the protection of children in the laws of Justinian, who, raised to the throne in 527 A.D., published a code of laws which have immortalized his name. Justinian proclaimed absolute liberty for foundling children, declaring that they were the property neither of the parents who exposed them nor of those who rescued them. The enactment of this legislation in the sixth century serves to indicate not only the obvious continuance of the practice, despite earlier decrees against it, but also the unending insistence upon its elimination.

CHILD SELLING

Child selling was another common and widespread custom in the early civilizations. In a sense, it was a substitute for infanticide and exposure. Naturally it came later in the course of history, for obviously its spread was impossible before economic conditions were such as to make children's labor valuable to the purchaser.

The sale of children early attained extensive proportions in the Orient. Both Chinese and Japanese reports bear witness to its prevalence and to efforts to suppress it. In Japan, for example, from 1624 to 1734, no less than eight enactments appeared declaring it a crime punishable by death; yet as late as the famine year of 1905 there are reports of its widespread practice.

In the days of the later Roman Empire, the spectacle of children being sold by the creditors of the parents was a common sight, it being the legal right of a creditor to satisfy his claim at the cost of the liberty of a son or the debauchery of a daughter. Among the Gauls, prior to their domination by the Franks, the heads of families that lacked food or the means to obtain it took their children to the market place and sold them as they would the veriest chattels. This traffic was common, and was carried on publicly in what is now France, Germany, Italy, and England. It was in this way that Saint Bathilde, afterward the wife of King Clovis II, became the slave of the mayor of the palace. The king saw her while she was at work in the mayor's household, and fell in love with her. The traffic attained such proportions in the British Isles that it became the principal object of a missionary expedition by Gregory, who became pope in 590.[7]

Various regulatory measures were passed during the period under consideration. In 391 A.D., Valentinian ordered that a child sold by its father become a free man after a certain period of servitude. In 451, it was decreed that a person who sold a free-born son for the purpose of having that son sold to the barbarians would be fined six ounces of gold. In 500, Theodoric ordered that when a father, because of poverty, was obliged to sell his child, the child was not to lose his liberty. The Justinian Code of 534 contained a provision by which a father whose poverty was extreme was allowed to sell his son or daughter at the moment of birth and to repurchase the child at a later date.

The nature of this legislation and its continuance through the centuries clearly indicate that it had at best only partial success. The sale of children occurred in many lands over a period of centuries, and persisted to comparatively recent times. It is the historic background that accounts for the popularity of the oft-used drama of the old homestead, the overdue mortgage, and the villainous mortgage holder who sought to barter his financial rights for the honor of an attractive and virtuous daughter. In modified form, the sale of children to satisfy the debts of their parents occurred in this country during the nineteenth century in the system of redemptioners. This was an arrangement whereby the children of immigrants who were brought here without money to pay for their passage were sold into service, as well as the immigrants themselves, for a number

[7] *Ibid.*, pp. 290 ff.

of years to persons who remunerated the carriers who had transported them across the seas.[8]

SUPPORT OF PARENTS

In all the early civilizations, and through the centuries since, children have been regarded by their parents as a form of social insurance, a kind of family old-age pension plan. Children must work for the benefit of their parents, and are to maintain them in their declining years. This motive is not always expressed directly or enjoined in specific commands; rather it is implied and taken for granted. It appears more often between than in the lines. Much of the emphasis upon respect for one's elders, with all its religious sanctions, was interpreted to mean economic support of the elders. It was for this reason, too, that the traditional differences in the values of boys and girls developed: girls left home and were of less value to the families which reared them. It is not mere coincidence that among the Chinese the greater value of the male child, the financial obligations of children to their parents, and the system of ancestor worship attained so high a degree of acceptance.[9]

The compact family life, the strong sense of family responsibility, the emphasis upon the economic duties of the younger toward the elder members all emerged from the larger socioeconomic situation. The struggle for existence was hard and uncertain, social welfare services and public treasuries were not as available as today, the health of middle-aged and older people was different from that of these groups today. The responsibility for the elders had to be carried by their young.

PARENTAL RIGHTS IN EARLY CIVILIZATIONS

The paradox of happy child life and parent-child relationships on the one hand, and of infanticide or exposure or child sale on the other, which have just been outlined, can be resolved into proper perspective if we think in terms of the basic status of childhood. In these earlier and older civilizations, children had little if any status as a separate age group in the population. Of affection between children and parents, of happy compensations in their daily lives, there was no doubt a great deal; but in the sense of having rights and privileges which were their distinctive own, there was no such thing. The child and few or no rights, per se. Not only under the Roman law, but in the old Persian, Egyptian, Greek, and Gallic legal codes, a father was given absolute power over his children. "While, generally speaking, fathers loved their children and did not desire to kill them or sell them or rule them in an arbitrary or selfish way,

[8] A. B. Faust, *The German Element in the United States,* The Steuben Society of America, New York, 1927.

[9] Cf. Pearl Buck, *The Good Earth,* John Day Co., Inc., New York, 1931; E. A. Ross, *The Changing Chinese,* D. Appleton-Century Company, Inc., New York, 1911.

they had the right to do so and the state enforced this right instead of interceding in behalf of the child."[10]

Particularly striking were the rights of the Roman father. His relation with his child was known as the *patria potestas;* and nowhere else, in a highly developed society, does one find anything just like it. It gave the father the right to reject his children: he could sell them, he could disinherit them, he could select their wives and husbands, he could mutilate them and put them to death. This absolute right did not end when the child reached his majority; it ceased only at death of if the father lost his right of Roman citizenship. "In the forum, the senate or the camp, the adult son of a Roman citizen enjoyed the public and private rights of a person; in his father's house, he was a mere thing, confounded by the laws with the movables, the cattle, and the slaves, whom the capricious master might alienate or destroy without being responsible to any earthly tribunal. . . . Neither age, nor rank, nor the consular office, nor the honors of a triumph, could exempt the most illustrious citizen from the bonds of filial subjection."[11]

The Child in Medieval Europe

The Middle Ages constitute an intriguing period in human history. On the ruins of the greatest nation and the highest civilization that the world had known, there was imposed the crude culture of the invading barbarian. For a thousand years civilization seemed to be stagnant. First deterioration, then its continuity, and ultimately its standardization in feudal society, stand out. Yet always there were hidden influences working imperceptibly to happier ends, resulting ultimately in the rebirth of civilization that is commonly called the Renaissance.

There is an extensive and imposing literature on the history of this period, with full accounts not only of political and national affairs, but also of the daily life of the people and the institutional forces that operated within the social structure. But one turns the pages of this literature endlessly and all but fruitlessly to find any information bearing upon the status of children. The omission is eloquent in its meaning.

The medieval pattern of childhood was the product of three sets of ideas and practices. First was the one that had existed in the Roman world, just referred to as the highest civilization in the world up to that time. In the pages immediately preceding, the child's status among the Romans was indicated. Second were the practices of the lusty Germanic invaders. Of them, Tacitus writes as follows: "In every house you see the

---

[10] Grace Abbott, *The Child and the State,* University of Chicago Press, Chicago, 1938, Vol. I, p. 3.

[11] Edward Gibbon, *The History of the Decline and Fall of the Roman Empire,* The Macmillan Company, New York, 1898, Vol. IV, pp. 473–474.

little boys, the sons of lords and peasants, equally sordid and ill-clothed, lying and playing promiscuously together on the ground and among the cattle, without any visible distinction. In this manner they grow up to that prodigious strength which we behold with admiration."[12] A healthy and disdainful disregard of children seems characteristic of these lusty ancestors of ours. The inhabitants of the northern part of Britain, prior to the inroduction of Christianity, did not give their sons names until after they had performed some brave deed or given some indication of their disposition and character; this is reminiscent of similar practices among primitive folk. The youth of Germany, Gaul, and Britain, according to Caesar, received scant attention until they approached the manly age, for when a son was younger it was held shameful for his father to be seen in his company.[13]

The third source of the medieval pattern of childhood undoubtedly is to be found in the influence of Christianity. These influences were strangely mixed. The early church fathers valued the ascetic life so strongly as to create almost an antagonism to married life. This, together with the lowered status accorded to women (despite the veneration of the Virgin) could not but have a marked influence upon family life and the status of the child. Children are seldom mentioned in the Christian writings of the second and third centuries, and almost nothing is said about their training. On the other hand, Christianity, from the first, condemned the practice of infanticide and denounced it as murder, thus becoming a powerful force for the protection of child life, of female children in particular. Out of this emphasis, and the general insecurity and poverty of the time, emerged the historic child policy of "easy come and easy go"—that is to say, a policy which insists upon natural and unlimited reproduction, accompanied by an excessively high child mortality.

Childhood in the Middle Ages was short. Betrothal and marriage took place at an early age, for boys customarily at 14 and for girls at 12. These ages, however, were often disregarded, children being married when even younger. Such matters were arranged by elders, and usually at their, not the children's, convenience. Another reason for the shortness of childhood was the early age at which people were put to work. An early marriage and an early age for work go hand in hand. Such early labor usually took the form of apprenticeship. The people of the Middle Ages accepted the fact that every child should be trained to do something. Boys of the upper classes were sent into the homes of nobles to serve a number of years in order to acquire the use of arms and become learned in the art of chivalry. Boys of the common classes were placed out under a master to

---

[12] Quoted from Oscar Chrisman, *The Historical Child*, Richard G. Badger, Boston, 1920, p. 288.
  [13] *Ibid.*, p. 288.

spend several years in learning a trade or to carry on agriculture. Children of the very poor were put to work at a particularly early age, and their plight was often very pitiful. Orphans had the hardest lot of all; for if parents treated their own children as has been indicated above, it is obvious that they treated other people's even worse. The basic principle in the work and training of young people in the Middle Ages was embodied in the apprentice system. This principle took legal form as time went on; and by the sixteenth century, in England for example, the law required every child to receive such training as would fit him for business, a trade, or agriculture. Only the parents who could prove that they were able to maintain their children if they did not work were exempt from this requirement.

One hesitates to generalize upon so intangible a matter, but there is much reason to believe that there was less affection between parent and child during the Middle Ages than we today take for granted as a normal condition. Part of the evidence leading to this conclusion is gained from bits of information about parent-child relationships; much of it is based on inferences from certain existing practices which show that children left home at such early ages that relatively little affection had an opportunity to develop. Children who were sent to boarding school spent the entire year there, save for a few holidays. There was the custom of boarding children out or sending them out to be servants or persons-in-waiting. There were the away-from-home implications of the apprenticeship system, already referred to. Finally, we cannot but speculate upon the extent of remarriage among the people of the Middle Ages, because of the high mortality rate among adults as well as other age groups.

Children were brought up with relative strictness during the Middle Ages. It was the theory of the time that every child needed corrective discipline which was both frequent and severe. Offenses of a rather minor character were often punished with marked severity. When knighthood was in flower, the youthful aspirant to chivalry was soundly thrashed for evidences of disobedience. Young noblemen, princes, and even kings were beaten, brutally at times, by their tutors. Henry IV of France expressly ordered his son's governess to whip the prince, since "there was nothing in the world more profitable for him." He who was crowned king of France in 1610, at the age of 9 years, had the following experiences, as evidenced in diaries relating to him:

October 9, 1603. Woke up about 8 o'clock. He was stubborn and was flogged for the first time. [He was born September 27th, 1601.]

March 4th, 1604. At eleven o'clock, he wishes to dine. When the dinner was brought in, he had it taken out again, then brought back. Troublesome, severely whipped.

May 14th, 1610. He was proclaimed king, went to Parliament, and received a delegation. For sundry offenses after his coronation, he was whipped. He reflects: "I would rather do without so much obeisance and honor, if they wouldn't have me whipped."[14]

The English Child in the Eighteenth Century

As every student of history knows, the eighteenth century was a period of tremendous upheaval and change which was particularly conspicuous in France and Great Britain. In France, these changes were most noteworthy in the realms of philosophy and politics, culminating in the French Revolution; in Great Britain, in the life and labor of the people, incidental to the development of the Industrial Revolution. It seems pertinent, therefore, to continue with a brief survey of child life in England in the eighteenth century, both because the changes in the life of the people were most pronounced in England, and also because of the more specific relationship of the English situation to that in the United States, with which we shall deal in the following chapter. In England in the latter half of the eighteenth century, the Industrial Revolution and the system of enclosures which was a forerunner to it brought poverty and misery to a great many people, and much wealth to a relative few. Any characterization of child life during this period must differentiate, then, between these two aspects of the picture.

For those elements who were on the upgrade, socially and economically, the century witnessed the appearance of new ideas in regard to social questions in general, and the problems of education and child status in particular. People began, says Mrs. Bayne-Powell, to take some interest in educational theories, to treat their offspring with less barbarity. A new spirit of humanity was creeping in. Parents were almost beginning to consider their children as of the same flesh and blood as themselves. Calvinism, with its theory of infant damnation and inherent juvenile depravity, was losing its hold. Complaints of indulgent parents multiplied. The old forms of address—"Sir" and "madam"—yielded to "papa" and "mamma." Portraits of children were painted, some at considerable cost. The lack of discipline within the home was bemoaned. Toward the end of the century a more serious spirit was manifest. Fathers and mothers, although still talking at length about the duty of children to their parents, had some idea also of the duty of parents to their children.[15]

These new ideas are brought into bold relief by the grimness of much of the old which still prevailed, even among the wealthier classes. Cruelty still existed, notably in the schools and among the rough and ignorant. Many parents were stern and harsh. Mary Wollstonecraft's father used

---

[14] Taken from Lowie, *op. cit.*, pp. 138–139.

[15] Rosamond Bayne-Powell, *The English Child in the Eighteenth Century*, E. P. Dutton & Co., Inc., New York, 1939, Chap. 1.

to flog his daughters regularly for no apparent reason except to satisfy his own whim. There is the story of a mother who always whipped her little boy when he fell downstairs. Susanna Wesley taught her babies of a year old and younger to fear the rod and cry softly. Many children wore iron collars round their neck, with backboards strapped over their shoulders. Families were large, unusually so; and the very abundance of children kept parents from regarding them individually or even looking upon their death with aught but equanimity. Boys and girls entered adult life very early. The introduction of girls to society, the termination of school training for boys, and marriage all occurred at an early age. On the whole, childhood was regarded as a tiresome stage which it was hoped would pass quickly and painlessly.

Naturally, for the great mass of the population, the penetration of new and softening ideas was slight, and the widespread poverty attending the revolutionizing changes of the era bore heavily upon the younger members of society. If childhood was short among the upper classes, it was doubly so among those less fortunately situated. Children went to work at a tender age. Defoe was delighted to find in the Taunton neighborhood that "there was not a child in the town or villages round it of above five years old, but, if it was not neglected by its parents, and untaught, could earn its bread."[16] Long before the industrial revolution young children were working in mill and mine, and its advent gave new impetus and opportunities to the extension of the practice. Industry was almost entirely unregulated during the century under consideration, and there developed those abuses—whereby, for example, very young persons worked for 14 and 16 hours a day—which are well known to all students of the history of the modern industrial system and which led to the nineteenth-century movement for regulation of hours and conditions of labor.

The apprentice system continued to operate on a large scale. Children could be apprenticed at the age of 8. In some instances, this system fulfilled its theory of a training process for the young; in others it was only a subterfuge for exploitation. Many persons took apprentices, but for the purpose of securing cheap and stable labor. There were many complaints about "these weary years of service." Virtually the only safeguard under the system was the fact that an apprentice could apply to the justices if he were starved or ill used, and, if convinced, the justice could order that his indenture be canceled. As a practical matter, such an application, while feasible in the rural areas, was scarcely effective in the towns, where justices were not only "harder-faced" as a rule, but also not so accessible or so likely to be known to an aggrieved apprentice.

Young children, particularly boys, were utilized extensively during the summer months to scare the birds from arable fields by running back and

[16] *Ibid.*, p. 32.

forth with a wooden clapper and making a noise. There were also sheep-
and cows to be watched in the open meadows. Such duties, while not
arduous, were apt to be monotonous and to extend over long hours.

> Where's the little boy that looks after the sheep?
> He's under the haycock, fast asleep.

Certain specific groups of children had a particularly unfortunate
status. One such group were the chimney sweeps. These boys, stolen in
many instances from their parents or inveigled out of workhouses, were
driven by beatings and torture to climb chimneys and do work which
left them bruised and injured; they were kept destitute of instruction and
moral teachings, and were in general as harshly treated as any children
of the time. Charles Kingsley wisely selected his hero for *The Water
Babies*. An official report on their plight was presented to Parliament in
1817. Another particularly unfortunate group were the pauper children
who were despatched in truck loads to work in the new factories in the
North and Midlands. "Probably no page in English history," says Mrs.
Bayne-Powell, "fills the reader with greater horror and pity than that on
which is described the misery of these helpless children."[17]

The legal status of children constitutes a tangible measure for the purposes of our study. The law of the eighteenth century dealt reversely with
children. They were imprisoned and hanged, for example, for offenses
with which probation officers now deal. Thus children from 6 to 14 years
of age were hung for theft and for other less serious offenses. To have
their helpless children convicted of a capital crime was for some parents
a convenient way of ridding themselves of unwanted children. There are
the all too numerous cases in which thieves and prostitutes "adopted"
children to aid them in their business or hired them out to beggars. References are not infrequent, in the eighteenth as in preceding centuries, to
the mutilation of the children used for begging, so as to increase their
pity-inciting appeal. The penalty for such mutilation, in an age which
hung offenders for theft, is highly relevant. In 1761, the Court of Hick's
Hall committed Anne Martin, alias Chapbury, to Newgate. Convicted
of putting out the eyes of children with whom she went begging about
the country, she was sentenced to two years' imprisonment! Other children languished in jail because their parents were confined there for non-
payment of debts. Large numbers were sent to America, as students of
our early history well know.

There were, to be sure, bright spots in the child life of the eighteenth
century. In a predominantly rural country, children had the liberty of
ranging gardens and fields. Such a setting, with the inevitable large families, made possible the enjoyment of simple pleasures, and for many
poor children these sufficed. In addition, however, there were a surprising

[17] *Ibid.*, p. 41.

number of other recreational facilities. The drama became exceedingly popular during the century, and the more careless parents might permit their children to accompany them to the theater. Puppet shows became prevalent during these years. A dictionary published in 1719 mentions the magic lantern. Fireworks, which have always delighted childish minds, were popular during the century. The country fair was an outstanding event for both young and old. Many of the children's games known to us were played by eighteenth-century children: blindman's buff, hide-and-seek (called hoop and hide), seesaw (known as teeter-totter), prisoner's base, cricket, hockey, and football. The rocking horse was brought to England from France during the century, and the music boxes and dolls which delighted children in those years are of interest to us yet.

Despite these lighter aspects, the status of child life in England in the eighteenth century was but little higher than it had been for centuries. "If an age is to be judged by its treatment of the weak and helpless, the eighteenth century merits our condemnation. It must be remembered, however, that those horrible cruelties were nothing new. They had unhappily been going on all through the centuries; the new thing was that people were beginning to take notice of them and to ask each other whether they could not and should not be prevented. The nascent humanitarianism of the eighteenth century produced the great reforms of the nineteenth."[18]

Factors in the History of Child Status

In the preceding pages of this chapter an effort was made to present a series of slides, as it were, from the history of childhood. These pictures vary considerably in their detail, but they agree in their basic implication that the child, through the long centuries of man's upward climb, was per se of little importance. The remainder of this chapter is devoted to an effort to generalize the factors which through the centuries have determined the status of childhood.

Detailed references to children and to adult practices relating to them contain much, both in overt phrase and by implication, that clarifies the motives which have operated in parent-child and society-child relationships over the centuries. When this material is brought together and reduced to its essential substance, four factors seem to emerge as the basic determinants of the status of childhood. They are: (1) the arithmetic of reproduction; (2) the prevailing economic situation, that is, what people can afford economically; (3) the ideological factor, that is, what people have been taught to believe; and (4) the familial factor, that is, the form and status of family life.

[18] *Ibid.,* p. 44.

THE ARITHMETIC OF REPRODUCTION

The term *arithmetic of reproduction* is used here to include the birth rate, the death rate, and the change in population resulting from the relation of these two rates to each other. The population data available through the centuries of human history show that for the most part, in most countries and for the great mass of people, the combination has been a high birth rate, a high death rate, and a slow rate of population growth, if there was any growth at all. These are commonplace facts to population students, but little attention has been given to their bearing on the welfare of children. The proposition advanced here is that they constitute a fundamental factor in determining the status of childhood.

The mathematics of population has meaning for the individual, and in many ways. Pearl Buck has written recently of one aspect of it. "In all those countries," she says, "where population is too abundant, the cause of the individual is lost. Democracy is impossible in an overpopulated country. One needs only to read history with this in mind to discover how inevitably as population increases the form of government changes from any semblance of democracy into some form of despotism."[19]

This is much the same thought as is implied here in regard to the significance of a high birth rate and a high infant and general mortality rate. They constitute the "easy come-easy go" method of reproduction. Life—infant life, child life—is cheap. Many children are born, many do not survive. Families are large, and the turnover within them is tremendous. It is the natural characteristic way of growth and reproduction in all forms of animal life.

The essential point to be recognized is this, that while the process of reproduction may be natural, its arithmetic is wasteful and its effect is a low value rating for the individual infant life. This individual fact, multiplied many times, dictates the relative status of infant and child life. Where the value of the individual unit is low, no group mores and programs based on a high status of child life are possible. As a social element in the population, children have little status because the individual child has little value.

Moreover, these effects are reinforced by the arithmetic of parenthood. Life for adults was considerably less certain in earlier centuries than it is today. The turnover among them was tremendous. The adult death rate was high. In particular, the birth of many children per family exacted a heavy toll from the mothers. Stepparents in earlier centuries were far more common than they now are. This affected parent-child relationships, for it meant that they could not be as individual or as stable as they are among us today. In other words, large families, a high turn-

[19] Pearl Buck, "Pearl Buck Writes on Birth Control," *Birth Control Review,* November, 1939, pp. 3–4.

over among parents and children, and short periods of infancy, all characteristic of earlier centuries, combined to these ends—shorter, less stable, less meaningful relationships between successive generations. Stated another way, the present high status of childhood was not possible until a more economical rate of reproduction and the small-family system came generally to prevail.

THE ECONOMIC FACTOR

A second and obvious factor in determining the status of childhood is the economic one, that is, what people can afford. Tersely put, the argument advanced is that the status of the child depends historically upon the aid he gives in the struggle for existence.

The contemporary American, with his high plane of living, finds it difficult to remain aware of the fact that for endless long centuries man was preoccupied wholly or largely with the stark struggle for existence. In this struggle, the society that was able to exist was the one that sacrificed the individual for the group. This fact is revealed clearly by the work of all students of societal history. In the early stages of human society, people were forced to function in rather compact groups. Kinship, real or fictitious, was the bond which held individuals together. The relation of the individual to his group was all or nothing. Individual capacity was used to the advantage of all the members of the group; but if it was considered a serious handicap to the group, it was eliminated, often with blunt ruthlessness. Only by group solidarity and mutual aid could survival be made possible in the conflict with unconquered nature and hostile groups.

In this struggle, the child naturally was low in the scale of value; and when a choice had to be made, he and not the able-bodied adult was selected for elimination or exploitation. In the simpler stages of societal development, the problems of existence were immediate and the answers invariably were direct. A child was born, there was no room or food for him, so the parents snuffed out his life. At first, here and there, this was a personal, individual reaction. Repeated and continued, it became a social observance, and the practice of infanticide was established. The extent of its use, the degree of its social acceptance, the forms which it took, and the substitutes which arose vary in place and with time, but all the students of it emphasize poverty as its basic, precipitating factor.[20] It is for this reason that infanticide and its harsh accompaniments are found extensively in countries like China and Japan when they reach a stage of marked populousness. The Greeks constantly emphasized this idea. "Why do you expose your child?" a Greek father was asked. "Because," he replied, "I love the children I have." Roman legislation against infanticide

[20] Edward Westermarck, *The Origin and Development of Moral Ideas*, Macmillan & Co., Ltd., London, 1906; Chrisman, *op. cit.*; Miller, *op. cit.*

and its substitutes clearly showed economic pressure as the chief causal factor. It is interesting to note, in passing, that some of the later emperors, in their awareness of this fact, attempted to strike at the problem by measures that were aimed at improving the condition of the parents.

What has been said about the relation of economic pressure to infanticide is equally true in regard to other practices which signify the status of childhood, or the lack of it. The heavy hand of economic want or scarcity lay heavy upon the heads of children through the ages. Parents loved their children, they indulged them when and as they could; but the institutionalized arrangements which determined the scope and scale of childhood were fixed by economic limits that were basic and distinct. It was and is not until the culture has reached the stage where economic surplus, or capital, is created that, first, individual parents in considerable numbers and, then, the social pattern are freed from the necessity of realizing present personal material gain from the child; only then can the parent and society afford to allow the child to devote himself to the development of his own individuality apart from parental demands.

THE IDEOLOGICAL FACTOR

Against the dictates of necessity growing out of the economic factor is that deep and mystic bond which binds parent and child. Whatever form of neural hypothesis one supports concerning what is psychically inborn—whether parental affection is an instinct or an acquired emotional habit—the fact remains that it is real, deep-seated, and widespread. How then, we may ask, was it possible for many of the historic forms of child treatment to develop? Why did sheer mother love not suffice to safeguard the child during the centuries, even in the face of economic pressure?

The answer to these questions is to be found in the history of the social process of innumerable social groups, and it is this: The leaders in society invented plausible excuses to justify such practices because they considered it necessary to maintain them for other reasons. This is one of the functions of leadership: to take action which is necessary for some effective but not appealing reason, and to justify it in terms that are effective and in forms that are socially acceptable.

Consider infanticide. Direct want dictates its use in individual cases. As time goes on, it becomes customary. But mother love in many cases struggles against the custom. Social leadership, which accepts its necessity, must find—invent if you will—acceptable justification. There is recourse to many subterfuges. What more effective answer to mother love than fear of the gods? "Mother, the gods have need of your child. You must sacrifice him. If you do not, they will be angry, and they will visit their wrath upon all of us." Such an argument served a triple purpose: It offered the strongest kind of counteracting influence, it gave supernatural sanction, and it socialized the practice by making the entire group interested in its acceptance.

To the student of cultural history it is obvious that the various social and parental practices involving children, considered in the preceding sections, arose as scattered individual reactions to urgent and immediate needs, and that as these "answers" proved acceptable and effective they became general and customary. Thus arose the folkways of child care. As time goes on, these folkways are examined, challenged, criticized, and defended. Social leadership, convinced of their value, is intent upon their maintenance. Searching for support, the leaders develop justifying ideologies. A powerful ideology is the religious one. Throughout history, supernatural sanction has been constantly brought to bear in order to bolster up the folkways that have grown up. The whole terrifying threat of the malignancy of the spirit world is let loose upon those who tend to dispute the power and to threaten the interests of the predominant sex, class, or group. Those who stray from the beaten path of custom become tainted with moral iniquity.[21]

Although religious ideology has been used for purposes of concrete presentation, the idea advanced is this: What people have been taught to believe about children is the third basic factor in determining child status. Whether this factor is primary in character and original in time, or whether it is secondary, reinforcing, and rationalizing, is after all of minor importance, once it has developed and found social acceptance.

The role of Christianity in the history of childhood offers an excellent example of what has just been said. Here was a new religion, arising in one of the least important provinces of the Roman Empire and started by a poor Jewish carpenter, which in three centuries pushed its doctrines to the end of the vast imperial domain and even conquered the imperial throne. Its teachings, which were steadfastly held up to cultured Roman and uncouth barbarian, had implications for children, and in time changed many practices in regard to their treatment.

Jesus, the founder of this new religion, considered children an integral part of society. "Suffer little children, and forbid them not, to come unto me: for of such is the kingdom of heaven." Among the most stirring passages in the recorded words of Jesus are His references to children. His attitude toward them was one of the many revolutions which His religion involved. The fathers of the early church were so much given to praise of the ascetic life as to appear almost antagonistic to marriage, and it is true that during the first century or two there were few references to children. From the beginning, however, certain general consequences of the new religion had significance for children. Its teachings had a liberalizing and softening effect, concretely in regard to legislation and generally in the new understanding of human problems it gave.

The first specific way in which Christianity affected the treatment of children was in its successful fight against infanticide and exposure,

[21] Miller, *op. cit.*, pp. 33–34.

which from the beginning it denounced as murder. The attack on these practices was based on the idea that every human being has a soul. This means that children had souls; and if this was true, then infanticide and exposure were murder. The Christian Church won its first fight for children when it convinced the Roman world that they have souls.

But the old incentives for these practices remained, and the church had to grapple with the problem in ways other than ideological. One of these ways was to accept the responsibility for many parentless children. It became the custom, early in church history, for mothers who felt that they were unable to rear their children to confide them to the church. By the door of many church buildings were placed marble receptacles in which mothers left the children they were forced to give up. Not only did this save many individual children, but its psychological implications were tremendous in that it identified the church with mother love.

Institutions for children flourished within the folds of the medieval church. The first one to take care of helpless children, a hospital for foundling children, was established by Daltheus, Archbishop of Milan, in 787. Many similar institutions developed during the fourteenth and fifteenth centuries. In the eleventh century, a monastic order was founded for the care of poor and abandoned children. Many institutions of the medieval church cared for children as an adjunct to their other work.

Against this brighter side is the fact that some of the doctrines developed in the name of the Christian Church had seriously handicapping effects upon children. One was the doctrine of child depravity. The child had a soul, but this soul was stained because of its origin. "By their carnal conception and nativity, they come into the world, steeped in sin and guilt, the heirs of hell." For centuries this gloomy declaration was considered a mere truism. It is easy, of course, to brush it tolerantly aside today as a mere theological theory, but the fact is that it colored practice and led to many forms of ill treatment of children. The puritanical trait of abnormal sternness and repression, which interpreted simple childish mischievousness as the work of the devil, is directly descended from the honest belief in the utter depravity of human nature. What people believe about children, we repeat, is a determining factor in the status they accord to children.

THE FAMILIAL FACTOR

The familial factor is the final one which may be said to have basic significance in determining the status of childhood, and the two aspects of the family that are of outstanding importance in this connection are the structure or form of its organization, and the relative importance accorded to it as a social institution. The family is, of course, not an independent social institution capable of being fashioned as one wills. It is part and parcel of the organic life of society. From this it follows that the family's role as a determinant of child status is not separate and distinct from other factors; it may be difficult to say which is the result of the influence of the family and which the result, let us say, of the economic factor. On the other hand, the family is the social vehicle through which the child customarily finds and makes his earlier way in the world; hence it seems obvious that what the family is and is not at any time and place in the history of a social group will have great meaning for the life and status of its children.

With reference to the form of the family, what all its historians have emphasized is the superiority of the monogamous type. The monogamous family has come to be the prevailing form because of its superiority over other historic competing forms. One of the bases of its superiority through the centuries of human experience is its high survival value. It is the best form of family life for children and the survival of child life. Polygyny, a competing form, is weak in its effect upon children. The care of the child tends, under this form, to rest more upon the mother. There is less biparental rearing of children.

In addition to the form, there is the relative importance of the family as a social institution. Among some peoples, the home and the family are of great significance, almost dwarfing at time other social institutions such as the state or the church. The family is the center of life and the outstanding vehicle for the transmission of the culture and values of the societal group. Because of this, the relationship between successive generations is closer and continues over a longer period of time than would otherwise obtain. On the other hand, there are and have been cultures in which the family seems of relatively minor importance. In ancient Sparta, for example, the state and not the family was considered paramount. In the Persia of classic times, the child remained with his mother until his fifth year; the father never saw him until then. At the end of this period, the boy left his mother and went under the care of the state to begin his physical training. But in China, through the centuries, the family has been of great importance and parental authority is strong, as a result of ancestor worship and the constant stress upon filial duty and piety. It is variations like these, in the relative position as well as the structure of family life, that have great basic meaning for the student of child problems.

Summary

1. The history of childhood presents special difficulties to the student, first because it is so inevitably bound up with every other aspect of life, and second, because of the relative dearth of historical data on childhood. This is in itself an index of the past status of children.

2. Children constituted a relatively large population element in primitive society. Although they were desired, abortion, infanticide, child spacing, short infancy, and early labor were common in the primitive cultures of the past.

3. Certain changes in the status of children can be noted in the civilizations of classic antiquity. Infanticide often softened into abandonment and exposure, child selling developed as a substitute for both, and emphasis on the duty of children to support their parents became common. However, there remained the sweeping and arbitrary rights of parents to use their child in whatever way was to their advantage.

4. The status of the medieval child was the product of a blending of Roman, German, and Christian influences. Childhood was short, rigorous work came early in life, and child rearing was coldly severe and harsh, even at the level of royalty.

5. Newer attitudes toward children appeared in England during the eighteenth century. Despite the retention of historic practices, parents began to show some conception of their duties to their children. Such changes, however, were limited in extent and scope.

6. Reviewing the general history of childhood, we see four factors as the basic determinants in its status: (a) the arithmetic of reproduction; (b) the prevailing economic situation; (c) the ideological factor; and (d) the familial factor.

Chapter 31

The Changing Status
of Childhood in the United States

In the preceding chapter the historical status of childhood was reviewed, with special reference to its development in western Europe, culminating in the England of the eighteenth century. This was emphasized because it constitutes the essential background for the story of the changing status of childhood in the United States, with which the present chapter is concerned. In an effort at effective presentation, this discussion is presented in three parts: (1) selected aspects of colonial child life, together with a summary statement regarding the status of the colonial child; (2) the status of childhood in contemporary America; and (3) the factors in the emancipation or changing status of childhood in this country. But first a brief reference to the early American reproduction of the European pattern of child status.

The Early American Reproduction of the European Pattern
of Child Status

More than 300 years ago, the United States began its history with scattered settlements of adventurous or disgruntled Europeans, chiefly English. The culture they established here did not arise *de novo;* it was the culture that prevailed in the Europe from which they came. And yet it was not, and could not be, exactly the same. The early settlers were mostly dissenters, which meant that they would make changes when opportunity afforded. In addition, they transplanted their culture to a new world, which meant that although the broad outlines and the general features of the European culture would be established here, there would be variations in the picture in adjusting to the new scene. Although much emphasis is given in popular thought to the seventeenth-century pioneers, the migration to colonial America was particularly heavy during the latter part of the seventeenth and the first half of the eighteenth centuries. These new and large-scale infusions tended to act, therefore, as a constant factor for the retention of the Old World ways and values.

What has just been said was true regarding the treatment of children, as it was about other aspects of life. Beginning with the same basic concepts of child status which obtained in the England and Europe from which the settlers of America came, the detailed expression of these basic concepts took form in terms of the minutiae of colonial American life. This is what is meant by the early American reproduction of the European pattern of child status.

Selected Aspects of Colonial Child Life

Colonial childhood is largely hidden in obscurity. "We know little," writes Mrs. Earle in her delightful volume on colonial child life, "of the childhood days of our forebears, and have scant opportunity to make comparisons or note progress. The child of colonial days was emphatically 'to be seen, not to be heard,'—nor was he even to be much in evidence to the eye. He was of as little importance in domestic, social, or ethical relations as his childish successor is of great importance today; it was deemed neither courteous, decorous, nor wise to make him appear of value or note in his own eyes, or in the eyes of his seniors. Hence there was none of that exhaustive study of the motives, thoughts, and acts of a child which is now so rife."[1] Scattered bits of evidence, however, are available, and they have been gathered together by social historians.[2] On the basis of their works, we are able to piece together the general outlines of the picture of child status. This picture is most clearly revealed in New England, first, because the forefathers there left comments and records to a greater extent than elsewhere, and second, because the greater homogeneity of the population made for a more distinct cultural pattern. It is estimated that at the opening of the Revolutionary War, 98 percent of the people of New England were English or unmixed descendants of the English. Nowhere else in the American colonies was there so homogeneous a population, or one of such uniformly high quality. Stoughton, the lieutenant governor of Massachusetts (1692–1701) said: "God sifted a whole nation, that he might send choice grain over into the wilderness."[3]

[1] Alice Morse Earle, *Child Life in Colonial Days,* The Macmillan Company, New York, 1899, p. vii.

[2] Particularly interesting and valuable in this connection are the works of Mrs. Earle and Dr. Calhoun. In addition to her *Child Life in Colonial Days,* Mrs. Earle has written *Home Life in Colonial Days* (The Macmillan Company, New York, 1898), *Colonial Days in Old New York* and *Customs and Fashions in Old New England,* the latter two published by Charles Scribner's Sons, New York, in 1896 and 1893 respectively. Dr. Arthur W. Calhoun's monumental three-volume work, *A Social History of the American Family* (Arthur H. Clark Company, Cleveland, 1919), is invaluable in this connection.

[3] Reuben G. Thwaites, *The Colonies, 1492–1750,* Longmans, Green & Company, Inc., New York, 1890, p. 181.

In turning, then, to a brief account of selected aspects of colonial child life, as we do at this point, we shall tell the story principally in terms of New England, but with comparisons with and references to circumstances in other sections of colonial America.

1. In pioneer days, when many forms of social organization have not yet reached a high state of development, the home and the family naturally are of great importance. Marriage occurred at an early age— for men more often under 20 than over; for girls, customarily at 16, often even younger. A man or woman without family ties was almost unthinkable. In case of the death of a husband or wife, remarriage was prompt.

2. The patriarchal form of family prevailed in colonial days. It was, speaking generally, a property-holding institution. In most parts of the colonies it was dominated by middle-class standards. It and the church were the two chief agencies of social control, and the family, in addition to being such an agency in its own right, was also important as the nursery of the church. It had, above all things, to be protected. "Ruin families and you ruin all."

3. Filled with Biblical traditions, there was in these families a cultivated desire for abundant posterity. Large ones were the rule. Families of 10 or 12 were quite common; 20 or 25 children in one family were not rare enough to occasion comment. Sir William Phips was one of 26 children, all with the same mother. Green, a Boston printer, had 30 children; Benjamin Franklin, another printer, came from a Boston family of 17. The Reverend Samuel Willard, the first minister of Groton, Massachusetts, had 20 children and was himself one of 17; the Reverend John Sherman, of Watertown, Massachusetts, had 26 children by two wives; the Reverend Moses Fiske had 16; and the Reverend Abigah Weld, of Attleboro, Massachusetts, with an annual salary of $220, had 15 children, reared a grandchild, lived with generous hospitality, and contributed to the needs of the poor. Special mention must be made of Mrs. Sara Thayer, whose death in 1751 led to the following poetic celebration of her fecund importance:

> Also she was a fruitful vine,
> The truth I may relate,—
> Fourteen was of her body born
> And lived to man's estate.
>
> From these did spring a numerous race,
> One hundred thirty-two;
> Sixty and six each sex alike,
> So I declare to you.

Nor must it be supposed that families of this size were limited to New England. The situation was similar in the other colonies. Patrick Henry was one of 19 children, and John Marshall was the first of 15; family magnitude in Maryland is shown by this revealing sentence: "Manor houses with outstretched wings were built to gather under their sheltering roofs the dozen or more little ones who usually came to break the stillness of the quiet days in that far-off time when there was more of maternity than nervous energy in the world."[4] Complementing this numerous progeny and further increasing the size of the family was the presence of relatives. Since women had few economic opportunities unless they were attached to some family, the typical family included several adult unmarried women—unpaid servants of their kindred.

4. As one would expect, maternal mortality in colonial America was high. Many women died exhausted by maternity and labor, to be succeeded by another and younger wife who carried on the torch of fecundity. Most of the large families of earlier times were the offspring of at least two wives, and marriages three and four deep were no rarity. We might be tempted to think of these marrying colonial husbands as a species of chronological Mormons.

5. Like maternal mortality, infant mortality was excessively high. Here, for example, is a portion of an early American family history that tells a story in itself:

In memory of
Mary the Daughter of John
and Effie Lewis who died 9th Nov. 1771
aged 4 years also
Seven children of Jno and Elizth Lewis

John Richard died	2d July 1787	aged 2 mo
Elizabeth	16th April 1789	11—
Richard	25th Feb 1791	7—
John	17th April 1795	1 yr
Eliza	24th July 1797	8 mo
Eliza	28th July 1800	3—
Jessy	3rd April 1805	4 yrs

Cases like these were not unusual. Of Cotton Mather's 15 children, only 2 survived him; of Judge Sewall's 14, only 3 survived.

There were obvious reasons for this high mortality rate among infants and young children. To begin with, for many years child rearing presented special difficulties in the New World. The climate was different from the historic habitat of the race, as were various items of diet. Distances were great, and physicians were not readily available; even if they were, the accepted treatment they gave for children's diseases was of doubtful value. Many of the ingredients and extracts used as medicines were incredibly revolting and absolutely ineffective, at best. Houses were not well built, and the roaring chimneys scorched within a distance of a few feet and left the rest of the house unheated. Then, too, many curious ideas prevailed about child rearing. One was that children

---

[4] Quoted from Calhoun, *op. cit.*, Vol. I, p. 286.

—at least parts of them—had to be toughened. One such part was their feet. Colonial New Englanders were always wetting children's feet with cold water to harden them. Children were deliberately made to wear thin-soled shoes so that the "wet may come freely in." Josiah Quincy writes that in his boyhood he sat more than half the time with wet feet. But above all, in its incredible uniqueness and selective significance, was the requirement, in New England at least, whereby all children had to be baptized in the meeting house the first Sunday after birth. The particular point about this requirement was the fact that New England meeting houses were unheated until after the Revolutionary War. Bearing this fact in mind, we are in a position to appreciate the full import of the following entry in the diary of Judge Sewall of Boston, under date of January 22, 1694: "A very extraordinary Storm by reason of the falling and driving of Snow. Few women could get to meeting. A child named Alexander was baptized in the afternoon." The ice in the baptismal font often had to be broken before the christening could proceed. Of a truth we can maintain with Mrs. Earle that such an ordeal may well have given rise to the expression "the survival of the fittest." Finally, other factors in the excessive infant mortality were the following: The laws of sanitation were disregarded, because unknown; disinfection, in the form of a scant sprinkling of vinegar, was but feebly practiced; drainage was both non-existent and deemed of no importance.

6. Large families and child labor go hand in hand, and colonial America was no exception. In fact, parents increased the size of their families with an eye to their children's future usefulness. As early as 1629, Higgeson wrote in his *New England's Plantation* that "little children here by setting of corne may earne much more than their own maintenance," and less than a decade later the people of Rowley were praised because they "built a fulling mill and caused their little ones to be very diligent in spinning cotton wool."

Fortunately, as happens at times, self-interest and religious precept dovetailed neatly with each other. Following their favorite model, the Hebrews, the Puritans conceived of idleness as a sin. Truly, they insisted, the devil did find work for idle hands. Moreover, the problem confronted all classes. Wrote Judge Sewall in 1725 concerning his grandson: "Sam Hirst got up betime in the morning, and took Ben Swett with him and went into the Common to play Wicket. Went before anybody was up, left the door open; Sam came not to prayer at which I was much displeased." Another entry in the Judge's diary, made two days later, gives further information concerning Sam and his grandfather. This entry reads: "Did the like again, but took not Ben with him. I told him he could not lodge here practising thus. So he lodged elsewhere."

The value of the tasks performed by children in colonial days is obvious. Although there were some small industries which employed children, most of the work was on the farm. Here there were the customary chores to do—bringing in fuel, cutting feed, watering horses, picking berries, gathering vegetables, sawing and chopping wood; then too they could sow seeds, weed flax fields, hetchel flax, comb wool, split shoe pegs, make brooms, and the like. The custom of making Saturday a school holiday grew out of the necessity of catching up with the week's work in preparation for the Sabbath.

While these tasks were varied and often interesting, and constituted a phase of education not yet replaced in our modern system, the fact is that children, little children, worked hard. But adults worked hard, too. Hard work was a colonial necessity for both. The struggle for existence in the New World was a stern reality.[5]

7. The well-being of the family was conceived to depend on rigid family discipline. The behavior of children toward their parents and elders was formal and meek. Parents were addressed as "esteemed parent" or "honored sir and madam"; a pert child was thought to be delirious and bewitched. Reading both between the lines and the lines themselves of the following letter, written by an 11-year-old Long Island miss to her grandfather, tells us a great deal:

Ever Honored Grandfather:
Sir: My long absence from you and my dear Grandmother has been not a little tedious to me. But what renders me a Vast Deal of pleasure is Being intensely happy with a Dear and Tender mother-in-law and frequent opportunities of hearing of your Health and Welfare which I pray God may long Continue. What I have more to add is to acquaint you that I have already made a Considerable Progress in Learning. I have already gone through some Rules of Arithmetic, and in a little Time shall be able of giving you a Better acct of my Learning, and in mean time I am Duty Bound to subscribe myself

Your most obedient and
Duty full Granddaughter
Pegga Treadwell[6]

The rod was universally accepted as the instrument of subjugation. John Robinson, the Pilgrim preacher, stated the prevailing philosophy in these words: "Surely there is in all children (tho not alike) a stubbernes and stoutnes of minde arising from naturall pride which must in the first place be broken and beaten down so that the foundation of their education being layd in humilitie and tractableness other virtues may in their time be built thereon. It is commendable in a horse that he be stout and stomackfull being never left to his own government, but always to have his rider on his back and his bit in his mouth, but who would have his child like his horse in his brutishnes?"[7]

[5] *Ibid.*, Vol. I, pp. 124–127, 286–288.
[6] Earle, *Colonial Days in Old New York*, pp. 16–17.
[7] Quoted from Calhoun, *op. cit.*, Vol. I, p. 112.

In this breaking and beating-down process, the school amply aided and abetted the home. Schools, like homes, resounded with strokes of the rod. Ferules, flat ladle-shaped pieces of wood to strike the palms of the pupils' hands, were a standard furnishing in colonial schoolhouses; birch rods, sold at goodly prices on the streets of London, were supplied in copious quantities on the New England hills; the flapper, a heavy piece of leather six inches in diameter, with a hole in the middle, and fastened to a pliable handle, was devised by a pitiless pedagogue of the times; and the cat-o'-nine-tails was widely known and used. Individual teachers, and no doubt particular parents, devised their own unique contributions to the corporal methodology of their day.

Colonial law was clear and positive in its support of paternal authority. For incorrigible disobedience to parents the death penalty was prescribed. The following law of New York, dating to the time that the colony passed from Dutch to English control, expresses the general attitude of the era: "If any Child or Children, above sixteen years of age, and of Sufficient understanding, shall smite their Natural Father or Mother, unless provoked and forct for their selfe preservation from Death of Mayming, at the Complaint of said Father or Mother, and not otherwise, they being Sufficient witness thereof, that Child, or those Children so offending shall be put to Death."[8] Punishment for lesser offenses of the kind were dealt with by the civil authorities. To deal with "divers children and servants" who "behave themselves disobediently and disorderly, towards their parents, masters and governors, to the disturbance of families," an early Massachusetts law gave authority to magistrates to "summon offenders and have them punished by whipping and otherwise."

8. A separate aspect of child life in colonial days, yet closely related to the matter of family discipline, was the marked emphasis upon manners and courtesy. This was a carry-over from the earlier days in old England when children were sent to school or placed in great men's houses to learn the courtesies and formalities of life, and when these things were considered more important elements in education than philosophy and the classics. In her delightful and penetrating chapter on manners and courtesy in her *Child Life in Colonial Days*, Mrs. Earle shows how, at a time when neighborhood life comprised the whole outside world, these refinements of human relations were what made life endurable, and that, viewed from this angle, the legislation and lawsuits involving lying, name calling, scandalmongering, and so on, were really essential to the keeping of the peace.

Authors and readers of modern books on etiquette need to be reminded that similar books existed in days far removed from the present. Various such printed books go back to the fifteenth and sixteenth centuries, and

---

[8] Quoted from Earle, *Colonial Days in Old New York*, p. 16.

these, together with those of later date written by colonial authors, were widely used. There was The Babees Book; the Lytill Children's Lytill Boke; the Boke of Curtasye; and the Schole of Vertue; and extracts of these will convey, as perhaps nothing else can, the emphases in child deportment in colonial days.

First follows an often-used list of instructions for table etiquette.

Never sit down at the table till asked, and after the blessing. Ask for nothing; tarry till it be offered thee. Speak not. Bite not thy bread but break it. Take salt only with a clean knife. Dip not the meat in the same. Hold not thy knife upright but sloping, and lay it down at right hand of plate with blade on plate. Look not earnestly at any other that is eating. When moderately satisfied leave the table. Sing not, hum not, wiggle not. Spit nowhere in the room but in the corner, and wipe it with thy foot.

Supplementing these are the following instructions:

Eat not too fast nor with Greedy Behavior. Eat not vastly but moderately. Make not a noise with thy Tongue, Mouth, Lips, or Breath in Thy Eating and Drinking. Smell not of thy Meat; nor put it to Thy Nose; turn it not the other side upward to view it upon thy Plate or Trencher. Foul not the napkin all over, but at one corner only. Gnaw not Bones at the Table, but clean them with thy knife and hold them not with the whole hand, but with two Fingers. When thou blowest thy Nose, let thy Handkerchief be used. . . .

Intriguing to the modern reader is the emphasis upon the long-neglected art of good listening: "When any speak to thee, stand up. Say not I have heard it before. Never endeavor to help him out if he tell it not right. Snigger not; never question the Truth of it."

Quite fashionable were the etiquette manuals which set forth their injunctions in verse, concessions no doubt to the progressive wing among parents and educators of the time. Part of one of these follows:

> Make cleane your shoes, and combe your head,
> And your cloathes button or lace;
> And see at no tyme you forget
> To wash your hands and face.
> . . . .
> Burnish no bones with your teeth,
> For that is unseemly;
> Rend not thy meate asunder,
> For that swarves from curtasye.
> Dip not thy meate in the Saltseller,
> But take it with thy knife.
> And sup not lowde of the Pottage,
> No tyme in all thy lyfe.
> Defile not thy lips with eating much,
> As a Pigge eating draffe;

> Eate softly and drinke mannerlye,
> Take heed you do not quaffe.
> Scratche not thy head with thy fyngers
> When thou art at thy meate;
> Nor spytte you over the table boorde;
> See thou dost not this forget.

Of all the directions for general deportment in these etiquette books —and there were many—probably none so appeals to the modern reader familiar with the ways of contemporary youth as the one indicating the proper behavior of a young person when spoken to by a grown person: "Not to lumischli cast thine head a-down, but with a sad cheer to look him in the face."

Perhaps the best general picture of the deportment expected of colonial youth is given by the kinsman biographer of David and John Brainerd, who were born in Connecticut in 1718 and 1720, respectively:

A boy was early taught a profound respect for his parents, teachers, and guardians, and implicit prompt obedience. If he undertook to rebel his will was broken by persistent and adequate punishment. He was taught that it was a sin to find fault with his meals, his apparel, his tasks or his lot in life. Courtesy was enjoined as a duty. He must be silent among his superiors. If addressed by older persons he must respond with a bow. He was to bow as he entered and left the school, and to every man and woman, old or young, rich or poor, black or white, whom he met on the road. Special punishment was visited upon him if he failed to show respect for the aged, the poor, the colored, or to any persons whatever whom God had visited with infirmities."[9]

9. From all that has been said concerning parental authority, it is easy to understand the desire of parents to control closely the courtship of their children, particularly their daughters, and that the right to do so was granted to them by law. The Puritan lawmaker, especially, who meddled with so many detailed aspects of life, could not leave untouched so vital a part of family and individual relationships, and the early age at which courtship and marriage customarily occurred gave to such legislation the sanction of common sense. Although there were many cases in which legal barriers to courtship were more honored in the breach than in the keeping, nevertheless the court records of the time are dotted with indictments, convictions, fines, imprisonments, and whipping-post treatments for those who took matters into their own hands. Let us relive, in imagination and for the sake of example, the drama of Jacob Murline and Sarah Tuttle. It happened in New Haven, Connecticut, on May Day in 1660. Sarah went to the neighboring Murline home to get some thread. Some loud jokes were exchanged with the two Murline misses when their brother Jacob entered the room, seized Sarah's gloves, and demanded the

[9] Earle, *Child Life in Colonial Days*, p. 224.

centuries-old forfeit of a kiss. "Whereupon, they sat down together; his arm being about her; and her arm upon his shoulder or about his neck; and hee kissed her, and shee kissed him, or they kissed one another, continuing in this posture about half an hour." Such kissing, let it be made clear at this point, was unauthorized. Moreover, Mr. Tuttle, Sarah's father, was a man of substance and of dignity. Promptly and angrily he brought suit against Jacob, the charge being that Jacob had inveigled his daughter's affections. The facts were established by adequate testimony. Finally the court asked Sarah whether Jacob had inveigled her, and she replied, "No." The court was outraged and baffled, for her answer precluded any judgment being rendered against Jacob. But the ends of justice had to be served, so the court fined Sarah, gave her a severe lecture, and called her a "Bould Virgin." Sarah was impressed. Demurely and piously she answered that she hoped that "God would help her to carry it Better for time to come." We cannot but be relieved, even after a lapse of three centuries, to find that she did learn to carry it better, for two years later the fine, still unpaid, was reduced by half.

It is not to be assumed, however, that parental control over courtship was supreme and unchallenged. Willful maids then as now overrode the parental mandate, and legal support for their independence was, at times, forthcoming. For above the parental authority was that of the general society or community. In a new country that needed population, discouragement of its legitimate increase by the personal motives of individual parents had to contend with the public interest; hence when parental prerogatives were exercised past a certain point to the undue delayment of marriage, the young people could appeal to the magistrates to bring their unruly parents to terms.

10. Looming large in the childhood of our forebears was the emphasis upon the religious aspects of life. The curing of souls began very early in life. For this there were two reasons. The first was the general tendency to regard the child as a miniature adult, which meant that the child's needs and experiences, and the procedure used with him, were the same as for the adult, an inference that was applied to spheres of life other than the religious. The second reason was the common acceptance of the idea of child depravity. Whitfield, the great preacher, likened children to rattlesnakes and alligators, which he said were likewise beautiful when small. Jonathan Edwards called them "young vipers." He said: "As innocent as children seem to be to us, yet, if they are out of Christ, they are not so in God's sight, but are young vipers, and are infinitely more hateful than vipers."[10]

The logical sequence of these two beliefs was a firm conviction regarding the necessity and propriety of infantile conversion. At the very out-

[10] Works of Jonathan Edwards, New York, 1881, Vol. III, p. 340.

set of their lives, children were confronted with the terrors of hell, from which escape was possible only by accepting the procedures prescribed by their pious elders. What this implied in outstanding homes of the times may be gathered from the following recorded instances. For example, Cotton Mather wrote:

> I took my little daughter Katy (aged four) into my study and there told my child that I am to dy shortly and she must, when I am dead, remember everything I now said to her. I sett before her the sinfull condition of her nature, and charged her to pray in secret places every day. That God for the sake of Jesus Christ would give her a new heart. . . . I gave her to understand that when I am taken from her she must look to meet with more humbling afflictions than she does now she has a tender father to provide for her."[11]

It is a relief to know that the Reverend Mather was spared to Katy for thirty years after this recorded conversation—indeed, he survived her.

That pillar of Boston colonial society, Judge Sewall, wrote with great feeling concerning his children. When Sam, his son, was 10 years old, there appeared this entry in the Judge's diary:

> Richard Durner, a flourishing youth of 9 years old, dies of the Small Pochs. I tell Sam of it and what need he had to prepare for Death, and therefore to endeavor really to pray, when he said over the Lord's Prayer; He seemed not much to mind, eating an Aple; but when he came to say Our Father he burst out into a bitter cry and said he was afraid he should die. I pray'd with him and read Scriptures comforting against Death, or O Death where is thy sting &c. All things yours. Life and Immortality brought to light by Christ.

"Stirred up more dreadfully to seek God," as the Judge put it, was his daughter Betty. The following entries concern her:

> When I came in, past 7 at night, my wife met me in the Entry and told me Betty had surprised them. I was surprised with the Abruptness of the relation. It seems Betty Sewall had given some signs of dejection and sorrow; but a little while after dinner she burst out into an amazing cry, which caus'd all the family to cry too; Her Mother ask'd the reason, she gave none; at last said she was afraid she should goe to Hell, her Sins were not pardon'd. She was first wounded by my reading a sermon of Mr. Norton's, Text, Ye shall seek me and shall not find me. And those words in the Sermon, Ye shall seek me and die in your Sins ran in her mind and terrified her greatly. And staying at home she read out of Mr. Cotton Mather—Why hath Satan filled thy Heart, which increased her Fear. Her Mother asked her whether she pray'd. She answered yes but fear'd her prayers were not heard because her sins were not pardon'd.

A fortnight later he wrote:

> Betty comes into me as soon as I was up and tells me the disquiet she had when wak'd; told me she was afraid she should go to Hell, was like Spira, not

[11] Calhoun, *op. cit.*, Vol. I, p. 108.

Elected. Ask'd her what I should pray for, she said that God would pardon her Sin and give her a new heart. I answer'd her Fears as well as I could and pray'd with many Tears on either part. Hope God heard us.

Three months later still he made this entry:

Betty can hardly read her chapter for weeping, tells me she is afraid she is gon back, does not taste that sweetness in reading the Word which once she did; fears that what was once upon her is worn off. I said what I could to her and in the evening pray'd with her along.

Betty, we must add, survived to marry and bear eight children before she died at the age of 35.[12]

One more example must suffice. Nathaniel Mather died at 19, but while he lived prayed thrice a day, not "slubbering over his prayers with hasty amputations, but wrestled in them for a good part of an hour." In his diary, in which he wrote out in detail his covenants with God, he included the following paragraph:

When very young I went astray from God and my mind was altogether taken with vanities and follies: such as the remembrance of them doth greatly abase my soul within me. Of the manifold sins which then I was guilty of, none so sticks upon me as that, being very young, I was *whitling* on the Sabbath-day; and for fear of being seen, I did it behind the *door*. A great *reproach* of God! a specimen of that *atheism* I brought into the world with me![13]

11. It would be wrong to suppose that life for colonial children was wholly drab. That there were lighter and joyous moments is clear, even if we had only the complaints of the Puritan theologians to go by. The mere size of many families was enough to insure some recreational developments. But there is much evidence that, in spite of parental authority and the repressive spirit of the time, colonial children, in their search for fun and their love for sport, were much like children today. Even the colonial meeting house, sacred as it was and central to the life of the community as were its services, was not safe from the surgings of youth. Boys and girls were pests to many a parson, and had to be put under town surveillance. King Philip's War was considered a judgment from God on the Massachusetts colony for the "disorder and rudeness of youth in many congregations in time of worship of God, whereby sin and profaneness is greatly increased."

In 1772 the following action was taken in Farmington: "Where as indecencies are practised by the young people in time of Publick Worship by frequently passing and repassing by one another in the galleries; intermingling of the sexes to the great disturbance of many serious and well minded persons—Resolved that each of us that are heads of families will use our utmost endeavors to suppress the evils."

[12] Earle, *Customs and Fashions in Old New England,* pp. 11–12.
[13] *Ibid.,* p. 15.

Despite the seriousness with which any levity at public worship was taken, the "wretched boys" presented a perennial problem, and many children were brought before the public authorities. The character of the misbehavior in such cases may be gathered from the record made by a Connecticut justice in 1750, regarding a small boy brought before him:

A rude and Idel Behaver in the meting hows Such as Smiling and Larfing and Intiseing others to the Same Evil

Such as Whispering and Larfing in the meting hows between metings

Such as Larfing or Smiling and pulling the hair of nayber benomi Simkins at the time of Publick Worship

Such as playing with her Hand and fingers at her hair

Such as throwing Sister penticost perkins on the ice it being Sabath day or Lord's day between the meting hows and his plaes of Abode.

Then there were the various games which colonial children played— tag, stone tag, and wood tag; honey pots; kite flying; marbles; hop, skip, and jump; cricket; leapfrog; hopscotch; squares; wicket; and many others. Coasting downhill became a most popular sport, although colonial youth had to win the right to enjoy it. A Massachusetts law of 1633 classified "common coasters, unprofitable fowlers and tabacco-takers" together as similarly detrimental. Even among the Dutch in Albany, the constables at one time were ordered to take the "small or great slees" in which "boys and girls ryde down the hills" and break them into pieces.

It is interesting to recall that football was played early in our history. In 1657, Boston passed a law which read: "Forasmuch as sundry complaints are made that several persons have received hurt by boys and young men playing at football in the streets, these therefore are to enjoin that none be found at that game in any of the streets, lanes or enclosures of this town under the penalty of 20s. for every such offence."

VARIATIONS IN THE COLONIAL SCENE

As was pointed out earlier in the chapter, this picture of colonial childhood has been drawn primarily with reference to New England. It was there that the lines of the picture are clearest and most distinct. In other parts of colonial America, the picture varied, even though, for the most part, the general features remained. These variations grew out of the cultural differences in the groups which settled the respective colonies. The Dutch who settled New York, for example, were a milder species of the genus to which the Puritans belonged. True, the tradition of paternal authority was as strong among the Dutch as in New England, and Dutch children were respectful and subdued in their manners; yet, on the whole, they were on more familiar terms with their parents and had more ample amusements. It is significant that schoolmasters, in complaining of youthful subordination, referred to maternal complicity in the children's mischief.

In the other middle colonies, paternal authority was likewise strictly upheld, although the minutiae of child life were much softer than in New England. The emphasis here was less upon worship and the restriction of play, and more upon work. Perhaps the outstanding fact in the history of the middle colonies was the unsettling influence of the heterogeneity of the population. Liberalizing influences operated from the beginning, but emphasis on work was an acceptable common denominator. Sons of wealthy Quakers in Pennsylvania and New Jersey were often indentured. Every man had to have a trade or occupation to follow. Daughters of wealthy Pennsylvania farmers worked as servants in other homes to complete their training in the domestic arts. This was their substitute for what in other places and times has been spoken of as a finishing school. The chief complaints against children and women in the middle colonies did not involve their religious activities and attitudes, as in New England, but "their going after fashions and ease to the neglect of butter-making, weaving, spinning and cooking."

Turning to the southern colonies, we find that the picture of early marriage, large families, excessive mortality, and youthful labor was much like that in New England. Concerning the spiritual and educational welfare of their children, colonial Southerners were solicitous to be sure, but the intensity was less and the vicissitudes were greater than among the Puritans. Family government in the southern colonies was patriarchal, but less harsh and forbidding than in other sections.

THE STATUS OF THE COLONIAL CHILD

Enough has been said, it is hoped, to enable the reader to picture the colonial scene as the children were related to it. The basic concept concerning the child which the early settlers brought with them was that which prevailed in the Europe from which they came. This concept may be stated in its simplest form in these words: The status of the child was distinctly subordinate. A study of parent-child relationships of the time shows much that is interesting and unique, but seldom do we find the idea of children treated with any thought of their individual needs, capacities, or potentialities. Only as they fitted into the pattern of adult life in the community, only as their abilities and interests contributed to the welfare and interests of their elders were they considered to be of any importance. In the postfeudal period, as under feudalism and slavery, the personal and affectional relations of children to their own parents and to other older people were a distinctly secondary consideration. The dead hand of historical tradition, the pioneer conditions of colonial America, the emptiness of the country, the constant shortage of hands for labor all combined to reëstablish the system of childhood exploitation in the early days of our history.

And yet, as we study this picture of colonial child life, we cannot but be impressed with the fact that, from the start, differences from the rigorousness of child life in Europe developed here in the New World, and that, as time went on, many of the harsh lines began to soften.

The Status of Childhood in Contemporary America

Against the picture set forth in the preceding pages stands the child in our contemporary society. Today, as can be readily perceived, the child and his interests and welfare are of prior and paramount importance. Not only is this the dictum of recent legislation and judicial decisions, it is the tacit assumption in the organization of the lives of millions of families and hundreds of communities. In the children's division of that new Magna Charta of human rights which a century and more of social struggle has evolved in our Western civilization, there are no emphases upon the rights of parents and relatively few upon the rights of society. Rather, they are upon the rights of children. Moreover, these rights are not simply new versions of the child's old prerogatives in the matter of food, shelter, and reasonable care; they are new rights, unknown and albeit inconceivable to parents and citizens of earlier centuries. The Children's Charter formulated by the third White House Conference on Child Health and Protection would have been as sacrilegious or unfathomable to the parents of a thousand years ago as the Declaration of Independence would have been to Louis XIV of France.

That the whole life of the modern child—all that is done and hoped and planned for him, either by individual parents or by organized social agencies—represents the opposite pole of the concept held 2000 or 200 years ago, is obvious; through the welter of changing circumstances and criteria we seek for the substance of the change. What is the essential change in the nature of the status of childhood?

The answer proposed is this: The essence of the change is the child's shift from a subordinate and incidental position in a family group dominated by an autocratic parent to one of acceptance as an equal with his own personality, needs, and problems of development. More tersely stated, it is a change from a position of subordination to one of equality, both in the family and in the larger social group. Use words to hide the truth as we will, the fact of the matter is that for centuries the child was dominated by his elders to be exploited in their interests. He had no rights, except as they fitted into the interests of his elders or his kinship group. That the bases of established authority upon which this exploitation rested came at various times and places to be clothed in ethical terms may confuse but does not alter the essential fact.

Today the child is recognized as a human personality in a peculiarly vital stage of development. He is a coequal personality in the emerging democracy of the family. The guarding of this personality is the child's precious right, and the dangers which threaten it are recognized social problems; the development of this personality is his most precious opportunity, and the furtherance and guidance of that development are the concern of his elders.

THE NATURE OF THE CHANGE

The great changes in human history occur, not in the mechanical gadgets which men use or in the institutionalized arrangements by which they live, but in their attitudes and in the values they accept. The revolutions of the past which have had great meaning for mankind are those which have taken place in the minds of men.

The outstanding change in the recent history of children has taken place in the minds of their elders. It has been essentially a change in the way in which older people, particularly parents, have come to regard children. This change has constituted a revolution in the life and status of children as a social element in the population.

Because this revolution has been achieved through gradual and voluntary concessions, rather than wrested by means of the more spectacular devices of bloodshed and riots, social historians have been slow to identify it or to appreciate its importance. Yet so profound and so far reaching in its consequences is this change in status proving to be that, viewed in the retrospect with a lengthened perspective, we may yet recognize it as one of the great revolutions of history.

Factors in the Emancipation of American Childhood

Having in mind the nature and the epoch-making scope of this change, we propose in the remainder of this chapter to analyze the factors in American life which have been responsible for this transformation. Following the outline of the factors identified in the general analyses in Chapter 30, we suggest that the emancipation of American childhood is the result primarily of four factors: the arithmetical, the economic, the ideological, and the familial. In each of these aspects of our life, great changes have occurred within the span of American history, and it is our purpose next to describe these changes and show their meaning for American childhood.

THE CHANGING ARITHMETIC OF REPRODUCTION

In Chapter 30 it was pointed out that the arithmetic of reproduction has operated through the ages as a basic factor in determining the status of childhood. Specifically, what was described there was the "easy-come and easy-go" method of reproduction—natural, wasteful, and involving a rather low value of the individual unit. This process, prevalent for centuries, was destined to change under the conditions attending the exploitation of the American continent and the emergence of the American culture. Although large families and high infant mortality rates continued in the New World for a time, the generally healthful conditions of life and the relative value of the individual resulting from the constant shortage of labor made for early emphasis on the conservation of child life. The result was the combination, for decades in our early history, of a high birth rate, a relatively low infant mortality rate, a rapid rate of population growth, and a high valuation of the individual unit. When, later, the birth rate began to decline but the demand for an ever larger population continued, the value of the individual unit increased even more. More detailed consideration will be given to this in a subsequent chapter; the two thoughts to be emphasized here are, first, the changing arithmetic of reproduction in our more recent history, and second, the fundamental significance of these changes for the status of American children.

THE ECONOMIC DEVELOPMENT OF THE UNITED STATES

More than three centuries ago, small settlements of Europeans were being established along the east coast of this country. They were the beginning of that epic instance of nation building which is the history of the United States. In the course of three centuries, these small, scattered settlements grew into a nation of 130 million, and the continent which they opened and developed proved to be of unparalleled richness in the resources which Western civilization needed. During this same period, the economic system was transformed from medieval landlordism with its prevailingly simple and rural pattern, to modern capitalism with its huge complex and interrelated processes and its gigantic cities. Considering this development objectively, it must be obvious that these factors, and their combination in point of time, are so unusual as to raise the question whether anything like it, in both nature and scale, can ever again happen in world history; conceived in its comprehensive enormity, it must be equally clear that such a development would loom large and with intimate constancy in relation to the other elements of our emerging culture. In other words, we cannot understand American life without understanding and keeping this economic background constantly in mind, because for three centuries it colored every phase of our national development.

Although every aspect of this changing economic pattern is important for our purposes, one in particular needs to be emphasized. This is the continued existence of the frontier. The direction and speed of our settlement of this continent, and the tremendous transcontinental distance involved, accounted for one of the distinguishing features of American life, namely, the constant rebirth of our civilization for the 300 years of its history. This process of rebirth we have sensed on the westward-moving frontier, and its significance has been made clear by Turner, Paxon, and other historians.[14] What sociologists have overlooked is the fact that for several decades the arrival of large numbers of immigrants and the rapid development of industrial urban centers created, especially in our larger cities, a series of urban-industrial frontiers with many of the basic features of the earlier western frontiers, which operated after the early frontier on the slopes of the Pacific had ceased to exist. This process of rebirth, usually associated with the western frontier, has actually continued in the urban East down to the present time.

The relationship between the changing economic background and the changing status of childhood is merely a phase of the larger story of the role of the economic factor in the development of our entire culture. It is well to keep this in mind here, for it means that while certain effects on the status of childhood were obvious and direct, many were indirect and touched child status only as it reacted to general changes in the culture as a whole. The discussion that follows, then, is meant to be selective and suggestive.

1. Migration is a highly selective process. This was particularly true in the case of colonial migration to the New World, for it involved a lengthy and uncertain voyage over an inadequately charted ocean to an unknown land beset with many dangers and difficulties. The bases of selection were bound to be definite and rigorous, and one of them clearly was a marked interest in the future. This interest would have to be more than a personal, self-centered one; it would be an interest in the family's future, in children, in the migrant's children, and in the future of society, which means other people's children. Selectivity on this basis meant that from the beginning the American colonist was relatively a lover of children. The whole process of colonial migration involved the continuing selection of persons sufficiently interested in the coming generations to make them exchange the certainties of the present for the prospect of the future. Building for the future is a child welfare process.

2. From the first days of our colonial history, children were wanted. All the social historians emphasize this fact. And the more the vastness of the unfolding continent and its needs impressed themselves upon the minds of the people, the more was the valuation of the child increased. It seems safe to make the generalization that in any situation in which the population is small and there are vast and valuable resources to be developed, children will tend to occupy an important position. Large families, under such circumstances, are an asset. The labor of grown sons and daughters is valuable. Children also give security against various foes and dangers—of man and beast and the forces of nature.

The continuing need for a rapidly growing population was a constant factor encouraging early marriage, large families, and a high status for

[14] F. J. Turner, *The Frontier in American History*, Henry Holt & Company, Inc., New York, 1920.

childhood. As has already been intimated, it led public authorities to be rather impatient with parents whose strictness with their adolescent children interfered with these ends. Parents had the right to supervise and control the courtship of their children, it was true, but only within reason, and not so as to interfere with the interests of society. Here, as so often happens, the interests of the community take precedence over private rights.

3. In an old, settled society, what has been is accorded respect. The conventions of life have crystallized and are emphasized, traditions are revered, the old are consulted and obeyed. In a new world, men think primarily in terms of the future. In the face of new situations, the opinions of the young count for as much as those of their elders. In fact, the young are less likely to be encumbered by vestigial thinking. The hold of ancestral and paternal prestige is diminished; the trend is toward the transference of power to the more youthful members of the group. If the new country is rich, there is engendered a social optimism which tends to measure people by their future prospects rather than by the tokens of the past.

Expressed in terms of the family, all this means thinking in terms of descendants rather than of ancestors. "For the children" became the motto of many a pioneer family who broke new ground and endured loneliness and privation and danger, always with an eye to the consoling fact that their children would have a better chance, would grow up with the country and enter into their inheritance.

4. There were other reasons why the thoughts of many families in the New World should be directed so largely to the future. Unpleasant as it may be to recall, many people who migrated to America had no family tree which they could regard with much pride or satisfaction. American historians are not inclined to take literally Dr. Samuel Johnson's reference to the colonists as "a race of convicts," yet it is well known that from time to time the English authorities emptied their prisons upon the shores of America. Although it is true that many of these persons were guilty of what are regarded today as rather petty offenses, the fact remains that the families they established here in the New World would emphasize almost exclusively their future prospects rather than their past status.

The same thought applies to many other early settlers as well as the later immigrants. They may not have had criminal records, but they were individuals who had not succeeded signally in the Old World. Their coming to America was a new deal, it gave them a fresh start, it meant turning over a new leaf, it involved essentially turning their back upon the old life and hopefully facing the new. Expressed in terms of family life, this meant that the children embodied their dream of the future—the children were the future.

5. The ease with which young people could make their own way, in-

dependent of aid from their families, was another powerful factor in the emancipation of American childhood and youth. Land was the basis of the prevailing economy, it was cheap, and for many years there was an abundance of unoccupied land. The equipment needed to cultivate it was scant. As soon as a young man had gathered a few dollars he could look forward confidently to establishing a family of his own. The customary wedding gift to a son was a horse, some farm implements, and some seed; a girl received a bed, a cow, some kitchen utensils, a table, and some chairs. The relatives might help in erecting a cabin and a crude stable. Life was simple, the prime necessities were abundant, subsistence was certain.

Such a situation made for self-sufficiency and independence at an early age. After their earliest years, children were not essentially dependent upon their parents. The tendency was toward the early loosening of the family bond. Undue prolongation of parental prerogatives was likely to result in estrangement. It was not that younger people always made their own way early in life, but that they so easily could, which was the emancipating factor.

As the nineteenth century wore on and land became less cheap and accessible, particularly in the older parts of the country, the factory system made its appearance, and many boys and girls went to work in these new industrial establishments at an early age. This development is usually referred to as part of the history of child labor, with rather definite condemnation of it. Whatever we may say about the employment of these children, measured by present-day standards, from the standpoint of our discussion here it had an emancipating influence in the relation of children and their elders. Give a child his own pay envelope, and the parent-child relationship is changed; have him share his wages with his parent, and he has gone a good part of the way in purchasing immunity to parental control.

6. The continuing process of vertical mobility in American society has been a far greater factor in parent-child relationships than is usually appreciated. Throughout their history, the people of the United States have been "on the up," economically speaking. Each generation has wanted to live better than preceding ones, and has succeeded so generally that such success has been accepted as natural and almost inevitable. This process has been viewed for the most part as an index of the economic progress of the country; what has only seldom been considered is its meaning in the relationship between these generations and their attitudes toward each other.

To speak more specifically, for 300 years the American child has been taught constantly to aim higher than his parents, to "begin where they left off." In this he has been aided and abetted, as a rule, by his parents, who have sacrificed, subordinated, driven themselves even, all to the end that he would have better advantages than they had. Even the un-lettered immigrant, preoccupied with his own problems of adjustment to the New World, has felt impelled to give his children better advan-tages—often much better—than he and his forebears had.

Desirable as certain features of this process may be, it is hardly favor-able to the development of a respect for parents. What has happened at best, in many cases, has been the undermining of parental prestige. Home after home, past and present, has been characterized by the following contrasts: parents preoccupied with business interests, children vying for social acceptance; parents whose own youth was one of poverty, pam-pered children living in the lap of luxury; parents trained to habits of simplicity and frugality, children thoughtlessly prodigal and wasteful; parents coming from simple rural American or European homes, children knowing naught else but the superficialities, sophistications, and cultural advantages of complex urban centers; children being given advantages which parents never have had, and able to act as the directive authorities in these matters for their parents.

7. Occupational mobility throughout the history of this country has played an important role in changing the status of childhood. Unlike the practice in older, more fixed civilizations, where a child customarily fol-lows the occupation of his father, the very nature and needs of our rapidly expanding economic development made this largely impossible. The overwhelming proportion of the workers in this country have gone into jobs different from those of their parents.

The significance of this for parent-child relationships is easy to grasp. American youth has been freed from parental supervision while at work, and since this form of supervision cannot always be separated from more comprehensive supervision, it has often meant freedom from parental supervision in general. Then, too, differences in the economic careers of parent and child have involved and facilitated divergence of interests, and this is part of the larger process of growing apart.

8. The American population has been relatively very mobile. The ex-ploitation of the continent would not have been possible by a race of "stay-at-homes." Earlier these movements were largely westward; but more recently, large-scale migrations in other directions have been taking place. Modern students, who may think that our mobility is a recent phenomenon, will be enlightened by the comments of a foreign observer in 1864: "The American family is like a covey of birds: the young escape as soon as they have wings to fly, and claws for defence. They forget the maternal nest, and often the parents themselves no longer recognize them. They have had the trouble of protecting them in their first feeble-ness, but, this task accomplished, their rights and their duties end to-

gether. It is the law of nature in all its crudity: the family association lasts only so long as it is indispensable to its members."[15]

The population movements which have been a feature of American history have had their counterparts in family histories. The expansion of the United States has been in large measure a series of westward jumps of successive generations. The Middle West was the New England and Middle Atlantic States of a later date; Colorado and Utah, the more intrepid of the next generation; the Pacific coast is the contemporary edition of all of them.

This entire process has, from one angle, been disruptive, tending to weaken family ties. Particularly was this true in the case of successive generations. Mobility of residence put space between them, just as differences of occupation made for divergence of interests. These two factors were peculiarly complementary in their effects; taken together, they were of continued and fundamental importance in changing the status of American youth.

9. Thus far, the discussion has been in terms of children, with no reference to any differences on a sex basis. From the very beginning, however, certain factors operated particularly to affect the status of girls. In a rough, wild, new country, it is evident that conventions and restraints concerning women which are natural and necessary in more staid cultures become untenable. Everyone, regardless of sex and, to some extent, age, must take a hand. The seclusion of women, for example, is not feasible. The frontier spirit is democratic, for young women as well as for the rest of the population; special treatment does not fit into the folkways.

Then, too, there was the effect of the arithmetic of the situation. For the greater part of our history, and particularly in the newer parts of the country, there has been a deficit of women. Between the older settled East and the more frontierlike West there went on, for decades, almost a commercial traffic in unmarried women. This shortage of wives, actual and potential, tended early toward the breakdown of the parental control of courtship and marriage, and where the control continued, young girls exercised considerable independence in their love affairs.

Other factors particularly affecting the status of girls might be mentioned, but enough has been said to indicate that from the beginning of our history the relative freedom of the American girl was the natural product of conditions of life in this country.

10. The final aspect of the role of the economic factor in the changing status of American childhood to be emphasized here is the transition from a state of deficit to one of surplus, economically speaking. The reference here is to the enlarging capacity of our nation to finance the

[15] Duvergier De Hauranne, *Huit mois en Amerique,* quoted from Calhoun, *op. cit.,* Vol. III, p. 163.

changing position and treatment of children, with special emphasis on the historical operation of this factor. Whether the surplus condition has passed permanently for the time being, whether it ceased with our large-scale discounting of the future in the huge borrowings during and since World War I—particularly since 1930—is an important question but has no bearing upon our historical analysis.

The rapid increase in the wealth of the United States, particularly between the Civil War and our entrance into World War I, is well known, and there can be no doubt of its fundamental importance in the transformation of our life. Of the general social implications of this transition no one has written with more insight perhaps than the late Simon N. Patten. His concept of a pain and a pleasure economy and of the process of the change from one to the other, although described almost a half century ago and not so well known to modern students, remains the most penetrating analysis of the fundamental changes involved. In an age of deficit, there exists what he called a pain economy. The primary purpose of this economy is the avoidance of pain, protection from enemies, the prevention of want, safety against destruction. The basis of the social institutions of such an economy is the fear of enemies and of pain. The purpose of its state is protection from enemies; of its morality, avoidance of destruction; of its religion, help from supernatural powers against foes; of its families, the satisfaction of primary physical needs. In a pleasure or surplus economy, the objectives of society are concerned with the promotion of welfare, with the enrichment and enlargement of the good life. Social values and ideals are recast and social institutions are remade to function toward these newer ends. The transition from a pain to a pleasure economy, Patten declared, was a difficult one, full of stresses and dangers.[16]

The child is a part of this economy and culture that is reconstructed as a result of this transition. In a pain economy, he is a pawn in the war against the constantly recurring threat of direct want, a pawn to be utilized, to be exploited. His function is to aid in the struggle for survival. Of affection between parents and child there may be a great deal, but life is hard and rigorous and imposes sharp and cruel limitations. In an age of surplus, the child becomes a luxury, the subject of social solicitude, the object of social planning. There is conscious promotion of his welfare. The question of how he can help in the struggle for survival is displaced by the question as to what can be done to develop him to the limit of his possibilities. The period of preparation for life is lengthened. Laws against child labor take form, and their age limitations are revised upward again and again. Schools multiply and the age of compulsory attendance is raised. Supplementary services and resources aimed at the more intensive cultivation of child capacities are developed. Children are reckoned in

[16] Simon N. Patten, "The Theory of Social Forces," *Publications of the American Academy of Political and Social Science,* 1896, Chap. 4.

terms of their future possibilities, and the expenditure of the social surplus on them is conceived as a promising investment.

THE IDEOLOGICAL FACTOR

American ideology is a colorful combination compounded of many elements. Some of these elements have changed from time to time throughout our history, others have remained rather constant. Our conception of and emphases on our ideology change too, for each generation recasts its ideas on the bases of its changing interests and needs. With this appreciation of the changing complexity of American ideology, the thesis is advanced here that this ideology has been compounded largely out of three basic and rather constant ingredients: humanitarianism, science, and democracy. The relationship of each of these to the changing status of childhood will be discussed briefly.

Humanitarianism and the child. There is an abundance of evidence that humanitarianism has increased greatly in its range in recent years. We need not go back more than a century and a half in the most advanced countries of Western culture to find a good deal of abuse of animals and human beings—the extensive existence of slavery, marked cruelties in the treatment of criminals, the brutal beating of small children, little interest in the poor except on the basis of personal almsgiving, incredible horrors in the treatment of the feeble-minded and insane. In the years since then, the condition of one after another of these groups has been transformed: the treatment of the sick, the insane, and various physically and mentally defective and sick persons has been humanized; there has been widespread amelioration in the condition of criminals; a large amount of social legislation has been passed to improve working conditions; slavery has been abolished; women have been placed more nearly on an equality with men; societies for the prevention of cruelty to animals have flourished; and extensive philanthropic movements have been directed toward the relief of distress and the reduction of poverty.[17]

Modern humanitarianism could not but affect the status of children. To begin with, children were bound to benefit from the ordinary implications of a general movement which affected the status and treatment of virtually all subject, exploited, and neglected groups. As one of these groups, children would naturally share in any general upward revision of the standards applied to such groups. But more than that, by their very nature they would be the particular beneficiaries of such a movement. After all, they were nearest and dearest to the persons who were influenced by these new humanitarian considerations, and no society could concern itself indefinitely with the freeing of slaves and better treatment for criminals without also taking thought of its children.

[17] Maurice Parmelee, *Poverty and Social Progress,* The Macmillan Company, New York, 1916, Chap. 17.

Science and the child. Science is the architect of our civilization. Its achievements dominate modern culture, and its spirit shapes the character of our intellectual and spiritual life. To the Western mind, all other expressions of the creative spirit seem somewhat futile. The final appeal in all problems and disputed points is to the scientist, and his judgments we consider to be altogether true and righteous.

The history of science is the story of its progressive application to an ever wider range of phenomena. First applied to the material objects of the nonliving world, with the consequent development of the physical sciences, the scientific method came in time to be applied successively to the field of organic life, with the resultant renaissance of the biological studies, and then to the realm of psychic phenomena, with the emergence of the modern psychological sciences. Finally, the most complex phase of human life, namely, human association, has come to be studied scientifically, with the gradual emergence of the social studies as scientific disciplines.

One phase of this most recent extension of the scientific method has been its application to the social welfare movement. Conceived originally with good intention and born at the dawn of human history out of an emotional concern for the unfortunate, this movement has been going to school, figuratively speaking, in the temple of science. The lessons learned in that temple, the methods utilized, the attitudes emphasized, are revolutionizing social welfare just as science has revolutionized other fields of human effort. We are concerned, at this point, in appraising in somewhat broad terms how the application of the scientific method to social phenomena in general and to the social welfare movement in particular has affected our attitude toward the child and his importance.

One definite way in which this application of the scientific method has affected the status of work with children has been through its emphasis upon the genetic point of view. The point of view of modern science is genetic. Since the time of Charles Darwin, and as a result of his work, all science, broadly speaking, has become biological. Every science sees its problems against an evolutionary background, which means that everything is viewed in the light of its historical development. In other words, when we say that the point of view of modern science is genetic, we mean that every science sees its problems in a historical perspective, and that if we want to understand anything we must understand its origin and development.

Such a point of view applied to problems of human life has revolutionary significance for childhood, for it makes this period of life of paramount importance. Childhood is the period of origins, the stage of beginnings. It is the period in which so many problems arise and are manifest in their incipient stages. This can be illustrated with particular aptness in the history of the science of psychology. G. Stanley Hall, the

Nestor of American psychology, was also its outstanding specialist in genetic psychology.

A second way in which the application of the scientific method to social phenomena and problems affects child study and work with children is through its emphasis on the principle of causation. The point of view of modern science is causal; its object is the establishment of causal relationships. This is saying horizontally much the same thing we say vertically when we point out that the point of view of modern science is genetic; either approach has the same significance for childhood.

This is, perhaps, the essential difference in the way our ancestors and ourselves regard the child. Our ancestors saw these earliest years as a negative period of life, a sort of necessary evil full of idle deviltry and cantankerous mischief; the child survived it and his parents endured it as best they could, until late adolescence when life hesitatingly began. We, of a later vintage, regard childhood as a foundation period of great importance, a period of twig bending during which the shape of the future tree is determined.

To be sure, students of human problems have emphasized causal antecedents for many years. Only recently, however, has come the knowledge that these causal relations are neither so few in number nor so simple in their operation as had previously been supposed. In the study of these relationships, there has been a transfer of interest and emphasis from the broadly obvious to the subtly effective. It is this that is essentially new in the contemporary approach to the study of behavior problems. Modern psychiatry and the psychoanalytic procedure have multiplied many times the significance of the earliest years. Theories regarding the causation of crime, mental disease, distorted character, economic failure, and domestic maladjustment have had to be reconstructed on the basis of the contributions of the modern sciences and resolved into elements of juvenile conditioning.

Under the suggestive influence of the genetic and causal points of view of modern science, the social welfare movement is coming to a new and better understanding of its task. The cumulative effect of recent discoveries in the life sciences has been to make the social welfare movement more "child-minded." The modern mind, wrestling with the problems of human welfare, finds them where Plato dreamed his ideal state —in the directed development of the next generation. Science now dictates what our tender sympathies long have counseled. Society's "acres of diamonds" lies revealed in the cradle inside the door, and social statesmanship finds its task in the heart of a child.

Modern democracy and the child. It is interesting to speculate on what the status of the child would be today in this country were it not for the rise and dominance of democracy. What effect would the other factors working to emancipate the child have had without the favoring support of this comprehensive, conditioning background? The emancipation of the American child must be considered, then, against the background, and as an integral part, of the general democratization of society. As such, it takes its place with other familial aspects of this democratizing process—the decay of patriarchism, the waning of paternal authority, and the greater freedom of and opportunities for women.

The most familiar instances of the operation of democracy are found in the political field. Political democracy has had direct and immediate significance for the status of children, for its basic tenet is to make the individual the ultimate unit of social development. The emancipation of the child, the decay of patriarchalism, the waning of the father's authority, and the changed status of the mother are all natural consequences of political democracy, which recognizes not clans or families, but individuals. "In a democracy the idea of superior fades before the idea of equal sovereignty. All men are sovereigns. Personality is exalted, and the political status overflows and democratizes family institutions."[18]

But democracy is more than a political creed or system. It is, in the ultimate analysis, an idea, an attitude, a value, a spirit, which permeates every phase of life. It expresses itself in and through our religious, economic, scientific, and social developments, as was pointed out in Chapter 4, and it is as a common core in these developments that it stimulated the changing status of childhood.

Perhaps all that has been said concerning the ideological factors—the rise of humanitarianism and the development of modern science and of the democratic way of life—comes to this: The current American ideology involves a new conception of the worth of the individual, and an appreciation of the child as the promise and hope of that individual.

THE FAMILIAL FACTOR

The child is so inextricably a part of the family that no discussion of a change in his status is complete without reference to changes in the family. Changes in the status as well as in the structure and functions of the family must be considered, then, as factors in the changing status of childhood. For a more complete study of the changing family, the reader is referred to the excellent books on the family which are now available. Here only selected aspects of these changes will be dealt with briefly.

Historic status of the American family.   "Families are the nurseries of the church and the commonwealth; ruin families and you ruin all." This maxim of the early colonial fathers is indicative of the high status which the family as a social institution enjoyed in those days. This status

[18] Calhoun, *op. cit.*, Vol. II, p. 53.

was the natural result of the conditions of colonial settlement, and certain factors inherent in our national development have tended to maintain and increase this relative status until comparatively recent years. These factors will be outlined briefly at this point.

The American colonist of English stock was a home builder from the beginning. It was his interest in his family, his home, and his children, and his belief that their future was circumscribed in the Old World which led to his migration to the New.

Some of the other nationality groups which figured prominently in the settlement of the United States were noted for their domesticity. This was particularly true of the German colonists. From the beginning, they manifested a distinctive fondness for home life. They gave America a distinct type of woman, interested primarily in the household arts. German husbands and fathers in colonial America were noted for their interest in home life and their participation in the simple pleasures of their family groups. Similarly, the Dutch in New York were mentioned repeatedly because of their conspicuous success with the marriage relationship. Both they and the Huguenots farther to the south were a liberalizing influence as far as family relationships were concerned. The Huguenots were particularly noted for their pleasant home life.

Migration is always a selective process, and from the standpoint of the present discussion it is significant that the English migration to colonial America, as well as that of the Germans, Huguenots, Dutch, and Swedes who settled among them, occurred in the form of family units. Moreover, this family character persisted in the immigration stream until far down into the nineteenth century, and among such groups as the Russian Jews, until into the twentieth century. It is this movement in terms of family units that makes these migrations differ from those of the French and Spanish to colonial America, and this distinction does much to explain the differences in the success of these respective groups as colonizers.

The relative lack of development of other institutions in the early centuries of our national existence favored the family. The whole historical background of these population movements, the experience of the colonists in their home countries, was not such as to favor any immediate development of a strong state, particularly because of the close connection of colonial governmental organizations with those of Europe. The school too, while not neglected, was relatively weak in those days. The church in New England, but apparently not so much so elsewhere, was the only social institution approaching the family in importance. The family was the one substantial social institution in a nation which had discarded hierarchical religion and reduced the power of government to a minimum. The entire colonizing process placed a premium upon the pioneers who moved in groups of families and tended to settle in areas contiguous enough to facilitate coöperation for defense, worship, and other prime social necessities, but for all other purposes utilized the family as the cradling and shaping agent of the new life.

What made possible this relative reliance upon the family was the self-sufficiency of the home as an economic unit. The almost complete self-sufficiency of the family in the economy of the time is pointed out by all economic and family historians. More will be said about this in the discussion of the functions of the family; the fact to be noted here is the importance of this self-sufficiency in support of the family's dominant role as a social institution.

Another factor of considerable importance was the relative isolation of the homes. This prevailed rather generally in the early history of this country, and in many cases persisted down to comparatively recent times. The general density of population for the greater part of our history and among our people has been very low. Rural settlements for the most part took the form of isolated homesteads rather than agricultural villages as in Europe. This isolation tended to throw the family upon itself, upon its own resources. It reduced tremendously the possibility or likelihood of much social control of the family, especially as far as detailed or continuing control was concerned.

Especially did the isolation of the frontier tend to turn the family within itself. The absence of social contacts, the silence and monotony, the lack of competing distractions, all characteristic of the frontier, made for strong family interests. This pioneer isolation tended not only to increase the importance of the family but also to soften and deepen its relationships. Husband and wife, parent and child, were partners in a common enterprise in work, and playmates in their recreational pursuits.

Effect upon the status of children. The relatively high status of the family as a social institution did not per se have a softening effect upon the treatment of children or tend to raise their status. Conceivably the importance of the family, coupled with the relative lack of importance of the state in the earlier centuries of our history, might have formed the basis of a highly repressive policy toward children. Conceivably the autocracy of the Roman parent might have been restored on the frontier. Who would there have been to say naught? Fortunately the other factors identified in this and the preceding chapter prevented that from happening. Neither the economic nor the ideological factors and incentives would have fitted in with such a turn of events. Rather they gave this strong family interest a liberalizing and democratic turn to aid still further in the emancipating process. The historic status of the American family operated, then, in the direction of a high level of parental interest in children, the mathematical, economic, and ideological factors and incentives combining to dictate the direction of that heightened interest toward more democratic objectives.

We must not be misunderstood when we say that the family today has a lower status in the institutional framework of society than it did in the earlier period of our history. In part this has been due to the rise to preeminence of other institutions, notably the state and the school. The status of both of these has been revolutionized within the past century; hence the relative position of the family would be altered, even if no changes had occurred in it. But there have been changes, principally in its structure and functions, and it is to these that we turn next.

Changing structure and functions. All students of the modern family agree that the family has been transformed in recent decades. In so far as its structure is concerned, the older, larger, semipatriarchal form has given way to the contemporary, smaller, democratic, companionship type. Many of the aspects and factors involved in this change have been alluded to in the preceding pages. They include: (1) the passing of the family function of economic production; (2) the gainful employment of women, particularly married women, outside the home; (3) the mechanization, and the consequent lightening of the burdens, of housekeeping; and (4) the small-family system and the resultant shrinkage in the physical basis of the home.[19]

With these changes in structure have come significant changes in the functions of the family. The decline of the home in the field of economic production has been accompanied by its increasing importance as a consumption unit, emphasizing rational consumption as a factor in the positive well-being of its members. In the area of protective functions, the rise of the civil authority and its agencies has led the family to shift its attention from dangers to life and limb to the protection of the interests of its members. The recreational needs of children tend to be satisfied less and less within the home, with the result that parents are concerned more with the selection, evaluation, supervision, guidance, and coördination of the family's recreational life. The responsibility for the education of children is now turned over to the school, the parents devoting themselves to the supervision and supplementation of the educational process. The small-family system makes possible the development of a more intensive parenthood.

From the standpoint of the child, the changing functions of the family have involved, first, the decline of its control over, and responsibility for, various phases of child development; second, the development of various specialized agencies to whom is transferred the responsibility for selected segments of the child-rearing process. The first has many consequences, but considered in relation to the status of childhood it tends to enable the family to give the child services that supplement those of the

[19] W. F. Ogburn and M. F. Nimkoff, *Technology and the Changing Family*, Houghton Mifflin Company, Boston, 1955.

specialized children's agencies, and to stimulate in an increasing proportion of families the development of an improved technique of parenthood. The second has led inevitably to the development of new vested interests concerned directly with the raising and maintenance of the status of childhood.

When this latter development is examined objectively and in terms of social process, the following steps emerge rather clearly: The creation of specialized child development agencies and services means, from the occupational standpoint, specialized jobs. This leads in turn to the development of specialized training facilities—schools, courses, institutes, and teaching personnel. Not only do these function to satisfy the demands for specialized training, but, naturally perhaps, they magnify the importance of the jobs for which they offer training. Time passes, and a specialized group of jobholders develops in a particular field; gradually, these jobholders become conscious of themselves and their common interests; ultimately they begin to organize, both to protect their interests and further to exploit their field. Thus arises a vested interest. The claim having been staked off, the developing resources having been organized, the next step is intensive cultivation. Against the background of a constantly increasing emphasis on its fundamental importance, refinements of specialized service are developed. They are labeled *the technique.* A literature specialized in scope and ambitious in tone is fostered; public interest and appreciation are cultivated. The leaders in the specialty now tend to be of the promoter type, rather than concerned with ideals of service or research. There is a growing intolerance of any critical analysis of task or technique. Jobs are at stake, budgets are imperiled, funds are threatened.

This brief account of the natural history of the development of a specialized service is sufficient to indicate that the parceling-out of the care of children to specialized service groups results, as time goes on, in the creation of various vested interests vitally concerned in promoting the importance of children, their needs, their welfare, and their status. For decades this factor has been operating silently and subtly in the development of ideas, programs, legislation, and so on, for children, thus involving an obvious rise in the status of childhood.

The history of many of these specialized service activities and groups shows that they begin in an experimental way, supported by private philanthropic means. But as time goes on and the service is established and is sold more and more to the public, public interest and discussion increase. Legislative aspects gradually emerge, and still further public discussion follows. Ultimately a public program takes form, the services are taken over as an obligation of the public treasury, and public agencies plan comprehensive programs to cover the particular field. All this means that the child, his needs and his importance, enter more and more into the public consciousness; standards of child care, which yesterday were the dreams of a few idealistic folk, tomorrow are the irreducible minimum below which no child must be allowed to live.

Finally, what has been described is a continuing process. These specialized types of child services are subject constantly to the forces of revision. New needs arise and stimulate new types of specialized services or modified forms of older ones. Sometimes these new types or modifications are added to those already established, resulting in marked growth and expansion of the range of the specialized services and agencies involved. This may proceed until the proportions attained are out of harmony with the group culture as a whole, raising problems of culture correlation such as are discussed in the closing pages of this volume. Or —and this is a second possibility—the new types of services may challenge the older, vested interests, with all the attendant evidences of conflict.

Summary

1. Colonial America reproduced, with certain modifications, the European pattern of child status. This pattern appeared most clearly in New England, and can best be studied there.

2. The colonial family had high status, was patriarchal in form and large in size. Maternal and infant mortality were high. Child labor was common, and from an early age. Family discipline was rigid, as was that of the school. Colonial law clearly supported both parent and teacher in their disciplinary measures. Manners and courtesy were markedly emphasized. Courtship was controlled closely by the parents. Religious experience was emphasized early in the lives of children. Large families seem, however, to have permitted some recreational developments, and references to children's games are numerous, even if sometimes in the form of complaints.

3. Contemporary America is seeing a revolutionary change in the status of children; they are viewed in terms of equality with other members of the family and recognized as coequal personalities in the emerging democracy of the family.

4. Four factors are primarily responsible for the emancipation of American childhood: the changing arithmetic of reproduction; the economic development of the United States; American ideology, a compound of humanitarianism, science, and democracy; and changes in the status, structure, and functions of the family.

Chapter **32**

Child Development:
Retrospect and Prospect

The preceding chapters have sought to summarize the changing status of children considered as a separate population element. Emphasis has been directed to the broad historic changes that have occurred and the basic factors that have been responsible. But broad social changes have a way of expressing themselves in specific movements and objectives, and the changing status of childhood has been no exception to this. The past two generations have witnessed the emergence and crystallization of a number of organized social efforts directed at changing particular aspects of the lives of children. The literature which has developed around these efforts has been sprinkled liberally with the phrase *rights of childhood*. The present chapter seeks to examine this concept of rights, its application to specific areas of child life, and finally, in a look to the future, some fundamental issues yet to be determined.

The Concept of Rights

The term *right* has long been used in the sense of designating that to which one has a just claim, that is, a privilege or immunity established by some form of authority, or valid to be maintained against authority. "From time immemorial," writes Merriam, "the rights of man derived from the laws of nature, from Christianity, from human experience, observation, and reflection, have been a refuge against human might, an altar to which men might flee, a rallying cry for resistance to tyranny or oppression or against arbitrary rule. As time went on, these rights were brought together in more systematic form. They found their way into the Roman Law; they flowered in the natural law when almost forgotten by governments; they became the basis of revolutionary movements against absolute despotism, the cornerstone of constitutional democracies everywhere, the foundation of twentieth century political progress."[1]

The best-known statement of human rights is the American Declaration of Independence. "We hold these truths to be self-evident, that all men are created equal, that they are endowed by their Creator with certain unalienable rights, that among these are life, liberty and the pursuit of happiness. That to secure these rights, governments are instituted among men, deriving their just powers from the consent of the governed." This statement, together with the French Declaration of the Rights of Man and of the Citizen (1789), marked the inauguration of the modern age and inspired the triumph of modern democracy.

Recent years have witnessed a resurgence of interest in the subject of human rights, and some notable attempts have been made to revise the historic formulations. These have been directed chiefly toward the inclusion of economic and social rights, on the basis of the claim that we are living in a new world in which the central problems arise from new pressures of power, production, and population which our forefathers did not face. The proposed new rights center about the development of personality, the basic implication being that there are certain social and economic rights which are as essential as the civil and political rights already established.

Several attempts to formulate these newer rights will be noted briefly. One was made by the United States National Resources Planning Board (1943). Nine rights were alleged, including the right to work; to fair pay; to adequate food, clothing, shelter, and medical care; to security; to live under a system of free enterprise; to come and go; to equality before the law; to education; and to rest, recreation, and adventure. Another attempt has been made by a committee of lawyers and political scientists, appointed by the American Law Institute and representing most of the principal cultures of the world. Their statement identifies 18 essential human rights: freedom of religion, of opinion, of expression, of peaceful assembly, to form associations, the right to safety from wrongful interference, fair trial, freedom from arbitrary detention, retroactive laws, the right to own property, to education, to work, to reasonable conditions of work, adequate food and housing, social security, participation in government, and equal protection before the law as "limited by the rights of others and by the just requirements of the democratic state." Finally, there is the Universal Declaration of Human Rights, approved by the United Nations General Assembly, 1948. This declaration is a statement of principles, not a treaty. It serves as a challenge to all peoples to promote world-wide respect for human rights. Article 24 of this dec-

[1] Charles E. Merriam, "Essential Human Rights," *Annals of the American Academy of Political and Social Science,* January, 1946, p. 11.

laration states that motherhood and childhood are entitled to special care and assistance.[2]

The concept of the rights of childhood is a product of the larger program of human rights. When first applied to children, the alleged rights were little more than claims which children were said to have upon the consideration of society, especially if that society was blessed with social feelings and intelligence. These rights might be spoken of as a series of ethical insistences. Gradually, however, these claims found expression in organized efforts, first private and then public; in the "amiable purposes" of the philanthropic; in goals formulated by professional workers; in standards set by official and quasi-official bodies, as the White House Conferences; and lastly, in legislative enactments.

It is often contended that these rights are not "true rights" and that they have no validity in scientific treatises or in government documents, at least not until they become the specific statement of some legislative act. To this Merriam replies as follows: "That rights have not yet been fully recognized or realized does not remove them from the field of the political, for politics deals with ideals as well as with realities. Ideals indeed are themselves realities. The rights of man provide the domain of faith and hope in government, the court of appeal which is never closed, the law beyond the law and the jurists, the lawmakers, the managers, and the adjudicators. The rights of man go deeper and higher than institutional devices for interpreting or applying them."[3]

To clarify the point of view in this volume, it will suffice to say that the rights of childhood are conceived of as social values in process of translation into the realities of daily living. This process begins with the crystallization of the ideas on which these values rest; it passes through many forms of social expression; and each manifestation in its history is but another index of the changing status of childhood. Some of these rights or social values will be considered briefly.

THE RIGHT TO LIFE

The basic right is the right to life. It involves the biological insistence for life expression, a social recognition of the eternal worth of the individual. It is primary to the development of all other rights, for these are merely subsequent devices which seek to give meaning to life. It seems proper, therefore, to begin a discussion of the emerging rights of childhood with the establishment of this primary one.

[2] Cf. Report, Committee of American Law Institute, "Statement of Essential Human Rights," January, 1946, pp. 18–26; United Nations Publications, *Universal Declaration of Human Rights,* U.N. Dept. of Public Information, March, 1949; Division of Historical Policy Research, Office of Public Affairs, U.S. Department of State, *Human Rights,* Washington, D.C., 1949.

[3] Merriam, *op. cit.,* p. 12.

Concretely, emphasis upon the child's right to life has been translated into the movement against infant mortality, one of the historic tragedies of childhood. Being a child has always been a dangerous occupation, and the earlier the stage in the life span, the greater has been the hazard. In all cultures and throughout the centuries, the first year was the most crucial one. A century ago, in this country, one out of every four babies born alive died before the end of the first year. As late as a generation ago, a baby born in the United States had less chance to live a week than a person 90 years old, and less chance to live a year than an individual 80 years of age.

Following the series of fundamental discoveries in the second half of the nineteenth century which laid the foundation for the modern science of bacteriology, individual leaders like Pierre Budin in France, Benjamin Broadbent in England, and L. Emmet Holt in the United States began to develop and advocate new techniques which revolutionized pediatric practice. These in turn led to organized movements, first developed through private initiative and financial support, like the Strauss milk depots in New York City, and then through publicly authorized and financed efforts, like the establishment of the federal Children's Bureau, the passage (1921) of the Sheppard-Towner Act, and the Social Security Acts, beginning in 1935. As a result of these efforts and changes in attitude which they indicated, infant mortality rates today are roughly one-sixth of what they were at the turn of the century. Social effort has gone far in guaranteeing the child's right to life.

THE RIGHT TO BE WANTED

Birth and death are two parts of one social process, and the establishment of the requirements of one inevitably raises the problem of corresponding needs for the other. The right of a child to be born under socially adequate circumstances seems as fundamental as the right of survival; in fact, it might easily be interpreted as of prior importance. Obviously, a child can have no say about his own birth, except as an after-the-fact reminder of what should have motivated his procreation. His right to be wanted, which may be taken as the first need in the protection of his birth, turns therefore into problems of the disposition, opportunity, and right of his parents to control and plan the introduction of his life into the social aggregate.

Consideration of the right to be wanted must begin with the reality of changes in the birth rate, that is, the number of births per year per unit of count, usually per 1,000 population. These changes, although complicated by periodic and other variations, show an overall long-term downward trend during the past 80 years throughout the Western world. There is general agreement that this decline represents a conscious and deliberate limitation of the number of children by parents in order to control the circumstances and conditions of family life as affected by the number of children. Apparently there has been no appreciable increase in the number of childless marriages but rather an extension of the small-family system.

The desire to control fertility apparently is age-old and universal, and it has taken a variety of forms. Once infanticide was widely practiced, with full consent of society and its leaders. The milder form of abandonment once was a recognized device. Abortion seems universal and frequent, by means of either bodily violence or internal concoctions. In primitive society, infanticide and abortion are the chief substitutes for control of conception. Most of the methods used are preventive, in that they seek control through the prevention of conception. These include celibacy, postponement of marriage, *coitus interruptus, coitus reservatus,* prolonged periods of nursing, belief in and observance of an infertile period, symbolic magic, sex perversions, abstention from intercourse, and castration. The prohibition of sexual relations between spouses over extended periods is well-nigh universal among primitive peoples. Chief among its forms are the taboo following childbirth, which may be in force as long as four years.[4]

In his *Medical History of Contraception*, Himes has gathered data on contraceptive techniques in the days of antiquity (for Western nations), during the Middle Ages in Eastern cultures, and in early modern times, which seem to warrant the following three conclusions: First, throughout these centuries and in all historic cultures, the idea of contraception has been known and accepted, much more so than is commonly supposed. Second, the techniques known, as compared to modern ones, were generally crude and had some reliance upon magic. Noteworthy exceptions existed, however. Thus two Greek physicians, Soranos and Aetios, carried the idea of contraception to a high degree of medical development, giving it a definite place in preventive medicine. Himes calls Soranos' treatment of technique the most brilliant until very late in modern times. Third, the use of such techniques was not widely diffused among the population. Especially limited was their practice during the Middle Ages, which constituted the era of greatest dominance by the Church. During this period particularly, the popular mores—economic, social, and religious—favored large families, and the prevailing high death rates prevented them from becoming too much of a problem.[5]

The past century and a quarter have witnessed marked changes in regard to the limitation of family size. First, there has been a marked im-

---

[4] For a detailed account of these methods, see Norman E. Himes, *Medical History of Contraception,* The Williams & Wilkins Company, Baltimore, 1936, pp. 3–59; Raymond Firth, *We, the Tikopia,* American Book Company, New York, 1936, Chaps. 12, 14.

[5] Himes, *op. cit.,* p. xii.

provement in the techniques of contraception, and in their effectiveness. The most widely used device was invented in 1880, and today more than 200 mechanical devices are now used in Western culture, in addition to chemical and other agents. Second has been the widespread diffusion and democratization of contraceptive knowledge, resulting both in its wider diffusion at upper-class levels and in its widespread penetration into the lower classes.

The third development has been the rise of cultural pressures favoring the limitation of family size. Particularly outstanding has been the stress upon its social and economic desirability. Such considerations scarcely antedate the nineteenth century, but by its close they assumed a position of prior importance. The factors involved are characteristic of our contemporary culture, and four of them are singled out for brief comment.

1. The modern industrialization process has created an economic system which has resulted in economic insecurity for many of its workers. The threat of unemployment and irregular employment have been widespread; the hazards of accident and sickness in a cash economy have been serious. In other words, the maintenance of a large family in our industrial culture has become much more precarious than under the older handicraft or agricultural system.

2. The value of a child to his parents has changed enormously within the past century. Formerly, the child, measured in economic terms, was an asset. His early and certain introduction to employment, often in his own family, resulted in his maintaining himself and being a source of income to his parents over a long period. Our contemporary industrial-urban pattern has changed all that. City life offers few opportunities for early and gradual employment. Industry eliminates the opportunities for homework. Child labor laws establish age limits for entering gainful occupations, and compulsory school requirements supplement these nonemployment factors. As a result, the child is today an economic liability to his parents, and definitely so, rather than an asset as formerly. There is reason to believe, as Karl Pearson suggested a number of years ago, that the effects of compulsory school and child labor legislation upon the birth rate are immediate and direct.

3. A relatively open class system is an important even if intangible factor. In any country where a considerable number of persons believe that they can raise their status by their own efforts, prudence combines with ambition to lead many families to seek to limit their size. Moreover, the competition in an open class system presses heavily upon those who wish merely to retain their status, so they too seek to plan the number of those they must maintain. The social democratic movement, the democratization of opportunity, rising and standardized planes of living—these are but so many phrases to describe the same basic process.

4. The status of women and their conception of their role in life has

changed greatly during the past century. In former times, the chief or one of their chief functions was to serve as a breeding machine. "Everything in woman is a riddle," said the philosopher Nietzsche, "and the answer to the riddle is childbearing." In recent decades many factors have revolutionized the status of women—education, employment opportunities, changing functions of the family, etc. This changed status has expressed itself nowhere more than in sex attitudes and behavior. The modern woman refuses to have her sex exploited. She has definite and often precise ideas concerning the number of children she will have, and the space that shall separate their births. In some cases, she is unwilling to accept even the birth of one child as the price of sex experience. Like the male, she insists that sex shall be a positive and contributing force in her development, not service rendered by a chattel. Significantly enough, modern methods of contraception are chiefly utilized by the woman rather than the man.

Progress in planned parenthood, to utilize the present term for this movement, has been complicated in the United States by several factors. One has been the existence of older laws against obscenity, and the like, which have been interpreted at times to include contraceptive information and agents. Another factor has been the inertia and seeming reluctance of some members of the legal and medical professions to face the issues involved. Finally, there has been the opposition from religious sources, chiefly from the Roman Catholic hierarchy which, following the encyclical of Pope Pius XI (December, 1930) has placed the subject beyond further controversy for all believing Roman Catholics.

THE CHILD'S RIGHT TO AN EDUCATION

The right to an education which prepares the child for life is perhaps the most completely established and accepted of all the rights accorded American children. Its development has been an integral part of our national history. While it had its beginning in the transplanting of English practices and systems, its subsequent unfolding came in answer to ideas and needs peculiar to the New World. For a long time, religious interest in the establishment of public education was paramount. Protestantism by its very nature tended to promote freedom of speech and thought; and the religious controversies of the post-Reformation period placed a premium upon the acquisition of intellectual tools which prepared the individual for participation in them. Learning, in other words, was prized so that men might read the Bible and acquire religious instruction. Denominational indoctrination characterized all education. Throughout the colonial and early national periods in our history, the sectarian and religious were the controlling motives in the establishment of education.

Following the Revolutionary War, the idea grew that the continuity and welfare of the new republic depended upon the enlightenment of its people, and that the nation must educate its youth as a duty to itself. By 1830, this idea had come to be widely accepted, and it became the task of the next generation (1830–1860) to develop the framework of a comprehensive public school system. "These thirty years," writes Mulhern, "saw the struggle for free public schools fought and won, and the right to support and control education vested in the people."[6] Tax-supported free schools were authorized by law as follows: Massachusetts, 1827; Delaware, 1829; Vermont, 1850; Ohio, 1853; Iowa, 1858; New York, 1867; Rhode Island, 1868; Connecticut, 1868; Michigan, 1869; and New Jersey, 1870. In Pennsylvania, school districts were permitted by a law of 1834 to establish free public schools, and in 1849 that permission changed to a requirement, although it was not until 1886 that all districts complied with the law. By 1900, the period of pioneering in public education was over, for it was required in nearly all states outside of the South. In the majority of the states, the age of compulsory attendance ranged from 8 to 14 years. The minimum length of the school year varied from eight weeks to eight months.

Statistical summaries of public education in the United States covering a period of years are available, and they show the progress and degree of completeness attained in the establishment of the child's right to an education. Various indices might be used in this connection, but it will suffice to state briefly three groups of facts. First, the percentage of the population 5 to 17 years of age enrolled in public and elementary schools has risen from 57.0 in 1870 to 73.5 in 1910 to 83.5 in 1953–1954. A second index is the number of persons graduated from high school per 100 persons 17 years of age. This number was 2.0 in 1869–1870, 8.8 in 1909–1910, and 60.0 in 1953–1954. A third index is the college enrollment per 100 persons 18 to 21 years of age. This has grown from 3 in 1889–1890 to 12 in 1929–1930 and to 25.7 in the fall of 1957.[7]

THE CHILD'S RIGHT TO HEALTH

The child's right to health may be said to be on the road to public acceptance. Compared with developments in public education, those in the field of child health make an unsatisfactory showing in large areas of this country; but when contrasted with the child health work of two or more generations ago, the advances made in recent years are striking. Two developments in the latter half of the nineteenth century in particular focused attention upon this aspect of child development. One was the evolution of public health work to the stage where the economy of the

[6] James Mulhern, *A History of Education*, The Ronald Press Company, New York, 1946, p. 472.

[7] Data compiled from *Biennial Survey of Education Reports*, published by the Office of Education, Federal Security Agency, Washington, D.C.

preventive approach was recognized. Once this approach was made, it was quickly seen that all the diseases which, from the point of view of medicine or public health, were known to be preventable, occurred in the early part of life; that to prevent disease, the beginnings must be made in the age span when it can be prevented; that if the individual's resistance was to be utilized to fight disease, this resistance must be built up in the years of childhood; and that if health education was to be made an effective instrument in public health work, the foundations for it had to be laid in the years when persons were most educable. These ideas, now seemingly so simple and obvious, were hailed in this earlier period with all the enthusiasm given a new discovery.[8]

The second early development that focused attention upon the basic importance of child health was the gathering of the children into the schools. As the dragnet of compulsory attendance brought more and more of them into the schools, and for longer periods of time, a number of problems with strong health implications came to be recognized. One was the necessity of safeguarding, from a health standpoint, the school buildings to which the children went. This problem of school sanitation was, as a matter of fact, the original compelling force in the development of school health work in several countries in Europe. Another problem involved the infections that were spread by contacts among the school children. This presented the direct danger of disease epidemics, and pointed to the obvious necessity of control measures. Another problem, which was recognized more slowly, was the importance of health for education. As the school year lengthened, as the number of years of required schooling increased, as the scope and standards of instruction were raised, schoolmen became increasingly concerned with the large number of children who could not keep step with their companions. In the search for causes, removable physical defects and other health conditions were recognized as an important factor. Gradually, the sound body and the sound mind came to be seen as inseparable aspects of the individual child, which meant of course that an educational program that ignored the children's health was doomed to at least partial failure. Finally, too, it came to be realized that the school environment and school pressures created health problems which it was society's simple and obvious duty to remedy, through the agency of the school. Small wonder, therefore, that the school has come to be recognized as the principal agency in the promotion of child health programs.

The school health program has taken definite form along five main lines.

School sanitation. School sanitation implies the provision of safe and healthful conditions in the school plant. It is recognized as of basic im-

[8] S. Josephine Baker, *Child Hygiene*, Harper & Brothers, New York, 1925.

portance, both as a direct requirement for health and as an object lesson. It is ironic at best to teach cleanliness in unclean schools, or conservation of sight in an ill-lighted schoolroom.

Health service.   Health service seeks actively and directly to promote the health of the school child. The conception of what this involves has changed completely in recent decades. Earlier, the purpose of health service in the schools was primarily to prevent the spread of communicable diseases, with an eye to protecting the community as well as the school children. It was developed as a legitimate exercise of the police power of the state, and was based on the same principle as quarantine laws, the establishment of pesthouses, and compulsory vaccination. Today, its chief purpose is to discover defects and physical abnormalities, and to promote measures directed at their removal to the end of securing and maintaining the health and vitality of the individual child. Such health work is now developed not as an exercise of the police power of the state but as a phase of its educational and social welfare program. The development of this program has involved the extensive use of school nurses; the maintenance of various types of school clinics, such as dental, eye, orthopedic, psychological, and nutrition clinics; and the development of various types of special classes for handicapped children. One of the chief problems in the furtherance of school health services is to secure the interest and cooperation of the parents of the children.

Health education.   Health education is concerned with imparting knowledge about how to preserve and promote health. In many states, instruction in the effects of the use of alcohol and narcotics is especially enjoyed. In more progressive school systems, the emphasis is upon health habits and healthful patterns of living.

Mental hygiene.   Childhood is the golden age for mental hygiene, and mental hygiene, like other aspects of health, involves essentially a way of living and of adjusting to other persons. This conception of mental health, and the approach to it during the child's school life and through the instrumentality of the school, seem so obvious that its recent recognition in school health work is particularly conspicuous. A beginning, but perhaps only that, has been made in this aspect of child health work in the schools.

Physical education.   The term *physical education* was formerly used to include all forms of health instruction but has come to be applied more specifically to instruction in the activities of the gymnasium and playground. Requirements for this type of instruction are rather general, particularly in city school systems, but the nature and degree of its integration with the rest of the school work vary a great deal.

THE CHILDREN'S CHARTER

Other rights have been advanced by various persons interested in child development. The standard statement of all of the rights of children is contained in the Children's Charter, drawn up in 1930 by the third White House Conference on Child Health and Protection. Its provisions follow:

I. For every child, spiritual and moral training to help him to stand firm under the pressure of life.

II. For every child, understanding and the guarding of his personality as his most precious right.

III. For every child, a home and that love and security which a home provides; and for that child who must receive foster care, the nearest substitute for his own home.

IV. For every child, full preparation for his birth, his mother receiving prenatal, natal, and postnatal care; and the establishment of such protective measures as will make childbearing safer.

V. For every child, health protection from birth through adolescence, including: periodical health examinations and, where needed, care of specialists and hospital treatment; regular dental examination and care of the teeth; protective and preventive measures against communicable diseases; the issuing of pure food, pure milk, and pure water.

VI. For every child, from birth through adolescence, promotion of health, including health instruction and a health program, wholesome physical and mental recreation, with teachers and leaders adequately trained.

VII. For every child, a dwelling place, safe, sanitary, and wholesome, with reasonable provisions for privacy, free from conditions which tend to thwart his development; and a home environment harmonious and enriching.

VIII. For every child, a school which is safe from hazards, sanitary, properly equipped, lighted, and ventilated. For younger children, nursery schools and kindergartens to supplement home care.

IX. For every child, a community which recognizes and plans for his needs; protects him against physical dangers, moral hazards, and disease; provides him with safe and wholesome places for play and recreation; and makes provision for his cultural and social needs.

X. For every child, an education which, through the discovery and development of his individual abilities, prepares him for life; and through training and vocational guidance prepares him for a living which will yield him the maximum of satisfaction.

XI. For every child, such teaching and training as will prepare him for successful parenthood, homemaking, and the rights of citizenship; and, for parents, supplementary training to fit them to deal wisely with the problem of parenthood.

XII. For every child, education for safety and protection against accidents to which modern conditions subject him—those to which he is directly exposed, and those which, through loss or maiming of his parents, affect him indirectly.

XIII. For every child who is blind, deaf, crippled, or otherwise physically handicapped, and for the child who is mentally handicapped, such measures as will early discover and diagnose his handicap, provide care and treatment, and so train him that he may become an asset to society rather than a liability. Expenses of these services should be borne publicly where they cannot be privately met.

XIV. For every child who is in conflict with society, the right to be dealt with intelligently as society's charge, not society's outcast; with the home, the school, the church, the court, and the institution when needed, shaped to return him whenever possible to the normal stream of life.

XV. For every child, the right to grow up in a family with an adequate standard of living and the security of a stable income as the surest safeguard against social handicaps.

XVI. For every child, protection against labor that stunts growth, either physical or mental, that limits education, that deprives children of the right of comradeship, of play, and of joy.

XVII. For every rural child, as satisfactory schooling and health services as for the city child, and an extension to rural families of social, recreational, and cultural facilities.

XVIII. To supplement the home and the school in the training of youth, and to return to them those interests of which modern life tends to cheat children, every stimulation and encouragement should be given to the extension and development of the voluntary youth organizations.

XIX. To make everywhere available these minimum protections of the health and welfare of children, there should be a district, county, or community organization for health, education, and welfare, with full-time officials, coordinating with a state-wide program which will be responsible to a nation-wide service of general information, statistics and scientific research. This should include: (a) Trained full-time public health officials, with public health nurses, sanitary inspection, and laboratory workers. (b) Available hospital beds. (c) Full-time public welfare service for the relief, aid, and guidance of children in special need due to poverty, misfortune, or behavior difficulties, and for the protection of children from abuse, neglect, exploitation, or moral hazard.

For every child these rights, regardless of race, or
color, or situation, wherever he may live
under the protection of the
American Flag.

The Problem of Financial Limitation

A basic problem involved in contemporary social programs for child development arises from the stubborn realities of financial limitations. Four recent trends combine to create this problem in its present urgent form. The first is the steady advances in virtually all fields of science. Such advances have been particularly phenomenal in the so-called life sciences. One result of them has been to open up almost endless vistas of human and social betterment. In virtually all the sciences that touch human life, there are available new insights and revealed possibilities which, if utilized and achieved, are almost boundless in their scope. Modern man, surveying the insights which scientists now give him, believes that he is only on the threshold of a new world which may be achieved through his own efforts.

Supplementing the insights and vistas for human development offered by the life sciences is the increasing emphasis upon the intensive treatment of the individual. This is often identified as the case method approach, and when applied to humans is defined as the differential treatment of the human personality. Its essential aim is to understand and deal with each case on the basis of its own distinctive aspects. The idea, to be sure, is not new. Five hundred years before the Christian era, Hippocrates, the father of medicine, made a series of case records of individual patients which have remained virtually without parallel to this day. What is novel about the case method today is the scope and intensity of its application in various aspects of human development.

A third related development is the increasing appearance of pressure and promoting forces in the social welfare field, and this includes child welfare. These forces stem from various sources: the vested interests of specialized jobholders eager to achieve occupational security and future promotions; the designs of go-getting, promoting types of welfare executives; the socially ambitious, who find welfare work a helpful avenue to social preferment and public esteem; and the politically astute, who promise all things to all strongly organized and vocal groups. Not all promoter types are occupied in the field of corporation finance; the social welfare field has its own featured individuals in these respects, and the child welfare phase of the work has been a particularly felicitous hunting ground for them.

Finally, there is in the background the rising level of public indebtedness. Many of the social welfare programs—particularly those aimed at child welfare—which are accepted as the minimum requirements of today, first took form or attained public recognition a generation ago, under belief in a supposed surplus of social income which could be utilized by persons interested in various forms of social improvement. Speaking of the advances of the 1920's, Murphy wrote: "We had money enough to do things for people, to get things for people, to introduce new baby carriages into neighborhoods where they had never been seen before. The whole nation had a kind of release from repressions; anybody who wanted a job could get one; everybody had money; married women could get work."[9] What careful students of finance now understand is that this supposed surplus was in reality fictitious, resulting from the financial discounting of the future in ways and to an extent which produced the eco-

[9] J. Prentice Murphy, "Certain Philosophical Contributions to Children's Case Work," *Annual Proceedings, National Conference of Social Work*, 1933, p. 77.

nomic crash of 1929 and the depression decade that followed.[10] Moreover, this discounting of the future through public borrowing has been continued, and on a scale unparalleled in human history, down to the year 1956. Some data on the increasing federal public debt will reveal the extent to which this discounting of the future has gone. In 1900, the debt of the federal government was 1.2 billion dollars; in 1932, it stood at 19.4 billion dollars. Following this, the New Deal policy of seeking prosperity through lavish public expenditures was put into operation. By 1937, the federal debt amounted to 36.5 billions. Then came the huge expenditures of the war period, until in 1946, the federal debt reached a total of 269 billions. Ten years later, after a decade of high prosperity, it was 272.7 billions. At the present writing (1958) it is about the same. In addition to this, there are the public indebtednesses of the respective states, some of which reach very large amounts; the debts of our cities, the interest payments on which in some cases require half their annual incomes; and the debts of private businesses, as expressed in their respective bond issues, mostly on a long-term basis. In 1956, the total public and private debt in the United States amounted to 683.8 billion dollars.

These huge debts, public and private, represent discounts or anticipation of future income which has been utilized for present expenditures. In modest and restricted amounts to facilitate the development of sound and long-range inprovements, and when limited in period of time to a single generation, the process of discounting the future presents no appreciable hardship. Our present indebtednesses, however, have gone far beyond this point. Especially significant is the changed debt structure of the federal government. Annual interest charges on the national debt alone amount to more than the total peacetime expenditures of the national government in any year before 1934. There is also the problem of the repayment of the principal. Annual payments of two billion dollars on the principal means that, with no future borrowing in the interval and with payments beginning now, the total will be liquidated in approximately 130 years from now. Interest charges during this period are, of course, additional.

This changing debt structure cannot but affect the life of every man, woman, and child in this country, and will continue to do so for a long time to come. It will influence the number of jobs open, the wages and incomes people receive, what and how much they can buy, and what their savings will be worth.[11] Obviously, too, it has great meaning for the status and development of the child element in the population. As pointed out in Chapter 30, the economic capacity of a society is a constant and

[10] James H. S. Bossard, *Social Change and Social Problems,* rev. ed., Harper & Brothers, New York, 1938, pp. 268–272.

[11] Committee on Public Debt Policy, *Our National Debt,* National Debt Series No. 1, 1946, p. iii.

fundamental factor in the determination of child status. Two outstanding aspects of this relationship in modern society will be noted briefly. First, it determines the nature and scope of the public financing of child development programs which is possible. The public treasury is not an inexhaustible reservoir. Over an appreciable period of time it presents a specific and inevitable problem in the balancing of income and expenditures. Moreover, all kinds of demands are made upon it: to maintain order within, to give protection against attacks from without, to conduct the ordinary business of government, to meet emergencies, and to promote the social welfare of the society. This last named category includes many programs other than those involving children—those for the aged, the sick, the mentally diseased, and many others. Time was, in the history of this country, when all these financial obligations of the public treasury were paid out of small-change levies on a generous citizenry; today they have become an integral problem in public finance, pressing heavily upon a taxpaying public increasingly resistant to existing demands. Because of the contemporary emphasis upon public responsibility for all kinds of social welfare programs, these facts about the basic conditions of public finance are of direct importance in child development.

In the second place, the existing tax structure, as well as its foreseeable form for some years to come, is also related to what individual families are able to do for their children. Federal income tax payments alone now exact, and will continue to do so for a number of years, a proportion of the family income which, until recently, financed many of the opportunities afforded to American children beyond those available to children in other lands. Our present standards of child care and education pose a relatively heavy financial obligation upon parents, and their maintenance over the period of the next generation at least constitutes a financial problem which many careful thinkers are considering with gravity.

The Proper Concern for Child Development

Another fundamental issue which needs to be faced involves the proper balance of adult concern for child development. How much should we do for our children? How much should we permit, and compel, them to do for themselves?

Two contrasting philosophies can readily be identified in the literature and discussions of recent years. One emphasizes the overwhelming responsibility of parents and society. Children are what we make them. They cannot be more, they dare not be less. Wise and adequate parenthood requires that parents assume the responsibility for child development, creating the necessary opportunities for their children to grow into healthy and happy adults. Wise statesmanship, through the public provision of the requisite conditions, seeks to supplement parental efforts in the controlled development of the next generation. The major responsibility for child development lies with parents and the larger society.

The opposite point of view is rather critical of this emphasis; it contends that too much concern has been shown for children in our contemporary society, that modern parents tend to pamper rather than discipline them, that society gives them too much and expects too little, and that proper child development calls for more emphasis upon child self-help. Adult life, it insists, is grim and hard, and adequate preparation for it dares not partake too much of the soft, the easy, and the effeminate. To show the broad front of this "harder" approach to the problems of child development, three comments regarding it will be presented. They were made by a psychiatrist, a former educator and journalist, and a sociologist, respectively.

The psychiatrist is Dr. E. A. Strecker, who served as special consultant to the Secretary of War and to Surgeons General of the Army and Navy in World War II. Emphasizing the fact that 1,825,000 men were rejected for military service in that war, that another 600,000 were discharged from the Army alone for neuropsychiatric reasons or their equivalent, and that another half million attempted to evade the draft, Dr. Strecker attributes the basic inability of these three groups out of 15 million persons to their immaturity, that is, to the fact that they had not grown up. This condition, he points out, is in turn the result in large measure of parental domination, of oversolicitous "moms," of lack of child weaning—in short, of the failure of parents to allow or compel their children to grow up. This one-fifth of the manhood of America failed to measure up to their country's crisis because their parents, particularly their mothers, did too much for them, and too long.[12]

The former teacher, later a research worker and writer, is Roy Helton. He also has expressed himself in unmistakable terms:

It is not that we do too much for our children, for we all agree that their health and education are vital responsibilities not yet fully discharged, but rather that we do permit them to do too much to us. We allow them to direct our taste in amusement, to control our time, and to determine our outlays. They compel us to insist on easy courses for them in their schools, and to badger educational authorities, not for the parental aim of better and more intensive education, but for the adolescent aim of better football teams. In short, they have so far taken over that a growing characteristic of modern life for the past twenty years has been not its youthfulness but its juvenility. . . .

An era of plain clothes for the young, an era of the divorcement of youth and gasoline, an era in which active and self-generated recreation is necessary as a prime condition, is the very beginning of a program for justice and intelligent help of our youth, in meeting the grave problems life is certain to present

[12] Edward A. Strecker, *Their Mothers' Sons,* J. B. Lippincott Company, Philadelphia 1946.

to them. Today we rob them of their future because we are too tender to deny them anything they now demand. We pity them, as we pick their pockets. We do too little for our children because we give them too much.[13]

Kingsley Davis, sociologist, has put it this way:

An individual's most important functions for society are performed when he is fully adult, not when he is immature. Hence, society's treatment of the child is chiefly preparatory and the evaluation of him mainly anticipatory (like a savings account). Any doctrine which views the child's needs as paramount and those of organized society as secondary is a sociological anomaly, although a personal evaluation of particular children above other ends (mainly by parents) is a normal phenomenon which fits the cultural system for socializing the young.[14]

The fundamental problem at issue in these conflicting points of view is that of relative responsibilities in the field of child development. How much parents and society should do for children, what they should do, when they should project themselves into the processes involved and when they should studiously withdraw from them, what status of childhood makes for its best development—these are moot questions. The answers to them cannot and should not be made arbitrarily. Some of them may be determined by scientific measuring sticks; others will come as by-products of the art of human living together. In the last analysis, child development means life, growth, development, socialization, adjustment—and these are the universals of each generation.

Child Development—For What?

There is a final group of questions which may not be out of place in this volume. These concern the complementary part of child development. For example, we have just discussed the rights of children. What now are their responsibilities? In return for the years of their rearing and preparation to play their role as adults, what do children owe in return? In contrast to the current emphasis upon the rights of children, the necessity for maintaining high standards for their development, and the need for ever prolonging the period of their preparation, one finds very little reference to reciprocal responsibilities. Is this a proper balance? Is life all take, and little or no give? What do children owe their parents? Their schools? Their college? Their community? The larger society? Are these questions not equal in importance to the standards of their development? Is not the price of early development that of subsequent responsibility? Does

---

[13] Roy Helton, "Are We Doing Too Much for Our Children?" *Annals of the American Academy of Political and Social Science*, November, 1940, pp. 233–234.

[14] Kingsley Davis, "The Child and the Social Structure," *Journal of Educational Sociology*, December, 1940, p. 217.

not the balance scale of life demand this? Does anything less spell inevitably the anomaly of social bankruptcy?

We talk constantly about the development of the child's patterns of response. Of what types? To become individualists, interested only or chiefly in their own interests and acquisitions? Theoretically, individualism means a series of rights guaranteeing the intensive development of the individual unit of society; actually, all too often its hard core is to place the individual ahead of the group and to guarantee a freedom in life's choices that ignores the frustrating burden of responsibility.[15] Or do we want to develop children to become "organization yes" adults in the rat race of a mass economy in which the highest virtue is not to get out of line?

Do we seek to develop scientific pioneers who will act as the cutting edge of change, creating gadgets and goods which will further material progress, and who will seek, while the known world is floundering about, to penetrate through outer space to still other worlds? Or are we to develop escapists into a dream world, like the ivory tower of the scholar, the Eden of the voluble semanticist, or the phantasy of a world "where life can be encompassed by one's bare hands, and where living goes forward to the rhythm of the tides and the seasons and in response to the heart's desire."[16]

Are there abiding verities in life which could serve as the basic goals of child development? Is self-discipline one of these? In a society in which the role of the intimate primary groups has given way largely to the impersonal specialized controls of secondary groups, must not much more reliance for the behavior of the individual rest upon the inner springs of conduct? Is consideration for one's family one of these verities? The family is not only a vehicle for the development of the personalities of its individual members, but it is also the connecting link between successive generations, a group device for the perpetuation both of life and of civilization. Can a society survive without the general acceptance of familism as a supreme value?

Is consideration of one's fellows one of the eternal verities? Is the revival and detailed expression of this the basic remedy to the "institutional chaos" and "moral anarchy" which modern scholars decry? Does the right to one's own development inevitably involve recognition of the rights of others to their growth and development? Is one possible, in the last analysis, without the other? After all, the developing individual is surrounded by other individuals who also seek their respective developments.

---

[15] Cf. James H. S. Bossard and Eleanor S. Boll, *Why Marriages Go Wrong*, The Ronald Press Company, New York, 1958, Chap. 7.

[16] Robert S. Lynd, *Knowledge for What?*, Princeton University Press, Princeton, 1939, p. 11.

The answers to these questions may seem patently plain. Perhaps their very obviousness poses the problem which they present. The argument for them is, to utilize the words of Archibald MacLeish in regard to another matter, "neither long nor sensational. . . . But such is the character of what everyone knows that no one knows it with enthusiasm."[17]

This problem of values is one which social scientists in general, and sociologists in particular, tend to evade. While the role of the learned man in the past was generally that of emphasizing and conserving traditional values, the modern scientist claims that values "may not be derived by science, and therefore science should have nothing to do with them. . . . It prefers to say that for science the word 'ought' ought never to be used, except in saying that it ought never to be used."[18]

Actually, this is a good deal of a pose, without foundation of fact. Values inhere in everything the scientist does—the problems which he selects, those which he avoids, his evaluation of data, his methods of research, and his treatment of conclusions. "Research without an actively selective point of view becomes the ditty bag of an idiot, filled with bits of pebbles, straws, feathers, and other random hoardings."[19]

Yielding to no one in the insistence that the sociologist be pure in his lack of bias and detached in his gathering and appraising of data, it still seems relevant to us to point out that the values of society are what give direction, scope, and significance to scientific analysis, whatever its particular value may be. The concepts, the methods, and the content of the sociology of child development all take meaning from their relation to the needs and values of children *and of the society* in which they live. The determination of these needs and values may well constitute the next stage in the development of the sociology of childhood.

Summary

1. Differences in the social acceptance of the rights of childhood, similar to those noted in the case of the child's right to life and his right to be well born, are found in contrasting the child's right to an education and the school child's right to health.

2. These contrasts suggest the existence of a lag on the part of some contemporary social movements involving the status of childhood, somewhat similar to the culture lags noted by sociological students of social change.

3. Efforts to raise the status of childhood are limited by economic capacities. The changing debt structure in the United States in recent

[17] Archibald MacLeish, *The Fall of the City*, Farrar & Rinehart, New York, 1937, p. ix.
[18] Lynd, *op. cit.*, p. 181.
[19] *Ibid.*, p. 183.

years is of particular significance in this connection. It has meaning both for the public maintenance of social standards of child development, and for what individual families are able to do for their children.

4. The identification and maintenance of the proper balance between those who want to do too much for children and those who want to do too little is one of the fundamental and abiding problems of child development.

Bibliography

Abbott, Grace, *The Child and the State*, University of Chicago Press, Chicago, 1938, Vols. I and II.

Ackerson, Luton, *Children's Behavior Problems*, University of Chicago Press, Chicago, 1942, Vols. I and II.

Adams, Romanzo, *Interracial Marriage in Hawaii*, The Macmillan Company, New York, 1937.

Adorno, T. W., and others, *The Authoritarian Personality*, Harper & Brothers, New York, 1950.

Allen, Frederick H., *Psychotherapy with Children*, W. W. Norton & Company, Inc., New York, 1942.

Allport, Gordon W., *Personality: A Psychological Interpretation*, Henry Holt & Company, Inc., New York, 1937.

Allport, Gordon W., *The Use of Personal Documents in Psychological Science*, Social Science Research Council, New York, 1942.

Anderson, Elin L., *We Americans*, Harvard University Press, Cambridge, 1938.

Anderson, John E., *The Psychology of Development and Personal Adjustment*, Henry Holt & Company, Inc., New York, 1949.

Anderson, John E., *The Young Child in the Home*, White House Conference on Child Health and Protection, D. Appleton-Century Company, Inc., New York, 1936.

Anderson, John P., *A Study of the Relationships Between Certain Aspects of Parental Behavior and Attitudes and the Behavior of Junior High School Pupils*, Bureau of Publications, Teachers College, New York, 1940.

Anderson, W. A., *Mobility of Rural Families*, Cornell University Agricultural Experiment Station, Ithaca, 1934.

Angyal, Andras, *Foundations for a Science of Personality*, Commonwealth Fund, New York, 1941.

Anshen, Ruth N. (ed.), *Language: An Inquiry into Its Meaning and Function*, Harper & Brothers, New York, 1957.

Anthony, Sylvia, *The Child's Discovery of Death*, Kegan Paul, Trench, Trubner and Company, London, 1940.

Argyle, Michael, *The Scientific Study of Social Behavior*, The Philosophical Library, New York, 1957.

Arlett, Ada H., *Family Relationships*, McGraw-Hill Book Company, Inc., New York, 1942.

Baker, Harry J., and Traphagen, Virginia, *The Diagnosis and Treatment of Behavior-Problem Children*, The Macmillan Company, New York, 1936.

Bales, Robert F., *Interaction Process Analysis: A Method for the Study of Small Groups*, Addison-Wesley Press, Cambridge, Mass., 1950.

Barber, Bernard, *Social Stratification,* Harcourt, Brace & Company, Inc., New York, 1957.

Barker, Roger G., and Wright, Herbert F., *Midwest and Its Children,* Row, Peterson and Company, Evanston, Ill. [n.d.].

Barnett, James, *Divorce and the American Divorce Novel, 1858–1937,* University of Pennsylvania thesis, Philadelphia, 1939.

Barron, Milton L., *People Who Intermarry,* Syracuse University Press, Syracuse, 1946.

Bateson, Gregory, and Mead, Margaret, *Balinese Character,* New York Academy of Sciences, New York, 1942.

Bayne-Powell, Rosamond, *The English Child in the Eighteenth Century,* E. P. Dutton & Co., Inc., New York, 1939.

Becker, Howard, *German Youth: Bond or Free,* Oxford University Press, New York, 1947.

Becker, Howard, and Hill, Reuben (eds.), *Family, Marriage, and Parenthood.* 2nd ed., D. C. Heath & Company, Boston, 1955.

Benedict, Ruth, *Patterns of Culture,* Houghton Mifflin Company, Boston, 1934.

Berenda, Ruth W., *The Influence of the Group on the Judgments of Children,* King's Crown Press, New York, 1950.

Bernard, Jessie, *American Family Behavior,* Harper & Brothers, New York, 1942.

Bernard, Jessie, *Remarriage,* The Dryden Press, New York, 1956.

Bernert, Eleanor H., *America's Children,* John Wiley & Sons, Inc., New York, 1958.

Bettelheim, Bruno, *Love Is Not Enough: The Treatment of Emotionally Disturbed Children,* Free Press, Glencoe, Ill., 1950.

Blake, Florence G., *The Child, His Parents and the Nurse,* J. B. Lippincott Company, Philadelphia, 1954.

Bloch, Herbert A., and Niederhoffer, Arthur, *The Gang,* The Philosophical Library, New York, 1958.

Blos, Peter, *The Adolescent Personality,* D. Appleton-Century Company, Inc., New York, 1941.

Bossard, James H. S., *Marriage and the Child,* University of Pennsylvania Press, Philadelphia, 1940.

Bossard, James H. S., *Parent and Child: Studies in Family Behavior,* University of Pennsylvania Press, Philadelphia, 1953.

Bossard, James H. S., *Philadelphia: A Series of Maps in Urban Ecology,* privately published and circulated.

Bossard, James H. S., *Social Change and Social Problems,* rev. ed., Harper & Brothers, New York, 1938.

Bossard, James H. S., and Boll, Eleanor S., *Family Situations,* University of Pennsylvania Press, Philadelphia, 1943.

Bossard, James H. S., and Boll, Eleanor S., *The Large Family System,* University of Pennsylvania Press, Philadelphia, 1956.

Bossard, James H. S., and Boll, Eleanor S., *One Marriage, Two Faiths,* The Ronald Press Company, New York, 1957.

Bossard, James H. S., and Boll, Eleanor S., *Ritual in Family Living,* University of Pennsylvania Press, Philadelphia, 1950.

Bossard, James H. S., and Boll, Eleanor S., *Why Marriages Go Wrong*, The Ronald Press Company, New York, 1958.

Bott, Helen, *Adult Attitudes to Children's Misdemeanors*, University of Toronto Press, Toronto, 1937.

Boulding, Kenneth E., *The Image*, University of Michigan Press, Ann Arbor, 1956.

Brooks, Lee Marshall and E. C., *Adventuring in Adoption*, University of North Carolina Press, Chapel Hill, 1939.

Brown, L. Guy, *Social Pathology*, F. S. Crofts & Co., New York, 1942.

Bruch, Hilde, *Don't Be Afraid of Your Child*, Farrar, Straus and Young, New York, 1952.

Brunner, Edmund de S., *Immigrant Farmers and Their Children*, Garden City Pub. Co., Inc., New York, 1929.

Brunner, Edmund de S., and Lorge, Irving, *Rural Trends in Depression Years*, Columbia University Press, New York, 1937.

Bühler, Charlotte, *The Child and His Family*, Harper & Brothers, New York, 1939.

Burgess, Ernest W., and Cottrell, Leonard S., Jr., *Predicting Success or Failure in Marriage*, Prentice-Hall, Inc., New York, 1939.

Burgess, Ernest W., and Locke, Harvey J., *The Family*, American Book Company, New York, 1945.

Bush, Robert Nelson, *The Teacher-Pupil Relationship*, Prentice-Hall, Inc., New York, 1954.

Calhoun, Arthur W., *A Social History of the American Family*, Arthur H. Clark Company, Cleveland, 1919.

Carr, Lowell J., *Delinquency Control*, Harper & Brothers, New York, 1940.

Carr, Lowell J., *Situational Analysis*, Harper & Brothers, New York, 1948.

Cavan, Ruth S., *The Family*, The Thomas Y. Crowell Company, New York, 1942.

Chesser, Eustace, *The Sexual, Marital and Family Relationships of the English Woman*, Roy Publishers, New York [n.d.].

Child, Irvin L., *Italian or American?* Yale University Press, New Haven, 1943.

Chrisman, Oscar, *The Historical Child*, Richard G. Badger, Boston, 1920.

Christensen, Harold T., *Marriage Analysis*, 2nd ed., The Ronald Press Company, New York, 1958.

Clemens, Alphonse H., *Marriage and the Family*, Prentice-Hall, Inc., Englewood Cliffs, N.J., 1957.

Cohen, Albert K., *Delinquent Boys*, Free Press, Glencoe, Ill., 1955.

Cole, Luella, *Psychology of Adolescence*, 3rd ed., Rinehart & Company, Inc., New York, 1948.

Cook, Lloyd A. and Elaine F., *A Sociological Approach to Education*, McGraw-Hill Book Company, Inc., New York, 1950.

Cooley, Charles H., *Human Nature and the Social Order*, Charles Scribner's Sons, New York, 1902.

Cooley, Charles H., *Social Organization*, Charles Scribner's Sons, New York, 1922.

Coutu, Walter, *Emergent Human Nature*, Alfred A. Knopf, New York, 1949.

Cowgill, Donald O., *Mobile Homes: A Study in Trailer Life*, American Council on Public Affairs, Washington, 1941.

Cowgill, Donald O., *Residential Mobility of an Urban Population*, Washington University Library, St. Louis, 1935.

Cronin, A. J., *The Green Years*, Little, Brown & Company, Boston, 1944.

Cunningham, Ruth; Elzi, Anna; Farrell, Marie; Hall, James A.; and Roberts, Madeline, *Understanding Group Behavior of Boys and Girls*, Bureau of Publications, Teachers College, New York, 1951.

Cutts, Norma E., and Moseley, Nicholas, *The Only Child*, G. P. Putnam's Sons, New York, 1954.

Dahlke, H. Otto, *Values in Culture and Classroom*, Harper & Brothers, New York, 1958.

Daly, Maureen (ed.), *Profile of Youth*, J. B. Lippincott Company, Philadelphia, 1951.

Davis, Allison, and Dollard, John, *Children of Bondage*, American Council on Education, Washington, 1940.

Davis, Allison; Gardner, B. B.; and Gardner, Mary R., *Deep South*, University of Chicago Press, Chicago, 1941.

Davis, Allison, and Havighurst, Robert J., *Father of the Man*, Houghton Mifflin Company, Boston, 1947.

Del Solar, Charlotte, *Parents and Teachers View the Child*, Bureau of Publications, Teachers College, New York, 1949.

Dennis, Wayne, *Readings in Child Psychology*, Prentice-Hall, Inc., New York, 1951.

Dollard, John F., *Caste and Class in a Southern Town*, Yale University Press, New Haven, 1937.

Dollard, John F., *Criteria for the Life History*, Yale University Press, New Haven, 1935.

Dollard, John F., and Miller, Neal E., *Social Learning and Imitation*, Yale University Press, New Haven, 1941.

Dollard, John F.; Doob, Leonard W.; and others, *Frustration and Aggression*, Yale University Press, New Haven, 1939.

Drysdale, C. V., *The Small Family System*, B. W. Huebsch, New York, 1913.

Du Bois, Cora, *The People of Alor*, University of Minnesota Press, Minneapolis, 1944.

Duvall, Evelyn M., *Family Development*, J. B. Lippincott Company, Philadelphia, 1957.

Duvall, Evelyn M., *In-Laws: Pro & Con*, Association Press, New York, 1954.

Duvall, Evelyn M., and Hill, Reuben, *When You Marry*, D. C. Heath & Company, Boston, 1945.

Earle, Alice Morse, *Child Life in Colonial Days*, The Macmillan Company, New York, 1899.

Earle, Alice Morse, *Colonial Days in Old New York*, Charles Scribner's Sons, New York, 1896.

Earle, Alice Morse, *Customs and Fashions in Old New England*, Charles Scribner's Sons, New York, 1893.

Earle, Alice Morse, *Home Life in Colonial Days*, The Macmillan Company, New York, 1898.

Edin, Karl A., and Hutchinson, Edward P., *Studies of Differential Fertility in Sweden*, P. S. King, London, 1935.

Elliott, Grace Loucks, *Understanding the Adolescent Girl*, Woman's Press, New York, 1949.

Elmer, Manuel, *The Sociology of Family Life*, Ginn & Company, Boston, 1944.

English, O. Spurgeon, and Foster, Constance J., *Fathers Are Parents, Too*, G. P. Putnam's Sons, New York, 1951.

English, O. Spurgeon, and Pearson, Gerald H. J., *Emotional Problems of Living*, W. W. Norton & Company, Inc., New York, 1945.

Erikson, Erik H., *Childhood and Society*, W. W. Norton & Company, Inc., New York, 1950.

Firth, Raymond, *We, the Tikopia*, American Book Company, New York, 1936.

Fishbein, Morris, and Kennedy, Ruby Jo Reeves (eds.), *Modern Marriage and Family Living*, Oxford University Press, New York, 1957.

Fisher, M. S., *Language Patterns of Preschool Children*, Child Development Monographs, Bureau of Publications, Teachers College, New York, 1934.

Flanagan, Edward Joseph, *Understanding Your Boy*, Rinehart & Company, Inc., New York, 1950.

Fleming, Sandford, *Children and Puritanism*, Yale University Press, New Haven, 1933.

Folsom, Joseph K., *The Family and Democratic Society*, John Wiley & Sons, Inc., New York, 1943.

Ford, Clellan S., and Beach, Frank A., *Patterns of Sexual Behavior*, Harper & Brothers, New York, 1951.

Foster, J. C., and Anderson, J. E., *The Young Child and His Parents*, University of Minnesota Press, Minneapolis, 1930.

Foster, Robert G., *Marriage and Family Relationships*, rev. ed., The Macmillan Company, New York, 1950.

Francis, Kenneth V., and Fillmore, Eva A., *The Influence of Environment upon the Personalities of Children*, University of Iowa Studies, Vol. IX, No. 2, 1934.

Frank, Lawrence K., *Nature and Human Nature*, Rutgers University Press, New Brunswick, 1951.

Frazier, E. Franklin, *The Negro Family in the United States*, rev. ed., The Dryden Press, New York, 1948.

Fredericksen, Hazel, *The Child and His Welfare*, W. H. Freeman & Company, San Francisco, 1948.

Fromm, Erich, *Psychoanalysis and Religion*, Yale University Press, New Haven, 1950.

Furfey, Paul H., *The Gang Age*, The Macmillan Company, New York, 1926.

Gennep, Arnold van, *Les rites de passage*, Nourry, Paris, 1909.

Gesell, Arnold, *The Guidance of Mental Growth in Infant and Child*, The Macmillan Company, New York, 1930.

Gesell, Arnold, and Ilg, Frances L., *The Child from Five to Ten*, Harper & Brothers, New York, 1946.

Gesell, Arnold; Ilg, Frances L.; and Ames, Louise Bates, *Youth: the Years from Ten to Sixteen*, Harper & Brothers, New York, 1956.

Gesell, Arnold; Ilg, Frances L.; and others, *Infant and Child in the Culture of Today*, Harper & Brothers, New York, 1943.

Glick, Paul C., *American Families*, John Wiley & Sons, Inc., New York, 1957.

Glueck, Sheldon and Eleanor T., *Criminal Careers in Retrospect*, Commonwealth Fund, New York, 1943.

Glueck, Sheldon and Eleanor T., *Delinquents in the Making: Paths to Prevention*, Harper & Brothers, New York, 1952.

Glueck, Sheldon and Eleanor T., *One Thousand Juvenile Delinquents*, Harvard University Press, Cambridge, 1934.

Glueck, Sheldon and Eleanor T., *Preventing Crime*, McGraw-Hill Book Company, Inc., New York, 1936.

Glueck, Sheldon and Eleanor T., *Unraveling Juvenile Delinquency*, Commonwealth Fund, New York, 1950.

Goff, Regina Mary, *Problems and Emotional Difficulties of Negro Children*, Bureau of Publications, Teachers College, New York, 1949.

Goode, William J., *After Divorce*, Free Press, Glencoe, Ill., 1956.

Gorer, Geoffrey, *The American People*, W. W. Norton & Company, Inc., New York, 1948.

Gottschalk, Louis; Kluckhohn, Clyde; and Angell, Robert, *The Use of Personal Documents in History, Anthropology and Sociology*, Social Science Research Council, Washington, 1945.

Groves, Ernest R., *The Family and Its Social Functions*, J. B. Lippincott Company, Philadelphia, 1940.

Gruber, Frederick C. (ed.), *The Emergence of the Modern Mind*, University of Pennsylvania Press, Philadelphia, 1958.

Gruenberg, Sidonie Matsner, *We, the Parents*, Harper & Brothers, New York, 1939.

Gruenberg, Sidonie Matsner and Benjamin C., *Parents, Children and Money*, The Viking Press, Inc., New York, 1933.

Hagood, Margaret J., *Mothers of the South*, University of North Carolina Press, Chapel Hill, 1939.

Hamilton, Gordon, *Psychotherapy in Child Guidance*, Columbia University Press, New York, 1947.

Hartley, Ruth E.; Frank, Lawrence K.; and Goldenson, Robert M., *Understanding Children's Play*, Columbia University Press, New York, 1952.

Havighurst, Robert J., and Neugarten, Bernice L., *Society and Education*, Allyn and Bacon, Inc., Boston, 1957.

Havighurst, Robert J., and Taba, Hilda, *Adolescent Character and Personality*, John Wiley & Sons, Inc., 1949.

Hayakawa, S. I., *Language in Action*, Harcourt, Brace & Company, Inc., New York, 1939.

Healy, William, *Personality in Formation and Action*, W. W. Norton & Company, Inc., New York, 1938.

Healy, William, and Bronner, Augusta F., *Delinquents and Criminals: Their Making and Unmaking*, The Macmillan Company, New York, 1926.

Healy, William, and Bronner, Augusta F., *New Light on Delinquency and Its Treatment*, Yale University Press, New Haven, 1936.

Hewitt, Lester E., and Jenkins, Richard L., *Fundamental Patterns of Malad-*

justment: the Dynamics of Their Origin, printed by authority of the State of Illinois, 1946.

Hill, Reuben, *Families Under Stress,* Harper & Brothers, New York, 1949.

Hill, Reuben, and Waller, Willard, *The Family,* rev. ed., The Dryden Press, New York, 1951.

Himes, Norman E., *Medical History of Contraception,* The Williams & Wilkins Company, Baltimore, 1936.

Hollingshead, A. B., *Elmtown's Youth,* John Wiley & Sons, Inc., New York, 1949.

Horney, Karen, *New Ways in Psychoanalysis,* W. W. Norton & Company, Inc., New York, 1939.

Hunt, J. McV., *Personality and the Behavior Disorders,* The Ronald Press Company, New York, 1944, Vols. I, II.

Hurlock, Elizabeth B., *Child Growth and Development,* 2nd ed., McGraw-Hill Book Company, Inc., New York, 1956.

Hutchinson, Dorothy, *In Quest of Foster Parents,* Columbia University Press, New York, 1943.

Hutchinson, Edward P., *Immigrants and Their Children, 1850–1950,* John Wiley & Sons, Inc., New York, 1956.

Hymes, James L., *Behavior and Misbehavior,* Prentice-Hall, Inc., New York, 1955.

Isaacs, Susan, *Troubles of Children and Parents,* Methuen & Company, Ltd., London, 1948.

Jersild, Arthur T.; Woodyard, Ella S.; and Del Solar, Charlotte (in collaboration with Ernest G. Osborne and Robert C. Challman), *Joys and Problems of Child Rearing,* Bureau of Publications, Teachers College, New York, 1949.

Josselyn, Irene M., *The Happy Child,* Random House, New York, 1955.

Kane, John J., *Marriage and the Family,* The Dryden Press, New York, 1952.

Kardiner, Abram, *The Psychological Frontiers of Society,* Columbia University Press, New York, 1945.

Kawin, Ethel, *Children of Pre-School Age,* University of Chicago Press, Chicago, 1934.

Kelley, Janet Agnes, *College Life and the Mores,* Bureau of Publications, Teachers College, New York, 1949.

Kiefer, Monica, *American Children Through Their Books,* University of Pennsylvania Press, Philadelphia, 1948.

Kluckhohn, Clyde; Murray, Henry A.; and Schneider, David M. (eds.), *Personality: In Nature, Society, and Culture,* Alfred A. Knopf, New York, 1952.

Koshuk, Ruth Pearson, *Social Influences Affecting the Behavior of Young Children,* Publications of the National Research Council, Washington, 1941.

Koster, Donald Nelson, *The Theme of Divorce in American Drama, 1871–1939,* University of Pennsylvania thesis, Philadelphia, 1942.

Kretschmer, E., *Physique and Character,* Harcourt, Brace & Company, Inc., New York, 1925.

Kuhn, Anne L., *The Mother's Role in Childhood Education,* Yale University Press, New Haven, 1947.

Lafitte, Paul, *The Person in Psychology: Reality or Abstraction,* The Philosophical Library, New York, 1957.

Landis, Judson T. and Mary G., *Building a Successful Marriage,* 2nd ed., Prentice-Hall, Inc., New York, 1953.

Landis, Judson T. and Mary G., *Personal Adjustment, Marriage and Family Living,* 2nd ed., Prentice-Hall, Inc., New York, 1955.

Landis, Paul H., *Adolescence and Youth,* McGraw-Hill Book Company, Inc., New York, 1945.

Landis, Paul H., *Understanding Teen-Agers,* Appleton-Century-Crofts, Inc., New York, 1955.

Lang, Olga, *Chinese Family and Society,* Yale University Press, New Haven, 1946.

Leighton, Dorothea, and Kluckhohn, Clyde, *Children of the People,* Harvard University Press, Cambridge, 1947.

LeMasters, E. E., *Modern Courtship and Marriage,* The Macmillan Company, New York, 1957.

Levy, David M., *Maternal Overprotection,* Columbia University Press, New York, 1943.

Levy, David M., *Studies in Sibling Rivalry,* Research Monograph No. 2, American Orthopsychiatric Association, New York, 1938.

Lindgren, Henry C., *Mental Health in Education,* Henry Holt & Company, Inc., New York, 1954.

Lindsay, Howard, and Crouse, Russel, *Clarence Day's Life with Father,* Alfred A. Knopf, New York, 1941.

Linsky, Leonard (ed.), *Semantics and the Philosophy of Language,* University of Illinois Press, Urbana, 1952.

Linton, Ralph, *The Cultural Background of Personality,* D. Appleton-Century Company, Inc., New York, 1945.

Linton, Ralph, *The Science of Man in the World Crisis,* Columbia University Press, New York, 1945.

Linton, Ralph, *The Study of Man,* D. Appleton-Century Company, Inc., New York, 1936.

Locke, Harvey J., *Predicting Adjustment in Marriage,* Henry Holt & Company, Inc., New York, 1951.

Loomis, Mary Jane, *The Preadolescent,* Appleton-Century-Crofts, Inc., New York, 1959.

Macardle, Dorothy, *Children of Europe,* Beacon Press, Boston, 1951.

Mangione, Jerre, *Mount Allegro,* Houghton Mifflin Company, Boston, 1942.

Marshall, Leon C., and May, Geoffrey, *The Divorce Court,* Johns Hopkins Press, Baltimore, Vol. I (Maryland), 1932; Vol. II (Ohio), 1933.

Martin, William E., and Stendler, Celia B., *Child Development,* Harcourt, Brace and Company, New York, 1953.

Martin, William E., and Stendler, Celia B. (eds.), *Readings in Child Development,* Harcourt, Brace & Company, Inc., New York, 1954.

Marzolf, Stanley S., *Psychological Diagnosis and Counseling in the Schools,* Henry Holt & Company, Inc., New York, 1956.

Mead, Margaret, *And Keep Your Powder Dry,* William Morrow & Company, Inc., New York, 1943.

Mead, Margaret, *From the South Seas,* William Morrow & Company, Inc., New York, 1939.

Mead, Margaret, *Male and Female,* William Morrow & Company, Inc., New York, 1949.

Mead, Margaret, *The School in American Culture,* Harvard University Press, Cambridge, 1951.

Mead, Margaret, and Wolfenstein, Martha, *Childhood in Contemporary Cultures,* University of Chicago Press, Chicago, 1955.

Mihanovich, Clement S.; Schnepp, Gerald J.; and Thomas, John L., *Marriage and the Family,* Bruce Publishing Company, Milwaukee, 1952.

Miller, Daniel R., and Swanson, Guy E., *The Changing American Parent,* John Wiley & Sons, Inc., New York, 1958.

Miller, George A., *Language and Communication,* McGraw-Hill Book Company, Inc., New York, 1951.

Mills, C. Wright, *White Collar,* Oxford University Press, New York, 1951.

Mohr, George J., and Despres, Marian A., *The Stormy Decade: Adolescence,* Random House, New York, 1958.

Moloney, James Clark, *The Battle for Mental Health,* The Philosophical Library, New York, 1952.

Money, John, *The Psychologic Study of Man,* Charles C. Thomas, Springfield, Ill., 1957.

Morgan, Edmund S., *The Puritan Family,* Trustees of the Public Library, Boston, 1944.

Morgan, Edmund S., *Virginians at Home,* Colonial Williamsburg, 1952.

Morris, C. W., *Signs, Language and Behavior,* Prentice-Hall, Inc., New York, 1946.

Mulhern, James, *A History of Education,* The Ronald Press Company, New York, 1946.

Murchison, C. (ed.), *A Handbook of Child Psychology,* rev. ed., Clark University Press, Worcester, 1933.

Murphy, Lois B., *Social Behavior and Child Personality,* Columbia University Press, New York, 1937.

Myers, Jerome K., and Roberts, Bertram H., *Family and Class Dynamics in Mental Illness,* John Wiley & Sons, Inc., New York, 1959.

Myers, Theodore R., *Intra-Family Relationships and Pupil Adjustment,* Bureau of Publications, Teachers College, New York, 1935.

Neisser, Edith G., *Brothers and Sisters,* Harper & Brothers, New York, 1951.

Neisser, Edith G., *Children in the Family: Rivals and Friends,* Bureau of Publications, Teachers College, New York, 1951.

Neisser, Edith G., *The Eldest Child,* Harper & Brothers, New York, 1957.

Newman, Horatio H.; Freeman, Frank M.; and Holzinger, Karl J., *Twins: A Study of Heredity and Environment,* University of Chicago Press, Chicago, 1937.

Ogburn, William F., and Nimkoff, Meyer F., *Technology and the Changing Family,* Houghton Mifflin Company, Boston, 1955.

Park, Robert E., and Miller, Herbert A., *Old World Traits Transplanted,* Harper & Brothers, New York, 1921.

Pavlov, I. P., *Conditioned Reflexes,* translated by G. V. Surep, Oxford University Press, London, 1927.

Payne, George Henry, *The Child in Human Progress,* G. P. Putnam's Sons, New York, 1916.

Pearson, Gerald H. J., *Emotional Disorders of Children,* W. W. Norton & Company, Inc., New York, 1949.

Phelps, Harold A., and Henderson, David, *Population in Its Human Aspects,* Appleton-Century-Crofts, Inc., New York, 1958.

Piaget, Jean, *The Language and Thought of the Child,* Harcourt, Brace & Company, Inc., New York, 1926.

Piaget, Jean, *The Moral Judgment of the Child,* Kegan Paul, London, 1932.

Pike, James A., *If You Marry Outside Your Faith,* Harper & Brothers, New York, 1954.

Plant, James S., *The Envelope,* Commonwealth Fund, New York, 1950.

Plant, James S., *Personality and the Cultural Pattern,* Commonwealth Fund, New York, 1937.

Podolsky, Edward, *The Jealous Child,* The Philosophical Library, New York, 1954.

Pollak, Otto, *Integrating Sociological and Psychoanalytic Concepts,* Russell Sage Foundation, New York, 1956.

Pollak, Otto, and collaborators, *Social Science and Psychotherapy for Children,* Russell Sage Foundation, New York, 1952.

Popenoe, Paul, *Modern Marriage,* The Macmillan Company, New York, 1927.

Powers, Edwin, and Witmer, Helen, *An Experiment in the Prevention of Delinquency: The Cambridge-Somerville Youth Study,* Columbia University Press, New York, 1951.

Queen, Stuart, and Adams, John B., *The Family in Various Cultures,* J. B. Lippincott Company, Philadelphia, 1952.

Redl, Fritz, and Wattenberg, William, *Mental Hygiene in Teaching,* Harcourt, Brace & Company, Inc., New York, 1951.

Ribble, Margaret A., *The Personality of the Young Child,* Columbia University Press, New York, 1955.

Ribble, Margaret A., *The Rights of Infants,* Columbia University Press, New York, 1943.

Roberts, Katherine Elliott, and Fleming, Virginia Van Dyne, *Persistence and Change in Personality Patterns,* Monograph of the Society for Research in Child Development, National Research Council, Washington, 1943.

Rockwood, Lemo D., and Ford, Mary E. M., *Youth, Marriage and Parenthood,* John Wiley & Sons, Inc., New York, 1945.

Ross, Murray G., *Religious Beliefs of Youth,* Association Press, New York, 1950.

Roucek, Joseph S. (ed.), *Juvenile Delinquency,* The Philosophical Library, New York, 1958.

Roucek, Joseph S., and others, *Sociological Foundations of Education,* The Thomas Y. Crowell Company, New York, 1942.

Sanger, Margaret, *My Fight for Birth Control,* Farrar & Rinehart, New York, 1931.

Santayana, George, *Persons and Places,* Charles Scribner's Sons, New York, 1944.

Schaffner, Bertram (ed.), *Group Processes,* Josiah Macy, Jr., Foundation, New York, 1957.

Sears, Robert R.; Maccoby, Eleanor E.; and Levin, Harry, *Patterns of Child Rearing*, Row, Peterson and Company, Evanston, Ill., 1957.

Shaw, Clifford, and McKay, Henry D., *Juvenile Delinquency and Urban Areas*, University of Chicago Press, Chicago, 1942.

Shaw, Clifford, and others, *Delinquency Areas*, University of Chicago Press, Chicago, 1929.

Shaw, Clifford, and others, *The Natural History of a Delinquent Career*, University of Chicago Press, Chicago, 1931.

Sheeley, Arlene; Landis, Paul H.; and Davies, Vernon, *Marital and Family Adjustment in Rural and Urban Families*, Bulletin No. 506, Institute of Agricultural Sciences, State College of Washington, Pullman, May, 1949.

Sheldon, William H., with the collaboration of Emil M. Hartl and Eugene McDermott, *Varieties of Delinquent Youth*, Harper & Brothers, New York, 1949.

Shuttleworth, Frank K., *The Adolescent Period: A Graphic Atlas*, Monographs of the Society for Research in Child Development, Vol. XIV, No. 49, Child Development Publications, Evanston, Ill., 1951.

Simpson, M., *Parent Preferences of Young Children*, Bureau of Publications, Teachers College, New York, 1935.

Slavson, Samuel R., *Child Psychotherapy*, Columbia University Press, New York, 1952.

Slotkin, J. S., *Personality Development*, Harper & Brothers, New York, 1952.

Smart, Mollie Stevens, and Smart, Russell Cook, *Living and Learning with Children*, Houghton Mifflin Company, Boston, 1949.

Smith, Betty, *A Tree Grows in Brooklyn*, Harper & Brothers, New York, 1943.

Smith, William C., *Americans in the Making*, D. Appleton-Century Company, Inc., New York, 1939.

Smith, William C., *The Stepchild*, University of Chicago Press, Chicago, 1953.

Sociological Foundations of the Psychiatric Disorders of Childhood, Proceeding of the Twelfth Institute of the Child Research Clinic of the Woods Schools, Langhorne, Pa., 1945.

Sorokin, Pitirim A., *Explorations in Altruistic Love and Behavior*, Beacon Press, Boston, 1950.

Stendler, Celia Burns, *Children of Brasstown*, Bureau of Research and Service, College of Education, University of Illinois, Urbana, 1949.

Stiles, Lindley J. (ed.), *The Teacher's Role in American Society*, John Dewey Society, Fourteenth Yearbook, 1957.

Stolz, Lois Meek, and others, *Father Relations of War-Born Children*, Stanford University Press, Stanford, 1954.

Stone, L. Joseph, and Church, Joseph, *Childhood and Adolescence*, Random House, New York, 1957.

Stonequist, Everett, *The Marginal Man: A Study in Personality and Culture Conflict*, Charles Scribner's Sons, New York, 1937.

Strang, Ruth, *The Adolescent Views Himself*, McGraw-Hill Book Company, Inc., New York, 1957.

Strang, Ruth, *An Introduction to Child Study*, 3rd ed., The Macmillan Company, New York, 1951.

Strecker, Edward A., *Their Mothers' Sons,* J. B. Lippincott Company, Philadelphia, 1946.

Strecker, Edward A., and Appel, Kenneth, *Discovering Ourselves,* The Macmillan Company, New York, 1931.

Sullenger, T. Earl, *Social Determinants in Juvenile Delinquency,* John Wiley & Sons, Inc., New York, 1936.

Taba, Hilda, *School Culture,* American Council on Education, Washington, D.C., 1955.

Terman, Lewis M., *Psychological Factors in Marital Happiness,* McGraw-Hill Book Company, Inc., New York, 1938.

Terman, Lewis M., and Oden, Melita H., *The Gifted Child Grows Up,* Stanford University Press, Stanford, 1947.

Thomas, John L., *The American Catholic Family,* Prentice-Hall, Inc., Englewood Cliffs, N.J., 1956.

Thomas, W. I., and Znaniecki, Florian, *The Polish Peasant,* Richard G. Badger, Boston, 1919.

Thrasher, Frederic M., *The Gang,* 2nd rev. ed., University of Chicago Press, Chicago, 1936.

Van de Water, Frederic F., *Fathers Are Funny,* John Day Company, New York, 1939.

Volkart, Edmund H., *Social Behavior and Personality,* Social Science Research Council, New York, 1951.

Wagenknecht, Edward (ed.), *When I Was a Child,* E. P. Dutton & Co., Inc., New York, 1946.

Waller, Willard, *The Sociology of Teaching,* John Wiley & Sons, Inc., New York, 1932.

Warner, W. Lloyd, and others, *Democracy in Jonesville,* Harper & Brothers, New York, 1949.

Warner, W. Lloyd, and Lunt, Paul, *The Social Life of a Modern Community,* Yale University Press, New Haven, 1941.

Warner, W. Lloyd; Meeker, Marchia; and Eells, Kenneth, *Social Class in America,* Science Research Associates, Chicago, 1949.

Warner, W. Lloyd, and Srole, Leo, *The Social Systems of American Ethnic Groups,* Yale University Press, New Haven, 1945.

Waters, Ethel, *His Eye Is on the Sparrow,* Doubleday & Company, Inc., New York, 1951.

Weill, Blanche C., *The Behavior of Young Children of the Same Family,* Harvard University Press, Cambridge, 1928.

Weill, Blanche C., *Through Children's Eyes,* Island Press, New York, 1940.

Wembridge, Eleanor R., *Other People's Daughters,* Houghton Mifflin Company, Boston, 1925.

Werner, Heinz, and Kaplan, Edith, *The Acquisition of Word Meanings: A Developmental Study,* Monographs of the Society for Research in Child Development, Vol. XV, No. 51, Child Development Publications, Evanston, Ill., 1952.

West, James, *Plainville, U.S.A.,* Columbia University Press, New York, 1945.

Whiting, John W. M., *Becoming a Kwoma,* Yale University Press, New Haven, 1941.

Whiting, John W. M., and Child, Irvin L., *Child Training and Personality*, Yale University Press, New Haven, 1953.

Wickman, E. K., *Children's Behavior and Teachers' Attitudes*, 6th printing, Commonwealth Fund, New York, 1937.

Winch, Robert F., *The Modern Family*, Henry Holt & Company, Inc., New York, 1952.

Witty, Paul (ed.), *The Gifted Child*, D. C. Heath & Company, Boston, 1951.

Wolf, Anna W. M., *Helping Your Child to Understand Death*, Child Study Association of America, New York, 1958.

Woods, Sister Frances Jerome, *The American Family System*, Harper & Brothers, New York, 1959.

Young, Pauline V., *The Pilgrims of Russian Town*, University of Chicago Press, Chicago, 1932.

Zachry, Caroline B., *Emotion and Conduct in Adolescence*, D. Appleton-Century Company, Inc., New York, 1940.

Zachry, Caroline B., *Personality Adjustments of School Children*, Charles Scribner's Sons, New York, 1929.

Zeligs, Rose, *Glimpses into Child Life*, William Morrow & Company, Inc., New York, 1942.

Zimmerman, Carle C. *Family and Civilization*, Harper & Brothers, New York, 1947.

Zimmerman, Carle C., *The Family of Tomorrow*, Harper & Brothers, New York, 1949.

Zimmerman, Carle C., and Du Wors, Richard E., *Graphic Regional Sociology*, The Phillips Book Store, Cambridge, Mass., 1952.

Zimmerman, Carle C., and Frampton, M. E., *Family and Society*, D. Van Nostrand Company, Inc., New York, 1935.

Articles

Aberle, David F., and Naegele, Kaspar D., "Middle-Class Fathers' Occupational Role and Attitudes Toward Children," *American Journal of Orthopsychiatry*, April, 1952, pp. 366–378.

Abrahamson, Stephen, "School Rewards and Social-Class Status," *Educational Research Bulletin*, January, 1952, pp. 8–15.

Ackerman, Nathan W., and Sobel, Raymond, "Family Diagnosis: An Approach to the Preschool Child," *American Journal of Orthopsychiatry*, October, 1950, pp. 744–753.

Albrecht, Ruth, "The Parental Responsibilities of Grandparents," *Marriage and Family Living*, August, 1954, pp. 201–204.

Albrecht, Ruth, "Relationships of Older Parents with Their Children," *Marriage and Family Living*, February, 1954, pp. 32–35.

Aldous, Joan, and Kell, Leone, "Child-Rearing Values of Mothers in Relation to Their Children's Perceptions of Their Mothers' Control: An Exploratory Study," *Marriage and Family Living*, February, 1956, pp. 72–74.

Alexander, Theron and Marie, "A Study of Personality and Social Status," *Child Development*, September, 1952, pp. 207–213.

Allen, Philip J., "Childhood Backgrounds of Success in a Profession," *American Sociological Review*, April, 1955, pp. 186–190.

Anderson, John E., "The Development of Social Behavior," *American Journal of Sociology*, May, 1939, pp. 839–857.

Anderson, John E., "The Development of Spoken Language," *38th Yearbook of the National Society for the Study of Education*, Public School Publishing Co., Bloomington, 1939.

Anderson, John E., "The Motivation of the Young Child," *Proceedings of the Mid-West Conference on Parent Education*, March, 1926, pp. 98–112.

Apple, Dorrian, "Learning Theory and Socialization," *American Sociological Review*, February, 1951, pp. 23–27.

Arsenian, Seth, "Bilingualism in the Post-War World," *Psychological Bulletin*, February, 1945, pp. 65–86.

Banham, Katharine M., "Obstinate Children Are Adaptable," *Mental Hygiene*, January, 1952, pp. 84–89.

Barker, Roger G., and Wright, Herbert F., "Psychological Ecology and the Problem of Psychosocial Development," *Child Development*, September, 1949, pp. 131–143.

Barron, Milton L., "Research on Intermarriage: A Survey of Accomplishments and Prospects," *American Journal of Sociology*, November, 1951, pp. 249–255.

Baruch, Dorothy W., "A Study of Reported Tension in Interparental Relationships as Co-Existent with the Behavior Adjustment in Young Children," *Journal of Experimental Education*, December, 1927, pp. 187–205.

Baxter, Celena A., "Sicilian Family Life," *The Family*, May, 1933, pp. 82–88.

Beach, Allen W. and Walter G., "Family Migratoriness and Child Behavior," *Sociology and Social Research*, July–August, 1937, pp. 503–523.

Beck, Annie G., "School Success as a Withdrawal Mechanism in Two Adolescents," *Journal of Abnormal and Social Psychology*, April–June, 1935, pp. 87–94.

Becker, Howard S., "The Career of the Chicago Public Schoolteacher," *American Journal of Sociology*, March, 1952, pp. 470–477.

Behrens, Marjorie L., "Child Rearing and the Character Structure of the Mother," *Child Development*, September, 1954, pp. 225–238.

Bell, Earl H., "Age Group Conflicts and Our Changing Culture," *Social Forces*, December, 1933, pp. 237–243.

Benedict, Ruth, "Child Rearing in Certain European Countries," *American Journal of Orthopsychiatry*, April, 1949, pp. 342–350.

Bernard, L. L., "A Classification of Environments," *American Journal of Sociology*, November, 1925, pp. 318–332.

Bernard, L. L., "The Significance of Environment as a Social Factor," *Publications of the American Sociological Society*, 1921, pp. 84–112.

Bettelheim, Bruno, and Sylvester, Emmy, "Notes on the Impact of Parental Occupations: Some Cultural Deteminants of Symptom Choice in Emotionally Disturbed Children," *American Journal of Orthopsychiatry*, October, 1950, pp. 785–795.

Blackey, Eileen, "The Social and Economic Adjustment of a Group of Special

Class Graduates," *Smith College Studies in Social Work,* December, 1930, pp. 160–179.

Block, Jack, "Personality Characteristics Associated with Fathers' Attitudes Toward Child-Rearing," *Child Development,* March, 1955, pp. 41–48.

Blood, Robert O., Jr., "Consequences of Permissiveness for Parents of Young Children," *Marriage and Family Living,* August, 1953, pp. 209–212.

Blumer, Herbert, "Social Attitudes and Nonsymbolic Interaction," *Journal of Educational Sociology,* May, 1936, pp. 515–523.

Bohannon, E. W., "The Only Child in a Family," *Pedagogical Seminary,* April, 1898, pp. 306–310.

Boll, Eleanor S., "The Child," *Annals of the American Academy of Political and Social Science,* September, 1943, pp. 69–79.

Boll, Eleanor S., "The Role of Preschool Playmates—A Situational Approach," *Child Development,* September, 1957, pp. 327–342.

Bossard, James H. S., "Child in Transition," *Educational Outlook,* January, 1931, pp. 34–40.

Bossard, James H. S., "Child Welfare and the Modern Mind," *Annals of the American Academy of Political and Social Science,* September, 1930, pp. 1–5.

Bossard, James H. S., "Children Are Human Beings," *Childhood Education,* September, 1944, pp. 6–10.

Bossard, James H. S. (ed.), "Children in a Depression Decade," *Annals of the American Academy of Political and Social Science,* November, 1940.

Bossard, James H. S., "Family Background of Wartime Adolescents," *Annals of the American Academy of Political and Social Science,* November, 1944, pp. 33–42.

Bossard, James H. S., "The Family in Past Wars," *Annals of the American Academy of Political and Social Science,* September, 1943, pp. 1–10.

Bossard, James H. S., "Family Problems in Wartime," *Psychiatry,* February, 1944, pp. 65–72.

Bossard, James H. S., "Family Problems of the Immediate Future," *Journal of Home Economics,* September, 1945, pp. 383–387.

Bossard, James H. S., "Family Situations and Child Behavior," *Journal of Educational Sociology,* February, 1944, pp. 323–337.

Bossard, James H. S., "Growing Up in a Large Family," *Child Study,* Fall, 1958, pp. 3–6.

Bossard, James H. S., "I Wrote About Dogs: A Mental-Hygiene Note," *Mental Hygiene,* July, 1950, pp. 385–390.

Bossard, James H. S., "The Impact of War on the Family," *Proceedings of the 8th Institute on Education and the Exceptional Child of the Child Research Clinic of the Woods Schools,* May, 1942.

Bossard, James H. S., "Large and Small Families—A Study in Contrasts," *Journal of the American Society of Chartered Life Underwriters,* Summer, 1959, pp. 222–240.

Bossard, James H. S., "Marriage as a Status-Achieving Device," *Sociology and Social Research,* September–October, 1944, pp. 3–10.

Bossard, James H. S., "The Mental Hygiene of Owning a Dog," *Mental Hygiene,* July, 1944, pp. 408–413.

Bossard, James H. S., "Nationality and Nativity as Factors in Marriage," *American Sociological Review,* December, 1939, pp. 792–798.

Bossard, James H. S., "Previous Conjugal Conditions," *Social Forces,* December, 1939, pp. 243–247.

Bossard, James H. S., "Process in Social Weaning: A Study of Childhood Visiting," *Child Development,* September, 1951, pp. 211–220.

Bossard, James H. S., "The Service Man and the Adolescent Girl," *National Parent-Teacher,* April, 1943, pp. 10–13.

Bossard, James H. S., "Sociological Fashions and Societal Planning," *Social Forces,* December, 1935, pp. 1–8.

Bossard, James H. S. (ed.), "Toward Family Stability," *Annals of the American Academy of Political and Social Science,* November, 1950.

Bossard, James H. S., "War and the Family," *American Sociological Review,* June, 1941, pp. 330–344.

Bossard, James H. S., "Welfare Objective and Scientific Concept," *Social Forces,* March, 1944, pp. 307–310.

Bossard, James H. S., "What Can We Do About Divorce?" *National Parent-Teacher,* October, 1945, pp. 4–7.

Bossard, James H. S., "Youth's Coming of Age," *Welfare Magazine,* November, 1928, pp. 1315–1320.

Bossard, James H. S., and Boll, Eleanor S. (eds.), "Adolescents in Wartime," *Annals of the American Academy of Political and Social Science,* November, 1944.

Bossard, James H. S., and Boll, Eleanor S., "Campus Marriages—For Better or for Worse," *The New York Times Magazine,* April 5, 1959, pp. 59, 83, 85, 86, 88.

Bossard, James H. S., and Boll, Eleanor S., "Child Behavior and the Empathic Complex," *Child Development,* March, 1957, pp. 37–42.

Bossard, James H. S., and Boll, Eleanor S., "The Immediate Family and the Kinship Group: A Research Report," *Social Forces,* May, 1946, pp. 379–384.

Bossard, James H. S., and Boll, Eleanor S., "Personality Roles in the Large Family," *Child Development,* March, 1955, pp. 71–78.

Bossard, James H. S., and Boll, Eleanor S., "Rite of Passage—A Contemporary Study," *Social Forces,* March, 1948, pp. 247–255.

Bossard, James H. S., and Boll, Eleanor S., "Ritual in Family Living," *American Sociological Review,* August, 1949, pp. 463–469.

Bossard, James H. S., and Boll, Eleanor S., "Security in the Large Family," *Mental Hygiene,* October, 1954, pp. 529–544.

Bossard, James H. S., and Boll, Eleanor S., "3 Wonderful Stages of Family Life," *House and Garden,* March, 1959, pp. 66–67, 110, 121.

Bossard, James H. S., and Dillon, Thelma, "The Spatial Distribution of Divorced Women," *American Journal of Sociology,* January, 1935, pp. 503–507.

Bossard, James H. S., and Letts, Harold C., "Mixed Marriages Involving Lutherans—A Research Report," *Marriage and Family Living,* November, 1956, pp. 308–310.

Bossard, James H. S., and Murphy, J. Prentice (eds.), "New Values in Child Welfare," *Annals of the American Academy of Political and Social Science,* September, 1925.

Bossard, James H. S., and Sanger, Winogene Pratt, "Children Have Insight, Too," *National Parent-Teacher,* January, 1949, pp. 27–29.

Bossard, James H. S., and Sanger, Winogene Pratt, "The Large Family System —A Research Report," *American Sociological Review,* February, 1952, pp. 3–9.

Bossard, James H. S., and Sanger, Winogene Pratt, "Social Mobility and the Child: A Case Study," *Journal of Abnormal and Social Psychology,* April, 1949, pp. 266–272.

Bossard, James H. S., and Weaver, W. Wallace (eds.), "The Prospect for Youth," *Annals of the American Academy of Political and Social Science,* November, 1937.

Bressler, Marvin, "Selected Family Patterns in W. I. Thomas' Unfinished Study of the Bintl Brief," *American Sociological Review,* October, 1952, pp. 563–571.

Bressler, Marvin, and Kephart, William M., "Marriage and Family Patterns of an Academic Group," *Marriage and Family Living,* May, 1954, pp. 121–127.

Brown, L. Guy, "The Development of Diverse Patterns of Behavior Among Children of the Same Family," *The Family,* April, 1928, pp. 35–39.

Brown, L. Guy, "The Family as a Universal Culture Pattern," *American Journal of Sociology,* May, 1948, pp. 460–463.

Brownfield, E. Dorothy, "Communication—Key to Dynamics of Family Interaction," *Marriage and Family Living,* November, 1953, pp. 316–319.

Burchinal, Lee G.; Hawkes, Glenn R.; and Gardner, Bruce, "Adjustment Characteristics of Rural and Urban Children," *American Sociological Review,* February, 1957, pp. 81–87.

Burgess, Ernest W., "The Cultural Approach to the Study of Personality," *Mental Hygiene,* April, 1930, pp. 307–325.

Burgess, Ernest W., "Environment and Education," *Supplementary Educational Monographs,* No. 54, March, 1942, pp. 1–15.

Burgess, Ernest W., "The Family and the Person," *Publications of the American Sociological Society,* 1928, pp. 133–143.

Burgess, Ernest W., "The Family as a Unit of Interacting Personalities," *The Family,* March, 1936, pp. 3–9.

Burgess, Ernest W., "Family Tradition and the Personality Development," *National Conference of Social Work,* 1928, pp. 322–330.

Burgess, Ernest W., "What Social Case Records Should Contain to Be Useful for Sociological Interpretation," *Social Forces,* June, 1928, pp. 524–534.

Burma, John H., "Research Note on the Measurement of Interracial Marriage," *American Journal of Sociology,* May, 1952, pp. 587–589.

Campisi, Paul J., "Ethnic Family Patterns: The Italian Family in the United States," *American Journal of Sociology,* May, 1948, pp. 443–449.

Carpenter, June, and Eisenberg, Philip, "Some Relations Between Family Background and Personality," *Journal of Psychology,* July, 1938, pp. 115–136.

Carter, Don C., "The Influence of Family Relations and Family Experiences on Personality," *Marriage and Family Living,* August, 1954, pp. 212–215.

Carter, Isabel Gordon, "Legislators Define Childhood," *Annals of the American Academy of Political and Social Science,* November, 1940, pp. 38–41.

Cavan, Ruth Shonle, "Regional Family Patterns: The Middle Western Family," *American Journal of Sociology,* May, 1948, pp. 430–431.

Centers, Richard, "Children of the New Deal: Social Stratification and Adolescent Attitudes," *International Journal of Opinion and Attitude Research,* Fall, 1950, pp. 315–335.

Centers, Richard, "Marital Selection and Occupational Strata," *American Journal of Sociology,* May, 1949, pp. 530–535.

Chambers, Bradford, "The Juvenile Gangs of New York," *American Mercury,* April, 1946.

Chapin, F. Stuart, "The Advantages of Experimental Sociology in the Study of Family Group Patterns," *Social Forces,* December, 1932, pp. 200–207.

Chapman, Stanley, "Church Schools," *Journal of Educational Sociology,* February, 1945, pp. 340–351.

Chin, Ai-Li S., "Some Problems of Chinese Youth in Transition," *American Journal of Sociology,* July, 1948, pp. 1–9.

Christensen, Harold T., "Dating Behavior as Evaluated by High-School Students," *American Journal of Sociology,* May, 1952, pp. 580–586.

Christensen, Harold T., "Mormon Fertility: A Survey of Student Opinion," *American Journal of Sociology,* January, 1948, pp. 270–275.

Clark, Robert E., "Psychoses, Income, and Occupational Prestige," *American Journal of Sociology,* March, 1949, pp. 433–440.

Clothier, Florence, "The Social Development of the Young Child," *Child Development,* September, 1938, pp. 285–291.

Cockrell, D. L., "A Study of the Play of Children of Preschool Age by an Unobserved Observer," *Genetic Psychology Monographs,* 1935, pp. 377–469.

Cohen, Lillian, "Family Characteristics of Homeowners," *American Journal of Sociology,* May, 1950, pp. 565–571.

Cottrell, Leonard S., Jr., "The Adjustment of the Individual to His Age and Sex Roles," *American Sociological Review,* October, 1942, pp. 617–621.

Cottrell, Leonard S., Jr., "Analysis of Situational Fields—A Theoretical Orientation for Social Psychology," *American Sociological Review,* June, 1942, pp. 370–383.

Cottrell, Leonard S., Jr., "The Case Study Method in Prediction," Sociometry, November, 1941, pp. 358–370.

Cottrell, Leonard S., Jr., and Gallagher, Ruth, "Important Developments in American Social Psychology During the Past Decade," *Sociometry,* May and August, 1941.

Crandall, Vaughn J., and Preston, Anne, "Patterns and Levels of Maternal Behavior," *Child Development,* December, 1955, pp. 267–277.

Crichton-Miller, Hugh, "The Significance of Parental Responsibility," *Mental Hygiene,* January, 1937, pp. 8–17.

Damrin, Dora E., "Family Size and Sibling Age, Sex, and Position as Related to Certain Aspects of Adjustment," *Journal of Social Psychology,* February, 1949, pp. 93–102.

Dashiell, J. F., "Experimental Studies of the Influence of Social Situations on the Behavior of Individual Human Adults," in Murchison, Carl, *A Handbook in Social Psychology,* Clark University Press, Worcester, 1935, Chap. 23.

Davis, Allison, "American Status Systems and the Socialization of the Child," *American Sociological Review,* June, 1941, pp. 345–354.

Davis, Allison, and Havighurst, Robert J., "Social Class and Color Differences in Child-Rearing," *American Sociological Review,* December, 1946, pp. 698–710.

Davis, Edith A., "The Mental and Linguistic Superiority of Only Girls," *Child Development,* March, 1937, pp. 139–143.

Davis, Kingsley, "The Child and the Social Structure," *Journal of Educational Sociology,* December, 1940, pp. 217–230.

Davis, Kingsley, "Children of Divorced Parents, Sociological and Statistical Analysis," *Law and Contemporary Problems,* Summer, 1944, pp. 713–714.

Davis, Kingsley, "Extreme Social Isolation in a Child," *American Journal of Sociology,* January, 1940, pp. 554–566.

Davis, Kingsley, "Final Note on a Case of Extreme Isolation," *American Journal of Sociology,* March, 1947, pp. 432–438.

Davis, Kingsley, "The Sociology of Parent-Youth Conflict," *American Sociological Review,* August, 1940, pp. 523–535.

Day, E. J., "The Development of Language in Twins: I. A Comparison of Twins and Single Children," *Child Development,* March, 1932, pp. 179–199.

Day, E. J., "The Development of Language in Twins: II. The Development of Twins: Their Resemblance and Differences," *Child Development,* March, 1932, pp. 298–316.

Devereux, George, "Maladjustment and Social Neurosis," *American Sociological Review,* December, 1939, pp. 844–851.

Dewey, Richard, "The Neighborhood, Urban Ecology, and City Planners," *American Sociological Review,* August, 1950, pp. 502–507.

Dollard, John F., "A Method for the Sociological Study of Infancy and Preschool Childhood," *Journal of Educational Sociology,* September, 1935, pp. 88–97.

Dollard, John F., "Needed Viewpoints in Family Research," *Social Forces,* October, 1935, pp. 109–113.

Dollard, John F., "The Psychotic Person Seen Culturally," *American Journal of Sociology,* March, 1934, pp. 637–648.

DuBois, Franklin S., "The Security of Discipline," *Mental Hygiene,* July, 1952, pp. 353–372.

Duvall, Evelyn Millis, "Conceptions of Parenthood," *American Journal of Sociology,* November, 1946, pp. 193–203.

Duvall, Everett W., "Child-Parent Social Distance," *Sociology and Social Research,* May–June, 1937, pp. 458–463.

Ellis, Albert, "Love and Family Relationships of American College Girls," *American Journal of Sociology,* May, 1950, pp. 550–558.

Ellis, Albert, and Beechley, Robert M., "A Comparison of Child Guidance Clinic Patients Coming from Large, Medium, and Small Families," *Journal of Genetic Psychology,* September, 1951, pp. 131–144.

Ellis, Albert, and Beechley, Robert M., "Assortative Mating in the Parents of Child Guidance Clinic Patients," *American Sociological Review,* October, 1949, pp. 678–679.

Escalona, Sibylle, "A Commentary upon Some Recent Changes in Child Rearing Practices," *Child Development,* September, 1949, pp. 157–162.

Fairchild, Mildred, "The Family in the Soviet Union," *American Sociological Review*, October, 1937, pp. 619–629.

Fenton, N., "The Only Child," *Pedagogical Seminary*, December, 1928, pp. 546–556.

Folsom, Joseph K., "Regional Family Patterns: The New England Family," *American Journal of Sociology*, May, 1948, pp. 423–425.

Foote, Nelson N., "A Neglected Member of the Family," *Marriage and Family Living*, August, 1956, pp. 213–218.

Form, William H., and Miller, Delbert C., "Occupational Career Pattern as a Sociological Instrument," *American Journal of Sociology*, January, 1949, pp. 317–329.

Frank, Lawrence K., "Fundamental Needs of the Child," *Mental Hygiene*, July, 1938, pp. 353–379.

Frazier, E. Franklin, "Ethnic Family Patterns: The Negro Family in the United States," *American Journal of Sociology*, May, 1948, pp. 435–438.

Furfey, Paul H., "The Group Life of the Adolescent," *Journal of Educational Sociology*, December, 1940, pp. 195–216.

Furfey, Paul H., "The Sociological Implications of Substandard English," *The American Catholic Sociological Review*, March, 1944.

Geiger, Kent, "Deprivation and Solidarity in the Soviet Urban Family," *American Sociological Review*, February, 1955, pp. 57–68.

Ginsburg, Ethel L., "The Relations of Parental Attitudes to Variations in Hyperactivity," *Smith College Studies in Social Work*, September, 1933, pp. 27–53.

Glick, Paul C., "The Family Cycle," *American Sociological Review*, April, 1947, pp. 164–174.

Glick, Paul C., "The Life Cycle of the Family," *Marriage and Family Living*, February, 1955, pp. 3–9.

Golden, Joseph, "Patterns of Negro-White Intermarriage," *American Sociological Review*, April, 1954, pp. 144–147.

Gough, Harrison G.; Harris, Dale B.; Martin, William E.; and Edwards, Marcia, "Children's Ethnic Attitudes: I. Relationship to Certain Personality Factors," *Child Development*, June, 1950, pp. 83–91.

Grace, Harry A., and Lohmann, Joan J., "Children's Reactions to Stories Depicting Parent-Child Conflict Situations," *Child Development*, March, 1952, pp. 61–74.

Grant, E. I., "The Effect of Certain Factors in the Home Environment upon Child Behavior," *University of Iowa Studies in Child Welfare*, Vol. XVI, No. 3, 1939, pp. 61–94.

Grant, J. R., "A Child's Vocabulary and Its Growth," *Pedagogical Seminary*, March, 1915, pp. 183–203.

Green, Arnold W., "Culture, Normality, and Personality Conflict," *American Anthropologist*, April, 1948, pp. 225–237.

Green, Arnold W., "The Middle Class Male Child and Neurosis," *American Sociological Review*, February, 1946, pp. 31–41.

Green, Arnold W., "The Social Situation in Personality Theory," *American Sociological Review*, June, 1942. pp. 388–393.

Gross, Llewellyn, "The Use of Class Concepts in Sociological Research," *American Journal of Sociology*, March, 1949, pp. 409–421.

Groves, Ernest R., "A Child Needs Two Parents," *Progressive Education*, October–November–December, 1926, pp. 300–304.

Gruenberg, Sidonie Matsner and Benjamin C., "Education of Children for Family Life," *Annals of the American Academy of Political and Social Science*, March, 1932, pp. 205–215.

Handel, Gerald, and Hess, Robert D., "The Family as an Emotional Organization," *Marriage and Family Living*, May, 1956, pp. 99–101.

Hardy, Martha C., "Social Recognition at the Elementary School Age," *Journal of Social Psychology*, August, 1937, pp. 365–384.

Hare, A. Paul, "A Study of Interaction and Consensus in Different Sized Groups," *American Sociological Review*, June, 1952, pp. 261–267.

Harris, Dale B.; Gough, Harrison G.; and Martin, William E., "Children's Ethnic Attitudes: II. Relationship to Parental Beliefs Concerning Child Training," *Child Development*, September, 1950, pp. 169–181.

Hatt, Paul K., "Occupation and Social Stratification," *American Journal of Sociology*, May, 1950, pp. 533–543.

Hattwick, Berta W., "Interrelations Between the Pre-School Child's Behavior and Certain Factors in the Home," *Child Development*, September, 1936, pp. 200–226.

Havighurst, Robert J., and Davis, Allison, "A Comparison of the Chicago and Harvard Studies of Social Class Differences in Child Rearing," *American Sociological Review*, August, 1955, pp. 438–442.

Hawkes, Glenn R., "The Child in the Family," *Marriage and Family Living*, February, 1957, pp. 46–53.

Hayner, Norman S., "Regional Family Patterns: The Western Family," *American Journal of Sociology*, May, 1948, pp. 432–434.

Heiman, Marcel, "The Relationship Between Man and Dog," *Psychoanalytic Quarterly*, Vol. XXV, 1956, pp. 568–585.

Helton, Roy, "Are We Doing Too Much for Our Children?" *Annals of the American Academy of Political and Social Science*, November, 1940, pp. 231–234.

Helton, Roy, "The Inner Threat: Our Own Softness," *Harper's Magazine*, September, 1940, pp. 337–343.

Henry, Jules, and Warson, Samuel, "Family Structure and Psychic Development," *American Journal of Orthopsychiatry*, January, 1951, pp. 59–73.

Henry, William E., "The Business Executive: The Psychodynamics of a Social Role," *American Journal of Sociology*, January, 1949, pp. 286–291.

Hess, Robert D., and Goldblatt, Irene, "The Status of Adolescents in American Society: A Problem in Social Identity," *Child Development*, December, 1957, pp. 459–468.

Hilgard, Josephine R., "Sibling Rivalry and Social Heredity," *Psychiatry*, November, 1951, pp. 375–385.

Hill, Patty Smith, "The Home and the School as Centers of Child Life," *Progressive Education*, July–August–September, 1928, pp. 211–217.

Horowitz, E. L., "Child-Adult Relationships in the Preschool Years," *Journal of Social Psychology*, February, 1940, pp. 41–58.

International Issue on the Family, *Marriage and Family Living,* November, 1954.

International Issue on Services to the Family," *Marriage and Family Living,* August, 1955.

James, John, "A Preliminary Study of the Size Determinant in Small Group Interaction," *American Sociological Review,* August, 1951, pp. 474–477.

Jameson, Samuel H., "Adjustment Problems of University Girls Because of Parental Patterns," *Sociology and Social Research,* January–February, 1940.

Jessner, Lucie, "Some Aspects of Permissiveness in Psychotherapy of Children," *Child Development,* March, 1950, pp. 13–18.

Johnson, Charles S., "Education and the Cultural Process," *American Journal of Sociology,* May, 1943, pp. 629–632.

Jones, Mary C., "Adolescent Development and the Junior High School Program," *The High School Journal,* November–December, 1949, pp. 237–239.

Jones, Mary C., and Bayley, Nancy, "Physical Maturing Among Boys as Related to Behavior," *Journal of Educational Psychology,* March, 1950, pp. 129–148.

Jones, Robert C., "Ethnic Family Patterns: The Mexican Family in the United States," *American Journal of Sociology,* May, 1948, pp. 450–452.

Kanner, Leo, "Unaware of Others," *Science News Letter,* August 11, 1945, p. 92.

Keller, Fred S., "Animals and Children," *Child Development,* March, 1950, pp. 7–12.

Kennedy, Ruby Jo Reeves, "Single or Triple Melting-Pot?" *American Journal of Sociology,* January, 1944, pp. 331–339.

Kennedy, Ruby Jo Reeves, "Single or Triple Melting-Pot? Intermarriage in New Haven, 1870–1950," *American Journal of Sociology,* July, 1952, pp. 56–59.

Kephart, William M., "A Quantitative Analysis of Intragroup Relationships," *American Journal of Sociology,* May, 1950, pp. 544–549.

King, Charles E., "Attitudes Toward Marriage and Motherhood of 183 College Women," *Social Forces,* October, 1943, pp. 89–91.

Kluckhohn, Florence R., "Dominant and Substitute Profiles of Cultural Orientations: Their Significance for the Analysis of Social Stratification," *Social Forces,* May, 1950, pp. 376–393.

Koch, Helen L., "The Relation in Young Children Between Characteristics of Their Playmates and Certain Attributes of Their Siblings," *Child Development,* June, 1957, pp. 175–202.

Koch, Helen L., "Some Emotional Attitudes of the Young Child in Relation to Characteristics of His Sibling," *Child Development,* December, 1956, pp. 393–426.

Koller, Marvin R., "Studies of Three-Generation Households," *Marriage and Family Living,* August, 1954, pp. 205–206.

Komarovsky, Mirra, "Functional Analysis of Sex Roles," *American Sociological Review,* August, 1950, pp. 508–516.

Kornhauser, William, "The Negro Union Official: A Study of Sponsorship and Control," *American Journal of Sociology,* March, 1952, pp. 443–452.

Koshuk, Ruth Pearson, "Problems for Sociological Research in Personality Development," *Journal of Educational Sociology,* April, 1937, pp. 464–469.

Landis, Judson T., "Marriages of Mixed and Non-Mixed Religious Faith," *American Sociological Review*, June, 1949, pp. 401–407.

Landis, Paul, "The Case for Mobility," *The Survey*, March, 1943, pp. 74–76.

Landis, Paul, "Sequential Marriage," *Journal of Home Economics*, October, 1950, pp. 625–628.

Lansing, John B., and Kish, Leslie, "Family Life Cycle as an Independent Variable," *American Sociological Review*, October, 1957, pp. 512–519.

Lasko, Joan K., "Parent Behavior Toward First and Second Children," *Genetic Psychology Monographs*, Vol. XLIX, 1954, pp. 97–137.

Lawton, George, "Can Adults Ever Really Understand Children?" *Childhood Education*, April, 1940, pp. 341–346.

Lees, J. P., "The Social Mobility of a Group of Eldest-Born and Intermediate Adult Males," *British Journal of Psychology*, July, 1952, pp. 210–221.

LeMasters, E. E., "Parenthood as Crisis," *Marriage and Family Living*, November, 1957, pp. 352–355.

LeMasters, E. E., "Social Class Mobility and Family Integration," *Marriage and Family Living*, August, 1954, pp. 226–232.

Levy, David M., "Maternal and Paternal Factors: Theories of Maternal Love," *Psychiatry*, November, 1939, pp. 571–597.

Levy, David M., "Sibling Rivalry Studies in Children of Primitive Groups," *American Journal of Orthopsychiatry*, January, 1939, pp. 205–214.

Linton, Ralph, "Age and Sex Categories," *American Sociological Review*, October, 1942, pp. 589–604.

Linton, Ralph, "A Neglected Aspect of Social Organization," *American Journal of Sociology*, May, 1940, pp. 870–887.

Lippitt, Ronald, "Group Dynamics and Personality Dynamics," *American Journal of Orthopsychiatry*, January, 1951, pp. 18–31.

Littman, Richard A.; Moore, Robert C. A.; and Pierce-Jones, John, "Social Class Differences in Child Rearing: A Third Community for Comparison with Chicago and Newton," *American Sociological Review*, December, 1957, pp. 694–704.

Locke, Harvey J., and Mackeprang, Muriel, "Marital Adjustment and the Employed Wife," *American Journal of Sociology*, May, 1949, pp. 536–538.

Lundberg, George A., and Dickson, Lenore, "Inter-Ethnic Relations in a High-School Population," *American Journal of Sociology*, July, 1952, pp. 1–10.

Maas, Henry S., "Some Social Class Differences in the Family Systems and Group Relations of Pre- and Early Adolescents," *Child Development*, June, 1951, pp. 145–152.

McCain, John Walker, Jr., "Some Small-Town Folk Beliefs of the Carolina Piedmont," *Social Forces*, March, 1934, pp. 418–420.

McCandless, Boyd, "Psychosocial Development of Personality," *Child Development*, September, 1949, pp. 123–129.

McCarthy, D., "A Comparison of Children's Language in Different Situations and Its Relation to Personality Traits," *Journal of Genetic Psychology*, December, 1929, pp. 583–591.

McClenahan, Bessie H., "The Child of the Relief Agency," *Social Forces*, May, 1935, pp. 560–567.

Macdonald, Margherita; McGuire, Carson; and Havighurst, Robert J., "Leisure Activities and the Socioeconomic Status of Children," *American Journal of Sociology,* May, 1949, pp. 505–519.

McFarland, Margaret B., "Relationships Between Young Sisters as Revealed in Their Overt Responses," *Journal of Experimental Education,* December, 1937, pp. 173–179.

MacFarlane, J. W., "Family Influences on Children's Personality Development," *Childhood Education,* October, 1938, pp. 55–59.

McGuire, Carson, and Clark, Rodney A., "Age-Mate Acceptance and Indices of Peer Status," *Child Development,* June, 1952, pp. 141–154.

Mack, Raymond W., "Occupational Ideology and the Determinate Role," *Social Forces,* October, 1957, pp. 37–44.

McKeown, James Edward, "The Behavior of Parents of Schizophrenic, Neurotic, and Normal Children," *American Journal of Sociology,* September, 1950, pp. 175–179.

Malinowski, Bronislaw, "The Pan African Problem of Culture Contact," *American Journal of Sociology,* May, 1943, pp. 649–666.

Martin, William E., "Effects of Early Training on Personality," *Marriage and Family Living,* February, 1957, pp. 39–45.

Maurer, Rose, "Recent Trends in the Soviet Family," *American Sociological Review,* June, 1944, pp. 242–249.

May, Mark A., and Hartshorne, H., "Personality and Character Tests," *Psychological Bulletin,* July, 1926, pp. 395–411.

Mead, Margaret, "Our Educational Emphasis in Primitive Perspective," *American Journal of Sociology,* May, 1943, pp. 633–639.

Meltzer, H., "Children's Attitudes to Parents," *American Journal of Orthopsychiatry,* July, 1935, pp. 244–265.

Meltzer, H., "Economic Security and Children's Attitudes to Parents," *American Journal of Orthopsychiatry,* October, 1936, pp. 590–608.

Melvin, Bruce, "Age and Sex Distribution in Relation to Rural Behavior," *Publications of the American Sociological Society,* 1929.

Menninger, Karl A., "Adaptation Difficulties in College Students," *Mental Hygiene,* July, 1927, pp. 519–535.

Merriam, Charles E., "The Content of an International Bill of Rights," *Annals of the American Academy of Political and Social Science,* January, 1946, pp. 11–17.

Miner, Horace, "The French-Canadian Family Cycle," *American Sociological Review,* October, 1938, pp. 700–708.

Mogey, J. M., "A Century of Declining Paternal Authority," *Marriage and Family Living,* August, 1957, pp. 234–239.

Moore, Madeline U., "The Treatment of Maternal Attitudes in Problems of Guidance," *American Journal of Orthopsychiatry,* April, 1933, pp. 113–127.

Moriyama, Iwao, and Grenville, Thomas N. E., "The Effect of Changing Birth Rates upon Infant Mortality Tables," Bureau of the Census, *Vital Statistics Special Reports,* November, 1944, pp. 399–412.

Moultin, Bryant E., "Some Causes of Delinquency in Relation to Family Attitudes," *American Journal of Orthopsychiatry,* January, 1931, pp. 173–177.

Mowrer, Harriet R., "The Study of Marital Adjustment as a Background for

Research in Child Behavior," *Journal of Educational Sociology*, April, 1937, pp. 487–492.

Mummery, Dorothy V., "Family Backgrounds of Assertive and Non-Assertive Children," *Child Development*, March, 1954, pp. 63–80.

Murphy, Lois B., and Gardner, "The Influence of Social Situations upon the Behavior of Children," in Murchison, Carl (ed.), *A Handbook in Social Psychiatry*, Clark University Press, Worcester, 1935, Chap. 22.

Myers, Garry C., "Our Children and Their Parents," *Parent Education*, May, 1932, pp. 27–60.

Myers, Garry C., "Parents Who Disagree Before Their Children," *Child Welfare*, April, 1929, pp. 409–413.

Myrdal, Alva, "Swedish Women in Industry and at Home," *Annals of the American Academy of Political and Social Science*, May, 1938, pp. 216–231.

Neal, Eva, "The Only Child," *Mental Hygiene Bulletin*, November, 1927, pp. 1–3.

Neugarten, Bernice, "Social Class and Friendship Among School Children," *American Journal of Sociology*, January, 1946, pp. 305–313.

Neumann, Frederika, "The Effects on the Child of an Unstable Home Situation," *Mental Hygiene*, October, 1928, pp. 742–751.

Neumann, Henry, "The Father's Responsibility in the Training of his Children," *Proceedings of the Mid-West Conference on Parent Education*, March, 1926, pp. 222–233.

Neumann, Sigmund, "The Conflict of Generations in Contemporary Europe from Versailles to Munich," *Vital Speeches of the Day*, August 1, 1939, pp. 623–628.

Newell, H. W., "A Further Study of Maternal Rejection," *American Journal of Orthopsychiatry*, October, 1936, pp. 576–689.

Newell, H. W., "Principles and Practices Used in Child Psychiatric Clinics," *Mental Hygiene*, October, 1951, pp. 571–580.

Nimkoff, Meyer F., "The Relation of Parental Dominance to Parent-Child Conflict," *Social Forces*, June, 1931.

Nimkoff, Meyer F., "Technology, Biology, and the Changing Family," *American Journal of Sociology*, July, 1951, pp. 20–26.

Nollen, John S., "The Child and His Home," *National Congress of Parents and Teachers, Proceedings of the Thirty-Eighth Annual Meeting*, May, 1934, pp. 62–69.

Nye, F. Ivan; Short, James F., Jr.; and Olson, Virgil J., "Socioeconomic Status and Delinquent Behavior," *American Journal of Sociology*, January, 1958, pp. 381–389.

Nye, Ivan, "Adolescent-Parent Adjustment—Socioeconomic Level as a Variable," *American Sociological Review*, June, 1951, pp. 341–349.

Ogburn, W. F., "Marital Separations," *American Journal of Sociology*, January, 1944, pp. 316–323.

Ogburn, W. F., "Marriages, Births, and Divorces," *Annals of the American Academy of Political and Social Science*, September, 1943, pp. 20–29.

Opler, Morris Edward, "Themes as Dynamic Forces in Culture," *American Journal of Sociology*, November, 1945, pp. 198–206.

Orgel, Samuel Z., "Bringing up Children," *Mental Hygiene,* July, 1937, pp. 436–451.

Parsons, Alice Beal, "How Changing Conditions Change Mothers," *Progressive Education,* October–November–December, 1926, pp. 295–330.

Parsons, Talcott, "Age and Sex in the Social Structure of the United States," *American Sociological Review,* October, 1942, pp. 604–617.

Phillips, E. Lakin, "Parent-Child Similarities in Personality Disturbances," *Journal of Clinical Psychology,* April, 1951, pp. 188–190.

Phillips, E. Lakin; Shenker, Shirley; and Revitz, Paula, "The Assimilation of the New Child into the Group," *Psychiatry,* August, 1951, pp. 319–325.

Plant, James S., "The Child as a Member of the Family," *Annals of the American Academy of Political and Social Science,* March, 1932, pp. 66–74.

Plant, James S., "Social Significance of War Impact on Adolescents," *Annals of the American Academy of Political and Social Science,* November, 1944, pp. 1–7.

Psathas, George, "Ethnicity, Social Class, and Adolescent Independence from Parental Control," *American Sociological Review,* August, 1957, pp. 415–423.

Queen, Stuart A., "Some Problems of the Situational Approach," *Social Forces,* June, 1931, pp. 480–481.

Rabban, Meyer, "Sex-Role Identification in Young Children in Two Diverse Social Groups," *Genetic Psychology Monographs,* Vol. XLII, 1950, pp. 81–158.

Radke-Yarrow, Marian; Trager, Helen; and Miller, Jean, "The Role of Parents in the Development of Children's Ethnic Attitudes," *Child Development,* March, 1952, pp. 13–53.

Rasey, Mabel, and Witmer, Helen, "Case Studies of Eight Well-Adjusted Families with Special Reference to the Childhood of the Parents," *Smith College Studies in Social Work,* September, 1936, pp. 46–91.

Rautman, Arthur L., "Youth in Search of a Standard," *Mental Hygiene,* October, 1946, pp. 597–605.

Rautman, Emily W. and Arthur L., "Is Your Child Well-Bred?" *Mental Hygiene,* April, 1950, pp. 228–240.

Rice, John A., "My Father's Folks," *Harper's Magazine,* September, 1940.

Rice, Stuart A., "Units and Their Definition in Social Science," *Social Forces,* June, 1931, pp. 475–479.

Rivlin, Harry M., "The Personality Problems of Teachers," *Mental Hygiene,* July, 1939, pp. 12–24.

Roff, Merrill, "Intra-Family Resemblances in Personality Characteristics," *Journal of Psychology,* July, 1950, pp. 199–227.

Rogers, Carl R., "The Nondirective Method as a Technique for Social Research," *American Journal of Sociology,* January, 1945, pp. 279–284.

Rose, Arnold M., and Warshay, Leon, "The Adjustment of Migrants to Cities," *Social Forces,* October, 1957, pp. 72–76.

Ross, Bertha M., "Some Traits Associated with Sibling Jealousy in Problem Children," *Smith College Studies in Social Work,* June, 1931, pp. 364–376.

Roucek, J. S., "The Problem of Becoming Americanized," *Sociology and Social Research,* January–February, 1933.

Roy, Katharine, "Parents' Attitudes Toward Their Children," *Journal of Home Economics,* October, 1950, pp. 652–653.

Ruesch, Jurgen, and Bateson, Gregory, "Structure and Process in Social Relations," *Psychiatry*, May, 1949, pp. 105–124.

Sanderson, D., and Foster, Robert, "A Sociological Case Study of Farm Families," *The Family*, June, 1930, pp. 107–114.

Sanford, Gilbert A., "A Research Note on Desired Family Size," *Social Forces*, October, 1943, pp. 87–89.

Sapir, Edward, "Personality," *Encyclopaedia of the Social Sciences*, The Macmillan Company, New York, Vol. XII, pp. 85–87.

Sapir, Edward, "Speech as a Personality Trait," *American Journal of Sociology*, May, 1927, pp. 892–908.

Schettler, Clarence, "Does Your Name Identify You?" *Social Forces*, December, 1942, pp. 172–176.

Schnepp, Gerald J., "Mixed Marriages," *The Family Today*, National Catholic Welfare Conference, Washington, 1945.

Schnepp, Gerald J., and Roberts, Louis A., "Residential Propinquity and Mate Selection on a Parish Basis," *American Journal of Sociology*, July, 1952, pp. 45–50.

Sears, Robert R., "Ordinal Position in the Family as a Psychological Variable," *American Sociological Review*, June, 1950, pp. 397–401.

Sears, Robert R., "Relation of Fantasy Aggression to Interpersonal Aggression," *Child Development*, March, 1950, pp. 5–6.

Sewell, William H., "Infant Training and the Personality of the Child," *American Journal of Sociology*, September, 1952, pp. 150–159.

Sewell, William H., and Mussen, Paul H., "The Effects of Feeding, Weaning, and Scheduling Procedures on Childhood Adjustment and the Formation of Oral Symptoms," *Child Development*, September, 1952, pp. 185–191.

Sewell, William H.; Mussen, Paul H.; and Harris, Chester W., "Relationships Among Child Training Practices," *American Sociological Review*, April, 1955, pp. 137–148.

Sheffield, Ada E., "Conditioning Patterns in the Family Circle," *Social Forces*, June, 1930, pp. 533–535.

Sheffield, Ada E., "The 'Situation' as a Unit of Family Case Study," *Social Forces*, June, 1931, pp. 465–474.

Sheldon, Sybil, "Bright Children Failing in School: St. Paul Child Guidance Clinic," *Smith College Studies in Social Work*, September, 1935, pp. 75–77.

Silverman, Baruch, "The Behavior of Children from Broken Homes," *American Journal of Orthopsychiatry*, January, 1935, pp. 11–18.

Sirjamaki, John, "Culture Configurations in the American Family," *American Journal of Sociology*, May, 1948, pp. 464–470.

Sletto, Raymond F., "Sibling Position and Juvenile Delinquency," *American Journal of Sociology*, March, 1934, pp. 657–669.

Slotkin, J. S., "Jewish-Gentile Intermarriage in Chicago," *American Sociological Review*, February, 1942, pp. 34–39.

Smalley, Ruth E., "The Influence of Differences in Age, Sex, and Intelligence in Determining the Attitudes of Siblings Toward Each Other," *Smith College Studies in Social Work*, September, 1930, pp. 23–40.

Smith, Madorah E., "A Comparison of Certain Personality Traits as Rated in the Same Individuals in Childhood and Fifty Years Later," *Child Development,* September, 1952, pp. 159–180.

Smith, William C., "The Stepchild," *American Sociological Review,* April, 1945, pp. 237–242.

Sowers, Alice, "Parent-Child Relationships from the Child's Point of View," *Journal of Experimental Education,* December, 1937, pp. 203–231.

Sperling, Melitta, "The Neurotic Child and His Mother: A Psychoanalytic Study," *American Journal of Orthopsychiatry,* April, 1951, pp. 351–364.

Spiro, Melford E., "Culture and Personality: The Natural History of a False Dichotomy," *Psychiatry,* February, 1951, pp. 19–46.

Spoerl, D. T., "Bilinguality and Emotional Adjustment," *Journal of Abnormal and Social Psychology,* January, 1943, pp. 37–57.

Stagner, Ross, "The Role of the Parent in the Development of Emotional Instability," *American Journal of Orthopsychiatry,* January, 1938, pp. 122–129.

Stanton, Howard R., "Mother Love in Foster Homes," *Marriage and Family Living,* November, 1956, pp. 301–307.

Staples, Ruth, and Smith, June Warden, "Attitudes of Grandmothers and Mothers Toward Child Rearing Practices," *Child Development,* June, 1954, pp. 91–97.

Stauffer, Marjorie, "Some Aspects of Treatment by Psychiatrist and Psychiatric Social Worker," *American Journal of Orthopsychiatry,* April, 1932, pp. 152–161.

Stendler, Celia Burns, "Critical Periods in Socialization and Overdependency," *Child Development,* March, 1952, pp. 3–12.

Stendler, Celia Burns, "Possible Causes of Overdependency in Young Children," *Child Development,* June, 1954, pp. 125–146.

Stendler, Celia Burns, "Sixty Years of Child Training Practices," *Journal of Pediatrics,* January, 1950, pp. 3–15.

Stendler, Celia Burns, "Social Class Differences in Parental Attitude Toward School at Grade 1 Level," *Child Development,* March, 1951, pp. 37–46.

Stendler, Celia Burns, "A Study of Some Socio-Moral Judgments of Junior High School Children," *Child Development,* March, 1949, pp. 15–28.

Stendler, Celia Burns, and Young, Norman, "The Impact of Beginning First Grade upon Socialization as Reported by Mothers," *Child Development,* December, 1950, pp. 241–260.

Stendler, Celia Burns, and Young, Norman, "Impact of First Grade Entrance upon the Socialization of the Child: Changes After Eight Months of School," *Child Development,* June, 1951, pp. 113–122.

Stevens, George C., "Autobiographical Material Concerning the Childhood Environments and the Effects on the After-Adjustment of One Hundred Recidivists and One Hundred College Freshmen," *American Journal of Orthopsychiatry,* July, 1932, pp. 279–303.

Stodgill, R. M., "The Measurement of Attitudes Toward Parental Control and the Social Adjustment of Children," *Journal of Applied Psychology,* June, 1936, pp. 359–367.

Stodgill, R. M., "Parental Attitudes and Mental Hygiene Standards," *Mental Hygiene,* October, 1931, pp. 813–827.

Stonequist, Everett, "The Problem of the Marginal Man," *American Journal of Sociology*, July, 1935, pp. 1–13.

Stouffer, George A. W., "Behavior Problems of Children as Viewed by Teachers and Mental Hygienists," *Mental Hygiene*, April, 1952, pp. 271–285.

Strauss, Anselm L., "The Development and Transformation of Monetary Meanings in the Child," *American Sociological Review*, June, 1952, pp. 275–286.

Strauss, Anselm L., "Strain and Harmony in American-Japanese War-Bride Marriages," *Marriage and Family Living*, May, 1954, pp. 99–106.

Strauss, Anselm L., and Schuessler, Karl, "Socialization, Logical Reasoning, and Concept Development in the Child," *American Sociological Review*, August, 1951, pp. 514–523.

Stroup, Atlee L., "Marital Adjustment of the Mother and the Personality of the Child," *Marriage and Family Living*, May, 1956, pp. 109–113.

Stubblefield, Robert L., "Children's Emotional Problems Aggravated by Family Moves," *American Journal of Orthopsychiatry*, January, 1955, pp. 120–126.

Sullivan, Harry Stack, "Conceptions of Modern Psychiatry," *Psychiatry*, February, 1940, pp. 1–13.

Sussman, Marvin B., "Family Continuity: Selective Factors Which Affect Relationships Between Families at Generational Levels," *Marriage and Family Living*, May, 1954, pp. 112–120.

Sutherland, E. H., "White Collar Criminality," *American Sociological Review*, February, 1940, pp. 1–12.

Swanson, G. E., "The Disturbances of Children in Urban Areas," *American Sociological Review*, October, 1949, pp. 676–678.

Symonds, P. M., "Personality Adjustment of Women Teachers," *American Journal of Orthopsychiatry*, January, 1941, pp. 14–20.

Tasch, Ruth Jacobson, "The Role of the Father in the Family," *Journal of Experimental Education*, June, 1952, pp. 319–361.

Thom, Douglas A., "Environment Factors and Their Relation to Social Adjustment," *Mental Hygiene*, July, 1939, pp. 379–414.

Thomas, John L., "The Factor of Religion in the Selection of Marriage Mates," *American Sociological Review*, August, 1951, pp. 487–491.

Thomas, John L., "Religious Training in the Roman Catholic Family," *American Journal of Sociology*, September, 1951, pp. 178–183.

Thomas, W. I., "The Behavior Pattern and the Situation," *Publications of the American Sociological Society*, 1928, pp. 1–13.

Thomas, W. I., "The Problem of Personality in the Urban Environment," *Publications of the American Sociological Society*, 1926, p. 31.

Thrasher, Frederic M., "Social Background and Informal Education," *Journal of Educational Sociology*, April, 1944.

Thurow, Mildred B., "A Study of Selected Factors in Family Life as Described in Life History Material," *Social Forces*, May, 1934, pp. 562–570.

Travis, L. E.; Johnson, W.; and Shover, J., "The Relation of Bilingualism to Stuttering," *Journal of Speech Disorders*, September, 1937, pp. 185–189.

Treudley, Mary B., "Mental Illness and Family Routines," *Mental Hygiene*, April, 1946, pp. 235–249.

Underwood, Virginia Van Meter, "Student Fathers with Their Children," *Marriage and Family Living*, Summer, 1949, p. 101.

Updegraff, Ruth, and Herbst, Esther K., "An Experimental Study of the Social Behavior Stimulated in Young Children by Certain Play Materials," *Journal of Genetic Psychology*, June, 1933, pp. 372–391.

Valien, Preston, and Fitzgerald, Alberta Price, "Attitudes of the Negro Mother Toward Birth Control," *American Journal of Sociology*, November, 1949, pp. 279–283.

Vance, Rupert B., "Regional Family Patterns: The Southern Family," *American Journal of Sociology*, May, 1948, pp. 426–429.

Vincent, Clark E., "Trends in Infant Care Ideas," *Child Development*, September, 1951, pp. 199–209.

Vollmer, Hermann, "The Grandmother: A Problem in Child-Rearing," *American Journal of Orthopsychiatry*, July, 1937, pp. 378–382.

Von Rhode, Carl, "The Suburban Mind," *Harper's Magazine*, April, 1946, pp. 289–299.

Walworth, Dorothy, "Just Married—And How," *Kiwanis Magazine*, October, 1942.

Ward, Anne, "The Only Child," *Smith College Studies in Social Work*, September, 1930, pp. 41–65.

Warner, W. Lloyd, *Environment and Education*, Supplementary Educational Monographs No. 59, University of Chicago Press, Chicago, 1942, pp. 16–28.

Warner, W. Lloyd, "Formal Education and the Social Structure," *Journal of Educational Sociology*, May, 1936.

Wessel, Bessie Bloom, "Ethnic Family Patterns: The American Jewish Family," *American Journal of Sociology*, May, 1948, pp. 439–442.

Wheeler, Olive A., "Variations in the Emotional Development of Normal Adolescents," *British Journal of Educational Psychology*, February, 1931, pp. 1–12.

White, Martha Sturm, "Social Class, Child Rearing Practices, and Child Behavior," *American Sociological Review*, December, 1957, pp. 704–712.

Whyte, William F., "A Slum Sex Code," *American Journal of Sociology*, July, 1943, pp. 24–31.

Williams, H. M.; and McFarland, M. L.; and Little, M. F., "Development of Language and Vocabulary in Young Children," *University of Iowa Studies in Child Welfare*, Vol. II, 1937.

Winch, Robert F., "Courtship in College Women," *American Journal of Sociology*, November, 1949, pp. 269–278.

Winker, James B., "Age Trends and Sex Differences in the Wishes, Identifications, Activities and Fears of Children," *Child Development*, December, 1949, pp. 191–200.

Wirth, Louis, "Urbanism as a Way of Life," *American Journal of Sociology*, July, 1938, pp. 1–24.

Witmer, Helen Leland, "The Childhood Personality and Parent-Child Relationships of Dementia-Praecox and Manic-Depressive Patients," *Smith College Studies in Social Work*, June, 1934, pp. 289–377.

Witmer, Helen Leland, "Parental Behavior as an Index to the Probable Outcome of Treatment in a Child Guidance Clinic," *American Journal of Orthopsychiatry*, October, 1933, pp. 431–444.

Witmer, Helen Leland, and others, "The Outcome of Treatment of Children

Rejected by Their Mothers," *Smith College Studies in Social Work*, 1938, pp. 187–234.

Woodhouse, Chase Going, "A Study of 250 Successful Families," *Social Forces*, June, 1930, pp. 511–533.

Wray, Donald E., "Marginal Men of Industry: The Foremen," *American Journal of Sociology*, January, 1949, pp. 298–301.

Young, Donald, "Some Effects of a Course in American Race Relations on the Race Prejudices of 450 Undergraduates at the University of Pennsylvania," *Journal of Abnormal and Social Psychology*, October–December, 1927, pp. 235–242.

Young, Kimball, "The Projection of Parental Ambitions," *The Family*, May, 1927.

Zachry, Caroline B., "A Challenge from Restless Youth," *New York Times Magazine*, May 2, 1942, p. 37, column 2.

Zeligs, Rose, "Children's Worries," *Sociology and Social Research*, September–October, 1939, pp. 23–32.

Zimmerman, Carle C., and Broderick, Carlfred B., "Nature and Role of Informal Family Groups," *Marriage and Family Living*, May, 1954, pp. 107–111.

Selected Sources of Reference

American Journal of Orthopsychiatry. Published quarterly by the American Orthopsychiatric Association, 1790 Broadway, New York 19, N.Y.

American Journal of Psychiatry. Published monthly by the American Psychiatric Association, 1270 Avenue of the Americas, New York 3, N.Y.

American Journal of Sociology. Published bimonthly, 1126 East 59th Street, Chicago 37, Ill.

American Sociological Review. Published bimonthly by the American Sociological Society, 4 Tyler Annex, Smith College, Northampton, Mass.

Bureau of Publications, Teachers College, Columbia University, New York, N.Y.

Child Development. Published quarterly by the Society for Research in Child Development, Inc., Purdue University, Lafayette, Ind.

Child Development Abstracts and Bibliography. Published three times a year, February through December, by the Society for Research in Child Development, Inc., Purdue University, Lafayette, Ind.

Childhood Education. Published monthly, September through May, by the Association for Childhood Education International, 1200 15th Street, N.W., Washington 5, D.C.

Family Life. Monthly service bulletin published by the American Institute of Family Relations, 5287 Sunset Boulevard, Los Angeles 27, Calif.

Journal of Abnormal and Social Psychology. Published bimonthly by the American Psychological Association, 1333 Sixteenth Street, N.W., Washington 6, D.C.

Journal of Educational Sociology. Published monthly, September through May, by the Payne Educational Sociological Foundation, Inc., 32 Washington Place, New York 3, N.Y.

Journal of Genetic Psychology. Published quarterly by the Journal Press, Provincetown, Mass.

Journal of Psychology. Published quarterly by the Journal Press, Provincetown, Mass.

Journal of Social Psychology. Published quarterly by the Journal Press, Provincetown, Mass.

Marriage and Family Living. Published quarterly by the National Council on Family Relations, 1219 University Avenue, S.E., Minneapolis 14, Minn.

Mental Hygiene. Published quarterly by the National Association for Mental Health, Inc., 10 Columbus Circle, New York 19, N.Y.

Monographs of the Society for Research in Child Development. Published by the Society for Research in Child Development, Inc., Purdue University, Lafayette, Ind.

National Parent-Teacher. Published monthly, September through June, by the National Congress of Parents and Teachers, 700 N. Rush Street, Chicago 11, Ill.

Psychiatry. Published quarterly by the William Alanson White Psychiatric Foundation, 1711 Rhode Island Avenue, N.W., Washington 6, D.C.

Research Relating to Children. Published annually by the Children's Bureau, U.S. Department of Health, Education, and Welfare, Washington, D.C.

Social Forces. Published four times a year by University of North Carolina Press, Chapel Hill, N.C.

Sociology and Social Research. Published bimonthly by the University of Southern California, Los Angeles 7, Calif.